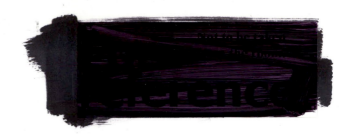

D0080944

# WHAT HAPPENED?
# AN ENCYCLOPEDIA OF EVENTS
# THAT CHANGED AMERICA FOREVER

# WHAT HAPPENED?

## An Encyclopedia of Events
## That Changed America Forever

VOLUME I:
THROUGH THE SEVENTEENTH CENTURY

**JOHN E. FINDLING AND
FRANK W. THACKERAY, EDITORS**

ABC-CLIO

Santa Barbara, California • Denver, Colorado • Oxford, England

Copyright 2011 by ABC-CLIO, LLC

**Library of Congress Cataloging-in-Publication Data**

What happened? : an encyclopedia of events that changed America forever / John E. Findling and Frank W. Thackeray, editors.
    p. cm.
  Includes bibliographical references and index.
  ISBN 978-1-59884-621-8 (set : alk. paper) — ISBN 978-1-59884-622-5 (set ebook)
1. United States—History—Encyclopedias.   I. Findling, John E.   II. Thackeray, Frank W.
  E174.W47   2011
  973.03—dc22      2010041518

ISBN: 978-1-59884-621-8
EISBN: 978-1-59884-622-5

15  14  13  12  11   1  2  3  4  5

This book is also available on the World Wide Web as an eBook.
Visit www.abc-clio.com for details.

ABC-CLIO, LLC
130 Cremona Drive, P.O. Box 1911
Santa Barbara, California 93116–1911

This book is printed on acid-free paper ∞

Manufactured in the United States of America

# CONTENTS

*Illustrations*                                                                    *ix*

*Preface and Acknowledgments*                                                       *xi*

## 1. FIRST ENCOUNTERS, ca. 40,000 BCE–CE 1492                                       1
Introduction                                                                         1
Interpretive Essay by Andrew Frank                                                   4
Algonquin                                                                           12
Anasazi Culture                                                                     13
Christopher Columbus (1451–1506)                                                    15
Hopewell Culture                                                                    17
Mississippian Culture                                                               17
Document: Journal of Christopher Columbus, 1492                                     18

## 2. THE FRENCH IN NORTH AMERICA, 1534–1701                                        33
Introduction                                                                        33
Interpretive Essay by John M. Hunt                                                  37
Jacques Cartier (1491–1557)                                                         45
Samuel de Champlain (ca. 1567–1635)                                                 47
French Fur Trade, Environmental Consequences of                                     48
Louis de Buade, Comte de Frontenac (1622–1698)                                       48
Louis Joliet (ca. 1645–1700)                                                        50
Jacques Marquette (1637–1675)                                                       51

## 3. THE EXPEDITION OF CORONADO, 1540–1542                                         55
Introduction                                                                        55
Interpretive Essay by Thomas Clarkin                                                58
Álvar Núñez Cabeza de Vaca (ca. 1490–1556/64)                                       67
Francisco Vásquez de Coronado (1510–1554)                                           68

Esteban (ca. 1503–1539) 69

Hopi 71

Spanish Colonization of the Americas 73

Zuni 76

**4. THE FOUNDING OF ST. AUGUSTINE, 1565** 79

Introduction 79

Interpretive Essay by Blake Beattie 82

Castillo de San Marcos 92

Hernando de Soto (ca. 1497–1542) 93

Florida 94

Juan Ponce de León (ca. 1470–1521) 97

**5. EARLY ENGLISH COLONIZATION EFFORTS, ca. 1584–1630** 99

Introduction 99

Interpretive Essay by Rick Kennedy 103

John Cabot (ca. 1450–1498) 110

Jamestown, Founding of (1607) 112

Pilgrims 112

Sir Walter Raleigh (ca. 1552–1618) 113

Roanoke Colonies (1585, 1587) 114

Document: Excerpt from Arthur Barlowe's "First Voyage to Roanoke," 1584 115

**6. EARLY EUROPEAN–NATIVE AMERICAN
ENCOUNTERS, 1607–1637** 117

Introduction 117

Interpretive Essay by Kathleen Perdisatt and Rick Kennedy 120

North American Smallpox Epidemic 128

Opechancanough (1545/56-ca. 1644) 129

Pequot War (1636–1637) 130

Pocahontas (ca. 1595–1617) 131

John Smith (ca. 1580–1631) 133

Squanto (1580–1622) 134

**7. THE INTRODUCTION OF SLAVERY INTO
NORTH AMERICA, 1619** 135

Introduction 135

Interpretive Essay by Julia A. Woods 138

African Slave Trade 148

Runaway Servants 154

Slavery 156

Slavery in Mid-18th-Century Colonial Virginia                    161
Document: Excerpt from Samuel Sewall's *The Selling of Joseph,* 1700    163

## 8. RELIGIOUS TOLERATION IN ENGLISH NORTH AMERICA, 1636–1701                                                    167
Introduction                                                    167
Interpretive Essay by Timothy L. Wood                            171
Cecil Calvert (1605–1675)                                        181
Anne Hutchinson (1591–1643)                                      183
Society of Friends (Quakers)                                     184
Roger Williams (1603–1683)                                       185
Document: Excerpt from Roger Williams's *Bloudy Tenent of Persecution,* 1644                                     187
Document: Maryland Act of Toleration, 1649                       189
Document: Excerpt from the Pennsylvania Charter of Privileges, 1701    192

## 9. THE SURRENDER OF NEW AMSTERDAM, 1664                      193
Introduction                                                    193
Interpretive Essay by Thomas A. Mackey                           197
Anglo-Dutch Wars                                                 206
Dutch East India Company                                         206
Dutch Reformed Church                                            207
Dutch West India Company                                         208
Peter Minuit (1580–1638)                                         210
Peter Stuyvesant (1610–1672)                                     211

## 10. KING PHILIP'S WAR, 1675–1676                             213
Introduction                                                    213
Interpretive Essay by Steven E. Siry                             216
Benjamin Church (1639–1718)                                      223
Metacom (ca. 1638–1676)                                          224
Narragansetts                                                    226
Mary Rowlandson (ca. 1635-ca. 1678)                             227
Wampanoags                                                       228
Document: Massasoit Peace Treaty, 1621                           230

## 11. THE GLORIOUS REVOLUTION IN AMERICA, 1688–1689            233
Introduction                                                    233
Interpretive Essay by P. D. Swiney                               237
Sir Edmund Andros (1637–1714)                                    246
Bacon's Rebellion (1676)                                         247

King William's War (1689–1697) 248

Jacob Leisler (1640–1691) 250

Document: English Bill of Rights, 1689 251

**12. THE SALEM WITCH TRIALS, 1692** 255

Introduction 255

Interpretive Essay by Frederick M. Stowell 259

Cotton Mather (1663–1728) 266

Increase Mather (1639–1723) 268

Puritan Family 269

Samuel Sewall (1652–1730) 271

Document: Cotton Mather: *Wonders of the Invisible World,* 1693 272

Document: Death Warrant of Five Women Convicted of Witchcraft in Salem, 1692 274

*Appendix A: Glossary of Terms and People* 277

*Appendix B: Timeline* 281

*About the Editors and Contributors* 283

*Index* I-1

# ILLUSTRATIONS

Columbus's flagship, the *Santa Maria*                                      3

Jacques Cartier claiming Canada for France                                 46

Coronado and his men in the southwestern desert                            56

An early view of the Saint Augustine area of Florida                       80

The Jamestown Tercentenary Exposition, 1607                               100

Pilgrims were idealized in the 1600s                                      119

The first Africans arriving in Virginia, 1619                             136

Roger Williams lands at Providence Plantation in 1636                     174

The Dutch surrender New Amsterdam, 1664                                   196

Indian wars in the 17th century featured fighting at close quarters       214

Nathaniel Bacon, leader of Bacon's Rebellion in Virginia                  234

Judicial proceedings during the Salem witch trials                        256

# PREFACE AND ACKNOWLEDGMENTS

This volume, which describes and evaluates the significance of 12 of the most important events in America prior to the 18th century, is the first in a multivolume series intended to acquaint readers with the seminal events of American history. Other volumes highlight events in the 18th, 19th, and 20th centuries, and the four volumes constitute a complete series. A companion series of volumes will address the global experience, "Events That Formed the Modern World."

Our collective classroom experience provided the inspiration for this project. Having encountered literally thousands of students whose knowledge of the history of their country was sadly deficient, we determined to prepare a series of books that would concentrate on the most important events affecting those students (and others as well) in the hope that they would better understand their country and how it came to be. Furthermore, we hope these books will stimulate the reader to delve further into the events covered in each volume and to take a greater interest in history in general.

The current volume is designed to serve two purposes. First, the editors have provided for each chapter an introduction that presents factual material about a particular topic in a clear, concise, chronological order. Second, each introduction is followed by a longer interpretive essay by a specialist exploring the background and/or the consequences of each event in a broader historical context. Each essay includes an annotated bibliography of the most important works about the event. Following the bibliography are a number of shorter essays featuring people or events closely related to the chapter topic. In some cases, there are primary source documents related to the topic as well. The 12 chapters are followed by two appendixes that provide additional information useful to the reader. Appendix A is a glossary of additional names, events, organizations, and terms mentioned but not fully explained in the introductions and interpretive essays that comprise each chapter. Appendix B is a timeline of key events corresponding to the time period this book covers. One editorial note: the spellings of the names of Indian tribes and individual Indians often varies among authorities. For example, one can spell the name of a New England tribe in various ways: Nipmucs, Nipmucks, Nipmets, and Neepmucks. We have attempted to employ the spelling used by the most recent and authoritative sources (which do not always agree among themselves!), including Frederick Hoxie, ed., *Encyclopedia of North American Indians*, Boston: Houghton Mifflin,

1996; Carl Waldman, *Encyclopedia of Native American Tribes*, New York: Facts On File, 1988; and Judith Nies, *Native American History*, New York: Ballantine Books, 1996.

The events covered in this volume were selected on the basis of our combined teaching and research activities. Of course, another pair of editors might have arrived at a somewhat different list than we did, but we believe that we have assembled a group of events that truly changed America before the 18th century.

As with all published works, numerous people behind the scenes deserve much of the credit for the final product. Barbara Rader, our editor at Greenwood Publishing Group, encouraged us as we prepared the first edition of this book in the late 1990s. Others who gave assistance to that edition included the staff of the Photographic Division of the Library of Congress, and our student research assistant, Bob Marshall. Brigette Adams, Carol Findling and Jo Ann Waterbury all helped with word processing in the final stage of the project. For this edition, we are grateful to James Stewart, John Wagner, Jennifer Boelter, and several others at ABC-CLIO who have answered our questions and addressed our concerns in a positive and timely manner. Special thanks go to Glenn Crothers and John Hunt, who helped us find excellent authors for several of the interpretive essays. We are also grateful to the authors of the shorter essays at the end of each chapter. These historians, provided by ABC-CLIO, wrote fine essays that significantly increased the value of each chapter. Among others who helped us in one way or another to make both the first edition and this one better books are John Newman, Sam Sloss, Sheila Anderson, Kim Pelle, Brook Taylor, Andrew Trout, and Deborah Bulleit. And, most important, we thank our authors, whose essays were well conceived and thoughtful and whose patience when the project seemed to lag was much appreciated.

Finally, we wish to express our appreciation to our spouses, Carol Findling and Kathy Thackeray, and to our children, Jamey and Jenny Findling and Alex, Max and Melanie Thackeray, whose patience with us and interest in our work made it all worthwhile.

John E. Findling
Frank W. Thackeray

# 1

# First Encounters, ca. 40,000 BCE–CE 1492

## INTRODUCTION

Scholars generally agree that human beings first came to what is now the United States from northeastern Asia, crossing overland at the point of the present-day Bering Sea. During this time, which archaeologists believe was between 40,000 and 70,000 years ago, the Ice Age had lowered ocean levels to the point where a wide stretch of land connected Asia with North America, creating a land geographers refer to as Beringia. Groups of nomadic people, searching for game or vegetation for sustenance, moved through Beringia into Alaska.

Later, as the glaciers retreated, Beringia fell below sea level and Asia and North America were separated. Those left in Alaska became North America's first indigenous people. Scholars do not agree on just when significant migrations into the more southern parts of North America took place, but all agree that people moved into the southern parts of North America at least 19,000 years ago and into South America at least 13,000 years ago.

The earliest indigenous peoples of North America were hunters and gatherers, killing bison, bear, deer, elk, and other game with increasingly sophisticated spear points and supplementing their diets with fish and berries. Archaeological evidence suggests that, after 6000 BCE, many Native people, while still hunters and gatherers, began living in larger houses and communities, making pottery, and adapting more creatively to their environment. Sometime after 5000 BCE, plant cultivation began in Mexico and spread northward unevenly, depending on the terrain and weather conditions. Corn, beans, gourds, and squash were among the first crops to be planted, although in some places this did not occur until 1000 BCE. At that point, the fundamental features of Native American culture were in place, and the years toward 1492 saw these cultures growing in social complexity and population.

Scholars disagree on the pre-1492 population of the Americas. Until the 1950s, the figures of 8 million for the entire Western Hemisphere and 1 million for North America were generally accepted, but more recent analyses of the available evidence suggest a much larger population. Many scholars now estimate that between 75 and 145 million people inhabited the Western Hemisphere in 1492, of whom between 12 and 18 million lived in North America. There may well have been more people living in the Americas at this time than lived in Europe and Russia combined.

For thousands of years, there was no contact whatsoever between Europe and the Americas. While Christopher Columbus is acknowledged to have been the first European to establish permanent settlements in the hemisphere, he was by no means the first visitor there. Legends and accounts from various northern European cultures, combined with archaeological evidence found in North America, inform us that Europeans knew of North America hundreds of years before Columbus set sail.

In the mid-sixth century, according to legend, an Irish monk known as St. Brendan (b. 489) took a long voyage and ended up in a magical place called the Land of Promise, where all the plants were in constant bloom, all the trees had delicious fruit, and all the stones were gems. Some other passages in the account suggest that St. Brendan sailed across the northern Atlantic, but no one seriously believes that St. Brendan or other Irish explorers after him ever got past Iceland.

The pagan Norse people began depredations in England in 793 and probably had established colonies in Iceland by 800. By 980, the Norse had settled Greenland's southeastern coast, just 500 miles from Labrador in northeastern Canada. Around the year 1000, Leif Eriksson made landfall on Baffin Island, north of Labrador, on Labrador itself, and at another land that he called Vinland, probably the northern peninsula of present-day Newfoundland. Eriksson's exploits led to four more voyages to Vinland shortly after this and to sporadic voyages and short-lived settlements for perhaps another 300 years after that. Norse accounts of these voyages are supported by scattered archaeological findings, but scholars still know very little about the extent and duration of these settlements. The Norse were never plentiful enough or well armed enough to forge a permanent colony in the midst of what was, even then, a significant Native American population.

Another legendary pre-Columbian settler was Madoc, a Welsh prince who, some believe, came to America in the 12th century and founded a number of colonies in locations as diverse as Newfoundland and Mexico. The Yarmouth Stone, a rock with mysterious inscriptions discovered in Nova Scotia, and the Newport Tower, a stone structure found in Rhode Island, have been advanced as evidence of Madoc's visits to America, but most scholars remain unconvinced. Others identify Madoc with Quetzalcoatl, a white man who in Aztec legend visited Mexico at about the same time Madoc is supposed to have come to America.

There is, however, credible evidence that ships were traveling from Norway to Iceland and Greenland fairly regularly by the 14th century, but if these vessels sailed any closer to the eastern shore of the Canadian arctic, they were just passing by and their crews made no effort to establish settlements. These contacts with Canada increased during the 15th century, and, at the end of that century, an Italian, Giovanni Caboto, better known as John Cabot, was probably the first European to sail along the coast of eastern North America and recognize it for what it was.

Although most of the pre-Columbian contacts with America had been with Canada, the first permanent European settlements were well to the south, in the islands of the Caribbean. This is where Christopher Columbus and the many Europeans who followed him first encountered the indigenous peoples of America with such devastating effects.

Born in 1451 in Genoa, an Italian port city, Columbus had only a rudimentary education and, as a boy and a young man, worked at several trades, including weaving. From an early age, however, he was fascinated by the sea and began working on Mediterranean merchant ships while still in his teens. In the mid-1470s, he went to Lisbon,

Portugal, where he took advantage of the maritime economy to become a much better sailor. In Lisbon, he learned much about earlier voyages and the search for a western route to Asia, and he married into a well-connected Portuguese family.

In 1485, when the Portuguese king would not sanction and support Columbus's plan for a voyage to find Asia by going west, Columbus went to Spain. By this time, Spain had been united by the marriage of Ferdinand and Isabella, and Columbus began seeking support for a voyage as early as 1486. At this time, however, Spain was fighting the Moorish stronghold of Granada, and Columbus's supplications were not approved until early 1492, and then only to keep him from going elsewhere.

In all, Columbus made four voyages to what came to be known as the New World. His first voyage, 1492–1493, took him to the Bahamas, Cuba, and Hispaniola (the island where Haiti and the Dominican Republic are located). On his second voyage, 1493–1496, he visited Guadeloupe, the Leeward Islands, the Virgin Islands, and Puerto Rico. His third voyage, 1498–1500, took him along the northeast coast of South America, to Trinidad and then to the established colony on Hispaniola. There he got into political trouble and was sent back to Spain a prisoner in chains. He regained royal favor and made a fourth and final visit, 1502–1504, sailing along the coast of Central America from Honduras to Panama and stopping at other Caribbean islands.

In recent years and especially during 1992, the observance of the quincentenary of Columbus's first voyage, scholars have fiercely attacked the reputations of Columbus and other early European explorers and colonizers in America. As the interpretive essay points out, the Europeans treated the indigenous peoples they encountered with great brutality as they attempted to enslave them, plunder their valuables, or simply exterminate them. Perhaps the epidemic diseases the Europeans brought with them to America killed even more Indians than did the guns and swords of the colonizers.

This photograph shows a 20th-century replica of Columbus's flagship, the *Santa Maria.* (Courtesy of the Library of Congress, Detroit Publishing Company Collection.)

Epidemic diseases, mostly smallpox, measles, and influenza, first began killing Amerindians (the name given to Indians living in the Caribbean at the time of the first encounters with Europeans) in 1493 with the arrival of the ships of Columbus's second voyage. Smallpox was especially deadly among the Indians on the various Caribbean islands, because they had no natural immunity to this strange new disease, and an epidemic in 1518 attracted much commentary among Spanish colonial writers.

Measles was first reported in force during the 1530s, when an African slave could have spread it. Known in Europe, measles did not kill many whites, as smallpox sometimes did, but 25 or 30 percent of the Indians who caught it died, a figure that remained constant throughout the colonial period. The 16th century is marked with a series of deadly epidemics, notably in the 1540s and the late 1550s and between 1576 and 1591. By the end of the century, typhus, mumps, and possibly bubonic plague had been added to the list of fatal diseases. Some scholars estimate that more than 90 percent of the Indians in the Americas died from European-introduced diseases.

## INTERPRETIVE ESSAY

ANDREW FRANK

"In fourteen hundred and ninety-two, Columbus sailed the ocean blue." Across the nation, countless schoolteachers annually recite these lines to commemorate the trans-Atlantic travels of Christopher Columbus and his "discovery" of the "New World" in October 1492. Indeed, American history often begins with a discussion of the Italian-born sailor, his financing from Spain's King Ferdinand and Queen Isabella, and his three ships, the *Niña,* the *Pinta,* and the *Santa Maria.* Columbus Day is currently celebrated as a national holiday in the United States, and most Americans believe that this journey to the New World initiated American history. Despite the poem that is often recited and the holiday celebrated in his name, Americans often miss the grand importance of Columbus's arrival in the New World. Rather than a beginning, the year 1492 marked a revolutionary turning point in world and American history.

The New World that Columbus and subsequent European explorers encountered was neither unsettled nor in need of discovery. For that matter, it was not even "new." Instead, the first human settlers migrated to North America 12,000 to 40,000 years before Columbus made his more famous journey. Rather than sailing across the Atlantic Ocean in three caravels, these small bands of early migrants crossed a land bridge that covered what is now the Bering Strait, a narrow stretch of water and ice that separates eastern Siberia from the western coast of Alaska. During the Ice Age, falling temperatures caused glaciers to grow and ocean levels to drop. This process exposed a stretch of land as wide as 1,000 miles. Scientists call this region, which now lies some 120 feet under water, Beringia. Bands of nomadic Asian hunters, consisting of approximately 25 people each, gradually crossed Beringia as they searched for and followed large game animals—especially the mammoth. These migrations brought an unknown number of nomadic hunters, or Paleo-Indians, deeper and deeper into the Americas.

There, on lands previously uninhabited by humans, they found new hunting territories, rich natural resources, and hospitable climates. When the ice melted and the ocean waters separated the continents once again, the migration ended. This trapped an unknown number of bands in the Americas. By 10,000 BCE, descendants of these migrants had settled almost all of North and South America.

Over the course of thousands of years, the Paleo-Indians adapted to their diverse surroundings and formed countless communities across the Americas. Almost all of these communities used kinship or family groups, often called clans, to determine social, economic, political, and religious obligations. Despite their common ancestry, each of these tribes eventually developed its own thriving and distinct culture. The Indians spoke hundreds of languages, used various tools, and often traced themselves back to different ancestors. Some lived in agrarian societies, while others hunted and gathered; some lived in permanent cities and villages, while others lived more nomadic lives. Pre-Columbian Indians fought wars with each other, traded goods with one another, and created specialized crafts and elaborate pieces of art. Columbus and his men stumbled upon a world thousands of years old, one whose peoples had established cultures rich in heritage and history.

In every region of the Americas, Indians had distinct cultures and lifestyles. In New England, for example, the region was filled with small Algonquian villages that normally contained fewer than 300 residents. These hunter-gatherers were divided into hundreds of tribes, among them the Abenakis, Mohegans, Wampanoags, Narragansetts, Nipmucs, Pocumtucks, Mohawks, and Mashpees. Kin groups in each of these small tribes followed a seasonal pattern of hunting, fishing, shellfish collecting, plant gathering, and small-scale agriculture. Coastal bands harvested salmon, shad, eel, sturgeon, and whale. Indians farther inland hunted moose, deer, black bear, and beaver. Rather than following hereditary chiefs, these Algonquians made political decisions by consensus and gave authority to those who could lead and persuade others to agree. Quite a different Indian culture emerged in what is now California. There, pre-Columbian Indians grew tobacco and harvested dozens of other foods that grew naturally in the area. The men hunted and fished, and the women prepared these foodstuffs for consumption and storage. These Indians typically lived in villages that numbered around 1,000 persons. Native peoples lived in even larger groups in what is today Florida. There, Indians lived in chiefdoms that numbered in the thousands. In these hierarchical societies, most villages paid tribute to the larger and more powerful chiefdoms. Most Indian men hunted, while women spent much of their time cultivating crops. Some of Florida's Indians used slash-and-burn techniques to ensure plentiful crops, and nearly all of the Indian communities in the Southeast grew the "holy trinity" of corn, beans, and squash. The emphasis on agriculture allowed many Indians in Florida to work as specialized artisans, full-time soldiers, or bureaucrats. In sum, pre-Columbian Indians did not share a single lifestyle.

Diversity also characterized the religions practiced by Indians in pre-Columbian America. Some Native Americans believed that spirits of gods inhabited the trees around them; others believed that they lived in a cosmic drama in which the gods competed for power. Some, like the northeastern Iroquois, believed that their ancestors had fallen from the sky, while others, like the southwestern Navajo, believed that their ancestors had emerged from the earth. The religious ceremonies and rituals of these diverse peoples involved altars and sacrifices, dances and songs, chants and potions. Many of these events took place on a seasonal calendar, especially those that celebrated the harvest, like the Cherokees' Green Corn Ceremony. Other ceremonies, like the Plains Indians' Sun Dance, were less tied to the calendar.

Estimates of the Native American population in 1492 vary widely for good reasons: no census was taken by Native peoples before the arrival of Europeans; archeological findings conflict with each other, are incomplete, or are difficult to assess; and European observers wrote only about the handful of peoples that they encountered in the decades after contact. Limited sources, as well as ethnocentric attitudes about Indians' culture that guided early scholarship, led most early 20th-century scholars to underestimate the Indian population on the eve of European contact. Until rather recently, most scholars believed that no more than 1 million Native Americans lived north of Mexico in 1492. In essence, they believed that the land that later became the United States was a "virgin land" untouched by human hands before the arrival of Europeans. In recent years, this description has been radically reassessed. The Smithsonian Institution, perhaps the most conservative participant in the debate, has doubled its estimate, claiming that there "may have been as many as two million" inhabitants in the region. Most recent scholars have offered more revolutionary reassessments of pre-Columbian America. These demographers have convincingly shown that before the arrival of Europeans, at least 12 to 18 million Indians made their homes in what is now the United States; North America was neither an empty nor an underpopulated continent,. In North and South America, the Native American population probably ranged between 43 and 65 million. Other scholars have asserted that the population for the Americas may have even approached 100 million or as much as one-fifth of the Earth's human population. Scholars have not reached consensus in demographic assessments of pre-Columbian America. This debate over numbers promises to continue, but the idea of the Americas as empty land has been universally dismissed. Scholars, even as they disagree over actual numbers, now agree that much of America was well populated by 1492.

Rather than virgin soil, the Americas became what historian Francis Jennings describes as "widowed land." America seemed empty to 16th-, 17th-, and 18th-century Europeans because most of its inhabitants had died. In the decades following contact, nearly all Native communities lost at least half of their population, and most communities suffered from even higher mortality rates. In the century after European contact, America's total Indian population dropped between 90 and 95 percent. This widespread depopulation began as a result of the arrival of Columbus and other European explorers and settlers. These European newcomers introduced a wide range of pathogens, flora, and fauna to American ecosystems in which they had never before existed. This Columbian exchange—the most important ramification of Columbus's journey—transferred countless pathogens, grains, grasses, large mammals, small rodents, insects, trees, shrubs, and birds. The introduction of European diseases to the Americas resulted in the rapid depopulation of Native populations. The arrival of American grains across the Atlantic fed a surging European population. New technology transformed Native society, and the introduction of sugar cane to the Americas was soon followed by the arrival of African slaves. In short, the disruption caused by this biological exchange between the continents irrevocably altered the lives of Native Americans and humanity at large.

Before most Native Americans actually met a European explorer or colonist or heard of their existence, they felt the impact of the Columbian exchange's deadly pathogens. Germs, viruses, and bacteria entered a world that they had not been in before. The lack of exposure to these European diseases left Native peoples without biological immunity, genetic resistance, or effective medical responses to the new pathogens. Indians suffered disproportionately when diseases hit their communities for the first time. As a result, smallpox, measles, influenza, chicken pox, whooping cough, malaria, amoebic dysentery, diphtheria, and the bubonic plague killed all or nearly all of the inhabitants of some Indian villages. After traveling in New Netherland in 1656, for example, Dutchman Adriaen Van der Donck wrote that "the Indians…affirm, that before the arrival of the Christians, and before the small pox broke out amongst them, they were ten times as numerous as they now are, and that their population had been melted down by this disease, whereof nine-tenths of them have died." Even though Columbus and other early explorers did not venture far from the Atlantic Coast, Native nations that lived as far west as California confronted the full force of the European diseases that spread across the Americas.

Those who survived the initial onslaught of the European diseases faced the nightmare of dealing with the sick, the infirm, and the deceased. After the loss of young adults to death and sickness, Indian villages could not meet their nutritional needs through hunting and farming. Throughout the Americas, the ensuing starvation and malnutrition simply added to the mounting death tolls. In the early 17th century, Gov. William Bradford found coastal New England to be nearly barren, the Indians "being dead & abundantly wasted in the last great mortality which fell in these parts about three years before the coming of the English, wherein thousands of them dyed." Bradford was further struck by the Indians "not being able to burie one another; their sculs and bones were found in many places lying still above ground, where their houses & dwellings had been."

The epidemics haunted Native Americans long after the initial contacts with European pathogens. Although Native Americans slowly built immunities to the new diseases, smallpox, measles, bubonic plague, and influenza continued to cripple the Native communities into the 18th and 19th centuries. Some Guale, Timucua, and Apalachee Indians, for example, survived the waves of disease that ravaged the Southeast in the 16th and 17th centuries, but newer epidemics had wiped them out by the American Revolution. Similarly, in 1763, Ottawa Indians suffered from smallpox after Lord Jeffrey Amherst gave them blankets that previously had been used to cover infected British soldiers. The disease quickly spread among the Delaware, Mingo, Miami, and several other Indian nations. Some 100,000 Indians lost their lives in this epidemic. Fatal disease, along with falling birth rates, increased warfare, and famine prevented Indian populations from returning to their previous numbers. The disruption of the Columbian exchange clearly outlived Columbus.

The widespread destruction of Native peoples caused a restructuring of tribal and national affiliations across the Americas. The creation of the Creek Confederacy in what later became Georgia and Florida typified this process. When Hernando de Soto plundered through the Southeast in 1540 looking for gold, he encountered dozens of individual Indian chiefdoms, including the Coosa, Apalachee, and the Alabama. There was no Creek Confederacy. The deadly European diseases that de Soto's Spanish forces left behind, however, resulted in the collapse in the region's Native population. Over the next century, the survivors regrouped and formed a new entity that eventually became known as the Creek Confederacy. Ethnic Muskogee Indians, later known as the Creeks, were at the core of this new polity. To bolster their size and strength, the Muskogees invited the remnants of other southeastern Indian nations and villages into their confederation. By the 18th century, thousands of non-Muskogee Indians from dozens of ethnic groups had made a home among the ever-expanding Confederacy. For this reason, the Creeks were the only Indian group to see its population expand in the 17th and 18th centuries.

Declining populations led to tribal restructuring throughout the Americas during the 16th and 17th centuries. For example, in New England, Indians who had earlier lived in small bands became dependent on the fur trade with French and English traders. This encouraged the region's small bands to create mechanisms of centralized power, or a single chief, to negotiate with the Europeans, who were hesitant to deal with countless leaders. Political restructuring also altered the Iroquois Confederacy. This Native alliance, also known as the Iroquois League or Five Nations, existed before the arrival of Europeans. Even so, the arrival of Europeans and Old World pathogens created new demands. By the 1680s, for the first time, village headmen from across the Iroquois League began consulting one another on a regular basis, and the Iroquois began speaking as a unified voice for the first time. In large part, this break from traditional forms of local authority resulted from the death of many prominent elders. As a group of Mohawk warriors asserted in 1691, "All those…who had sense are dead." The diseases of the Columbian exchange had taken their toll.

The Columbian exchange brought more than new diseases to the Americas. It also introduced new plants and animals that reshaped the American environment and Indian economies. After 1492, the flora and fauna of the Americas and of Europe, whose plants and animals had existed isolated from each other, slowly became more alike. Indeed, the ecosystem of 15th-century America seemed to be radically different from the European scenery to which Columbus had become accustomed. Columbus wrote, "I saw neither sheep nor goats nor any other beast. If there were any I couldn't have failed to see them." Columbus did not encounter domesticated animals in his travels, and the animals that he did observe were often unlike anything he had seen before. Generations of European settlers and scientists confirmed these initial observations. The New World alligators and crocodiles startled the Europeans, as the Old World had no reptiles larger than the iguana. Even stranger to European sensibilities were the electric eels and flesh-eating piranhas found in the Americas. The exotic American scenery also included monkeys that could swing from their tails, snakes with rattles on their tails, and huge bison and buffalo. The range of insects, the size of the rodents, and the plethora of freshwater fish similarly surprised the Europeans.

The arrival of European animals to the Americas transformed the American countryside. In addition to cattle and swine, Europeans also brought chickens, sheep, horses, and domesticated dogs and cats. Sometimes Europeans transplanted the new animals to fit their uniquely European needs. Members of the 17-century Virginian gentry, for example, introduced red foxes to the Chesapeake region to participate in English-style hunting. Similarly, some Dutch and English settlers introduced honeybees to the Americas to provide an Old World sweetener for their diet. Other imports came as unintentional stowaways on the trans-Atlantic vessels that brought explorers and colonists. In this way, English sparrows filled the skies of colonial America, and the American cockroach, brought over on slave ships from Africa, infested colonial homes.

The European plants of the Columbian exchange further changed the American countryside. Soon after his arrival in the New World, Columbus observed that "all the trees were so different from ours as day from night, and so the fruits, the herbage, the rocks, and all things." Within decades, America contained much of what Columbus believed it lacked. Like the first wave of disease and some of the animals, much of the flora that came to the Americas accidentally took root in America. Colonists unwittingly transported seeds for grasses and clovers in the textiles, blankets, and dirty boots brought from Europe. In this way, Europeans transformed much of the countryside. By 1700, for example, a European bluegrass covered Kentucky. Daisies and dandelions, not indigenous to the Americas, also spread across the countryside.

Many other plants made their way into the New World because of the conscious designs of explorers and settlers. Indeed, almost immediately after their arrival in the Americas, Europeans worked to change the New World to fit their image of the Old World. Spanish friars, for example, introduced wheat to grow the grain needed to make communion wafers. Europeans also imported and planted chickpeas, melons, onions, radishes, grapes, olives, and bananas. These crops changed the landscape and helped dictate the path that colonization would take. Perhaps most important to the development of the early colonies, European settlers introduced sugar cane in the Caribbean and South America. The ramifications of this import were felt worldwide as Europeans turned to African slaves to tend to the highly profitable crop. In the centuries that followed, slave traders brought at least 11 million enslaved Africans to the Americas to cultivate this and other labor-intensive crops.

The incorporation of new animals in Native societies was not necessarily a smooth process. On one hand, many Indian people took advantage of the new animals. Plains Indians, such as the Comanche and Cheyenne, used horses to hunt buffalo and other large game. Navajo and Pueblo Indians incorporated sheep and goats into their diets and economies. Cherokee, Creek, and Choctaw Indians domesticated cattle. At the same time, however, the arrival of some new animals disrupted many traditional patterns. Newly introduced range animals competed with indigenous game for scarce grazing grounds and water supplies and also trampled over Indian cornfields. At times, disputes over animals resulted in warfare. Southeastern Indians, even as they incorporated domesticated animals into their diet, constantly complained to the colonial governments of Georgia and South Carolina about the damage done by the free-range pigs and cattle that the English had introduced. Similarly, in 17th-century New England, many Indians incorporated domesticated pigs into their lifestyles. The ensuing disputes over grazing rights resulted in many small skirmishes that contributed to the outbreak of King Philip's War in 1675–1676.

The Columbian exchange also brought new technology and products to the New World. These products, which included metal tools, guns, and liquor, reshaped the lifestyle of the Native Americans. Most Indians quickly replaced tools made of bone and wood with metallic versions. Europeans traders offered steel axes and knives, iron kettles, woolen clothing, blankets, linen shirts, jackets, scissors, thimbles, needles and thread in return for valuable animal pelts, furs, and skins. The demand for European items created networks of trade between European and Indian communities. In many Native communities, the demand for European goods resulted in the increased "production" of animal furs. With men spending more time hunting and women spending more time preparing pelts for trade, Indian peoples became increasingly dependent on Europeans for food and clothing. This dependence often resulted in greater demands by European traders, increased prices for trade goods, new political loyalties, and occasionally the sale of tribal lands to pay off mounting debts. At times, Indians sold their enemies to European slave traders in return for desired trade goods.

The Indian trade often resulted in the entrance of European settlers into Indian villages. Thousands of intermarriages between Indian women and European men occurred in colonial America, especially in the Great Lakes region and in the lower Southeast. Native wives proved to be invaluable assets to European traders because they provided companionship and residences, solicited business, and informed them about the community's general temperature. Furthermore, traders benefited from the labor of their wives, who interpreted for them, collected debts from Indians, prepared animal skins for market, and, as British traveler John Lawson explained, "instruct[ed] [th]em in the Affairs and Customs of the Country."

Intermarriages in the lower south, especially within the Creek, Cherokee, and Choctaw Nations, created generations of "mixed" individuals. Often these so-called half breeds became proponents of acculturation. They helped bring African slaves, cotton cultivation, centralized forms of government, and written laws to Native society. By the early 19th century, the Cherokees had a tribal government that reflected European systems. The new tribal government contained a bicameral legislature, elected officials, an elected head chief with a limited term of power, and a court system.

Among the new ideas that Europeans brought to the New World, perhaps the most intrusive was Christianity. Few Europeans saw anything in Indian society that they recognized as organized religion. At best, they saw Indians as unchurched individuals immersed in superstition; at worst, they believed Indians practiced devil worship. In either case, Europeans viewed Indians as prime candidates for "the work tending to the enlargement of the Kingdom of Jesus Christ." European missionaries attempted to convert Indians throughout North and South America. In almost every case, Indian peoples saw these attempts as hostile assaults on their traditional beliefs and customs.

Only a handful of 17th-century Christian missionaries successfully converted many Indian peoples in what later became the United States. Puritan ministers, led by John Eliot, established "praying towns" for the conversion of New England's Wampanoag Indians in 1646. The most successful of these missions was established at Martha's Vineyard, where 282 Indians entered the covenant and an Indian church was established. The Massachusetts Bay Company used the power of the law to coerce neighboring Indians into converting, but even this could not convince most of New England's Natives to accept Christianity. By the end of the 17th century, only four of the original "praying towns" remained. Farther south, Spain established more than 150 missions in Florida. Spanish friars obtained the allegiance of thousands of Guale, Timucua, and Apalachee Indians and extracted the labor of their parishioners. Most of these missions were short lived, however, and by 1700 there were no remaining Guale or Timucua converts. Within a few decades, Spain had to abandon nearly all of its missions among the Apalachee Indians.

Apart from these short-lived successes, most Christian missionaries had difficulty converting Indian peoples. This frustrated many religious leaders, who, instead of looking at the intrusive behavior of the Christian missionaries, found fault in the "Indian's character." Methodist leader John Wesley, for example, believed that the Indians' "insatiate love of drink, as well as other European vices" made conversion an impossible task. The Indians, he stated, "show no inclination to learn anything, but least of all Christianity." Indeed, as many Europeans noticed, so-called converted Indians never fully accepted Christianity on the missionaries' terms. In most cases, Indians blended Christian doctrines with their traditional beliefs and formed new syncretic faiths. British commissioner George Cartwright observed that in New England, "those whom they say are converted cannot be distinguished by their lives, manners, or habits from those who are not."

While Indian peoples suffered massive depopulation and cultural disruption, the Columbian exchange helped Europe's population to flourish. The Americas provided an endless list of new food, including maize (or corn), several kinds of beans, potatoes, sweet potatoes, peanuts, tomatoes, pumpkins, papaya, squash, guava, avocados, pineapples, chili peppers, and cocoa beans. These agricultural products eventually turned the Americas into the breadbox of the world and allowed European farmers to increase their ability to feed themselves. These food products helped to put an end to the famine and fear of famine that had kept European populations in relative check in previous centuries. Europe, whose population hovered slightly above 100 million from 1450 to 1650, saw its population explode to 144 million in 1740 and 192 million in 1800. The introduction of American vegetables also affected the traditional foods of European cultures. Ireland adopted the potato as its central caloric source by the 18th century. Similarly, generations after it arrived in Europe, the tomato transformed Italian cuisine. Some nonedible crops transformed Europe, as well. The Americas provided the world with tobacco, rubber, and most forms of cotton. These exports remained among the most lucrative for American farmers. Just as fortunate to the development of Europe, America did not export a deadly range of pathogens. Although some suggest that syphilis may have been transported to Europe from the Americas, there were no New World counterparts to smallpox, measles, or the bubonic plague. In comparison to the Americas, where Native peoples primarily suffered from the Columbian exchange, Europeans generally prospered from the "new" American foods and raw materials.

In 1540, a mere five decades after the arrival of Columbus, a southeastern chief struggled to describe what the collision with the Old World meant to his people: "The things that seldom happen bring astonishment. Think, then, what must be the effect on me and mine, the sight of you and your people, whom we have at no time seen, stride the fierce brutes, your horses, entering with such speed and fury into my country, that we had not tidings of your coming." Astonishment, he admitted, hardly approached a description of what had happened after 1492 or of the impact the forces that Columbus's "discovery" unleashed. In the decades that preceded and followed this statement, Native societies witnessed waves of epidemics across the Americas, the alteration of their traditional diet and customs, a change in their trading and hunting patterns across the Americas, and a cultural assault on their religious belief systems by Christian missionaries. The Columbian exchange resulted in the population explosion of Europe and Asia, the massive population movement across the Atlantic, the rise of a trans-Atlantic slave trade, and the expansion of world trade. In short, Columbus may not have found a continent in need of "discovery," but he did make 1492 a turning point in world history.

## SELECTED BIBLIOGRAPHY

Axtell, James. *Beyond 1492: Encounters in Colonial North America.* New York: Oxford University Press, 1992. A book of essays dealing with the first encounters between Europeans and Native Americans and the historical treatment of that event since 1492.

Bray, Warwick, et al. *The New World.* Oxford, England: Elsevier-Phaidon, 1975. A heavily illustrated survey of the archeological and ethnological history of North America before 1492.

Cook, Noble David. *Born to Die: Disease and New World Conquest, 1492–1650.* Cambridge: Cambridge University Press, 1998. A survey of the various epidemics of smallpox, measles, typhus, and other diseases that proved fatal to millions of American Indians.

Denevan, William M., ed. *The Native Populations of the Americas in 1492.* 2nd ed. Madison: University of Wisconsin Press, 1992. First published in 1976 as a pioneer demographic study, this book has been updated and its conclusions altered based on more recent population studies.

Fernandez-Armesto, Filipe. *Columbus.* New York: Oxford University Press, 1992. Short, balanced account of the explorer's life and career.

Jennings, Francis. *The Invasion of America: Indians, Colonialism, and the Cant of Conquest.* Chapel Hill: University of North Carolina Press, 1975. Jennings was one of the first historians to look at European colonization from an Indian viewpoint.

Josephy, Alvin, M., Jr., ed. *America in 1492: The World of the Indian People Before the Arrival of Columbus.* New York: Knopf, 1992. A collection of scholarly articles on the various American Indian groups and their cultures in the 15th century.

———. *The Indian Heritage of America.* Rev. ed. Boston: Houghton-Mifflin, 1991. Josephy, a titan of American Indian history, devotes fully half of this survey history to the pre-conquest era.

Morison, Samuel Eliot. *Admiral of the Ocean Sea: A Life of Christopher Columbus.* Boston: Little, Brown, 1942. For many years, this book stood as the definitive life of Columbus, but it is now outdated in its interpretation.

Oleson, Tryggvi J. *Early Voyages and Northern Approaches, 1000–1632.* Toronto: McClellan and Stewart, 1963. A history of the early voyages from Scandinavia and the British Isles to Iceland, Greenland, and North America.

Phillips, William D., Jr., and Carla Rahn Phillips. *The Worlds of Christopher Columbus.* Cambridge: Cambridge University Press, 1992. A study of Columbus and his times that treats him neither as a hero nor an unprincipled villain.

Stannard, David E. *American Holocaust: Columbus and the Conquest of the New World.* New York: Oxford University Press, 1992. A detailed history of the early encounters between Europeans and American Indians, with emphasis on the destructive effects of the diseases and purposeful violence that the Europeans brought.

Thornton, Russell. *American Indian Holocaust and Survival: A Population History since 1492.* Norman: University of Oklahoma Press, 1987. A demographic study of the decline in Indian population from 1492 to 1900 and its rise since then.

# ALGONQUIN

"Algonquin" or "Algonkin" probably comes from a Micmac word meaning "at the place of spearing fish and eels from the bow of a canoe." It is the name of a northeastern group of bands that also gave its name to an important language family. The original self-designation was *Anishinabeg,* or "true men." Principal Algonquin bands included the Weskarinis (the Algonquins proper), Abitibis, and Temiskamings. In the early 17th century, Algonquins lived in the Ottawa Valley of Quebec and Ontario, particularly along the northern tributary rivers. Algonquins spoke an Algonquin language.

The people believed in a great creator spirit and a host of lesser spirits, both good and evil. Both shamans and hunters sought guardian spirits to help them with their work, which included interpreting dreams and healing the sick. Small bands were composed of one or more clans with local chiefs. People smoked tobacco silently before council meetings. Algonquins entertained visitors with the annual Feast of the Dead, a dance with a war theme. When entertaining guests, the host did not eat. Clan descent as well as the inheritance of hunting territories may have been patrilineal. Bands tended to come together in the summer and disperse in the winter. People lived in cone-shaped, teepee-like dwellings. They also built rectangular birchbark hunting shelters.

Men fished in both the summer and winter (through holes cut in the ice). They hunted game such as moose, deer, caribou, and beaver. Agricultural crops played a small role in their diet. Important material items included birchbark containers sewn with spruce roots, basswood bags and mats, wooden cradle boards, bows and arrows, and double-headed drums. Algonquins imported fish nets and cornmeal from the Hurons and traded extensively with Iroquoian tribes. They traded animal pelts and porcupine quills to nearby groups in exchange for corn, tobacco, fishing gear, and wampum.

Men made birchbark canoes, snowshoes, and toboggans. Dress varied according to location. Most clothing was made of buckskin or moose skin. Clothing included breech-clouts, skirts, ponchos, leggings, robes, and moccasins; moccasins were often dyed black. Fur garments were added in cold weather.

Algonquins lived on the north shore of the Saint Lawrence River from about 1550 to 1650. They began trading with the French in the early 16th century and later provoked a war with the Mohawks. The Algonquins won that skirmish with the assistance provided by the French in order to maintain an important trade partner.

However, the French had made a powerful enemy in the Mohawks, and within a few decades the local military situation had been reversed, with the Iroquois now firmly in control. Meanwhile, the Hurons had replaced the Algonquins as the key French trade partner. The Mohawks, needing to expand their trapping area, soon attacked again. The Algonquins were forced to abandon the upper Saint Lawrence and, after about 1650, the Ottawa Valley. They returned in the 1660s, when peace was reestablished. An epidemic in the 1670s left them further weakened.

During the late 17th century, some Algonquin bands merged with the Ottawa Indians. French trading posts were established, and missionaries became a permanent presence in their territory by the early 18th century. Some Algonquins traveled to the far west to trap for Canadian companies. After the final French defeat, in 1763, the Algonquins became staunch British allies. Reserves for the group were created in the 19th century, when their lands were overrun by British settlers. The decline of the fur trade and of their hunting grounds (mainly owing to local logging operations), as well as a growing dependence on non-Natives, led many Algonquins to adopt a sedentary lifestyle.

BARRY M. PRITZKER

## ANASAZI CULTURE

The Anasazi culture refers to a North American tradition that emerged around CE 100 in the area where the borders of present-day Arizona, Colorado, New Mexico, and Utah intersect. The word "Anasazi" comes from the Navajo word for "old ones." The Anasazi evolved from a semisedentary culture characterized by its basketry (in the period from CE 100 to CE 700) into a village and town-based culture known for its large cliff dwellings and multistory structures (until the late 13th century). As agriculture developed around 600, the Anasazi became more sedentary. The Anasazi abandoned their large communities by the 14th century and merged with other Native American cultures in the Southwest.

The origins of the Anasazi remain uncertain, but they were related culturally to the neighboring Mogollon and Hohokam cultures. For the first two stages of their development (Basket Maker and Modified Basket Maker), from 100 to 750, the Anasazi were hunter-gatherers who lived in caves or in simple pole-and-mud structures built over pits. They adopted the bow and arrow, and, as could be expected of a people who had only recently given up a nomadic lifestyle, hunting remained important. The Anasazi culture also produced some excellent basketry crafted from plant fibers in a wide variety of shapes and sizes, often with elaborate designs.

In the next two stages of development (Developmental and Classic Pueblo), from 700 to 1300, the Anasazi began building sandstone block dwellings, replacing the older pole-and-mud pit construction. Archaeological evidence suggests that when the Anasazi economy shifted to agriculture, above-ground architectural innovations followed. The Anasazi gradually became more dependent on farming maize and beans. A noticeable increase in food production created a greater need to store those crops, which above-ground masonry provided. Continuous ecological changes, including droughts, created a further need for long-term storage.

As they moved above ground, they began using their old underground living chambers, called kivas, as places to hold ceremonies. The physical area of the Anasazi occupation shrank during that time; however, the population increased as more people concentrated in larger towns.

In some places, the Anasazi became cliff dwellers and built their villages into cliff faces. In other locations, they built multistory, freestanding apartment-like structures against mesa or canyon walls. Two of the most well-known Anasazi towns were the settlement at Chaco Canyon and the Mesa Verde Cliff Palace.

The Anasazi towns were linked by a 400-mile network of roads. They carried on a vibrant long-distance trade with other groups of Mesoamerican people as far away as the Gulf of Mexico and the Pacific Ocean. Agriculture became more sophisticated with the development of terracing and irrigation systems, and pottery gradually replaced baskets for many uses in Anasazi life.

During the early 12th century, frequent droughts occurred, especially at Chaco Canyon. Scholars contend that, after the severe droughts, the Anasazi lost confidence in their priests, who had been responsible for calling on the rain deities. Thus, dispersion may have been attributed to both ecological and sociocultural factors.

Later in the 13th century, the Anasazi began abandoning their large villages and towns after a long drought and raids by aggressive Apache. Most of the Anasazi moved west and south and joined other traditions throughout the American Southwest.

They gradually merged with other Native American peoples who are now known collectively as the Pueblo Indians. Modern-day descendants of the Anasazi peoples include

Acoma, Hopi, Isleta, Jemez, Keres, San Ildefonso, Taos, Tewa, and Zuni. Many of the crafts and skills developed by the Anasazi culture continue in modified forms today.

KEVIN MARSH

## CHRISTOPHER COLUMBUS (1451–1506)

Navigator of the first recorded European expedition to cross the Atlantic Ocean in search of the elusive route to Asia, Christopher Columbus landed instead on islands in the Caribbean Sea. His voyage, which was well publicized in Europe, stimulated exploration of what was for 15th-century Europeans an undiscovered world, the Americas. Although Columbus's discovery of the Americas presented undreamed of opportunities for Europeans, it also marked the beginning of several centuries of famine, disease, dislocation, and violence for the Native American peoples already living in the Western Hemisphere.

Columbus was born Cristoforo Columbo in Genoa, Italy, in 1451, to Domenico Columbo, a master weaver and part-time wine shop owner, and Suzanna Fontanarossa. He received little or no formal education in his youth. He never wrote in Italian but did learn to read and write in Spanish and Portuguese. Columbus spent much of his youth working as an apprentice to his father's trade, but, by his own account, he took to the sea at a "tender age." His earliest trading voyages were likely to have been to collect supplies of wool or wine.

At the age of 19, Columbus made his first trading voyage in the Aegean Sea. In his early twenties, he began to make longer voyages to Marseilles and Tunis, as well as to the Greek island of Chios (then a Genoese colony). In 1476, Columbus set out for Flanders and England, but his vessel was sunk by French privateers. He landed penniless in Portugal and was taken in by one of many Genoese living in Lisbon, which was then the principal European center of overseas exploration. At Lisbon, Columbus acquired most of his knowledge of navigation.

In 1479, Columbus married Felipa Perestrello e Moniz, the daughter of a widow of a distinguished family who had inherited property in Madeira and an interest in the hereditary captaincy of the island of Porto Santo. By this marriage, he had a son, Diego, who was born in 1480. In Madeira, Columbus learned about island discovery and settlement and caught the optimistic enthusiasm for charting new islands that was characteristic of the time.

Columbus's idea of sailing west to the Indies seems to have been inspired by three sources: Florentine cosmographer Paolo Toscanelli, Cardinal Pierre d'Ailly's *Image of the World,* and Marco Polo's account of the Far East. Columbus theorized that the world was predominately covered in land and that the distance to Asia was much shorter than previously thought. Although he clearly sought adventure, his primary motivations were most likely the pursuit of honor and wealth. When the king of Portugal rejected Columbus's proposal to finance the voyage, he turned to Spain, where he received high praise and royal patronage for his proposed adventure.

In April 1492, King Ferdinand V and Queen Isabella I of Spain agreed to sponsor the expedition. On the first voyage, Columbus commanded three ships: the *Santa Maria,* the *Pinta,* and the *Niña.* The fleet departed on August 3, 1492, from Palos, Spain. The length of the voyage tested the will of the new explorers, but on October 12, the expedition sighted Guanahaní, an island in the Bahamas. Columbus renamed the island San Salvador and claimed it for Spain. The expedition also landed on Cuba and Española (later called Hispaniola, which now comprises the Dominican Republic and Haiti), where Columbus left 40 men before returning to Spain to an enthusiastic welcome in 1493.

On his return, Isabella commanded Columbus to sail again immediately. Columbus embarked on a second expedition with 17 ships and 1,000 colonists in September 1493. Upon returning to Española, he discovered that the men he had left behind had been killed by the Natives. On this second voyage, Columbus landed on the islands of Dominica, Guadeloupe, and Antigua and established the first European settlement in the Americas—the colony of Isabella, near what is now Cape Isabella, in the Dominican Republic. He explored the coast of Cuba in the spring of 1494 and, before returning to Spain in June 1496, established a new capital on Española that he called Santo Domingo. It was at the end of this second voyage that many colonists who had sailed with him and then returned to Spain began to express criticism of Columbus and his ventures, but the queen continued to support him.

In May 1498, Columbus set out on his third expedition. He landed on the island of Trinidad and sighted what is now Venezuela, discovering South America. When he arrived in Santo Domingo, Columbus found the colony of Española in revolt. Across the Atlantic in Spain, discontented colonists finally managed to persuade the reigning monarchs that Española demanded a new governor. The king and queen removed Columbus in May 1499 and appointed Francisco de Bobadilla to establish order in the colony. Columbus was subsequently arrested and sent back to Spain in chains. On his return, the queen pardoned Columbus but refused to restore his office as governor of Española.

In May 1502, Columbus ventured on his fourth and final expedition. Hampered by hurricane damage to the fleet, he managed to reach Honduras and searched in vain for nearly six months along the Central American coast for the passage across the continent to Asia. In January 1503, Columbus landed at Panama and established a colony. In June of that same year, his fleet became marooned near Jamaica. Columbus summoned help from Española, but the stranded expedition waited nearly one year for rescue.

After returning to Spain in 1504, Columbus found he had lost not only his title as governor of the Indies but his chief support in the person of Isabella, who had died earlier that year, on November 26. Suffering from arthritis, humiliated, and frustrated by the elusive fame and wealth that he so fiercely sought through his discoveries, Columbus died in Valladolid on May 20, 1506. His remains were ultimately laid to rest, alongside those of his son Diego, at the cathedral of Santo Domingo in 1542.

Columbus was not the first European to land in the Americas. Navigators from Norway, Iceland, or Greenland had settled briefly in Newfoundland in the late 10th or early 11th century. Evidence also exists to suggest that English fishermen may have sighted some part of North America prior to Columbus's first voyage. Columbus's discoveries in the Western Hemisphere, however, are distinguished from those of other adventurers by their consequences, mainly that they were followed by rapid, widespread, and permanent European settlement.

## HOPEWELL CULTURE

Hopewell culture, which flourished from 200 BCE to CE 400, was a period of development in the Native American woodland civilization centered in the Ohio and Mississippi river valleys. The Hopewell were the first Native American peoples fully committed to agriculture. Along with the adoption of agriculture, Hopewell civilization developed long-distance trade networks that contributed to the growth of religion and ritual.

The name "Hopewell" is taken from the farm name in Ross County, Ohio, where the first site of the people's burial mounds were studied. The people were first known as the Mound Builders, but it was later concluded that the Hopewell were only one of many such aboriginal cultures to build extensive mound structures for various uses.

Sometime around the turn of the first century CE, Hopewell culture improved agricultural techniques that Native Americans had been experimenting with since 3000 BCE. Archaic Native American agriculture was traditionally used to supplemental food obtained by foraging (hunting and gathering). Hopewell culture no longer foraged full time but chose to develop farms that cultivated seed-bearing plants like sunflowers and squash; the introduction of maize and bean agriculture was still limited. Although there were regional variations, Hopewell agriculturalists contributed to the development of social stratification.

In a sense, the Hopewell adopted agriculture because of an increase in population and the expansion of exchange networks, those informal trade networks that developed tied Hopewell culture to Native peoples in the regions of Wyoming, the Great Lakes, and the Gulf of Mexico. Archaeologists have shown that the elaborate network of rivers—notably the Mississippi, Missouri, Ohio, and Tennessee—facilitated the growth of trade.

Hopewell sophistication and geographic expansion surpassed those of the preceding Adena culture. The Hopewell were noted for splendid funerary art, discovered in the hundreds of burial and ritual mounds found throughout the region. Such ritual earthworks as the Great Serpent Mound, in Ohio, indicate the growing importance of religion as well as the Hopewell's capacity to organize relatively large groups of people for cooperative efforts. The use of unsmelted copper in tools and art was also refined, as was the spread of utensils and pottery for feasts and religious ritual.

By roughly CE 400, the Hopewell trading network had collapsed, shattering the cultural continuity and agricultural communities. Over the next 400 years, the woodland civilization continued, but the people were divided into numerous small regional cultures with limited interaction.

TIM BARNARD

## MISSISSIPPIAN CULTURE

The Mississippian culture, renowned for its distinctive mound dwellings, dominated its region for a period of nearly 700 years. The nascent Mississippian culture first arose along the fertile banks of the Mississippi River of North America sometime around CE 800. At its height, the Mississippian culture extended across vast tracts of the American Southeast and Midwest. Mississippian culture also moved northward to the Minnesota region and eventually westward into the Great Plains. That expansion was due to several factors, including a frequent cycle of warfare with neighboring tribes and a propensity for forging diplomatic and trade alliances.

The most telling indication of the geographical extent of the Mississippian culture is its renowned temple mounds. Those massive earthen structures—the largest of which spans 14 acres at its base and reaches heights of 100 feet—formed the center of large-scale temple complexes. Located in present-day Illinois, Monks Mound, which is a part of Cahokia Mounds, is widely acknowledged as the most illustrious example of Mississippian architecture. The urban centers that were supported by extensive satellite villages and farming communities were autonomous, well-organized political entities, although alliances and fluid confederacies with like-minded neighboring city-states were not uncommon.

An abundantly industrious people, the Mississippians excelled at stone carving, pottery, woodwork, weaponry, and agriculture. Maize cultivation formed the backbone of the Mississippian economy, although Mississippians also produced squash and beans. Overcultivation, shorter growing seasons, and shortages of arable land were among the key factors contributing to the decline of the Mississippian culture ca. 1500.

When European explorers encroached on the Americas in the early 16th century, the waning Mississippian societies were dealt a traumatic blow. Unable to successfully fend off the invaders, the Mississippian peoples were ravaged by diseases contracted from the Spanish conquistadors. The combination of disease, dispersal, and foreign invasion, coupled with the depletion of natural resources, brought about the rapid demise of the once-dominant culture.

The Mississippians represent the last Native American culture to dominate the North American continent immediately prior to the European conquest. Despite their decline, many contemporary tribes descend from the Mississippians, including the Natchez.

CARTER MCBEATH

## DOCUMENT: JOURNAL OF CHRISTOPHER COLUMBUS, 1492

> *The discoverer of the "New World," the Italian Christopher Columbus, landed in the West Indies in October 1492 and proclaimed the region the property of the king and queen of Spain. Columbus's well-publicized discovery fueled the mania for exploration that was sweeping over European adventurers, initiating a period in which various European powers attempted to claim vast tracts of territory in both North and South America. Columbus kept the following journal of his historic voyage. (Columbus, Christopher, The Journal of Christopher Columbus: During His First Voyage, 1492–93, translated by Sir Clements Robert Markham [London: Hakluyt Society, 1893].)*

## IN THE NAME OF OUR LORD JESUS CHRIST

Whereas, Most Christian, High, Excellent, and Powerful Princes, King and Queen of Spain and of the Islands of the Sea, our Sovereigns, this present year 1492, after your

Highnesses had terminated the war with the Moors reigning in Europe, the same having been brought to an end in the great city of Granada, where on the second day of January, this present year, I saw the royal banners of your Highnesses planted by force of arms upon the towers of the Alhambra, which is the fortress of that city, and saw the Moorish king come out at the gate of the city and kiss the hands of your Highnesses, and of the Prince my Sovereign; and in the present month, in consequence of the information which I had given your Highnesses respecting the countries of India and of a Prince, called Great Can, which in our language signifies King of Kings, how, at many times he, and his predecessors had sent to Rome soliciting instructors who might teach him our holy faith, and the holy Father had never granted his request, whereby great numbers of people were lost, believing in idolatry and doctrines of perdition. Your Highnesses, as Catholic Christians, and princes who love and promote the holy Christian faith, and are enemies of the doctrine of Mahomet, and of all idolatry and heresy, determined to send me, Christopher Columbus, to the above-mentioned countries of India, to see the said princes, people, and territories, and to learn their disposition and the proper method of converting them to our holy faith; and furthermore directed that I should not proceed by land to the East, as is customary, but by a Westerly route, in which direction we have hitherto no certain evidence that any one has gone. So after having expelled the Jews from your dominions, your Highnesses, in the same month of January, ordered me to proceed with a sufficient armament to the said regions of India, and for that purpose granted me great favors, and ennobled me that thenceforth I might call myself Don, and be High Admiral of the Sea, and perpetual Viceroy and Governor in all the islands and continents which I might discover and acquire, or which may hereafter he discovered and acquired in the ocean; and that this dignity should be inherited by my eldest son, and thus descend from degree to degree forever. Hereupon I left the city of Granada, on Saturday, the twelfth day of May, 1492, and proceeded to Palos, a seaport, where I armed three vessels, very fit for such an enterprise, and having provided myself with abundance of stores and seamen, I set sail from the port, on Friday, the third of August, half an hour before sunrise, and steered for the Canary Islands of your Highnesses which are in the said ocean, thence to take my departure and proceed till I arrived at the Indies, and perform the embassy of your Highnesses to the Princes there, and discharge the orders given me. For this purpose I determined to keep an account of the voyage, and to write down punctually every thing we performed or saw from day to day, as will hereafter appear. Moreover, Sovereign Princes, besides describing every night the occurrences of the day, and every day those of the preceding night, I intend to draw up a nautical chart, which shall contain the several parts of the ocean and land in their proper situations; and also to compose a book to represent the whole by picture with latitudes and longitudes, on all which accounts it behooves me to abstain from my sleep, and make many trials in navigation, which things will demand much labor.

Friday, 3 August, 1492. Set sail from the bar of Saltes at 8 o'clock, and proceeded with a strong breeze till sunset, sixty miles or fifteen leagues south, afterwards southwest and south by west, which is the direction of the Canaries.

Monday, 6 August. The rudder of the caravel Pinta became loose, being broken or unshipped. It was believed that this happened by the contrivance of Gomez Rascon and Christopher Quintero, who were on board the caravel, because they disliked the voyage. The Admiral says he had found them in an unfavorable disposition before setting out.

He was in much anxiety at not being able to afford any assistance in this case, but says that it somewhat quieted his apprehensions to know that Martin Alonzo Pinzon, Captain of the Pinta, was a man of courage and capacity. Made a progress, day and night, of twenty-nine leagues.

Thursday, 9 August. The Admiral did not succeed in reaching the island of Gomera till Sunday night. Martin Alonzo remained at Grand Canary by command of the Admiral, he being unable to keep the other vessels company. The Admiral afterwards returned to Grand Canary, and there with much labor repaired the Pinta, being assisted by Martin Alonzo and the others; finally they sailed to Gomera. They saw a great eruption of names from the Peak of Teneriffe, a lofty mountain. The Pinta, which before had carried latine sails, they altered and made her square-rigged. Returned to Gomera, Sunday, 2 September, with the Pinta repaired.

The Admiral says that he was assured by many respectable Spaniards, inhabitants of the island of Ferro, who were at Gomera with Dona Inez Peraza, mother of Guillen Peraza, afterwards first Count of Gomera, that every year they saw land to the west of the Canaries; and others of Gomera affirmed the same with the like assurances. The Admiral here says that he remembers, while he was in Portugal, in 1484, there came a person to the King from the island of Madeira, soliciting for a vessel to go in quest of land, which he affirmed he saw every year, and always of the same appearance. He also says that he remembers the same was said by the inhabitants of the Azores and described as in a similar direction, and of the same shape and size. Having taken in food, water, meat and other provisions, which had been provided by the men which he left ashore on departing for Grand Canary to repair the Pinta, the Admiral took his final departure from Gomera with the three vessels on Thursday, September 6.

Sunday, 9 September. Sailed this day nineteen leagues, and determined to count less than the true number, that the crew might not be dismayed if the voyage should prove long. In the night sailed one hundred and twenty miles, at the rate of ten miles an hour, which make thirty leagues. The sailors steered badly, causing the vessels to fall to leeward toward the northeast, for which the Admiral reprimanded them repeatedly.

Monday, 10 September. This day and night sailed sixty leagues, at the rate of ten miles an hour, which are two leagues and a half. Reckoned only forty-eight leagues, that the men might not be terrified if they should be long upon the voyage.

Tuesday, 11 September. Steered their course west and sailed above twenty leagues; saw a large fragment of the mast of a vessel, apparently of a hundred and twenty tons, but could not pick it up. In the night sailed about twenty leagues, and reckoned only sixteen, for the cause above stated.

Friday, 14 September. Steered this day and night west twenty leagues; reckoned somewhat less. The crew of the Nina stated that they had seen a grajao, and a tropic bird, or water-wagtail, which birds never go farther than twenty-five leagues from the land.

Sunday, 16 September. Sailed day and night, west thirty-nine leagues, and reckoned only thirty-six. Some clouds arose and it drizzled. The Admiral here says that from this time they experienced very pleasant weather, and that the mornings were most delightful, wanting nothing but the melody of the nightingales. He compares the weather to that of Andalusia in April. Here they began to meet with large patches of weeds very green, and which appeared to have been recently washed away from the land; on which account they all judged themselves to be near some island, though not a continent, according to the opinion of the Admiral, who says, "the continent we shall find further ahead."

Monday, 17 September. Steered west and sailed, day and night, above fifty leagues; wrote down only forty-seven; the current favored them. They saw a great deal of weed which proved to be rockweed, it came from the west and they met with it very frequently. They were of opinion that land was near. The pilots took the sun's amplitude, and found that the needles varied to the northwest a whole point of the compass; the seamen were terrified, and dismayed without saying why. The Admiral discovered the cause, and ordered them to take the amplitude again the next morning, when they found that the needles were true; the cause was that the star moved from its place, while the needles remained stationary. At dawn they saw many more weeds, apparently river weeds, and among them a live crab, which the Admiral kept, and says that these are sure signs of land, being never found eighty leagues out at sea. They found the sea-water less salt since they left the Canaries, and the air more mild. They were all very cheerful, and strove which vessel should outsail the others, and be the first to discover land; they saw many tunnies, and the crew of the Nina killed one. The Admiral here says that these signs were from the west, "where I hope that high God in whose hand is all victory will speedily direct us to land." This morning he says he saw a white bird called a water-wagtail, or tropic bird, which does not sleep at sea.

19 September. Continued on, and sailed, day and night, twenty- five leagues, experiencing a calm. Wrote down twenty-two. This day at ten o'clock a pelican came on board, and in the evening another; these birds are not accustomed to go twenty leagues from land. It drizzled without wind, which is a sure sign of land. The Admiral was unwilling to remain here, beating about in search of land, but he held it for certain that there were islands to the north and south, which in fact was the case and he was sailing in the midst of them. His wish was to proceed on to the Indies, having such fair weather, for if it please God, as the Admiral says, we shall examine these parts upon our return. Here the pilots found their places upon the chart: the reckoning of the Nina made her four hundred and forty leagues distant from the Canaries, that of the Pinta four hundred and twenty, that of the Admiral four hundred.

Thursday, 20 September. Steered west by north, varying with alternate changes of the wind and calms; made seven or eight leagues' progress. Two pelicans came on board, and afterwards another,—a sign of the neighborhood of land. Saw large quantities of weeds today, though none was observed yesterday. Caught a bird similar to a grajao; it was a river and not a marine bird, with feet like those of a gull. Towards night two or three land birds came to the ship, singing; they disappeared before sunrise. Afterwards saw a pelican coming from west-northwest and flying to the southwest; an evidence of land to the westward, as these birds sleep on shore, and go to sea in the morning in search of food, never proceeding twenty leagues from the land.

Friday, 21 September. Most of the day calm, afterwards a little wind. Steered their course day and night, sailing less than thirteen leagues. In the morning found such abundance of weeds that the ocean seemed to be covered with them; they came from the west. Saw a pelican; the sea smooth as a river, and the finest air in the world. Saw a whale, an indication of land, as they always keep near the coast.

Saturday, 22 September. Steered about west-northwest varying their course, and making thirty leagues' progress. Saw few weeds. Some pardelas were seen, and another bird. The Admiral here says "this headwind was very necessary to me, for my crew had grown much alarmed, dreading that they never should meet in these seas with a fair wind to return to Spain." Part of the day saw no weeds, afterwards great plenty of it.

Sunday, 23 September. Sailed northwest and northwest by north and at times west nearly twenty-two leagues. Saw a turtle dove, a pelican, a river bird, and other white fowl;—weeds in abundance with crabs among them. The sea being smooth and tranquil, the sailors murmured, saying that they had got into smooth water, where it would never blow to carry them back to Spain; but afterwards the sea rose without wind, which astonished them. The Admiral says on this occasion "the rising of the sea was very favorable to me, as it happened formerly to Moses when he led the Jews from Egypt."

Tuesday, 25 September. Very calm this day; afterwards the wind rose. Continued their course west till night. The Admiral held a conversation with Martin Alonzo Pinzon, captain of the Pinta, respecting a chart which the Admiral had sent him three days before, in which it appears he had marked down certain islands in that sea; Martin Alonzo was of opinion that they were in their neighborhood, and the Admiral replied that he thought the same, but as they had not met with them, it must have been owing to the currents which had carried them to the northeast and that they had not made such progress as the pilots stated. The Admiral directed him to return the chart, when he traced their course upon it in presence of the pilot and sailors.

At sunset Martin Alonzo called out with great joy from his vessel that he saw land, and demanded of the Admiral a reward for his intelligence. The Admiral says, when he heard him declare this, he fell on his knees and returned thanks to God, and Martin Alonzo with his crew repeated Gloria in excelsis Deo, as did the crew of the Admiral. Those on board the Nina ascended the rigging, and all declared they saw land. The Admiral also thought it was land, and about twenty-five leagues distant. They remained all night repeating these affirmations, and the Admiral ordered their course to be shifted from west to southwest where the land appeared to lie. They sailed that day four leagues and a half west and in the night seventeen leagues southwest, in all twenty-one and a half: told the crew thirteen leagues, making it a point to keep them from knowing how far they had sailed; in this manner two reckonings were kept, the shorter one falsified, and the other being the true account. The sea was very smooth and many of the sailors went in it to bathe, saw many dories and other fish.

Wednesday, 26 September. Continued their course west till the afternoon, then southwest and discovered that what they had taken for land was nothing but clouds. Sailed, day and night, thirty-one leagues; reckoned to the crew twenty-four. The sea was like a river, the air soft and mild.

Sunday, 30 September. Continued their course west and sailed day and night in calms, fourteen leagues; reckoned eleven.—Four tropic birds came to the ship, which is a very clear sign of land, for so many birds of one sort together show that they are not straying about, having lost themselves. Twice, saw two pelicans; many weeds. The constellation called Las Gallardias, which at evening appeared in a westerly direction, was seen in the northeast the next morning, making no more progress in a night of nine hours, this was the case every night, as says the Admiral. At night the needles varied a point towards the northwest, in the morning they were true, by which it appears that the polar star moves, like the others, and the needles are always right.

Monday, 1 October. Continued their course west and sailed twenty-five leagues; reckoned to the crew twenty. Experienced a heavy shower. The pilot of the Admiral began to fear this morning that they were five hundred and seventy-eight leagues west of the island of Ferro. The short reckoning which the Admiral showed his crew gave five hundred and eighty-four, but the true one which he kept to himself was seven hundred and seven leagues.

Saturday, 6 October. Continued their course west and sailed forty leagues day and night; reckoned to the crew thirty-three. This night Martin Alonzo gave it as his opinion that they had better steer from west to southwest. The Admiral thought from this that Martin Alonzo did not wish to proceed onward to Cipango; but he considered it best to keep on his course, as he should probably reach the land sooner in that direction, preferring to visit the continent first, and then the islands.

Sunday, 7 October. Continued their course west and sailed twelve miles an hour, for two hours, then eight miles an hour. Sailed till an hour after sunrise, twenty-three leagues; reckoned to the crew eighteen. At sunrise the caravel Nina, who kept ahead on account of her swiftness in sailing, while all the vessels were striving to outsail one another, and gain the reward promised by the King and Queen by first discovering land—hoisted a flag at her mast head, and fired a lombarda, as a signal that she had discovered land, for the Admiral had given orders to that effect. He had also ordered that the ships should keep in close company at sunrise and sunset, as the air was more favorable at those times for seeing at a distance. Towards evening seeing nothing of the land which the Nina had made signals for, and observing large flocks of birds coming from the North and making for the southwest, whereby it was rendered probable that they were either going to land to pass the night, or abandoning the countries of the north, on account of the approaching winter, he determined to alter his course, knowing also that the Portuguese had discovered most of the islands they possessed by attending to the flight of birds. The Admiral accordingly shifted his course from west to west-southwest, with a resolution to continue two days ill that direction. This was done about an hour after sunset. Sailed in the night nearly five leagues, and twenty-three in the day. In all twenty-eight.

8 October. Steered west-southwest and sailed day and night eleven or twelve leagues; at times during the night, fifteen miles an hour, if the account can be depended upon. Found the sea like the river at Seville, "thanks to God," says the Admiral. The air soft as that of Seville in April, and so fragrant that it was delicious to breathe it. The weeds appeared very fresh. Many land birds, one of which they took, flying towards the southwest; also grajaos, ducks, and a pelican were seen.

Tuesday, 9 October. Sailed southwest five leagues, when the wind changed, and they stood west by north four leagues. Sailed in the whole day and night, twenty leagues and a half; reckoned to the crew seventeen. All night heard birds passing.

Wednesday, 10 October. Steered west-southwest and sailed at times ten miles an hour, at others twelve, and at others, seven; day and night made fifty-nine leagues' progress; reckoned to the crew but forty-four. Here the men lost all patience, and complained of the length of the voyage, but the Admiral encouraged them in the best manner he could, representing the profits they were about to acquire, and adding that it was to no purpose to complain, having come so far, they had nothing to do but continue on to the Indies, till with the help of our Lord, they should arrive there.

Thursday, 11 October. Steered west-southwest; and encountered a heavier sea than they had met with before in the whole voyage. Saw pardelas and a green rush near the vessel. The crew of the Pinta saw a cane and a log; they also picked up a stick which appeared to have been carved with an iron tool, a piece of cane, a plant which grows on land, and a board. The crew of the Nina saw other signs of land, and a stalk loaded with rose berries. These signs encouraged them, and they all grew cheerful. Sailed this day till sunset, twenty-seven leagues.

After sunset steered their original course west and sailed twelve miles an hour till two hours after midnight, going ninety miles, which are twenty-two leagues and a half; and as the Pinta was the swiftest sailer, and kept ahead of the Admiral, she discovered land and made the signals which had been ordered. The land was first seen by a sailor called Rodrigo de Triana, although the Admiral at ten o'clock that evening standing on the quarter-deck saw a light, but so small a body that he could not affirm it to be land; calling to Pero Gutierrez, groom of the King's wardrobe, he told him he saw a light, and bid him look that way, which he did and saw it; he did the same to Rodrigo Sanchez of Segovia, whom the King and Queen had sent with the squadron as comptroller, but he was unable to see it from his situation. The Admiral again perceived it once or twice, appearing like the light of a wax candle moving up and down, which some thought an indication of land. But the Admiral held it for certain that land was near; for which reason, after they had said the Salve which the seamen are accustomed to repeat and chant after their fashion, the Admiral directed them to keep a strict watch upon the forecastle and look out diligently for land, and to him who should first discover it he promised a silken jacket, besides the reward which the King and Queen had offered, which was an annuity of ten thousand maravedis. At two o'clock in the morning the land was discovered, at two leagues' distance; they took in sail and remained under the square-sail lying to till day, which was Friday, when they found themselves near a small island, one of the Lucayos, called in the Indian language Guanahani. Presently they descried people, naked, and the Admiral landed in the boat, which was armed, along with Martin Alonzo Pinzon, and Vincent Yanez his brother, captain of the Nina. The Admiral bore the royal standard, and the two captains each a banner of the Green Cross, which all the ships had carried; this contained the initials of the names of the King and Queen each side of the cross, and a crown over each letter Arrived on shore, they saw trees very green many streams of water, and diverse sorts of fruits. The Admiral called upon the two Captains, and the rest of the crew who landed, as also to Rodrigo de Escovedo notary of the fleet, and Rodrigo Sanchez, of Segovia, to bear witness that he before all others took possession (as in fact he did) of that island for the King and Queen his sovereigns, making the requisite declarations, which are more at large set down here in writing. Numbers of the people of the island straightway collected together. Here follow the precise words of the Admiral: "As I saw that they were very friendly to us, and perceived that they could be much more easily converted to our holy faith by gentle means than by force, I presented them with some red caps, and strings of beads to wear upon the neck, and many other trifles of small value, wherewith they were much delighted, and became wonderfully attached to us. Afterwards they came swimming to the boats, bringing parrots, balls of cotton thread, javelins, and many other things which they exchanged for articles we gave them, such as glass beads, and hawk's bells; which trade was carried on with the utmost good will. But they seemed on the whole to me, to be a very poor people. They all go completely naked, even the women, though I saw but one girl. All whom I saw were young, not above thirty years of age, well made, with fine shapes and faces; their hair short, and coarse like that of a horse's tail, combed toward the forehead, except a small portion which they suffer to hang down behind, and never cut. Some paint themselves with black, which makes them appear like those of the Canaries, neither black nor white; others with white, others with red, and others with such colors as they can find. Some paint the face, and some the whole body; others only the eyes, and others the nose. Weapons they have none, nor are acquainted with them, for I showed them swords which they grasped by the blades, and cut themselves through ignorance. They have no iron, their javelins being without it, and nothing more than sticks, though some have fish-bones or other things at the ends. They are all of a good size and stature, and handsomely formed. I saw some with scars of wounds upon their bodies, and demanded by signs the origins of them; they answered me in the same way, that there came people from the other islands in the neighborhood who endeavored to make prisoners of them, and they defended themselves. I thought then, and still believe, that these were from the continent. It appears to me, that the people are ingenious, and would be good servants and I am of opinion that they would very readily become Christians, as they appear to have no religion. They very quickly learn such words as are spoken to them. If it please our Lord, I intend at my return to carry home six of them to your Highnesses, that they may learn our language. I saw no beasts in the island, nor any sort of animals except parrots." These are the words of the Admiral.

Saturday, 13 October. At daybreak great multitudes of men came to the shore, all young and of fine shapes, very handsome; their hair not curled but straight and coarse like horse-hair, and all with foreheads and heads much broader than any people I had hitherto seen; their eyes were large and very beautiful; they were not black, but the color of the inhabitants of the Canaries, which is a very natural circumstance, they being in the same latitude with the island of Ferro in the Canaries. They were straight-limbed without exception, and not with prominent bellies but handsomely shaped. They came to the ship in canoes, made of a single trunk of a tree, wrought in a wonderful manner considering the country; some of them large enough to contain forty or forty-five men, others of different sizes down to those fitted to hold but a single person. They rowed with an oar like a baker's peel, and wonderfully swift. If they happen to upset, they all jump into the sea, and swim till they have righted their canoe and emptied it with the calabashes they carry with them. They came loaded with balls of cotton, parrots, javelins, and other things too numerous to mention; these they exchanged for whatever we chose to give them. I was very attentive to them, and strove to learn if they had any gold. Seeing some of them with little bits of this metal hanging at their noses, I gathered from them by signs that by going southward or steering round the island in that direction, there would be found a king who possessed large vessels of gold, and in great quantities. I endeavored to procure them to lead the way thither, but found they were unacquainted with the route. I determined to stay here till the evening of the next day, and then sail for the southwest; for according to what I could learn from them, there was land at the south as well as at the southwest and northwest and those from the northwest came many times and fought with them and proceeded on to the southwest in search of gold and precious stones. This is a large and level island, with trees extremely flourishing, and streams of water; there is a large lake in the middle of the island, but no mountains: the whole is completely covered with verdure and delightful to behold. The natives are an inoffensive people, and so desirous to possess any thing they saw with us, that they kept swimming off to the ships with whatever they could find, and readily bartered for any article we saw fit to give them in return, even such as broken platters and fragments of glass. I saw in this manner sixteen balls of cotton thread which weighed above twenty-five pounds, given for three Portuguese ceutis. This traffic I forbade, and suffered no one to take their cotton from them, unless I should order it to be procured for your Highnesses, if proper quantities could be met with. It grows in this island, but from my short stay here I could not satisfy myself fully concerning it; the gold, also, which they wear in their noses, is found here, but not to lose time, I am determined to proceed onward and ascertain whether I can reach Cipango. At night they all went on shore with their canoes.

Sunday, 14 October. In the morning, I ordered the boats to be got ready, and coasted along the island toward the north-northeast to examine that part of it, we having landed first at the eastern part. Presently we discovered two or three villages, and the people all came down to the shore, calling out to us, and giving thanks to God. Some brought us water, and others victuals: others seeing that I was not disposed to land, plunged into the sea and swam out to us, and we perceived that they interrogated us if we had come from heaven. An old man came on board my boat; the others, both men and women cried with loud voices—"Come and see the men who have come from heavens. Bring them victuals and drink." There came many of both sexes, every one bringing something, giving thanks to God, prostrating themselves on the earth, and lifting up their hands to heaven. They called out to us loudly to come to land, but I was apprehensive on account of a reef of rocks, which surrounds the whole island, although within there is depth of water and room sufficient for all the ships of Christendom, with a very narrow entrance. There are some shoals withinside, but the water is as smooth as a pond. It was to view these parts that I set out in the morning, for I wished to give a complete relation to your Highnesses, as also to find where a fort might be built. I discovered a tongue of land which appeared like an island though it was not, but might be cut through and made so in two days; it contained six houses. I do not, however, see the necessity of fortifying the place, as the people here are simple in war-like matters, as your Highnesses will see by those seven which I have ordered to be taken and carried to Spain in order to learn our language and return, unless your Highnesses should choose to have them all transported to Castile, or held captive in the island. I could conquer the whole of them with fifty men, and govern them as I pleased. Near the islet I have mentioned were groves of trees, the most beautiful I have ever seen, with their foliage as verdant as we see in Castile in April and May. There were also many streams. After having taken a survey of these parts, I returned to the ship, and setting sail, discovered such a number of islands that I knew not which first to visit; the natives whom I had taken on board informed me by signs that there were so many of them that they could not be numbered; they repeated the names of more than a hundred. I determined to steer for the largest, which is about five leagues from San Salvador; the others were some at a greater, and some at a less distance from that island. They are all very level, without mountains, exceedingly fertile and populous, the inhabitants living at war with one another, although a simple race, and with delicate bodies.

15 October. Stood off and on during the night, determining not to come to anchor till morning, fearing to meet with shoals; continued our course in the morning; and as the island was found to be six or seven leagues distant, and the tide was against us, it was noon when we arrived there. I found that part of it towards San Salvador extending from north to south five leagues, and the other side which we coasted along, ran from east to west more than ten leagues. From this island espying a still larger one to the west, I set sail in that direction and kept on till night without reaching the western extremity of the island, where I gave it the name of Santa Maria de la Concepcion. About sunset we anchored near the cape which terminates the island towards the west to enquire for gold, for the natives we had taken from San Salvador told me that the people here wore golden bracelets upon their arms and legs. I believed pretty confidently that they had invented this story in order to find means to escape from us, still I determined to pass none of these islands without taking possession, because being once taken, it would answer for all times. We anchored and remained till Tuesday, when at daybreak I went ashore with the boats armed. The people we found naked like those of San Salvador, and of the same disposition. They suffered us to traverse the island, and gave us what we asked of them. As the wind blew southeast upon the shore where the vessels lay, I determined not to remain, and set out for the ship. A large canoe being near the caravel Nina, one of the San Salvador natives leaped overboard and swam to her; (another had made his escape the night before,) the canoe being reached by the fugitive, the natives rowed for the land too swiftly to be overtaken; having landed, some of my men went ashore in pursuit of them, when they abandoned the canoe and fled with precipitation; the canoe which they had left was brought on board the Nina, where from another quarter had arrived a small canoe with a single man, who came to barter some cotton; some of the sailors finding him unwilling to go on board the vessel, jumped into the sea and took him. I was upon the quarter deck of my ship, and seeing the whole, sent for him, and gave him a red cap, put some glass beads upon his arms, and two hawk's bells upon his ears. I then ordered his canoe to be returned to him, and dispatched him back to land.

I now set sail for the other large island to the west and gave orders for the canoe which the Nina had in tow to be set adrift. I had refused to receive the cotton from the native whom I sent on shore, although he pressed it upon me. I looked out after him and saw upon his landing that the others all ran to meet him with much wonder. It appeared to them that we were honest people, and that the man who had escaped from us had done us some injury, for which we kept him in custody. It was in order to favor this notion that I ordered the canoe to be set adrift, and gave the man the presents above mentioned, that when your Highnesses send another expedition to these parts it may meet with a friendly reception. All I gave the man was not worth four maravedis. We set sail about ten o'clock, with the wind southeast and stood southerly for the island I mentioned above, which is a very large one, and where according to the account of the natives on board, there is much gold, the inhabitants wearing it in bracelets upon their arms, legs, and necks, as well as in their ears and at their noses. This island is nine leagues distant from Santa Maria in a westerly direction. This part of it extends from northwest, to southeast and appears to be twenty-eight leagues long, very level, without any mountains, like San Salvador and Santa Maria, having a good shore and not rocky, except a few ledges under water, which renders it necessary to anchor at some distance, although the water is very clear, and the bottom may be seen. Two shots of a lombarda from the land, the water is so deep that it cannot be sounded; this is the case in all these islands. They are all extremely verdant and fertile, with the air agreeable, and probably contain many things of which I am ignorant, not inclining to stay here, but visit other islands in search of gold. And considering the indications of it among the natives who wear it upon their arms and legs, and having ascertained that it is the true metal by showing them some pieces of it which I have with me, I cannot fail, with the help of our Lord, to find the place which produces it.

Being at sea, about midway between Santa Maria and the large island, which I name Fernandina, we met a man in a canoe going from Santa Maria to Fernandina; he had with him a piece of the bread which the natives make, as big as one's fist, a calabash of water, a quantity of reddish earth, pulverized and afterwards kneaded up, and some dried leaves which are in high value among them, for a quantity of it was brought to me at San Salvador; he had besides a little basket made after their fashion, containing some glass beads, and two blancas by all which I knew he had come from San Salvador, and had passed from thence to Santa Maria. He came to the ship and I caused him to be taken on board, as he requested it; we took his canoe also on board and took care of his things. I ordered him to be presented with bread and honey, and drink, and shall carry him to Fernandina and give him his property, that he may carry a good report of us, so that if it please our Lord when your Highnesses shall send again to these regions, those who arrive here may receive honor, and procure what the natives may be found to possess.

Tuesday, 16 October. Set sail from Santa Maria about noon, for Fernandina which appeared very large in the west; sailed all the day with calms, and could not arrive soon enough to view the shore and select a good anchorage, for great care must be taken in this particular, lest the anchors be lost. Beat up and down all night, and in the morning arrived at a village and anchored. This was the place to which the man whom we had picked up at sea had gone, when we set him on shore. He had given such a favorable account of us, that all night there were great numbers of canoes coming off to us, who brought us water and other things. I ordered each man to be presented with something, as strings of ten or a dozen glass beads apiece, and thongs of leather, all which they estimated highly; those which came on board I directed should be fed with molasses. At three o'clock, I sent the boat on shore for water; the natives with great good will directed the men where to find it, assisted them in carrying the casks full of it to the boat, and seemed to take great pleasure in serving us. This is a very large island, and I have resolved to coast it about, for as I understand, in, or near the island, there is a mine of gold. It is eight leagues west of Santa Maria, and the cape where we have arrived, and all this coast extends from north-northwest to south-southeast. I have seen twenty leagues of it, but not the end. Now, writing this, I set sail with a southerly wind to circumnavigate the island, and search till we can find Samoet, which is the island or city where the gold is, according to the account of those who come on board the ship, to which the relation of those of San Salvador and Santa Maria corresponds. These people are similar to those of the islands just mentioned, and have the same language and customs; with the exception that they appear somewhat more civilized, showing themselves more subtle in their dealings with us, bartering their cotton and other articles with more profit than the others had experienced. Here we saw cotton cloth, and perceived the people more decent, the women wearing a slight covering of cotton over the nudities. The island is verdant, level and fertile to a high degree; and I doubt not that grain is sowed and reaped the whole year round, as well as all other productions of the place. I saw many trees, very dissimilar to those of our country, and many of them had branches of different sorts upon the same trunk; and such a diversity was among them that it was the greatest wonder in the world to behold. Thus, for instance, one branch of a tree bore leaves like those of a cane, another branch of the same tree, leaves similar to those of the lentisk. In this manner a single tree bears five or six different kinds. Nor is this done by grafting, for that is a work of art, whereas these trees grow wild, and the natives take no care about them. They have no religion, and I believe that they would very readily become Christians, as they have a good understanding. Here the fish are so dissimilar to ours that it is wonderful. Some are shaped like dories, of the finest hues in the world, blue, yellow, red, and every other color, some variegated with a thousand different tints, so beautiful that no one on beholding them could fail to express the highest wonder and admiration. Here are also whales. Beasts, we saw none, nor any creatures on land save parrots and lizards, but a boy told me he saw a large snake. No sheep nor goats were seen, and although our stay here has been short, it being now noon, yet were there any, I could hardly have failed of seeing them. The circumnavigation of the island I shall describe afterward.

Wednesday, 17 October. At noon set sail from the village where we had anchored and watered. Kept on our course to sail round the island; the wind southwest and south. My intention was to follow the coast of the island to the southeast as it runs in that direction, being informed by the Indians I have on board, besides another whom I met with here, that in such a course I should meet with the island which they call Samoet, where gold is found. I was further informed by Martin Alonzo Pinzon, captain of the Pinta, on board of which I had sent three of the Indians, that he had been assured by one of them I might sail round the island much sooner by the northwest. Seeing that the wind would not enable me to proceed in the direction I first contemplated, and finding it favorable for the one thus recommended me, I steered to the northwest and arriving at the extremity of the island at two leagues' distance, I discovered a remarkable haven with two entrances, formed by an island at its mouth, both very narrow, the inside capacious enough for a hundred ships, were there sufficient depth of water. I thought it advisable to examine it, and therefore anchored outside, and went with the boats to sound it, but found the water shallow. As I had first imagined it to be the mouth of a river, I had directed the casks to be carried ashore for water, which being done we discovered eight or ten men who straightway came up to us, and directed us to a village in the neighborhood; I accordingly dispatched the crews thither in quest of water, part of them armed, and the rest with the casks, and the place being at some distance it detained me here a couple of hours. In the meantime I strayed about among the groves, which present the most enchanting sight ever witnessed, a degree of verdure prevailing like that of May in Andalusia, the trees as different from those of our country as day is from night, and the same may be said of the fruit, the weeds, the stones and everything else. A few of the trees, however, seemed to be of a species similar to some that are to be found in Castile, though still with a great dissimilarity, but the others so unlike, that it is impossible to find any resemblance in them to those of our land. The natives we found like those already described, as to personal appearance and manners, and naked like the rest. Whatever they possessed, they bartered for what we chose to give them. I saw a boy of the crew purchasing javelins of them with bits of platters and broken glass. Those who went for water informed me that they had entered their houses and found them very clean and neat, with beds and coverings of cotton nets. Their houses are all built in the shape of tents, with very high chimneys. None of the villages which I saw contained more than twelve or fifteen of them. Here it was remarked that the married women wore cotton breeches, but the younger females were without them, except a few who were as old as eighteen years. Dogs were seen of a large and small size, and one of the men had hanging at his nose a piece of gold half as big as a castellailo, with letters upon it. I endeavored to purchase it of them in order to ascertain what sort of money it was but they refused to part with it. Having taken our water on board, I set sail and proceeded northwest till I had surveyed the coast to the point where it begins to run from east to west. Here the Indians gave me to understand that this island was smaller than that of Samoet, and that I had better return in order to reach it the sooner. The wind died away, and then sprang up from the west-northwest which was contrary to the course we were pursuing, we therefore hove about and steered various courses through the night from east to south standing off from the land, the weather being cloudy and thick. It rained violently from midnight till near day, and the sky still remains clouded; we remain off the southeast part of the island, where I expect to anchor and stay till the weather grows clear, when I shall steer for the other islands I am in quest of. Every day that I have been in these Indies it has rained more or less. I assure your Highnesses that these lands are the most fertile, temperate, level and beautiful countries in the world.

Thursday, 18 October. As soon as the sky grew clear, we set sail and went as far round the island as we could, anchoring when we found it inconvenient to proceed. I did not, however, land. In the morning set sail again.

Friday, 19 October. In the morning we got under weigh, and I ordered the Pinta to steer east and southeast and the Nina south-southeast; proceeding myself to the south-east the other vessels I directed to keep on the courses prescribed till noon, and then to rejoin me. Within three hours we descried an island to the east toward which we directed our course, and arrived all three, before noon, at the northern extremity, where a rocky islet and reef extend toward the North, with another between them and the main island. The Indians on board the ships called this island Saomete. I named it Isabela. It lies westerly from the island of Fernandina, and the coast extends from the islet twelve leagues, west, to a cape which I called Cabo Hermoso, it being a beautiful, round headland with a bold shore free from shoals. Part of the shore is rocky, but the rest of it, like most of the coast here, a sandy beach. Here we anchored till morning. This island is the most beautiful that I have yet seen, the trees in great number, flourishing and lofty; the land is higher than the other islands, and exhibits an eminence, which though it cannot be called a mountain, yet adds a beauty to its appearance, and gives an indication of streams of water in the interior. From this part toward the northeast is an extensive bay with many large and thick groves. I wished to anchor there, and land, that I might examine those delightful regions, but found the coast shoal, without a possibility of casting anchor except at a distance from the shore. The wind being favorable, I came to the Cape, which I named Hermoso, where I anchored today. This is so beautiful a place, as well as the neighboring regions, that I know not in which course to proceed first; my eyes are never tired with viewing such delightful verdure, and of a species so new and dissimilar to that of our country, and I have no doubt there are trees and herbs here which would be of great value in Spain, as dyeing materials, medicine, spicery, etc., but I am mortified that I have no acquaintance with them. Upon our arrival here we experienced the most sweet and delightful odor from the flowers or trees of the island. Tomorrow morning before we depart, I intend to land and see what can be found in the neighborhood. Here is no village, but farther within the island is one, where our Indians inform us we shall find the king, and that he has much gold. I shall penetrate so far as to reach the village and see or speak with the king, who, as they tell us, governs all these islands, and goes dressed, with a great deal of gold about him. I do not, however, give much credit to these accounts, as I understand the natives but imperfectly, and perceive them to be so poor that a trifling quantity of gold appears to them a great amount. This island appears to me to be a separate one from that of Saomete, and I even think there may be others between them. I am not solicitous to examine particularly everything here, which indeed could not be done in fifty years, because my desire is to make all possible discoveries, and return to your Highnesses, if it please our Lord, in April. But in truth, should I meet with gold or spices in great quantity, I shall remain till I collect as much as possible, and for this purpose I am proceeding solely in quest of them.

Saturday, 20 October. At sunrise we weighed anchor, and stood to the northeast and east along the south side of this island, which I named Isabela, and the cape where we anchored, Cabo de la Laguna; in this direction I expected from the account of our Indians to find the capital and king of the island. I found the coast very shallow, and offering every obstacle to our navigation, and perceiving that our course this way must be very circuitous, I determined to return to the westward. The wind failed us, and we were unable to get near the shore before night; and as it is very dangerous anchoring here in the dark, when it is impossible to discern among so many shoals and reefs whether the ground be suitable, I stood off and on all night. The other vessels came to anchor, having reached the shore in season. As was customary among us, they made signals to me to stand in and anchor, but I determined to remain at sea.

Sunday, 21 October. At 10 o'clock, we arrived at a cape of the island, and anchored, the other vessels in company. After having dispatched a meal, I went ashore, and found no habitation save a single house, and that without an occupant; we had no doubt that the people had fled in terror at our approach, as the house was completely furnished. I suffered nothing to be touched, and went with my captains and some of the crew to view the country. This island even exceeds the others in beauty and fertility. Groves of lofty and flourishing trees are abundant, as also large lakes, surrounded and overhung by the foliage, in a most enchanting manner. Everything looked as green as in April in Andalusia. The melody of the birds was so exquisite that one was never willing to part from the spot, and the flocks of parrots obscured the heavens. The diversity in the appearance of the feathered tribe from those of our country is extremely curious. A thousand different sorts of trees, with their fruit were to be met with, and of a wonderfully delicious odor. It was a great affliction to me to be ignorant of their natures, for I am very certain they are all valuable; specimens of them and of the plants I have preserved. Going round one of these lakes, I saw a snake, which we killed, and I have kept the skin for your Highnesses; upon being discovered he took to the water, whither we followed him, as it was not deep, and dispatched him with our lances; he was seven spans in length; I think there are many more such about here. I discovered also the aloe tree, and am determined to take on board the ship tomorrow, ten quintals of it, as I am told it is valuable. While we were in search of some good water, we came upon a village of the natives about half a league from the place where the ships lay; the inhabitants on discovering us abandoned their houses, and took to flight, carrying of their goods to the mountain. I ordered that nothing which they had left should be taken, not even the value of a pin. Presently we saw several of the natives advancing towards our party, and one of them came up to us, to whom we gave some hawk's bells and glass beads, with which he was delighted. We asked him in return, for water, and after I had gone on board the ship, the natives came down to the shore with their calabashes full, and showed great pleasure in presenting us with it. I ordered more glass beads to be given them, and they promised to return the next day. It is my wish to fill all the water casks of the ships at this place, which being executed, I shall depart immediately, if the weather serve, and sail round the island, till I succeed in meeting with the king, in order to see if I can acquire any of the gold, which I hear he possesses. Afterwards I shall set sail for another very large island which I believe to be Cipango, according to the indications I receive from the Indians on board. They call the Island Colba, and say there are many large ships, and sailors there. This other island they name Bosio, and inform me that it is very large; the others which lie in our course, I shall examine on the passage, and according as I find gold or spices in abundance, I shall determine what to do; at all events I am determined to proceed on to the continent, and visit the city of Guisay, where I shall deliver the letters of your Highnesses to the Great Can, and demand an answer, with which I shall return.

# 2

# The French in North America, 1534–1701

## INTRODUCTION

During the last portion of the 15th century, mariners sailing under the flags of Portugal and Spain inaugurated what became known as the European Age of Discovery. The Portuguese directed their energies southward along the western coast of Africa and, at the end of the century (1498), Vasco de Gama sailed around the Cape of Good Hope and through the Indian Ocean to India itself. Spain took a more westward route as shown by Christopher Columbus's famous 1492 voyage that resulted in the European discovery of the New World. Both Portugal and Spain continued to explore and colonize throughout the 16th century with spectacularly favorable results.

Curiously, perhaps, during the 16th century, England and France, the other two major states bordering the Atlantic Ocean jumping-off point, failed to emulate the Iberian nations. In the French case, domestic unrest featuring a near collapse of royal authority provoked a civil war. Much of the unrest arose from intense religious conflict. Together, the political confusion and the religious strife paralyzed the state and squelched any serious thought of state-sponsored trans-Atlantic exploration and colonization.

France's descent into chaos began under the reign of Francis I (1515–1547). Although intelligent enough and blessed with a winning and forceful personality, Francis spent his entire reign unsuccessfully fighting against a burgeoning Spain for control of the Italian peninsula as well as the provinces of Artois, Burgundy, Navarre, and Flanders. The failed effort served to wreck France's finances. It also heightened an already well-developed sense of independence among the French nobility despite the many steps Francis took to strengthen the monarchy. This downward spiral accelerated under Henry II (1547–1559). Henry was less intelligent and able than his father; however, he continued to challenge Spain without any positive results. Ultimately, he accepted the inevitable with the Treaty of Cateau-Cambresis, signed shortly before his death, in 1559.

Henry II's death opened a Pandora's box for France. In succession, the Crown passed to his three sons, none of whom proved up to the task. The oldest son, Francis II, died in 1560; the next eldest, Charles IX, reigned until 1574; the youngest, Henry III, ruled until his death, in 1589. Not only was France handicapped by these woefully weak and incompetent rulers, but also a resurgent nobility, often divided into warring factions, undermined what was left of central authority, thereby bringing France to a state of anarchy.

One major source of this dreadful situation was religious conflict. During the first half of the 16th century, the Protestant revolt against the Roman Catholic Church had made significant headway in France. Notably, the French lawyer John Calvin's brand of Protestantism attracted Frenchmen from all walks of life, but especially from the nobility, who saw in Calvinism an opportunity to assert their independence from any authority, secular or religious. Moreover, Calvinism was a particularly unbending form of Protestantism, and that greatly diminished the chances of compromise. The French Protestants, known as Huguenots, remained a minority in a Catholic country. However, they were too numerous to be crushed, although just such an attempt was made with the infamous Saint Bartholomew's Day Massacre in 1572, when more than 3,000 Huguenot leaders were massacred in Paris and an additional 15,000 or so were killed throughout the country.

The first French attempt to settle in North America arose from the ongoing religious strife. The driving force behind this effort was Gaspard de Coligny, a prominent French admiral and a Huguenot, who sought to establish colonies as refuges for his coreligionists. Allegedly advised by John Calvin himself, de Coligny first planted a colony of Huguenots in what is today Brazil. However, the Portuguese who dominated that area destroyed the colony.

Undaunted, de Coligny enlisted Jean Ribault, a fellow naval officer, to help him establish a Huguenot colony in North America. In 1562, Ribault and 150 Huguenots from Normandy settled near Parris Island, in present-day South Carolina. This colony failed, but two years later de Coligny convinced Ribault to try again. This time the French set up a colony at Fort Caroline, near present-day Jacksonville, Florida. However, Spain objected to a French Protestant presence in what it regarded as its sphere of influence. It also feared that the French would prey on the Spanish treasure ships that passed nearby. Consequently, Spain sent Don Pedro Menendez de Aviles north from the fort at Saint Augustine to destroy the French outpost. Amid much bloodshed, Aviles succeeded, and, with de Coligny's murder during the 1572 Saint Bartholomew's Day Massacre, a permanent French presence in North America was delayed for several more decades.

During the 1580s, civil war once again shook France. Sometimes known as the War of the Three Henrys, since all three contenders for power had the first name Henry, the conflict ended in 1589 with the triumph of Henry of Navarre. Taking the crown as Henry IV, Henry of Navarre was the first of the Bourbon dynasty that ruled France until the French Revolution of 1789. With the fortunes of the French monarchy at a low point, Henry IV set about restoring the monarchy's power and prestige. To that end, he turned his attention to the all-important religious question. Although a Protestant, Henry was not a fanatic. Upon taking the Crown, he converted to Catholicism, supposedly remarking that "Paris is worth a Mass." Then, in 1598, he calmed his Protestant supporters when he issued the Edict of Nantes, which served to protect the Huguenots.

With something resembling normalcy returned to France under Henry IV, the French state rather belatedly turned its attention to the Atlantic and the possibilities of exploration and colonization. Not surprisingly, perhaps, it turned its gaze toward the northern reaches of North America.

Well before France descended into chaos in the middle of the 16th century, Frenchmen had been familiarizing themselves with North America. The first to do so were French fishermen who fished the rich waters of the Grand Banks laying off the coasts of Newfoundland and Labrador. Often, these fishermen put ashore to repair their nets and to dry their catch. In doing so, they came in contact with the Natives as goods and stories were exchanged.

This attracted the attention of the French monarchy, and, in 1523, Francis I sponsored an unsuccessful expedition, led by Giovanni da Verrazano, to find a water route to the Far East. Several years later, in 1534, the king commissioned Jacques Cartier to explore the northern reaches. Spurred on by stories of riches awaiting an intrepid explorer, Cartier made several voyages, claiming what today is maritime Canada for the French Crown. However, he failed to find the legendary kingdom of Saguenay, despite discovering the Saint Lawrence River and sailing upstream as far as today's Montreal. In 1542, Cartier returned empty-handed to France.

Despite the difficult situation that prevailed in France during the later years of the 16th century, individual Frenchmen made their way to the Saint Lawrence to trade for furs; however, it would not be until the early 17th century that the French Crown ventured to return to what would be New France, or Canada. Even then, it did so in an uncoordinated and unfocused manner, leaving most of the task to private individuals or companies sponsored by the Crown but controlled by merchants.

The most intrepid of this new generation of French explorers was Samuel de Champlain, who first sailed to New France in 1603 and remained the dominant French figure there until his death, in 1635. Champlain was instrumental in founding Port Royal on the Bay of Fundy in 1605 and, three years later, establishing a post at Quebec City that would serve as his headquarters.

As the 17th century unfolded, it became increasingly evident that France's stake in North America would be that of an empire of trade rather than an empire of settlement as pursued by Spain and, increasingly, France's greatest rival, England. Several factors account for this. The lands that made up New France were desolate, chilly, and not particularly fertile—hardly an attractive destination for a European settler. Moreover, the French Crown rarely if ever went out of its way to encourage settlement. In fact, as the century wore on, it actively discouraged Huguenots from relocating to New France. This stood in stark contrast to the situation in England, where religious malcontents had London's blessing to resettle in North America. Finally, among the French settlers who did make their way to New France, there was a tendency to replicate France's rural socioeconomic structure, which featured peasants, "*les habitants,*" living and working on lands granted by the Crown to members of the French nobility. In other words, there were neither economic nor social incentives for large numbers of Frenchmen to immigrate to New France.

Since theirs was an empire based on the fur trade, the French in Canada cultivated good relations with their Native American trading partners. This was particularly true of the Huron, whom the French backed against their traditional enemy, the Five Nation Iroquois Confederation. It was no coincidence that the Huron dominated the Great Lakes region, which was rich in furs. Typically, a handful of intrepid French traders would trek into the backwoods with Indian guides at their side to return many months later laden down with valuable furs. Because there was continual interaction between the French and the Native Americans, and because there were very few French women in Canada, the French trappers and traders tended to intermarry with the Indians and in many cases assimilated Indian ways as they left behind their native European culture.

During the 17th century, these *"coureurs de bois,"* or "runners of the forest," slowly moved down the valley of the Saint Lawrence and then made their way along the Great Lakes to the upper reaches of the Mississippi River. As they moved inland, they established tiny posts and forts that reinforced their claims to the land as well as facilitating trade.

However, the *coureurs de bois* and their Indian colleagues were not always alone. With the assassination of Henry IV in 1610, and the subsequent ascendancy of Marie de Medici, the queen mother, and Cardinal Richelieu, the French monarchy reaffirmed its commitment to its version of Roman Catholicism. Although New France was not a priority by any stretch of the imagination, this new orientation was reflected not only in the policy of discouraging Huguenot emigration to Canada but also in the encouragement of Catholic, primarily Jesuit, missionaries. The first Jesuits arrived in Canada in 1625. Although few in number, these brave and determined souls traveled into the wilds of New France where they attempted to convert the Indians. The missionaries were astute enough and flexible enough to tailor their message to fit the needs and the cultural dimensions of the Native Americans. Moreover, they treated the Indians as equals and made a real effort to learn the languages and the customs of those they would convert. Consequently, despite some horrific setbacks, the Jesuits generally succeeded in converting the Native Americans.

Undoubtedly, the most famous Jesuit missionary was Father Jacques Marquette, who teamed with the French-Canadian explorer Louis Joliet to navigate the Mississippi River as far south as the mouth of the Arkansas River in 1673. Nine years later, René-Robert Cavelier, Sieur de La Salle, reached the mouth of the Mississippi and claimed for France the mighty river's entire watershed from the Appalachian Mountains in the east to the Rocky Mountains in the west. This opened up a new area of exploration and colonization. The French settled Biloxi and Mobile, and in 1699 Pierre le Moyne established a settlement that would grow into present-day New Orleans. Slowly, a French presence began to wend its way north on the Mississippi as French colonists both settled and traded. Many agrarian communities that hugged the Gulf of Mexico and the Mississippi River as far as Baton Rouge and Natchez developed a plantation-style economy that in turn gave rise to African slavery to meet the unrelenting demand for labor.

Although Montreal had been founded in 1642, Quebec City remained Canada's most important settlement. In 1674, a bishopric was established there, and the royal governor, who exercised great power as a consequence of the highly centralized administrative system that France employed, maintained his headquarters there.

Nevertheless, at the turn of the 18th century, the French position in North America remained rather tenuous. Although France maintained a string of posts and forts in a huge arc ranging from the mouth of the Saint Lawrence through the Great Lakes and down the Mississippi and Ohio river valleys, and although France claimed the bulk of the North American continent's interior, the actual French presence paled in comparison with that of the English and Spanish. For example, most estimates conclude that in 1700 there were perhaps 15,000 Frenchmen in all of North America, as opposed to 285,000 English colonists settled on the North American East Coast at that time, a population almost 20 times that of New France! Obviously, this imbalance pointed toward a potentially uncertain future for France in North America.

## INTERPRETIVE ESSAY

JOHN M. HUNT

In 1534, the Breton sea captain Jacques Cartier sailed down the Gulf of Saint Lawrence, where he encountered the Iroquois at what is now Quebec City. Cartier, unimpressed with the Indians, wrote that "[t]his people may be called savage, for they are the sorriest folk there can be in the world, and the whole lot of them had nothing above the value of five *sous,* their canoes and fishing-nets excepted." Cartier was more interested in discovering a western passage to China and the East Indies and in finding gold and silver than in establishing a permanent base in the Saint Lawrence Valley. To prove he had sailed to the New World and to pique the interest of the French king, Francis I, Cartier kidnapped several Iroquois warriors to take back to France. Although the Natives died in captivity, Cartier did persuade the French king to finance another expedition to the New World. Thus began the inauspicious story of French colonialism in North America—an enterprise fraught with failure and setbacks for most of the 16th century. French imperialism, when compared to the spectacular success of the Spanish and Portuguese in South and Central America, proved to be rather disappointing. Cartier's first encounter with the Iroquois also established the tone of Franco-Indian relations for the next two and half centuries. The French entered North America as equals to the Indians, rather than as conquerors.

Indeed, the French virtually made no headway in establishing a permanent colony in North America throughout the 16th century. In 1535–1536, Cartier returned with three ships and a crew of more than 100 men to the Gulf of Saint Lawrence. This trip again stirred the interest of Francis I, who in 1541–1542 sent Cartier out on a larger expedition under the command of the Huguenot nobleman and corsair Jean-François de La Rocque de Roberval. Cartier and Roberval quickly butted heads: Roberval proved more interested in piracy, while Cartier sailed to the Iroquois settlement of Stadacona and founded the fortified colony of Charlesbourg-Royal. Discovering what he thought to be gold (really iron pyrites), Cartier left in September 1541 on a reconnaissance mission to discover the kingdom of Saguenay, the source of this wealth according to local Indian legend. On his return from the mission, he discovered Charlesbourg-Royal in a dire situation. The cold Laurentian winter had reduced the number of settlers, and the once friendly Iroquois, who had taught the French wilderness survival skills, had now begun to attack colonists who left the protection of the fortress. Cartier decided to return to France with his wealth. On his return trip, he encountered Roberval, who had just decided to rendezvous with the main party of the expedition. Roberval and his men remained in the colony, but the harsh conditions of boreal North America, coupled with repeated Iroquoian raids, made life thoroughly miserable for them. In 1543, when the relief party arrived, Roberval decided to abandon the colony and return to France.

Deterred by the harsh winter conditions and the lack of success in the north, the French concentrated their colonization efforts on Brazil and, later, Florida. The Saint Lawrence River Valley was left to hardy French fishermen. But the Brazilian and Floridian expeditions—spearheaded by Huguenots in search of a place to practice their Calvinist faith—ended in failure, as well. Only with the cessation of the French Wars of

Religion in 1589 and the stability brought about by the ascent of Henri Bourbon of Navarre as Henry IV did the French government again attempt to colonize North America. This time, the mariner Samuel de Champlain undertook numerous expeditions in the Saint Lawrence River Valley and its environs. His encounter with the Huron and the Algonquin tribes of that region set a precedent in Franco-Indian relations. Rather than seeing Champlain and his men as subjugators, the Indians, particularly the Huron, treated them as equals, making use of them and their arquebuses in skirmishes with their enemies, the Iroquois. In return, Champlain made use of Indian guides and their canoes in exploring the region.

In 1608, Champlain founded Quebec City, the first permanent French settlement in North America, before continuing with his exploration of what was to become New France. In its first 50 years, Quebec City hung by a thread. Receiving little support from the French state and attracting only a handful of settlers per year, the town and the colony remained pitifully underpopulated throughout these years. In spite of this unpromising beginning, the population of New France grew slowly. In 1640, 359 colonists lived in Quebec City. Twenty years later, the city had 2,000 inhabitants. Two other cities were subsequently founded: Trois Rivières, in 1634, and Montreal, in 1642. Nevertheless, despite the presence of a royal governor at Quebec City, the state played only a small role in the day-to-day existence of the settlers in New France, who were for the most part either fur traders or Jesuit missionaries. To encourage immigration, Cardinal Richelieu introduced the seigneurial system to New France in 1627. Essentially a late form of feudalism, the system installed by Richelieu divided land around the Saint Lawrence into long, narrow strips. These strips belonged to the king but were managed by *seigneurs,* or landlords, who in turn had settlers called *habitants* work the land. The *habitants* paid taxes to the *seigneurs* and also owed them three days of labor a year. Although this succeeded in attracting a few peasants seeking a better life, the majority of settlers nevertheless came to New France to take part in the lucrative fur trade.

Due to the lack of state support, the French experiment in colonization differed greatly from those of the Spanish in South and Central America and the Portuguese in Brazil. Lacking supplies, troops, and other resources, the French had to rely on Indian allies to survive the harsh winter, to find food, and to acquire beaver pelts and other furs. The French needed the Indians more than the Indians needed the French. This relationship colored the encounters between the French and the Indians—predominantly Algonquians, a group of Native Americans that included the Algonquin, Ottawa, and Mi'maq Indians who occupied the regions of the Saint Lawrence River Valley. The Algonquians shared a related language and lived as hunter-gatherers. Their way of life differed greatly from that of the Iroquoian Indian groups, who lived primarily in fortified villages and who included the various Iroquois nations and the Huron. Throughout the 17th century, the French and their allies among the Algonquians developed a relationship based on negotiation and trade. Historian Richard White calls this relationship the "Middle Ground" because neither side truly held an advantage over the other. Instead, both the French and the Indians met as equals and learned from each other.

The principal bond of this relationship was the fur trade. By the late 16th century, the broad-brimmed beaver felt hat had become quite fashionable in Europe. The European beaver, however, had become extinct at this time. Hence, the North American beaver quickly became an important commodity, particularly because its fur was thicker and better suited to the production of hats. The French eagerly participated in this trade—centered on the Saint Lawrence—either as official merchants with permits from the provincial government or as illicit traders called *coureurs de bois,* or woodland runners, so named because they often lived with and adapted to the cultural ways of the Indian allies. The fur trade proved quite profitable and was the mainstay of New France's economy well until the 18th century. The Indians provided the French traders with the beaver pelts; in return, the French gave the Indians manufactured implements, mirrors and glass beads (both of which the Indians believed to have magical powers), alcohol, and, after the mid-17th century, guns.

Trade was not the only connection between the French and the Indians. To solidify relations with each other, they often took part in elaborate rituals, often of Indian origin. One of these was the calumet ceremony, or the smoking of a peace pipe. The joint smoking of the pipe between two rival Indians nations had long been a tradition among both the Algonquians and the Iroquois. The Indians introduced it to the French as a symbolic way to seal diplomatic alliances, marriage proposals, and trade relations. Another method of negotiation between Indians and Frenchmen was the gift exchange, an ancient custom of the Indians that helped keep the peace between rival nations. The Indians saw the gift exchange as imparting status and power on both the giver and the recipient. The actual monetary worth of the objects exchanged mattered less to them. It was a way to form friendships and to gain social capital. Although the French adopted this mode of exchange, they nevertheless brought their notions of trade to their economic dealings with the Indians. The value of the furs mattered to them, and many unscrupulous French traders swindled the Indians by obtaining them in exchange for a few bottles of cheap brandy. Nevertheless, the calumet ceremony and the ritual exchange of gifts indicate that the Indians saw the French as equals, rather than oppressors.

This can also be seen in the marriages between the French and the Indians, which constituted another form of negotiated exchange between the two groups. The vast majority of the settlers of New France were men, particularly adventurers without wives. Few French or European women made the perilous journey to New France. Oddly enough, a skewed sex ratio existed among the Algonquians. Women outnumbered men among the Indians, with the result that polygamy was common among them. Frenchmen took advantage of the situation by taking Indian concubines and wives. In turn, this facilitated friendships and trade relationships between the French and the Indians. Indian fathers often married their daughters to prominent fur traders and *coureurs de bois* as a means of consolidating trade relationships and increasing their status. Frenchmen took Indian brides to gain their knowledge of the fur trade and to act as liaisons between the French and Indian worlds. Through marriage, Frenchmen were treated as kin of the Indians and gained social capital among the nations of their brides. Indeed, many *coureurs de bois* went Native after marrying Indian brides.

Yet, Franco-Indian relationships were not always harmonious. Although the activities of the French were relatively peaceful when compared to the Spanish and English examples of colonization in the New World, warfare and periodic episodes of violence also marked the encounter between the French and the Indians of North America. This was due to the fact that the French permanently entered the Saint Lawrence River Valley exactly when the Iroquois and their confederacy (situated in what is now northern New York and southern Ontario) had begun to go on the offense against the Huron and the various Algonquian nations. This inter-Indian hostility was rooted in a contest over limited hunting grounds. Before the arrival of the French in the 17th century, a tentative equilibrium had existed among the various Indian groups. With the arrival of the French and the subsequent boom in the fur trade, hostilities among the Indians exploded over control of that trade. The French played a careful game of allying with the Algonquians and the Huron in opposition to the more aggressive Iroquois. The French needed their Native American allies to help them procure beaver pelts. They feared that the Huron would submit to the Iroquois, thereby causing them to lose their tentative monopoly of the fur trade. For their part, the Iroquois allied themselves first with the Dutch and, later, with the English. Both the Dutch and the English supported Iroquois raids on the Algonquians and the Huron by selling guns to them. This upset the balance between the Indians of the Saint Lawrence River Valley because the French government refused to sell firearms to their allies.

In the midst of this burgeoning storm of war, an epidemic struck the Indians of the Saint Lawrence River Valley. Unused to European diseases—especially smallpox—the Indians were devastated by diseases brought to the New World by the French during the 1630s and 1640s. Smallpox and influenza wreaked havoc among the Huron. The epidemic of 1636–1639 reduced the Huron population by half—from 20,000 to about 10,000. Already weakened by disease, the Huron could not stop the Iroquois from initiating a violent campaign against them in 1649. Within months, the Iroquois had destroyed the entire Huron village system, killing many women and children as well as warriors. The refugees sought assistance from the French Jesuits in the region or moved westward to avoid further Iroquois hostility.

This was only the opening salvo in a series of raids and wars that pitted the French and their Algonquian allies against the Iroquois that was to last until 1701. At the start of these wars—known collectively as the Fur Trade Wars or Beaver Wars—the Iroquois had the advantage. Terrorizing their opponents, they destroyed numerous Algonquian villages, killed the Jesuit priests administering to their needs, and massacred their women and children. They tortured Algonquian warriors that they captured and supposedly ate their dead foes. The violence of the Iroquois had a profound impact on the demographic regime of the Saint Lawrence River Valley. The Iroquois aggression pushed the remnants of the shattered Algonquian nations westward into what the French called the *pays d'en haut*—the western Great Lakes region that encompassed parts of modern-day Michigan, Illinois, Indiana, and Ohio. Native Americans from different nations gathered together in refugee villages, creating a new society wherein diverse cultural traditions amalgamated into a new synthesis. The French supported these refugees. The Jesuits, in particular, were able to win many converts among these scattered tribes.

Iroquois aggression and the Algonquian Diaspora had the subsequent consequence of pushing the fur trade between the French and the Indians further west into the *pays d'en haut*. By 1650, Montreal had become the center of the fur trade, but the Diaspora, coupled with the efforts of the *coureurs de bois* to find new trading partners and sources of beaver pelts, relocated the locus of the fur trade in the west. Despite opposition from the governor of New France, the royal finance minister, Jean-Baptiste Colbert, tacitly supported these efforts to further the extent of the French empire in the New World. A famous example of the French push westward can be seen in the noble adventurer and explorer René-Robert Cavelier, Sieur de La Salle. Besides searching for a westward passage to China and the East Indies, La Salle also hoped to establish a trading connection with the western Indians, thereby moving the fur trade from the Saint Lawrence-Montreal axis to the Great Lakes-Mississippi River watershed. His efforts, as well as those of countless *coureurs de bois,* underlined the growing importance of the West to the French and thus ensured that North America west of the Appalachian Mountains would remain in French hands until the end of the French and Indian War (1756–1763).

The Fur Trade Wars continued into the beginning of the 18th century, ending only with the 1701 Great Treaty of Montreal when the Iroquois, exhausted after nearly a century of constant war, sued for peace. The Iroquois, fearful of the growing English presence in New York and Pennsylvania, sought to maneuver between the two European powers. The French, however, maintained their traditional alliance with the Algonquians. This would serve the French well in the 18th century, when hostilities between the French and the English would flare up over control of North America between the Mississippi River and the Appalachian Mountains. The Iroquois would ultimately side with the English in the French and Indian War.

The "Middle Ground" is the most important and lasting legacy of French colonialism in North America. For two centuries, the experiment in cultural fusion developed between the French and the Native peoples of the Saint Lawrence River Valley and the *pays d'en haut.* This relationship was centered not on dominance but on negotiation. The French state did not adequately support the colonists with troops and money until 1681, when New France was officially made a province of the royal domain. Until then, it was up to fur traders and the *coureurs de bois* to regulate their own affairs and to negotiate with the Native Americans. And, without the infrastructure of a state or, at least, an army to back them up, they could never negotiate with the Indians as superiors until the Iroquois onslaught reduced the Huron and Algonquians to shattered wanderers. Until then, the French remained heavily indebted to the Indians for pelts, survival techniques, and women. A complaint of Jesuit missionaries in New France was that Frenchmen were all too ready to live among the Indians, marry their women, and drop the accoutrements of civilization.

But the avenue of influence was not a one-way street. The French influence over their Native American allies was equal to, if not greater than, the Natives' influence over the French. They introduced European manufactured goods to the Indians. The gun altered traditional Indian warfare, making it easier for warring nations to kill each other. The Iroquois, in particular, made aggressive use of the guns they bought from the Dutch and English. The gun fundamentally changed the nature of war among the Indians. Rather than occasional skirmishes over hunting grounds, the Indians now used guns to fight a total war for control of the fur trade. Alcohol also had a tremendous impact on the Indian way of life. It quickly became a popular drink among warriors, who, as a result of its intoxicating effects, thought they were invincible and went on berserk killing sprees. The fur trade capitalized an item—the beaver pelt—that the Indians had never valued in monetary terms. Thus, the French brought the Indians of the Saint Lawrence River Valley and the *pays d'en haut* into the emerging global economy.

Another important impact of French colonialism in North America was the eventual conversion of the Algonquian and Iroquoian Indian groups to Roman Catholicism. As with all early modern colonial efforts, the thirst for profit went hand and hand with the thirst for souls. The goal of the French mission in North America was given particular impetus due to Europe's Wars of Religion of the 16th century, as well as the renewal of the Catholic faith after the Council of Trent. Both events, coupled with a nascent desire to bring more Christian subjects under the Crown's control, imparted a particular crusading zeal to the French state. In 1627, Louis XIII, advised by Cardinal Richelieu, issued a decree along with the land reorganization act that made New France completely a Catholic bastion—no longer was it to be a haven for Huguenots.

The early efforts of the French to convert the Indians of North America failed entirely. This was due to the fact that most of the early colonists of the 16th and early 17th centuries were corsairs, *coureurs de bois* and other young adventurers, rather than priests and friars. The first true attempt to proselytize among the Indians of New France occurred in 1615, when a handful of Recollets—French reformed Franciscans—settled in Quebec City. The Recollets—too few in numbers, inexperienced with the Native Americans, and a bit aloof—never had much success.

It took the Jesuits to establish a permanent mission in New France. They arrived in 1625 and quickly set about trying to proselytize among the Indians and meeting the religious needs of the Frenchmen in the wilds of Canada. The Jesuits saw New France as a kind of challenge—an inhospitable region of wild forests, harsh, cold winters, and warring Indian nations. Individual Jesuits saw New France as a testing ground of their faith and hoped to find their martyrdoms at the hands of the marauding Iroquois. This attitude is best preserved in the self-written hagiography of the first Jesuit martyr, Isaac Jogues, who suffered twice at the hands of the Mohawk tribe of the Iroquois nation. In 1642, Jogues and a mixed party of Huron and Frenchmen were captured and tortured by the Mohawks. At first, Jogues concealed himself among some brush once the Mohawk war party had surrounded his companions. But, rather than save himself, he surrendered to his enemies, ready to die a martyr's death, as his memoir testifies. He asked himself the following:

> Could I really…abandon our French and leave those good neophytes and those poor catechumens, without giving them the succor that the church of my God had entrusted to me. Flight seemed horrible to me. It must be, I said in my heart, that my body suffer the fire of earth in order to deliver these poor souls from the flames of Hell. It must die a transient death, in order to procure for them an eternal life.

After surrendering, he was tortured by his captors, who maimed his hands permanently and made him a living martyr of the Church. Undaunted, Jogues continued his mission among the Iroquois and, in 1646, got his wish for martyrdom when a band of Mohawks, blaming him and his fellow Jesuits for the epidemics that had wreaked havoc among the Indians, beheaded him and several companions in present-day upstate New York.

The French Jesuits in North America employed tactics similar to those used by Jesuits in China and Japan at the same time. That is, they sought to understand the people they were proselytizing by learning as much as they could of their customs and religious practices and by making accommodations to these traditions. The Jesuits lived in the Algonquian and Huron villages, learned their languages and dialects, and harmonized their beliefs with Christian teachings (while simultaneously criticizing them as superstitious). Despite their practical approach, the first two decades failed to harvest many

Indian souls for the Catholic Church. The Indians believed that the "black robes" were sorcerers who killed them with their dark magic. This stemmed from the fact that many Jesuits presided over deathbed conversions of Indians laid low by the epidemics of the 1630s and 1640s.

The Jesuits had better success among the Huron in the wake of their virtual destruction at the hands of the Iroquois. The Huron, with nowhere else to turn, came to the Jesuits to beg for their aid and protection. The Jesuits used the opportunity to baptize them and to introduce them to the Catholic faith. The Jesuits saw the Iroquois as the hand of God. The Jesuit Superior, Paul Raguereau, wrote that the Iroquois had served a purpose in Providence's master plan because they had "delivered many souls from the fires of Hell, while burning their bodies in an elemental fire."

The Jesuits also enjoyed success among refugees during the Fur Trade Wars, particularly among the Native Americans who had settled in the *pays d'en haut* region. This success had much to do with the devastation wrought by the Iroquois but was also due to the role Indian women played in converting family members. According to historian Susan Sleeper-Smith, Christianity presented Indian women of the Great Lakes region with an opportunity to escape some of the harsher aspects of Indian society by allowing them to avoid polygamous arrangements and by giving them the ability to choose their husbands, whether Indian or French. After the Council of Trent, the Catholic Church emphasized the sacramental role of marriage and the sanctity of marriage appealed to many Indian women. Jesuits, at first wary of the challenge Indian women presented to male authority, acquiesced when they saw the benefits that accrued from using these women as mediators between the French and Indian worlds. They helped convert family members and chastised reprobate husbands.

The Jesuits recorded their successes and failures in annual reports called *Relations*, which were printed in Paris from 1632 to 1673. The *Relations* not only chronicle the hardships of the missions, the raids of the Iroquois, and the outbreak of epidemics among the Algonquians but also provide detailed descriptions of customs and life-ways of the eastern woodland Indians. The reports found an audience among the pious in France. The *Relations* were intended to drum up financial and political support for the Jesuits missionary enterprise among wealthy patrons, as well as the state. Without this support, the missions would not have been as successful as they were by the end of the century.

The French experiment in colonization contrasted greatly with the efforts of the Spanish, Portuguese, and English. Getting a late start, the French state did not enjoy the heady success that the Spanish and Portuguese did in Central and South America. Unlike the Spanish and Portuguese, the French did not rapidly come to dominate the Indians of the Saint Lawrence River Valley. Instead, they encountered the Indians as equals, creating a world based on negotiation and cultural amalgamation. This contrasted sharply with English colonialism. The English, land-hungry farmers rather than fur traders, remained aloof from the Native Americans and fought them for their land. The French instead traded with the Indians, learned from them, and married their women. Rather than trying to conquer the lands of the Indians, the French were content with creating a network of trading posts throughout New France. In turn, the Indians adopted western ways and manufactured goods. The fur trade served as the lynchpin of the Franco-Indian world, which proved nevertheless to be ephemeral. The 18th century saw Europeans fighting all over the world for political and economic hegemony. North

America did not escape the clash of empires, as the French and the English increasingly skirmished with each other and with their Indian allies. This culminated in the English victory over the French and their Indian allies in the French and Indian War. The stipulations of the Treaty of Paris (1763) gave the English much of the territory of New France, including the Saint Lawrence River Valley and the *pays d'en haut.* At the first, the English sought to keep the French policy of giving the Indians their space by forbidding immigration past the Appalachian Mountains, but the English colonists pushed westward, initiating the further decline of this negotiated world. However, the disintegration of this world would be completed only in the years after the American Revolution.

## SELECTED BIBLIOGRAPHY

Anderson, Fred. *The War that Made America: A Short History of the French and Indian War.* New York: Viking, 2005. A succinct introduction to the French and Indian War.

Anderson, Karen. *Chain Her by One Foot: The Subjugation of Women in Seventeenth-Century New France.* London: Routledge, 1991. A feminist critique of the Jesuit mission among the Huron.

Briggs, Robin. *Early Modern France, 1560–1715.* 2nd ed. Oxford: Oxford University Press, 1998. The standard introduction to early modern France.

Delâge, Denys. *Bitter Feast: Amerindians and Europeans in Northeast North America, 1600–64.* Vancouver: University of British Columbia Press, 1993. A more traditional approach to French and Indian encounters.

Dickason, Olive P. *The Myth of the Savage and the Beginnings of French Colonialism in the Americas.* Edmonton: University of Alberta Press, 1984. Recounts the early encounters between the French and the Indians, both in Canada and Brazil.

Eccles, William J. *The Canadian Frontier, 1534–1760.* New York: Holt, Rinehart and Winston, 1969. A classic study of the Saint Lawrence River Valley and the Canadian Great Lakes.

Grant, John Webster. *Moon of Wintertime: Missionaries and the Indians of Canada in Encounter since 1534.* Toronto: University of Toronto Press, 1984. A thorough study of the relations between Catholic missionaries and the Indians of North America since the time of Jacques Cartier.

Greer, Alan, ed. *The Jesuit Relations: Natives and Missionaries in Seventeenth-Century North America.* Boston: Bedford/St. Martin's, 2000. A selection of Jesuit reports describing their missions among the Indians of North America.

Jennings, Francis. *The Ambiguous Iroquois Empire: The Covenant Chain Confederation of Indian Tribes with English Colonies from Its Beginnings to the Laurentian Treaty of 1744.* New York: W. W. Norton, 1984. A detailed account of the Iroquois encounter with the British, Dutch, and French.

Monet, Jacques. "The Jesuits in New France." In *Cambridge Companion to the Jesuits.* Edited by Thomas Worcester. Cambridge: Cambridge University Press, 2008. A concise account of the Jesuit mission in New France.

O'Malley, John W. *The First Jesuits.* Cambridge, MA: Harvard University Press, 1995. An excellent history of the missionary ethos of the early Jesuits.

Podruchny, Carolyn. *Making the Voyageur World: Travelers and Traders in the North American Fur Trade.* Toronto: University of Toronto Press, 2006. Although mostly concerned with the 18th and 19th centuries, this is a good introduction to the world of fur traders and the *coureurs de bois.*

Sleeper-Smith, Susan. *Indian Women and French Men: Rethinking Cultural Encounter in the Western Great Lakes.* Amherst: University of Massachusetts Press, 2001. An interesting analysis of the role of Indian women in Franco-Indian relations; compare to Anderson's argument.

———. *Rethinking the Fur Trade: Cultures of Exchange in an Atlantic World.* Lincoln: University of Nebraska, 2009. A collection of essays reassessing the role of the fur trade in the Atlantic World.

Trudel, Marcel. *Introduction to New France.* New York: Holt, Rinehart and Winston, 1968. As the title implies, this is a solid introduction to the history of New France.

Warhentin, Germaine, and Carolyn Padruchny, eds. *Decentering the Renaissance: Canada and Europe in Multidisciplinary Perspective, 1500–1700.* Toronto: University of Toronto Press, 2001. A collection of essays that assesses the French experience in North America.

White, Richard. *The Middle Ground: Indians, Empires, and Republics in the Great Lakes Region, 1650–1815.* Cambridge: Cambridge University Press, 1991. An important study that examines the negotiated relationship between the French and the Indians.

# JACQUES CARTIER (1491–1557)

During three voyages in which he—like several adventurers before him—hoped to find a short ocean passage from Europe to China, Jacques Cartier of France explored the Saint Lawrence River. His discoveries eventually led to the French colonization of Canada.

Cartier was born in 1491 in the seaport town of Saint Malo, France. Little is known about his youth, but there is evidence that he spent his early adulthood at sea on trading voyages to Brazil. Some historians believe that he accompanied the Italian explorer Giovanni da Verrazano to North America in 1524.

By the 1530s, Spain, England, and Portugal had already sponsored sea voyages to find a westward route to Asia, known as the Northwest Passage. Such a route remained elusive, but, in the process, parts of the North American continent and nearby islands had been discovered. In 1533, King Francis I of France, who had already commissioned Verrazano's voyage, authorized Cartier to make a voyage to the New World.

On April 20, 1534, Cartier sailed from Saint Malo with two small ships. The weather was cooperative, and he crossed the Atlantic Ocean in a short three weeks, approaching the coast of northern Newfoundland. He passed through the Strait of Belle Isle, sailing southward to Prince Edward Island, before heading northwest past the New Brunswick coast. A bout of stormy weather forced him to anchor his ships in a cove off the Gaspe Peninsula. He went ashore and planted a cross, claiming all the land he saw for King Francis.

While near shore, Cartier became one of the first Europeans to encounter North American Indians. He established friendly relations with Chief Donnacona, the head of an Iroquois tribe, who permitted two of his sons to return with Cartier to France. Cartier's little fleet arrived in Saint Malo in September 1534. Cartier, however, was eager to return to the New World. The Native Americans had told him of an area that was rich in gold and silver, and Cartier was convinced that the waterway to this land would prove to be the Northwest Passage to Asia.

In May 1535, Cartier went back to the Canadian coast with three ships. In early August, he entered a bay near the Gaspe Peninsula that he named the Bay of Saint Lawrence, because the ships had arrived there on the saint's feast day. He sailed up the Saint Lawrence River until he reached the foot of a mountain, which he named Mont Real (Mount Royal)—the future site of the city of Montreal. No precious metals were found.

Jacques Cartier claiming Canada for France at Gaspé in 1534. (Courtesy of the National Archives of Canada.)

The two Native American boys who had acted as his guides were returned to their father. Cartier and his crew spent the winter at a base camp in the area, where conditions were harsh. Before the winter was over, 25 of the 110 men had died.

During the winter months, relations between the French and the Native Americans deteriorated and became violent. Cartier seized 10 Native Americans, including Chief Donnacona, as hostages to ward off tribal attacks. He forced the Native Americans to accompany him during his summer return to France, where he brought them before Francis I. Cartier hoped that the Native Americans' accounts of gold and riches in Canada would persuade the king to sponsor a third expedition.

Five years passed, however, before another trip was organized. By then, all of the Native Americans had died, except for one little girl. Francis I commissioned a nobleman, Jean-François de La Rocque de Roberval, to set up permanent French colonies in the New World, and he gave Cartier a subordinate role. After Roberval's departure was delayed, however, Cartier set sail in May 1541 as the commander of five ships. Returning to the Saint Lawrence, he continued down the river, past Mount Royal, to search (vainly) for gold before setting up camp in what is now Quebec City for the winter.

The Iroquois, angry that their tribe members had not returned, attacked Cartier's camp and killed several crew members. Once the winter was over, Cartier set sail for France again. As he passed Newfoundland, he encountered Roberval, who was finally on his way to establish a colony, although the colony ultimately failed. The nobleman ordered Cartier to remain in Canada, but Cartier refused and continued back to Saint Malo, where he lived until his death in 1557.

## SAMUEL DE CHAMPLAIN (ca. 1567–1635)

Samuel de Champlain was a French explorer who founded the Canadian city of Quebec and discovered the lake in upstate New York that bears his name. Because of his efforts to colonize Canada, which was called New France in the 17th century, he is often called the father of New France.

Champlain was born around 1567 in Brouage, France, a seaport town on the Bay of Biscay. As a boy, he learned about sailing, navigating, and mapmaking from his father, who was a sea captain. By the time he was a young man, he was an experienced seaman.

From about 1593 to 1598, during the Protestant-Catholic wars in France, Champlain fought on land and sea under the command of Henry of Navarre (who later became King Henry IV of France). In 1599, after the wars were over, Champlain made his way to Spain, where his uncle was organizing a trading expedition to the Spanish colonies in the West Indies and Central America. Champlain went along and spent 22 months sailing the Caribbean and the south Atlantic. He kept a detailed record—which he illustrated with watercolors—of the land, people, and animals he saw during the long voyage.

King Henry IV was greatly impressed by Champlain's written account of the New World. Soon afterward, the king decided to establish colonies in the area of North America (present-day Canada) that French explorer Jacques Cartier had discovered in the early to mid-16th century. In 1603, Champlain, who had been named the royal geographer by the king, went on the first of several expeditions to Canada. He sailed up the Saint Lawrence River as far as the site of modern-day Montreal before returning to France laden with furs that he had traded for with Native Americans.

Champlain sailed back to Canada in 1604 and mapped the eastern coast of North America as far south as Cape Cod. In 1605, he helped establish a small colony in present-day Nova Scotia. He stayed on the continent until 1606, making at least two more voyages along the New England coastline, looking for a better place for a settlement.

In 1607, all the colonists were ordered back to France by the king, who had grown impatient with their slow progress in establishing outposts. Champlain pleaded with the king for one more chance, which was granted in 1608. With little time to waste, Champlain sailed back to the Saint Lawrence to set up a colony along the river, which he named Quebec. The crew built a fort and a storehouse to live in during the winter, but the weather was extremely harsh, and many of the men died.

To prevent Indian attacks on the small settlement, Champlain befriended the local Algonquian and Huron tribes. In return for their friendship, the Native Americans asked the Frenchmen to help them defeat their enemies, the Iroquois. In 1609, Champlain and two settlers went on a raid with the Algonquians and Hurons to Iroquois territory in upstate New York. As the Iroquois raised their bows and arrows, the Frenchmen fired their muskets, killing three chieftains who were standing alongside one another. Terrified by the white men's "thunder sticks," which they had never seen before, the Iroquois fled. Thereafter, the Iroquois were the bitter enemies of the French. During this raid, Champlain came upon an area with a lake so lovely that he named it after himself—Lake Champlain.

From 1610 to 1615, Champlain explored the waterways along what today is the Canadian-New York border, reaching Lake Ontario. His friendship with the Algonquians and Hurons continued. During a skirmish with the Iroquois in 1615, he was seriously wounded by an arrow but was nursed back to health by the Hurons. After 1616, he served as the governor of Quebec and made several trips back and forth to France, seeking assistance for the growing colony.

In 1628, England and France went to war. English ships blockaded Quebec, and Champlain was forced to surrender the settlement to the English a year later, after the settlers had run out of food and gunpowder. He was taken to England as a prisoner but released in 1632, when Quebec was returned to France in a peace treaty. Champlain made his last trip across the Atlantic in 1633 and spent the last two years of his life in Quebec trying to rebuild the colony. He died there on December 25, 1635.

## FRENCH FUR TRADE, ENVIRONMENTAL CONSEQUENCES OF

In the 17th and 18th centuries, the French used the fur trade to bring Hurons and Algonquians into the French trade network and make them dependent on (and thus allies with) the French. Therefore, they would be less likely to trade with and create alliances with other foreign powers.

Unfortunately, to remain a trade partner, tribes had to find furs that they could trade. As the years progressed, Indian tribes trapped all of the available beaver pelts in their rivers and drainage basins, requiring that they enlist other tribes farther west or south into trading and then become middlemen in the trade system themselves or move from their traditional homelands and move farther upriver to hunt and trap. However, the lands to which they relocated were not unoccupied, and intertribal conflict arose between tribes competing for resources.

With French guns, the westward-moving tribes easily dominated the tribes they encountered, and those tribes joined the trade network, fought and paid dearly for their unwillingness to join, or relocated (thereby causing other displacements or potentially uniting tribes that had been diminished by the diseases that also came with French trade goods). Besides disrupting entire communities and river systems, these changes altered the long-established balance of power throughout the western regions. Often those who came out on top were those with French guns and trade goods.

Moreover, the balance of nature was also irreparably damaged. Beaver no longer built their dams, and existing dams eroded, thereby causing water systems to be greatly affected in each watershed. The food chain, or, rather, pyramid, was irrevocably altered, and the lasting impact of that on the region cannot be overstated. The result was a shift in plant and animal life that is still being studied by botanists and zoologists.

SANDRA K. MATHEWS

## LOUIS DE BUADE, COMTE DE FRONTENAC (1622–1698)

Louis de Buade, Comte de Frontenac and Comte de Palluau, was a French soldier, nobleman, and courtier who became governor of New France, present-day French-speaking Canada. A flamboyant and charismatic figure, Frontenac is well known for his famous stand in October 1690 against the English during the siege of Quebec City, during which his wit and daring allowed the French forces to defeat a superior English army.

Frontenac was born on May 22, 1622, in Saint-Germain-en-Laye, near Paris, France. He was the son of Henri de Buade and Anne Phélypeau de Ponchartrain, both aristocrats.

His father—also Comte de Frontenac, a baron, and later Comte de Palluau—was a colonel in the regiment of Navarre and a member of King Louis XIII's entourage. Frontenac combined in himself the two branches of nobility then existing in France. From his father's side, he descended from the old nobility of the sword—the old knights—while on his mother's side, he came from the increasingly powerful nobility of the robe—the new, self-made nobility that owed its power to money and connections.

The young Frontenac received a good education, probably at the hands of the Jesuits, which may explain his hostility to that order later in his life. He entered the French Army in his teens and served in the Thirty Years' War. In 1643, by age 21, he had achieved the rank of colonel of the regiment of Normandie; three years later, he was appointed *maréchal de camp,* a position equivalent to that of brigadier general. When he was not in active duty, Frontenac spent his time at court, where his great personal charm gave him great influence. Unscrupulous and extravagant in his tastes, Frontenac incurred debts of more than 350,000 livres, which he never paid.

When his father died, Frontenac inherited his titles and lands and became known as the Comte de Frontenac. In 1648, he clandestinely married Anna de la Grange, a hot-headed beauty and daughter of a wealthy judge. The bride's father, convinced that Frontenac was a fortune hunter, prevented both son-in-law and daughter from ever inheriting any of his wealth. Frontenac, hounded more and more by his creditors, got a commission to fight with the Venetian forces defending Crete against the Turks but was dismissed from his post of lieutenant general for plotting against his superior officers and making a nuisance of himself. Back in France and still hounded by the creditors, Frontenac secured an appointment as governor general of New France and arrived in Quebec in the autumn of 1672 without his wife.

When Frontenac arrived in Quebec, the intendant, Jean Tallon, had been recalled to France, which left the colony without an administrator to look after the police, justice, and finances. Frontenac quickly appropriated the position for himself and began a despotic rule by quarreling constantly with the members of the Sovereign Council and imprisoning and deporting those who opposed him. The move proved foolish. Back in France, the deported officials brought a plaint before Jean-Batiste Colbert, the secretary of state responsible for the colonies, who, unlike King Louis XIV, did not have any sympathy for Frontenac. He curtailed Frontenac's powers, but, in his usual manner, Frontenac took no heed.

Frontenac had established a fur-trading post on Lake Ontario within a year of his arrival. The fur trade was the main source of income, and Frontenac wanted to cash in on it as much as possible. Colbert's policy for the colony, however, was to develop farming, timber, and ship building in order to create a strong, stable, and defendable colony. Frontenac, who associated himself with the explorer René-Robert Cavelier, Sieur de La Salle, kept establishing new trade posts until he brought the colony into a head-on confrontation with the powerful Iroquois Confederacy, which then challenged the French over control of the Ohio Valley. Before the conflict broke out, Frontenac was recalled to France in 1682 to answer for his chaotic administration of the colony, which he claimed was in perfect peace. He was stripped of his properties but was later reappointed governor general of New France in 1689.

When Frontenac arrived in Quebec, King William's War, which pitted France against England and the Iroquois, was under way, and the English and Iroquois seemed to have the upper hand. Frontenac's military command proved as disastrous as his administration. In January 1690, he launched an attack on three frontier settlements in New England and a village in New York and destroyed them all. Those attacks had some unexpected results, as the English colonies united the following year, determined to conquer French-held Canada once and for all.

When the siege of Quebec began, on October 16, 1690, Sir William Phips, a magistrate in the provincial government of Massachusetts, sent an envoy to ask Frontenac to surrender. In his usual arrogant and flamboyant style, Frontenac told the envoy, "I have no reply to make to your general other than from the mouths of my cannon and muskets." The bluff paid off, and the superior British forces were routed and suffered a humiliating defeat.

After the failed Quebec siege, the Anglo-Americans left the fighting to their Iroquois allies, who suffered heavy losses. When King William's War ended, in 1697, the English colonies finally abandoned the Iroquois, who were forced to sue for peace. Frontenac remained at his post until his death, on November 28, 1698.

JOSE VALENTE

## LOUIS JOLIET (ca. 1645–1700)

Louis Joliet was a French cartographer, trader, and adventurer who explored the Mississippi River Valley. Although Joliet is a very well-known explorer of North America, many pieces of his life are unknown. Joliet and Father Jacques Marquette came down the Wisconsin River to be the first Europeans to encounter the Mississippi River.

Louis was the third child of Jehan Joliet and Marie d'Abancourt dite La Caille and was born outside Québec around September 21, 1645. Joliet lost his father before the age of six. Joliet studied in the Jesuit College of Québec and spent his early years after college working as a musician within the seminary. In 1667, Joliet left the seminary and sailed for France under the support of Bishop Laval. The following year, he returned to Canada, where he began his career as an explorer.

Joliet made his first journey for Intendant Talon, who hired Louis and his brother Adrien to take supplies to Jean Pere, then searching for copper in the area of Lake Superior. While Talon paid Adrien 1,400 livres for expenses, he simultaneously sent René-Robert Cavelier, Sieur de La Salle, in search for the Great River. La Salle was known as a great woodsman and knew the area well, and he traveled with a large company in the same direction as the Joliet brothers. The La Salle journey turned dreadful—many priests became ill, they journeyed off route, and food became scarce. The Joliets met up with the La Salle party shortly after its return from Lake Superior. Adrien impressed the party with his knowledge of the area, which infuriated La Salle. Many of the La Salle party continued on the journey with the directions Adrien had supplied. La Salle refused to join the party, and he left to travel southwest.

Joliet never made contact with Jean Pere and returned to Québec in 1671. Although Joliet's first mission had been a failure, Talon next sent him to locate the Sea of the South, refusing to pay him in advance because of his lack of success on his first expedition.

On the trip, Joliet surpassed his brother by becoming an excellent mapmaker, a successful fur trader, and an expert at the use of a compass astrolabe. He then made a second voyage west sometime in 1670 and another in 1671. Because he had not received funds from the foreign minister, Talon instead gave Joliet and his party trading and trapping rights in the area they explored. The expedition included not only many strong and experienced woodsmen but also Marquette, an adventurous priest whose duty on the journey consisted of carrying the faith to Native Americans met along the way.

Throughout the winter of 1673, Joliet and Marquette collaborated on plans for a journey down the Wisconsin River. Joliet and his associates combined their money in order to purchase the equipment and necessary supplies needed; the associates would be guaranteed a share of the profits gained from pelts acquired on the trip. The voyagers left on May 17, 1673, with five men and two canoes. With the aid of Native Americans, the company continued the journey through Wisconsin until June 17, 1673, when it came upon the Mississippi River. The explorers took the Mississippi River all the way to Arkansas and then turned back toward Illinois.

Joliet and Marquette followed the advice of Peoria Indians they met and returned north by following the Illinois River. Enchanted by the Illinois River's abundance of wildlife, gentle, sloping hills, and quiet water, the voyagers enjoyed this portion of the journey even more than the trip along the banks of the Mississippi. Joliet's passion for the area made him consider returning to the Illinois region for a possible colonization. He truly intended to return to the Illinois River Valley and maintained that throughout all of his travels in North America, he had found Illinois to be the most splendid.

From the Illinois River Valley, the party continued up through Illinois territory, stopping at Kaskaskia, where Marquette christened the mission in Kaskaskia "Mission of Conception." The explorers continued to Des Plaines and then onward to the Chicago portage. Throughout the entire trip from Kakaskia to Chicago, Joliet continued to keep detailed maps of the area, especially mapping the minerals and stones of the area, which included iron, copper, and coal. In the fall of 1763, the party reached the Saint Xavier mission, where Marquette spent the remainder of his life. Joliet spent the winter exploring the Lake Michigan region. On his return trip to Canada, his canoe overturned in rapids above Montreal. Destroyed by the rapids, his journals and maps were never recovered. Joliet returned to Canada and reproduced some of his maps by memory and presented them to Quebec's legislators.

Joliet tried to obtain permission from Quebec and the King of France to start a settlement in the Illinois territory that he had explored. Denied permission to start the colony, Joliet never again traveled to the Illinois River Valley. He obtained some land in the lower Saint Lawrence, which included the island of Anticosti, married Claire Bissot, and started a homestead. Joliet continued his voyages in the Saint Lawrence area and became the royal hydrographer for Canada in 1697. Joliet died sometime between May 4 and October 18, 1700.

MICHELLE HINTON

## JACQUES MARQUETTE (1637–1675)

Father Jacques Marquette was one of the first Europeans to explore the Mississippi River. Yet, his voyage of discovery with Canadian fur trader Louis Joliet did much more than survey a great estuary—it symbolized the role of the Jesuit missionary in North

America. Marquette's mission required great courage, faith, and religious zeal, and the resulting toll on his personal constitution merely satisfied the missionary's penchant for stoic self-sacrifice and endurance, while providing a martyr and example for the next generation.

Born to aristocratic parents in Laon, France, on June 10, 1637, Marquette seemed predisposed to the priesthood from an early age. Contemporaries noted his easygoing, open disposition, his aptitude for learning languages, and his ardent desire to spread the Catholic faith. Such qualities were strong prerequisites for becoming a successful missionary. At age 17, Marquette entered a seminary in order to join the Society of Jesus, or Jesuit, order. The Jesuits, founded by a former soldier, Ignatius Loyola, organized themselves in a military-style hierarchy, with each priest being ultimately responsible only to the Pope, rather than to any secular authorities. They stressed rhetorical debating skills and philosophy in their training, as well as classical languages—skills that would prove useful in arguing with (and, it was hoped, converting) nonbelievers. Furthermore, the Jesuits placed great value on self-sacrifice and endurance in the face of earthly trials and tribulations. These traits proved indispensable in North America, where the Natives were not eager to relinquish their own religious traditions and might well torture or kill outsiders who obstinately pressed their own views.

Since 1611, the Jesuits had sought to convert the Natives of New France (Canada), and this challenge held great appeal for Marquette. After nearly a decade of study and tutoring, he received permission to travel to the New World, satisfying both his love of travel and his religious missionary zeal. He particularly hoped that he might get the opportunity to convert "new" Indians, who had not yet been visited by missionaries. The answer to Marquette's prayers came when his superior, Father Claud Dablon, ordered him to accompany Canadian-born fur trader Joliet on a journey into the unexplored territory to the southwest of Lake Michigan.

Joliet, a former clergyman himself, had traded in his black robe for a fur trader's life and was hoping to capitalize on new markets. Having heard of a mighty river that divided the continent, he hoped to use this superhighway as a means of extending his trade to the Indians. On May 17, 1673, Marquette, Joliet, and five other Canadian *voyageurs* (fur traders) whose names have been lost to history, set out on their historic expedition.

Traveling in two fragile yet versatile birch bark canoes, the party set out from Saint Ignace (in present-day Michigan's upper peninsula) and paddled down the Fox River to the Wisconsin. After seven days traveling through rather marshy water, the expedition reached the Mississippi River. The party paddled down the Mississippi for approximately 300 miles. The relatively few Indians encountered greeted the men amicably. At the mouth of the Arkansas River, Natives warned them of treacherous waters downstream, so Joliet decided to turn the mission around and head back upstream. Having been told by Illinois Indians that the Illinois River provided a shortcut back to the Great Lakes, he led the expedition up the river; the explorers then carried their canoes across what would become Chicago to reach Lake Michigan.

In addition to trade and religious conversion, Marquette and Joliet also took interest in the flora and fauna they encountered. They noted vast prairies and unfamiliar animals and were especially interested in the "wild cattle" they encountered. Marquette's journal entries concerning the buffalo and how they were processed and utilized by

Indians remain among the earliest European eyewitness accounts of the animals. Marquette's journal of the voyage, as well as a surprisingly accurate map he drew of the territory explored, would prove of significant value to later French expeditions.

The mission constituted a fine success, yet the upriver canoeing and portaging proved exhausting, particularly for Marquette. Whereas he had previously seemed indefatigable to his peers, apparently he never fully recovered from the rigors of the expedition. He spent an entire year recovering at the Saint Francis Mission in what is now De Pere, Wisconsin. Yet the missionary zeal that had characterized his life again overtook him. In late 1674, he canoed to the Chicago River to establish a mission among the local Indians. Marquette's linguistic gift allowed him to become sufficiently fluent in the local languages and enabled him to preach to the Natives for several weeks, but severe illness led him to try to return to the Saint Ignace mission. He died en route on the shores of Lake Michigan, taken with fevers and the "bloody flux" (probably amoebic dysentery). The following year, Christianized Ottawa Indians followed Marquette's trail and collected his remains for a Native funeral rite, and later that year his remains were taken to Saint Ignace to be buried.

# 3

# The Expedition of Coronado, 1540–1542

## INTRODUCTION

Coronado's expedition into the present-day southwest and south central United States was the most elaborate and far-reaching Spanish expedition into North America in the 16th century. But a number of other Spanish explorers paved the way for Coronado by sailing to the mainland of North America and spending months, sometimes years, trekking across unknown landscapes and sometimes enduring great hardships.

Juan Ponce de León arrived in the West Indies in 1508 and became governor of the island of San Juan (now Puerto Rico) in 1509. There he found some gold, and, by 1512, he had amassed a considerable fortune. That year, King Ferdinand granted him permission to explore the islands to the north, in what is now the Bahamas. Natives from the north spoke of a spring that restored youth to those who drank from it. Such a spring was, however, unknown in the Bahamas, and the legend probably referred to limestone springs in Florida, which was then thought of as an island. But Ponce de León was far more interested in capturing slaves and enhancing his wealth than in spending his money seeking a fountain of youth. He left Puerto Rico in March 1513 and sailed northward through the Bahamas, reaching the Saint Augustine area of Florida during Easter week or the Feast of Flowers, from which the place name is derived.

Turning south at that point, Ponce sailed back along the coast to the southern tip of Florida, then up the west coast to San Carlos Bay, where a skirmish with hostile Indians drove him back out to sea. The expedition returned to Puerto Rico in August 1513. In 1514, the king gave Ponce a contract to occupy and govern Florida, although he had found nothing of value there. Probably because of the slim prospect of finding wealth, Ponce did not return to Florida until 1521, when news of the great treasures being found in Mexico encouraged him to try again. His expedition made landfall in southwest Florida; there, a fight with Indians resulted in a Spanish defeat and a fatal arrow wound for Ponce himself. His death, along with that of Francisco de Garay, another explorer who had died on a journey to the Gulf Coast, placed Spanish claims to the southeastern part of the United States in abeyance, waiting for the next, more successful expedition. Garay had approached the Gulf Coast on his way to Mexico, where Hernán Cortés was busy extending Spanish dominance on his own terms. After Cortés had reached Veracruz in 1519 on his way to plunder the Aztecs and assume control of Mexico, he broke ranks with Gov. Diego Velásquez in Hispaniola. He had proclaimed himself de facto

Coronado's expedition took him and his men through endless miles of barren countryside in the southwestern desert in search of fabulous treasure. (Courtesy of the Library of Congress.)

Spanish governor of Mexico, in effect seceding from Spanish colonial authority in the Caribbean and affirming his loyalty directly to the king.

Velásquez did not take this affront to his authority lightly and declared Cortés and his followers traitors. He authorized Garay to lead an expedition to displace Cortés or at least limit the territory that the rebel was claiming and offered Garay the governorship of the land north and east of Mexico as a reward. Garay's expedition took him first to Florida and then along the Gulf Coast to Pánuco, in northern Mexico. This was the first recorded voyage of the Spanish to that area. Garay's efforts to subdue Cortés failed in 1523, when most of the men in an expedition he led against Cortés chose to join the rebel's forces. The unlucky Garay was captured and died in captivity.

In 1526, still annoyed by Cortés' independence, Velásquez commissioned Pánfilo de Narváez to take control of a large area along the northern coast of the Gulf of Mexico west to the Rio de las Palmas, well into Cortés's domain. Narváez received political authority over a vast territory from which he was expected to threaten Cortés. Narváez left Spain in June 1527 with five ships and 600 men, although about 140 stayed in Santo Domingo when the expedition stopped to resupply. After wintering in Cuba, they landed at Tampa Bay in April 1528. Interested in finding gold rather than Cortés, Narváez took the main body of his men ashore and set off toward the north, occasionally encountering Indians but finding no treasure. In June, they reached the Tallahassee area, where food was more plentiful, and then continued moving west. In August, they decided to build some boats and sail across the Gulf of Mexico to the safe port of Pánuco. Setting sail in September, they followed the coast, encountering storms and antagonizing resident Indians. Somewhere off the coast of Louisiana, three of the five ships were lost, including the one carrying Narváez; the other two were beached at Galveston Bay in November, stranding about 90 men there.

In one of the great odysseys of history, about a dozen of these men survived and roamed the southwestern countryside for more than seven years. They traveled as far west as southern New Mexico. The last four survivors crossed the Rio Grande River and made their way to Mexico City, arriving in the summer of 1536. One of the survivors, Álvar Núñez Cabeza de Vaca, wrote expansively about his experience, and his account opened the eyes of Spanish leaders to the possibilities of wealth that might lie north of Mexico.

Cabeza de Vaca and his fellow travelers told stories gleaned from indigenous people they had met about other people farther north who lived in large dwellings and had turquoise, emeralds, and tropical birds. Spanish authorities were impressed and decided to send Hernando de Soto to learn more. De Soto had received Narváez's title to the Gulf Coast territory in 1537 after a profitable career as a conquistador in Peru, and the Spanish were still interested in staking a permanent claim to the area. De Soto's expedition set out from Spain in April 1538 with more than 600 men. After a winter in Cuba, the expedition landed at Tampa Bay at the end of May 1539 and moved north by land, much as Narváez had done. It had frequent clashes with the Indians as it moved into northern Florida. After a winter in Tallahassee, the explorers continued north into present-day Georgia, then northeast into South Carolina, and finally west toward Chattanooga, Tennessee. They arrived there in June 1540, turned south, and moved through Alabama all the way to Matula, just north of Mobile, where they fought a major battle with local Indians. That forced de Soto back toward the north, and the expedition spent its third winter on the road in northeastern Mississippi. In the spring of 1541, the party continued westward, crossing the Mississippi River in June and spending most of the rest of that year and the next winter in present-day Arkansas.

By the spring of 1542, the weary de Soto had apparently abandoned his search for turquoise, emeralds, and tropical birds, and the expedition moved south toward the Gulf. Fighting Indians was still a common occurrence. De Soto died in May of a fever, and the survivors agreed to try to get to Pánuco. They wintered in northeastern Louisiana, near the Mississippi River, built barges, and floated down the river in the spring, and, after still more conflict with Indians, they reached the Gulf of Mexico in July and Pánuco in September.

Meanwhile, back in Mexico, the viceroy, Antonio de Mendoza, appointed Francisco Vásquez de Coronado governor of Nuevo Galicia, a recently created province on Mexico's west coast. In 1539, Mendoza and Coronado dispatched a missionary, Marcos de Niza, who had also been in Peru, to the north to see what he could find in the way of cities or treasures.

De Niza, ably assisted by a black slave and translator, Esteban de Dorantes, returned in August with reports about a place called the Seven Cities of Cíbola, comparing it to the fabled Inca cities in Peru. Encouraged, Mendoza and Coronado sent another expedition, this time headed by Melchior Diaz, a military officer, northward. He, too, reported positively about Cíbola when he returned, and his report convinced Coronado to take an army himself in search of Cíbola.

Coronado's force numbered about 350 Spaniards, of whom more than 200 were mounted. In addition, Coronado had 1,300 Indians, an unknown number of additional servants and slaves, and 1,500 horses and mules. Herds of cattle and sheep were brought along to ensure a supply of fresh meat. More supplies were sent by ship up the coast of the Gulf of California. The expedition arrived at Culiacan on March 28, 1540, and at the town of Hawikuh, supposedly a Cíbolan site, on July 7, taking routes that are still in dispute among historians and archaeologists. Although the supply voyage sailed to the junction of the Gila and Colorado rivers in the summer of 1540, the expedition never made contact with it. Another supply expedition the next year was aborted by a Mixton Indian rebellion in Jalisco.

Meanwhile, Coronado and his men made contact with a smaller group headed by Hernando de Alvarado that included a Pawnee Indian whom the Spanish named "the Turk." The Turk told the Spanish about other sources of great wealth. Coronado stationed the main body of his expedition in the Sonora Valley in the fall of 1540 prior to moving to winter quarters in the Rio Grande Valley. But he took 30 men with him and continued the search in what is now southeastern Socorro, finding nothing of value.

By early 1541, the lack of supplies had become a serious problem. The Spanish demanded clothes and food from Indian villages and burned and looted them when the Indians proved uncooperative. In April, Coronado directed the expedition toward another rumored golden city, Quivira, leaving the unhappy Indians behind. His force, now numbering about 1,700, moved to the Pecos River, where it met hostile Indians. After diplomacy failed, Coronado bridged the river, continued eastward, and found large herds of bison. The expedition spent the summer of 1541 in the Arkansas River valley, not too far from where de Soto's expedition was exploring, but again it found nothing of consequence.

Coronado planned to continue his wanderings in 1542, still certain he would find gold and the lost city of Quivira. Early in the year, however, he was seriously injured in a riding accident, and, after receiving word that another Spanish expedition had been nearly wiped out in an Indian uprising, he decided to return to Mexico, leaving several small parties behind to continue the search. Not until the 1580s did the Spanish mount a large-scale expedition to this area again.

## INTERPRETIVE ESSAY

THOMAS CLARKIN

On Sunday, February 22, 1540, the viceroy of New Spain, Antonio de Mendoza, watched as an expeditionary force assembled for an official review before it set forth to explore *la Tierra Nueva,* the New Land, the unexplored territory to the north of the Spanish Empire. Commanded by Francisco Vásquez de Coronado, the small army of adventurers included some 300 European soldiers, perhaps 1,000 or more Indian allies, and between four and six friars. Fifteen hundred animals, including packhorses and mules to carry supplies and tow the six brass cannons and sheep and cattle for food accompanied the expedition. After celebrating Mass, the force gathered to hear Viceroy Mendoza offer a speech in which he spoke of the expeditions goals: the conquest of new lands that would bring the soldiers and Spain great wealth and the opportunity to bring new souls to God. The men then swore an oath of loyalty to Coronado. The following day, they began the journey known as the *entrada* that would last more than two years and reveal the peoples and places of the American Southwest to European eyes for the first time. More than 400 years after the *entrada*, Coronado's grand failure remains an exciting tale of adventure and exploration that endures as an essential part of the history of the American Southwest.

Mendoza spoke of saving souls, and, while converting Indians to Christianity was always important to the Spanish, it was the lure of riches that drew men to scramble for a place in the expedition. The viceroy had promised each soldier a land grant in the territory that they claimed for Spain, and the Indians had been guaranteed their fair share. But Coronado's force did not set forth into *la Tierra Nueva* out of a desire for land. It sought the Seven Cities of Cíbola, a civilization of amazing wealth that the explorers believed lay somewhere to the north.

By the time of Coronado, the legend of the Seven Cities was several centuries old. During the eighth century, so the story went, seven Christian bishops fled from invading Moors, sailing west over the ocean. When they reached the distant island of Antillia, each bishop constructed a magnificent city of gold. In the minds of many Europeans, the story of the Seven Cities of Antillia was no mere folktale. Mapmakers included Antillia on their maps, and during the 15th century at least one sea captain planned a voyage to discover the island's exact location.

Upon arriving in the Western Hemisphere, Europeans assumed they were close to Antillia. They did not find the cities of gold, but hope remained, and their dreams gained new life when Álvar Núñez Cabeza de Vaca and his three companions arrived in Mexico City in July 1536. Members of an ill-fated expedition that had landed in Florida in 1528, Cabeza de Vaca and his friends were shipwrecked on the Texas coast later that year. For the next eight years, they lived among the Indians, wandering through the region until they encountered a party of Spaniards, in March 1536. Their arrival astounded the Spanish, who eagerly listened to Cabeza de Vaca's tales of enormous cities to the north, where the people traded turquoise and emeralds for the feathers of tropical birds. He did not claim to have seen such cities, only to have heard of them from Indians that he encountered. Despite Cabeza de Vaca's cautious reports, New Spain was gripped with excitement at the prospect of discovering and conquering what surely must be the Seven Cities.

What were the Indians referring to when they told Cabeza de Vaca of the distant cities of wealth? They may have been referring to trading cultures and kingdoms that existed in various locations in North America, including those of the people known as the Anasazi or pre-Puebloans in the Southwest. In addition, historians have pointed out that American Indians had their own myths and legends, one of which concerned a city called the Seven Caves. It is possible that Indians were sharing their own legends with Cabeza de Vaca, who understood them in terms with which he was familiar.

Whatever their origin, the Indian tales of distant lands that Cabeza de Vaca shared held a great appeal for the people of New Spain, who had good reason beyond their belief in the legend of Antillia to accept those rumors as fact. The New World had already yielded a fabulous trove of treasure. Cortés had plundered the cities of the Aztecs less than two decades earlier, and only five years had passed since Francisco Pizarro had conquered the Inca Empire to the south, again capturing vast riches. Surely kingdoms of great wealth and beauty would be found in the north, ripe for the conquistadors bold enough to venture into unknown lands.

Viceroy Mendoza believed so, and, in March 1539, he sent the Franciscan friar Marcos de Niza (Fray Marcos) to investigate. One of Cabeza de Vaca's companions, Estevánico, an African, accompanied Fray Marcos, as did a small group of Indians. Fray Marcos returned that summer with thrilling news. He had seen but not entered a city larger than Mexico City that the inhabitants called Cíbola. The people lived in houses that were several stories high and had turquoise decorations on the doorways. In his official report, Marcos noted that there were a total of seven such cities. Although he had not seen gold, Indians claimed it was common to the region. Privately, Fray Marcos told people that he had seen idols covered with precious stones.

Fray Marcos did not enter the city because Estevánico, who had gone ahead, had been murdered there. His contemporaries and later generations of scholars have expressed doubts about Fray Marcos and his report. Hernán Cortés dismissed Fray Marcos as a liar, and some historians have claimed that he never saw the city, fleeing in panic when he received word of Estevánico's death and fabricating the details that he later recounted. Others maintain that Fray Marcos probably saw a pueblo, a city constructed by the Indians. The word "Cíbola" is in all likelihood a mispronunciation of the Zuni word for the area that Fray Marcos visited.

Whether falsehoods or exaggerations, Fray Marcos's reports included two crucial pieces of misinformation. First, the friar portrayed Cíbola as a region of considerable wealth, a depiction certain to fire the Spanish desire to conquer the territory immediately. Second, Fray Marcos claimed that Cíbola was near the sea. This observation led Coronado to rely upon a small convoy of ships following Mexico's western coast to resupply his expedition as he headed northward.

Fray Marcos had been to Peru and seen the riches of the Incas, and his word was enough to generate rumors of golden cities among the inhabitants of New Spain. When Mendoza learned that the conquistador Hernando de Soto was organizing an expedition to search for the Seven Cities by way of Florida, he knew he had to act quickly to be the first to lay claim to the riches. He selected Coronado to mount a major expedition into *la Tierra Nueva*. Born in Spain in 1510, Coronado had accompanied Mendoza to New Spain and had served as a provincial governor, a military commander, and a member of the council in Mexico City. While Coronado organized the land expedition, Hernando de Alarcón prepared the supply fleet. In the meantime, Melchior Diaz led a small party north in an effort to confirm Fray Marcos's reports.

The Coronado expedition departed on February 23, 1540. Less than a month later, Diaz met the expedition with some troubling news. Poor weather had prevented him from reaching Cíbola, but the Indians he interviewed made it clear that the settlements were small and contained no gold. Fray Marcos, who was present, argued that Diaz had not gone far enough north and assured Coronado that they would see the riches of Cíbola in the coming weeks. Satisfied with Fray Marcos's explanation, Coronado ordered Diaz to join the expedition, which in late March reached the Spanish settlement at Culiacán, where the group rested for nearly a month.

While at Culiacán, Coronado decided to split the expedition into two groups. He would lead a small party of perhaps 100 men north, while the main body, which moved slowly under the weight of supplies, followed at a slower pace. Coronado's force made good time and entered into the present-day state of Arizona in late May. However, supplies were running low, and doubts regarding Fray Marcos's reporting skills grew as the party encountered no evidence that the friar had told the truth. Several men and horses died in the uninhabited region, which the Spaniards called the *despoblado*, the wasteland or uninhabited region. Weary and facing starvation, the advance force encountered Zuni Indians in early July. Finally, on July 7, Coronado and his men laid eyes on Cíbola, and their disappointment knew no bounds.

Schooled in the legends of Antillia, bolstered by the tales of Fray Marcos, and led on by their own greed, Coronado and his soldiers anticipated a city of gold and silver and turquoise. Instead, they saw a small city of stone, the Zuni pueblo of Hawikuh in modern New Mexico. One member of the expedition later recalled that the first reaction of the men was to curse the friar. Despite the crushing realization that he had been misled, Coronado prepared to claim the pueblo for Spain.

Informed by scouts of the approach of the strangers, the Zunis had prepared for the worst. Women and children were sent away, and the ground in front of the pueblo was patterned with lines made from sacred golden cornmeal as a warning not to pass this way. The Zuni men lined the walls of the town as a small group of Spaniards moved toward the town to read aloud a document known as the *requirimiento.* Spanish law required the conquistadors to explain their mission to the Native peoples by reading the *requirimiento,* which informed the Indians that they must accept Christianity and recognize the Spanish Crown. If they agreed, all would be well. If they refused, their lands would be taken and they would be killed or taken as slaves. The reading of the *requirimiento* satisfied the Spaniards but meant nothing to people who could not understand Spanish or, in the event that it was translated, make any sense of it. In any case, the Zunis were unwilling to submit to the demands of strangers whom they regarded as dangerous. When Coronado's men went forth to read the proclamation, the Zunis shot arrows at them.

Why did the Zunis respond with hostility to Coronado's expedition, which at this point was clearly in poor shape after making the arduous journey to the pueblo? Although the Zunis probably had no firsthand acquaintance with these foreigners (other than the unfortunate Estevánico, whom they had killed the year before), they probably knew about the strangers clad in metal. A slave-trading network had developed in New Spain, and Indians throughout the region feared the armored soldiers who kidnapped their people and never returned them. Coronado's men met with arrows because their reputation had preceded them.

Historians have offered an additional reason for the Zunis' refusal to receive the Spaniards with open arms. The expedition arrived during summer ceremonies related to the harvest. The Zunis may have believed that the interruption of the sacred rituals might result in a poor harvest; thus, Coronado unknowingly posed a threat to the well-being of the entire community when he arrived on that summer day in 1540.

The clash at Hawikuh was yet another instance of the collision of European and Indian cultures that was repeated again and again along the Spanish frontier. Although the specifics of each encounter differed in some respects, the meetings between these two very different cultures often resulted in misunderstandings, disagreements, and, finally, bloodshed. Indians usually suffered the most as a result of these meetings for a number of reasons. The introduction of European diseases decimated their populations and disrupted the social order, and they did not possess weapons such as the crossbow, the harquebus, and the cannon, which the Europeans used. However, Coronado did not gain much advantage from these two factors. There is no record of widespread epidemic in the region that would have weakened the Indians prior to his arrival. Cannons would prove ineffective against the walls of the pueblos, which were designed as defensive strongholds.

Organization was the key to Coronado's successes against the Indians, and it carried the day at Hawikuh. He ordered his forces to surround the pueblo to prevent any Indians from escaping and had his archers clear the pueblo's terraces of defenders. Although Coronado was knocked unconscious by a stone, his men rallied and, through a determined effort, entered the pueblo. The Zunis surrendered and departed, and the famished Spaniards found a treasure more valuable than gold, food stores, which they immediately plundered.

Coronado occupied Hawikuh and negotiated a peace with the Zunis, who for the most part kept their distance by staying at pueblos to the east. Determined to achieve success, Coronado had no intention of abandoning his quest. In the following weeks, he sent out several small parties to continue exploring. He ordered Melchior Diaz to head south and contact the main body of the expedition. Diaz did so and then headed west in hopes of finding Alarcón and the supply fleet. Contrary to Fray Marcos's report, Cíbola (now renamed Granada in honor of the hometown of Viceroy Mendoza) was nowhere near water, and the expedition had lost contact with the fleet months earlier.

Diaz reached the Colorado River, where he met Indians who told him they had sighted boats downriver weeks earlier. Diaz and his men hurried south, where they discovered carvings on a tree indicating that letters were buried in a box there. They learned that Alarcón had sailed up the Gulf of California and had taken small boats several miles up the Colorado River about two months earlier. However, worms were eating the boats, and Alarcón had no choice but to return to New Spain. The expedition would not receive badly needed winter supplies; to make matters worse, Diaz, a trusted and reliable officer, was killed in a freak accident on the return journey.

Meanwhile, Coronado sent a second expedition to investigate rumors of another seven cities to the west. In what is today northeastern Arizona, Pedro de Tovar and his soldiers met the Hopi Indians, who, like the Zunis, were not receptive to the strangers. A short battle ensued, after which the defeated Hopis offered assistance to the invaders. Tovar returned to Hawikuh without gold but with news of a great river farther to the west. Coronado then dispatched García López de Cárdenas to find the river and follow it downstream, probably in hopes that he might encounter Alarcón. With the aid of Hopi guides, Cárdenas reached the Colorado River in late September 1540.

He saw what he later described as a brook about six feet wide. The Hopis insisted that it was a mighty river, and indeed it was. Cárdenas was viewing the Colorado from the rim of the Grand Canyon, the first European to do so. The Spaniard was unable to fathom the enormous size of the canyon and believed the river to be closer than it was.

Today the Grand Canyon is recognized as one of the natural marvels on the Earth, and, as a part of the U.S. National Park system, it draws visitors from all over the world. However, Cárdenas and his men left no record indicating that the natural beauty of the canyon awed them. Instead, they regarded it as a gaping wound in the earth that stopped their advance and prevented them from reaching the river. For three days, they traveled along the rim of the canyon searching for a path down, until, ironically, a shortage of water forced them to retreat.

Coronado sent a final exploration party to the east. When two Indians arrived from the east offering their friendship, Coronado authorized Hernando de Alvarado to return with them. Today, they are remembered only by the nicknames given them by the Spaniards, Cacique and Bigotes. These two men spoke of villages that lined a great river and of large herds of wild cattle. With the capable assistance of Bigotes, Alvarado and his men met with no opposition from the Indians they encountered on their journey. They visited the pueblo at Acoma and then proceeded to the river now called the Rio Grande. They named that region, which is now the site of the city of Albuquerque, the province of Tiguex, after the Tigua Indians who lived there. The party then headed north but soon returned to Tiguex and again headed east.

Alvarado's men visited the home of Bigotes, the pueblo at Pecos, and, while there, they met an Indian who altered the future and the fate of Coronado's expedition. The man, who was probably a Pawnee captured by the people at Pecos, was nicknamed the Turk by the Spaniards. The Turk traveled east with the party, perhaps reaching the border of modern Texas, where the Spaniards first saw the amazing herds of buffalo that ruled the grasslands of the high plains. Along the way, the Turk told the strangers of great kingdoms to the east that were filled with gold. Unwilling to learn their lesson, the Spaniards seized on these stories as evidence of the fabled Seven Cities.

Historians believe that the Turk was describing Indian communities of the Mississippian culture, which were indeed impressive but did not possess gold. Perhaps the Turk mentioned the imaginary gold to persuade Alvarado to continue eastward, thus giving the Turk the opportunity to return home. However, Alvarado rushed back to inform Coronado, and, as he hurried west, he brought with him the Turk, Cacique, and Bigotes in chains to ensure their cooperation.

Coronado had taken a small party south while the main force of the expedition established winter quarters at Tiguex. The Spaniards forced the Indians from one pueblo for their own use. Faced with a serious shortage of supplies because of the failure to meet with Alarcon's fleet, expedition members seized food and clothing from the Tiguas. Relations between the Spaniards and the Indians rapidly worsened, and Cárdenas, who was in charge during Coronado's absence, ordered his men to destroy one pueblo and burn any survivors at the stake. Throughout the winter and into the early spring, a brutal war raged along the northern Rio Grande, resulting in the destruction of many villages and the enslavement of an unknown number of Tiguas. The war ended in April, when Coronado set out to Quivira, the golden kingdom of which the Turk had spoken.

With the Turk acting as a guide, the expedition, which included more than 1,700 men, headed east, soon reaching the grasslands of modern Texas. The monotonous landscape offered no markers to measure the distances traveled each day, and Coronado and his men grew disoriented as they crossed the plains. Their confusion was compounded by the fact that the Turk was intentionally leading them astray, hoping to lose them in the vast wilderness so that they would never return to harm his people. As a result, to this day historians are uncertain as to the route the expedition took through Texas.

Frustrated by the apparent lack of progress toward Quivira, Coronado confronted the Turk, who admitted his deception. Coronado ordered the main body of the expedition to return to Tiguex and prepare for another winter. He selected a small group of men to continue the search for Quivira, following the directions of an Indian named Ysopete, who insisted that the city lay to the north. After several days of travel, the party arrived in what is now central Kansas. There they discovered Quivira, several small villages belonging to the Wichita Indians, whom Coronado dismissed as barbarians. When he discovered that the Turk, who was brought along in chains, was attempting to convince the Wichitas to kill the Spaniards' horses, Coronado had him executed.

Coronado spent three weeks exploring Quivira. Fearing the approach of winter weather, he led his men south back to Tiguex in August. During the harsh and unpleasant months of inactivity, Coronado debated a return to Quivira. Yet another Indian, a Wichita called Xabe, insisted that the Spaniards had not searched long enough because there was indeed gold to be found there. But another foray was not to be. Cárdenas left the expedition to fulfill family obligations in New Spain, but he soon returned with bad news. Indians in northern Mexico had destroyed the town of Corazones, and the route back to New Spain was in peril. A final stroke of bad luck, a riding accident in which Coronado was almost killed, ensured the end of the expedition, which headed back to New Spain in April 1542.

The expedition, which had departed with great ceremony just two years earlier, was received with little enthusiasm in New Spain. Mounting the expedition had been an expensive effort, and investors discovered that their profits were nonexistent. Coronado returned with only discouraging news of the north. There were no great cities, no gold to plunder, no fortunes to be made. An official investigation of the expedition determined that Coronado had acted responsibly, and no charges were brought against him. Although he again held government positions, the expedition ruined his career and his health. His contemporaries regarded him as a failure, and many noted a change in his personality and a loss of the leadership qualities he had once possessed. He was also weakened physically and died in 1554 at the age of 44.

Was the expedition a failure? If measured by the dreams that Coronado and his men set forth with in 1540, it was surely no success. They intended to find and conquer the Seven Cities of legend, known variously as Antillia, Cíbola, and, finally, Quivira. The soldiers suffered two years away from family and friends, facing the hardships of travel in unknown territory, hunger, and the danger posed by Indians. All these sacrifices were made for nothing, and, although he was officially held blameless, many citizens of New Spain held Coronado to be at fault.

However, it is difficult to find failure in an expedition with goals that were founded in legend and rumor. Coronado could not find the fabulous cities of gold because they did not exist, and Viceroy Mendoza, despite his disappointment, knew this. The myth of the Seven Cities lingered on for a while—a 1578 map shows Cíbola in all its golden glory, and at times French and English explorers pondered the existence of a land of wealth in the Western Hemisphere. However, for the most part the dream died with the return of the dusty and bedraggled men who marched back to New Spain in 1542.

The long-term consequences of the expedition's discoveries were minimal. Although accounts of the expedition were written, they were not readily available in New Spain, and within three decades the information that Coronado had brought back with him was largely forgotten. The people of New Spain focused their energies on activities closer to home, especially exploiting the vast silver mines that were discovered in Mexico. The lands to the north were again places of mystery.

The expedition had little impact on the world of the American Indians in the Southwest. Archaeologists have discovered no evidence that they adopted any Spanish technology, either in the form of weapons or in the making of other material objects such as pottery. Moreover, efforts to convert Indians do not appear to have had any long-lasting effect, and Christianity did not take root among the peoples who listened to the friars during the *entrada.*

Modern scholars have explored two facets of the Coronado expedition, one a curiosity of minor importance, the other more significant. The question of Coronado's route has long been a great historical puzzle, and professional and amateur historians have invested time and effort in retracing his steps. While these studies have revealed the location of pueblos and of certain Indian communities in Texas and Kansas, they tend to satisfy the curiosity more than they offer insight into the Spanish frontier in the 16th century.

Coronado's interactions with the Indians of the Southwest provide a useful means of understanding the cultural clashes that marked the European arrival in the Americas. Coronado was a conqueror, both in his intent and in his method. He wanted to acquire the legendary gold of the north, and he ventured forth with a military force ready to subdue the Native peoples if necessary. His predecessor, Cabeza de Vaca, had been forced to live with the Indians, and in so doing he learned about their cultures and their ways of interacting with the environment. As a result, he gained a great appreciation for the Indians. When he returned to New Spain, he denounced the trade in Indian slaves as unchristian, and he soon earned a reputation for being too kind to Indians.

Coronado and his men depended upon the Indians in a different manner, relying upon their food stocks when their own supplies dwindled. Because they did not respect the Indians, they never learned from them, and the European and American cultures remained distinct and antagonistic. The expedition left in its wake a hatred for the Spanish, which would sour relations between the two peoples for centuries.

However, Spanish attitudes toward the Indians were ambivalent. On the one hand, they were a people to conquer and to enslave. On the other hand, they were human beings who possessed souls and needed to be converted to Christianity. These conflicting viewpoints resulted in actions that seem odd or even contradictory today, such as the reading of the *requirimiento* before attacking Indian communities. Two minor events connected to the Coronado expedition reveal the tensions in the Spanish attitudes toward American Indians.

The first was the fate of García López de Cárdenas, who commanded the expedition during Coronado's absence and started the war with the Tigua during the winter of 1541–1542. Cárdenas was found guilty of mistreating the Indians, and he spent seven years in prison for his crimes. The second was the decision of Friar Luis de Ubeda to remain at Pecos to minister to the Indians there. (Another friar, Juan de Padilla, returned to Quivira, but historians suspect he was more interested in searching for gold than in saving souls.) About Ubeda there are no such doubts, because Pecos offered no riches.

Given the fact that the Indians at Pecos were angry with the Spaniards, Ubeda's decision reflected great courage and dedication to his cause. His fate remains a mystery, but his act reflects a commitment to his faith and to the mission of bringing Christianity to the Indians. Spaniards such as Friar Ubeda make the history of the Spanish frontier a complex tale of which Coronado's *entrada* is a fascinating component.

## SELECTED BIBLIOGRAPHY

Bolton, Herbert E. *Coronado on the Turquoise Trail: Knight of Pueblos and Plains.* Albuquerque: University of New Mexico Press, 1949. Bolton's entertaining account of the expedition is considered a classic of historical writing.

Chavez, Angelico. *Coronado's Friars.* Washington, DC: Academy of American Franciscan History, 1968. The *entrada* from the perspective of the friars who accompanied the expedition.

Clissold, Stephen. *The Seven Cities of Cíbola.* London: Eyre and Spottiswoode, 1961. A well-written account of efforts to find the fabled seven cities.

Day, A. Grove. *Coronado's Quest: The Discovery of the Southwestern States.* Berkeley: University of California Press, 1964. A biography of Coronado that focuses on the *entrada*.

Flint, Richard, and Shirley Cushing Flint, eds. *The Coronado Expedition to Tierra Nueva: The 1540–1542 Route across the Southwest.* Niwot: University Press of Colorado, 1997. This collection of essays continues the debate over the route that Coronado took.

Hallenbeck, Cleve. *The Journey of Friar Marcos de Niza.* Dallas: Southern Methodist University Press, 1987. Contains a translation of Friar Marcos's account of his 1539 journey and an essay that is highly critical of Marcos.

Hodge, Frederick W., and Theodore H. Lewis, eds. *Spanish Explorers in the Southern United States, 1528–1543.* Austin: Texas State Historical Association, 1984. This volume contains a translation of Pedro de Castaneda's chronicle of the *entrada*.

Kessell, John L. *Kiva, Cross, and Crown: The Pecos Indians and New Mexico, 1540–1840.* Albuquerque: University of New Mexico Press, 1979. The opening chapter examines the impact of Coronado upon the Pecos Indians.

Morris, John Miller. *El Llano Estacado: Exploration and Imagination on the High Plains of Texas and New Mexico, 1536–1860.* Austin: Texas State Historical Association, 1997. Places Coronado's expedition into a much broader historical context.

Riley, Carroll L. *Rio del Norte: People of the Upper Rio Grande from Earliest Times to the Pueblo Revolt.* Salt Lake City: University of Utah Press, 1995. This history of American Indians includes chapters on the *entrada*.

Sauer, Carl Ortwin. *Sixteenth Century North America: The Land and the People as Seen by the Europeans.* Berkeley: University of California Press, 1971. A standard source that includes chapters on Spanish exploration and Coronado.

Speck, Gordon. *Myths and New World Explorations.* Fairfield, WA: Ye Galleon Press, 1979. Readable discussion of the role of myth that includes black-and-white photographs.

Terrell, John Upton. *Search for the Seven Cities: The Opening of the American Southwest.* New York: Harcourt Brace Jovanovich, 1970. This account is most appropriate for younger readers.

Udall, Stewart L. *Majestic Journey: Coronado's Inland Empire.* Santa Fe: Museum of New Mexico Press, 1987. Places the expedition into the larger context of Spanish exploration and includes beautiful color photographs of locations that the expedition visited.

Weber, David J. *The Spanish Frontier in North America.* New Haven, CT: Yale University Press, 1992. While the discussion of Coronado is brief, this work provides an excellent overview of the Spanish frontier for interested students.

## ÁLVAR NÚÑEZ CABEZA DE VACA (ca. 1490–1556/64)

Starting on Galveston Island in November 1528 and ending on the Pacific coast of Mexico nearly eight years later, Álvar Núñez Cabeza de Vaca and his three surviving companions were the first Europeans to cross the North American continent on foot. Cabeza de Vaca's account of his journey and life during these years contains the first descriptions of Texas geography, flora, fauna, and Native culture. The explorer also brought back rumors of fabulous riches that encouraged further Spanish expeditions into what is now the United States.

Cabeza de Vaca was born around 1490 in the Andalusian region of Spain in the town of Jerez de la Frontera to Francisco de Vera, an alderman of the town, and Teresa Cabeza de Vaca. He took his mother's surname, which means "cow's head," because of her more distinguished ancestry. Her family had been members of the nobility since 1212, when a shepherd named Martín Alhaja revealed to King Sancho of Navarre an unguarded mountain pass that allowed him to surprise and defeat a Moorish army. As a reward for his services, the king ennobled Alhaja and bestowed the new surname on him and his descendants in memory of the cow's skull with which the shepherd had marked the hidden pass.

Following in his medieval forebear's footsteps, Cabeza de Vaca became a soldier for the king of Spain, serving on campaigns against the French and Italians from 1511 to the 1520s. In June 1527, he departed Spain as treasurer of the expedition to Florida led by Pánfilo de Narváez. After spending the winter in Cuba, the expedition anchored off the Gulf Coast of Florida near present-day Tampa in April 1528. Narváez then led 300 men, including his treasurer, on a long foray into the interior of the peninsula.

Several months later, with food supplies running low and conflicts with the indigenous breaking out, Narváez and his men fled westward along the coast in makeshift barges. Violent storms west of the Mississippi delta sank several of the vessels, including that of Narváez, and deposited Cabeza de Vaca and several dozen others near present-day Galveston, Texas, on November 6, 1528. The castaways lived on the island for approximately a year, after which most of them headed south toward Spanish settlements on the Gulf Coast of Mexico. Only two remained behind: Cabeza de Vaca, whom the other Spaniards believed to be lost, and Lope de Oviedo, who was too afraid of the risks to make the journey.

Actually, Cabeza de Vaca was not lost but was living with a group of Indians and was too ill to follow the other Spaniards. After recovering from his illness, Cabeza de Vaca lived an extraordinary life, trading shells, dried beans, hides, and red ochre with the various Indian tribes in the Galveston region, which had come to hold him in high regard because of his ability to perform healing miracles. In 1532, he started south, having finally persuaded Oviedo to leave. Oviedo eventually turned back, however, and Cabeza de Vaca was captured by the Mariame Indians, who reunited him with the three surviving members of the group of castaways who had left Galveston in 1529.

With these three, Andrés de Dorantes de Carranza, his African slave Esteban, and Alonso Castillo Maldonado, Cabeza de Vaca planned an escape. They fled southward in 1534, 18 months after Cabeza de Vaca had been captured, and crossed the Rio Grande River near Falcon Lake. They then headed west across northern Mexico, desiring both to avoid the hostile coastal tribes and to explore unknown territory. They reached Culiacán, a Spanish outpost near the Pacific coast, in 1536. Cabeza de Vaca then returned to Spain, where he published an account of his life and journey in Texas and Mexico in 1542.

The narrative is noteworthy for its detailed descriptions of Texas plant life, animal life, and geography and for its sympathetic treatment of Native Americans. In 1540, Spain's King Charles V appointed Cabeza de Vaca governor of Spanish possessions stretching from Peru to the Strait of Magellan. His progressive rule, however, especially his protection of local Indians, angered wealthy Spanish colonists. Spanish authorities arrested Cabeza de Vaca in 1544 after his policies provoked a revolt among the colonists.

In 1551, after a lengthy trial, Cabeza de Vaca was banished to North Africa, which did not stop him from publishing a second edition of his Texas adventure in 1555. By 1556, he had returned from exile; in that year, King Charles appointed him to be chief justice of Seville, Spain. He probably died there some time between 1556 and 1564.

MICHAEL CONNALLY

## FRANCISCO VÁSQUEZ DE CORONADO (1510–1554)

Francisco Vásquez de Coronado, who sought mythical cities of gold, led a treacherous two-year expedition through Sonoran Mexico and into the territory that eventually became the states of Arizona, New Mexico, Texas, Oklahoma, and Kansas. His soldiers were the first Europeans to see the Grand Canyon and navigate the Colorado River.

Coronado seemed destined to poverty; he was born in 1510 as the second son of four children and inherited nothing from his father's entailed estate in Salamanca, Spain. However, he luckily made rich and powerful friends, as he traveled to Mexico in 1535 with the newly appointed viceroy of New Spain, Antonio de Mendoza. That personal connection helped Coronado advance his position. He married the wealthy Beatriz de Estrada, daughter of the treasurer of New Spain, and, in 1539, Mendoza appointed Coronado governor of Nueva Galicia, in northern Mexico.

Soon after he took office, rumors reached Coronado of rich cities of gold to the north. The Spaniards believed those cities were seven mythical cities of gold called the Seven Cities of Cíbola. Hernán Cortés and other conquistadors competed for the chance to discover a new rich empire like Mexico. As the viceroy's favorite, in 1540, Coronado was granted the title captain general of the Seven Cities of Cíbola and any people he might find there, including the Hopi, Acoma, and Zuni civilizations. With the help of his wife and Mendoza, Coronado personally financed an army of about 350 men with perhaps four to five times as many support people, along with three Franciscan friars and 1,000 slaves taken from the already conquered population of central Mexico; almost all had horses. He set out with that army to conquer the territories to the north and to convert to Christianity the indigenous peoples they encountered.

By the time they crossed into present-day Arizona, many men and horses had died of starvation because the journey was far longer than the Spaniards had estimated. Coronado divided the group. Some turned west, eventually encountered the Grand Canyon, and navigated a portion of the Colorado River.

Coronado led a second group, which traveled east. They found the first of the seven cities, a Zuni town or pueblo of 500 families. There, Coronado suffered injuries in a battle with the Zuni. The Spaniards admired the well-built city with its secure multi-storied houses constructed of adobe. However, they found no wealth there, only much-needed food, which included corn and turkeys.

The Spaniards spent the winter of 1540–1541 with the Zuni near Albuquerque and lived off their resources, which included literally taking the clothes off their backs. Coronado tried to find information about richer cities while he attempted to establish military domination over the Zuni. Finally, the Zuni rebelled, and several pueblos were destroyed. The Spaniards moved east toward a settlement on the site of present-day Taos.

As the Spaniards moved further east, they met a man they called the Turk. He told Coronado of a city called Quivira, which straddled a huge river full of enormous fish. The Turk pointed out the Spaniards' gold ornaments and said they were common in Quivira. He offered those temptations to the Spaniards to encourage them to leave the region and end the destruction of the pueblos.

Following the rumors of wealth spread by the Turk, Coronado and his soldiers followed their indigenous guide to the southeast through what is today Texas and Oklahoma, and the group survived off the meat of massive buffalo herds on the way. After much futile searching for wealthy cities, the Spaniards began to distrust the Turk. A nomadic people following the buffaloes finally disabused the Spaniards. The Turk maintained that Quivira supposedly existed further to the north, in Kansas. What the Spaniards did not know was that the duplicitous guide had been entrusted by his people to lead the Spaniards astray since he knew they could not survive on the barren plains. Once the Spaniards became convinced of the Turk's treachery, they strangled him to death.

The discouraged army went north and found more poor mud villages where only the chief possessed even a bronze necklace. Although the Spaniards neglected to make good maps of their wanderings, they traveled more than 2,500 miles. By a direct route, they were only half that distance from Mexico, but they had explored much of the Great Plains of North America.

After suffering a debilitating fall from his horse, Coronado lost control of his followers. He discovered a mutinous petition that the Spanish soldiers had drawn up demanding their return to Mexico. In 1542, Coronado was carried on a stretcher as he returned to Mexico with fewer than 100 men. He left the friars behind to work to convert the indigenous populations to the north. Mendoza treated the expedition as a complete failure and investigated Coronado for corruption and mistreatment of the Zuni. Coronado's injuries and the loss of his fortune on the expensive expedition made him a poverty-stricken invalid. He suffered in disgrace until 1551, when he was finally given an estate and a seat on the governmental council in Mexico City. He died on September 22, 1554.

NICOLE VON GERMETEN

## ESTEBAN (ca. 1503–1539)

Esteban, also known as Estevánico the Moor, was a North African slave and explorer who participated in several Spanish expeditions to North America in the 16th century.

Esteban was born in the North African port city of Azemmour, Morocco, in around 1503. The city was captured by the Portuguese in 1513 after a fierce battle, but keeping it proved equally difficult. During a particularly harsh drought during 1520–1521, the Portuguese sold many of the prisoners into slavery in Europe in an effort to raise money. Esteban was sold to a Spanish nobleman, Andrés de Dorantes de Carranza, and became his personal servant. In time, master and servant developed a close relationship and became friends. When Dorantes de Carranza joined an expedition to Florida, he took Esteban with him. Among the leaders of the expedition was Álvar Núñez Cabeza de Vaca, who wrote a detailed account of the ill-fated expedition in the *Relación*, published in 1542.

The expedition, 300 men strong, landed in Florida on April 12, 1528, and began inland exploration. The harsh environment and constant Indian attacks quickly brought their numbers down. In desperation to save themselves, the survivors made crude barges and set out to sea in an attempt to reach the coast of Mexico. They were shipwrecked off the Texas coast, near Galveston Island. Esteban was among the eight survivors. They remained captives of the Natives for five years. Four survivors—Esteban, Dorantes de Carranza, Cabeza de Vaca, and Alonso Castillo—were able to escape inland in 1534 and began a long overland trek.

The four men arrived in Tenochtitlán, Mexico in July 1536. They had survived the long, perilous journey by passing themselves off as Christian medicine men. They gained a reputation as healers among the different tribes along the way. Many of the local people in the Southwest desert began to follow them, building an ever larger retinue that provided the four explorers with food and other commodities. When they finally made it to Spanish-controlled territory, Cabeza de Vaca and Castillo returned to Spain, while Dorantes de Carranza and Esteban remained in Mexico.

The viceroy of Mexico was very interested in the account of the journey and wanted to send an expedition back into Arizona and New Mexico. In February 1539, Esteban accompanied the expedition leader, the Franciscan Fray Marcos de Niza, to carry out a survey of the lands they had previously crossed. Esteban and Fray Marcos did not get along, however, and Esteban decided to go ahead of the expedition's main body and prepare the local people for the arrival of the Spaniards.

As described in the *Relación de la Jornada de Cíbola*, by Pedro de Castañeda, a member of the Coronado expedition that followed in the steps of Fray Marcos, Esteban was motivated by greed, not piety, in his effort to establish first contact with the Natives. According to Castañeda, Esteban claimed to have the power to protect the Natives and demanded in return women and turquoise as payment. He presented himself to the Natives ornately dressed with clusters of feathers and bells, his chest covered with amulets and necklaces. Charismatic and casting a powerful impression on those who saw him, Esteban built up an entourage of admiring women, who followed him from place to place.

Esteban's way of dealing with the Natives by presenting himself as a healer and precursor of powerful messengers seems to have worked well until he arrived among the Zuni, who saw him as a threat. It is also believed that Esteban's medicine gourd, decorated with owl feathers and which he had carried for a long time with him, was seen as a bad omen by the Zunis, who believed that owls symbolized death. Esteban was murdered in 1539 by the followers of Hanikuh, a Zuni leader, who failed to be impressed by Esteban's display of miraculous power. According to some accounts, the Zunis had his body cut into several pieces and sent to several nearby towns to prove that Esteban did not have any superhuman powers, but the incident is probably apocryphal.

Fray Marcos, who feared for his own safety, returned to New Spain. To avoid criticism for having abandoned the expedition, he passed on to Coronado the stories Esteban had told him about the mythical and gold-covered Seven Cities of Cíbola and thus ensured a continuous presence of Spanish explorers in the area.

JOSE VALENTE

## HOPI

The word "Hopi" comes from *Hopituh Shi-nu-mu*, "Peaceful People." They were formerly called the Moki (or Moqui) Indians, a name probably taken from a Zuni epithet. The Hopis are the westernmost of the Pueblo peoples. First, Second, and Third Mesas are all part of Black Mesa, located on the Colorado Plateau between the Colorado River and the Rio Grande, in northeast Arizona. Of the several Hopi villages, all but Old Oraibi are of relatively recent construction. Hopi, a Shoshonean language, is a member of the Uto-Aztecan language family.

According to legend, the Hopis agreed to act as caretakers of this Fourth World in exchange for permission to live here. Over centuries of a stable existence based on farming, they evolved an extremely rich ceremonial life. The Hopi Way, whose purpose is to maintain a balance between nature and people in every aspect of life, is ensured by the celebration of their ceremonies.

The Hopis recognize two major ceremonial cycles, masked (January or February until July) and unmasked, which are determined by the position of the sun and by the lunar calendar. The purpose of most ceremonies is to bring rain. As the symbol of life and well-being, corn, a staple crop, is the focus of many ceremonies. All great ceremonies last nine days, including a preliminary day. Each ceremony is controlled by a clan or several clans. Central to Hopi ceremonialism is the kiva, or underground chamber, which is seen as a doorway to the cave world from whence their ancestors originally came.

Katsinas are guardian spirits, or intermediaries between the creator and the people. They are said to dwell at the San Francisco peaks and at other holy places. Every year at the winter solstice, they travel to inhabit people's bodies and remain until after the summer solstice. Re-created in dolls and masks, they deliver the blessings of life and teach people the proper way to live. Katsina societies are associated with clan ancestors and with rain gods. All Hopis are initiated into katsina societies, although only men play an active part in them.

Perhaps the most important ceremony of the year is Soyal, or the winter solstice, which celebrates the Hopi worldview and recounts their legends. Another important ceremony is Niman, the harvest festival. The August snake dance has become a well-known Hopi ceremony.

Like other Pueblo peoples, the Hopis recognize a dual division of time and space between the upper world of the living and the lower world of the dead. Prayer may be seen as a mediation between the upper and the lower, or the human and the supernatural, worlds. These worlds coexist at the same time and may be seen in oppositions such as summer and winter, day and night, life and death. In all aspects of Hopi ritual, ideas of space, time, color, and number are all interrelated in such a way as to provide order to the Hopi world.

Traditionally, the Hopis favored a weak government coupled with a strong matrilineal, matrilocal clan system. They were not a tribe in the usual sense of the word but were characterized by an elaborate social structure, each village having its own organization and each individual his or her own place in the community. The "tribe" was "invented" in 1936, when the non-Native Oliver La Farge wrote their constitution. Although a tribal council exists, many people's allegiance remains with the village *kikmongwi* (*cacique*). A *kikmongwi* is appointed for life and rules in matters of traditional religion. Major villages include Walpi (First Mesa), Shungopavi (Second Mesa), and Oraibi (Third Mesa).

Hopi children learn their traditions through katsina dolls, including scare-katsinas, as well as through social pressure, along with an abundance of love and attention. This approach tends to encourage friendliness and sharing in Hopi children. In general, women owned (and built) the houses and other material resources, whereas men farmed and hunted away from the village. Special societies included katsina and other men's and women's organizations concerned with curing, clowning, weather control, and war.

Distinctive one- or two-floor pueblo housing featured sandstone and adobe walls and roof beams of pine and juniper, gathered from afar. The dwellings were entered via ladders through openings in the roofs and were arranged around a central plaza. This architectural arrangement reflects and reinforces cosmological ideas concerning emergence from an underworld through successive world levels.

Hopis have been expert dry farmers for centuries, growing corn, beans, squash, cotton, and tobacco on floodplains and sand dunes or, with the use of irrigation, near springs. The Spanish brought crops such as wheat, chilies, peaches, melons, and other fruit. Men were the farmers and hunters of game such as deer, antelope, elk, and rabbits. The Hopi also kept domesticated turkeys. Women gathered wild food and herbs, such as pine nuts, prickly pear, yucca, berries, currants, nuts, and seeds. Crops were dried and stored against drought and famine.

Farming technology included digging sticks (later the horse and plow), small rock or brush-and-dirt dams and sage windbreaks, and an accurate calendar on which each year's planting time was based. Grinding tools were made of stone. Men wove clothing and women made pottery, which was used for many purposes. Men also hunted with the bow and arrow and used snares and nets to trap animals.

The Hopis are probably descended from the prehistoric Ancestral Puebloan culture. Ancestors of the Hopis have been in roughly the same location for at least 10,000 years. During the 14th century, the Hopis became one of three centers of Pueblo culture, along with the Zuni/Acoma and Rio Grande Pueblos. Between the 14th and 16th centuries, three traits in particular distinguished the Hopi culture: a highly specialized agriculture, including selective breeding and various forms of irrigation; a pronounced artistic impulse, as seen in mural and pottery painting; and the mining and use of coal (after which the Hopi returned to using wood for fuel and sheep dung for firing pottery).

The Hopis first met non-Native Americans when members of Francisco Vásquez de Coronado's party came into their country, in 1540. The first missionary arrived in 1629, at Awatovi. Although the Spanish did not colonize Hopis, they did make the Indians swear allegiance to the Spanish Crown and attempted to undermine their religious beliefs. For this reason, the Hopis joined the Pueblo Revolt of 1680. They destroyed all local missions and established new pueblos at the top of Black Mesa that were easier to defend. The Spanish reconquest of 1692 did not reach Hopi land, and the Hopis welcomed refugees from other pueblos who sought to live free of Spanish influence. In 1700, the Hopis destroyed Awatovi, the only village with an active mission, and remained free of Christianity for almost 200 years thereafter.

During the 19th century, the Hopis endured an increase in Navajo raiding. Later in the century, they again encountered non-Natives, this time permanently. The U.S. government established a Hopi reservation in 1882, and the railroad began bringing in trading posts, tourists, missionaries, and scholars. The new visitors in turn brought disease epidemics that reduced the Hopi population dramatically.

Like many tribes, the Hopis struggled to deal with the upheaval brought about by these new circumstances. Following the Dawes Act (1887), surveyors came in preparation for parceling the land into individual allotments; the Hopis met them with armed resistance. Although there was no fighting, Hopi leaders were imprisoned. They were imprisoned as well for their general refusal to send their children to the new schools, which were known for brutal discipline and policies geared toward cultural genocide. Hopi children were kidnapped and sent to the schools anyway.

Factionalism also took a toll on Hopi life. Ceremonial societies split between "friendly" and "hostile" factions. This development led, in 1906, to the division of Oraibi, which had been continuously occupied since at least 1100, into five villages. Contact with the outside world increased significantly after the two world wars. By the 1930s, the Hopi economy and traditional ceremonial life were in shambles (yet perhaps the latter remained more intact than that of any other U.S. tribe). Most people who could find work worked for wages or the tourist trade. For the first time, alcoholism became a problem.

In 1943, a U.S. decision to divide the Hopi and Navajo reservations into grazing districts resulted in the loss of most Hopi land. This sparked a major disagreement between the tribes and the government that continues to this day. Following World War II, the "hostile" traditionalists emerged as the caretakers of land, resisting Cold War–related policies such as mineral development and nuclear testing and mining. The official ("friendly") tribal council, however, instituted policies that favored the exploitation of the land, notably permitting Peabody Coal to strip-mine Black Mesa, beginning in 1970.

BARRY M. PRITZKER

## SPANISH COLONIZATION OF THE AMERICAS

The first of the European powers to reach the New World, Spain remained a dominant force there for more than a century after the arrival of Christopher Columbus. The empire Spain amassed in North America included at one time or another Central America, Mexico, and a significant portion of what is now the central and southwestern United States.

Spain's heritage was one of conquest or, more correctly, reconquest (*reconquista*), as the preceding seven centuries had been spent driving the Moors out of Spain. Following the ousting of the Moors, King Ferdinand V found himself with a large number of Spanish soldiers ill equipped for civilian life. In 1493, Columbus, whose expeditions to find new trade routes had been sponsored by Spain, returned with news of vast unexplored land, which brought purpose to Ferdinand's unemployed soldiers.

The first of the Spanish arrivals in the New World were primarily Castilians with a threefold mission: God, Spain, and gold—not always necessarily in that order. Through exploration, missionaries hoped to spread Catholicism, Spain hoped to expand its empire, and merchants hoped to acquire new wealth. The soldiers' goals, particularly the acquisition of personal wealth and glory, were deemed ample justification for subjugating the indigenous inhabitants of the new land, often in a brutal fashion not at all in keeping with the directives of the Spanish Crown. However, in the far-flung reaches of the New World frontier, it was the hidalgo, or noble representative of Spain, who ruled. With few exceptions, the oppressive treatment of Native peoples established a pattern of mistrust and hatred that would be passed on to subsequent generations.

Spanish conflict with indigenous populations in the Americas commenced almost immediately, when the fortified camp of Villa de la Navidad (Town of the Nativity), erected by Columbus on Hispaniola prior to his return to Spain in 1493, was attacked and destroyed by Natives of the area in retaliation for brutal treatment. With minor variations, it was a scenario that would repeat itself in the years to follow. However, the indigenous peoples were just as likely to be defending themselves against the Spaniards as to be initiating the aggression, if not more likely.

After his arrival on the Yucatán Peninsula in 1519, for example, Hernán Cortés heard of the Aztec Empire and immediately set out for it. With the help of other local indigenous tribes that were either conquered by Cortés or more afraid of the Aztecs than the Spanish, Cortés and his army took the Aztec capital, Tenochtitlán. The Aztecs soon ousted the Spanish, but Cortés returned in 1521 and retook the empire. The Spanish built Mexico City on the ruins of Tenochtitlán and made the Aztecs their laborers. Mexico, with its plentiful silver mines, became one of Spain's most valuable possessions in the New World; three centuries later, as the United States and Great Britain took over North America, it was Mexico that Spain fought hardest to keep.

The success of Cortés and Francisco Pizarro, who discovered and conquered the Inca Empire, led the Spanish to believe that even greater wealth awaited them in the lands to the north. Accordingly, between 1513 and 1563, a dozen expeditions of varying sizes landed along the southeastern and Gulf Coast areas of what is today the United States. Those efforts were mostly directed at Florida by Juan Ponce de León, who discovered the area on Easter Sunday in 1513. Ponce de León was searching the swamps and everglades of Florida for the mythical Fountain of Youth, a spring that rejuvenated and cured those who drank from it. Several other expeditions, however, ranged as far north as present-day Georgia and the Carolinas.

Notwithstanding the presence of women, children, slave labor, and a retinue of friars and priests, the expeditions were decidedly military in character. Typically, they consisted of mounted lancers armed with both lances and swords and supported by infantry equipped with pikes, crossbows, and harquebuses (an early matchlock shoulder weapon). The heavily armed professional soldiers, calling themselves conquistadores (conquerors), were proud and reckless, with a lust for power and an aversion to discipline. They were also legendary for their capacity to endure heat, cold, hunger, and pain. Their expeditions were usually financed and led by a Spanish hidalgo. The object of the expedition was to make an armed entrance, or *entrada,* into the interior of the country and create a fortified base camp, called a presidio, from which to carry out the mission.

Most of those expeditions clashed with the indigenous people that they encountered; in some instances, resistance from the latter was fierce and, in view of Spanish behavior, completely understandable. Native villages were plundered, women raped, and people forced into slavery. A favorite Spanish tactic was to lure the chief or village head into a council setting and then hold him hostage to ensure that the expedition's needs were met. In one instance, expedition leader Pánfilo de Narváez ordered the nose of a Timucua chief to be cut off and the chief's mother thrown to savage dogs to be torn apart.

Major confrontations between the Spanish conquistadores and indigenous peoples included fights around San Carlos Bay, Florida, with the Spanish led by Francisco Hernández de Córdoba in 1517 and Ponce de León in 1521. Hernando de Soto's 1541 clash with Choctaws in the Battle of Mabila (near present-day Selma, Alabama) was probably the largest single engagement of the period. Hernández de Córdoba, Ponce de León, and de Soto eventually died from wounds sustained during their fights with the indigenous.

Another expedition that had its share of fighting was that of the hidalgo Narváez. Landing on the west coast of Florida in 1527, Narváez, after sending his ships in search of a better harbor, headed overland. After first fighting Timucuas, they clashed with Apalachees. Continuing on, the hard-pressed and exhausted contingent was constantly harried by the indigenous people. After discovering that their ships were not waiting at the expected place (the ships had been there and, believing the expedition lost, departed for Mexico), they finally reached Mobile Bay and crossed the Mississippi River. Of the 300 who began the ordeal, only 4 survived to reach Mexico. The saga of their incredible ordeal, later recounted in the journal of a survivor, Álvar Núñez Cabeza de Vaca, became one of the epics of history.

Spanish efforts were not limited to the Southeast, however. In April 1540, Francisco Vásquez de Coronado set out in search of the fabled Seven Cities of Cíbola. In large part, Coronado's expedition was inspired by Cabeza de Vaca's reports. During the two-year expedition, Coronado failed to find the rumored golden cities but did explore much of what is now the southwestern United States, including Arizona and Colorado, and penetrated as far east as Kansas and northern Texas. The expedition also marked the first time Europeans reached the Grand Canyon and the Colorado River. In the process of exploring, Coronado managed to capture the Zuni pueblo at Hawikuh as well as other Hopi and Zuni pueblo communities in Arizona and New Mexico. Later, Spanish expeditions in the Southwest resulted in Juan de Oñate's brutal attack on the Acoma pueblo in 1599, followed by the bloody Pueblo Revolt of 1680.

Meanwhile, during the last half of the 16th century, the Spanish continued to send expeditions into the interior of Florida in an effort to strengthen their position there. As earlier, ill treatment of Native peoples, particularly in the form of forced labor, continued to produce clashes between the two cultures, although an increased emphasis on the establishment of missions met with some success. Perhaps the most notable Spanish achievement in the area was the creation of San Agustín, now Saint Augustine, the oldest city in the United States settled by Europeans. Spanish presence in Florida continued until 1763, when the territory was given over to Britain in exchange for Cuba.

The conquest of indigenous peoples in the Americas was ultimately accomplished due to disease brought to the New World by Europeans, the superiority of their weapons, and, at times, brutal massacres. Although the Spanish legacy in the New World is one of harsh treatment and exploitation, Spain's contribution to architecture, the arts, and language in the Americas cannot be overlooked.

JERRY KEENAN

## ZUNI

"Zuni," from the Spanish, is the name of both a people and a pueblo. The Zuni Pueblo's original name was *Ashiwi,* which might have meant "the flesh." The Zuni consisted of six pueblos along the north bank of the upper Zuni River, in western New Mexico, at least 800 years ago. They are presently in the same location. Perhaps as many as 20,000 people lived there in 1500. Zuni is a language unlike that spoken at other pueblos. Scientists speculate about a possible link to the Penutian language family.

Zunis and their ancestors, the Mogollon and the Ancestral Puebloans, and perhaps Mexican Indians as well, have lived in the Southwest for well over 2,000 years. By the 11th century, the "village of the great kiva," near Zuni, had been built. In the 14th and 15th centuries, a large number of villages existed in the Zuni Valley. By 1650, the number of Zuni villages had shrunk to six.

Zuni was probably the first Native North American village visited by Spaniards, who had heard tales of great wealth in the Kingdom of Cíbola. In 1539, Estevánico, a black man in the advance guard of Fray Marcos de Niza's party, visited Zuni. He was killed as a spy, and his group quickly retreated. The following year, Francisco Vásquez de Coronado visited the pueblos, ranging all the way to present-day Kansas, in search of the mythical Cíbola. The Zunis resisted his demands and fled to a nearby mesa top. Other Spanish came in Coronado's wake. The first mission was established at Hawikuh in 1629. In 1632, the Zunis attacked and killed a number of missionaries, but the Spanish built a new mission, Halona, in 1643.

The Zuni participated in the Pueblo Revolt of 1680. Their main grievances were being forced to supply the Spanish with corn, women, and labor and being punished harshly for practicing their religion. At that time, the Zunis lived in three of the original six pueblos. They fled to escape the Spanish, and in 1693 they returned to the village at Halona on the Zuni River. A new church was built there but was soon abandoned, the Zunis preferring their own religion to Christianity. The ancient site of Halona is now modern Zuni.

Left on their own by the Spanish, the Zuni Pueblo was open to raids from Apaches, Navajos, and Plains tribes. As of 1850, it was still self-sufficient, although, because it was on important trade routes, it was increasingly raided by both Indians and Anglos. The U.S. government officially recognized a Zuni reservation in 1877, although one far too small to support traditional agriculture. Three outlying summer villages established in the early 19th century became permanent in the 1880s, and a fourth such village was established in 1912 or 1914. In the late 19th and early 20th centuries, the Zuni economy shifted from agriculture to sheep and cattle herding. With the decline of warfare, their

Bow society turned to warfare against supposed Zuni witches. The Bureau of Indian Affairs soon called in troops to suppress witchcraft trials, destroying the power of the Bow priests and the entire traditional government.

The opposition of tribal members as well as the failure of the government's Black Rock Reservation and Dam combined to block the implementation of the allotment process at Zuni. Erosion of arable land has been a considerable problem, especially since the debacle of counterproductive, government-mandated canal irrigation projects in the early 20th century. By the 1930s, the government was promoting livestock as an alternative to agriculture. After World War II, the continuing shift in political power from priests to politicians led to the growth of political parties and the increased importance of the tribal council.

Religion, including membership in religious and ceremonial organizations, was at the core of Zuni existence. The sun priest was highly revered; in charge of solstice ceremonies as well as the calendar, he was held responsible for the community's welfare. The Zunis recognized six points of orientation, which corresponded to the cardinal directions as well as to mythological events. Each had its own color, position, kiva group, medicine societies and priesthoods, and ceremonies. Kivas were rectangular and aboveground.

Katsinas, or benevolent guardian spirits, played a key part in Zuni religion. Katsinas represented the rain gods as well as Zuni ancestors. All boys between the ages of 11 and 14 underwent initiation into the Katsina Society. At death, one was said to join the katsinas, especially if one was closely associated with the cult. Both men and women could join the curing cult of the beast gods. Its focus was on animals of prey who lived in the east.

The Zuni new year began at the winter solstice. A 20-day period during this time was known as *Itiwana*, or cleansing and preparing the village for the new year. Winter dances took place from February through April. Summer dances began at the solstice and lasted into September, concluding with the fertility ritual called Olowishkia. In late November or early December, the Zunis celebrated Shalako, a reenactment by katsina priests of the creation and migration of the Zuni people. The people built six to eight Shalako houses and attended the Shalako katsinas—giant-sized messengers of the rain gods. This festival was accompanied by spectacular dancing and closed the Zuni year. Molawai, or the ritual dramatization of the loss and recovery of corn maidens, immediately followed Shalako.

Ruled by heads of various priesthoods and societies, the Zuni pueblo was a theocracy. Bow priests enforced the rules from at least the 17th century on. A tribal council played a minor role in the 19th century but a more powerful one in the 20th century. The Zunis accepted the Indian Reorganization Act and an elected tribal council in 1934 (they ratified a constitution in 1970).

During the 18th century, a parallel, secular government developed at Zuni to handle mundane problems. Based on the Spanish model, it was appointed by and responsible to the religious leaders. Offices included a governor, two lieutenant governors, a sheriff, and fiscales (church assistants). These officers acted as liaisons between the pueblo and the outside world and kept order within the pueblo. Metal-topped canes with a Spanish cross served as symbols of authority. Through the years, these were augmented by more Spanish canes, Mexican canes, and then canes given by President Lincoln to reward the pueblo for its neutrality in the Civil War.

Zunis were divided into two groups: people of the north (also characterized as winter or rain) and people of the south (also characterized as summer or sun). Matrilineal clans affected ceremonial roles and certain behaviors. In general, however, ritual activity went through the father's family, and economic activity went through the mother's. There were also a number of secret cults and societies, some highly complex, each responsible for certain ceremonies. Zunis traditionally cremated their dead. In modern times, the dead are buried, with their possessions burned or buried after four days, following a ceremony that includes prayer sticks and cornmeal. With the exception of certain clan and family taboos, marriage was a matter between the two people involved and was traditionally preceded by a trial period of cohabitation. Divorce was simple and easy.

Like other Pueblo Indians, Zunis lived in multistoried houses (pueblos). Men built the structures of stone and plaster, not the adobe bricks used in the pueblos to the east. Ladders led to the upper stories. Floors were of packed adobe and roofs of willow boughs, brush, and packed earth. Women kept the outsides whitewashed. Tiny windows and outside beehive ovens were introduced in the 16th century.

Farming was the chief Zuni mode of subsistence. Men grew at least six varieties of corn, as well as beans, squash, and cotton. The Spanish introduced crops such as wheat, chilies, oats, and peaches. Zunis used dams and sage windbreaks for irrigation. Corn was dried, ground into flour or meal, and served as mush or baked into breads. Food was also obtained by hunting (deer, antelope, and rabbits), fishing, and gathering wild plants (women were the gatherers, and they also kept small garden plots).

BARRY M. PRITZKER

# 4

# The Founding of
# St. Augustine, 1565

## INTRODUCTION

The first Spanish explorer to set foot in Florida was Juan Ponce de León in March 1513. He named what he thought to be an island La Florida, because, in the Spanish religious calendar, March was the time of the Feast of Flowers. At the time of Ponce de León's arrival, about 25,000 Indians, spread among four major tribes, lived in Florida. These were the Calusa, who lived in southwest Florida; the Tekesta, from southeast Florida; the Timucua, from northeast Florida; and the Apalachee, from northwest Florida, the area known today as the Florida panhandle.

The Calusa were seagoing Indians who fished and sailed small boats as far away as Cuba and Hispaniola. They did not cultivate crops, although they did gather roots, dry them, and pound them into flour to make into bread. The Calusa developed a fairly sophisticated social structure, with authority vested in a king who resided in a centrally located village protected by extensive fortifications. The tribe also used slaves, who were members of other tribes taken captive in battle. Within their domain, they developed a system of food storage and distribution, so villages that experienced food shortages could be supplied with dried food from other villages. They were not receptive to Spanish encroachment, killing some of Ponce de León's men in 1513 and Ponce de León himself in 1521, during his second voyage to Florida.

The Timucua, whose culture can be traced back to 500 BCE, built villages along rivers or next to lakes. These villages were fortified and included ceremonial sites, granaries, and public buildings. They ate game and fish, planted small gardens, and collected berries and acorns. Like the Calusa, the Timucua developed a social structure based on matriarchal clans, a system of intertribal alliances, and a class system based on a nobility and commoners.

Of the other two Florida tribes, we know less. The Tekesta Indians lived in southeast Florida. They also harassed the Spanish, although fewer attempts were made to settle in that part of Florida than in other parts. Missionaries claimed some success in converting the Tekesta, but the Indians were still reputed to have killed Spanish sailors shipwrecked in their territory, and those Spaniards who escaped them reported that they were cruel and untrustworthy. Near Pensacola in northwest Florida were the Apalachee, a powerful and united tribe whose antagonism toward Europeans helped prevent the success of colonization efforts in that area.

**This German book illustration from the late 16th century gives some idea of what the French saw when they first arrived in the Saint Augustine area in 1564. (Courtesy of the Library of Congress.)**

Attempts to colonize Florida before 1565 had failed, costing Spain many lives and ships and much money. Spanish explorers spent too much time and energy looking for gold and other symbols of immediate wealth, failed to pacify the Indians, and suffered in the hostile climate and environment. The ill-fated but far-ranging expeditions of both Pánfilo de Narváez and Hernando de Soto in the 1520s and 1530s began as Florida colonization efforts. Narváez, who passed through Florida in 1528, found both the land and the Indians inhospitable. De Soto, whose expedition landed near Tampa Bay in May 1539, also encountered difficulty with Indians and found nothing of value. The dismal fates of these two expeditions led Spain to regard Florida as relatively unimportant in their colonial policies, although the strategic location of the territory and the missionary opportunities among Indians remained factors to be considered.

In 1549, the second of those two factors was recognized with the mission of Fray Luis Cancer de Barbastro to Florida. He was put ashore near Tampa Bay and killed on the beach in sight of the ship that had taken him there. While Cancer's death encouraged some to want revenge against the Indians, the increasing incidence of shipwrecks off the Atlantic Coast of Florida was also a concern, since nothing could be recovered from these wrecks without settlements on the shore.

The first serious attempt to colonize Pensacola occurred in 1561 when an expedition headed by Tristán de Luna y Arellano arrived. Renaming the place Santa Maria, the de Luna expedition left settlers behind, but, two years later, after most of a fleet was destroyed in a storm, the Spanish abandoned Santa Maria, and King Philip II decided to make no further attempts to colonize the inhospitable territory. But when the king learned that an expedition of French Huguenots was on its way to set up a colony in Florida, he changed his mind.

René Goulaine de Laudonnière founded the French colony in Florida. The French foreign minister, Gaspard de Coligny, had sponsored the expedition in the hope that the colony could be used as a base from which French ships could raid Spanish fleets carrying treasure back to Europe. Laudonnière and 300 colonists, many of whom were French Huguenots, arrived at the mouth of the Saint John's River (which they named the River of May) in April 1564, established good relations with the Indians, and built a fort on the river bank, naming it Fort Caroline in honor of the French king, Charles IX.

Despite its auspicious beginnings, the French colony soon encountered serious problems. Laudonnière proved to be an autocratic leader who also angered the Indians by meddling in their affairs. By December, some colonists were ready to go home, while others were refitting two ships to harass the Spanish. Before they could leave, however, another French fleet, led by Jean Ribault, arrived to reinforce Fort Caroline. Ribault, moreover, had come to replace the discredited Laudonnière, who had been recalled to France.

Philip II, concerned about the threat to Spanish shipping that the French colony represented, dispatched an expedition under Captain-General Pedro Menéndez de Avilés to Florida to oust the French and establish a Spanish colony in the same area. Menéndez de Avilés left Santo Domingo, the Spanish settlement on Hispaniola, in August 1565 with five ships and 800 people, mostly soldiers and sailors.

Menéndez de Avilés and his party arrived at a place 35 miles south of the French settlement on September 5, 1565, and founded a colony called Saint Augustine, named for the saint on whose day they first sighted the place. There they met members of a Timucua Indian tribe, who hated the French for having allied themselves with a rival tribe. The Timucua gave Menéndez de Avilés information about the French settlement, and the Spanish captain sailed up the coast to the mouth of the Saint John's River. Four French ships, under Ribault's command, hastily set sail from the French settlement, and a conflict was avoided when the faster French ships escaped. Ribault then decided to attack the Spanish at their landfall, Saint Augustine. He nearly succeeded in destroying the Spanish ships, but at a crucial moment, a sudden storm developed and forced the French ships away.

Menéndez de Avilés then took his troops across land with an Indian guide, surprised the French, and captured Fort Caroline, killing everyone except women and children under the age of 15 in the process. Meanwhile, a hurricane had driven the four French ships onto the beach several miles away, where they were wrecked. The survivors appealed to Menéndez de Avilés for mercy, but the Spaniard ordered most of them killed. Altogether 358 of the 544 French sailors, including the unlucky Ribault, were summarily executed on a sand dune that became known as Matanzas, or Place of Killing. With these executions, the French presence in Florida was ended, and Spanish control of the Saint Augustine area was ensured. Fort Caroline was rebuilt and renamed San Mateo.

Although the Spanish colony at Saint Augustine survived, other attempts at colonization in Florida did not, and Menéndez de Avilés's efforts to ally himself with other Indian tribes were also unsuccessful. Menéndez de Avilés, who had financed much of the expense of colonizing Saint Augustine with his own money, had to be sustained in his last years by a royal subsidy and died in poverty in 1574.

The Jesuits first undertook religious conversion in Florida, but they left in 1572, and Franciscan monks took their place. The Franciscans claimed to have won 13,000 souls for Christ, but many clerics lost their lives in the process, and the Indians never were assimilated into Spanish colonial life, as they were in other parts of Spanish America.

As happened everywhere else in the Spanish American empire, disease took a heavy toll on the Indian population. Prior to the settlement of Saint Augustine, other efforts to create a permanent settlement in Florida had brought deadly disease to Indians in the Pensacola area. In Saint Augustine, in 1586, the captain of the *Primrose*, a ship in Sir Francis Drake's English fleet, reported, "The wilde people at first comminge of our men died verie fast and said amongst themselves, it was the Englisshe God that made them die so fast" (quoted in Cook, p. 95). Since many of Drake's men died at the same time, this epidemic was probably typhus, a disease to which Europeans had no special immunity.

Saint Augustine experienced other epidemics in 1596, 1613–1617, and 1649. Franciscans missionaries reported that the epidemic that broke out in 1613 killed perhaps half the population of some tribes, noting that "these deaths have taken great harvests of souls for heaven" (quoted in Cook, p. 192). The 1649 epidemic, an outbreak of yellow fever, killed the governor of Florida, two treasury officials, and a number of military officers and missionaries in addition to countless numbers of Indians.

For most of the colonial period, Saint Augustine was little more than a large, stout fort, and the inhabitants were quite dependent on the home government for most of their supplies. Not until the late 17th century did the Spanish colonists discover the economic feasibility of cattle raising inland from the fortress town.

## INTERPRETIVE ESSAY

BLAKE BEATTIE

For most Americans, "colonial America" remains a distant and unvisited country, known chiefly through a few vivid images emblazoned on the American mythic consciousness. The legend of Pocahontas; the first Thanksgiving; the Salem witch trials: these are the remembered emblems of a national formation that played itself out in Virginia plantations and quaint New England villages lying under the white steeples of austere Congregational churches, guided by men with names like John Alden, William Bradford, Roger Williams, and John Smith. Simply put, while few Americans have more than a passing acquaintance with the history of America's European settlement, most would agree that the process began when the first English settlers arrived in Jamestown in 1607 and the Pilgrims landed at Plymouth Rock in 1620, inaugurating an American colonial experience that is essentially English, centered in New England and Virginia, and vigorously Protestant.

This perception has been challenged over the past generation by historians who stress the importance of groups like America's Native peoples and African slaves in shaping American nationhood. Yet, even the revisionists, with their heightened consciousness of the "other" in the national history, often overlook the fact that the critically important process of European exploration and settlement, by which America became possible as an historical and a political entity, began not in the north with the English but in the south with the Spaniards. The first permanent European settlement in what would become the United States of America was a fort christened San Augustin or Saint Augustine, by a Founding Father named Pedro Menéndez de Avilés. Two decades would pass before the English settled Roanoke Island. By the time Virginia Dare was born at that ill-fated colony, becoming the first English child born in the Americas, a generation had grown up in Spanish Florida, and it would still be there long after Virginia and the other 117 Roanoke settlers vanished from history the following year. If it is true that Spain eventually lost the contest for North America to France and especially England, its cultural legacy has endured without interruption in the American Southwest and parts of the Southeast for four centuries. More important, the contest for North America might never have taken place without Menéndez de Avilés's *empresa en la Florida* and the establishment of a Spanish foothold in the New World north of the Rio Grande.

Ironically, the foundation of Saint Augustine came about almost accidentally, as an act of desperation, three years *after* the king of Spain had decided to abandon efforts to settle Florida. The Spaniards had attempted to colonize the territory they called La Florida ever since the expedition of Juan Ponce de León in 1513. Contrary to popular belief, the aging veteran of Columbus's second voyage sought not a legendary fountain of youth but a discovery that would make him as famous as Columbus. What he found instead was financial ruin and a fatal wound from an Indian arrow in 1521. Ponce de León's experience proved portentous for the next two generations of Florida's would-be conquistadores. Pánfilo de Narváez (d. 1528) and Hernando de Soto (d. 1542) squandered fortunes, reputations, and, ultimately, their own lives in picaresque but fruitless quests for gold-laden cities like the ones that Narváez had seen in Mexico and de Soto had plundered while serving under Pizarro in Peru. In 1549, the Dominican friar Luis Cancer de Barbastro and three confrères were martyred while attempting to missionize the Timucua Indians. A decade later, the viceroy of Mexico, Luis de Velasco, sent Tristán de Luna y Arellano to found a settlement near Pensacola Bay. Luna lost a third of his 1,500 men and 5 of his 13 ships before he was relieved of his command; his successor, Angel de Villafane, abandoned the colony after a hurricane ravaged his fleet in June 1561. In the aftermath of the debacle, Spain's King Philip II reluctantly declared, in September 1561, that the Crown would no longer sponsor colonial initiatives in La Florida.

Spain's involvement in Florida might well have ended then had not the exigencies of dynastic politics driven Philip's French rivals to take advantage of the situation. Since the time of Philip's father, Charles of Habsburg (1500–1558), France and Spain had been divided by a bitter enmity. Charles stood heir to a remarkable inheritance: from his maternal grandparents, the famous Spanish monarchs Isabella of Castile and Ferdinand II of Aragon, he inherited the Spanish Crown in 1516; after the death of his paternal grandfather, Emperor Maximilian I, he ruled the Holy Roman Empire as Emperor Charles V. The sum of Charles's inheritances—the largest in European history—entailed a collection of satellite states throughout central and eastern Europe and a colonial empire with holdings on four other continents. The vast scope of Charles's power alarmed his European contemporaries, but none more than the Valois kings of France, who found themselves hemmed in by Habsburg patrimonies to the south and to the east. King Francis I fought—and lost—four wars against Charles over disputed territories in Burgundy and in Italy. Discouraged by the spread of Lutheranism in the empire, the devoutly Catholic

Charles abdicated his constellation of thrones in 1556, leaving the empire to his brother Ferdinand and Spain to Philip. But the division of Charles's inheritance brought no relief to France. Spain was emerging as Europe's greatest military power at a time when France was dangerously destabilized by conflicts between the Catholic majority and the increasingly powerful and assertive Huguenots (French Protestants who followed the teachings of John Calvin). In 1559, Henry II made peace with Philip II at Cateau-Cambrésis, acknowledging Spanish supremacy in Italy in exchange for Burgundy and a much-needed promise of Spanish nonaggression.

Any hope of a rapprochement was extinguished when poor Henry was killed in a joust during the celebrations for the treaty. Franco-Spanish relations deteriorated rapidly in the successive reigns of Henry's three weak sons, particularly during the political ascendancy of Prince Gaspard de Coligny (1519–1572), the ambitious and stridently anti-Spanish admiral of France who came to exercise a great influence over young Charles IX between 1560 and 1574. Coligny was a vigorous promoter of overseas colonization who believed that France had done too little to develop its colonial interests in the Americas since Jacques Cartier explored the Saint Lawrence basin of eastern Canada in the 1530s and 1540s. He was also a calculating statesman who hoped to strike a blow at Spain's imperial might before it became insuperable. As a Huguenot, he hoped to avert a civil war by uniting France's Catholics and Protestants against their common enemy, Habsburg Spain. For Coligny, the Spanish moratorium on settlement in La Florida was an opportunity too tempting to pass up.

Coligny easily secured royal approval and dispatched a fleet to Florida under Jean Ribaut (1520–1565), one of France's ablest seamen. On May 1, 1562, Ribaut founded the settlement of Mayport on an island in the Saint John's River; a few days later he sailed to Parris Island, off the coast of South Carolina, and established a tiny settlement named Charlesfort, in honor of France's 12-year-old sovereign. When he returned to France to obtain supplies, however, Ribaut found the kingdom rent by sectarian strife and Coligny out of favor at court. The Huguenot Ribaut eventually decided to try his luck in Protestant England. But Queen Elizabeth I had no desire to be drawn into France's struggle with Spain and had Ribaut cast into prison.

Without material relief, Ribaut's settlements foundered. Charlesfort was abandoned after a fire destroyed its few remaining supplies, and a mutiny broke out at Mayport. The French settlement was on the brink of abandonment when Coligny, restored to royal favor after the Peace of Amboise in March 1563, sent forth a relief expedition under the Huguenot nobleman René Goulaine de Laudonnière, a veteran of Ribaut's first voyage. Upon his arrival, in April 1564, Laudonnière immediately set about the construction of a stout, triangular fort not far from Mayport, on a low bluff overlooking the south bank of the Saint John's River.

Philip II had long been aware of the French expeditions into Spanish Florida and made no secret of his outrage at Colingy's audacity. Still, prior to the Laudonnière expedition, Philip had hoped to resolve the matter diplomatically. The construction of Fort Caroline, however, forced him to act more decisively. A fortress on Florida's strategic northeast coast would provide a base from which swift French corsairs could strike at sluggish Spanish treasure fleets in the Gulf of Mexico. Reversing his decision of September 1561, Philip now concluded that the French fort had to be destroyed and Florida secured for Spain, at all costs.

The man he selected to lead the venture was Pedro Menéndez de Avilés (1519–1574). One of 20 children born to a noble family from Asturias, Menéndez de Avilés had little to expect from the division of his family's modest estate and entered Spain's maritime service as a very young man. With his meager inheritance, he purchased a small patrol vessel and quickly established himself as the scourge of the French and Moorish pirates who bedeviled Spanish ships along Spain's Atlantic coast. In 1554, he escorted the future King Philip II to England for his wedding to Queen Mary I; five years later, he commanded the royal guard, which conducted the king safely from Flanders to Spain after the negotiations at Cateau-Cambrésis. In 1559, a grateful Philip II named him captain general of Spain's East Indian fleet. But Menéndez de Avilés had powerful enemies in the merchants' guilds and in the *Casa de Contratación*, the regulatory council founded by Queen Isabella in 1503 to oversee all trade conducted between Spain and the Spanish West Indies. At their instigation, Menéndez de Avilés was arrested on a charge of smuggling upon his return to Spain in June 1563. He was languishing in a Seville prison, on the brink of political and financial ruin, when he managed to convince his royal patron to grant him the license to settle La Florida in March 1565.

The conquistadores of the previous generation claimed to have acted *por dios, oro y gloria*—for God, gold, and glory. Like them, Menéndez de Avilés was driven by official, personal, and spiritual motives. As *adelantado* (the military-governor of a frontier province), he meant to secure La Florida for Spain; as a father, he desperately hoped to find his only son, Juan, who had disappeared while commanding a royal armada near Bermuda in 1563; as a fervent Catholic and a commander of the ancient crusading order of the Knights of Santiago de Compostela, he intended to expel the French heretics from lands that had belonged to Spain for more than 50 years. And so, on June 29, 1565, Menéndez de Avilés boarded his 900-ton flagship, *San Pelayo*, and led a magnificent fleet of 19 ships and 1,500 souls out of the harbor at Cádiz.

Initially, Menéndez de Avilés seemed no more likely to succeed than any of his predecessors in La Florida. In July, his armada was dispersed by storms in the mid-Atlantic; only five of his ships managed to reach Puerto Rico at the beginning of August. Moreover, the indefatigable Ribaut, released from his English prison, had beaten Menéndez de Avilés in a desperate race across the Atlantic and assumed command of Fort Caroline. When Menéndez de Avilés reached the mouth of the Saint John's River, at the end of August, he was dismayed to find the French fort defended by five bristling warships. In no position to engage the French ships, Menéndez de Avilés withdrew to a natural harbor some 40 miles to the south. He had first seen the site on August 28—the feast day of Saint Augustine—and so he named his camp San Augustin. When the armada's Franciscan chaplain Francisco López Mendoza de Grajales celebrated Mass there on September 8, America's oldest continually inhabited city was born.

But the Spaniards had not heard the last of Ribaut. Determined to destroy the Spanish fleet, he sailed into the mouth of San Augustin harbor and might well have defeated the unprepared Spaniards but for a sudden storm, which drove his ships far to the south and wrecked them along Cape Canaveral. Now utterly convinced of God's favor, Menéndez de Avilés took the offensive with a spectacular exploit. Leaving his brother Bartolomé in charge of the camp, Menéndez de Avilés led 500 soldiers on a grueling four-day march through torrential rains and waist-deep swamps to Fort Caroline. At dawn on the fifth day, the Spaniards attacked, completely overwhelming the unsuspecting French garrison. The women and children were spared, but some 130 French soldiers were put to the sword. Only a handful of men, including Ribaut's son and the rather unheroic Laudonnière, managed to escape by sea. Menéndez de Avilés rechristened the fort San Mateo to honor the apostle on whose feast day (September 21) it had been captured.

The final stages of the conflict were swift, bloody, and predictably one-sided. The survivors of Ribaut's wrecked fleet, unaware that Fort Caroline had fallen and hoping to rejoin their comrades, managed to come within 20 miles of San Augustin before the Spaniards fell upon them in early October. A few managed to escape into the wilderness, only to be captured a month later; the rest of the exhausted French party surrendered in two groups to the smaller Spanish force with only minimal resistance. Menéndez de Avilés and his vice admiral, Diego Flores de Valdéz, had the French prisoners marched across the sand dunes in groups of 10 and executed. Of between 150 and 300 men, only 12 Catholics and 12 military musicians were spared. The valiant Ribaut was dispatched with a knife to the belly and a pike thrust through the heart. The site still recalls the ferocity of the Spanish victory in the name Matanzas (Spanish for "massacres") Inlet. La Florida was Spanish once again.

In the conquest of Florida, Menéndez de Avilés brought to bear all of the ruthlessness and daring what had established him as the greatest Spanish naval commander of his day. He soon discovered, however, that the development of a colony there would require more than the skills of a conquistador. Each of the Florida settlements founded by Menéndez de Avilés's predecessors had fallen into dereliction within a very short time of its establishment. The failure of the Florida settlements baffled and frustrated their sponsors in Mexico City and Madrid. How could Spain subdue the great empires of the Aztecs and Incas so quickly, yet fail repeatedly in its attempts to colonize a land as comparatively backward and underdeveloped as La Florida?

In fact, the answer lay in that very backwardness, which the Spaniards attributed to Florida. Cortés and Pizarro had overwhelmed advanced, urbanized pre-Columbian states, at least in part with superior military technologies. The subsequent administration of those states was relatively easy, for both Mexico and Peru had sophisticated, centralized governmental systems not unlike the one that existed in 16th-century Spain. In Mexico, peoples scattered over thousands of square miles had rendered tribute and obedience for centuries to the emperor in Tenochtitlán; the Inca cities created social and political unity all along the Andean spine of Peru. Once the Aztec and Inca rulers had been defeated, the Spaniards could assume their place and impose their own colonial administration on the vanquished states.

The peoples of Florida had no such tradition of extended political unity. The Tallahassee hills of the north were home to the agrarian Apalachee. The more warlike Timucua inhabited much of the central peninsula. The Ais, Jeaga, and Tekesta lived along the southeastern coast, while the fierce, seagoing Calusa dominated the Southwest. Each nation was further divided into scores of independent villages. Some *caciques* (tribal leaders), especially among the Timucua and Calusa, managed to unite groups of villages into regional confederations, but rivalries within confederations were often as bitter as those between them. The divisiveness and localism of Florida's peoples made it easy for Narváez and de Soto to cut a bloody swath through the peninsula but quite impossible to subdue whole tribes in a single, decisive stroke. And, unlike Mexico or Peru, the Native societies of Florida offered no preexisting administrative infrastructures that could be adapted to Spain's colonial strategy.

Menéndez de Avilés proved more than equal to the challenges before him. Certainly, he was the first of the Florida conquistadores to demonstrate an active interest in the survival of his settlement. He expended nearly all of his considerable fortune on the Florida enterprise; by one contemporary account, Menéndez de Avilés spent almost a million ducats on his expeditionary fleet alone. He was also tireless in soliciting material support from the *grandes* of the Spanish court. Though he held the governorship of Florida for life, Menéndez de Avilés spent most of his time after 1568 in Spain courting wealthy investors; indeed, at the time of his death, he was in Spain on a fundraising campaign. Unlike his predecessors, who quickly sacrificed their perfunctory settlements to the quest for gold, Menéndez de Avilés remained committed to his Florida colony throughout his life.

To maintain his colony, Menéndez de Avilés developed an extended organizational scheme centered on the heavily fortified towns of San Augustin and San Mateo, each with a garrison of 250 men. On the South Carolina coast, the Spaniards constructed a third fort, Santa Elena, with a garrison of 150, to guard against French attempts to rebuild Charlesfort. Initially, San Augustin appeared the least viable of the three, with its marshy terrain and open, vulnerable harbor. But, in 1568, the French privateer Dominique de Gourgues attacked and destroyed San Mateo; the fort was rebuilt and reoccupied, but only briefly. Twenty years later, Santa Elena was abandoned and destroyed by its own garrison after Spain accepted the inevitability of an English settlement in the Carolinas. By 1600, San Augustin was the only major fortified settlement in the territories of Spanish Florida and the uncontested center of the Spanish colonial network there.

The demographics of 16th-century San Augustin betray the town's essentially military character and function. The population included a significant number of artisans and specialized craftsmen, and virtually every family maintained a small farm with livestock; indeed, in a report of 1602, Governor Gonzalo Mendéz de Canço complained about the herds of cattle that ran free through San Augustin's muddy streets. As elsewhere in the Spanish New World, San Augustin's population was ethnically diverse. It included two distinct groups of Spaniards: immigrants from Spain, who typically held the principal military and civil posts in the community, and *criollos*, Spaniards whose birth in "the provinces" entailed a somewhat humbler social station. Spanish expeditions to Florida had always included a few fearless women, but they were invariably far outnumbered by Spanish men. From the outset, intermarriage and ethnic intermixing (*mestizaje*) were essential to San Augustin's survival, though less so than in other parts of New Spain, and Hispano-Indian mestizos quickly came to comprise a substantial group within the community. At San Augustin, the population also included Native Floridians and Africans, many but by no means all of whom were slaves. But, for all its professional and ethnic diversity, San Augustin remained first and foremost a soldier's town. As of 1598, more than a third of the 625 inhabitants were professional soldiers, and virtually the entire male population, with the exception of the clergy, was expected to bear arms in times of crisis. Compared to the English colonies that later grew up in North America, the settlements of Spanish Florida were distinguished by an ethnic diversity still discernible in many parts of the American Southeast, yet rarely managed to move much beyond their principally military foundations.

Though San Augustin was hardly a major colonial center on par with Mexico City, Lima, or Havana, it nevertheless commanded the chain of smaller, dependent outposts that Menéndez de Avilés founded to secure Spain's foothold in what would become the southeastern United States. In the immediate vicinity, San Augustin was defended by a blockhouse at Matanzas Inlet, a watchtower on Anastasia Island, and three small forts (Picolata, San Francisco de Pupo, and Diego) along the Saint John's River. Farther afield, the Spaniards maintained a network of less permanent outposts whose location shifted over time according to military exigency. The first were a series of watchtowers, erected by Menéndez de Avilés and his immediate successors along Cape Canaveral and Biscayne Bay to provide an early warning against the incursions of French pirates. A century later, the Spaniards raised a new line of forts on the Gulf Coast and Pensacola Bay when the French began moving into the Mississippi Delta in the 1680s and 1690s. Regardless of their location, however, the coastal forts remained under the authority of the governor at San Augustin as part of an extended colonial system intended for the maintenance and consolidation of Spanish power on the northern rim of the Caribbean basin.

Following the example of Ribaut, Menéndez de Avilés hoped to guarantee the security of his settlements further by cultivating peaceful relations with Florida's Native population. He enlisted Timucua scouts in the struggle against Fort Caroline and spent much of the next year traveling throughout the peninsula making contact with Native leaders. But Menéndez de Avilés was haunted by the brutal legacy of earlier conquistadores, from whom the Florida Indians had learned to fear Spaniards. In the vicinity of San Augustin, he had to contend with the hostility of the formidable Timucua chief Saturiba, an ally of the French who joined forces with Dominique de Gourgues to destroy San Mateo in 1568. Though Menéndez de Avilés managed to establish cordial relations with the Ais, he failed completely to come to terms with the Calusa. He invested considerable time and energy in negotiating a trade compact with the colorful young Calusa *cacique* whom the Spaniards called Carlos. In 1566, Menéndez de Avilés went so far as to feign a marriage to Carlos's sister, "Doña Antonia"—in spite of the fact that he already had a wife in Spain! But Menéndez de Avilés's efforts came to nothing. In the spring of 1567, the Spaniards learned that Carlos was planning a secret attack and killed the unreliable *cacique.* The rival they raised up to take his place, "Don Felipe," quickly proved as hostile as Carlos had been: he was executed at the orders of the *adelantado*'s nephew, Pedro Menéndez de Marqués, for plotting to destroy the missionary settlement of San Antonio in 1570.

Catholic missions, through which the Spaniards hoped to produce both converts and allies, played an important role in New World colonial strategies. Jesuit friars who accompanied the devout Menéndez de Avilés on his voyage established the first successful Spanish missions in La Florida. At the *adelantado*'s urging, and often with his personal participation, major Jesuit missions were founded at Guale (in southeastern Georgia) and at Orista; in 1570, friar Juan Baptista de Segura led a missionary party as far north as Chesapeake Bay. Menéndez de Avilés provided each missionary with a daily stipend of three *reales* for subsistence, taken from the *adelantado*'s own pocket. Within just a few years of their arrival, the Jesuits had established 10 mission centers in La Florida, before a series of setbacks, including the massacre of Segura and his companions, in February 1571, convinced them to withdraw from their mission contract in 1572.

The Franciscans who took up their burden the following year proved considerably more tenacious. Though nominally subject to the bishop of Havana, the Florida missions were effectively autonomous; in the century following Menéndez de Avilés's death, the only bishops to visit the province were Juan de los Cabejos Altimirano, in 1606, and Gabriel Dias Vara Calderón, who undertook a census of the missions in 1674. Freedom from outside interference enabled the Franciscans in Florida to devise missionary techniques that responded to the peculiar circumstances of the region. Preaching a simplified version of the gospel, the friars often adopted Native customs as part of their missionary strategy. In 1595, the Franciscans undertook a more systematic missionary program based on the *encomiendas* (mission-farms built on royal land-grants), where resident Indians received instruction in Catholic doctrine, often from mestizo friars, and sustained the community through collective agricultural labor. By 1655, 70 friars were claiming to minister to more than 25,000 Native Christians in La Florida, chiefly among the Apalachee and the Timucua. In fact, the Spanish mission system was never as successful as the Spaniards had hoped. Most Indian converts were at best tenuously Catholic, and missionaries never managed to secure a permanent foothold south of San Augustin. Even apparently secure mission centers were prone to Indian uprisings like the one that destroyed the important Guale mission in 1597. By 1705, the Spanish mission system had collapsed altogether under pressure from British colonial militias in the Carolinas, leaving only traces of a Spanish Catholic influence on Florida's Native peoples.

The mixed fortunes of the Spanish missions in Florida may be seen as symbolic for the Florida colony as a whole. To a considerable extent, history and geography conspired to keep the Florida colony from evolving beyond a collection of semipermanent frontier forts. In 1570, Florida was placed under the supreme authority of the viceroys of Mexico, who never saw the territory as anything but a first line of defense against French and English aggression in the Caribbean Sea and Gulf of Mexico. The sweeping powers Menéndez de Avilés enjoyed as *adelantado* were not passed on his to successors; as terminally appointed subordinates to the governor-general of Cuba, later governors of Florida were simply unable to operate with the freedom and initiative of their colony's founder. Moreover, fires, famines, storms, and a general mortality rate that prevented population increase for a century consistently plagued the Florida settlements. In 1600, King Philip III ordered the governor of Cuba to conduct hearings into the feasibility of maintaining the struggling Florida settlements at all; only the perennial threat of French or English attack kept colonial authorities from abandoning Florida altogether.

Most critical was the failure of the Florida colony to develop an effectively independent economy. Without gold, silver, and other mineral resources, La Florida failed to excite much interest from wealthy investors in Madrid and Mexico City; the Spaniards seem not to have appreciated the agricultural potential of Florida's lush, subtropical climate. By 1600, the overwhelming majority of Florida's sparse colonial population lived within the walls of San Augustin, leaving the land beyond largely uncultivated and Florida's natural resources untapped. The *encomiendas* supplied the colony with fruit, grain, and cotton; otherwise, La Florida was entirely dependent on the royal *situado* (subsidy), disbursed annually after 1570 to provide for the colony's defenses and for the missions. The *situado* was wholly inadequate for more significant colonial development; at times, its payment failed altogether, and the Florida colonists were forced to borrow from officials in Havana, creating a debt whose full repayment remained forever beyond the colony's capacity.

More than a generation after its founding, San Augustin was still a small and primitive frontier settlement of 120 thatched houses; even the Franciscan church, the town's largest and most important building, was built in part of palmetto leaves and straw. Major building projects in the town were invariably military in character and came in response to foreign attacks from the sea, which reinforced the prevailing view in Mexico City and Havana that Florida was a strategically essential but economically marginal frontier on the peripheries of Spain's New World empire. After Sir Francis Drake attacked and burned the town, in 1586, Governor Hernando de Miranda began the costly fortification of the harbor; the massive stone fortress of San Marcos, which still stands watch over the harbor today, was built at the command of Governor Francisco de la Guerra y de la Vega after the destructive raid of the English pirate Robert Searles in 1668. So long as they remained essentially military posts, neither San Augustin nor its dependent settlements could develop the diversified and professionally specialized population base necessary to colonial self-sufficiency.

But even if Spanish Florida never quite lived up to its founder's expectations, it would nevertheless be a mistake to underestimate the colony's significance. Animated by the tenacious spirit of its founder, San Augustin endured often astonishing hardships to become—as any inhabitant of Saint Augustine will proudly attest—the oldest continually inhabited city north of the Rio Grande. While more ambitious colonial ventures elsewhere in North America collapsed in the face of lesser adversities, La Florida weathered remarkable hardships to retain its institutional integrity for two centuries. Pedro Menéndez de Avilés was followed by a succession of 40 royally appointed governors who ruled Spanish Florida from 1565 until the British took control of the territory under the Peace of Paris in 1763. After the American Revolutionary War, Florida was returned to nominal Spanish control by the Treaty of Paris (1783), until the territory was annexed in the Adams-Onis Treaty of 1819. Until then, San Augustin and its satellites offered incontrovertible evidence that the North American wilderness could sustain a European colony, so long as its colonists were willing to endure the attendant challenges. Soon after San Augustin's foundation, the wealth of the colonial empire La Florida helped to defend would all but compel Spain's European neighbors to seek their own colonial fortunes in North America. While none of Spain's colonial rivals in the Americas would adopt the Florida model outright, all of them would borrow elements of Spanish colonial government (particularly in terms of military administration), and all would profit from the lessons of the Spanish experiment. Most important, as the French, the Dutch, and, above all, the British came to challenge Spain's domination in the New World, they would create global empires that would not only redefine the bases of power in Europe but, in the process, lay the foundations of American nationhood.

## SELECTED BIBLIOGRAPHY

Axtell, James. *The Indians' New South: Cultural Change in the Colonial Southeast.* Baton Rouge: Louisiana State University Press, 1997. A study of the impact of the Europeans on the southeastern Indians between 1500 and 1700.

Barrientos, Bartolomé. *Pedro Menéndez de Avilés, Founder of Florida*. Trans. Anthony Kerrigan. Gainesville: University of Florida Press, 1965. Composed by a prominent Spanish scholar in 1568, this lively and highly informative biography traces Menéndez's life and career up to December 1567.

Cook, Noble David. *Born to Die: Disease and New World Conquest, 1492–1650*. Cambridge: Cambridge University Press, 1998. A careful analysis of the depopulating impact of European disease on Native Americans.

Deagan, Kathleen, et al. *Spanish St. Augustine: the Archaeology of a Colonial Creole Community*. New York: Academic Press, 1983. Seven archaeologists examine different aspects of settlement and society in Saint Augustine from the 16th through the 18th centuries.

Galloway, Patricia, ed. *The Hernando de Soto Expedition: History, Historiography, and "Discovery" in the Southeast*. Lincoln: University of Nebraska Press, 1997. Collection of essays on different aspects of de Soto's expedition through the American Southeast.

Laudonnière, René. *Three Voyages*. Trans. Charles E. Bennet. Gainesville: University Presses of Florida, 1975. Laudonnière's thorough and fascinating account of the French experience in Florida provides a valuable corrective to Barrientos's panegyric of Menéndez.

Lorant, Stefan. *The New World; the first pictures of America, made by John White and Jacques Le Moyne and engraved by Theodore De Bry, with contemporary narratives of the Huguenot settlement in Florida, 1562–1565, and the Virginia colony, 1585–1590*. New York: Duell, Sloan and Pierce, 1946. This interesting collection of materials includes two eyewitness accounts of the French colony in Florida by the artist Jacques LeMoyne and the carpenter Nicolas LeChalleux, illustrated with 43 marvelous engravings of Florida's Indians and fauna by Theodore De Bry, based on LeMoyne's own paintings.

Lowery, Woodbury. *The Spanish Settlements within the Present Limits of the United States. Florida, 1562–1574*. New York: Russell and Russell, 1959. First published in 1911, Lowery's comprehensive account, based on extensive consultation of the materials in Ruidíaz's *La Florida*, remains the definitive narrative of the establishment of the Spanish colony in Florida.

Lyon, Eugene. *The Enterprise of Florida: Pedro Menéndez de Avilés and the Spanish Conquest of 1565–1568*. Gainesville: University Press of Florida, 1976. This extremely well-researched monograph examines both the founding of the Spanish colony in Florida and the political processes that underlay it.

McEwan, Bonnie G., ed. *The Spanish Missions of La Florida*. Gainesville: University Press of Florida, 1993. This collection of 16 essays by archaeologists examines a wide range of topics concerning life in the Spanish missions.

Milanich, Jerald T. *Florida Indians and the Invasion from Europe*. Gainesville: University Press of Florida, 1995. Examines the European settlement of Florida from the Indian perspective on the basis of extensive archaeological research.

Reitz, Elizabeth Jean, and C. Margaret Scarry. *Reconstructing Historic Subsistence, with an Example from Sixteenth-Century Spanish Florida*. Glassboro, NJ: Society for Historical Archaeology, 1985. This relatively short monograph offers a fascinating and thorough, though highly technical, investigation of the relationship between environment and diet in early Spanish Florida.

Sauer, Carl O. *Sixteenth-Century North America. The Land and the People as Seen by the Europeans*. Berkeley: University of California Press, 1971. A general survey that draws heavily from contemporary accounts; Part III is most useful for those interested in the Spanish foundation of Saint Augustine.

Tebeau, Charlton W. *A History of Florida*. Coral Gables, FL: University of Miami Press, 1971. Chapters 2, 3, and 4 provide a concise discussion of the Spanish experience in Florida, placed in the larger context of the state's history.

Weber, David J. *The Spanish Frontier in North America.* New Haven, CT: Yale University Press, 1992. This lively, well-researched, and eminently accessible work tells the story of the Spanish presence and significance in North America.

## CASTILLO DE SAN MARCOS

Erected at Saint Augustine, Florida, the Castillo de San Marcos is the oldest stone block fort in the continental United States. The Castillo de San Marcos was constructed between 1672 and 1695 and protected the Spanish settlement at Saint Augustine for centuries.

Located on the Florida peninsula, Saint Augustine became an important link in the protection of the great Spanish commercial route that joined its rich Latin American colonies with Spain itself. The route followed by the Spanish treasure ships sailing in the Bahama Channel on their way to Spain passed close by the tip of Florida. It was thus essential that Spain establish a strong presence at Saint Augustine to prevent Florida from falling under the control of its enemies, who might then establish bases there and mount attacks against the treasure ships. England's 1670 colonization of nearby Carolina brought the opposing sides closer. The proximity of the two enemies further magnified Florida's need to construct strong and modern defenses.

Construction of the fort began in 1672, just four years after English pirate Robert Searles attacked Saint Augustine. Florida's governor retained the services of Ignacio Daza, a military engineer responsible for the design and construction of fortifications throughout the Spanish Empire, including the forts at Havana and at San Juan, Puerto Rico. Construction began on October 2, 1672, at the site of Saint Augustine's ninth and final wooden fort. Located on the bank of the Matanzas River and overlooking Anastasia Island and the entrance to the harbor, the site had been used as a military outpost for more than a century when construction began.

The fort's design called for a structure approximately 33 feet tall, with four-sided bastions jutting out of each corner. The top of each bastion was painted red and white, Spain's traditional colors. Because of the shape of the bastions, the fort appeared triangular. A water-filled moat surrounded the fort, and beyond that stood a secondary wall that created a partial sea wall. A stone-like substance composed of compressed sea shells and sand called coquina provided the material to build the fort. Workers quarried sufficient coquina locally to complete the project. In the 18th century, engineers added an additional wall, known as the Cubo line. This extension began at the fort's edge and ended west of the city at the San Sebastian River. By 1695, much of the fort was complete, and the outpost housed approximately 350 soldiers. When completed, the fort made Saint Augustine the heaviest guarded city in what is now the United States.

In 1702, Carolina governor James Moore provided the first test for the fort when his troops sacked and burned Saint Augustine. During the invasion, Florida residents found protection inside the walls of the Castillo. When the attack ended, Saint Augustine remained in Spanish hands only because the English could not breach the walls of the fort. In 1740, the English again attacked Saint Augustine but again failed to capture the fort.

In 1763, Britain assumed control of Florida as a result of the French and Indian War. Initially, the British did not make much use of the fort until they faced the possibility of a colonial revolution. In 1775, the British renovated the fort in preparation for the coming American Revolution. In 1783, Spain regained possession of Florida. During the second Spanish period, the Spaniards made additional repairs to the Castillo, but the fort proved an unnecessary fortification for the small outpost. On July 10, 1821, the United States assumed control of Florida and the Castillo de San Marcos.

SHANE RUNYON

## HERNANDO DE SOTO (ca. 1497–1542)

Hernando de Soto was a Spanish explorer and conquistador in the 16th century who participated in the conquest of the Inca Empire and conducted extensive explorations of present-day Florida and the southern United States from 1539 to 1542.

De Soto was born in about 1497 in Jeréz de los Caballeros. in the province of Estremadura, Spain, an area noted for producing many of the Spanish conquistadors. His parents, Francisco Méndez de Soto and Leonor Arías Tinoco, were *hidalgos*, or members of the Spanish upper class, and wanted their son to become a lawyer. Because of his social standing, de Soto was literate and educated, although not much is known about his youth.

Evidence suggests that. by 1514, de Soto was in the Americas. In 1519, he was part of the force under Pedro Arias de Ávila (usually known as Pedrarias) on the second expedition to Darién, a city founded in 1513 by the Spanish explorer Vasco Núñez de Balboa on the isthmus of Panama. (De Ávila later became governor of Darién by displacing Balboa and ordering him beheaded.) Throughout the 1520s, de Soto participated in numerous military expeditions in Panama and Nicaragua. As a result of his exploits, he amassed a great deal of wealth from slave trading and plunder captured from Native Americans.

From 1531 to 1535, de Soto led a group of men who assisted Francisco Pizarro in his conquest of Peru. De Soto and his men helped to found the first Spanish settlement in Peru, named San Miguel, and then to seize and subsequently guard the Inca emperor Atahualpa. In 1536, de Soto returned to Spain with a massive fortune of 180,000 ducats from the conquest of the Inca Empire that was divided among the Spanish conquistadors. That newly acquired wealth allowed de Soto to marry Isabela de Bobadilla, the daughter of his old commander de Ávila.

In Spain, de Soto attempted to persuade Holy Roman emperor Charles V to grant him lands in either Ecuador, Colombia, or Guatemala, but Charles refused. However, stories of adventure and wealth inspired de Soto to try his hand at the exploration of Florida. On April 20, 1537, he obtained a royal grant from Charles that named him governor of Cuba and *adelantado* (the king's "advance agent") in the lands of Florida. In order to mount the expedition to Florida, de Soto sold part of his property and gathered a force of 750 men. In April 1538, the group set sail from Spain.

De Soto's first stop in North America was Havana, Cuba, where he established a base of operations and completed the organization of his expedition to Florida. On May 18, 1539, he and his men left Cuba, and, seven days later, they arrived on the west coast of Florida near present-day Tampa Bay. There they made contact with a village of Uzita. Among the people who traveled with de Soto were two women, a trumpeter, priests, servants, shoemakers, a notary, cavalry, and infantry. The total size of the de Soto expedition to Florida was between 600 and 700 people. Furthermore, he had 220 horses and a large number of pigs for food.

De Soto searched for gold and riches for almost four years. During that time, he and his men traveled through present-day Georgia, Alabama, Mississippi, Louisiana, and Arkansas. They went as far north as the Appalachian Mountains in present-day North Carolina and Tennessee and encountered numerous groups of Native Americans: Tequesta, Calusa, Moscoso, Urriparacoxi, Tocobaga, and Utina. In 1541, de Soto and his entourage sighted the Mississippi River. Despite de Soto's lengthy stay in the region, no lasting settlement was established.

As with other Spanish expeditions, treatment of Native inhabitants was harsh and often brutal. De Soto's strategy was to capture the chief or head of each village through which they passed. The captive would then be ransomed to ensure that Spanish demands for food, women, and slaves were met. If the demands were satisfied, the captive would be released when the expedition approached the next village, where the process was repeated.

In one instance, however, the strategy had unexpected repercussions when the captive, a Choctaw chief named Taskaloosa (Tuscaloosa), orchestrated an offensive in response, which at first sent the Spanish reeling. In the ensuing fight, known as the Battle of Mabila (near present-day Selma, Alabama), de Soto's troops eventually regained the initiative and inflicted an estimated 2,500 casualties. Following the Battle of Mabila, de Soto headed northwest, where, in 1541, his winter encampment was attacked and burned by Chickasaws.

In the spring of 1542, the expedition moved west across the Mississippi River, where de Soto died of fever on May 21. The survivors of the nearly four-year-old expedition were finally driven out of the New World by Native Americans from the kingdom of Quigualtam. De Soto's men, now under the command of Luís Moscoso de Alvarado, sailed down the Mississippi to the Gulf of Mexico. In September 1543, approximately 300 survivors of the expedition arrived at Panuco on the west coast of Mexico, near Tampico.

## FLORIDA

The area that makes up the state of Florida was inhabited as early as 12,000 years ago. In the last centuries before contact with other cultures, Native Americans in the area developed complex societies, practiced agriculture, developed extensive trade networks, and built large temple mounds. When Europeans arrived, in the 16th century, the dominant peoples in the region were the Calusa, who lived on the southwestern coast; the Timucua, who lived in the northern half of the Florida peninsula; the Tekesta, who lived in the southeastern part of Florida and included present-day Miami in its territory; and the Apalachee, who lived in the northwestern extreme of the peninsula and adjacent parts of the adjacent parts of what is now the Florida panhandle.

Juan Ponce de León, who gave Florida its name after leading an expedition of Spaniards that landed near present-day Saint Augustine in 1513, is often credited with being the first European to visit the region. Ponce de León returned in 1521 and was unsuccessful in his attempts to found a colony near present-day Fort Myers. Over the next several decades, subsequent Spanish expeditions to Florida, including those by Pánfilo de Narváez and Hernando de Soto, were brief. Consequences were severe for Native Americans, nonetheless, as they died in large numbers from diseases that Europeans brought.

French establishment of a fort at the mouth of the Saint Johns River in 1564 led to more serious Spanish attempts to establish a presence. Pedro Menéndez de Avilés founded Saint Augustine in 1565 and attacked the French settlement to the north, slaughtering most of the residents. Over the next 200 years, the Spanish were in regular conflict with another enemy, the English, who established the colonies of Georgia and South Carolina to the north. The Battle of Bloody Marsh, in 1742, in which settlers from Georgia defeated the Spanish, caused the northern border of Florida to be established at the Saint Marys River. By this time, the Native inhabitants of Florida had largely been wiped out and were replaced by Creeks and other southeastern peoples who moved into the area and became known as the Seminoles.

The Spanish ceded Florida to Great Britain after the French and Indian War in 1763, but the British ceded it back to Spain in 1783, at the end of the American Revolution. Over the next 12 years, Spain and the newly founded United States were at odds over the northern boundary of West Florida, which was finally established by treaty in 1795. U.S. influence increased in the area as many Americans were drawn to Florida by the opportunity to own land. During the War of 1812, Andrew Jackson led U.S. soldiers into the area and took Pensacola, where Spain had allowed the British to set up a naval base. Jackson brought U.S. troops to Florida again in 1819, retaliating for Seminole raids during the First Seminole War. That year, Spain ceded Florida to the United States. Florida became a territory in 1821, minus the lands along that Gulf of Mexico that Spain had ceded in 1810 and that became parts of the states of Mississippi and Alabama.

The southern plantation system, based on the labor of enslaved Africans, became established during Florida's territorial period. Tobacco and cotton were the major crops grown in Florida. As white settlement increased, the Seminoles were increasingly and more brutally displaced from their lands. Attempts to remove them from Florida to Indian Territory resulted in the Second Seminole War, during 1835–1842, which ended with most Seminoles being killed or removed and a few others retreating to the swamps of the Everglades. Florida became a state in 1845 and quickly allied itself with the other slave states in the growing tensions between the slave South and the free North. After the election to the presidency, in 1860, of Abraham Lincoln, a member of the antislavery Republican Party, Florida seceded from the Union. It joined other secessionist slave states in the Confederate States of America several weeks later.

During the Civil War, no decisive battles were fought in Florida. The Union occupied many coastal towns in the state, but the Confederacy controlled the interior. After the war, Florida, like most other former Confederate states, was placed under military rule in 1868, and former Confederate leaders were kept out of political office. Blacks, most of whom were recently freed from slavery, gained the right to vote, and the Republican Party gained control of state politics. As in other parts of the South, Florida Democrats eventually regained control of its state legislature in the 1870s and reversed many of the gains made by blacks. In the years after the Civil War, Florida followed a Southern trend in agriculture, as tenant farming, or sharecropping, replaced the plantation system. The tenant farming system caused many farmers to go into debt to large landowners and to live in extreme poverty. This compelled many poor farmers to join such populist organizations as the Farmers' Alliance and the People's Party (also known as the Populist Party), which advocated policies friendly to small farmers. The Alliance was particularly successful in influencing the policies of the Democratic Party in the late 19th century.

While many events in Florida mirrored events in the South in general, other changes helped the state become unique among former Confederate states. An expanding system of railroads brought new settlers and many tourists from the North, and the first big real estate boom in the South began. Northern capitalists like Henry Flagler profited by building both railroads and such tourist facilities as hotels. New lands were also opened to agriculture in the southern part of the state, and citrus and cattle raising became important industries. Manufacturing also spread during this time, particularly the cigar industry.

Florida entered a period of progressive politics in the early part of the century, particularly under governors William Sherman Jennings, elected in 1900, and Napoleon Bonaparte Broward, elected in 1904. Broward made his name as a corporate and railroad watchdog. During his tenure, higher education was boosted and the government commission charged with monitoring the powerful railroads was strengthened. Florida passed legislation prohibiting the manufacture, sale, and use of alcohol before nationwide prohibition under the Eighteenth Amendment to the U.S. Constitution.

After World War I, Florida experienced its greatest land boom. As the tourist industry expanded, Florida's population grew four times faster in the early 1920s than that of any other state. After several years, the demand for land declined, and the largely inflated land prices plummeted. Though Florida's early land boom ended in 1926, tourism has remained a dominant industry in the state. Following the end of the boom times, several other disasters struck the state. Major hurricanes brought devastation in the late 1920s, and in 1929 the Mediterranean fruit fly caused a 60 percent drop in citrus production. Also in 1929, the Great Depression hit the United States. It would take the better part of the next decade for federal and state programs to help boost the state's economy and improve the lot of its citizens. Also during this time, wood pulp and paper production developed as important industries.

Following the U.S. entry into World War II, in 1941, the establishment of military bases helped bring real prosperity back to Florida. After the war, the state's economy and population resumed their rapid growth. The seemingly limitless water supply and the mild climate of Florida brought business and people. An important new industry was aerospace. The U.S. Air Force Missile Test Center was established at Cape Canaveral in 1949, and this site later became a center for space exploration, with the Cape serving as the site for satellite launches beginning in 1958 and manned space launches beginning in the 1960s.

Florida's population has changed dramatically since the 1950s. Many new Floridians came from the North or other parts of the United States, and many came from the Caribbean, especially Cuba. The Cuban Revolution in the late 1950s touched off a flood of refugees who began arriving in 1958. Another wave of Cuban refugees hit Florida in 1980, when Cuban leader Fidel Castro allowed a large flotilla of privately owned boats to shuttle emigrants from the Cuban port of Mariel. In 1991, a military coup in the Caribbean nation of Haiti caused many Haitians to flee to Florida. In the late 20th century, Miami, heavily influenced by the refugee flow from the Caribbean, became a major media and trade center for Latin America.

The influx of refugees from the Caribbean has been paralleled by the steady movement of Americans from outside Florida, particularly the northeastern states, into the state. Many of these new residents are retirees, large numbers of which have settled in communities like Saint Petersburg and West Palm Beach.

Together, foreign refugees and northern migrants transformed state politics. The massive movement of Cuban refugees into southern Florida made Cuban immigrants a major political force in that part of the state. African Americans, already socially and politically disadvantaged, suffered a further loss of power as a result. Frustrated over their impoverished condition and angered by their treatment from police, many African Americans rioted in Miami in 1980, resulting in 18 deaths and $100 million in property damage. Meanwhile, with the growth of the Cuban community transforming southern Florida, the arrival of many new voters from outside the Democratic south changed statewide voting patterns. Republican candidates have won the governor's office regularly since the 1960s, and Florida voted Republican in nearly every presidential election from 1952 to 1996.

DAVE COMPTON

## JUAN PONCE DE LEÓN (ca. 1470–1521)

Juan Ponce de León was the first European to navigate the southeastern tip of the United States. In 1513, he discovered the peninsula that is today part of the state of Florida. In 1521, Ponce de León made an unsuccessful trip to return and settle there.

Ponce de León was born to noble parents in around 1470 in San Servas, in the province of León, Spain. He served as a soldier all his life, beginning with campaigns in Granada that drove the Moors out of Spain in 1492. The next year, he accompanied Christopher Columbus on his second voyage to America.

Ponce de León joined the rebellion against Columbus's rule in the West Indies. In 1508, Nicolas de Ovando, governor of Hispaniola, appointed Ponce de León the lieutenant of the eastern side of the island. Looking east from his territories, Ponce de León could see another island that the Spanish had not yet conquered (present-day Puerto Rico). In 1509, he invaded it and secured it for the Spanish Crown. Ponce de León competed with Columbus's son Diego Columbus for the governorship of the new territory. Finally, King Ferdinand V granted the position to Ponce de León, and he settled with his wife and children in the new capital of San Juan.

In Puerto Rico, Ponce de León heard rumors of a land to the north called Biminy that was thought to be part of Asia. The rumors promised that the new land contained great wealth in gold and slaves. In 1511, he appealed to the king for the authority to conquer that unexplored area. The king granted Ponce de León lifetime rule over any territories he should discover. Ponce de León outfitted three ships at his own expense and sailed northwest from Puerto Rico in 1513.

The ships navigated through the Bahamas and landed on the future site of Saint Augustine, on the eastern coast of Florida, on Easter Sunday, 1513. Ponce de León called the country Pascua Florida after the Spanish word for Easter. Ponce de León fought strong currents to navigate around Cape Canaveral, where he set up a stone cross after defeating some hostile Native Americans in the area. Ponce de León and his ships traveled an unknown distance north up the coast of Florida, possibly to Charlotte Harbor, and then returned to Puerto Rico.

Soon after his return to Puerto Rico, Ponce de León left for Spain to report on his explorations and strengthen his authority over the conquered areas. The king granted

Ponce de León the title of *adelantado* (or military governor) over Florida and also permitted him to wage war against the Native Americans in the territory, which enabled Ponce de León to make slaves of any Indians who resisted conversion to Catholicism. Before Ponce de León could return to Florida in 1515, the king gave him command of a mission to fight the Caribs, a warlike people who were invading the islands around Puerto Rico. Ponce de León further delayed his explorations to Florida by arranging the marriages of his daughters and building up his finances after losing significant funds on his first expedition in the Spanish colony.

In 1521, Ponce de León heard of the incredible wealth of the Mexican Aztec Empire, which had been conquered by Hernán Cortés. Ponce de León hoped to discover similar great civilizations in Florida and believed that the territory promised to be plentiful in tropical fruits, gold, and pearls. Thinking the peninsula was an island, Ponce de León appealed to the king to finance settlement of that area and also to support the search for the mainland. He recruited 200 settlers for that second expedition and also brought tools, livestock, seeds, and missionaries. His two ships made a difficult trip to the area of Tampa Bay, where they began to build a colony. Shortly thereafter, in an attack by the Calusas Indians, Ponce de León suffered an arrow wound.

Leaving the settlers there, the injured Ponce de León returned to Cuba and died soon after, in May 1521. In the next several years, many other Spanish expeditions explored Florida. Eventually, Spain built forts and missions on the peninsula, but they always conflicted with local Indian tribes. Because of Spain's nearly continuous warfare with other European powers, Florida would pass in and out of its control for the next 300 years.

NICOLE VON GERMETEN

# 5

# Early English Colonization Efforts, ca. 1584–1630

## INTRODUCTION

The first sanctioned English venture to America came with the voyages of an Italian, Giovanni Caboto, better known as John Cabot, at the end of the 15th century. Cabot was probably the first European to sail along the coast of eastern North America and to recognize it for what it was, a previously unknown continent. As a young man living in Italy, Cabot plied the Mediterranean as a merchant seaman. He went to England around 1484 (some scholars believe it was as late as 1495) and settled in Bristol, already an important seafaring community, where he learned about Iceland and Greenland and the possibility of a passage to the rich lands of the Orient.

In 1496, King Henry VII of England sanctioned Cabot's first voyage of exploration. That year, he made a relatively short voyage that probably did not take him farther than Iceland. In 1497 and 1498, he made two longer voyages in search of a route to Asia. During his first voyage, from May to August 1497, Cabot reached Labrador and, possibly, Newfoundland. On his 1498 voyage, sponsored by King Henry and a group of English merchants, he sailed farther to the south and reached the East Coast of what is now the United States. Cabot died on this voyage, but his son Sebastian returned to England and spent the rest of his life aggrandizing his own accomplishments at the expense of his father's and thoroughly confusing the historical record. Nevertheless, Cabot's voyages did open the door to the possibility for English exploitation of the New World. England, however, was not yet ready to take that step.

By the middle of the 16th century, England was on the verge of having the capability to colonize overseas. An economic revival in Europe increased demand for cloth, which at that time meant wool. England was ideally suited for raising sheep, and the process of creating enclosed pastureland began. This displaced serfs who had been utilized as farm laborers and contributed to a late-16th-century phenomenon of excess labor and insufficient food. Wool exports, meanwhile, were creating a surplus of capital in England that could be used for investing in, say, a colonization venture.

This economic situation helped create the conditions that produced colonizing efforts in competition with other states in Europe. By the late 16th century, English merchants were also involved heavily in the export of finished cloth, a more expansive market than wool. They were also developing coastal and overseas shipping operations and, ultimately, de facto control of England's foreign trade. This made the merchant

A world's fair known as the Jamestown Tercentenary Exposition celebrated the tercentenary of the founding of Jamestown in 1607. (Courtesy of the Library of Congress.)

class a powerful force in English society and the element necessary for successful colonization.

Not only did the merchants provide the means for colonization, but they also determined the nature and purpose of the colonies that would be established. When it became apparent that England's colonies were not going to yield the treasures in gold and silver that the Spanish colonies did, commerce was the only practical rationale for establishing colonies. From the beginning, English merchants assumed that their colonies would provide raw materials for England's manufacturing economy and markets for England's finished products.

Colonization efforts on the part of the English might have come earlier had it not been for the religious situation in Europe in the mid-16th century. Europe was in the midst of the Protestant Reformation, which was producing much political instability because of the intense rivalry between Protestants and Catholics. As a newly Protestant state, thanks to Henry VIII's insistence on several marriages to try to produce a male heir, England was divided between those like Elizabeth I (queen 1558–1603), who was loyal to her father's religion, and Catholics, who continued to place their faith in Rome. Given the domestic situation, as well as the threat posed by Catholic Spain and Catholics in France (itself rent by religious strife), Elizabeth had no time for or interest in colonial ventures early in her reign. Toward the latter years of the century, however, the situation within England stabilized, while the rivalry with Spain intensified and grew hostile, factors that produced more interest in extending the competition with Spain into the colonial area.

At the same time, however, Spain was England's best foreign trade customer, and, until English merchants found other markets, Spain had to be mollified. These new markets could be developed with American colonies, and, as interest in that alternative grew, so did the deterioration of Anglo-Spanish relations, culminating in the defeat of the Spanish Armada in 1588.

By 1588, English sea captains were finding their way to North America in increasing numbers. In the 1570s, Francis Drake and Martin Frobisher skirted the Western

Hemisphere in the elusive search for more treasures beyond. The first serious effort to establish a colony in North America was that of Sir Walter Raleigh, who launched an expedition in April 1584. Sailing north of their intended course, the colonists passed the North Carolina coast and made landfall north of Cape Hatteras near Roanoke Island. The local Indians were hospitable, the food was good and plentiful, and the prospects for a successful colony appeared excellent.

The following year, seven ships under the command of Richard Grenville landed at nearby Pimlico Sound. This time, the loss of a silver cup led to the burning of an Indian village and continued trouble with the Natives. A party was left over the winter of 1585–1586, however, and survived quite well. In 1586, the Indians' hospitality began to wear thin, and, when Drake arrived in June with a veritable fleet of 23 ships, the Pimlico settlers chose to return to England.

In July 1587, a new band of colonists came to Roanoke Island. Poorly supplied and inexperienced, they were left to their own devices. By the time a relief expedition returned to Roanoke Island in August 1590, there was no trace of the colony or any of its inhabitants. This put a damper on new colonization efforts for a number of years, although much interest had been generated by the efforts that were made.

Between the 1580s and the formation of the Virginia Company, in 1606, the geographer Richard Hakluyt kept interest in colonization alive through his writings about the subject and its importance to England's future national greatness. Only colonies could free England from economic dependence on Spain and provide security by allowing the construction of strategic outposts to protect shipping. The idea of converting Natives to Christianity and thus pleasing God also worked its way into the equation.

The goal was finally satisfied with the chartering, in 1606, of the Virginia Company. The company's purpose was to establish colonies along the Atlantic Coast of America between 34 and 45 degrees north latitude. In 1607, the first representatives of this company landed near the mouth of the James River in present-day Virginia and named their settlement Jamestown, after King James I. On their agenda were the multiple objectives of searching for valuable minerals, looking for a northwest passage to the riches of the Orient, persuading the Indians to be good neighbors, customers, and Christians, and laying the groundwork through agriculture and town-building for a permanent community. When neither gold, nor silver, nor a northwest passage was found in the first year or so, the company changed course and concluded that the only way Jamestown could survive was through a much greater infusion of both capital and settlers. In 1609, the Virginia Company became a public joint-stock company to raise both money and potential settlers. By advertising financial incentives and hinting that investors would participate in the decisions of the company, the Virginia Company eventually attracted the people and money it needed to survive, especially after the move toward extensive tobacco production in 1617. The rapidly growing market for tobacco in England created interest in acquiring land in Virginia, and, between 1617 and 1622, the colony grew from 400 to 4,500 people.

If commerce was the principal motivation for the Virginia settlers, religion served to inspire the earliest New England settlements, although that was not the original intention. In 1602, the *Concord,* captained by Bartholomew Gosnold, anchored off the coast of present-day Maine. This expedition, the first since the disappearance of the Roanoke Island colonists, intended to establish a colony through which the economic resources of the surrounding area could be exploited. The small band of colonists encountered friendly Indians almost immediately, but the task that lay before them was simply overwhelming, and they sailed home after five weeks ashore.

Gosnold made a positive report about the land he had seen, however, and, in 1607, another expedition made its way to the shores of Maine, making landfall near the Kennebec River. The colonists built a small fortified village and entered into trade with local Indians, but they were unable to cope with the severe winter weather and returned to England the following spring.

Thus, it was the fate of the Pilgrims to create the first permanent settlement in New England in 1620. The Pilgrims were religious refugees who were known as Separatists in England. They believed that the split from the Roman Catholic Church that King Henry VIII had engineered had not gone far enough in liturgical reform. They wanted to "purify" the Church by eliminating all ceremonies reminiscent of Catholicism. Some Puritans preferred to fight for reform from within the Church, while others felt it necessary to separate themselves from the established Church and form their own Church. This was not acceptable to the English government. One group of Separatists, after a good deal of legal harassment, found its way to the Netherlands, where freedom of worship was accepted. They stayed in the Netherlands for 11 years but always felt like exiles and consequently determined to go to America.

The Pilgrims, as they called themselves, appealed to the Virginia Company of London for a patent, which would give them the right to settle within the territory the company controlled. They also made some financial arrangements with Thomas Weston, a London ironmonger who was seeking investment opportunities. Weston helped the Pilgrims obtain their patent from the Virginia Company and offered to subsidize their expedition, but in return he demanded joint ownership of everything built or produced in the colony for a period of seven years. The details of the arrangement were still unsettled when the Pilgrims left the Netherlands for England, where their ship, the *Mayflower*, was being prepared. Last-minute negotiations with Weston broke down, and he withdrew further financial support. The determined Pilgrims proceeded on their own.

The *Mayflower* arrived in Provincetown harbor, at the tip of Cape Cod, on November 11, 1620, but the company moved to Plymouth Bay in early December. During the winter that followed, nearly half the 102 men and women died, and the settlement barely eked out an existence. With the help of friendly Indians, the Plymouth colony did better the next year and was heartened when a group of 36 new settlers arrived in November. But the newcomers, who had brought no supplies with them, depleted the available food, and the colony passed another difficult winter. After 1622, however, its fortunes improved, and its survival was ensured.

In 1630, another Puritan colony was established under the auspices of the Massachusetts Bay Company. Here the motive for colonization was again less commercial and more religious. Led by John Winthrop, whose vision for the colony is explored in the interpretive essay for this chapter, the Massachusetts Bay colony grew rapidly in the 1630s, finding its success in good planning, substantial capital, and political influence back in England. Even so, the colonists needed aid from Indians occasionally when crop yields were low. Still, the colony attracted thousands of new settlers during its first decade, and new villages sprung up along the Massachusetts coast and the rivers that emptied into the bays. Settlers spread into present-day Connecticut and, in 1643, the four Puritan colonies of Massachusetts Bay, Plymouth, Connecticut, and New Haven loosely organized themselves into the New England Confederation to cooperate in regional defense matters against the French to the north, the Dutch to the west, and the Indians all around them.

## INTERPRETIVE ESSAY

RICK KENNEDY

In the spring of 1630, John Winthrop composed and delivered one of the most famous speeches in American history, "A Model of Christian Charity." Winthrop was the head of the Massachusetts Bay Company, a corporation that organized a crossing of the Atlantic to establish an English colony. His goal, at its core, was simple. He wanted to create a society out of towns that were economically, politically, and religiously prosperous, thereby serving as a model to the world. Adopting an image used by Jesus, his colony was to be a "City upon a Hill" where "the eyes of all people are upon us." Although initially delivered as a speech, "A Model of Christian Charity" was subsequently printed as an essay and widely distributed.

The idea of a watching world may seem a bit egomaniacal; however, a bigger world than Winthrop ever imagined has continued to watch for 370 years. Popular histories of Winthrop's company began to be written within a half-century. Within another century, English Whigs and American revolutionaries were regularly referring to the motives and actions of the Puritan migration as they questioned the relationship between England and her colonies. In the 19th century, the world really was watching America, and Winthrop's speech came to be thought of as prophecy. In the early 20th century, Puritan studies became a major cottage industry at American universities, and interest in Puritan society and culture has continued throughout the century. Ronald Reagan, in his first presidential inaugural address, quoted Winthrop's famous sentence: "For we must consider that we shall be as a City upon a Hill, the eyes of all people are upon us."

The Puritans of Massachusetts Bay, next to our national Founding Fathers, are probably the most highly studied and talked about group of people in American history. If we consider this, Winthrop and his Puritans are more a city on a hill now than they were then. In this light, it behooves us to look at the "Model of Christian Charity" and see what is in it and in the Massachusetts Bay Company's implementation of it that has such lasting power.

John Winthrop was born in 1588, the year the Spanish Armada fell to the English navy. England was proud and confident during the first decades of his life. Queen Elizabeth's greatness was clear. She had made a weak and fractious country strong and stable. Without recourse to ruinous taxation, military oppression, or draconian politics, Elizabeth had guided the country to greatness by compromise and moderation.

When John Winthrop went to Cambridge University, he joined with other pious young men who enjoyed the benefits of Elizabeth's England but were uncomfortable with Elizabethan complacency and compromise. For the young men of Cambridge, Elizabethan wealth and stability left them yearning for something still better. Winthrop and many of his friends became part of an informal network of dynamic people called Puritans, who wanted to reform England. The members of this informal network would eventually be leaders in a migration to America and a revolution in England.

After college, John Winthrop owned a village named Groton out in what might be called the Kansas of England. Winthrop was a typical village owner. He rented lands to farmers on long-term leases, owned and operated the church, hired the minister, settled local disputes, and encouraged education, family life, and care for any in the community who became destitute. Winthrop was a member of the conscientious ruling elite of England. Men such as he were the backbone of what made rural England good and virtuous. They considered themselves and the people they looked after to be free.

After Elizabeth died, in 1603, the Stuart family came to the throne. To people like Winthrop, there appeared to be an increase in political corruption. Economic decline seemed rampant. The second Stuart king, Charles I, began, in 1625, to implement policies that diminished the independence of villages like Groton. Under the king's authority, the archbishop of Canterbury began to interfere with the local churches, including those like Winthrop's that were managed and funded by the local manor lord.

In 1629, Winthrop sold his village and joined with a network of Puritan friends, many of them connected through Cambridge University, in purchasing stock in the Massachusetts Bay Company. Winthrop set sail aboard the *Arbella* and reached Salem in June 1630. As the stockholders of a company to set up a community in America, Winthrop and his friends regained an extensive amount of economic, political, and religious independence. Although villages in England were losing their autonomy under Charles I's policy of political and religious centralization, company charters to America did not receive the same close oversight.

The stockholders elected the 41-year-old Winthrop their governor. Hundreds of farmers and trades people joined the expedition as workers—many of them people who had previously rented from or worked for the stockholders. At this time, Winthrop composed his "Model of Christian Charity." Although much would later be said about the motivation for religious freedom that spurred the Puritans to this moment, the essay itself is just as much about politics, economics, and, specifically, the need to reclaim local autonomy and responsibility against the centralizing tendency of the king.

The greatness of Winthrop's essay, and the Puritan migration in general, is that, though Winthrop and the Puritans sought to regain lost freedom, they succeeded in doing so much more with the freedom they gained than they ever would have been able to do in England even if they had never lost their Elizabethan freedom. The call of Winthrop's words and the actions he led in Massachusetts far exceeded any selfish attempt of a threatened owner of a village to gain control of a new village.

The conclusion of "A Model of Christian Charity" is the most important part of Winthrop's essay. "It rests now to make some application," he declared. First, those who claim to be Christians should be "knit together" in a "bond of Love." Second, church and town governments must work together, and the public good must "oversway all private respects." Third, the goal is "to improve our lives, to do more service to the Lord." Fourth, and most significant, "Whatsoever we did or ought to have done when we lived in England, the same must we do and more also where we go."

Winthrop declared a contract between the Puritans and God. God has "ratified" the contract and further commissioned the Puritans to get to work. God, Winthrop threatened, "will expect strict performance." Given this threat, there is only one way to success: "to do justly, to love mercy, to walk humbly with our God."

It is in this context that Winthrop then closes with the "city upon a hill" line. But note that the line is in the context of failure, not success:

> For we must consider that we shall be as a City upon a Hill, the eyes of all people are upon us; so that if we shall deal falsely with our God in this work we have undertaken, and so cause Him to withdraw His present help from us, we shall be a by-word through the world.

With such a speech about such a contract and such a commission, how could anyone expect Winthrop and the Puritans to succeed? In fact, they did not succeed—in the long run. In his own diary, Winthrop reported the frustrations and failures. "As the people increased," he wrote 12 years after arriving in New England, "so sin abounded."

But, early on, Winthrop and his company made an heroic effort to succeed. The story of the initial implementation of Winthrop's speech makes it amazing that he did succeed. Winthrop turned his directorship into an annually elected position. Voting was extended more widely among the people than ever before in England. Renters became landowners. Rich people took less than they could have demanded. Local government was given autonomy. Ministers restrained their political power. Public education was ensured to all children. Virtuous economics was encouraged and price-gouging punished. Surely anyone watching had to admit that the Puritans used their increased freedom to do more political, economic, and religious good in America than was ever possible in England.

Take first the change in Winthrop's position from company director to governor and the extension of voting rights. The stockholders of the Massachusetts Bay Company were a relatively small number of men who were given extensive powers to run their business. Winthrop was elected director by these stockholders. Normal expectation would have the on-site stockholders set up shop in America as an all-powerful aristocracy. Communities of utopian dreamers tend to centralize power, rather than disperse it. Winthrop and the stockholders, however, began almost immediately to reinterpret their royal charter so as to set up a little Puritan republic rather than the business venture that it legally was.

On October 19, 1630, Winthrop and seven stockholders met in an open meeting, as Edmund Morgan writes, to implement "a revolution that was to affect the history of Massachusetts from that time forward" (Morgan, p. 90). Essentially, ownership was extended out to "the people"—that vague term that at that time meant most of the adult males in Massachusetts. What used to be a company was now a self-governing commonwealth, with "the people" having the power to elect a legislature, which, in turn, had the power to appoint yearly a governor and deputy governor.

The only way to understand such a move is to see that Winthrop and his colleagues were serious about what was said in "A Model of Christian Charity." If the Puritans were supposed to be "knit together" with everybody responsible for the success or failure of the enterprise, then Winthrop and the stockholders had to share responsibility and control with those who had not initially put up any money.

Next, consider the fact that renters became landowners and rich people willingly took less than they might have. When migrating to America, a large number of small farmers and townspeople joined the endeavor. Although many of these people had sold their land in England and were prepared to buy in America, there were also many people who had not owned any land. Many farmers in England held long-term leases from men like Winthrop, who, we must remember, owned the whole village of Groton and the surrounding farms. Winthrop could have easily expected a similar deal for himself in America, expecting the poorer immigrants to rent land from him and the other company owners. Even the Quaker William Penn, famous for being nice to Indians and religiously tolerant, held on to his legal right of landownership when he and the Quakers came to Pennsylvania in the 1680s. Penn and his family required a "quitrent" from colonists for the use of the land. Penn also built for himself a mansion on a large estate outside his "city of brotherly love."

Winthrop and his fellow stockholders never tried to rent land. They encouraged land ownership. Land was given away to immigrants. Former renters and poor tradespeople received a town lot upon which to build a house and a field lot upon which to farm. Winthrop built himself a nice house, but it was certainly no mansion. He lived on a town lot in Boston. None of the original stockholders demanded a huge estate in return for their investment.

We must understand that Winthrop and the Puritans were not egalitarian, but they did believe in community responsibility. Winthrop's "Model of Christian Charity" begins with the simple distinction that there are two ranks of people: the rich and the poor. When giving out land, the Puritans tended to give the people who had been richer in England a little more than the formerly landless. The Puritans did not want to undermine social distinctions. Responsibility was what they were after, not equality. In his speech, Winthrop offered several biblical precedents for "enlargement towards others, and less respect towards our selves and our own right."

Here again, we must see the reality behind the rhetoric of Winthrop's call to do "whatsoever we did or ought to have done when we lived in England, the same must we do and more also where we go." Only this way could the Puritans "improve our lives, to do more service to the Lord." Winthrop wanted everyone in Massachusetts to start "rich" and not "poor." Being "rich" he defined not by estate and servants but rather as the ability "to live comfortably by their own means." The Puritan contract with God needed everyone to have such basic comfort so that all people could be "knit together" and spend their days improving Massachusetts instead of worrying about subsistence.

Next in the list of applications rooted in Winthrop's "Model of Christian Charity" is the encouragement of local autonomy and the restraint of ministerial power. The English people had a long history of believing that their freedom was rooted in local autonomy. A well-functioning England depended not on centralized authority but on well-functioning parts making up the whole. In the book of I Corinthians, Paul had advocated a view of the church as different body parts working together as a whole. The Puritans had much to draw from when thinking of autonomous parts making up strong wholes. Winthrop in his speech said it this way: "There is no body but consists of parts, and that which knits these parts together gives the body perfection."

For the Puritans, Massachusetts must consist of multilayered covenants. The marriage covenant was the root of a family covenant, which was the root of church, and town covenants, which were the blossoms in the bouquet of Massachusetts Bay Colony's convenant with God. The whole needed the parts to function well. No king or bishop at the center could make society function well; only the autonomous parts could make the whole work. There was, therefore, much emphasis on independent towns and churches. In fact, people were not allowed to live alone either as individuals or as families. Nobody was given land unless he was part of a family covenant, and the family had to live on a town lot. Unmarried men were thought to be dangerous. People without responsibilities to other people were hard to knit into the fabric of society. Families had to be knit together with other families. A family living out on a farm, far from other families, was useless in building a city on a hill. Families must be gathered together in towns and churches. Only then could everybody watch over everybody else. Wife-beaters could be revealed, sick mothers could be helped with their children, and barns could be raised. Talented children could be identified, and patrons could be organized to send them to college. Only in a town and church could sinners be punished and the saints encouraged.

So when immigrants arrived, they were told to organize themselves into towns and to form churches before they were allotted land. Every town had to have a minister, and ministers had to be educated. Many ministers were part of the Cambridge University Puritan network. It would have been easy to have given the ministers special power in the towns, but that was not the Puritan way. The ministers actually encouraged a restriction of their power. Puritans believed in separation of church and state. Roman Catholics and Anglicans mixed their clergy and government bureaucracy so much that the Puritans believed this helped cause impurity in both church and state. The Puritans liked to call themselves a "New English Israel," which to them indicated a strict differentiation between the roles of magistrate and minister. In Winthrop's speech, he delineated two types of law: Moral Law and the Law of the Gospel. The two must work together in society, but they were divided into the separate realms of state and church.

Where church and state connected in Puritan Massachusetts was in town government and with the voters. Only church members in good standing could vote. This was the crucial link between the highest Christian ideals of the colony and its political structure. The link was not at the top of the pyramid of government but at the base. Church membership was based on a declaration of one's experience of Christ's mercy and a recognition of one's sinfulness.

The whole structure and purpose of the Massachusetts Bay Colony rested on the vitality of towns and churches—and especially the education that towns and churches were supposed to supply. Within the first decade in America, the Puritans passed laws requiring towns to supply public education for Bible literacy, and Harvard College was created to grow a crop of highly educated Puritan leaders. The educated ministers in the towns usually took the responsibility of teaching Latin and Greek to college-bound boys.

Not all towns were able to keep schools at all times, but the Puritans never lost their passion for the connection of politics, religion, and education. Whenever Puritan vitality seemed to be waning, colonial leaders took up the call for increased education. Cotton Mather reminisced about "the ardour with which I once heard" a minister pray at a regional gathering of the clergy: "Lord, for schools every where among us! That our schools may flourish! That every member of this assembly may go home and procure a good school to be encouraged in the town where he lives!" Winthrop's "Model of Christian Charity" says nothing directly about education, but its rational structure and reliance on biblical and legal assumptions leaves no doubt that he expected education to be the foundation of the social model he was describing.

With respect to economics, Winthrop advocated a virtuous business world that condemned pricing anything by what the market will bear. He had no vision of a capitalistic system of individuals working for their own benefit. "The care of the public," he declared, "must oversway all private respects." The goal certainly was "to improve our lives," but only for the purpose of doing "more service to the Lord."

In 1639, Winthrop as governor had to face capitalism in the ideas of a Christian merchant named Robert Keayne, who was fined by the legislature for overcharging. Merchants were supposed to profit according to their level of wit and energy but not at the expense of the community fairness. Winthrop recorded in his diary a sermon on false economic principles given soon after by a Boston minister:

Some false principles were these:—
That a man might sell as dear as he can, and buy as cheap as he can.
If a man lose by casualty of sea, etc. in some of his commodities, he may raise the price of the rest.
That he may sell as he bought, though he paid too dear, etc. and though the commodity be fallen, etc.
That as a man may take the advantage of his own skill or ability, so he may of another's ignorance or necessity.

The city on a hill as preached in "A Model of Christian Charity" was not a utopia. Utopias usually depend on the belief that human nature is good and that a bad environment is what keeps most societies from attaining purity. The Puritan city on a hill was a republic of Christian voters gathered in towns and churches where individual sinfulness could be inhibited by peer pressure. Puritans believed in the inherent sinfulness of individuals and had no illusions about their colony attaining purity.

Using the language of later founding fathers, Winthrop wanted to create a "more perfect" society. As he said in the speech, he wanted to take the politics, religion, and economics of village life in England and make it better. The end product would be a model to the world.

An often-stated irony about the Puritans is that they wanted religious toleration for themselves but refused to extend it to others. While this is superficially true, we should recognize that Winthrop's speech never said anything about religious liberty or toleration. Winthrop's speech was about knitting together people into a web of politics, religion, and economics with underlying assumptions about education. The Puritan creation of a loose republic rooted in independent towns and churches established the web. Those who refused to fully participate in the web were punished in much the same way English towns punished those unwilling to abide by the social contract.

In 1680, more than a half-century after the founding of the colony, England imposed religious toleration on Massachusetts and demanded that voting no longer be restricted to church members. But the loose town and church structure of the commonwealth was becoming too loose anyway. Success was killing them. As Winthrop noted early: "As people increased, so sin abounded." Too many people wanted to come to the city upon a hill, thus turning it into nothing more than a dynamic English colony. When English imperial policy demanded a break between church membership and the right to vote, the key innovation of the city upon a hill was destroyed. What was left was just the shell of Winthop's model.

But even the shell of the plan has long been influential. By the time of Samuel and John Adams, in the 1770s, towns remained the most powerful force in Massachusetts politics. Calling a "town meeting" is still a catch-phrase of participatory democracy. A good case could be made today that it is not Winthrop's speech that is important in American history; rather, it is simply the line about being a city upon a hill: that our town-based, participatory democracy should be exported to the rest of the world.

On the other hand, the deep ideas contained in the "Model of Christian Charity" and their implementation in colonial Massachusetts are inspiring. John Winthrop and his fellow stockholders led one of the greatest events in American history. A small band of rich Protestant men voluntarily diminished their own power to launch a social experiment they hoped would inspire the world.

## SELECTED BIBLIOGRAPHY

Axtell, James. *The Invasion Within: The Contest of Cultures in Colonial North America*. New York: Oxford University Press, 1985. This study of Indian, French, and British contact emphasizes how New France's better relations with Indians long made up for the problem of a few French colonists.

Bailyn, Bernard. *The Peopling of British North America: An Introduction*. New York: Knopf, 1986. Probably the most important historian of colonial America of the generation after Edmund S. Morgan, Bailyn does not emphasize the role of towns. This book, however, is an overview of the immigration patterns that served to fill the towns of America.

Bradford, William. *Of Plymouth Plantation, 1620–1647*. Edited by Samuel Eliot Morison. New York: The Modern Library, 1967. Bradford, a governor of Plymouth Colony, wrote this very readable history of his colony's early years.

Breen, T. H. *Puritans and Adventurers: Change and Persistence in Early America*. New York: Oxford University Press, 1980. An excellent collection of essays comparing northern and southern town life, government, and immigration.

Bridenbaugh, Carl. *Cities in the Wilderness: The First Century of Urban Life in America, 1625–1742*. New York: Oxford University Press, 1938. A fundamental study of town life in British America.

Dawson, Hugh J. "John Winthrop's Rite of Passage: The Origins of the 'Christian Charitie' Discourse," *Early American Literature* 26 (1991): 219–231. Dawson argues that Winthrop wrote and delivered his speech before leaving land in England. The oldest testimony to the speech, however, says it was written on board the *Arbella*.

Fischer, David Hackett. *Albion's Seed: Four British Folkways in America*. New York: Oxford University Press, 1989. Fischer analyzes folkways that manifest the deep social connection between Britain and its colonies.

Fries, Sylvia Doughty. *The Urban Ideal in Colonial America*. Philadelphia: Temple University Press, 1977. Fries emphasizes the ideals involved in founding Boston, New Haven, Philadelphia, Williamsburg, and Savannah.

Goodwin, Rutherford. *A Brief & True Report concerning Williamsburg in Virginia*. Williamsburg, VA: Colonial Williamsburg Inc., 1941. A good study of the founding.

Horn, James. *A Land As God Made It: Jamestown and the Birth of America.* New York: Basic Books, 2005. Comprehensive study of the colonization effort at Jamestown in 1607.

Lockridge, Kenneth A. *A New England Town: The First Hundred Years.* New York: W. W. Norton, 1970. Lockridge builds up the utopianism of the Puritan settlement ideal so that he can then emphasize the fall. Powell's *Puritan Village* is better because it has less of an axe to grind, but both are key studies of the intricacy of a 17th-century town.

Mather, Cotton. *Magnalia Christi Americana.* First published in London in 1702. Anonymously edited with translations in 1853 and reproduced in Carlisle, PA: Banner of Truth, 1979. Any serious student of colonial New England must read Mather's history.

Morgan, Edmund S. *American Slavery American Freedom: The Ordeal of Colonial Virginia.* New York: W. W. Norton, 1975. This classic work emphasizes the British idealism of the Virginia Company and the work of Edwin Sandys.

———. *The Puritan Dilemma: The Story of John Winthrop.* Boston: Little, Brown, 1958. This classic studies the Puritan governor's dilemma of how to separate without separating, how to be exclusive without being exclusive, and how to lead while encouraging self-government.

Morison, Samuel E. *Samuel de Champlain: Father of New France.* Boston: Little, Brown, 1972. Champlain, the founder of Quebec, did as much as he could to encourage stable town life in New France.

Powell, Sumner Chilton. *Puritan Village: The Formation of a New England Town.* Middletown, CT: Wesleyan University Press, 1963. In this Pulitzer Prize winning study, Powell thoroughly discusses English town ideals.

Price, David A. *Love and Hate in Jamestown: John Smith, Pocahontas, and the Heart of a New Nation.* New York: Knopf, 2003. Popular account focusing on the life of John Smith as well as English colonization ventures along the East Coast of North America prior to 1620.

Richter, Daniel K. *Facing East from Indian Country.* Cambridge, MA: Harvard University Press, 2001. Discusses Indian attitudes toward early English attempts at settlement in North America.

Smith, John. *Captain John Smith: A Select Edition of His Writings.* Edited by Karen Ordahl Kupperman. Williamsburg, VA: Institute of Early American History and Culture and Chapel Hill: University of North Carolina Press, 1988. An excellent short collection of Smith's writings, divided into categories of autobiography, Jamestown, relations with Indians, and relation to the environment.

Winthrop, John. *The Journal of John Winthrop, 1630–1649.* Edited by Richard S. Dunn and Laetitia Yeandle. Cambridge, MA: Harvard University Press, 1996. A recent abridged edition of Winthrop's own view of the founding years.

## JOHN CABOT (ca. 1450–1498)

John Cabot's historic voyage to North America in 1497 became the basis for England's claim to the New World and led to the establishment of the British colonies. Ironically, Cabot never knew that he was the first European since the Vikings to step on the uncharted American continent—he thought he had landed on the coast of Asia.

Cabot was born about 1450 in Genoa, Italy. His real name was Giovanni Caboto, although he later anglicized it to John Cabot. When he was still a boy, his family moved to Venice, Italy, which was one of the great shipping ports of Europe at that time.

As a young man, Cabot worked as a sailor, mapmaker, and navigator. Eventually, he became the captain of his own ship and sailed the Mediterranean Sea between Venice and Egypt, trading Italian goods for spices, silks, and jewels from the Far East. Curious as to where the Oriental merchandise came from, Cabot traveled on at least one occasion to Mecca, Saudi Arabia, where Arabian merchants brought the precious goods after long, overland journeys from Asia and India.

Cabot was convinced that it would be easier and cheaper to import Eastern goods to Europe by sea. Other people had the same idea, too, but most thought that the only way to get to Asia from Europe was to sail around the African continent and continue eastward—a very long and perilous journey. Cabot, like Christopher Columbus, believed that it was possible for a ship to reach Asia by sailing west, instead of east.

By the mid-1480s, Cabot had moved with his wife and children to England. He had tried to persuade the kings of Spain and Portugal to commission a voyage to Asia, but they turned him down. Then, in 1496, he convinced King Henry VII of England to grant him a charter to sail west and claim new lands for the English Crown. His plan was to sail farther north on the Atlantic Ocean than Columbus had in 1492, which Cabot believed was a faster way to Asia.

In 1496, Cabot set sail from Bristol, England, but was forced to turn back because of poor weather and dissension among the crew. On May 2, 1497, he set off again, on a single small ship called the *Matthew* (named after his Italian wife, Mattea), with a crew of 18. He headed out directly west, around the coast of Ireland, and then stayed on a northwest course. Five weeks into the trip, on June 24, he sighted land and went ashore.

No one knows exactly where on the North American continent Cabot landed, but it was probably somewhere in what is now known as Newfoundland or Nova Scotia. Cabot planted the English and Venetian flags on the "New Founde Lande," and he claimed it in the name of the English king. He was convinced that he had landed somewhere on the eastern coast of Asia.

Cabot and his crew explored inland for a short distance. They did not discover the source of Oriental spices and jewels as they had hoped, but they did find verdant land and fertile fishing grounds. Although he and his crew did not see any people or animals, they saw signs that the land was inhabited, including cut trees and the remnants of campfires. Cabot returned to the ship and sailed eastward, exploring the coastline. He remained convinced that he had found the Asian continent or an island off the coast of Asia and that further exploration westward was necessary. With only one small ship and dwindling supplies, however, he decided to return home. After a quick, 15-day crossing across the Atlantic, the *Matthew* sailed back into Bristol in early August.

Cabot was greeted in England as a returning hero. He had no trouble convincing Henry VII to commission five ships for another, bigger exploration. Cabot's plan was to return to his original landfall and continue sailing southwest until he found the source of "all the spices in the world," as Marco Polo had written about the Orient.

In 1498, Cabot's fleet set sail from Bristol once again. One ship was damaged soon after the fleet left and anchored in Ireland. The fate of the other four ships remains a mystery. Some historians believe that Cabot reached North America and explored the eastern coast of the continent before he died. Most historians, however, think Cabot died at sea, when his fleet was hit by storms.

In any event, it appears certain that Cabot perished without knowing his true value to history. Although his dream of a westward route to Asia went unfulfilled, his journey spurred others, including his son Sebastian, to follow him and continue the exploration of the North American continent.

## JAMESTOWN, FOUNDING OF (1607)

The colony of Jamestown, Virginia, was the first permanent English settlement in America. In June 1606, the Virginia Company of London was granted a charter to establish a colony in the New World in order to exploit the area's mineral resources. Three ships, the *Susan Constant,* the *Discovery,* and the *Godspeed,* carried 108 adventurers and indentured servants across the Atlantic Ocean to the North American continent. The expedition first anchored at Cape Comfort (present-day Old Point Comfort in Hampton, Virginia) on April 30, 1607.

As prescribed by the charter, a president was to be elected by the council, and Edward Maria Wingfield was chosen. It was his determination to land at the site of Jamestown (named for King James I). However, other colonists, like Capt. Bartholomew Gosnold, opposed the selection. Nonetheless, the new colonists established their fort and settlement on May 14, 1607.

From its very beginnings, Jamestown was largely a failure. The swampy, low-lying site had impure drinking water and was host to a variety of diseases, and, within a year, almost two-thirds of the settlers, including Gosnold, had died from illness or malnutrition. The worst part of all, as far as the Virginia Company was concerned, was that there was no gold or other minerals to be found. The colonists, particularly Capt. John Smith, had become increasingly at odds with Wingfield's leadership. In September 1607, the council was able to displace Wingfield from his position.

Smith managed to hold the colony together when he assumed command of Jamestown, in 1608, but Smith returned to London in 1609, and Jamestown reached its lowest point during the winter of 1609–1610, when it suffered disease, starvation, and Indian attacks. Only the arrival of additional colonists in 1610 saved the colony. Gradually, the settlers learned which crops could be grown, especially tobacco and corn, for export, and the colony eventually achieved a solid economic footing. In 1619, Jamestown was the location of the first meeting of the Virginia House of Burgesses, which was the first representative legislative body in the New World.

The town was destroyed in 1676 during Bacon's Rebellion, and, although it was rebuilt, it was succeeded by Williamsburg as the capital in 1699. Eventually, the course of the James River created an island of the original site, which is today preserved as part of the Colonial National Historic Park System administered by the National Park Service.

STEVEN STROM, KAREN MEAD, AND ELIZABETH DUBRULLE

## PILGRIMS

The Pilgrims were Separatists from the Church of England who left England in 1620 to establish a colony in what is now Plymouth, Massachusetts. The Separatists were Puritans, but, unlike the main body of Puritans, who chose to remain within the Church of England in order to enact reforms, the Pilgrims did not believe that the church could be purified of its lingering Roman Catholic liturgy and theology, and they separated to form their own church.

The Pilgrims were persecuted by the English government as nonconformists, and, in 1608, some of them emigrated to Holland in search of religious freedom. After a few years in Holland, however, many Pilgrims grew concerned about the cultural influence of the Dutch and the possibility of a war between Holland and Spain. A movement began to establish a colony in the New World in order to have the freedom to worship as they thought proper. By 1620, the Pilgrims had obtained financial backing for their venture, and, on September 16 of that year, 102 Pilgrims left Plymouth, England, in their ship, the *Mayflower.* After a sea voyage of 65 days, they sighted North America on November 10. The night before they embarked in the New World, the groups' leaders drafted the Mayflower Compact to provide some form of government for the settlement.

The Pilgrims originally landed at Cape Cod, Massachusetts, on November 11 but decided that the terrain was not suitable for farming. Following explorations of the surrounding countryside, they chose a site on the western side of Cape Cod Bay on which to establish their settlement, named Plymouth Plantation, on December 21. The Pilgrim settlement barely survived its first winter in the New World, but, over the course of the next 10 years, it stabilized and grew. The Pilgrims were adamant about protecting their autonomy once the Puritans founded the Massachusetts Bay Colony in Boston, just to the north of Plymouth Plantation. They remained separate from the Puritans and Massachusetts for the rest of the century but eventually assimilated with the other settlers in New England.

## SIR WALTER RALEIGH (ca. 1552–1618)

A poet, courtier, soldier, and historian, Sir Walter Raleigh did more than any other Elizabethan to promote English exploration and colonization of North America. Born into a Devonshire gentry family, Raleigh (he favored the spelling Ralegh) was educated at Oxford. He spent the early 1570s in France fighting with the Huguenots as part of a contingent of Devonshire volunteers. In the late 1570s, he helped his half-brother Sir Humphrey Gilbert fight rebels in Ireland and outfit privateering expeditions against Spanish shipping. After 1581, he was mostly at court, where he was much favored by the queen, who knighted him in 1584 and appointed him captain of her guards in 1587. Between 1583 and 1589, he invested more than £40,000 in six colonizing expeditions to North America, having received a grant from Elizabeth to plant colonies along the eastern coast of the continent, which area Raleigh named Virginia, for the "Virgin Queen."

Although responsible for introducing potatoes and tobacco to England and Ireland, Raleigh's ventures were unsuccessful in establishing a permanent English colony in America. Raleigh was briefly imprisoned in 1592 for his unauthorized marriage to Elizabeth Throckmorton, one of the queen's ladies-in-waiting. He was forbidden the queen's presence for a time but was back in favor by 1595, when he set off on a fruitless search for the legendary Eldorado, supposedly to be found in Guyana. He was part of the successful English attack on Cadiz in 1596 and the unsuccessful Islands Expedition of 1597. He quarreled with the royal favorite Robert Devereux, Earl of Essex, in 1597, and thereafter was a consistent opponent of the earl and much blamed for his downfall.

In 1603, James I, persuaded by Raleigh's many enemies that the Devon gentleman was a dangerous conspirator, had Raleigh arrested and tried for treason. From 1603 to 1616, Raleigh lay in the Tower of London, where he composed poetry and wrote his *History of the World.* Released to search for gold along the Orinoco in South America, Raleigh found none but burned a Spanish settlement and was rearrested upon his return on the insistence of the Spanish king, with whom James was attempting to negotiate a marriage for his son. Raleigh was executed on October 29, 1618.

## ROANOKE COLONIES (1585, 1587)

In 1584, Walter Raleigh obtained a six-year grant from Queen Elizabeth to establish an English colony in North America. Raleigh immediately sent out the Amadas-Barlowe expedition to explore the East Coast of the continent and locate a likely settlement site. After exploring Roanoke and Hatarask Islands, and claiming the region for England, the expedition returned with a glowing description of the islands and two Indians named Manteo and Wanchese. Hoping to secure the queen's financial backing for his colonization efforts, Raleigh named the newly explored region Virginia, after the Virgin Queen. When this ploy failed, Raleigh attracted private backers by claiming the region could supply England with commodities then only available from the Spanish-controlled Mediterranean.

In April 1585, six vessels carrying 600 men left Plymouth under the command of Sir Richard Grenville, Raleigh's cousin. By July, the expedition had, with the aid of Manteo and Wanchese, established friendly relations with the Roanoke chief Wingina, who allowed the Englishmen to settle on the northern end of Roanoke Island. Because much of the colony's food supply had been lost when one of the ships ran aground, Grenville decided in August to leave a settlement of only about 100 men under Ralph Lane and to return to England with the rest of the colonists. Seeking sources of immediate wealth, Lane began to explore the surrounding region and, in the fall, discovered Chesapeake Bay. In the spring, Lane determined to move the colony to Chesapeake when he heard reports from the Indians that pearls and metals that sounded like gold and copper could be found in the area. The coming of spring brought hostilities with the Indians.

Having arrived too late to plant crops, the colonists bartered for food with the Indians, whose willingness to trade declined with their own food supplies. In June, having learned through Manteo of Indian plans to attack the settlement, Lane launched a preemptive raid on the Roanoke village that left Wingina dead. One week later, a relief expedition of 29 vessels under Sir Francis Drake reached Roanoke after a successful raid on the Spanish West Indies. Given the precarious state of the colony's food supply and its relations with its Roanoke neighbors, Lane and the surviving colonists left for England with Drake on June 18, 1586.

After the voluntary return of the first Roanoke colonists in 1586, Sir Walter Raleigh sent out a second colonization expedition in 1587. Unlike the all-male first colony, the new venture, under the governorship of John White, a member of the first colony, included whole families. Three vessels carrying 89 men, 17 women, and 11 children departed Plymouth on May 8, 1587. Although intending to settle on Chesapeake Bay, the settlers were forced on July 22 to take up the first colony's site on Roanoke Island (off present-day North Carolina) when the ships' crews, eager to raid in the Spanish West Indies, refused to sail up the Chesapeake. The ill will the previous colonists had left among the Roanoke Indians led quickly to tragedy. On July 28, George Howe, who had gone alone to catch crabs, was found murdered, perhaps an act of revenge for the previous colony's killing of the Roanoke chief Wingina. Attempts to reestablish relations with the Indians through Manteo, one of the Indians who had gone to England with the Amadas-Barlowe expedition in 1584, failed.

On August 18, White's daughter Eleanor, the wife of Ananias Dare, gave birth to a daughter. The first English child born in North America, the child was christened Virginia Dare by her grandfather. The unfriendliness of the Indians meant that the colony was totally dependent on England for supplies, and the colonists decided that White was best suited to ensuring that Raleigh sent regular provisions and that the English public remained aware of and interested in the colony. Accordingly, White set sail on August 27 and reached England on October 16. In April 1588, White set out with two relief ships but had to turn back when the crews' taste for piracy led to an unfortunate encounter with a Spanish vessel.

The Armada crisis of 1588 tied up all shipping and prevented White from returning to Virginia until 1590. On August 16, he landed on Roanoke but found no trace of the colony, only the word "Croatoan" carved on a tree. This seemed to indicate the colony's removal to nearby Croatoan Island, but storms prevented investigation, and White returned to England without ever knowing what became of his family and the "lost colony" of Roanoke.

## DOCUMENT: EXCERPT FROM ARTHUR BARLOWE'S "FIRST VOYAGE TO ROANOKE," 1584

*In April 1584, Philip Amadas and Arthur Barlowe, two gentlemen of Sir Walter Raleigh's household, set sail from Plymouth in command of two vessels bound for the New World. Having just secured a grant from Queen Elizabeth to establish an English colony in America, Raleigh charged the two men with reconnoitering the American coast to find a good settlement site and learn something of the Natives, climate, and products of the area. The expedition sailed along the coasts of the modern-day states of Georgia, South Carolina, and North Carolina and then landed on Hatteras Island where they made friendly contact with the nearby Roanoke Indians. Below is an excerpt from the report that Barlowe wrote of the trip, which Raleigh used to stimulate investment and encourage settlement in his planned colony.* (Barlowe, Arthur, *First Voyage to Roanoke,* edited by Increase N. Tarbox, *Sir Walter Ralegh and His Colony in America* [Boston: Printed for the Prince Society by John Wilson and Son, 1884], pp. 110–112, 119, 121.)

[We] cast anchor about three harquebus-shots within the haven's mouth, on the left hand of the same: and after thanks given to God for our safe arrival thither, we manned our boats, and went to view the land next adjoining, and to take possession of the same, in the right of the Queen's most excellent Majesty, and rightful Queen, and Princess of the same, and after delivered the same over to your use, according to her Majesty's grant, and letters patents, under her Highness great seal. Which being performed, according to the ceremonies used in such enterprises, we viewed the land about us, being, whereas we first landed, very sandy and low towards the waters side, but so full of grapes, as the very beating and surge of the Sea overflowed them, of which we found such plenty, as well there as in all places else, both on the sand and on the green soil on the hills, as in the plains, as well on every little shrub, as also climbing towards the tops of high Cedars, that I think in all the world the like abundance is not to be found: and myself having seen those parts of Europe that most abound, find such difference as were incredible to be written.

We passed from the Sea side towards the tops of those hills next adjoining, being but of mean height, and from thence we beheld the Sea on both sides to the North, and to the South, finding no end any of both ways. This land lay stretching itself to the West, which after we found to be but an Island of twenty miles long, and not above six miles broad. Under the bank or hill whereon we stood, we beheld the valleys replenished with goodly Cedar trees, and having discharged our harquebus-shot, such a flock of Cranes (the most part white), arose under us, with such a cry redoubled by many echoes, as if an army of men had shouted all together.

This Island had many goodly woods full of Deer, Conies, Hares, and Fowl, even in the middle of Summer in incredible abundance. The woods are not such as you find in Bohemia [or] Muscovy . . . barren and fruitless, but the highest and reddest Cedars of the world, far bettering the Cedars of the Azores, of the Indies, or Lebanon, Pines, Cypress, Sassafras . . . Mastic . . . and many other of excellent smell and quality. . . .

[The brother of Wingina, the local chief] sent us every day a brace or two of fat Bucks, Conies, Hares, Fish the best of the world. He sent us divers kinds of fruits, Melons, Walnuts, Cucumbers, Gourds, Peas, and divers roots, and fruits very excellent good, and of their Country corn, which is very white, fair and well tasted, and grows three times in five months: in May they sow, in July they reap, in June they sow, in August they reap: in July they sow, in September they reap: only they cast the corn into the ground, breaking a little of the soft turf with a wooden mattock, or pickaxe; ourselves proved the soil, and put some of our Peas in the ground, and in ten days they were of fourteen inches high: they have also Beans very fair of divers colors and wonderful plenty: some growing naturally, and some in their gardens, and so have they both wheat and oats.

The soil is the most plentiful, sweet, fruitful and wholesome of all the world: there are above fourteen several sweet smelling timber trees, and the most part of their underwoods are Bays and such like: they have those Oaks that we have, but far greater and better. . . .

[By the people] [w]e were entertained with all love and kindness, and with as much bounty, after their manner, as they could possibly devise. We found the people most gentle, loving and faithful, void of all guile and treason, and such as live after the manner of the golden age.

# 6

# Early European–Native American Encounters, 1607–1637

## INTRODUCTION

The English who first colonized North America received their earliest perceptions about American Indians, or Native Americans, from the Spanish, who, with the exception of Bartolomé de las Casas (infrequently read in England), characterized the Natives in the most unflattering terms. The first book in English on America was seen in 1511, and it described Indians as "lyke beasts without any resonablenes.... And they ete also on[e] another, the man ete his wyf his children.... They hange also the bodyes or persons fleshe in the smoke as men do with us swynes fleshe" (quoted in Stannard, p. 226).

To philosophers and intellectuals of the day, such people were barely human; indeed, some believed them to be satanic progeny of a human-animal coupling. Thus, the vast majority of Englishmen came to North America predisposed to treat Indians with undisguised hostility. As Robert Gray, an early Virginia settler, put it in 1609, "[They are] incredibly rude, they worship the divell, offer their young children in sacrifice to him, wander up and down like beasts, and in manners and conditions, differ very little from beasts" (quoted in Stannard, p. 227).

By the late 16th century, most Europeans had concluded that Indians probably were human but that they were still godless and lawless.

English treatment of Indians worsened as the colonial experiment wore on and settlers saw that the Natives were not going to submit either to their religion or their laws. For them to reject those basic tenets of English culture meant that they must be "less than rational and thus less than human" (Stannard, p. 229).

The English colonists simply had difficulty accepting Indians for what they were; they were too conscious of the racial differences and, as a consequence, instinctively antagonistic. As the interpretive essay for this chapter points out, there were exceptions. Thomas Mayhew got along well with the Indians on Martha's Vineyard for many years. John Eliot spent 15 years learning the Algonquin language and then translating the Bible into Algonquin before going out to do missionary work among the Indians. After 30 years, he claimed that there were 1,500 "praying Indians" and another 1,000 converted Natives living in special villages throughout the Plymouth Colony.

Much of the European concern for Indians involved a desire to convert them to Christianity, as John Eliot spent much of life doing. But, in general, the Church of England and its Puritan offspring did not make much of a concerted effort to win the souls of the Indians. Clergy were reluctant to do missionary work among the tribes when the pay was low and the conditions uncomfortable and occasionally dangerous. Most preferred the traditional life of serving a parish in a colonial town.

The French were better able to adapt to the Indians. Although the French Jesuit missionaries thought that the Natives were barbarians, they still wanted to convert them to Catholicism. Perhaps the Catholic faith appealed more to the Indians, or perhaps the Jesuits were better prepared for their task. They often knew the Indian dialect, for example, while Protestant missionaries seldom had any formal preparation.

On the other hand, Dutch relations with the Indians were strictly commercial. Early on in the Dutch colonial experience, perhaps around 1618, informal trade with the Mohawk Indians began. The Indians brought furs to the Dutch and in return received muskets at a rate of 20 beaver pelts for one gun. At first, relatively few muskets fell into Indian hands by means of this trade, but, by the 1640s, when French-English rivalry accelerated the pace of war, the Mohawks, part of the Iroquois federation, had acquired many more muskets. When the English replaced the Dutch as trading partners with the Indians, they, too, supplied guns for furs.

In general, Dutch relations with Indians were good from the beginning of their settlement. The colony of New Netherland grew quite slowly and thus was less threatening to the Indians than the rapidly expanding English colonies in New England. Before the 1620s, the Dutch were always careful to treat the Indians with dignity and to pay them for their land. The Dutch West India Company stipulated that "everyone should be strict in dealing with the Indians—no one should give offense to their person, their womenfolk, or their possessions" (quoted in Edmonds, p. 168).

By the late 1620s, this attitude was changing. The Indians were less in awe of the Dutch, who began to consider the Indians a nuisance. Jonas Michaelius, one of the first pastors to come to New Netherland, thought that the Indians were "stupid as posts, proficient in all wickedness and godlessness . . . thievish and treacherous as they are tall" (quoted in Edmonds, p. 168). Perhaps this is why Dutch-Indian relations were strictly commercial.

The first phase of English–Native American relations ended with the brutal Pequot War of 1637. The Pequots were a Connecticut tribe that before the 1630s had had little contact with either the English or the Dutch. They had been involved in fighting other nearby tribes, but they did not perceive the English or the Dutch as threats to their security or territory.

Indian-white distrust in New England began in 1615, even before the first permanent settlement, when an English sea captain, Thomas Hunt, captured 15 Indians while loading fish and sold them to the Spanish as slaves. Out of this group came Squanto, educated and converted by the Jesuits and a friend later to the English. Prior to Squanto's return, in the early 1620s, however, word of the kidnapping spread among different Indian groups, and, when a smallpox epidemic accompanied the rumors, killing many Natives, the Indians could not have viewed the white people in a favorable light. The English, on the other hand, saw the epidemic as a mark of God's favor.

The Pilgrims were idealized and romanticized in early American history, as this 19th-century illustration shows. (Courtesy of the Library of Congress.)

The Pequots were not affected by the smallpox epidemic; at that time, they were still too isolated from contact with Europeans. After the English began coming to New England in the 1620s, the Pequots did have occasion to deal with the newcomers, and they were considered peaceful and honorable in those dealings. Described as "stately and warlike," they were known to engage in wars with their Indians neighbors, such as the Mohawks.

Trouble between the English and the Pequots began in 1633 when a renegade band of Pequots killed a trading party led by Captain John Stone, something of a renegade himself and a person whose immoral behavior had caused the Massachusetts Bay Colony authorities to expel him on two separate occasions. Sassacus, the Pequot chief, was concerned enough about this incident to send a delegation to Boston to seek a treaty of friendship with the English. The Indians succeeded in convincing the colonists that there had been no profit to them for the deed; indeed, 8 of the 10 Indians involved had soon after died of smallpox. The Pequots agreed to turn over the two surviving attackers, but they never did.

Nonetheless, the incident was apparently forgotten, and there was a period of calm until 1636, when another incident, even worse than the John Stone affair, took place, near Block Island, off the Connecticut coast. A ship belonging to John Oldham was seen adrift, with Indians on deck, who fled when a ship commanded by John Gallup approached. Gallup's ship rammed Oldham's, and several Indians who had not previously fled jumped (or fell) overboard and drowned. Gallup boarded Oldham's ship, found two more Indians and took them prisoner, and then found Oldham's body, his head, hands, and feet cut off. In addition, most of the cargo was missing.

Massachusetts Bay Colony governor Henry Vane learned that several Indians who had managed to escape from Oldham's ship had gone to the Pequots, who were apparently protecting them. Vane sent a delegation to the Pequots, who surrendered two boys who had been members of Oldham's crew and promised to return the stolen cargo. The Indians evidently felt that this was a reasonable compromise, but the colonists were not satisfied. There were a few minor skirmishes over the matter, but the violence was minimal.

After a difficult winter in 1636–1637, marked by Pequot raids on colonial settlements and the kidnapping of two teenage girls, who were later released unhurt, New England leaders decided that the Pequots had to be eliminated, and a force of 90 colonists and 70 Mohegan Indians (enemies of the Pequot) set out for Pequot territory. They were later joined by an indeterminate number of Narragansetts, who were also enemies of the Pequots. The combined force managed to approach a sizable Pequot town without detection and attacked late at night, setting the town afire and firing musket volleys at Indians trying to flee. By dawn, the town was in ashes, and all but 14 of the 700 Pequots who had lived there were dead. A month later, another English force invaded Pequot country and killed several hundred more Indians. When the Mohawks killed Sassacus, who had fled to them for protection, the war, such as it was, ended, and the Pequot nation was dead. Most English settlers saw the whole affair as another indication of God's working his will.

If English muskets failed to kill Indians, their diseases made up for it. As in the Spanish world, European diseases proved fatal to thousands of Indians in the early years of colonization in New England. A smallpox epidemic in 1616–1617, apparently brought by fishing vessels trading with Indians, killed enough Natives to eliminate them as a major threat to the Plymouth Colony after 1620. Smallpox continued to be a health problem in the 1630s, killing substantial numbers of settlers but many more Indians. A major epidemic in 1639–1640 in the Saint Lawrence River Valley and nearby areas killed many Huron Indians, reducing that tribe's population to 10,000 from the 20,000 to 35,000 it had been at the beginning of the century. The Iroquois were similarly decimated in the 1660s.

The English could have quarantined smallpox patients and made an effort to reduce the spread of the disease, as the Spanish and Portuguese tried to do (though without great success). But the English were not concerned with the physical well-being of the Indians and, indeed, welcomed what they considered an obvious manifestation of God's blessings upon them.

## INTERPRETIVE ESSAY

KATHLEEN PERDISATT AND RICK KENNEDY

Seventeenth-century North American history is the story of a contest for domination. In that contest, the Native Americans ultimately lost and British culture won. The greatest failure in 17th-century America was the inability of Natives and the settlers to construct a mutually beneficial life together in North America. From the grand perspective of the history of our nation, it is appropriate to emphasize the tragic and doomed battles of the Indians against dispossession as European disease, population growth, and land-grabbing proved unstoppable. Within the largely tragic story, however, there are many small stories of creative people trying to work against the tide. In the 17th century, Pocahontas, Squanto, and Hiacoomes, along with settlers in the regions surrounding Jamestown, Virginia, and Cape Cod, Massachusetts, tried to create the biracial relationship that might have undercut the beginnings of the contest for domination.

Pocahontas was a young woman who aspired to do what Americans throughout history have never been able to do: create productive cross-cultural relations between Native and non-Native Americans. Pocahontas was the daughter of Wahunsonacock, who also went by the name Powhatan. Wahunsonacock was the dynamic emperor of eastern Virginia. He ruled 30 separate tribes that were together called the Powhatans. Pocahontas was a favored daughter who shared her father's vivacity and leadership abilities.

With the founding of Jamestown by the British, in 1607, misunderstandings and distrust abounded. Wahunsonacock apparently thought that the English, with their guns and technology, could be useful to Powhatan imperial expansion. On the English side, the unruly but talented John Smith was sure he was dealing with savages who could not be trusted. He and his fellow English invaders were much too suspicious of the surrounding Indians to think much about what they were doing and what was happening.

Edmund S. Morgan calls the British situation in Jamestown a "fiasco" of organization and direction. Wahunsonacock and the Powhatans willingly supplied Jamestown with food and help, but Smith, distrustful of this arrangement, tells us that he would come armed to get these gifts. Smith reported that in one encounter Wahunsonacock told him that he need not bring weapons "for here they are needlesse we being friends." Smith refused to believe the chief and, shortly after, even pointed his gun at and demanded supplies from Opechancanough, the king's brother and eventual successor. Opechancanough was already opposed to his brother's way of handling the British, and Smith succeeded only in justifying Opechancanough's own paranoia.

The climate of distrust continued when, in 1608, Smith was "captured" by the Powhatans. Smith described his situation as follows:

> A long consultation was held, but the conclusion was, two great stones were brought before [Wahunsonacock]: then as many as could lay hands on [me], dragged [me] to them, and thereon laid [my] head, and being ready with their clubs, to beate out [my] braines, Pocahontas the Kings dearest daughter, when no intreaty could prevaile, got [my] head in her armes, and laid her owne upon [mine] to save [me] from death: whereat the Emperour was contented [I] should live.

Two days later, Wahunsonacock, ceremonially dressed in imperial garb, came to Smith and "told him now they were friends" and sent him back to Jamestown.

Smith thought that Pocahontas had saved his life and that her tricky father had some plan up his sleeve. In truth, we do not know what really happened; however, it appears that John Smith had been not a prisoner but an honored—if coerced—guest. The Powhatan emperor had ceremoniously inducted Smith and Jamestown into his empire. John Smith, after a ceremony of submission, was now a subchief of the Powhatans and was sent back to his people. Pocahontas, an 11- or 12-year-old girl at that time, was either playing a role in the ceremony or trying to calm Smith.

Pocahontas was also at the center of another confusion: Wahunsonacock's coronation as a subject-king under the king of England. Smith tells us that after Wahunsonacock was asked to come to Jamestown, some English soldiers were surprised by a "hydeous noise" coming from the woods. Smith and the colonists grabbed their guns, thinking the Natives were attacking, "but presently Pocahontas came, willing him to kill her if any hurt were intended." Pocahontas then joined with 30 other young women in a dance. The next day, Wahunsonacock arrived. The colonists attempted to explain what was happening, and the emperor did not readily participate. "Foule trouble there was to make him kneele to receive his Crowne," Smith wrote.

In the midst of two coerced ceremonies of subjection was a young girl who may have understood the big picture better than either her father or Smith. As the Powhatans and the British vied ceremonially to make each the subchief of the other, Pocahontas played the role of mediator. Many children's stories and cartoons have completely distorted the story of Pocahontas; however, they usually have the main point right. Pocahontas, the loving and fearless child, represents the possibility of a relationship of trust between the invaders and the ruling empire.

Between 1608 and 1610, Pocahontas was a welcome visitor in Jamestown, often carrying messages to and from her father. Smith and other leaders of Jamestown had sown much distrust, but young Pocahontas was oblivious to the danger. In 1610, however, war broke out between Powhatans and the colonists, and in 1613 the colonists captured Pocahontas and brought her to Jamestown. She became a diplomatic hostage but does not seem to have thought of herself as a hostage. She freely converted to Christianity and consented to marry John Rolfe in 1614. She may have helped Rolfe and the English learn to grow tobacco during this time. Wahunsonacock consented to the marriage, which brought the war to an end.

Pocahontas apparently loved Rolfe. She could have escaped. Eventually, she bore a child who became a symbol for the possibility of mutually beneficial biracial relations. Pocahontas and Rolfe agreed to sail to England to publicize the possibility of peace, but, sadly, Pocahontas died in England in 1617 from a European disease. Many people have written about Pocahontas as a victim sacrificed to a British farce. But this is too cynical. The British had high hopes of bringing peace after the fiasco in Jamestown, and Pocahontas's marriage and child symbolized the best possibility. She seems to have willingly embraced the people of Jamestown and accepted the role of peacemaker between the English and her people. She died pursuing her aspiration.

Her father died two years later, leaving Opechancanough to spread his distrust. The relationship between Opechancanough and Smith, not that between Pocahontas and Rolfe, became the model for 17th-century Virginia. In March 1622, Opechancanough orchestrated widespread attacks on English settlements. The attacks, however, did not stop immigration and only encouraged distrust.

Business relationships between the Indians and the British in Virginia continued throughout the 17th century; however, hope for sharing the land, intermarriage, and raising mixed-blood children was gone. By the 1670s, the Natives had been pushed across the Blue Ridge Mountains. British settlers on the Virginia frontier for the rest of the century fueled more hatred and distrust in ongoing skirmishes.

*Assimilation* was the term eventually adopted in the 18th century as the answer to the "the Indian problem." By then, assimilation clearly meant the destruction of the weaker culture in favor of the adoption of the stronger. In the 17th century, assimilation still could have meant something more benign and mutually beneficial. Pocahontas hoped for this type of assimilation. Squanto (also known as Tisquantum), the Patuxet who taught the Pilgrims to fertilize their corn with fish, also aspired to assimilate Natives and non-Natives into a mutually beneficial relationship.

Squanto was a highly intelligent and versatile native of Patuxet, a thriving town of some 2,000 people on what is now Plymouth Bay, Massachusetts. At the time of Jamestown's founding (1607), Patuxet and other coastal New England towns were developing a trading relationship with European ships fishing for cod. John Smith, after leaving Jamestown in 1608, sailed to Cape Cod in 1614 and gave the region the name New England. A companion ship with Smith was captained by a man who wanted to make some extra money by capturing some Indians to sell as slaves in Spain. Squanto and 20 other Wampanoags from Patuxet were lured on board and placed in chains.

A Spanish priest later freed Squanto, but, finding himself now in Europe, Squanto began learning what he could from the Europeans while working toward getting home. Not much is known about his travels in Europe, but we know that after three years he was living in London, helping prospective colonists and explorers with information about New England. Five years after leaving America, he found a chance to go back by sailing with a colonizing mission. The mission failed, but Squanto returned home in 1619.

However, New England had been ravaged by European diseases while Squanto was away. The Bostonian Cotton Mather would later write that God had "wonderfully prepared" the New World for Puritan "entertainment, by a sweeping mortality that had lately been among the natives." Mather wrote that only one-tenth, even one-twentieth, of the Natives remained "so that the woods were almost cleared of those pernicious creatures, to make room for a better growth." William Bradford, one of the founding Pilgrims of Plymouth Colony, was more respectful of what he called "the late great mortality." Bradford reported that "skulls and bones were found in many places lying still above the ground where their houses and dwellings had been, a very sad spectacle to behold." Such was the spectacle Squanto beheld upon his return. But again Squanto did not fall into despair.

When Bradford and the Pilgrims arrived at Squanto's hometown in 1620, they were understandably fearful of Indian attack. Initially, the Natives kept their distance except for stealing some tools. On March 16, an Indian from the north named Samoset who spoke broken English walked out of the woods to greet the English. Samoset later returned with several local Wampanoags carrying the Pilgrims' stolen goods. With the Wampanoags was Squanto and their sachem (Indian chief), Massasoit. After some "friendly entertainments," the Pilgrims and the Wampanoags then negotiated a long-lasting peace agreement:

1. That neither he nor any of his should injure or do hurt to any of their people.
   That if any of his did hurt to any of theirs, he should send the offender, that they might punish him.
   That if anything were taken away from any of theirs, he should cause it to be restored; and they should do the like to his.
   If any did unjustly war against him, they would aid him; if any did war against them, he should aid them.

He should send to his neighbours confederates to certify them of this, that they might not wrong them, but might be likewise comprised in the conditions of peace.

That when their men came to them, they should leave their bows and arrows behind them. (Bartett, p. 188)

Governor Bradford described Squanto as "a special instrument sent of God for their good beyond their expectation." He was the intermediary in negotiating the peace treaty and chose to settle with the English. His teaching the Pilgrims to grow corn is one of the great traditions of American education. He was the key figure in making possible the first Thanksgiving celebration, when Massasoit and 90 Wampanoags joined the Pilgrims for three days of happy feasting. Squanto spent most of his time brokering deals between various tribes and the English. He died of an "Indian fever" in 1622 on a trading mission helping Miles Standish. In his last days, Squanto gave gifts to his English friends and "remembrances of his love."

Squanto, after the loss of his own town, was able to embrace both the Natives and the non-Natives of Plymouth Bay. He was by far the most well-traveled, broadly experienced, linguistically versatile person in New England. Cynics have disparaged him as weak, but they fail to give Squanto the credit he deserves. He was a townless Indian who seems to have been able to see beyond the tribal distrust and animosities of other Natives and non-Natives.

At one point, Squanto seems to have made an attempt at centralizing power in himself as an intertribal leader. All we know of this story is William Bradford's version, which says that Squanto told the Pakanokets to abandon Massasoit's leadership while, at the same time, encouraging the English to think Massasoit was going to betray them. Squanto, Bradford believed, was trying to undermine Massasoit's political position.

The story shows the complexity of Squanto's work brokering relations between local power centers. If Bradford's history is right and Squanto was making a power play for himself at that point, it raises the possibility that the person who had orchestrated the first peace treaty and Thanksgiving feast was attempting to do even greater good.

But Squanto did not gain an intertribal leadership position, and, 15 years after his death, the Pequot War broke out. Governor Winthrop in Boston wrote to Governor Bradford in Plymouth: "we conceive that you look at the Pequots and all other Indians as a common enemy." Thirty years later, Massasoit's son, Metacom, believed the leaders of Plymouth Colony poisoned his brother. He and the English no longer upheld the treaty written with Squanto's help. In the 1670s, Metacom galvanized Indian resistance to the English and died in New England's most devastating civil war.

Pocahontas and Squanto died just at the point they might have done something great for relations between Natives and non-Natives. Maybe it is significant that both were "outsiders" in the sense that one was a girl and young woman—a weak position in foreign affairs—and the other was homeless. Hiacoomes was also an outsider, but he did not die young. His story, along with that of the Mayhew family, represents the best hope in the 17th century for a mutually beneficial relationship between the British and the Indians.

Hiacoomes and the Mayhew family were the most influential people on the island of Martha's Vineyard. In 1641, Thomas Mayhew Sr. became, in the presumptuous fashion of the English, the "owner" and governor of Nantucket and Martha's Vineyard, which are islands near the southern coast of Cape Cod. The island Indians were Wampanoags related to those under Massasoit's rule on the mainland. The Native government of Martha's Vineyard, the larger island, was hierarchical, with four sachems ruling separate districts. Mayhew, breaking from the Puritan tradition and not wanting to fall fully into the presumptuous land-grabbing of the English, insisted on "purchasing" land from the Natives as he began the process of encouraging British colonization.

In 1643, Thomas Mayhew Jr., son of the governor, moved onto the island with his family as a farmer and missionary. The younger Mayhew had learned to speak the Algonquian dialect of the Wampanoags and hoped to create Puritan towns where Indians and British Christians could live together.

Hiacoomes was Mayhew's first convert. Hiacoomes was somewhat of an outcast from the Wampanoag community and was open to the Christian gospel. Beginning in 1643, Mayhew trained Hiacoomes as a co-missionary working toward the creation of a church and covenanted Christian town. Given the relative strength of the Native culture on the island and the weakness of the Mayhews, there was no extreme pressure for Indians to convert; however, many Indians eventually converted, founded, or joined churches and moved into "praying towns." After an epidemic in 1645, a large number of Indians came to Hiacoomes "to be instructed by him; and some Persons of Quality, such as before had despised him, sent for him to come and instruct them."

By 1651, Hiacoomes was the co-minister of his own church of 199 professed believers. Sharing the leadership was Momonequem, one of Hiacoomes's converts. In 1652, the Wampanoags asked Thomas Mayhew Jr. to draw up a town covenant similar to other Puritan town covenants. We are told "Mr. *Mayhew* drew up an excellent *Covenant* in their native Language, which he often read and made plain to them: and they all with free Consent and Thankfulness united in it, and desired the Grace and Help of GOD to keep it faithfully."

The mutually beneficial relationship of Natives and non-Natives that developed on Martha's Vineyard is best seen in the churches founded. From 1667 to 1684, there were no British clergy living on the island, only ordained Indian pastors. Natives and non-Natives gathered in bilingual church services under the leadership of these Indian pastors for nearly two decades. Mayhew remembered from boyhood these church services and later reported to one of the ministers that the English "very chearfuly received the Lord's Supper from him."

The whole line of Mayhews on Martha's Vineyard from 1643 to 1806 should be remembered for the way they respected the rights of Indians. The Vineyard sachems had no desire to reduce their authority and let the British take over the island. From the beginning, Thomas Mayhew Sr. assured the sachems that the British had no desire to undermine their political jurisdiction and that they would respect the rights of any Natives who chose not to become Christians. He assured them that "Religion and Government were distinct things." Throughout the 17th century, the Natives were not dispossessed of their land or authority, while Christian and non-Christian Natives shared political power.

By the end of the 17th century, six "praying towns" were established where Christian Wampanoags were encouraged to covenant together. Native towns, "praying towns," and Puritan towns existed peacefully together on the small island throughout the

17th century. Puritan political and religious theory was focused on the creation of towns with churches at the center. The Wampanoags of Martha's Vineyard had a similar focus on towns held together by deep religious commitments. Isolated from the pressures of mainland British immigration, the Puritans and the Wampanoags developed a mode of appreciating each other. When in the 1670s Massasoit's son Metacom led the mainland Wampanoags into a brutal war against the Puritans, the Wampanoags of Martha's Vineyard refused to join and actually protected the British colonists on their island.

Hiacoomes and the Mayhews also joined in encouraging English education for whites and Indians. From 1650 to 1672, intellectually promising Indian boys were sent to grammar school on the mainland to learn the Latin and Greek required at Harvard College. Hiacoomes and Thomas Mayhew Jr. sent their sons Joel and Matthew together to the Cambridge grammar school. Four other Wampanoags accompanied them. Sadly, two of these Indian boys died from British diseases contracted in the residential situation of the school. Diseases always flourish in the closed atmosphere of schools, and Indian mortality rates at schools were high in early America. In 1663, Joel, Matthew, and Caleb Cheshchaamog, the son of a Vineyard sachem, entered Harvard College, three of probably only five Indians to attend Harvard College in the 17th century. Tragically, Joel was murdered by some Indians on Nantucket Island just a few months before graduation. Caleb Cheshchaamog was the only Native to graduate from Harvard in the 17th century.

Along with Hiacoomes's initial openness and long-term support, much credit should be given the Mayhew family who made the forging of an Indian-British community into a multigeneration family business. Thomas Mayhew Jr. was recognized in his own day, along with mainlander John Eliot, as someone who not only "understood" the Natives but also loved them. In 1658, he disappeared at sea, and his father, Thomas Mayhew Sr., took up the responsibility of keeping the good relations and Christian hope going. More politically oriented, the elder Mayhew helped the Wampanoags reform their governing system, including instituting councils for conflict resolution and juries for criminal trials. The Mayhews continued to share leadership on the island with Wampanoag officials for more than 150 years. By the time of the American Revolution, most of the Natives were Christians, but in the 1760s an epidemic ravaged the Wampanoag population. After the Revolution, the Natives were very weak and barely hung onto their past role on the island. Today, the island is a resort.

In the big picture of British-Indian relations, the stories of Pocahontas, Squanto, and Hiacoomes are accounts of only small and marginal successes. In all three stories, there was a minimum requirement of religious toleration and openness. Certainly, British Christians were always trying to convert Indians; however, John Smith, Governor Bradford, and the Mayhews did not limit good relations only to those who converted. Most important, in all three stories, the Natives and the settlers *wanted to get along* in the hope of some mutually beneficial end. Pocahontas, Squanto, and Hiacoomes *wanted* to construct something beneficial to all involved and persuaded John Rolfe, Governor Bradford, and the Mayhews to agree with them. All involved *wanted* peace.

Also, Pocahontas, Squanto, and Hiacoomes were outsiders cut off from the main lines of power. Pocahontas was a woman. Squanto had lost all family and community ties. Hiacoomes was not part of the hierarchical order of Martha's Vineyard. The Vineyard itself was an island cut off from the mainland and not subject to the same immigration pressures. Each Indian understood that greater opportunity and maybe even strength would come from developing relations with the British. As for the Englishmen most open to the Indians, John Rolfe needed a wife in a largely womanless community, Governor Bradford understood fully that his people could be easily massacred by Massasoit's warriors, and the Mayhews were owners of nearly worthless property who could not even keep a Puritan minister employed.

Perhaps mutually beneficial relations between peoples depend on weakness rather than strength. The stories of Pocahontas, Squanto, and Hiacoomes are indicators that, in the 17th century, a mutually beneficial relationship between the British and the Indians was possible. By the 1670s, however, the opportunity had passed.

## SELECTED BIBLIOGRAPHY

Axtell, James. *The Invasion Within: The Contest of Cultures in Colonial North America.* New York: Oxford University Press, 1985. The most authoritative book on French, British, and Indian relations in the 17th century.

Banks, Charles Edward. *The History of Martha's Vineyard Dukes County Massachusetts in Three Volumes.* Edgartown, MA: Dukes County Historical Society, 1966. This extensive work on Martha's Vineyard includes several chapters dedicated to the missionary efforts of the Mayhew family and the history of the Native American population on the island.

Barbour, Philip L. *Pocahontas and Her World.* Boston: Houghton Mifflin, 1970. Presently the standard biography on Pocahontas. Primary documents relating to her are weak and leave a broad range of interpretation as to her character and motives. No one biography can be considered authoritative.

Bartlett, Robert M. *The Faith of the Pilgrims.* New York: United Church Press, 1978. Primarily a history of the Pilgrims' religious beliefs, this book also touches on their relationship with Indians.

Bradford, William. *Of Plymouth Plantation.* Edited by Samuel Eliot Morison. New York: Modern Library, 1952. The classic history. Virtually everything we know about Squanto comes from this book.

Bross, Kristina. *Dry Bones and Indian Sermons.* Ithaca, NY: Cornell University Press, 2004. Study of the contact between Native Americans and British missionaries in 17th-century North America.

Edmonds, Walter D. *The Musket and the Cross.* Boston: Little, Brown, 1968. A study of the French and English struggle for North American colonial dominance.

Hauptman, Laurence M., and James D. Wherry, eds. *The Pequots in Southern New England: The Fall and Rise of an American Indian Nation.* Norman: University of Oklahoma Press, 1990. The Pequot war shows the Puritans at their worst. Gov. John Winthrop in Boston never felt the weakness of Governor Bradford, nor did he have the assistance of such a talented Native as Squanto.

Jennings, Francis. *The Invasion of America: Indians, Colonialism, and the Cant of Conquest.* Chapel Hill: University of North Carolina Press, 1975. As the title indicates, Jennings considers British rhetoric about desiring good relations with Natives to be hypocritical. Although largely true, the book is overly cynical.

Johnson, Margery Ruth. *The Mayhew Mission to the Indians, 1643–1806.* Ann Arbor, MI: University Microfilms, 1976. Johnson's unpublished dissertation on the Mayhew family is the most exhaustive history of the family found in my research of the clan. Her use of extensive primary sources gives her writing authority.

Mather, Cotton. *Magnalia Christi Americana: or the Ecclesiastical History of New England.* Edited by Raymond J. Cunningham. New York: F. Ungar, 1970. Originally published in 1702, this history written close to the sources offers a biographical chapter on John Eliot, "The Apostle to the Indians." Eliot, who worked closely with the Mayhews, has always been more famous than the Mayhews because of this book.

Morgan, Edmund S. *American Slavery American Freedom: The Ordeal of Colonial Virginia.* New York: W.W. Norton, 1975. Very readable detailed account of the establishment of English settlements in Virginia during the 17th century.

Morrison, Dane. *A Praying People.* New York: Peter Lang, 1995. Morrison's work is a general text describing the work of Puritan missionaries in New England that focuses on the impact of missionaries on the Native culture.

Rountree, Helen C. *The Powhatan Indians of Virginia: Their Traditional Culture.* Norman: University of Oklahoma Press, 1989. This is the standard scholarly study of the Powhatans. The focus is on their own culture rather than relations with the British.

Salisbury, Neal. "Squanto: Last of the Patuxets." In *Struggle and Survival in Colonial America.* Edited by David G. Sweet and Gary B. Nash. Berkeley: University of California Press, 1981. This is an excellent short biography of the notable Native American.

Segal, Charles M., and David C. Stineback. *Puritans, Indians, and Manifest Destiny.* New York: G. P. Putnam's Sons, 1977. The distinction of Segal and Stineback's book is its use of extensive quotations from primary sources.

Smith, John. *Captain John Smith: A Select Edition of His Writings.* Edited by Karen Ordahl Kupperman. Williamsburg, VA, and Chapel Hill, NC: Institute of Early American History and Culture and the University of North Carolina Press, 1988. Smith wrote of his adventures with the Powhatans in two versions. Kupperman brings the two versions together and includes excellent footnotes.

Stannard, David. *American Holocaust.* New York: Oxford University Press, 1992. A detailed history of the early encounters between Europeans and American Indians, with emphasis on the destructive effects of the diseases and purposeful violence that the Europeans brought.

# NORTH AMERICAN SMALLPOX EPIDEMIC

During the 1600s, American Indians living in North America encountered a new and deadly pathogen—smallpox. Brought unknowingly by European capitalists and conquerors sailing on ships from across the Atlantic Ocean, the disease helped British, French, and Spanish governments gain a foothold and eventually dominate indigenous societies across the continent.

Isolated from the Eastern Hemisphere, North American Indians lacked immunity to pathogens common in Europe, Africa, and the Far East and thus experienced smallpox epidemics that devastated their populations. It is estimated that more than 90 percent of precontact Indian populations in Mexico perished between 1519 and 1619, while Indians living in the more northern portions of North America suffered a similar fate throughout the 17th century. The number of Indian deaths from smallpox parallels those from the Holocaust during World War II.

In the 17th century, 17 known outbreaks of smallpox and related pathogens surfaced in North America. Based on the records of explorers and priests, that number represents only a fraction of the number of unreported cases of smallpox within the inland regions of the continent.

In the early part of that century, Portuguese sailors fishing off the northeastern coast of North America spread smallpox to the coastal Indian population, which touched off a wave of disease that spread to inland Native societies. When Spanish explorers began exploring the coast of North Carolina in the 1610s, they encountered abandoned villages scattered with the bones of the dead.

In one particularly devastating case, smallpox attacked Indians living in the Northeast and in the Great Lakes region in 1633. That outbreak was followed by a wave of scarlet fever and another round of smallpox two years later. The resulting massive population loss meant the removal of the Indians as a military threat to English settlers in what is now Massachusetts.

Smallpox spread quickly throughout Native American societies because of the dense populations of people, extensive trade routes, and Indian ignorance of the disease. Some scholars argue that the high numbers of deaths from 17th-century smallpox epidemics stemmed from the lack of people to care for the sick, who often died of malnutrition and dehydration because the entire village was incapacitated and unable to care for its ill members. Adults suffered a higher death rate than children; often a few children were the only survivors in a village attacked by the disease. They had acquired a life-long immunity due to exposure, but they often succumbed to other waves of such contagious diseases as measles, influenza, or the plague.

Like other virgin soil epidemics, smallpox returned intermittently to Indian populations for the next several decades. Smallpox was reported again in 1649, 1662, 1669, and 1687. Until vaccination for Indians on reservations became common, in the 1870s, smallpox continued to erupt throughout the 18th century and the first half of the 19th century.

JASON NEWMAN

## OPECHANCANOUGH (1545/56-ca. 1644)

Opechancanough (spelled variously as Opechankino, Apechancanough, Appochankeno, and Apitchan-kihneu and meaning "sharp opposition") was a leader of the Powhatan Confederacy in Virginia and the younger brother of Powhatan, the powerful sachem who ruled his vast Native American empire around the Chesapeake Bay. An important negotiator with the English settlers in Virginia during the early 17th century, Opechancanough later led raids against them.

Opechancanough was most likely born at Powhatan Village, near present-day Richmond, Virginia, in either 1545 or around 1556 (historians have not been able to agree on the date). His father's ancestry may have been Mexican; perhaps he was one of the Native Americans brought north by the de Soto expedition in the 1540s. The Spanish were attempting to build a stronghold in Virginia and to establish Jesuit missions in the area. Opechancanough's high-ranking lineage among the Powhatans most likely came from his mother's side of the family. Two of Opechancanough's brothers, Opitchapam and Katataugh, were called "the two kings of Pamaunke" by Capt. John Smith because they presided over a village at the eastern tip of Pamunkey Neck in Virginia. Sometime before 1607, Opechancanough himself became the acknowledged leader of the Pamunkey River region.

Distrustful of the Jamestown settlers, Opechancanough and 300 of his men ambushed a party of explorers on the Chickahominy River in 1607. Only Smith, who had been away from his group hunting with his Native American guides, escaped and survived. Opechancanough took Smith back to his village and then to Powhatan's village on the York River. There, legend has it, Pocahontas interceded to save Smith's life. Smith's extensive journals about his experiences with this tribe show a mutual respect between Opechancanough and himself.

During 1607–1618, Opechancanough's relations with the English settlers were uneasy, but he served as a chief negotiator for his people. He refused to accept Smith's offer of trade in 1608, which led to hard feelings between the two men, but Opechancanough sided with the English during a dispute with the Chickahominy people in 1616, granting a Chickahominy town to the settlers as ransom for the killing of five Englishmen. When Powhatan, the great leader of the Algonquian-speaking tribes of the Tidewater region, died in 1618, Opechancanough rose as the active leader and diplomat to the English, although his brother Opitchapam was the nominal chief.

Over the next years, the colonists' demands for goods and land increased, especially as they depleted the soil with tobacco farming. Opechancanough became disgusted with their greed, particularly as traditional hunting lands were cleared for tobacco farming. When one of his people was murdered by a white colonist in 1622, Opechancanough led a surprise attack on the Jamestown settlers, killing 347 people in one day. Battles and raids raged for 10 years, with the English sending out regular patrols to destroy Native American villages and the Powhatan Indians retaliating. In 1632, a peace treaty brought a 12-year truce to the region.

White settlers continued to intrude on Native American territory, however, and the tribes were forced further inland each year. In frustration, Opechancanough led another raid on the settlers in April 1644, killing 500 of the 8,000 inhabitants of Jamestown. He was an old man by this time, possibly close to 100 years old, and accounts state that his men had to carry him on a litter into battle. Soon after, he was captured and killed, and his people were pushed further inland and away from the colony.

## PEQUOT WAR (1636–1637)

The issues surrounding the Pequot War are among the more complex in the history of the confrontations between American Indian peoples and European colonists. Rooted in land ownership, the volatile conflict was exacerbated by a power struggle between rival English settlements and an ongoing struggle for dominance among various Indian tribes.

Although the Pequot War began in 1636, its genesis was actually two years earlier, when English trader John Stone was killed by Indians in retaliation for his kidnapping and otherwise brutal treatment of them. The Pequots bore the onus for the act, even though those responsible for Stone's death were later proved to be the neighboring Niantics. Separately, the Pequots, who were cut off from trade with the Dutch, began trading with the Massachusetts Bay Company.

Massachusetts Bay authorities figured Stone's murder might be used to political advantage and demanded the surrender of Stone's killers and a large wampum payment, to which the Pequots agreed. Subsequently, only a portion of the tribute was paid, and the

Pequots explained that only two of the killers were still alive, whereabouts unknown. For whatever reason, the English did not press the matter until 1636, when Mohegan chief Uncas reported the Pequots were preparing for war.

Worsening the situation, a second trader was killed, probably by the Narragansetts. The Pequots' involvement in this second murder was apparently irrelevant; the English wanted to take action. Massachusetts Bay organized a strike force and proceeded to Fort Saybrook, where they met Pequot sachems and demanded a confrontation on the field of battle. When the Pequots, who likely did not understand the demand, failed to show, the strike force vented its wrath on their villages and crops. Thus provoked, the Pequots laid siege to Fort Saybrook.

In April 1637, after their attempt to ally with the Narragansetts was quashed by Roger Williams, Pequots raided the settlement at Wethersfield (near present-day Hartford). In response, the English settlements joined together, and a mixed force of colonists and Mohegans moved against the Pequots. After minimal success on the first attempt, the expedition added more colonists and some 500 Narragansett and Niantic allies and moved a second time. What followed on May 26, 1637, was a massacre.

The strike force surrounded the Pequot village on Mystic River, set it afire, and slaughtered Pequots as they attempted to escape. Warriors from the main Pequot stronghold hastened to help their brethren but arrived too late. In all, an estimated 300 to 700 Pequots—whose numbers had already been reduced by as much as 75 percent due to a smallpox epidemic in 1633—died in the Mystic River Massacre.

After months of being hunted by the English and Narragansetts, in July 1637, the remaining Pequots were surrounded near present-day New Haven, their power decidedly broken. The Treaty of Hartford delineated the terms of the English-Narragansett victory, and surviving Pequots sought refuge with other tribes. Ironically, during King Philip's War, nearly four decades later, the Pequots allied with the English.

JERRY KEENAN

## POCAHONTAS (ca. 1595–1617)

The daughter of a powerful chief of a confederation of tribes in the tidewater region of Virginia, Pocahontas played a crucial role in negotiating a stable relationship between the Jamestown colonists and the Powhatan Confederacy, thus ensuring the survival of the English colony. More interesting is the myth that has evolved around Pocahontas that emerged during the colonial era and has continued into the present day.

Historians are unsure about Pocahontas's exact date or place of birth, but rough estimates suggest the year 1595. She was the daughter of Powhatan, chief of the Powhatan confederation, a powerful alliance that united many of the tribes in Virginia at this time. Pocahontas was first noted by the English colonists in 1607 when she sauntered into Jamestown as a young girl. The storybook version of Pocahontas relates the tale of Capt. John Smith's capture by Powhatan's brother, Opechancanough, when Smith raided the Powhatan territory in search of food. Pocahontas rescued Smith, 16 years her senior, from certain death. As Smith later told the story, just when he was about to meet his death from two warriors with clubs, Pocahontas placed her head on Smith's. He thus always credited Pocahontas with saving his life. Historians have recently posited that Pocahontas was actually participating in an elaborate adoption ritual that Smith simply misinterpreted. Regardless, the story that Pocahontas saved Smith is the story that has endured.

After Smith's rescue, Pocahontas continued to visit the settlement of Jamestown over the next year and a half. She often advised the colonists on which Indian tribes were the friendliest and taught the English how to bargain for food. Pocahontas also rescued several other colonists in 1610. First, she helped an English boy, Richard Wiffin, run away from his father, who sought to kill him. Then, she warned Smith and his men that several Native Americans were plotting to murder them. Forewarned, Smith and his companions escaped.

Relations between the Powhatans and the English remained shaky, however. Capt. Samuel Argall kidnapped Pocahontas in 1613 in hopes of exchanging her for the return of English prisoners, food, and weapons that the Powhatans had taken. The plan fell through when Pocahontas's father refused to meet their demands and sent only a small portion of what the English demanded.

Pocahontas remained with the English and soon adjusted to her new circumstances. By 1614, with the help of Rev. Alexander Whitaker and colonist John Rolfe, Pocahontas rejected her tribal religious beliefs and converted to Christianity. She was baptized and renamed "Rebecca." In the meantime, Rolfe, who would earn fame by developing a new strain of tobacco plant, had fallen in love with Pocahontas while he was instructing her in the Christian faith. Rolfe convinced the deputy governor of Virginia and representatives of the Church of England that his marriage would prove that the Native tribes could be civilized and Christianized for "our Country's good, the benefit of this Plantation, and for the converting [of] an irregenerate to regeneration." With Powhatan's assent, Pocahontas married Rolfe on April 5, 1614. Their marriage brought a brief period of peace between the Powhatans and the colonists, as well as the birth of a son, Thomas.

The Virginia Company of London, in hopes of capitalizing on the marriage between a Native American and an Englishman, arranged a tour of England for the Rolfe family in June 1616. They made a number of appearances, including at the court of King James I. Pocahontas also sat for a portrait, the only one known of her. The Rolfes left London in March 1617 for Rolfe's new job as secretary of the Virginia colony. While en route to a port city so that they could return to Virginia, Pocahontas fell gravely ill. She died on March 21, 1617, in Gravesend, where she was buried.

The myth of Pocahontas, the "Indian Princess," has been propagated since the 18th century and has captured the imagination of generations of Americans. Artists have devoted countless poems, novels, biographies, and paintings to Pocahontas, each telling and contributing to the myth. One of the most prominent stories—that Pocahontas and Smith were romantically involved or that at least she was "enamoured" of Smith—had emerged by the mid-19th century. Amidst fears of miscegenation, the emphasis shifted from the tale of Pocahontas's marriage to John Rolfe, once seen as an honorable and worthy event, to her rescue of John Smith. In the process, Pocahontas changed from a real historical figure and mother to a heroic protector, thus removing the troubling stigma of her son, Thomas. This presentation of her as the heroic, mythic protector is the way that she is most often portrayed.

## JOHN SMITH (ca. 1580–1631)

The English soldier and adventurer Capt. John Smith not only helped to found the Virginia colony but also, through his bold and vigorous leadership, played a crucial role in its survival.

Born the son of a farmer in Willoughby, England, in 1579 or 1580, Smith left home at an early age to seek adventure as a soldier in Europe. While serving with the eastern European forces that were fighting the Turks, he was captured and sold into slavery. After a dramatic escape and further adventures abroad, Smith returned to England. There, by his own account, he helped organize the Virginia Company of London for the purpose of starting a colony in Virginia. In December 1606, Smith was one of the 108 colonists who sailed for America in three ships.

Landing in Virginia in May 1607, the colonists founded a settlement at Jamestown, 40 miles up the James River. From the start, Jamestown was wracked by disease and internal dissension. Unlike Smith, who at the age of 27 was already a tough and experienced captain, most of the settlers were ill prepared for the serious business of establishing a colony. They had come expecting to make their fortunes through the discovery of gold and silver and were unwilling to work to feed and defend themselves. As a later settler observed, the colonists "would rather starve in idleness...than feast in labor."

Smith quickly emerged as a natural leader by virtue of his energy and resourcefulness. He traded with the Powhatan Confederacy for corn to feed the starving settlers and went on several voyages to explore the Potomac and Rappahannock rivers and the Chesapeake Bay. On one expedition, undertaken in December 1607, Smith and seven companions were ambushed by Native Americans, and Smith was taken prisoner and brought before their chief, Powhatan. According to Smith, he was saved from death through the intervention of Powhatan's 11-year-old daughter, Pocahontas.

In this and subsequent dealings with the Native Americans, Smith showed himself a shrewd strategist. He drove a hard bargain and generally got what he wanted through bluff and a show of force but very little bloodshed.

Upon his return to Jamestown in January 1608, Smith found that rival leaders had assumed control. Held responsible for the deaths of two of his men, he was arrested, tried, and sentenced to hang. Only the timely arrival of a supply-laden English ship, with a high official on board (who restored Smith as a leader of the colony), saved Smith from the gallows.

The following fall, Smith managed to defeat his rivals and get himself elected president of Jamestown's governing council. He soon put the colony under what amounted to martial law. Declaring that the settlers "must be more industrious or starve," Smith made them farm and work at other constructive tasks, including strengthening the settlement's defenses against Indian attack.

Smith's term as president lasted just a year. In September 1609, he returned to England. That winter, the colony was nearly wiped out by starvation and Indian attacks. In 1614, Smith again sailed for America, this time to explore the area around Cape Cod, which he named "New England." He returned with a valuable cargo of fish and furs, along with accurate maps of the region. Smith's second and last voyage to America ended when he was captured by pirates. Escaping and making his way back to England, he devoted himself to writing accounts of his travels. His most important book was *The*

*Generall Historie of Virginia, New-England, and the Summer Isles* (1624). In it, Smith emphasized the importance of products like fish, furs, and timber; criticized the fruitless quest for gold and silver; and urged that future colonists be willing to work hard. His information and maps were most helpful to later settlers.

A colorful, near-legendary figure, Smith has inevitably been the subject of much controversy. Although in the past historians discounted Smith's overblown accounts of his exploits, modern research has largely substantiated his claims to fame. Smith died in England on June 21, 1631.

WILLIAM McGUIRE AND LESLIE WHEELER

## SQUANTO (1580–1622)

A member of the Patuxet Indian tribe, Squanto was kidnapped by English explorers in the early 17th century and sold into slavery. He managed to escape and, despite the cruelty he suffered, became one of the first Native Americans to befriend the Pilgrims at Plymouth Colony. He taught them invaluable survival skills.

Squanto was born in 1580 in what is now Plymouth, Massachusetts. In 1615, he and about 20 other Patuxets were abducted by English seamen who had come to explore the New World. The Native Americans were taken to Malaga, an island off the Mediterranean coast of Spain, where they were sold into slavery. Squanto somehow escaped, and a clergyman helped him get to England, where he spent at least two years. According to one account, he worked for a rich merchant while learning the English language. In 1619, Squanto managed to get passage on a trading ship and returned to North America. When he got home, he discovered that his tribe had been wiped out by disease and that he was the sole survivor.

When the *Mayflower* arrived in New England, in 1620, Squanto surprised the settlers by greeting them in English. He quickly established friendly relations with the new immigrants and lived among them for long periods of time. When the Pilgrims failed in their attempts to grow the seeds of English wheat, barley, and peas, Squanto showed them how to plant corn, using dead herring as fertilizer. He also taught them the fishing and hunting techniques that had been developed by his people. Without Squanto's help, it is doubtful that the settlers would have survived their first winter in America.

Squanto also acted as an interpreter and cultural mediator between the Pilgrims and the local Wampanoag tribe, on whose territory the English had settled. Historians believe that Squanto was instrumental in negotiating the 1621 peace treaty between the new immigrants and Massasoit, the chief of the Wampanoags. The treaty included provisions for a trading partnership and a pledge to assist each other in case of attack by a third party. It was also in 1621 that the Pilgrims celebrated their first Thanksgiving feast in the New World with about 90 Native American guests. Massasoit was listed in colonial accounts as one of those who attended, and Squanto may very well have participated, as well.

Unlike the Wampanoags, several other tribes grew wary of the increasing English presence in New England. To ease the tension, Squanto stepped in as a peacemaker. In 1622, he began negotiating a trade agreement between the Pilgrims and the Narragansetts. Before a pact was reached, however, he contracted smallpox and died in November 1622 near Chatham, Massachusetts.

# 7

# The Introduction of Slavery into North America, 1619

## INTRODUCTION

From the beginning of African history, the diverse cultures of that continent practiced slavery, although it frequently was not based on racial differences. Cultures in Egypt, Greece, and Rome forced captives from wars into slavery without regard for race or ethnicity. As Muslims settled North Africa, they took African men and women as slaves and harem subjects and shipped others to Islamic lands in the Middle East. There, these slaves worked mainly as servants and were an indicator of their master's wealth and social position.

As W. E. B. Du Bois and John Hope Franklin have pointed out, the Renaissance gave Europeans the opportunity to break away from old customs and traditions and to search for ways to improve themselves both spiritually and physically. With this new freedom, however, there was no concomitant sense of social responsibility. To be free, one could justifiably take away the freedom of others. Along with this came the development of commerce-based economies founded on the accumulation of capital and the drive to exploit resources for purely economic gain. These resources came to include other human beings.

By the end of the 1300s, slaves were being brought from the west coast of Africa and sold in Europe. The Portuguese were the first to see the advantages of the slave trade, a practice that they and others occasionally justified as part of the struggle to win souls for Christ. They believed that a Christian slave, no matter how bad his or her lot, was better off than a heathen free person.

Europe, however, did not have much economic use for slaves. Most sectors of the European economies were not labor-intensive, and there was a surplus of white labor because of the enclosure movement, which limited farming opportunities.

Africans went to the Americas with the Spanish as early as 1501, fighting and working alongside their white colleagues. They also accompanied the French in some of their early explorations into what is now Canada and the Mississippi River valley. In neither case were the Africans considered to be slaves. It was different with the English. Africans did not come with them on their earliest exploration efforts to America.

When a need for a labor supply first became apparent, the Spanish enslaved indigenous Indians, to the great detriment of native societies, especially in the Caribbean.

The first Africans to come to America as slaves arrived in Jamestown, Virginia, in 1619. (Courtesy of the Library of Congress.)

The combination of cruel treatment, disease, and the Indians' inability to adjust to the discipline demanded by their masters led to the deaths of thousands.

After the Indian experiment had failed, Europeans, and especially the English, looked to poor whites as the solution to their labor needs. In England, a common source of labor during the 17th century was indentured servitude. Typically, a person wishing to come to America would contract with a sponsor (or master) to work for a certain number of years, usually between four and seven, in return for his or her passage to the colonies and upkeep during the time of servitude. Such servants could be sold to another master, and colonies passed laws regulating the master-servant relationship, including the provision of "freedom dues," clothes, and other goods received at the end of a person's term of servitude. In many cases, this system proved unsatisfactory, as indentured servants were bound to their masters for only a limited number of years, and many ran away, never to be recovered, before their terms had expired.

Africans, however, were easier to deal with. They could be purchased outright, their skin color made them distinctive, and their heathen background made it easier to subject them to harsh treatment. Finally, there appeared to be a never-ending supply that would provide labor for all who needed it.

The Spanish began importing African slaves into America in 1517, and, by 1540, some 10,000 were arriving in the West Indies every year. But it was the Dutch, French, and ultimately the English who dominated the slave trade in the 17th century. In 1621, the Dutch States General chartered the Dutch West India Company and gave it a monopoly over the African and West Indian trade. The Dutch challenged the Portuguese for control of the West African slave trade in midcentury, but frequent wars with both France and England weakened them after 1675. The French began organizing a slave trade in the 1630s with the founding of the French Company of the West Indies, but it was never economically successful. By the end of the 17th century, the French were just holding onto a small share of the African slave trade.

At the dawn of the colonial era, slavery as such did not exist in England. Medieval serfs were bound in certain ways to their feudal lords, but they still enjoyed some legal rights. In the 16th century, England began to place stricter controls on vagrants, beggars, and others who seemed to have no constructive role in society. These controls included branding and servitude for a period of years to the person who had turned the misfit in. Strict punishment awaited those who attempted to escape.

By the beginning of the 17th century, the concept of slavery was understood in England. A slave's freedom was nonexistent, and a slave was a slave in perpetuity rather than for a limited number of years. To some English thinkers, this equated to a loss of humanity, such as one might think of a captive taken in battle. An important factor here is that captives were strangers, people from another place, and they were often infidels. As it developed in the early colonial years, blacks from Africa fit the definition of a slave perfectly.

England first began carrying slaves from Africa to Spanish America in 1562, but the trade was not profitable until 1618, when King James I chartered the Company of Adventurers of London to engage in African slave trade. The Adventurers were not successful, however, and the Dutch brought most of the earliest slaves to the English settlements in North America. In 1672, Charles II chartered the Royal African Company and gave it a monopoly over England's slave trade. The company worked hard to drive the Dutch and French out of Africa and to suppress independent English slave traders. Ultimately, it, too, was unsuccessful, and it lost its charter in 1698. With other companies free to involve themselves in the slave trade, the slave population in the English colonies rose significantly after 1698.

The first slaves to come to the English colonies in North America arrived in Jamestown on a Dutch vessel in 1619. Few were concerned about the legal status of these Africans, and, in the earliest censuses in Virginia, they were listed as servants, even to the point of having a limited term of servitude before achieving freedom. There were very few Africans in Virginia at this time, perhaps only 300 in 1650. Not until 1661 did the Virginia assembly give legal recognition to slavery, although, after 1640, Africans were no longer indentured and thus had no likelihood of achieving their freedom. For Virginia planters, it was an economic question, a way to solve the perpetual labor shortage problem.

In the middle colonies, and especially in New Netherland, slavery was instituted in the 1620s. The Dutch, who were active slave traders, used African slaves on their Hudson River valley plantations and continued to do so until 1664, when the English took control of the colony. On the whole, the Dutch treated their slaves humanely and occasionally gave them their freedom as a reward for long or loyal service. After 1664, slavery continued in New York as the English sought commercial advantages from their colonies, although the number of slaves remained small in the 17th century. In 1698, there were 2,170 slaves in New York, out of a total population of more than 18,000. Under English rule, slaves were more restricted in their freedom than they had been under the Dutch; one consequence of this was a serious slave uprising in 1712, which led to even more restrictive laws. The situation was different in Pennsylvania, where the Quaker influence dampened the enthusiasm for slavery. But slavery certainly existed in the colony, and even William Penn said that Negro slaves were preferable to white servants because of the control that could be exerted over them.

In New England, the first blacks came as servants rather than slaves. While slaves were present in New England during the entire 17th century, it was the slave trade and not the slaves themselves that suited the region's businessmen, with their commercial orientation. Competition with European slave traders was difficult, however, and some New England traders went as far as Madagascar to find their cargoes of slaves. Late in the century, the slave-trading prospects of New England improved with the decline of the Dutch and the removal, in 1698, of the English Royal African Company's monopoly. New England slave traders enjoyed their most profitable years in the early 18th century.

Although there were fewer slaves in New England than in other parts of colonial North America, Puritans justified the institution on religious grounds; slavery was a vehicle for Christianizing the heathen African, who would surely benefit in the long run from the grace of God. There were short-term benefits, as well—Puritans recognized the sacrament of marriage for slaves and did not make them work on Sundays.

By 1700, the question of race became central to understanding the particular evil of slavery in America. That Africans were "black" had a profound influence on the English. From well before their first encounters with Africans, the English had placed negative connotations on the word black. Black meant dirty; it meant having "dark or deadly purposes"; it was the color of evil. White, on the other hand, was linked with purity, light, and cleanliness.

Black people confused scientists who could not understand why some American Indians living at the same equatorial latitudes as Africans were not also black or why blacks brought to Europe failed to turn white after a while. To answer these questions, some turned to the Bible and concluded that either the "mark of Cain" or God's curse on Noah's son Ham and his descendants was the origin of black people, which made them God's cursed race. Although many refuted this notion, it persisted into the 19th century, when slavery proponents used it to justify slavery in the years before the Civil War.

Other factors that supposedly made black Africans suitable for slavery to the English in the 17th century were their heathenism and their perceived uncivilized behavior. Although the English were not much interested in converting Africans, despite the Puritans' claims to the contrary, they did claim that Africans' heathen beliefs were defects that distanced them from the English Christians. The perceived uncivilized nature of Africans, seen in the way they lived their lives, was also something that marked them as quite different from the English. Englishmen frequently likened Africans to beasts. This was seen in the way in which the slave trade was managed. Potential slaves were herded together, examined, and bought and sold, just like livestock.

## INTERPRETIVE ESSAY

JULIA A. WOODS

Slavery was introduced into the English colonies of North America almost by accident in 1619, when a group of Africans arrived in Virginia, which was then a struggling English colony. These Africans are mysterious figures. We know of them only because John Rolfe, a leader of the Jamestown colony, wrote to a treasurer of the Virginia Company, and in that letter he noted casually that a Dutch man-of-war had arrived five months before at nearby Point Comfort, in the Chesapeake Bay, and the settlers had traded provisions for "20. and odd Negroes" (meaning some number greater than 20). It is not known whether the Africans came to Virginia directly from Africa or after a period of residence in the Dutch sugar islands in the Caribbean, nor is it known what happened to them after their arrival in Virginia. Their status as slaves was unclear, since the institution of slavery was not clearly defined by their English masters, who were more familiar with the practice of indentured servitude. (Much of the labor in the colony at that time was performed by English indentured servants, people who exchanged a period of service, usually five or so years, for the price of their passage from England to the New World. The person to whom labor was owed could trade or sell the labor contract like any other valuable commodity, so indentured servants could be "sold" during their period of service.) The 20 or so Africans in the Jamestown colony were the first arrivals in a huge migration of workers brought to the Virginia colony to work in the enormously profitable tobacco-growing business. The colonists at the time did not seem to be aware of the importance of that first transaction in 1619, which would ultimately have a profound effect on the future of Virginia and the rest of North America.

Slavery in Virginia did not start out as an important part of the colony's society. The institution changed as the need for laborers to work the tobacco fields became more acute and as fewer English people were willing to undertake the risks inherent in settling in Virginia. As the numbers of Africans and people of African descent in Virginia increased, the leadership of the colony began to regard them as a potential source of trouble and took steps to see to it that legal and social institutions existed to keep them subordinate. In time, slaves found that their status had become permanent and absolute, encompassing every aspect of their lives; in the end, slavery would be ended only by a bloody civil war.

We can only guess what had happened to them before their arrival in Virginia, but try to imagine these things happening to you: you are kidnapped by strangers who force you to walk many miles from your home to a coastline you have never seen before. You may be sick, since the diseases here on the coast are new to you and you have no resistance to them. You are held here for a while, then put on an enormous ship, the likes of which you have never seen before. On the ship are men who look so strange to you they scarcely seem human. You are taken across an unbelievably vast body of water, tossed about in the tiny space allotted to you below the deck. The smell is horrible, a combination of unwashed bodies, feces, blood, vomit, and urine. You may know some of your fellow captives or at least speak the same language, or they may all be foreign and speak some assortment of languages unrecognizable to you. Some of your fellow captives may have tried to escape by flinging themselves into the water, even though they know they will drown in that enormous sea. The slavers may order a blacksmith to pull out all the teeth of some especially stubborn slaves who fought back by biting. Many of your fellow captives will have died during this voyage. When you at last arrive at land, it is unlike any other place you have ever been: either an island covered with mile after mile of sugarcane, worked by people who look like your fellow captives at the command of people who look like the slavers, or a densely wooded, swampy-looking shore where, you soon learn, you are going to help your English "masters" become rich by working long hours to grow a plant called tobacco.

The English were trying to establish a colony in Virginia for a very basic reason: they wanted to improve their own situation in this life and in the next one. European powers had been sending ships and men to remote parts of the world to trade, bringing back exotic goods that could be sold at high profit. Ships returning with spices from India made their investors rich. Spanish explorers had made themselves and their country rich, bringing home gold and silver from Mexico and South America. The English sought to benefit similarly from colonies in North America. Both the Spanish and the English were also motivated by the desire to spread their religion, which would bring God's favor to themselves and their nation. Spanish friars worked hard to convert the native population of Mexico and South America, and the English similarly sought to expand their own Protestant religion in North America. It did not seem at all odd to them that their financial and religious interests were so closely related; instead, they assumed that God was on their side and would reward their efforts on behalf of the one true faith.

Most of the slaves brought to the English colonies in North America were from the coast and adjacent interior of western and west central Africa, brought by English traders either directly from Africa or after some time in the West Indies. English traders usually bought slaves in coastal trade centers along the West African coast, between the present-day countries of Senegal and Angola. This region was very diverse and difficult to describe in general: it included both densely forested areas and grasslands and supported several hundred different ethnic groups, some as culturally and linguistically different from each other as they were from Europeans. Some raised cattle, and others were farmers. Some people lived in relative isolation, while others had ties, by friendship, political alliance, or trade, throughout the continent and beyond.

The smallest and most basic social unit in African societies was usually the household. This group would include parents, children, grandparents, and other relatives. The household also included any slaves, who may have, by long association with the family, been treated well and been recognized members of the household, though never quite the same as family. A person could be enslaved by violent means, either kidnapped or captured in warfare, and then was usually transported far from home to prevent future escape. One could also be enslaved by a judicial or religious proceeding, as punishment for a crime. More rarely, a person might enslave himself voluntarily because he could no longer afford to take care of himself, thus choosing dependence over starvation.

Slave trading in Africa has a long history. Extensive trade networks crisscrossed the continent. Beginning around CE 700 and continuing into the 20th century, slaves were traded north, across the Sahara. There were also slave trade routes east toward the Indian Ocean. Long-distance traders traveled from one trading center to another, dealing with agents who had their own local networks. Slaves were only part of a huge trade: ivory, copper, and hides from central Africa; metalware, figs, and dates from North Africa; palm cloth and salt from the coast. Europeans bought these goods and many more, including gold from the Gold Coast, but mostly they were interested in slaves.

When European traders appeared on the West African coast in the 16th century, the scale of the slave trade increased dramatically. They traded cloth, metalware, horses, brandy, and rum for slaves. Though the statistics have been disputed, the most reliable indicate that, between the 16th and the 19th centuries, as many as 15 million people were exported from Africa's Atlantic coast and more than 9 million arrived in the New

World, with some 1.5 million dying during the sea passage in between. This involuntary migration of people, known to historians as the Black Diaspora, scattered an astonishingly large number of people throughout the world. Though the number of slaves taken to the English colonies in North America was relatively low, around 5 percent of the total, this trade represented a substantial proportion of the English slave trade from around 1650 to 1800. (As it happens, the 20 or so slaves taken to Virginia in 1619 were not the first Africans to set foot in North America, as some had traveled with the Spanish conquistadores in their travels in Mexico and Florida.) While the English entered the slave trade after the Spanish and Portuguese, they were quick to see the potential profits in the trade. Later, American merchants based in New England took up the trade.

From the beginning, Englishmen were fascinated by West Africans. They had no firsthand knowledge of West Africa before 1530, when the first Englishmen went to Africa and returned to publish a detailed account of the journey. The descriptions of black-skinned people and their strange ways were of great interest to English readers. The differences between Africans and Europeans are important because they helped make it possible for Europeans to tolerate (and profit from) slavery. Historians have debated whether racism existed first, before slavery, or whether slavery, in all its dehumanizing cruelty, made the enslaver racist as a response. This debate is important to those seeking to understand the origins and meaning of present-day racism. Englishmen had long associated the word "black" with negative ideas, using the term to describe things they regarded with dread. Englishmen did not like the fact that West Africans were not Christian and not interested in converting. Also, English observers found West African culture shocking and strange; they often saw cultural differences as signs of immorality and inferiority rather than as simply differences. Some historians have focused on these cultural differences to explain racism, while other historians looked more closely at English attitudes toward gender. They pointed out that Englishmen began, unconsciously, to regard people and places they encountered during their explorations with the same attitude with which they regarded women: they spoke of "virgin land" and described both the land and the people using words strikingly similar to words that they used to describe women. And, in English culture at that time, women were entirely subordinate to men, legally and socially. Thus, it is argued, it seemed completely natural that these strange lands and people would need to be controlled and dominated, just as women were. Whatever one may conclude about this debate, it serves as a useful example of how historians grapple with difficult issues, including the shadowy origins of modern problems and the elusive nature of human evil.

Ironically, Englishmen, before they began to profit from slavery, had regarded the practice with disdain. They saw the institution as the business of Portuguese and Spanish, people the English tended to regard with scorn. They were aware of the role of slavery in the past. For example, slavery had been an important institution in Greece and the Roman Empire, and slavery is also mentioned in the Bible. Unfree labor, in the form of serfdom, had existed in feudal England, but serfs had some traditional rights, while slaves were simply property, with no rights whatsoever. In the European view, slaves were outsiders, non-Christians, and usually captives taken in wars, such as during the Crusades. It would simply not have occurred to an Englishman to enslave a fellow Englishman, and any person to be enslaved would have to appear to be very different from himself. From the perspective of an Englishman, the human world was arranged, metaphorically speaking, as a series of outwardly expanding circles: at the center were the English people, who represented the ideal of humanity; the next circle included non-English white Protestants, such as the Dutch, who fell short of perfection only by not being English. The people become more alien and imperfect as the rings moved outward, with successive circles including European Catholics, such as the Spanish and Portuguese, and then perhaps North African and Turkish Muslims (whom the English tended to lump together under the term "Moors"), then finally reaching such people as non-Christian, dark-skinned West Africans, whose cultures and religious practices were utterly alien to an Englishman in the year 1500.

Englishmen were familiar with the institution of slavery but were not necessarily morally opposed to the practice. Slavery became more important to Europeans with the discovery that tremendous profits could be made from growing sugarcane, first in the Canary Islands and later in the Caribbean. Sugarcane is a very labor-intensive crop, requiring year-round backbreaking work to plant and harvest. The most practical (and profitable) way to grow sugarcane was to use workers who could be forced to the point of exhaustion and who had no right to quit their jobs. The high profit to be made in the west was of great interest to ambitious Europeans. The Spanish had found great mineral wealth. There was big money in sugar, and the goal of most European monarchs was to claim some of this wealth and keep it out of the hands of their enemies. One of the problems with this plan was the difficulty of finding workers to extract the wealth from the land. The local indigenous population (called Indians, perpetuating Columbus's confusion about the exact location of the Caribbean islands and nearby North America) tended to fare badly when put to work, dying in large numbers from European diseases in some areas. It was difficult to bring enough European workers to the New World, though the English tried. How, then, could they make the colonies profitable?

The Virginia colony was settled with the idea that profits could be made even as Englishmen spread the Protestant faith and kept out their rivals, the Catholic Spanish and French. The English practice was for the monarch to grant the right to explore, settle, and extract profits to a group of wealthy investors, who paid the expenses of colonizing an area. The Virginia Company, for example, hoped to recoup its investments and make a profit from the settlement in Virginia. When Rolfe wrote his letter to the treasurer of the Virginia Company regarding the 20-some Africans, he was essentially reporting to his employers. While the Virginia Company expected eventually to settle families in the Virginia colonies, the first settlers were mostly young men of middle-class origin. Company officials were not sure exactly how the colony could be made profitable, but every possibility was explored. The local Indians did not wear lots of gemstones or gold or silver ornaments, which indicated that there was not the sort of mineral wealth here that the Spanish had found in Mexico and the Andes. Still, the possibilities seemed endless in this vast land.

The first settlers had trouble getting successfully settled at first. The colony at Roanoke, in present-day North Carolina, had failed entirely, and the Jamestown colony had problems of its own. There is some evidence of a terrible drought that made both water and food scarce and also that the first settlers were not always the most hardworking or knowledgeable farmers. Nearby swamps, with the associated mosquitoes, meant that mosquito-borne illnesses were rampant among the colonists. The difficulty of finding good water sources meant that water-borne illnesses were also common. Further, the local Indians, organized under the Powhatan Confederacy, sensed correctly that the Englishmen intended to move into their territory. They attacked from time to time, often causing large numbers of casualties. For the first few years, colonists subsisted mostly on foodstuffs brought from England or traded from the Indians. The colony might have failed entirely if the English had not learned how to grow tobacco.

Growing tobacco became an enormously profitable undertaking in Virginia. The English market for tobacco brought high prices as more people became addicted to smoking. But growing tobacco required an enormous amount of work. First the seeds had to be planted; then the seedlings were thinned and transplanted into rows, with each plant set into a mound of dirt that had to be first loosened and piled up by someone wielding a hoe. The rows had to be kept weeded so that the young plants were not choked out by weeds. As the plants got larger, the tobacco planter had to worry about the weather, as hail or heavy winds and rain could tear up the leaves, rendering them worthless because tobacco buyers would not buy leaves that were not whole. When harvest time arrived, the leaves had to be handled carefully to prevent tearing. The bottom leaves of each plant were picked first, and the harvest continued for weeks as the slower-maturing upper leaves were picked, the pickers working their way up the plant until only a stem and the topmost leaves remained. As they were picked, the leaves were bundled and dried. The dried leaves were carefully packed into enormous barrels called hogsheads, which were rolled to the nearest river or navigable creek and onto boats for transport. There were very few roads suitable for transporting large loads in the Chesapeake region, so the ownership of land with water access was an important requirement for successful tobacco farming. Growing tobacco required year-round work, as the winter months, after the barrels had been shipped and before the next planting, were usually spent clearing new fields and repairing fences and tools. The backbreaking work of clearing fields, hoeing the rows, and picking the leaves required a substantial labor force. Most of the first settlers in Virginia were young men without families, so they did not have wives and children to help work in the fields. They needed workers who could be forced to put in long hours in the fields.

The system of indentured servitude had worked well for settling the colonies, and between 75 and 80 percent of the people who left England for the Chesapeake during the 17th century were indentured servants. Indentured servants were young, in their mid-teens to early twenties, and were drawn from the ranks of unemployed farm and factory workers. There were far more men than women among their ranks. Their motive for going to Virginia was typically simple: in Virginia, after they served their term of servitude, they could hope to buy land. In England, an island where land was limited, land ownership was the basis for membership in the ranks of the land-owning, voting English elite; a landowner in Virginia would have the same rights. Indentured servants presented some problems to those seeking workers for their plantations. The unhealthful climate in Virginia meant that many Englishmen became ill and died, especially the hardworking and underfed servants. After the term of service had expired, few were willing to sign on for another term, so the period of servitude was limited. The low ratio of women to men meant that there were few children being born to the servant class, so there were no native-born English children to employ on plantations. The system required a constant flow of servants from England, but, as economic conditions improved there, fewer people were willing to sign on to such a risky endeavor as servitude in Virginia. Another group of people who represented a potential source of labor, the Indians in Virginia, was unwilling to work for the English and could easily resist any attempt to enslave them, either by armed resistance or by disappearing into the vast wilderness.

Africans as laborers had some important advantages over English servants. To some extent, they were resistant to the diseases that killed or incapacitated whites. White servants were likely to run away, and some managed to reach other English colonies, where they disappeared into the white population. Africans' dark skin made it impossible for them to do likewise. Running away into the backcountry was also difficult, since Indians were willing to return a runaway slave or servant for a bounty. Slavery proved to be more economically stable than servitude: a slave can be made to work for the rest of his life, not just for a period of years. Furthermore, a Virginia law passed in 1662 declared that the status of children follows that of their mothers, so female slaves could potentially generate additional property for their owners, since their children would also be their owners' slaves. One can only imagine the feelings of a slave mother on the birth of a child, knowing as she did that her baby was also her owner's property, a slave for the rest of his or her life. A slave could hope to raise enough money to buy freedom for herself or her children, but that was extremely difficult. Later laws would make it more difficult for a slave to become free, either by self-purchase or through the kindness of a master, who might have freed a slave for faithful service.

As the English presence became more solidly established in the Virginia colony, the social order began to change. As the English population increased, the availability of land decreased. The best land, located along navigable waterways, had long been claimed. Movement into the backcountry was restricted by hostile Indians. One result was the appearance of a class of landless white men, unmarried because of the unfavorable ratio of men to women and landless because there was no land available. These men were angry that the wealthy tobacco growers along the coast made little effort on their behalf to open up the frontier. This anger led to Bacon's Rebellion, in 1676, a series of skirmishes between poor frontiersmen and wealthier coastal residents. The rebellion persuaded many tobacco planters that African slaves were a better source of labor than white indentured servants, who presented a potential source of trouble after their term of service was up. Slaves, they reasoned, were never freed and so could be controlled. Another conclusion that they reached was that relationships between slaves or free blacks and poor whites were potentially very threatening. What if the two groups allied themselves in armed rebellion against the authorities? The prospect was alarming. Slaves had already demonstrated that they were capable of resisting their masters in a wide array of strategies, including committing violent acts, running away for a few days, breaking tools, feigning illness, sabotaging crops, or other means.

Changes in the laws regarding slavery tightened the restrictions on slaves and clarified the differences in status between slaves and servants. The law tended to follow behind social practices: the first law making it clear that some "servants" were bound for life was passed in 1660, even though slaves had existed in the colony for some time. Another law, passed in 1667, made it clear that a slave could not be made free by converting to Christianity; this law meant that, for the first time, the essential difference between slave and master was race, not religion, since one Christian could now legally own another. The harsh treatment of slaves is apparent in another law, passed in 1669, that declared that should a master kill a slave in the course of punishment for failure to obey orders, the master would not be charged with a crime, as the law presumes that no one would willfully destroy his property. Laws passed in the 1700s placed greater restrictions on slaves and free blacks, punishing whites who socialized with blacks and white women who bore children by black men and prohibiting marriage between blacks and whites. The result of these laws is that a master literally had the power of life and death over his slaves. Another result was an increasing sense of white solidarity; poor whites who did not own slaves identified themselves more with the wealthier slave-owning class than with black slaves, with whom they were strongly discouraged from socializing.

Historians have considered how it was possible that slavery became so important so quickly in the English colonies. Some argue that slavery was simply an economically rational solution to a labor problem: African slaves filled a need for labor on the sugar plantations and in the tobacco fields that otherwise could not be met. They point out that the uncertain status of the first Africans in the New World indicates that racism was not an important motivation in the initial decision to use unfree African labor. Other historians disagree: while slavery solved an economic problem, it was also based on an awareness of ethnic differences between Europeans and Africans that hardened rapidly into racial hatred; the fact that slavery was a status reserved for people of West African ancestry supports this argument.

The events of the 17th century set the stage for the next 200 years, though no one at the time could have expected the results. Slavery became increasingly important to the agricultural economy of the South and less so in the North, where industrialization meant that agriculture was not as important and immigration ensured that labor was more readily available. During the Revolution, some of the colonists feared that the British government was determined to reduce them to the equivalent of slaves, and Thomas Jefferson, himself a slaveholder, wrote that "all men are created equal" and that a government that threatened the rights that every man possessed was doomed to failure. How can we reconcile these beliefs to the fact that so many revolutionaries themselves owned slaves? Some historians argue that it was this fact that helped make these men revolutionaries, that the daily presence of slaves and their powerlessness in the face of the utter control of slave owners served as an inescapable negative example. A slave owner did not think that he, personally, could be enslaved, but he would be the one who determined that no man, no government, would ever have that degree of power over him. And he would be prepared to risk a revolution to prevent such a thing from happening.

There were, of course, other reasons for the Revolution besides some slaveholders' anxiety about being reduced to helplessness. The Enlightenment, an intellectual current in European thought that, among other things, asserted that all institutions should be evaluated on the basis of their reasonableness, not merely respected as part of tradition. Every human being, Enlightenment philosophers insisted, had a right to be treated justly by a reasonable and humane government. American revolutionaries, unhappy with their treatment at the hands of the British colonial authorities, found those ideas tremendously appealing. And they were not oblivious to the irony of slave ownership in their midst. They repealed laws making it difficult or expensive for a master to free his slaves. Thomas Jefferson himself agonized about the cruelties of slavery and devised schemes to gradually end the institution in Virginia, yet he personally freed only a handful of slaves, too deeply in debt to risk the financial setback of the loss of his slaves. George Washington, himself a rich man, freed his slaves in his will, as did a number of lesser-known revolutionaries. Some, like Washington, were motivated by the obvious contradiction between revolutionary principles and slave ownership, and others were also inspired by a deep Christian faith and the desire to do right by their human property. Slaves themselves took action: many fled to the British lines during the war in response to promises of freedom if they deserted their masters. Many observers soon after the Revolution believed that slavery was a doomed institution, that a long-term decline in tobacco production would make slavery unprofitable.

Slave owners had a more practical reason to regard slavery with dismay: the slaves on the island of San Domingue, a French sugar island, rebelled, defeated the French army, and created their own nation, the Republic of Haiti. No sensible slave owner could regard his own slaves the same way after the news of that revolution. The news from San Domingue/Haiti caused some slaveholders to consider freeing their human property and others to seek to tighten control over their potentially rebellious slaves. What they could not anticipate was the invention of the cotton gin. The gin, which removed the seeds from the fuzz in cotton bolls, made it profitable to grow a variety of cotton plants that thrived throughout the South. Cotton is a labor-intensive crop and, in the days before mechanized farming, was most profitable when grown with the use of slave labor.

In the end, those who sought to control slaves more closely won. Slaveholders would continue to guard their rights with particular care, with the thought that weakness in the institution of slavery could lead to the situation that had resulted in the Haitian revolution. Throughout the 19th century, Southern politicians would seek to ensure that the institution would be allowed to expand westward with the growth of the nation and that laws would ensure that runaway slaves would be returned as swiftly as possible. They believed that the right to move into western territories with their slaves was essential to preventing the high ratio of black to white population that existed in Haiti before the revolution by diffusing the slave population westward. Northern politicians became less sympathetic to these Southern demands; slavery in the North had been ended, and they saw the West as a land of opportunity for small farmers, not as a place set aside for plantations worked by slaves. These differing views of the West and, by extension, of the American dream itself were an essential source of regional conflict, a struggle that would eventually be settled by a bloody Civil War.

## SELECTED BIBLIOGRAPHY

Berlin, Ira. *Many Thousands Gone: The First Two Centuries of Slavery in North America.* Cambridge, MA: Belknap, 1998. This book focuses on slavery from the perspective of the slaves and what they did every day, in the Chesapeake, South Carolina, and the Mississippi Delta.

Boles, John B. *Black Southerners, 1619–1869.* Lexington: University Press of Kentucky, 1984. As the title suggests, this book looks at African Americans in the cultural context of the Old South.

Brown, Kathleen M. *Good Wives, Nasty Wenches, and Anxious Patriarchs: Gender, Race and Power in Colonial Virginia.* Chapel Hill: University of North Carolina Press, 1996. Brown uses gender analysis in her approach to slavery and Virginia society. From this perspective, issues of race, gender, and religion take on whole new meanings.

Davis, David Brion. *The Problem of Slavery in the Golden Age of Revolution, 1770–1823*. Ithaca, NY: Cornell University Press, 1975. Davis addresses the conflicts between the rhetoric of the revolution and the ownership of slaves.

Degler, Carl N. *Neither Black nor White: Slavery and Race Relations in Brazil and the United States*. New York: Macmillan, 1971. The comparative approach adopted in this book provides an unusually insightful view of the subject of slavery.

Du Bois, W. E. B. *The Souls of Black Folk*. 1903. Reprint ed. New York: Penguin, 1996. Written by one of the most influential African American leaders in the first half of the 20th century, this book is part sociological and historical analysis and part manifesto. It is also prophetic: "The problem of the twentieth century is the problem of the color line."

Elkins, Stanley. *Slavery: A Problem in American Institutional and Intellectual Life*. Chicago: University of Chicago Press, 1959. Elkins created a storm of criticism when he depicted slavery as such a total system of oppression that slaves were reduced to childlike "sambos." His use of an analogy to World War II concentration camps was especially controversial.

Fogel, Robert, and Stanley Engerman. *Time on the Cross: The Economics of American Negro Slavery*. 1974. New ed. New York: W. W. Norton. 1995. This book is controversial both for the conclusion—that slavery was not as oppressive as others had depicted it—and for its approach, a purely numeric economic analysis based on slaveholders' records.

Fox-Genovese, Elizabeth. *Within the Plantation Household: Black and White Women of the Old South*. Chapel Hill: University of North Carolina Press, 1988. This book considers relationships between white and black women, concluding that the shared ties of womanhood were not enough to transcend the institution of slavery.

Franklin, John Hope. *From Slavery to Freedom: A History of African Americans*, 1947. 7th ed. New York: Knopf, 1994. This book is an authoritative and comprehensive history of African Americans from African civilizations up to the present.

Genovese, Eugene. *Roll, Jordan, Roll: The World the Slaves Made*. New York: Pantheon, 1974. This landmark book places greater emphasis on slave autonomy and culture, while not neglecting the essential oppressiveness of the institution itself.

Gutman, Herbert G. *The Black Family in Slavery and Freedom, 1750–1925*. New York: Pantheon, 1976. This well-researched book is a good choice for a reader interested in a longer view of the subject.

Hine, Darlene Clark, and Kathleen Thompson. *A Shining Thread of Hope: The History of Black Women in America*. New York: Broadway Books, 1990. A narrative survey covering four centuries of history, including individual stories of black women's struggles and accomplishments. It is well written and lively, a fascinating read.

Isaac, Rhys. *The Transformation of Virginia: 1740–1790*. New York: W. W. Norton, 1988. A fascinating and well-written book, useful for anyone interested in understanding colonial and Revolutionary-era Virginia.

Jordan, Winthrop. *White over Black: American Attitudes toward the Negro, 1550–1812*. New ed. New York: W. W. Norton, 1995. Originally published in 1969, this book explores the cultural and psychological origins of slavery and racism. Jordan's conclusions have been debated and criticized, yet his ideas remain compelling.

Kolchin, Peter. *American Slavery: 1619–1877*. New York: Hill and Wang, 1993. This clear and succinct book covers slavery not only in the United States but also in the Caribbean and in Brazil, providing a description of how slavery developed and evolved.

Morgan, Edmund S. *American Slavery American Freedom: The Ordeal of Colonial Virginia*. New ed. New York: W. W. Norton, 1995. This book presents a good, brief coverage of slavery in the colonial era. It also offers a clear explanation of the connections between slaveholding and revolutionary ideology.

Parish, Peter J. *Slavery: History and Historians.* New York: Harper and Row, 1989. Parish presents a useful summary of the debates among historians about slavery.

Smith, Patricia. *Africans in America: America's Journey through Slavery.* New York: Harcourt Brace, 1998. This book is the accompanying volume to the PBS television series and covers slavery from Africa, to the Atlantic crossing, and throughout the Caribbean and America up to emancipation.

Wood, Betty. *The Origins of American Slavery.* New York: Hill and Wang, 1997. This book provides a helpful and succinct presentation of its subject, covering not only Virginia but also Africa and the Caribbean.

Wood, Peter. *Black Majority: Negroes in Colonial South Carolina from 1670 through the Stono Rebellion.* New York: Knopf, 1974. This book offers an excellent survey of slavery in South Carolina in the colonial period, including the Stono Rebellion, one of the most fascinating episodes.

Wright, Donald R. *African Americans in the Colonial Era: From African Origins through the American Revolution.* Arlington Heights, IL: Harlan Davidson, 1990. This book contains a useful and brief summary of colonial slavery, with interesting background information about slavery in Africa and the Caribbean.

## AFRICAN SLAVE TRADE

When Olaudah Equiano was 12 years old, he was captured in his home in the interior of West Africa and marched west across a large river, probably the Niger River. He lived at the mercy of several different masters and was eventually sold to slave traders, who sold Equiano to Europeans at the West African coast. At the coast, Equiano fainted after boarding a slave ship that was bound for the West Indies. In his autobiography, published in 1789, he remembered:

> Such were the horrors of my views and fears at the moment, that if ten thousand worlds had been my own, I would have freely parted with them all to have exchanged my condition with that of the meanest slave of my own country. When I looked around the ship and saw a large furnace of copper boiling, and a multitude of black people of every description chained together, every one of their countenances expressing dejection and sorrow, I no longer doubted my fate. Quite overpowered with horror and anguish, I fell motionless on the deck and fainted.

Equiano intensely feared the Europeans, the ship, and the unfamiliar objects. He thought that the Europeans wanted to eat the Africans and that the ocean and the ship were magic, until several Africans speaking the Igbo language comforted him. During the voyage, Equiano and others were beaten severely, and some Africans jumped overboard to their deaths.

An African slave trade existed since the days of ancient Egypt, when Nubian captives were brought from the Nile Valley to work for the pharaohs. Slaves were an important trade item in the trans-Saharan trade that flourished between North Africa and West Africa after the 10th century, and slaves had been traded into the Indian Ocean world from East Africa for centuries. However, the most significant African slave trade was that initiated by Europeans in West Africa during the 16th century. Over three centuries, the Atlantic slave trade forcibly removed millions of Africans to plantations throughout the

New World. In doing so, it left an indelible imprint on the histories of North America, South America, Europe, and Africa.

Portuguese mariners began trading with states along the West African coast in the middle of the 15th century. In 1470, Portuguese merchants began buying slaves from the Kingdom of Benin (in modern Nigeria) to trade with the Akan peoples to the west (in modern Ghana). There, they were exchanged for gold and put to work in mines. In the 1480s, the Portuguese established sugar plantations on the Atlantic islands of São Tomé and Principe, which were located off of the west coast of Africa. Those were modeled after plantations in the Mediterranean and southern Europe, which used North African and Eastern European slaves to undertake the arduous work of harvesting and processing the sugar. The proximity of those new sugar plantations to the mainland encouraged sugar planters to purchase slave labor from African traders. The African slaves worked in large gangs and were supervised by European overseers.

When the Iberian powers began establishing sugar plantations in the New World after 1492, they adopted the plantation model used on the African islands. As the plantation economy of the New World expanded, it developed an insatiable appetite for African slave labor. European criminals imported to work on plantations quickly succumbed to tropical diseases, and Native American peoples were all but exterminated by harsh treatment at the hands of Europeans and exposure to new strains of disease. Beginning in 1532, slaves from West Africa were imported directly to the New World in a system that would last more than three centuries and ultimately enslave and transport millions of victims.

The conditions of enslavement, transportation, and servitude were horrifying. After being captured in Africa, slaves were chained and kept in port until they were purchased by European traders. The trip across the Atlantic was extremely hazardous, with many slaves perishing from disease or even being thrown overboard to their death when a ship's provisions ran low. Equiano wrote of the beginnings of his journey on the slave ship:

> I inquired of these what was to be done with us. They gave me to understand we were to be carried to these white people's country to work for them. I then was a little revived, and thought if it were no worse than working, my situation was not so desperate. But still I feared that I should be put to death, the white people looked and acted in so savage a manner. I have never seen among my people such instances of brutal cruelty, and this not only shown towards us blacks, but also to some of the whites themselves.

This was the Middle Passage, the middle part of the three-part journey taken by slave traders in the 17th and 18th centuries. The traders first carried goods to Africa, then traded the goods for slaves and started across the Atlantic Ocean to the Americas, where they exchanged the slaves for other goods and departed again for Europe. The middle part of the voyage saw the newly enslaved Africans shackled and packed tightly into tiny areas where they were subject to disease. Valuable cargo, slaves who would not eat or attempted suicide were often tortured. Mortality rates were high; it is estimated that between 10 percent and 20 percent of Africans transported through the Middle Passage lost their lives. "The closeness of the place and the heat of the climate, added to the number of the ship, which was so crowded that each had scarcely room to turn himself, almost suffocated us," Equiano wrote.

This produced copious perspiration so that the air became unfit for respiration from a variety of loathsome smells and brought on a sickness among the slaves, of which many died—thus falling victims to the improvident avarice, as I may call it, of their purchasers. This wretched situation was again aggravated by the galling of the chains, which now became insupportable, and the filth of the necessary tubs [toilets] into which the children often fell and were almost suffocated. The shrieks of the women and the groans of the dying rendered the whole a scene of horror almost inconceivable.

While historians debate the volume of slaves transported during this era, it is evident that at least 10 million African slaves arrived in the New World. Given the vast number who died during the notorious Middle Passage (estimates range in the low millions) and the number sent to other regions (like South Africa), the total number of people ensnared in the system would have been much greater.

Portuguese domination of the trade ended in the 17th century as merchants from several European states began supplanting them. By the mid-18th century, British, French, and Dutch merchants were transporting upward of 100,000 slaves out of West Africa annually. Those slaves worked in mines in South America, on coffee and sugar plantations in Brazil, on sugar plantations in the Caribbean, and on cotton plantations in the American south. Life expectancy on those plantations was short due to overwork and disease, creating a constant demand for more slave labor.

Once his ship docked in Barbados, Equiano was sold to a merchant who took him to Virginia, where the introduction of tobacco had been the primary stimulus for the adoption of slavery in the North American colonies. The arrival of the first slaves in the North American colonies, in 1619, began what would become an economic and cultural institution in the United States. Profit drove that entrenchment of slavery. Tobacco, cotton, and westward expansion were all key economic catalysts used to justify such forced labor.

After tobacco was introduced in Virginia, tobacco growers soon recognized the profit potential from the use of slave labor and attributed that potential to several reasons: Africans were more acclimated to the brutal, hot weather and could labor longer than their white immigrant counterparts; as they came from different regions and spoke different languages, it was hard for them to organize resistance; and they were too far away from their homeland to run away. The use of slaves in the tobacco industry marked the beginning of more than two centuries of slavery in the United States.

By the late 17th and early 18th centuries, slavery was firmly established as the principal labor system in the South, although it did exist to a lesser extent in the North. Even when tobacco began to yield fewer returns in the late 18th century and slavery appeared to be declining, the institution had already become enmeshed in U.S. culture. Racism was part of that culture, as most white Americans believed that Africans were inferior and that slaves were better off being provided for in captivity than they would be if they were free. Because they believed that slavery was an important part of American life, the delegates to the Constitutional Convention in 1787 ensured its continuance in the U.S. Constitution.

While tobacco was on the decline, another cash crop greatly impacted the institution of slavery in the United States—cotton. Eli Whitney's introduction of the cotton gin in 1794 at the time of the Industrial Revolution, during which large-scale manufacturing greatly increased the demand for cotton, propelled a resurgence in the need for slavery. Settlers, along with slaves purchased from failing tobacco planters, migrated to the South to establish large cotton plantations in such states as Mississippi, Louisiana, and Georgia. Thus, the institution of slavery in the United States was revived and once again became essential to Southern economic concerns.

Different regions of West Africa participated in the slave commerce to varying degrees. The Senegambia region was an important supplier in the early days of the trade, as was Angola. Later, the west coast of modern Nigeria became the focus of the trade, earning the region the nickname the "slave coast." The coast of modern Ghana was also an area with a high concentration of European slave trading posts. At the slave trade's peak in the 18th century, virtually every port along the West African coast was participating in the trade.

The role of African rulers and merchants in the trade has been a subject of much controversy. Most people who were sold to Europeans were captives from wars or criminals. Before the advent of the Atlantic trade, captives would have been returned home after ransom was paid or enslaved. Criminals would have been either executed or enslaved. However, slavery in that context meant something quite different from what it would come to mean in the New World. A slave in West African communities was frequently considered a member of a family. In many cases, slaves were eligible to own and inherit property, and their children would often be freed. Thus, while forms of slavery can be said to have existed in West Africa before the advent of the Atlantic slave trade, the chattel slavery of the New World, which viewed slaves as private property and beasts of burden, was rare in Africa.

Americans and Europeans did not have the resources or inclination to capture slaves themselves, and they acted for the most part as buyers in slave markets along the African coast. However, merchants proved willing and able to encourage conflict among African states, as they did in Angola and the Kongo Empire in the 16th century, in order to maximize the pool of available captives. In general, the demand for slaves appears to have encouraged conflict among African states and to have transformed the nature of warfare. Where victory would have once encouraged rulers to exact tribute from the vanquished, the slave trade encouraged the victors to destroy and enslave weaker communities.

The slave trade also had significant demographic and social consequences in West Africa. Traders preferred to purchase men rather than women because they were seen as better suited to survive the grueling Atlantic crossing and the arduous labor of the plantations. That preference left many regions of Africa with a disproportionate number of women, many of whom were enslaved by African rulers. It also robbed local economies of their most productive members, who were exchanged for manufactured goods like alcohol, cloth, and guns that had little if any productive value. The plantation system also gradually took hold in West Africa, and, by the 19th century, large plantations run by slave labor were producing palm oil and other products desired by traders. Thus, the chattel slavery of the New World came to transform slave relations in Africa.

During the 18th century, the Atlantic slave trade reached its zenith. Developments in Europe during the century, however, were laying the foundations for the system's demise. In the late 18th century, European intellectuals, influenced by the Enlightenment, began calling for an end to the trade. Some of those critics were inspired by the French philosophes' ideas of the equality and dignity of all people, while others were influenced by the economic arguments of Adam Smith and other physiocrats, who maintained that slavery was an inefficient economic institution.

At the same time, Christian evangelicals in Great Britain and the United States began arguing for abolition on the grounds that the traffic in human beings was immoral. Many of the abolitionists were freed slaves or repentant slave traders. Initially, the abolition movement focused its attention on the slave trade itself. The abolitionists reasoned that the Middle Passage was the most dangerous aspect of the system for those enslaved and that, if the supply of slaves dried up, the owners in the New World would be forced to treat their slaves more humanely. Many abolitionists were also hesitant to support the cause of manumission, which was seen as an infringement on the property rights of slave owners.

The campaign for abolition coincided with important changes in the political economy of the Atlantic world. A glut in world sugar production in the 18th century, combined with the rising price of slaves on the West African coast, cut into the profits of plantation owners and slavers. Meanwhile, the rising manufacturing class of Great Britain (many of whom were staunch abolitionists) was beginning to view Africa as a potential source of raw materials and markets, rather than as a reserve of human labor.

Abolitionists were further aided by the growing specter of slave revolts. The Haitian slave uprising, or Haitian Revolution, of 1791 was the most prominent and successful such rising. Other resistance movements proliferated throughout the New World. In the New York slave revolt of 1712, slaves in New York City armed themselves with guns and clubs and revolted. The leaders of the revolt were newly arrived from Africa. In 1800, a slave named Gabriel Prosser led slaves in what became known as Gabriel's Rebellion, followed in 1831 by Nat Turner's Rebellion, led by a slave named Nat Turner. Slaves in Brazil and Jamaica formed self-governing communities outside European control. Such movements made slave trading an increasingly precarious investment and helped pave the path toward abolition.

The abolitionist cause was strongest in France, where the trade was outlawed by the French revolutionaries after 1789, and in Great Britain, where the British Parliament abolished the British slave trade in 1807. The United States abolished the trade in the same year when President Thomas Jefferson signed the Act to Prohibit the Importation of Slaves (1807) into law. An illegal slave trade continued until the Civil War, however, with the Compromise of 1850 calling for an end to the slave trade in Washington, D.C.

At the conclusion of the Napoleonic Wars, Great Britain was able to get several of the remaining powers of Europe to agree to a ban on the trade. The restored French monarchy refused to agree to the ban on slave trading, although, by 1831, the nation had effectively ended its participation in the trade. Spain was the one European nation that continued to ignore the ban, and many slave ships began using Spanish or Cuban flags. The trade between Africa and the New World plantations of Cuba and Brazil was ended only in 1867.

With trade in slaves forbidden, the U.S. and British governments determined to prevent rival powers from benefiting from the use of slave labor. Cooperation between Secretary of State Daniel Webster and Lord Ashburton of Great Britain resulted in the Webster-Ashburton Treaty (1842), which settled the boundaries between the United

States and Canada but also aimed to suppress the slave trade. The treaty called for the two countries to equip and maintain naval vessels on the coast of Africa with the explicit purpose of ending the trade of slaves. "The Parties to this Treaty agree that they will unite in all becoming representations and remonstrances, with any and all Powers within whose dominions such markets are allowed to exist; and that they will urge upon all such Powers the propriety and duty of closing such markets effectually at once and forever," it stated.

Therefore, the U.S. Navy began patrolling the coast of West Africa, intercepting slave ships and liberating slaves. Admirals Andrew H. Foote and Matthew Perry, among others, sailed along the African coast, stopping ships suspected of trading in slaves. The British Royal Navy plied the waters along the eastern African coast, where Swahili and Arab slave traders continued to export slaves to the Middle East and Asia.

Ironically, the abolition of the slave trade actually increased the incidence of slavery in West Africa in the short term. African states that had grown wealthy by supplying slaves to coastal traders were slow to abandon their economic livelihood. With the U.S. Navy and the Royal Navy closing off the export of slaves from the coast, vast reservoirs of slaves accumulated in ports. Missionaries and merchants attempted to encourage African states to replace slave trading with "legitimate commerce," the production of tropical foodstuffs for export to the European and North American markets. However, those new products were produced on large plantations that still used slave labor.

In the late 19th century, European powers justified their conquest of Africa in part by promising that colonial rule would end the traffic in human beings once and for all. However, European administrators soon found that, without slave labor, many colonies would not be economically self-sufficient, and they often turned a blind eye toward the practice. Though slavery had been eradicated throughout much of Africa by 1930, it continues to exist in some areas of the continent.

With the American south one of the chief cotton producers of the world and with westward expansion offering more land for cotton and tobacco cultivation, slavery was more entrenched than ever in the United States even after the end of the slave trade. It would remain so until the end of the Civil War.

Before Equiano had been in Virginia long, he was purchased by a British Royal Navy lieutenant and taken to England. There, he learned to read, changed masters many times, and began working aboard ships. He traveled between the Caribbean islands and North America and then to Italy, Turkey, Portugal, the West Indies, and the Arctic. He was finally allowed to trade in order to earn money, and, in 1766, he presented his master with £40 sterling and received the papers for his manumission.

All the while, Equiano did not waver from his mission to end the slave trade. During 1788–1789, he published his autobiography, *Equiano's Travels: His Autobiography or The Interesting Narrative of the Life of Olaudah Equiano or Gustavus Vassa, the African.* He concluded the account of his own experiences and his observations of the brutality of slavery with an appeal to the British legislature to end the slave trade. "I hope," he wrote, "to have the satisfaction of seeing the renovation of liberty and justice resting on the British government to vindicate the honour of our common nature." It was not to happen. Equiano died in obscurity in either 1797 or 1801.

JAMES BURNS

## RUNAWAY SERVANTS

Rebellion and escape from indentured servitude was common throughout the colonial period. The most common acts of rebellion involved breaking tools, feigning sickness, or shirking work duties, but there are some examples of servants sabotaging their master's crops, burning his home, poisoning his food, or killing his livestock. In the most egregious cases, they even committed acts of violence against their masters. In one gruesome example, a young Virginia servant murdered his master and his wife in their sleep with an axe. The servant, who was trained as a bookseller and raised in a middle-class English family, was angry that his master had reneged on a promise he had made to make him a tutor to his children. Instead, the servant found himself working in the tobacco fields for long hours of the day, toiling in the heat of the sun without adequate food and water. He was angry at his mistress, too. She "would not only rail, swear, and curse at him," but she haunted him "like a live ghost" while he was doing the "most irksome" work in the field. Such incidents reveal that servants had limits to the abuse they were willing to take.

Running away was also a common method of rebellion. Because masters had invested so much time and money in their servants, they did not look upon runaways favorably. Often they placed detailed ads in the local newspapers describing who had run away, what the person was wearing, and, most important, certain physical features that would make them recognizable. They offered a reward as well. This advertisement in *The Pennsylvania Journal,* dated May 10, 1775, is a typical example:

Race-street, an English Servant Man named John Watts, a Brass-founder by trade, about 22 years old, 5 feet 5 inches high; he came to this place in December last with Capt. Cook, from London; he has a long face, white grey eyes, black curled hair very thin on his head, a childish but hoarse voice; and says, since he has been here, he ran-away, from his uncle in London, to come to this country. He had on when he went away, a felt hat, a black silk cravat, Check Shirt, an old peachblossom-coloured waistcoat, of cotton velvet, the back parts of different stuff, and a coating upper-jacket, the lining of white woolen stuff, blue duffel trousers, blue and white mixed stockings very little worn, new neat's leather shoes with silver plated buckles.— Whoever takes up said Servant, and secures him so that his Master may have him again, shall have the above Reward of FIVE POUNDS, and reasonable charges, paid by me Frederick Weckerly, Brass-founder.

There is no way of knowing how many runaways successfully escaped, but, if Maryland can be used as an example, the number is high. Over a three-year period from 1685 to 1688, the *Maryland Gazette* published an average of 450 advertisements for runaways, but county court records recorded that not more than four or five were captured.

While escape from abusive masters was the most common reason for fleeing, it was not the only one. The majority of runaways in Pennsylvania were from rural areas where they often worked in isolation, cut off from the social networks that urban servants seemed to enjoy. Most of them ran away with other servants and occasionally slaves. A number of them went to Connecticut, a colony that did not have laws compelling the return of runaways. Some went to other colonies, such as South Carolina, where it was believed runaways would be sheltered. Others, during times of war, joined the British army. Wherever they went, though, they were difficult to catch.

Runaways who were caught or who returned home paid dearly: they had their indentures extended, usually for twice the time lost to their master. In Pennsylvania and Maryland, the ratios were 5 to 1 and 10 to 1, respectively, but that did not seem to deter runaways: in Pennsylvania, nearly a quarter of servants ran away in the first half of the 18th century. In addition to having their contracts extended, runaways were often whipped. When Thomas Wood, a seven-year-old servant from Virginia, ran away from his master's farm in the summer of 1640, his master, who was known in the community as "a cruell man," vowed to flog him if he returned. The young boy returned, and the master made good on his word. He hired a man, one Samuel Lucas, to whip the boy, and, when Lucas finished the deed, Wood's master took a turn at cracking the whip, beating the boy with a rope "about the bignes of a finger." The boy died shortly after his beating, but it was not clear whether he died from sickness or from the abuse he suffered from his attackers.

One of the reasons servants were treated so harshly is that they were not considered to be part of the master's family, as they were in England, where they were treated with greater care. English masters took great pride in looking after the comfort, health, and well-being of their servants, much as they would their own children. They purchased their servants in small face-to-face gatherings, where they got to know them and their families. Most servants were bound to households, usually in localities close to their own homes, for a period of one year, which made many young men and women view themselves as hired labor rather than indentured servants. Furthermore, these servants received wages and acquired property once their contracts were up. This was not always the case in the colonies.

In the colonies, servitude was often impersonal and inhumane. Servants were sold at large auction blocks to the highest bidder, and the bidders looked on their new labor recruits as nothing more than property. In addition, most colonial servants could be bought and sold, rented out at their master's discretion, or doled away in a will to a destitute family member. Servants also risked losing their freedom dues if their master felt particularly stingy that year or if he didn't like his servant. There were no remedies to such injustices, other than filing a petition to the court, but, as already noted, such appeals did not usually go in the servants' favor. For these and other reasons, servants often compared their plight to that of slaves. James Revel, an indentured servant in Virginia, captured this feeling in a poem he wrote: "we and the Negroes both alike did fare / Of work and food we had an equal share."

Not surprisingly, Europeans who visited the colonies were horrified at how servants were treated. One such visitor, William Eddis, who arrived in Maryland in 1769, believed slaves were treated better than servants. "Generally speaking," he observed, "they groan beneath a worse than Egyptian bondage." Servants said as much, too. "As is too commonly the case," one Connecticut servant bitterly noted, "I was rather considered a slave than a member of the family, and, instead of allowing me the privilege of common hospitality, and a claim to that kind of protection due to the helpless and indigent children, I was treated by my master as his property and not as his fellow mortal."

What especially galled servants was the fact that they were bought and sold like slaves. "My Master Atkins," wrote one disgruntled servant from Virginia in 1623, "hath sold me for a £150 sterling like a damned slave." A servant from Pennsylvania complained that his master had sold him for a "yoke of bulls" valued at £12, which was nothing more than the price a slave would fetch. But most degrading was how they were sold. In most colonial cities, they were herded off at large auctions, "driven," as one servant explained, "in tens and twenties like cattle to a…market and exposed to sale in public fairs as so many brute beasts." Like slaves, they were poked and prodded at the auctions, demeaned and humiliated, as one servant put it, "in the vilest of ways."

JOHN A. GRIGG

## SLAVERY

The most brutal institution in American history, slavery existed in the United States from the early 17th century until 1865, when Congress enacted the Thirteenth Amendment shortly after the Union victory over the Confederacy in the Civil War. By that point, more than 4 million African American slaves lived in the United States. Although their communities thrived and multiplied, these people were subject to harsh living conditions and enjoyed none of the rights or freedoms so fiercely protected by white Americans.

Native Americans were the first enslaved people in North America. Many aboriginal societies had practiced different forms of slavery for thousands of years before they had ever seen Europeans. The practice, however, represented a temporary condition and was used more as a badge of status than a moneymaking enterprise. Most Indian slaves were women and children either purchased or captured as prizes in warfare. Some were adopted into their new tribe over time, their offspring being free persons who could even rise to positions of leadership. Slavery, therefore, was not a hereditary condition, nor was it based on race.

Europeans continued the practice of enslaving Indians after their arrival in the New World in the late 15th century. Spanish, English, and French colonists broadened the scope of Indian slavery by selling Indians, including men, into bondage in other colonies as punishment for warfare or rebellion. The Spanish, in particular, erected a vast system of slave labor in their colonies in Latin America.

The English and French enslaved Native Americans much less frequently and seldom held Indian slaves to labor among them. Rather, they sold Indian captives south to the West Indies, as Connecticut colonists did to surviving Native American women and children following the Pequot War of 1636–1637, which virtually annihilated the Pequots from New England. In general, the British colonists found it difficult to enslave Native Americans, who had great opportunities to escape from bondage and rejoin their tribes.

The system of chattel slavery that developed in the New World and focused on African Americans was different from the slavery practiced against Native Americans. The first group of African slaves, numbering four men and women, arrived aboard a Dutch ship at Jamestown, Virginia, in 1619.

English planters like John Rolfe quickly realized the enormous profits to be had from importing unfree laborers. Rolfe's introduction of a viable tobacco plant in Virginia served as a major impetus for the adoption of African slavery as the region's main labor system. Tobacco was an extremely labor-intensive crop, requiring field hands to spend long hours bending over plants under the blazing hot sun. Most whites proved entirely unsuited for this labor, in part because they were unused to such hot and humid weather conditions and in part because they flat out refused to do such work. Some white indentured servants were forced to work in the fields, but, as the 17th century progressed, it proved more and more difficult to convince Europeans to immigrate under these conditions.

African slaves solved many of these problems. Physically, Africans were more used to such brutal weather conditions and capable of laboring in them for longer periods than whites. As African slaves represented a diversity of nations and spoke a wide variety of languages, they also found it difficult to communicate with one another and organize resistance to their forced bondage. And, unlike the Native Americans, Africans were too far from their homeland to run away from their white masters. Finally, some West African leaders proved extremely receptive to the idea of selling other Africans into slavery for profit, so most of the kidnapping of Africans and forcing them into bondage was actually done by other Africans, reducing the effort on the part of whites necessary to perpetuate the system. For all these reasons, African slavery quickly emerged as a desirable and profitable labor system.

Throughout the course of the 17th century, the various British North American colonies erected a series of laws and social conventions that served to entrench African slavery at the heart of colonial society, particularly in the south. Although African slavery spread to all of the colonies, it never took hold in the northern colonies as it did in the southern, primarily because of the nature of the work required. Northern colonies were populated with small family farms, and the rocky terrain proved inhospitable for crops like tobacco. Slaves certainly existed in the northern colonies but not in nearly such large numbers as in their southern counterparts.

During the colonial period, nowhere did slavery become more firmly entrenched than in Virginia, and the slave system that Virginia developed during this period served as a model for all other slave societies in the years to come. At first, in the 1620s, the rules governing slavery were ill defined, and some masters treated the Africans more like indentured servants than slaves. Several Africans even labored for specified amounts of time and then secured their freedom. By the 1640s, however, the idea that African slavery should be both perpetual and hereditary had begun to take hold, as the labor required to keep large plantations functioning and profitable grew scarce and the price of slaves rose.

The Virginia House of Burgesses passed a series of laws in the second half of the 17th century that legitimized African slavery. Perhaps most important, the legislature grounded slavery on a strict definition of race, ensuring that anyone with even as little as one-eighth of African blood was likely to be a slave. The laws also clearly classified slaves as property, according them no rights or protections under the law. Masters were free to do with their slaves as they pleased. Although the legislature would pass other laws in the coming decades to refine the slave-labor system, its essentials were in place by 1700.

By that point, slavery was firmly entrenched as the primary labor system of the South. White indentured servants from Europe became increasingly scarce, while African imports rose dramatically beginning in 1680. New England shipping firms profited immensely from the trade by transporting Africans from their homeland to America. Known as the Middle Passage, the journey across the Atlantic Ocean in slave ships was a brutal one, with the Africans being held below decks, chained together in cramped conditions, and suffering from disease, starvation, and outrageously poor sanitary conditions. Although mortality rates on the Middle Passage were alarmingly high, most Africans reached North America and were quickly sold into perpetual bondage with no hope of ever attaining their freedom or returning home.

Once sold to their new masters, slaves were forced to assimilate into American life very quickly. They learned English with amazing speed and proved fast students of American culture, as well. Often they were aided by other slaves working on the same plantation, who informally introduced the Africans to their new way of life. In the slave quarters, a whole new culture emerged that combined elements of African life with American features, giving rise to a unique African American culture.

Living conditions for slaves were hard, with long work hours and little material comfort. Few masters recognized the sanctity of the slave family and sold off children from their parents, or vice versa, as they pleased. Slave marriages were not recognized by any white institution, either legal or religious, and masters, rather than slave parents, had the ultimate power to discipline slave children. Nevertheless, historians have recently conjectured that slave families did exist and managed to exert a tremendous influence on African American life while avoiding the watchful eyes of white overlords.

Slaves were subject to harsh punishment for even minor offenses, depending on the character and temperament of each individual master. The relatively high purchase price for slaves did not protect them from mistreatment. If a master chose, he could even murder his slaves with impunity, although it would mark a significant financial loss for him if he did so. Whippings and beatings were not uncommon, however, and some masters became adept at inflicting physical punishments on their slaves that did not hinder their ability to work.

Slaves performed a wide variety of work in the South. The majority served as field hands or house servants. A privileged few were taught such trades as carpentry or blacksmithing. Some slaves even became preachers, presiding over many of the religious aspects of slave life.

Religion, in fact, was a pillar of African American life during this period. Whites had long boasted that slavery allowed them an opportunity to Christianize African "heathens," and many whites actively encouraged the spread of religion among slaves, pushing in particular biblical injunctions for slaves to obey their masters and accept their condition in life. As with other aspects of slave culture, African Americans accepted Christianity but modified it, combining with it some aspects of traditional African religions. Because slaves were prohibited by law from learning how to read or write, slave preachers played a particularly important role in African American religion and were often the center of slave communities.

In recent years, historians have focused more and more attention on the dynamics of slave communities and whether or not the majority of slaves accepted their condition in life or worked to undermine their bondage. A series of slave rebellions and revolts throughout American history, most notably the Stono Rebellion of 1739 and Nat Turner's Rebellion of 1831, alarmed whites and illustrated that not all slaves complacently accepted their status. Currently, though, historians have been hypothesizing that a majority of slaves most likely sought to undermine the system through a series of small, passive-aggressive acts—like working as slowly as possible in the fields or surreptitiously ruining crops. For many, such acts were the only way to show their discontent without suffering tremendous retribution at the hands of their masters.

Short of fomenting a rebellion, the most common measure to undermine the institution of slavery was for a slave to run away. Some fled to Native American communities in the West, which sometimes offered a haven for African Americans. Others made the arduous journey to Canada. Still others opted to take their chances in the North, hoping to melt into one of the many communities of free African Americans living in northern cities.

The chance of recapture was extremely high, both for those in flight and for those who fled to the North. Slaves caught attempting to run away met with particularly harsh punishments, sometimes even death, at the hands of southern authorities. Some southern communities even maintained slave patrols, complete with tracking dogs, to discourage runaways. Slave catchers—privately employed agents who returned slaves to their masters for a fee—were particularly feared among slaves for their brutality.

Despite the often cruel conditions of slavery, American slaves enjoyed a higher standard of living than any other enslaved people, higher even than many of the laboring free classes around the world. Natural increase of the American slave population, through high birth rates and relatively low death rates, was marked throughout slavery's existence.

By the outbreak of the American Revolution, more than a half-million slaves lived in the British colonies, almost all of them in the South. As tobacco proved less and less profitable, however, slavery seemed to be on the decline. The delegates at the Continental Congress even briefly discussed abolishing slavery, although strenuous objections from southern delegates, whose constituents had enormous sums tied up in slave property, brought such talk to a close quickly.

The idea that the colonists could be fighting the British for their freedom at the same time they held a half-million people in bondage troubled many Americans, but the issue of race played a tremendous role in assuaging their consciences. For centuries, Africans had been seen as an inferior people, and most white Americans, in both the North and the South, managed to convince themselves that slaves were better off and better cared for in bondage than they would be with their freedom.

Adhering to the belief that slavery was an important aspect of American life, the delegates of the Constitutional Convention enshrined the institution of slavery in the U.S. Constitution in 1787, ensuring its continuance in the United States despite any qualms Americans might be feeling about it. However, the convention did incorporate a ban on the international slave trade, to be implemented in 1808. This ban on importation did little to lessen the strength of slavery as an institution, however, as the slave population in America was thriving on its own, and the lack of new imports served to keep the price of slaves high.

By this point, slavery had geographically split the country, with the southern states relying on it heavily while many of the northern states abolished it or passed laws to phase it out. Many Americans in both regions thought that slavery would eventually disappear from the entire country, as it was becoming less profitable for southern tobacco planters.

In 1794, however, Eli Whitney introduced the cotton gin, a labor-saving machine that transformed cotton from a ridiculously high-labor crop into a profitable one. Growing cotton still required a tremendous amount of labor, but its rewards proved greater after the advent of the cotton gin.

Almost immediately, settlers pushed into the southwest to establish large cotton plantations in Mississippi, Louisiana, and Georgia. Into these new regions, they took thousands of slaves, purchased from failing tobacco planters in Virginia who were happy to convert their slave property into ready cash. Suddenly, the institution of slavery was reborn, reestablishing itself as the backbone of southern financial interests once again. With the South emerging as one of the chief cotton regions of the world, slavery was more entrenched than ever.

The spread of slavery to new states ignited a "fire bell in the night," according to the elderly Thomas Jefferson in 1820. Jefferson in the 1770s had attempted to put slavery on a course of destruction. However, by the first decades of the 19th century, Jefferson, like other leading southern statesmen, proclaimed the need to protect the institution to save the southern way of life. Indeed, slavery became the most abiding and powerful symbol of that way of life.

Increasingly, northern and southern politicians came to view each other as members of hostile camps, representing two opposing images of American life: one based on free labor and the other based on slave labor. As a result, the issue of admitting new states that either prohibited slavery or allowed it emerged as one of vital political significance. Southerners saw the admission of a free state as a tangible sign of growing northern political power, and vice versa. The advent of a vocal and controversial abolition movement in the North only heightened southern fears of a plot to destroy slavery and the South's political power.

The result was increasing sectional tension between the two regions as more and more territories petitioned for statehood in the federal Union during the first half of the 19th century. The adoption of a series of compromises, most notably the Missouri Compromise of 1820 and the Compromise of 1850, offered only temporary relief for these tensions, which eventually culminated in the secession of 11 southern states and the outbreak of the Civil War, in 1861.

During the war, President Abraham Lincoln adhered to his position that the conflict was not over slavery but rather over the issue of states' rights and the sanctity of the federal Union. In 1862, he issued the Emancipation Proclamation, which freed all slaves in the rebelling states. Although abolitionists praised the move, Lincoln still held that it had been a war measure, prompted by the fact that slaves were directly contributing to the South's fighting capabilities by manning the home front and freeing up more whites for service on the battlefield. The wording of the proclamation was also important, as it essentially freed only the slaves in areas not under the federal government's control, while leaving slaves in bondage in other regions.

Nevertheless, by the end of the war, the South's defeat brought slavery to a de facto end, as hundreds of thousands of slaves fled to the victorious Union troops. Congress officially declared slavery dead with the passage of the Thirteenth Amendment, in 1865. The struggle for equal rights for African Americans was another whole issue, and one that most white Americans chose not to tackle in the aftermath of the war. By the end of Reconstruction, white southerners had reestablished their control over African

Americans through a series of laws and restrictions that severely curtailed their rights and opportunities. It was not until the civil rights movement of the 1950s and 1960s that African Americans were truly able to throw off this new form of control, which in many ways proved even more confining than the bondage of slavery.

JASON NEWMAN

## SLAVERY IN MID-18TH-CENTURY COLONIAL VIRGINIA

On the eve of the American Revolution, the life of a slave in colonial Virginia was dictated by the same crop that had dictated the lives of countless other slaves before him—tobacco. The colony's primary staple throughout the colonial era, tobacco was best produced on a small scale and on land that required careful cultivation and management. For these reasons, tobacco plantations tended to be far smaller than the rice plantations of the low country. Most tobacco farmers needed the labor of just a few slaves to make a profit. The lives of slaves in the Chesapeake were determined by the seasonal demands of the crop. To bring a tobacco crop successfully to market, small bands of slaves and their overseers toiled ceaselessly between the months of January and September. In the early spring, slaves cleared the land and planted seeds. As the seedlings matured, slaves weeded, hoed, and transplanted the seedlings to fields prepared to nurture them. In late summer, the intricate process of harvesting began. Leaves were first cut, then cured, then rolled, and finally packed for delivery. Because the crop could be ruined by the carelessness of its harvesters, plantation owners or their hired overseers closely supervised the work of their slaves, who typically worked in small groups, or "gangs." Slaves in such gang units were often ordered to keep pace with the most efficient and practiced hand among them, to prevent the "lazier" or less capable slaves in their midst from slowing down the progress of the harvest. Those who did not keep up with the relentless pace could expect some form of punishment.

The system of gang labor that dominated the tobacco plantations of Virginia left slaves little free time of their own. During the peak seasons of planting and harvesting, slaves toiled from early dawn into the late hours of the night. Their few hours of rest were spent in quarters or cabins set some distance away from the master's home. Slaves spent their limited free time on recreation or on the more practical activities of tending to their own small gardens or livestock. Observing plantation life at the home of one of Virginia's wealthiest planters, Philip Vickers Fithian wrote in his diary: "Before Breakfast, I saw a Ring of Negroes at the Stable, fighting Cocks, and in several parts of the plantation they are digging up their small Lots of ground allow'd by their Master for Potatoes, peas etc. All such work for themselves they constantly do on Sundays, as they are otherwise employed on every other Day." Here, Fithian might have been describing any number of slave plantation scenes in Virginia, as the Sabbath was typically the slave's only day for rest and recreation.

The distance between the typical Virginian plantation home and its slave quarters allowed slaves the chance to create a world of their own, a world that was, to a limited extent, shielded from the constant scrutiny of whites. Within this world, slaves found spouses, raised children, looked after the old and infirm, and tended their homes and gardens. Few slaves, however, were content to make this world their only sphere of social interaction. Despite the prohibitions against their going abroad without the permission of their masters, slaves in Virginia traveled widely across the countryside, mostly under the cover of night. Slaves renounced sleep and risked severe punishment for a number of different reasons: to visit kinfolk and friends living on other plantations; to pilfer food and provisions from neighboring farms, to hunt and feast with companions in the stillness of the night; and, last but certainly not least, to taste the liberty that was not theirs by daylight. The Virginia landscape, a patchwork of irregularly shaped fields separated by borders of forest and dense undergrowth, lent itself to their nocturnal sojourning; to escape detection, slaves created alternative routes and paths between adjoining plantations that allowed them to avoid the established roads that were frequented by whites. Their determination to expand their social networks often led to marriages that tenuously united different plantations. To minimize the possibility of separation, a husband might appeal to his master to purchase his wife so that they might be united on the same plantation. On some occasions, masters were willing to accommodate such wishes, seeing the benefits of such an arrangement. Often, though, slaveholders had little sympathy for the bonds that none but slaves recognized. In many cases, runaway slaves were not running away from masters but running to wives, husbands, and children who had just been torn from them.

Slaves' living arrangements on Virginia plantations provided for some measure of privacy, but they did little to protect or shield them from the inherent violence of chattel slavery. Despite their spatial separation on the plantation, slaves and Virginia slaveholders were often in close and intimate contact with one another. Slave women were particularly vulnerable to the predations of white men, including their masters. Virginia law strictly prohibited sexual relations and marriages between blacks and whites, but such prohibitions did not prevent sexual violence against slave women. Rape was a common crime on Virginia slave plantations, but slave women had no protections under colonial law. In her study of race, gender, and power in 18th-century Virginia, Kathleen M. Brown points out that the rape of a slave woman was not recognized as a crime because of the particular status of the victim. Any crime visited on a female slave was considered an economic crime against her master, who owned the rights to her body, her labor, and any children she might bear. Because her master did not suffer any economic hardship as a result of a rape, there was, at least in the eyes of the law, no crime to report. Slave women suffered under their mistresses, as well. Jealous of the attention their husbands paid to female slaves, plantation mistresses were known to punish, maim, torture, and even murder their domestic slaves. Just as eager to assert their authority over their property as their husbands, mistresses publicly humiliated and brutalized their female slaves to establish and maintain their power within the household.

Slave men were at the mercy of the white overseers who supervised their labor in the field. Fithian recounted the methods of one overseer who boasted of his success in handling slaves:

> He said that whipping of any kind does them no good, for they will laugh at your greatest Severity; But he told us he had invented two things, and by several experiments had proved their success.—For Sulleness, Obstinacy, or Idleness, says he, Take a Negro, strip him, tie him fast to a post; take then a sharp Curry-Comb, & curry him severely til he is well scrap'd; & call a Boy with some dry Hay, and make

the Boy rub him down for several Minutes, then salt him, & unlose him. He will attend to his Business, (said the inhuman Infidel) afterwards!—But savage Cruelty does not exceed His next diabolical Invention—To get a Secret from a Negro, says he, take the following Method—Lay upon your Floor a large thick plank, having a peg about eighteen Inches long, of hard wood, & very Sharp, on the upper end, fixed fast in the plank—then strip the Negro, tie the Cord to a staple in the Ceiling, so as that his foot may just rest on the sharpened Peg, then turn him briskly round, and you would laugh (said our informer) at the Dexterity of the Negro, while he was releiving his Feet on the sharpen'd Peg!

That this overseer found satisfaction in discovering such extreme ways to coerce his slaves into submission suggested that whites were at times powerless to control their slaves. Indeed, the overseer's extraordinary inventiveness might be read as a determined response to the slaves' derisive laughter that challenged and even overturned his authority.

JOHN A. GRIGG

## DOCUMENT: EXCERPT FROM SAMUEL SEWALL'S *THE SELLING OF JOSEPH*, 1700

*One of the earliest antislavery tracts,* The Selling of Joseph *was written by famed Massachusetts legal scholar and judge Samuel Sewall in 1700. Below is an excerpt of the work.* (Sewall, Samuel, *The Selling of Joseph: A Memorial* [Boston: Printed by Bartholomew Green and John Allen, June 24, 1700].)

Forasmuch as Liberty is in real value next unto Life: None ought to part with it themselves, or deprive others of it, but upon most mature Consideration.

The Numerousness of Slaves at this day in the Province, and the Uneasiness of them under their Slavery, hath put many upon thinking whether the Foundation of it be firmly and well laid; so as to sustain the Vast Weight that is built upon it. It is most certain that all Men, as they are the Sons of Adam, are; and have equal Right unto Liberty, and all other outward Comforts of Life. God hath the Earth with all its Commodities unto the Sons of Adam. (Psalms 115:16) And hath made of One Blood, all Nations of Men, for to dwell on all the face of the earth, and hat determined the Times before appointed, and the bounds of their habitation: That they should seek the Lord. Forasmuch then as we are the Offspring of GOD. (Acts 17:26, 27, 29) Now although the Title given by the last ADAM, doth infinitely better Mens Estates, respecting GOD and themselves; and grants them a most beneficial and inviolable Lease under the Broad Seal of Heaven, who were before only Tenants at Will: Yet through the Indulgence of GOD to our First Parents after the Fall, the outward Estate of all and every of the children, remains the same, as to one another. So that Originally, and Naturally, there is no such thing as Slavery. Joseph was rightfully no more a Slave to his Brethren, then they were to him: and they had no more Authority to Sell him, than they had to Slay him. And if they had nothing to do to Sell him; the Ishmaelites bargaining with them, and paying down Twenty pieces of Silver, could not make a Title. Neither could Potiphar have any better Interest in him than the Ishmaelites had. (Genesis 37:20, 27, 28) For he that shall in this case plead Alteration of Property, seems to have forfeited a great part of his own claim to Humanity. There is no proportion between Twenty Pieces of Silver, and LIBERTY. The Commodity it self is the Claimer. If Arabian Gold be imported in any quantities, most are afraid to meddle with it, though they might have it at easy rates; lest if it should have been wrongfully taken from the Owners, it should kindle a fire to the Consumption of their whole estate. 'Tis a pity there should be more Caution used in buying a Horse, or a little lifeless dust; than there is in purchasing Men and Women.... And seeing GOD hath said, He that stealeth a Man and Selleth him, or if he be found in his hand, he shall surely be put to Death. (Exodus 12.16) This Law being of Everlasting Equity, wherein Man Stealing is ranked amongst the most atrocious of Capital Crimes: What louder Cry can there be made of the Celebrated Warning, Caveat Emptor!

And all thing considered, it would conduce more to the Welfare of the Province, to have White Servants for a Term of Years, than to have Slaves for Life. Few can endure to hear of a Negro's being made free; and indeed they can seldom use their freedom well; yet their continual aspiring after the forbidden, renders them Unwilling Servants. And there is such a disparity in their Conditions, Color & Hair, that they can never embody with us, and grow up into orderly Families, to the Peopling of the Land: but still remain in our Body Politic as a kind of extravagant Blood. As many Negro men as there are among us, so many empty places there are in our Train Bands, and the places taken up of Men that might make Husbands for our Daughters. And the Sons and Daughters of New England would become more like Jacob, and Rachel, if this Slavery were thrust quite out of doors. Moreover it is too well known what Temptations Masters are under, to connive at the Fornification of their Slaves; lest they should be obliged to find them Wives, or pay their Fines. It seems to be practically pleaded that they might be Lawless; 'tis thought much of, that the Law should have Satisfaction for their Thefts, and other Immoralities; by which means, Holiness to the Lord, is more rarely engraven upon this sort of Servitude. It is likewise most lamentable to think, how in taking Negros out of Africa, and selling of them here, That which GOD has joined together men to boldly rend asunder; Men from their Country, Husbands from their Wives, Parents from their Children. How horrible is the Uncleanness, Mortality, if not Murder, that the Ships are guilty of that bring great Crowds of these miserable Men, and Women. Methinks, when we are bemoaning the barbarous Usage of our Friends and Kinsfolk in Africa: it might not be unseasonable to enquire whether we are not culpable in forcing the Africans to become Slaves amongst our selves. And it may be a question whether all the Benefit received by Negro Slaves, will balance the Accompt of Cash laid out upon them; and for the Redemption of our own enslaved Friends out of Africa. Besides all the Persons and Estates that have perished there.

Objection 1: These Blackamores are of the Posterity of Ham, and therefore are under the Curse of Slavery. (Genesis 9:25, 26, 27)

Answer: Of all Offices, one would not beg this one. Uncall'd for, to be an Executioner for the Vindictive Wrath of God; the extent and duration of which is to us uncertain. If this ever was a Commission; How do we know but that it is long since out of date? Many have found it to their Cost, that a Prophetical Denunciation of Judgement against a Person or People, would not warrant them to inflict that evil. If it would, Hazael might justify himself in all he did against his Master, and the Israelites, from 2 Kings 8:10, 12.

But it is possible that by cursory reading, this Text may have been mistaken. For Canaan is the Person Cursed three times over, without the mentioning of Ham. Good Expositors suppose the Curse entailed on him, and that this Prophesie was accomplished in the Extirpation of the Canaanites, and in the Servitude of the Gibeonites. *Vide Pareum.* Whereas the Blackamores are not descended of Canaan, but of Cush. (Psalms 68:31) Princes shall come our to Egypt [Mizraim] Ethopia [Cush] shall soon stretch out her hands unto God. Under which Names, all Africa may be comprehended; and the Promised Conversion ought to be prayed for. (Jeremiah 13:23) Can the Ethiopian change his skin? This shows that Black Men are the Posterity of Cush: who time out of mind have been distinguished by their Colour....

Objection 2: The Nigers are brought out of a pagan country, into places where the Gospel is Preached.

Answer: Evil must not be done, that good may come of it. The extraordinary and comprehensive Benefit accruing to the Church of God, and to Joseph personally, did not rectify his brethrens Sale of him.

Objection 3: The Africans have Wars with one another: our Ships bring lawful Captives taken in those Wars.

Answer: For ought is known, their Wars are much such as were between Jacob's Sons and their brother Joseph. If they be between Town and Town; Provincial, or National: Every War is upon one side Unjust. As Unlawful War can't make lawful Captives. And by Receiving, we are in danger to promote, and partake in their Barbarous Cruelties. I am sure, if some Gentlemen should go down to the Brewsters to take the Air and Fish: And a stronger party from Hull should Surprise them, and Sell them for Slaves to a Ship outward bound: they would think themselves unjustly dealt with; both by Sellers and Buyers. And yet 'tis to be feared, we have no other kind of Title to our Nigers. Therefore all things whatsoever ye would that men should do to you, do ye even so to them: for this is the Law and the Prophets. (Matthew 7:12)

Objection 4: Abraham had servants bought with his Money, and born in his House.

Answer: Until the Circumstances of Abraham's purchase be recorded, no Argument can be drawn from it. In the mean time, Charity obliges us to conclude, that He knew it was lawful and good.

It is Observable that the Israelites were strictly forbidden the buying, or selling of one another for Slaves. (Leviticus 25:39, 46. Jeremiah 34.8–22) And GOD gauges His Blessing in lieu of any loss they might conceive they suffered thereby. (Deuteronomy 15:18) And since the partition Wall is broken down, inordinate Self love should likewise be demolished. GOD expects that Christians should be of a more Ingenuous and benign frame of spirit.

Christians should carry it to all the World, as the Israelites were to carry it one towards another. And for men obstinately to persist in holding their Neighbours and Brethren under the Rigor of perpetual Bondage, seems to be no proper way of gaining Assurance that God has given them Spiritual Freedom. Our Blessed Saviour has altered the Measures of the Ancient Love-Song, and set it to a most Excellent New Tune, which all ought to be ambitious of Learning. (Matthew 5:43, 44. John 13:34) These Ethiopians, as black as they are; seeing they are the Sons and Daughters of the First Adam, the Brethren and Sister of the Last ADAM, and the Offspring of GOD; They ought to be treated with Respect agreeable....

# 8

# Religious Toleration in English North America, 1636–1701

## INTRODUCTION

At the start of the 16th century, the Roman Catholic or Latin Christian Church dominated Europe in much the same manner that it had done so for hundreds of years. This is not to say that the Church's rule had gone unchallenged. During the earlier centuries, barbarians and non-Christians such as the Muslims had repeatedly threatened its very existence. Later, secular figures, including powerful feudal princes and medieval kings, unsuccessfully sought to bring the Church under their control. One of the best-known examples featured the ambitious but incompetent English king John I (r. 1199–1216), whose challenge to the papacy brought about his excommunication. Even more damaging to John's aspirations, the Church placed England under an interdict, an order denying English Christians the sacraments and solemn services including baptism, marriage, and last rites. Fearing for their souls, English people everywhere blamed the king. Ultimately, John relented and swore allegiance to the pope as his liege lord.

However, with Martin Luther's 1517 rebellion, the Church's primacy came to an abrupt end. Luther, a German monk become a professor of theology, cited massive corruption within the Church's leadership and demanded a thorough reform. When this was not forthcoming, Luther broke with Rome, an act that initiated the Protestant Reformation that shattered Western Europe's Christian unity and ended the undisputed sway of the Roman Catholic Church.

Beyond Luther's quest for moral purity, there were many secular factors that explained the Reformation's initial success. In the case of England, the Reformation had virtually nothing to do with morality or theology and everything to do with dynastic continuity, power, and national stability. The Tudor dynasty had forcibly seized the throne in 1485. While the Tudors were not common folk, clearly they were usurpers, and the question of their legitimacy always loomed large in their minds. The first Tudor, Henry VII, ruled wisely and frugally. He left to his son, Henry VIII, a full treasury and a fairly tranquil and united kingdom.

Henry VIII, who ruled from 1509 until his death in 1547, was most certainly not the buffoon that one sometimes encounters on movie screens. He was an intelligent and thoughtful if at times unruly and boisterous monarch. Nevertheless, he could be ruthless and forceful when the occasion demanded. He also possessed a personality that was larger than life. Henry, the father of the Reformation in England, remained committed to Roman Catholic theology and ritual throughout his life. In fact, Pope Leo X bestowed upon him the honorific Defender of the Faith for a 1520 religious tract in which the king condemned Luther's theology.

However, Henry was increasingly desperate for a male heir in order to avoid the chaos that would inevitably follow if he died without a son. While he and his wife of many years, Catherine of Aragon, had produced numerous children, only one, a girl named Mary, survived. Thus, Henry petitioned Pope Clement VII for an annulment or divorce. Because Catherine was the aunt of Holy Roman emperor Charles V and because Charles V had come to dominate papal affairs and opposed the annulment, Clement refused Henry's request. At this juncture, Henry took matters into his own hands. Using a pliant Parliament as his vehicle, over several years he separated England from papal lordship, naming himself "Supreme Head" of the Church in England. However, in terms of ritual and dogma, this Church of England remained indistinguishable from the Roman Catholic Church.

Throughout the remainder of the 16th century, a knotty problem confronted England's rulers: how to pacify those Englishmen who continued loyal to Rome while simultaneously retaining the support of the growing number of English people who increasingly embraced the more austere versions of Protestantism emanating from continental Europe. During the latter part of the century, Henry's second surviving daughter, ruling as Queen Elizabeth I, seemed to hit upon a workable resolution of the dilemma. In the Thirty-Nine Articles (1563), Elizabeth reaffirmed the fundamental rules governing the Church of England. Purposefully, she left them so imprecise and ambiguous that virtually all of England could find a home in the national church. Only the irreconcilables, Roman Catholic and Protestant alike, rejected this Elizabethan Compromise. Insignificant at first, the irreconcilables grew into a major force during the 17th century.

Among the most resolute of the irreconcilables were the Puritans, an English version of the stern continental Calvinists who sought to purify the Anglican Church of its Roman Catholic features. During the 17th century, Puritan dissatisfaction with the Elizabethan Compromise, which they saw as too conciliatory to Roman Catholicism, only increased. Ultimately, this led to civil war and the execution of Charles I in 1649. Subsequently, the religious issue helped to unseat a second monarch, James II, during the Glorious Revolution of 1688–1689. However, well before the outbreak of civil war in 1642, some Puritans—despairing of their prospects of success in England—looked across the Atlantic Ocean to North America. In 1629, the Crown granted a royal charter to a group of prosperous Puritans who intended to plant a colony in New England where they might practice their version of Christianity unimpeded. Within a decade, this Massachusetts Bay Company transported more than 20,000 people from England to New England. Radiating out from Boston, which was founded in 1630, the Puritans quickly came to dominate the landscape as far as the eye could see and beyond.

The self-proclaimed "saints" who ruled over the Massachusetts Bay Colony were hardly a tolerant lot. Firmly believing that God had selected them for salvation while damning all others, the Calvinist Puritans imposed their ideas and ideals on all the colonists despite the fact that they constituted only a minority. However, in 1631, the arrival of Roger Williams challenged the Puritan monopoly. By all accounts, Williams was a bright, energetic, and exceptionally likable man. He was also a Separatist, that is, a member of a religious movement very similar to Puritanism except in its conviction that the Church of England was beyond reform, or purification. Williams preached his beliefs from the pulpit of his church in Salem.

The views articulated by Williams soon brought him into conflict with the colony's power brokers, including its leader, the respected John Winthrop. Among other things, Williams objected to the Puritan habit of seizing Indian land rather than bargaining in good faith with the Native Americans. Most important, perhaps, he quarreled with the colony's leadership over the issue of enfranchisement. The complexities of this argument, rooted in the murky mysteries of Calvinistic predestination thought, need not detain us. However, the practical consequences of Williams's ideas would have been to end absolute Puritan control over the affairs of the colony. More obliquely, based on his interpretation of Calvinist doctrine, Williams was groping his way toward the very radical concepts of separation of church and state and religious toleration.

The Puritan leaders rejected Williams's argument and, their patience at an end, prepared to return him to England. Williams was warned of this likelihood by Winthrop himself, who continued to respect Williams while disagreeing with him on almost every issue. Consequently, Williams and his supporters fled Massachusetts in 1635. After a harsh winter with the Indians, the following year they founded the town of Providence in what would become Rhode Island. Several years later, Williams returned to England, where he secured formal recognition for his settlement from the Puritan dominated Parliament. At that time, he wrote in favor of religious toleration and indicated that this principle would prevail in Rhode Island.

Massachusetts's Puritans despised Williams's colony, calling it "the sewer of New England." However, Rhode Island served a practical purpose for the Puritans as a dumping ground for malcontents and religious radicals, such as Anne Hutchinson, who challenged their authority. While Rhode Island survived as a haven for those who marched to the beat of a different drummer, it never really prospered. Only 7,000 people lived there at the opening of the 18th century.

Almost 30 years after Williams founded his colony, another major step toward religious toleration was taken. With royal power restored in England, in 1663 John Clarke, one of Rhode Island's most important figures, returned to London, where he persuaded King Charles II to confirm the Parliamentary charter issued in 1644. This time, the charter explicitly endorsed freedom of conscience and guaranteed against harassment or punishment attributable to one's religious beliefs.

If the Puritans were Protestants who would not reconcile themselves with the Elizabethan Compromise, the same could be said of unbending English Catholics. Such irreconcilable Catholics were relatively few in number; however, they carried disproportionate weight, since many were wealthy and influential aristocrats. Moreover, with Elizabeth's death, in 1603, the Scottish Stuarts inherited the throne of England. Both James I (1603–1625) and Charles I (1625–1649), if not professing Roman Catholics, were sympathetic to the cause. However, the tide was running against Catholicism in England. The civil war (1642–1649) dethroned and executed Charles, and the victorious Puritans led by Oliver Cromwell held sway until the restoration of the monarchy in 1660. The new Stuart king, Charles II (1660–1685), while a Catholic himself, was wise enough to downplay the religious issue, although his brother and successor, James II (1685–1688), flaunted his Catholicism and, as a consequence, lost his throne.

In part, the quest to find a refuge for England's Roman Catholics led Charles I to grant a proprietary colony to the Calvert family, the Lords Baltimore, in 1632. George Calvert, a wealthy landowner and high government official under James I, had converted to Catholicism in 1624. His son, Cecilius or Cecil, oversaw the establishment of the colony, named Maryland in honor of Charles's wife, Henrietta Maria. The land grant covered 10 million acres on the northern shores of the Chesapeake Bay. The first settlement, St. Mary's, was established in 1634; however, the town of Baltimore, further north on the Bay, eventually became the colony's hub.

Calvert specifically invited Catholics to settle there, and he sent Jesuit priests with the first colonists. However, he also allowed Protestants to settle, and almost from the beginning they outnumbered the Catholics. Despite their minority status, Roman Catholic settlers initially dominated the colony. Nevertheless, their primacy was short-lived as the majority Protestants soon gained the upper hand in the colony's House of Delegates. Fearing for his co-religionists, in 1649 Cecil approved the Act of Toleration that called for religious toleration for almost all Christian faiths. Although Puritanical Protestants gained control of the colony and repealed the Act in 1654, it was reinstated several years later.

This formal declaration of religious toleration was not a sweeping one; Jews and freethinkers, or atheists, were excluded. Nevertheless, the Act provided that no Christian could "...be any wais troubled, molested, or discountenanced for or in respect of his or her religion nor in the free exercise thereof."

In addition to irreconcilables such as Puritans, Separatists, and Roman Catholics, 17th-century England witnessed the rise of several religiously oriented sects that defied the norm. These included the communistic Diggers and the Fifth Monarchy Men, who believed that the end of the world was nigh. The Society of Friends, or Quakers, also fit this description. They rejected all earthly authority in both political and religious matters, proclaiming instead that the light of God resided in each individual. That being the case, hierarchy—both religious and political—should play no role in a person's life. Furthermore, the Quakers—called Quakers because they tended to shake when filled with the spirit of God during their religious services—were pacifists, treated women equally, and adopted a generally egalitarian attitude at a time of great social stratification. These exceptionally radical ideas for the time earned the Quakers both a growing number of adherents and the wrath of the established church and state, which did not hesitate to persecute these evident misfits.

William Penn was a Quaker, but an unusual one in that he came from the English aristocracy and his family was well connected at court during the reign of Charles II (most Quakers were poor and undistinguished). At least in part to establish a refuge for his coreligionists and to create a Quaker vision of an earthly paradise, in 1681 Penn secured a grant of several million acres from Charles II. Charles, who was no friend of the Quakers, issued this grant in order to pay off a debt of gratitude owed to Penn's father and, possibly, to rid his kingdom of yet another group of religious malcontents.

After receiving the grant, Penn went immediately to work, advertising his colony in both England and continental Europe as an ideal place to migrate, especially for those who were Quakers or held similar beliefs. In fact, he called his vision a "Holy Experiment." Certainly, Penn did not grossly exaggerate his colony's earthly potential. With good farmland and access to the Atlantic Ocean, Pennsylvania, or Penn's Woods, showed great promise that it quickly fulfilled. When Penn first arrived in his colony, in 1682, there were already 4,000 settlers, and by 1720 Philadelphia, the city of brotherly love, boasted a population of 10,000, well on its way to becoming the largest city in the 13 colonies.

In governing Pennsylvania, Penn encountered numerous difficulties that ultimately proved insurmountable. However, Penn succeeded in creating a haven of religious toleration. His greatest triumph in his quest for religious toleration was his Frame of Government, which he drafted in 1682. Although a disaster from a political perspective because of its contradictory and ambiguous nature, the Frame of Government provided for unimpeded freedom of conscience and the right to worship as one saw fit. Many of Penn's adversaries were Quakers themselves; however, as much as they opposed Penn politically and economically, they remained true to their Quaker belief in religious toleration. Although these men forced many changes in the Frame of Government and re-placed it altogether in 1701 with the Charter of Liberties, they allowed the principle of religious toleration to remain untouched and in the process made Pennsylvania a sanc-tuary for practitioners of all religions, including Judaism.

## INTERPRETIVE ESSAY

TIMOTHY L. WOOD

In 1802, President Thomas Jefferson penned the following famous words to the Dan-bury Baptist Association in Connecticut:

> Believing with you that religion is a matter which lies solely between Man and his God, that he owes account to none other for his faith or his worship, that the legiti-mate powers of government reach actions only, and not opinions, I contemplate with sovereign reverence that act of the whole American people which declared that their legislature should "make no law respecting an establishment of religion, or prohibiting the free exercise thereof," thus building a wall of separation between Church and State.

However, the concept of religious freedom in America did not originate with Jef-ferson, or even with the First Amendment. Instead, the first American experiments in religious liberty date back to the colonial period and were products of the religious tur-moil that racked England and its colonies during the 17th century. Founded by religious minorities that faced persecution in both Europe and America, the colonies of Rhode Island, Maryland, and Pennsylvania became three of the most important English out-posts in America to embrace the principles of freedom of conscience and the separation of church and state.

Since the United States has not had any type of religious establishment since the early 19th century, many Americans are unfamiliar with the concept. An established church (also known as a state or national church) is one that is financially supported by the government through taxation. During the 1600s, that financial support was fre-quently coupled with a willingness to use the legal and judicial mechanisms of the state to enforce moral and religious law. For instance, the government might require people to observe the Sabbath or criminalize certain types of sexual behavior. Sometimes people were punished by the state for holding "heretical" beliefs contrary to the official teachings of the church. In return, the church lent its moral authority to the state by promoting ethical behavior, public order, good citizenship, obedience to the law, and loyalty to the nation and its rulers.

Certainly, the concept of the church and the state working in tandem in religious matters did not originate in the American colonies. Since the time of the Roman emperors Constantine and Theodosius, the Christian church had enjoyed the patronage of secular government. Once the Reformation commenced in 1517, the idea of the church and state sharing jurisdiction in both the spiritual and secular realms was quickly encoded into Protestant doctrine and its understanding of scripture by such major reformers as Martin Luther and John Calvin.

That interplay between politics and religion played a huge role in the formation of the Church of England. Unable to produce a male heir with his wife Catherine of Aragon, England's King Henry VIII petitioned Pope Clement VII for an annulment dissolving the marriage. When Henry's petition was denied, he proclaimed himself head of the Church of England and officially severed ties with the Roman Catholic Church in 1534. Taking advantage of the opportunity that this religious realignment presented, Henry began liquidating the property of the Catholic Church and seizing its English assets, all the while punishing government officials who refused to recognize his new role as head of the national church. Under Henry's daughter, Queen Elizabeth I, the Church of England continued to be a politically savvy institution, seeking the wide middle ground between Catholicism and Protestantism to ensure that most English people were theologically comfortable within its domain (and thus loyal to the monarch that controlled it).

Indeed, the alliance between church and state that characterized European politics and religion in the 17th century became the template for colonial American society. The first three permanent English colonies founded in America featured a religious establishment. Virginia (1607) established the Church of England, while the governments of Plymouth (1620) and Massachusetts Bay (1630) both supported the Congregationalist Church.

However, out of the religious establishments of colonial America there emerged an important reaction to the principle of church-state union. In several of the North American colonies founded by England during the 17th century, the idea of religious liberty and the separation of church and state prevailed. By examining the development of Rhode Island, Maryland, and Pennsylvania, one can begin to appreciate how radical that idea was during the 1600s and how it eventually grew into one of the bedrock principles of the American political system.

The figure most responsible for bringing religious freedom to what would become the colony of Rhode Island was Roger Williams. Like many of the architects of religious liberty in colonial America, Williams hailed from a persecuted religious sect. In this case, Williams was a Separatist. Like the Puritans, the Separatists adhered to a Calvinistic theology that viewed salvation as an act of divine predestination. Like the Puritans, Separatists were suspicious of ritual and ceremony within the church and advocated simplicity in worship. Like the Puritans, the Separatists believed that no ecclesiastical authority existed beyond the local church; church hierarchies composed of bishops and archbishops were, in their view, unbiblical. However, one difference remained between the two groups. While Puritans regarded the Church of England as a genuine church in need of reform, Separatists believed that the Church of England had become irredeemably corrupt and that true Christians were duty bound to renounce and leave it. Remaining even technically in fellowship with England's established church threatened the spiritual purity of the various Separatist fellowships.

Williams first arrived in the Massachusetts Bay Colony in 1631. Although the colony's leaders were happy to see him at first, it soon became apparent that Williams's Separatism did not sit well with the Puritan leadership. Williams soon began to preach that the colony's churches must formally and publicly condemn the Church of England for its sins and sever all ties with the mother church. This offended many Puritans who still hoped that the Church of England might be redeemed and that their efforts in America might even spearhead the needed reformation.

Williams's concern for purity within the church eventually led him to an even more radical set of opinions regarding religious freedom and the need for a divorce between church and state. In later years, when Americans like Thomas Jefferson argued for the separation of church and state, their main concern was that hidden religious agendas might taint the government. But for Williams, the separation of church and state was about safeguarding the spiritual purity of the church from the worldliness inherent in politics. The only pure church was a completely voluntary one free from coercion. Williams's political opponents were apt to argue that laws making people attend church were a commonsense measure that improved life in the colony by exposing citizens to Christian morality. The Rhode Island founder begged to differ. Laws that forced people to participate in religious exercises against their will actually increased the amount of evil within that society because it forced men and women into the sin of hypocrisy.

By 1635, Williams's religious views led to his expulsion from the Massachusetts Bay Colony. Early in 1636, he made his way south to the Narragansett Bay and founded the settlement of Providence, the first town in what would become the colony of Rhode Island. Once in Providence, Williams had the opportunity to begin building a society from scratch. As Rhode Island grew up around him, Williams was meticulous in insisting that this new colony provide freedom of religion and the complete separation of church and state. In fact, by 1637 the town of Providence had encoded into law the belief that "wee agree, as formerly hath been the liberties of the town, so still, to hold forth liberty of Conscience."

However, this was not always an easy task. Religious persecution would now have to be opposed by force of law. For instance, in 1637, Providence resident Joshua Verin was convicted of "breach-of a covenant for restraining liberty of conscience" and was sentenced to "be withheld from the libertie of voting till he shall declare the contrarie." However, these pioneering efforts to define the boundaries of religious freedom often led to confusion and controversy. What if one's religion demanded that its teachings be imposed on others? Concerning the Verin case, Massachusetts governor John Winthrop remarked in his journal as follows:

> At Providence…Williams and the rest did make an order, that no man should be molested for his conscience, now men's wives, and children, and servants,

Roger Williams lands at Providence Plantation in 1636 and is greeted by members of the Narragansett tribe. (Courtesy of the Library of Congress.)

claimed liberty hereby to go to all religious meetings ...; and because one Verin refused to let his wife go to Mr. Williams...they required to have him censured. But there stood up one Arnold...telling them that, when he consented to that order, he never intended it should extend to the breach of any ordinance of God, such as the subjugation of wives to their husbands..., and gave divers solid reasons against it....In conclusion, when they would have censured Verin, Arnold told them, that it was against their own order, for Verin did that he did out of conscience: and their order was that no man should be censured for his conscience.

In the end, episodes like the Joshua Verin case clarified that religious freedom would be defined individually, not collectively. Religious freedom would come to be understood as the right of individuals to follow their own religious beliefs, rather than the freedom of religious groups to engage in coercive activities.

In the meantime, the towns that sprang up around Providence seemed determined to chart their own destiny. The town of Portsmouth, on Aquidneck Island, founded by fellow Massachusetts exiles Anne and William Hutchinson and the ambitious merchant William Coddington, at first appeared bent on re-creating some version of Massachusetts's religious establishment. However, the Hutchinsons and Coddington soon had a falling out, and in 1639 Coddington left Portsmouth and founded a new settlement at Newport. Two years later, Portsmouth and Newport had reunited under Coddington's leadership, this time proclaiming a policy of religious freedom.

The arrival, in 1637, of Samuel Gorton complicated matters even further. A "heretic" by most standards of the 17th century, Gorton rejected organized forms of religion, believed in the divinity of humankind, and for years had been the object of unrelenting persecution because of his beliefs. Expelled from Massachusetts Bay, Gorton eventually landed in Portsmouth, although he refused to recognize the legitimacy of that town's government since it was not officially chartered by the king. He eventually obtained the permission of the Crown to settle in what would become Warwick and created a government there based on the principles of religious toleration.

The diversity of early Rhode Island often made the colony difficult to govern. Although most Rhode Islanders had come to embrace the concept of religious liberty, that freedom alone was not enough to create harmony among the colony's contentious citizens. Some residents convinced themselves that their freedom from religious coercion also meant that they were not bound by any political authority, either. In January 1655, an exasperated Williams responded as follows to those who held this position:

> That I ever should speak or write a tittle, that tends to such an infinite liberty of conscience, is a mistake, and which I have ever disclaimed and abhorred. To prevent such mistakes, I shall at present only propose this case: There goes many a ship to sea, with many hundred souls in one ship, whose weal and woe is common, and is a true picture of a commonwealth....[S]ometimes...both papists and protestants, Jews and Turks, may be embarked in one ship; upon which I affirm, that all the liberty of conscience, that I ever pleaded for, turns upon these two hinges—that none of the papists, protestants, Jews, or Turks, be forced to come to the ship's prayers or worship, nor compelled from their own particular prayers or worship, if they practice any. I further add, that I never denied, that notwithstanding this liberty, the commander of this ship ought to command the ship's course, yea, and also command that justice, peace, and sobriety, be kept and practiced, both among the seamen and the passengers. If any of the seamen refuse to perform their services, or passengers to pay their freight; if any refuse to help, in person or purse, toward the common charge or defence [*sic*]; if any refuse to obey the common laws and orders of the ship, concerning their common peace and preservation; if any shall mutiny and rise up against their commanders and officers; if any should preach or write that there ought to be no commanders and officers, because all are equal in Christ, therefore no masters nor officers, no laws nor orders, no corrections nor punishments;—I say...in such cases...the commander may judge, resist, compel, and punish such transgressors, according to their deserts and merits.

Such social chaos was exactly what those who favored a strong church-state alliance would have predicted within a society that practiced religious freedom. But Williams insisted that religious liberty did not imply anarchy and worked diligently to prove that a just and effective civil government could function in a society based on religious toleration.

By the 1640s, Williams had become increasingly concerned that the autonomous nature of the Rhode Island settlements left them vulnerable to outside interference. Indeed, over the years, such neighbors as Massachusetts Bay and Connecticut had frequently demonstrated a willingness to violate Rhode Island's territorial integrity. In 1643, Williams traveled back to England, and the following year the English government formally recognized what would become the colony of Rhode Island and Providence Plantations, with Williams himself serving as president of the colony from 1654 until 1657. However, an official royal charter signed by the king would elude them until 1663, when John Clarke, one of the colony's leading citizens, convinced King Charles II to affix his name to a new governing document. Tellingly, Rhode Island's new charter stipulated that "a most flourishing civil state may stand and best be maintained...with a full liberty in religious concernments."

The second major experiment in religious freedom in 17th-century America was the colony of Maryland. Like Rhode Island, Maryland's commitment to religious liberty sprang from its founder's own experience with religious dissent—in this case Roman Catholicism. There can be little doubt that Catholics were even less popular than Puritans or Separatists in England during the early 1600s. After the English Reformation and Henry VIII's official departure from the Catholic fold, refusal to renounce one's allegiance to the pope and acknowledge the English monarch as head of the church was viewed as treason. Adherence to the old faith dangerously divided the loyalty of English Catholics, since during the 1600s the pope was not only a spiritual leader but also a foreign prince who ruled a vast kingdom in central Italy. In the years after the Reformation, English society was gripped by the fear that the island's Catholic population owed its ultimate allegiance to the pope and systematically sought to undermine the nation's legitimate government in London. Historian Ronald Dufour provided the following statistics:

There were about fifty thousand Catholics in England, and during the late Elizabethan period, they had suffered persecution, torture, and death. Between 1588 and 1603, sixty-one priests, forty-seven laymen, and two women were executed. Some Jesuits had been hung, drawn, and quartered, having been convicted of high treason simply by virtue of their being Catholic. Catholics who refused to declare their allegiance to the Church of England were fined twenty pounds a month or had most of their property confiscated.

Despite the hazards of being a Catholic in England during the 17th century, some members of the English aristocracy continued to be faithful to the Roman Church. Such was the case with George Calvert, first Baron of Baltimore. Calvert was a former member of the House of Commons who was serving as King James I's secretary of state in 1624 when he announced that he had converted to the Catholic faith. Although his decision required his departure from government service, Calvert nonetheless retained the king's goodwill and was given his title of nobility as he left the royal court.

Colonization also interested Calvert. During an earlier sojourn in America, Calvert had been impressed by the living conditions in Virginia. Cashing in on any favor he might still have at court, he soon requested a colonial charter in the region immediately north of Virginia. Although George Calvert died in 1632, later that year King Charles I finally granted a charter for Maryland to his son Cecilius, the second Lord Baltimore. By now, Cecilius had begun to envision Maryland as a place of refuge for England's persecuted Catholic population. By 1634, Cecilius had named his younger brother, Leonard Calvert, governor of Maryland, and the first group of settlers landed in the Chesapeake.

In religious matters, the Calverts walked a fine line in Maryland. The colonial charter stipulated that all churches founded in the colony be in compliance with English law, so the establishment of the Catholic Church was out of the question. Moreover, Catholic migration to the colony tended to be lighter than expected, meaning that Roman Catholics would end up being a minority once again, thus reinforcing the need for some system of religious coexistence in Maryland. As historian John D. Krugler observed:

> Cecil Calvert rejected the beliefs that his colonists had to profess his religious faith and that he had to control their religious practices....His novel concept that religion was a private matter, free from government assistance or restraint, marked a significant break with the dogmas of the age. When he removed the prop of religious uniformity, which contemporary rulers considered essential for political stability, he was calling on the immigrants to behave in radically different ways. Their culture distrusted religious differences, but he urged them to put their differences aside, to act with Christian charity toward one another, and to prosper.

Consequently, in 1649 the colonial legislature passed a law guaranteeing limited religious freedom within Maryland's borders, stating that no individual "professing to believe in Jesus Christ, shall from henceforth bee any waies troubled, Molested, or discountenanced for or in respect of his or her religion nor in the free exercise thereof." However, the leaders of Maryland still viewed religious toleration strictly in Christian terms. Residents must confess belief in the Trinity or face the death penalty. Blasphemy against the Virgin Mary or the saints, failure to observe the Sabbath, or giving anybody an unflattering nickname ("heretic, schismatic, idolater, Puritan") because of their religion earned a lesser punishment. In fact, in 1638, when the non-Catholic servants of a Jesuit priest named William Lewis complained that their master refused to allow them to read any form of Protestant literature, Lewis was found guilty of disturbing the peace. He was fined five hundred pounds of tobacco and ordered to refrain from such provocative behavior in the future. As Krugler remarked:

> Once the [Lewis] dispute became public, the government treated it seriously. Maryland authorities moved quickly to prevent the social fabric from being torn apart by religious dissension, much as Massachusetts officials had done in the [case] of Roger Williams....But the leaders of the Maryland colony added a curious twist. In this instance the dominant element took action against one of its own who had violated the principles enunciated by Baltimore.

But even Maryland's constrained view of religious toleration remained a contentious idea. In 1654, in the aftermath of Parliament's victory in the English Civil War, delegates from England appeared in the capital announcing that a new Puritan government under the leadership of William Fuller was being imposed on the colony by order of London. Under this new regime, practice of the Roman Catholic faith would be illegal.

This takeover of the colony would ultimately lead to bloodshed. Upon hearing of the new government that had supplanted his family's proprietary claims, Leonard Calvert appealed to England's new Puritan ruler, Oliver Cromwell, who verified the Calvert family's control over Maryland. In 1655, Calvert sent an army under the command of William Stone back to Maryland to challenge Fuller and the Puritan cabal that controlled the colony. In March 1655, on the banks of the Severn River, Calvert's forces suffered a humiliating defeat. Only through negotiations would the Calvert family be able to regain any of its lost influence. In 1657, both parties crafted a compromise in which Lord Baltimore's ownership of the colony and his system of religious toleration was restored in exchange for some land concessions to the Protestant party.

However, the Calverts' system of religious toleration began to collapse once and for all in 1689. Maryland's disgruntled Protestant population once again rebelled, and this time its plea for vast political and religious change in Maryland found a receptive audience with the newly crowned English monarchs, King William III and Queen Mary II. By 1692, Cecilius's son, Charles Calvert, the third Lord Baltimore, had lost his claim to his father's New World dominion, and Maryland officially became a royal colony. Along with these political changes came the formal establishment of the Church of England. By 1704, Maryland authorities had passed a series of laws restricting Catholic worship and education. Although in 1715 the colony would be returned to the fourth Lord Baltimore, Benedict Leonard Calvert, the price was his conversion to the Church of England. Involvement in the Maryland project now carried certain religious expectations. By the beginning of the 18th century, religious freedom in colonial Maryland was dead.

Pennsylvania, founded in 1682 by William Penn, stands as a third American prototype of a society based upon religious freedom. It is impossible to understand Pennsylvania's adherence to the principles of religious liberty without delving into Penn's own spiritual background. Penn was a member of a Christian movement known as Quakerism (more formally, the Religious Society of Friends). Quakerism first emerged in England during the 17th century under the leadership of an itinerant preacher named George Fox (1624–1691). From its birth, it was a deeply countercultural movement that stressed presence of the inner light of Christ within the believer. As historian Thomas D. Hamm described it, early Quakers believed that

> all people had within them a certain measure of the Light of Christ. If they heeded it, that Inward Light would show them their sinful conditions and their need for Christ, and would lead them to salvation. But if they ignored it or failed to heed its admonitions, they would be lost and ultimately damned.

From that theological wellspring flowed a number of tenets that did not endear Quakers to the greater part of the population of 17th-century England. First of all, Quakers practiced pacifism, viewing Jesus as a man of peace and refusing to take up arms in defense of king and country. Nor would they agree to swear any oath, even when called upon to do so by the state. Next, because of the intense persecution that they had endured because of their faith, Quakers were advocates of religious toleration.

Furthermore, they defied social convention by stressing the spiritual equality of men and women and often recognized the divine calling of women who felt inspired to take positions of leadership within their church. Finally, Quakers exhibited a steadfast refusal to acknowledge the social superiority of the upper classes, insisting on the equality of all people in the eyes of God. As historians T. H. Breen and Timothy Hall quipped, this conviction "generally annoyed people of rank and achievement." Such beliefs made early Friends the object of much derision and persecution in the Old World.

As a young man, William Penn found himself drawn to the teachings of Quakerism (much to the horror of his respectable family). Indeed, he found himself imprisoned multiple times due to his insistence on preaching and writing about the Quaker religion. Like Cecilius Calvert before him, Penn became convinced that America might offer a safe haven for his embattled coreligionists. Although he had become something of a pariah, his father had been a prominent naval officer and had helped restore King Charles II to the throne in 1660. Consequently, in order to repay his debt to Penn's father, in March 1681 the king granted Penn a vast tract of real estate in the New World amounting to about 600,000 square miles—the future Pennsylvania.

The following year, Penn and the first settlers arrived in America. In accordance with his religious convictions, Penn made no attempt to grant the Society of Friends any privileged position within the government of this new colony—although wealthy Quakers did eventually come to dominate the colony's political institutions. Instead, he created yet another society based on the principle of religious freedom for almost all people. (However, like the Calverts, Penn had his limits; atheists and nonbelievers were still considered persona non grata in colonial Pennsylvania). As historian Melvin B. Endy remarked, Penn's

> basic contention . . . was his belief that a man's religious life was authentic only when he willingly and spontaneously granted his allegiance to God on the basis of understanding and conviction and without the base motives introduced by coercion.
>
> . . . Although he often argued for toleration by holding that religious beliefs had nothing to do with political and socio-economic matters, Penn was hardly a secularizer. He did not believe that religion should . . . be kept out of public life or that political judgments suffered when religious considerations influenced them. He believed, rather, that religion was the best bond of human society. . . . But such uniformity had to come by consent, not constraint.

Unlike Maryland, where religious freedom remained a controversial proposition, Pennsylvania thrived under the system. The principle of religious toleration allowed Penn to recruit settlers from all across Europe, with the new immigrants being secure in the knowledge that they would not face persecution for their faith. Penn's Quaker humility also served him well in dealing with Native Americans. Whereas most colonies had an adversarial relationship with the Indians that lived within their borders, Penn viewed the natives as fully human, proper objects of Christian love, and worthy of honest and fair treatment. Thus, he went out of his way to pay a fair price for the land that the settlers were soon to occupy. As he put it, "the king of the Country where I live, hath given me a great Province, but I desire to enjoy it with [the Delaware Indians] Love and Consent, that we may always be together as Neighbors and friends."

Although Penn was sincere in his adherence to the values of the Society of Friends, the government he established in America retained more than a hint of aristocratic privilege. Penn served as governor by virtue of his role as proprietor, regarded himself as the feudal lord of Pennsylvania and demanded quitrents (annual payments acknowledging a landowner's obligation to a higher authority) from settlers, and did not permit the lower (and larger) house of the bicameral colonial assembly to introduce legislation. As Endy observed:

[Penn's] society, although largely noncoercive, was to combine…consentualism with hierarchical social and even political patterns.… [H]e expected that unanimity would be achieved through the leadership of a responsible elite.… The colony was to be governed by a combination of democracy, aristocracy, and monarchy precisely as England was ruled.

However, the Quaker emphasis on equality and democracy eventually contributed to Penn's loss of day-to-day control over the colony. In 1701, Penn signed the Charter of Privileges, in which he forfeited his right to be involved in the lawmaking process within the colony except through the use of the veto. As proprietor, his only remaining power would be the power to appoint the governor and his advisers. In the end, even Penn could not contain the egalitarian forces that Quakerism unleashed in Pennsylvania.

Religious freedom had become an important theme in America long before the drafting of the First Amendment or Thomas Jefferson's ruminations on the separation of church and state. Rhode Island, Maryland, and Pennsylvania all present different models of how that institution grew in the soil of colonial America. Rhode Island emerged in revolt against the rigid religious establishment of Massachusetts Bay. For Roger Williams, the greatest challenge was to protect freedom of conscience while still maintaining civil order within an extremely unruly society. In Maryland, the Calvert family endeavored to create a refuge for Catholic Christians by severing the link between one's religious life and one's civic responsibilities. However, Maryland's Protestant population never fully bought into Lord Baltimore's vision, and by the 18th century the colony returned to the familiar ideas of an established church and legal restrictions on the activities of Roman Catholics. Finally, in Pennsylvania the ideal of religious freedom quickly took root, creating a diverse and prosperous colony that was nevertheless informally shaped by Quaker beliefs and attitudes. Although those colonies began as three vastly different experiments in religious liberty that—in the short run—seemed to yield three quite different outcomes, ultimately those separate histories converged into an unquestionably "American" perspective on the subject. That outlook would eventually find expression in the opening sentence of the Bill of Rights: "Congress shall make no law respecting an establishment of religion, or prohibiting the free exercise thereof." The intellectual thread that proved to be so radical and controversial for Williams, Penn, and the Calverts had now been woven into the tapestry of a new nation.

## SELECTED BIBLIOGRAPHY

Breen, T. H., and Timothy Hall. *Colonial America in an Atlantic World.* New York: Pearson Longman, 2004. Breen and Hall offer a textbook-style overview of the development of colonial America, emphasizing the connections between the Old World and the New.

Bremer, Francis J. *The Puritan Experiment: New England Society from Bradford to Edwards.* Hanover, NH: University Press of New England, 1995. This book takes a geographic approach to the subject of colonial America, focusing in on the development of the New England colonies, including Rhode Island.

Dufour, Ronald. *Colonial America.* Minneapolis: West Publishing Company, 1994. Probably one of the best and most detailed surveys of colonial American history.

Endy, Melvin B., Jr. *William Penn and Early Quakerism.* Princeton, NJ: Princeton University Press, 1973. This study offers an in-depth look at the thought of William Penn and the ways in which it was reflected in the founding of Pennsylvania.

Gaustad, Edwin S. *Liberty of Conscience: Roger Williams in America.* Grand Rapids, MI: William B. Eerdmans Publishing Company, 1991. This biography of Roger Williams emphasizes the role that the idea of religious freedom played in his life and career.

Hamm, Thomas D. *The Quakers in America.* New York: Columbia University Press, 2003. An excellent overview of American Quakerism penned by one of the most recognized scholars in the field.

James, Sydney V. *John Clarke and His Legacies: Religion and Law in Colonial Rhode Island, 1638–1750.* University Park: The Pennsylvania State University Press, 1999. This study presents a detailed look at the development of the Rhode Island colony through the life of John Clarke, the Baptist leader and close associate of Williams.

Krugler, John D. *English and Catholic: The Lords Baltimore in the Seventeenth Century.* Baltimore: Johns Hopkins University Press, 2004. This monograph examines the development of the Maryland colony through the lens of the Calvert family.

Miller, Perry. *Roger Williams: His Contributions to the American Tradition.* New York: Atheneum, 1953. This book presents an analysis of the thought of Roger Williams by the scholar who became the patriarch of 20th-century Puritan studies.

Morgan, Edmund S. *Roger Williams: The Church and the State.* New York: Harcourt, Brace, and World, 1967. Here Morgan analyzes the origins and development of the Rhode Island founder's view on religious freedom and church-state relations—the major recurring themes of Williams' career.

## CECIL CALVERT (1605–1675)

As the second Lord Baltimore and the first lord proprietor of Maryland from 1632 to 1675, Cecil Calvert played an important role in establishing the foundations of government and society in the British colony of Maryland. He is often called its founder, although he himself never traveled to America. The outstanding achievement of his lifetime was the establishment of a form of government in Maryland where all Christian religious sects were equal before the law.

Calvert was born in 1605 in England. He was son of George Calvert, the first Lord Baltimore. He entered Trinity College, Oxford, in 1621, but there is no record of his graduation. An explanation for this can be found in the fact that Oxford was a university set apart for the Church of England, and Calvert had converted to Catholicism just before he would have graduated. In 1628, he married Lady Anne Arundel, the daughter of Thomas Arundel (Lord of Wardour), a well-known Catholic peer.

Calvert's father had for years campaigned vigorously for a land grant in the Americas from King Charles I. The Maryland charter was granted by the king a few days before George Calvert's death, on April 15, 1632, and so was issued instead to Calvert on June 20, 1632. The charter set the boundaries of Maryland from the Atlantic Ocean along the 40th parallel "unto the true meridian of the first fountain of the river of

Pattowmack," thence along the south bank of the river to a point "when it disembogues" into the Chesapeake Bay, and then eastward along the parallel that runs through Watkin's Point to the Atlantic Ocean. This grant gave Calvert practically free rein to do as he pleased in the colony. Thus, at the age of 26, Calvert became the second Lord Baltimore and the sole lord proprietor of the colony of Maryland.

Because of the poor treatment of Catholics in England at the time, Calvert had a hard time recruiting non-Catholics to take part in the expedition, partly because they did not want to go to the Americas with Catholics and partly because they did not want to be ruled by a Catholic. It took him nearly 18 months to organize an expedition. His two ships, the *Ark* and the *Dove,* left England in November 1633 and reached the colony in March 1634, although Calvert, beset by personal and political enemies, was unable to leave England and join the expedition. In his place, he delegated direct administration to his younger brother, Leonard, who left with the first group of settlers and became the first governor of Maryland.

To guide the colony, Calvert prepared a letter of instructions that Leonard carried with him on the voyage. Among the rules regarding the governing of the colony, he articulated his policy of religious tolerance, instructing each man—when it came to the matter of religion—to "mind his own business." To illustrate his earnestness regarding religious toleration, Calvert dictated that all governors of the colony take an oath to protect religious freedom and promote toleration.

In February 1635, the first legislative assembly of Maryland met in St. Mary's, the capital of the colony. Calvert, however, insisting that only he had the right to propose laws and that the assembly was to act merely as a rubber stamp for such legislation, nullified their acts once they had been transmitted to him in England. No effective legislation was enacted in Maryland until the second session, held at St. Mary's in January 1638. Calvert again nullified the legislation passed by the assembly, and the laws he sent to the colony were subsequently rejected by the assembly in turn. Convinced that the freemen of Maryland were determined that he should not exercise his right to rule and because he wanted to avoid a major confrontation, Calvert yielded the right to initiate legislation to the assembly the following year. In this concession, he had laid the foundation for self-government in Maryland.

In England, civil strife jeopardized the Maryland settlement in the 1640s. King Charles I (and his Catholic wife) had long displayed a degree of religious toleration for Catholics that made many of his Protestant subjects uncomfortable. When civil war erupted in England between Charles and the Protestant-dominated Parliament, Catholicism was a primary source of contention between the two sides. Parliament ultimately prevailed and executed Charles in 1649, establishing in the place of the monarchy a Puritan-dominated military government (known as the Commonwealth and led by Oliver Cromwell).

Throughout this turbulent decade, Calvert faced increasing hostility toward himself and his American colony because of his persistent devotion to Catholicism and religious toleration. In addition, his contact with the colony became disrupted, first by the civil war in England and then by the appearance of Leonard, who traveled to England to consult with Calvert in 1643, leaving the colony in the hands of the lieutenant governor.

In Leonard's absence, the government of Maryland was seized by anti-Catholic rebels, who ran the colonial government for more than three years and ensured that the colony was entirely out of Calvert's hands. After Leonard returned to America, he was able to reclaim control of Maryland by force with the military aid of the governor of Virginia in 1646. In England, despite the ascendancy of Cromwell, Calvert was able to retain his charter to the colony through skillful diplomatic maneuvering.

To calm the situation in Maryland, Calvert appointed a Protestant, William Stone, as governor in 1649 (Leonard had died in 1647 but had appointed a Catholic as his successor). In addition, he presented the Maryland Assembly with the "Act of Toleration" that did not positively affirm religious toleration but made intolerance a crime among Christians. The act was the first legislation in the English-speaking world explicitly granting toleration to all Christians. Unfortunately, the measure served to exacerbate tensions, since the Puritan newcomers (invited by Baltimore to flee persecution from Anglicans in Virginia) were interested only in toleration for themselves.

With Calvert's support in England tenuous, the Puritans managed to gain control of Maryland once again, instituting a regime of religious intolerance, particularly against Catholics. Violence erupted in Maryland as Catholics fought for their rights. After almost a decade of civil war in Maryland, Calvert managed to secure a compromise settlement with the Puritan government in Maryland in 1657. By the terms of the compromise, he was reinstated as proprietor, and he agreed to pardon the Puritan rebels in Maryland. The Puritans, in return, agreed to accept the Act of Toleration.

Although minor disturbances continued in Maryland for several years regarding religious toleration, Calvert secured the support of England's King Charles II (restored to the English throne in 1660), which ensured his control over the colony's government.

With his power once again secure in Maryland, Calvert concentrated on encouraging settlement and peopling the province. He died on November 30, 1675, without ever visiting Maryland, although, roughly 50 years after his death, the colony would found a town (Baltimore) in his family's honor, and the state's flag bears his family crest even today. At the time of his death, Maryland was a prosperous and populous colony, containing settlers employed in agriculture and trade. He was succeeded by his son, Charles Calvert, as lord proprietor of Maryland and the third Lord Baltimore.

JEFFREY M. CHWEIROTH

## ANNE HUTCHINSON (1591–1643)

Anne Hutchinson may indeed be the first figure in American culture in whom dissent becomes associated with female empowerment and, more specifically, with public speaking by a woman. Her opponents accused her of stepping out of her place, encouraging other women to do the same, and circulating her ideas too freely and too publicly. Hutchinson had come to the Massachusetts Bay Colony to secure religious liberty. However, she found that, when her ideas did not match those of the majority, she had no such liberty and instead was banished from the colony.

Wife of William Hutchinson and mother of 15 children, Anne Hutchinson immigrated with her family to the New World in 1634. They joined the Massachusetts Bay Colony at Boston. Once she arrived in the New World, she began to speak publicly of her religious beliefs. At first, she spoke at meetings organized among Boston women to discuss that week's sermon and the Bible; after a while, many leaders of the community began to come to hear her. She believed that people could be saved by complete faith in God, that their faith was more important than their actions. In contrast, the Puritan church espoused a belief in salvation through good deeds or good works. By placing responsibility for a person's actions directly on the person himself, rather than tying the actions to the demands of the church, she caused a great political controversy in the colony. While this was partly due to her voicing her religious beliefs, it was also partly due to her challenge to the traditional subordinate role of women. The accepted belief of the day was that intelligence and understanding was given to men, not to women, so a woman's chief duty as a wife was to her husband and children. Indeed, Puritan minister John Cotton warned her, saying, "Here it be tactful to hold one's tongue."

The Puritans feared that Hutchinson would instigate an outbreak of individualism that would threaten the very foundation of their social order. She supported a covenant of grace theology that ensured that one's salvation was located within oneself. They thought she carried the Puritan conception of grace to such an extreme that it translated into an overall abandonment of any structured church. They also thought she advocated anti-intellectualism, which was taken to indicate the irrelevance of scholarship and of study of the Bible. In essence, they feared she was advocating the abandonment of a Puritan society.

As a result of this controversy, Hutchinson was brought to trial twice—once in civil court in 1637 and then again by the church in 1638. Deputy Governor Thomas Dudley stated that he was "fully persuaded that Mrs. Hutchinson is deluded by the devil." He feared that she would encourage her "hearers to take up arms against their prince and to cut the throats one of another." Cotton at first supported Hutchinson and then turned against her, saying of her, "Your opinions frett like a Grangrene and spread like a Leprosie, and infect farr and near, and will eate out the very Bowells of Religion, and hath soe infected the Churches that God knowes when thay will be cured." The governor of the colony, John Winthrop, was a particularly strong opponent. He made himself attorney general, foreman of the jury, and chief justice at the trial.

Hutchinson was found guilty, excommunicated, and banished from the colony. She and her family moved to Aquidneck, which is now part of Rhode Island. Today, Hutchinson is recognized as a great leader in the cause of religious toleration in America and the advancement of women in society.

## SOCIETY OF FRIENDS (QUAKERS)

The Quakers, or Society of Friends, were adherents of a Protestant religious movement founded in England in the mid-17th century. Standing out from British society, they attracted much persecution and migrated in large numbers to North America, particularly Rhode Island and Pennsylvania.

The Quakers were founded by George Fox in England in the 1650s. Although raised an Anglican, Fox began to preach in 1647 after a spiritual vision inspired him to minister. He called for a profound spiritual renewal within England, supported the prohibition of alcohol, and preached against holidays, sports, and all other activities that diverted attention from the spirit. Fox supported peace, and, when he was imprisoned for his beliefs, he converted his jailer.

The group that arose around Fox professed the belief that Christ provided individuals with an inner light, so that believers could experience personal illumination from God in their daily lives. Followers of Fox became known as Quakers because they reportedly shook when filled with the Holy Spirit. As part of what was considered a radical fringe, the Quakers attracted much persecution in England and the New World. They especially stood apart with their distinctive code of dress and manners and their refusal to observe status distinctions, swear oaths, or pay tithes to the established church. They were helped somewhat by the Toleration Act of 1689, which modified laws against dissenters.

The Quakers had no clergy, so church services consisted of long periods of sitting together in silence, waiting for the Holy Spirit to move someone to speak. Initially, men and women met together for religious services, and women were often moved to speak. By the 18th century, the Friends held segregated meetings, and, from 1737 on, Quakers followed a yearly "Book of Discipline" designed to provide church cohesion and instruct followers in proper behavior.

Rhode Island was an early refuge for Quakers in North America and sheltered William Penn during the 1660s. When Penn received the large tract of land that is now Pennsylvania, it provided Quakers with plenty of land in which to practice religious freedom and from which to gain a comfortable living. Although the Quakers were never an established church or officially linked to the colony's government, the importance of individual Quakers among the early proprietors gave them considerable power in the colonial assembly long after they ceased to be a majority of the population.

Quakers used that power to pursue the abolition of African slavery, to minister to Native American groups in the region, and to pursue peaceful relations. Slave importation to Pennsylvania was outlawed in 1711. In England, Quakers were prominent in antislavery and prison reform campaigns. John Woolman, an influential leader during the first half of the 18th century, preached that war and slavery were inherently evil and that the materialism of non-Quakers showed spiritual degradation. When the French and Indian War began, 21 Friends opposed the payment of taxes in 1755, since their tax revenue went to finance the war. As the American Revolution approached, Quakers again refused to pay taxes or to support the war effort in any way.

During the 19th century, Quakers abandoned the strict code of dress they had previously followed, which helped them assimilate into contemporary society. Their antiwar stance and pacifist commitment further set them apart in the 20th century, however, when they were again seen as radicals.

## ROGER WILLIAMS (1603–1683)

The religious intellectual Roger Williams established the colony of Rhode Island and left a legacy of respect for the principle of religious freedom in America. Williams was born on January 16, 1603, in London, England. A protege of Sir Edward Coke, he attended Charterhouse. After graduating from Pembroke College, Cambridge, England, in 1627, he became an Anglican chaplain. In 1629, he participated in the Puritan conference at Sempringham called to decide whether the Puritans should immigrate to New England. Williams arrived in the Massachusetts Bay Colony in February 1631. Although offered the chance to preach in Salem, he decided that the Puritans were not "separated" enough in their beliefs from the Church of England and settled instead in Plymouth. After only a year in Plymouth, however, he decided that conditions were no better there and accepted a second offer in 1633 to preach in Salem.

In Salem, Williams immediately caused a furor by arguing that the Puritans' Massachusetts Bay royal charter was invalid because the king could not give away land that belonged to the Indians without their consent. He compounded his unpopularity by writing a letter to King Charles I accusing him of being an ally of the Devil. Reprimanded by the Massachusetts General Court, Williams apologized for his actions. He was back before the court in 1635 for his belief that no government had the right to punish people for violating the first four commandments, nor could it administer an oath to a nonbeliever. When he refused to back down from these positions, he was banished from Massachusetts.

In April 1636, the unrepentant Williams decided to found a new colony, Providence, Rhode Island, upon land he secured from the Narragansett Indians. He attracted settlers to his colony by generously distributing land to anyone willing to accept his belief that "no man should be molested for his conscience." Williams's good relations with the Narragansetts even helped the Puritans who had exiled him when he agreed to negotiate an end to the Pequot War in 1637. During the hostilities, the colonists nearly wiped out the Pequot tribe, which had fought back against the continuing takeover of the lands by Europeans.

In 1639, Williams briefly joined the Baptist Church. He quickly left the Baptists, and for the rest of his life he considered himself a "Seeker"—someone who accepted no creed but believed in the fundamental truth of Christianity. To protect his new colony from being crushed by the hostile Puritans or usurped by another colonizer, Williams returned to England in 1642 to secure a royal charter. On the journey, he wrote *A Key into the Language of America* (1643), which illustrated his appreciation for American Indian cultures. In England, he also published *Mr. Cotton's Letter Lately Printed, Examined, and Answered* (1644), in which he rebutted the Puritan clergyman John Cotton's claim that those who encouraged groups of settlers to separate from the New England Puritan colonies threatened the ability of the Puritans to establish a reform church. Williams argued that no government had the right to persecute a man for his religious beliefs.

Williams secured his charter and returned to Providence in March 1644, committed to establishing a democratic government. He was forced to return once again to England in 1651 to defend the validity of his charter against another claimant. He succeeded and, upon his return to Providence, was elected to the first of three terms as president of the colony.

Although Williams had saved the colony from court intrigue, he was unable to prevent the catastrophic Indian uprising known as King Philip's War in 1675. For three years, the Wampanoags, under the leadership of a chief known as King Philip, terrorized some New England towns in retaliation for the taking of their lands. Eventually the Wampanoags, and what power they still wielded, were destroyed. The situation was so desperate that even Williams, now more than 72 years old, shouldered a musket and participated as a militia captain in military maneuvers during the war. The devastation of the conflict wiped out Williams's personal fortune and ended his vision of peaceful coexistence between the European and the Native American cultures.

In his last years, Williams defended the right of Quakers to practice their religion unimpeded in Rhode Island. This did not, however, prevent him from publishing *George Fox Digg'd Out of His Burrowes* in 1676 to illustrate the error of Quaker theology. Williams hoped that the religious fanaticism of the Quakers might reinvigorate interest in Puritan theology. The increasingly secular preoccupations of the inhabitants of New England troubled his deeply religious soul. Williams died on March 15, 1683.

WILLIAM McGUIRE AND LESLIE WHEELER

## DOCUMENT: EXCERPT FROM ROGER WILLIAMS'S *BLOUDY TENENT OF PERSECUTION*, 1644

*Although many Puritans came to America to gain religious liberty for themselves, many of them were not keen on extending such liberty to others. Roger Williams, at various times an Anglican, a Baptist, and a Seeker, was among those eventually expelled from the Massachusetts Bay Colony, in part for his view that civil authorities had no right to try to extend their control over the human conscience by adopting legislation over religious matters. Williams subsequently founded Providence Plantation in present-day Rhode Island. Among the most famous of Williams's writings is his* **Bloudy Tenent of Persecution,** *which he authored in 1644 while applying for a charter for Rhode Island in England. With a clear view of the toll that religious persecution had taken in human lives, Williams's essay is one of the earliest defenses of what is today called separation of church and state. More than a century later, similar arguments would be made by more secularly oriented thinkers like Thomas Jefferson and James Madison on behalf of religious liberties. Such concerns eventually found their way into the First Amendment. Below is an excerpt from Williams's work.* (Williams, Roger, *The Bloudy Tenent of Persecution, for the Cause of Conscience, Discussed in a Conference Between Truth and Peace* [London, 1644].)

First, that the blood of so many hundred thousand souls of Protestants and Papists, spilt in the wars of present and former ages, for their respective consciences, is not required nor accepted by Jesus Christ the Prince of Peace.

Secondly, pregnant scriptures and arguments are throughout the work proposed against the doctrine of persecution for cause of conscience.

Thirdly, satisfactory answers are given to scriptures, and objections produced by Mr. Calvin, Beza, Mr. Cotton, and the ministers of New English churches and others former and late, tending to prove the doctrine of persecution for cause of conscience.

Fourthly, the doctrine of persecution for cause of conscience is proved guilty of all the blood of the souls crying for vengeance under the altar.

Fifthly, all civil states with their officers of justice in their respective constitutions and administrations are proved essentially civil, and therefore not judges, governors, or defenders of the spiritual or Christian state and worship.

Sixthly, it is the will and command of God that (since the coming of his Son the Lord Jesus) a permission of the most paganish, Jewish, Turkish, or antichristian consciences and worships, be granted to all men in all nations and countries; and they are only to be fought against with that sword which is only (in soul matters) able to conquer, to wit, the sword of God's spirit, the Word of God.

Seventhly, the state of the Land of Israel, the kings and people thereof in peace and war, is proved figurative and ceremonial, and no pattern nor president for any kingdom or civil state in the world to follow.

Eighthly, God requireth not a uniformity of religion to be enacted and enforced in any civil state; which enforced uniformity (sooner or later) is the greatest occasion of civil war, ravishing of conscience, persecution of Christ Jesus in his servants, and of the hypocrisy and destruction of millions of souls.

Ninthly, in holding an enforced uniformity of religion in a civil state, we must necessarily disclaim our desires and hopes of the Jew's conversion to Christ.

Tenthly, an enforced uniformity of religion throughout a nation or civil state, confounds the civil and religious, denies the principles of Christianity and civility, and that Jesus Christ is come in the flesh.

Eleventhly, the permission of other consciences and worships than a state professeth only can (according to God) procure a firm and lasting peace (good assurance being taken according to the wisdom of the civil state for uniformity of civil obedience from all forts).

Twelfthly, lastly, true civility and Christianity may both flourish in a state or kingdom, notwithstanding the permission of divers and contrary consciences, either of Jew or Gentile....

*First,* the proper means whereby the civil power may and should attain its end are only political, and principally these five.

First, the erecting and establishing what form of civil government may seem in wisdom most meet, according to general rules of the world, and state of the people.

Secondly, the making, publishing, and establishing of wholesome civil laws, not only such as concern civil justice, but also the free passage of true religion; for outward civil peace ariseth and is maintained from them both, from the latter as well as from the former.

Civil peace cannot stand entire, where religion is corrupted (2 Chron. 15. 3. 5. 6; and Judges 8). And yet such laws, though conversant about religion, may still be counted civil laws, as, on the contrary, an oath doth still remain religious though conversant about civil matters.

Thirdly, election and appointment of civil offices to see execution to those laws.

Fourthly, civil punishments and rewards of transgressors and observers of these laws.

Fifthly, taking up arms against the enemies of civil peace.

*Secondly,* the means whereby the church may and should attain her ends are only ecclesiastical, which are chiefly five.

First, setting up that form of church government only of which Christ hath given them a pattern in his Word.

Secondly, acknowledging and admitting of no lawgiver in the church but Christ and the publishing of His laws.

Thirdly, electing and ordaining of such officers only, as Christ hath appointed in his Word.

Fourthly, to receive into their fellowship them that are approved and inflicting spiritual censures against them that offend.

Fifthly, prayer and patience in suffering any evil from them that be without, who disturb their peace.

So that magistrates as magistrates, have no power of setting up the form of church government, electing church officers, punishing with church censures, but to see that the church does her duty herein. And on the other side, the churches as churches, have no power (though as members of the commonwealth they may have power) of erecting or altering forms of civil government, electing of civil officers, inflicting civil punishments (not on persons excommunicate) as by deposing magistrates from their civil authority, or withdrawing the hearts of the people against them, to their laws, no more than to discharge wives, or children, or servants, from due obedience to their husbands, parents, or masters; or by taking up arms against their magistrates, though he persecute them for conscience: for though members of churches who are public officers also of the civil state may suppress by force the violence of usurpers, as Iehoiada did Athaliah, yet this they do not as members of the church but as officers of the civil state.

## DOCUMENT: MARYLAND ACT OF TOLERATION, 1649

*Drafted by Maryland's founder Lord Baltimore early in 1649 and passed by the Maryland legislature in April of that year, the Maryland Toleration Act offered religious freedom for all Christians who accepted the Divine Trinity but did not extend this same toleration to non-Christians or to Christians who denied the Trinity. The act was particularly intended to protect Catholics from persecution in a colony with a large Protestant population, as well. Despite the somewhat limited extent of the toleration granted, it was among the most liberal acts of its kind in colonial America.* (Maryland Toleration Act of 1649. From Browne, William H., ed., *The Archives of Maryland,* vol. I [Baltimore: Maryland Historical Society, 1883], pp. 244–247.)

## AN ACT CONCERNING RELIGION

Forasmuch as in a well governed and Christian Common Wealth matters concerning Religion and the honor of God ought in the first place to bee taken, into serious consideracion and endeavoured to bee settled, Be it therefore ordered and enacted by the Right Honourable Cecilius Lord Baron of Baltemore absolute Lord and Proprietary of this Province with the advise and consent of this Generall Assembly:

That whatsoever person or persons within this Province and the Islands thereunto belonging shall from henceforth blaspheme God, that is Curse him, or deny our Saviour Jesus Christ to bee the sonne of God, or shall deny the holy Trinity the father sonne and holy Ghost, or the Godhead of any of the said Three persons of the Trinity or the Unity of the Godhead, or shall use or utter any reproachfull Speeches, words or language concerning the said Holy Trinity, or any of the said three persons thereof, shalbe punished with death and confiscation or forfeiture of all his or her lands and goods to the Lord Proprietary and his heires.

And bee it also Enacted by the Authority and with the advise and assent aforesaid, That whatsoever person or persons shall from henceforth use or utter any reproachfull words or Speeches concerning the blessed Virgin Mary the Mother of our Saviour or the holy Apostles or Evangelists or any of them shall in such case for the first offence forfeit to the said Lord Proprietary and his heirs Lords and Proprietaries of this Province the summe of five pound Sterling or the value thereof to be Levyed on the goods and chattells of every such person soe offending, but in case such Offender or Offenders, shall not then have goods and chattells sufficient for the satisfyeing of such forfeiture, or that the same bee not otherwise speedily satisfyed that then such Offender or Offenders shalbe publiquely whipt and bee imprisoned during the pleasure of the Lord Proprietary or the Lieutenant or cheife Governor of this Province for the time being. And that every such Offender or Offenders for every second offence shall forfeit tenne pound sterling or the value thereof to bee levyed as aforesaid, or in case such offender or Offenders shall not then have goods and chattells within this Province sufficient for that purpose then to bee publiquely and severely whipt and imprisoned as before is expressed. And that every person or persons before mentioned offending herein the third time, shall for such third Offence forfeit all his lands and Goods and bee for ever banished and expelled out of this Province.

And be it also further Enacted by the same authority advise and assent that whatsoever person or persons shall from henceforth uppon any occasion of Offence or otherwise in a reproachful manner or Way declare call or denominate any person or persons whatsoever inhabiting, residing, traffiqueing, trading or comerceing within this Province or within any the Ports, Harbors, Creeks or Havens to the same belonging an heritick, Scismatick, Idolator, puritan, Independant, Prespiterian popish prest, Jesuite, Jesuited papist, Lutheran, Calvenist, Anabaptist, Brownist, Antinomian, Barrowist, Roundhead, Separatist, or any other name or terme in a reproachfull manner relating to matter of Religion shall for every such Offence forfeit and loose the somme of tenne shillings sterling or the value thereof to bee levyed on the goods and chattells of every such Offender and Offenders, the one half thereof to be forfeited and paid unto the person and persons of whom such reproachfull words are or shalbe spoken or uttered, and the other half thereof to the Lord Proprietary and his heires Lords and Proprietaries of this Province. But if such person or persons who shall at any time utter or speake any such reproachfull words or Language shall not have Goods or Chattells sufficient and overt within this Province to bee taken to satisfie the penalty aforesaid or that the same bee not otherwise speedily satisfyed, that then the person or persons soe offending shalbe publickly whipt, and shall suffer imprisonment without baile or maineprise untill hee, shee or they respectively shall satisfy the party soe offended or greived by such reproachfull Language by asking him or her respectively forgivenes publiquely for such his Offence before the Magistrate of cheife Officer or Officers of the Towne or place where such Offence shalbe given.

And be it further likewise Enacted by the Authority and consent aforesaid That every person and persons within this Province that shall at any time hereafter prophane the Sabbath or Lords day called Sunday by frequent swearing, drunkennes or by any uncivill or disorderly recreacion, or by working on that day when absolute necessity doth not require it shall for every such first offence forfeit 2s 6d sterling or the value thereof, and for the second offence 5s sterling or the value thereof, and for the third offence and soe for every time he shall offend in like manner afterwards 10s sterling or the value thereof. And in case such offender and offenders shall not have sufficient goods or chattells within this Province to satisfy any of the said Penalties respectively hereby imposed for prophaning the Sabbath or Lords day called Sunday as aforesaid, That in Every such case the partie soe offending shall for the first and second offence in that kinde be imprisoned till hee or shee shall publickly in open Court before the cheife Commander Judge or Magistrate, of that County Towne or precinct where such offence shalbe committed acknowledg the Scandall and offence he hath in that respect given against God and the good and civill Governement of this Province, And for the third offence and for every time after shall also bee publickly whipt.

And whereas the inforceing of the conscience in matters of Religion hath frequently fallen out to be of dangerous Consequence in those commonwealthes where it hath been practised, And for the more quiett and peaceable governement of this Province, and the better to preserve mutuall Love and amity amongst the Inhabitants thereof, Be it Therefore also by the Lord Proprietary with the advise and consent of this Assembly Ordeyned and enacted (except as in this present Act is before Declared and sett forth) that noe person or persons whatsoever within this Province, or the Islands, Ports, Harbors, Creekes, or havens thereunto belonging professing to beleive in Jesus Christ, shall from henceforth bee any waies troubled, Molested or discountenanced for or in respect of his or her religion nor in the free exercise thereof within this Province or the Islands thereunto belonging nor any way compelled to the beleife or exercise of any other Religion against his or her consent, soe as they be not unfaithfull to the Lord Proprietary, or molest or conspire against the civill Governement established or to bee established in this Province under him or his heires. And that all and every person and persons that shall presume Contrary to this Act and the true intent and meaning thereof directly or indirectly either in person or estate willfully to wrong disturbe trouble or molest any person whatsoever within this Province professing to beleive in Jesus Christ for or in respect of his or her religion or the free exercise thereof within this Province other than is provided for in this Act that such person or persons soe offending, shalbe compelled to pay trebble damages to the party soe wronged or molested, and for every such offence shall also forfeit 20s sterling in money or the value thereof, half thereof for the use of the Lord Proprietary, and his heires Lords and Proprietaries of this Province, and the other half for the use of the party soe wronged or molested as aforesaid, Or if the partie soe offending as aforesaid shall refuse or bee unable to recompense the party soe wronged, or to satisfy such fyne or forfeiture, then such Offender shalbe severely punished by publick whipping and imprisonment during the pleasure of the Lord Proprietary, or his Lieutenant or cheife Governor of this Province for the tyme being without baile or maineprise.

And bee it further alsoe Enacted by the authority and consent aforesaid That the Sheriff or other Officer or Officers from time to time to bee appointed and authorized for that purpose, of the County Towne or precinct where every particular offence in this present Act conteyned shall happen at any time to bee committed and whereupon there is hereby a forfeiture fyne or penalty imposed shall from time to time distraine and seise the goods and estate of every such person soe offending as aforesaid against this present

Act or any part thereof, and sell the same or any part thereof for the full satisfaccion of such forfeiture, fine, or penalty as aforesaid, Restoring unto the partie soe offending the Remainder or overplus of the said goods or estate after such satisfaccion soe made as aforesaid.

The freemen have assented.

## DOCUMENT: EXCERPT FROM THE PENNSYLVANIA CHARTER OF PRIVILEGES, 1701

*Adopted by William Penn in 1701, the Pennsylvania Charter of Privileges guaranteed religious freedom for those who believed in God. This charter states that all believers in God have the right to serve in the government and should not be discriminated against in their "Person or Estate."* (Penn, William, Pennsylvania Charter of Privileges, 1701.)

Because no People can be truly happy, though under the greatest Enjoyment of Civil Liberties, if abridged of the Freedom of their Consciences, as to their Religious Profession and Worship: And Almighty God being the only Lord of Conscience, Father of Lights and Spirits; and the Author as well as the Object of all divine Knowledge, Faith and Worship, who only doth enlighten the Minds, and persuade and convince the Understanding of People, I do hereby grant and declare, That no Person or Persons, inhabiting in this province or Territories, who shall confess and acknowledge One almighty God, the Creator, Upholder and Ruler of the World; and profess him or themselves obliged to live quietly under the Civil Government, shall be in any Case molested or prejudiced, in his or their Person or Estate, because of his or their conscientious Persuasion or Practice, nor be compelled to frequent or maintain any religious Worship, Place or Ministry, contrary to his or their Mind, or to do or suffer any other Act or Thing, contrary to their religious Persuasion.

AND that all Persons who also profess to believe in Jesus Christ, the Savior of the World, shall be capable (notwithstanding their other Persuasions and Practices in Point of Conscience and Religion) to serve this Government in any Capacity, both legislatively and executively, he or they solemnly promising, when lawfully required, Allegiance to the King as Sovereign, and Fidelity to the Proprietary and Governor, and taking the Attests as now established by the Law.

# 9

# The Surrender of New Amsterdam, 1664

## INTRODUCTION

The Dutch explorer Henry Hudson first sailed up what is now known as the Hudson River in 1609, but his third voyage, in 1610, was particularly important because it proved to the Dutch government that the North (Hudson) River was a good place for settlement and trade and that there was no water route extending from the river to the "western sea," where China and its fabulous treasures were supposed to be.

One of the first detailed geographical descriptions of the Dutch area of settlement was Johannes de Loet's *New World, or a Description of West-India*, published in 1625. De Loet was involved in Dutch business ventures in America, and his book appeared after the States-General (the Dutch legislature) had chartered the Dutch West India Company, in 1621. The company, which remained in control of New Netherland until 1664, enjoyed a trade monopoly among the Netherlands, the west coast of Africa, and all of America and could ally itself with Native tribes and administer colonial government. In its earliest years, the Dutch West India Company was more interested in maintaining Brazil as a colony. In the early 1650s, the Dutch battled the Portuguese for control of Brazil and lost in 1654.

Despite its interest in Brazil, the Dutch West India Company began sending settlers to New Netherland in 1624, and, the following year, it appointed Willem Verhulst director general. Verhulst, however, took advantage of the distance between New Netherland and company headquarters to abuse his powers. A local advisory council he had established objected to his behavior and banished him from the colony. The council replaced Verhulst with Peter Minuit, a surveyor who had arrived in New Netherland with Verhulst.

The governmental and commercial center of the colony was New Amsterdam, located on the site of present-day New York City. New Amsterdam, like the rest of the colony, remained small during the early years of settlement. By 1643, its population was still fewer than 500 permanent residents, although there was considerable ethnic and religious diversity. The port facilities were busy, but many who worked there were transients. In the late 1620s, Minuit tried to attract more colonists by initiating brick manufacturing and timber-cutting enterprises and by ordering the building of a ship larger than any then in the Dutch fleet. The ship, which probably weighed 800 tons, was finished in 1630 and christened the *New Netherland*. The ship became a part of the West India Company's transoceanic fleet, but the company directors never forgot how expensive the ship was to build, and the experiment contributed to Minuit's recall, in 1631. Not long afterward, the Swedish government employed Minuit to lead New Sweden, its colonization venture in North America.

When the New Netherland colony did not become self-sufficient, as had been expected, the company introduced new initiatives to encourage greater immigration and economic activity. In 1629, company officials implemented the patroonship plan. Under this plan, one could become a *patroon* (a patron) if, over the course of three years, one brought 50 new settlers to New Netherland. In return, the company granted the patroon four leagues (about 18 miles) of land along one side of the Hudson River or two leagues along each side of the river. Settlers could move inland from the river as far as it was practical or safe. Within this domain, the patroon exercised administrative and judicial authority, although a colonist could appeal to the company in matters regarding serious offenses. Patroons were permitted to trade with anyone up and down the coast of North America by paying a 5 percent tax to the company for the concession. In addition, all trade within the colony or between the Dutch and other colonists was supposed to flow through New Amsterdam so that the director general could keep track of it for tax purposes, but this was virtually impossible to enforce.

Several prominent investors applied for patroonships, but only the van Rensselaer family possessed the wealth to establish a functioning community. In 1630, Kiliaen van Rensselaer established the patroonship of Rensselaerswyck. Several others tried but failed to create successful patroonships and sold their land back to the company. Although van Rensselaer remained prominent in New Netherland affairs for many years, the patroonship plan did not result in a significant increase in either the population or the prosperity of New Netherland.

Although New Netherland was not founded for religious reasons, the Dutch West India Company was concerned about the spiritual needs of its settlers. The company established a Reformed Church in the colony, basically Presbyterian in nature. Congregations had a good deal of control over their own affairs, although they were nominally under the supervision of a body called the classis, which consisted of all the ministers in a particular district. The classis could install and remove ministers from their churches. Above the classis was the synod, a group of church leaders, which had broad supervisory authority. The first minister sent to the colony was Jonas Jansen Michielase, whose name was Latinized to Jonas Johannes Michaelius. He arrived in April 1628 and organized a church in Manhattan, the settlement near the port.

In addition, the patroonship arrangement also required patroons to provide a religious opportunity for the settlers within the domain, and van Rensselaer eventually called a minister to his patroonship. Johannes Megapolensis arrived in 1642 under a six-year contract. Megapolensis enjoyed the full confidence of van Rensselaer, who often consulted him on important administrative issues. In 1643, Megapolensis was one of the first Christian ministers to go out and preach to the Indians. After leaving Rensselaerswyck in, 1649, Megapolensis was persuaded to preach in New Amsterdam and stayed there until his death, in 1669.

After the controversy about the *New Netherland*, the Dutch West India Company replaced Minuit with Bastiaen Jansen Krol, who served only a year. The next director general was Wouter Van Twiller. The fourth director general of New Netherland was not a notable colonial administrator, but his physical presence was remarkable, if the description of fictional chronicler Diedrich Knickerbocker is to be believed:

> He was exactly five feet six inches in height and six feet five inches in circumference. His head was a perfect sphere, and of such stupendous dimensions that Dame Nature, with all her sex's ingenuity, would have been puzzled to construct a neck capable of supporting it; whereupon she wisely declined the attempt and settled it firmly on the top of his backbone, just between the shoulders. . . . His legs were short, but strictly in proportion to the weight they had to sustain, so that when erect he had not a little the appearance of a beer barrel on skids. (Quoted in Irving, p. 141)

Van Twiller's service in New Netherland lasted five years, all the while plagued by his alcoholism and ineffectiveness. In 1638, he was replaced by Willem Kieft, a hard-driving, ambitious director general whose eight years in the colony were marked by worsening relations with the Indians of the region. The economy and society of New Netherland were badly damaged by a series of Indian wars between 1643 and 1647. At the end of these wars, Peter Stuyvesant replaced Kieft as director general of New Netherland. He was the last Dutch director general of the colony, honest and capable but authoritarian to the point of being tyrannical.

As director general, Stuyvesant was interested in defending New Netherland against its English and Swedish neighbors, in reining in the independent patroons, like van Rensselaer, and in suppressing illegal trading with the Indians, who were acquiring guns in that way. In 1650, to pay for his policies, Stuyvesant convened representatives of the people, known as the Board of Nine Men, to secure their assent to levy taxes. The Board of Nine Men came to represent a kind of political opposition to the director general, expressing their displeasure over various issues and requesting mediation in the Netherlands States-General.

Stuyvesant opposed this challenge to his authority and tried to suppress the Board of Nine Men, but they petitioned the States-General, which, since it was involved with Brazilian matters at the time, did nothing about the dispute. Ultimately, Stuyvesant relented somewhat, gave "village rights," including the right to establish local courts, to 12 settlements, and, in 1653, allowed New Amsterdam, the largest settlement, a limited municipal government.

Stuyvesant's most important military action was the capture of Swedish settlements on the Delaware River in 1655. New Sweden was founded in 1638 with some help from Dutch merchants, who could envision a profitable trade relationship with the traditionally friendly Swedes. The Swedish South Company, responsible for the settling of New Sweden, sent Peter Minuit to direct the new colony. Early Dutch-Swedish relations were good; each colony controlled a bank of the Delaware River. Conflict arose, however, over Indian trade, disputed purchases of Indian lands, and the aggressiveness of Stuyvesant's administration. In 1651, he ordered the construction of a new fort on the South River very near the Swedes' Fort Christina. Relations worsened, and, in 1654, New Sweden received a large number of reinforcements from Sweden, but further efforts to strengthen the colony's defenses were too late.

The Dutch surrender New Amsterdam, September 8, 1664. (Courtesy of the Library of Congress.)

The Dutch West India Company ordered Stuyvesant to drive the Swedes out of their territory, and, in August 1655, Stuyvesant organized the largest military force yet seen in any of the colonies along the Atlantic Coast. The Dutch forces sailed to the Delaware River in early September and forced the surrender of Fort Casimir on September 11. Ironically, the Dutch had built Fort Casimir in 1651, but the Swedes had captured it a year later. On September 24, Fort Christina capitulated, effectively ending the conflict and the Swedish presence in North America.

Conflict between the Dutch and the English over New Netherland dated back to 1621. The Dutch claimed the territory by virtue of prior discovery and occupation, while the English pointed to the proclamation of King James I in 1606 that granted the Virginia Company the right to colonize anywhere between 34 and 45 degrees north latitude, an area that easily encompassed New Netherland. English pressure mounted as the New England colonies grew much more rapidly than did New Netherland, and boundary disputes were frequent. Eventually, New Netherland was outmatched by the English presence, and directors general in the 1650s and 1660s permitted English settlements like New Haven to be established on territory the Dutch had originally claimed. A similar conflict regarding English settlement occurred on Long Island, although Stuyvesant did not object to independent English settlers coming to New Netherland.

In 1650, Stuyvesant and the English negotiated a treaty establishing a boundary running through both Long Island and present-day Connecticut. Although not ratified by the Dutch government until 1656 and never ratified by the English, the agreement worked to keep the peace for several years. After the restoration of King Charles II, in

1660, however, the English government sought to streamline their North American colonial administration. Removing the Dutch from New Netherland would give the English control of the entire coastline, now that the Dutch themselves had eliminated New Sweden.

In 1662, Connecticut was given a new charter that extended its domain well into parts of New Netherland, ignoring the 1650 treaty. In the following year, Charles II, ignoring totally the existence of New Netherland, granted the land from the Connecticut River to the Delaware River to his younger brother James, then Duke of York. James organized a military force under the command of Colonel Richard Nicolls to go to New Netherland and secure his land. In late August 1664, Nicolls's forces landed in the harbor at New Amsterdam and demanded that Stuyvesant surrender the city, a move with which many Dutch people, aware of the futility of a fight, agreed. Stuyvesant held out for several days but finally yielded to the English on September 8, 1664.

New Netherland became the English colony of New York, except for a brief period in 1673, when, during an Anglo-Dutch war, the Dutch navy captured New York. The city (if not the entire colony) remained under Dutch control for about 15 months until the treaty ending the war returned New York to England.

## INTERPRETIVE ESSAY

THOMAS A. MACKEY

While walking through the concrete, steel, and glass canyons of lower Manhattan today, it is difficult to believe that one walks in the footsteps of the original Dutch settlers of New Netherland where a wall separated the wilds of Manhattan from the Dutch city of New Amsterdam. Although Dutch heritage is difficult to find in lower Manhattan, a few Dutch place names survive, such as Wall Street and Bowling Green. In other places in greater New York and up the Hudson River, the Dutch presence can be heard in names such as "Breukelyn" (Brooklyn) and "Haerlem" (Harlem). An Indian trail ran the length of Manhattan Island, ending at the Dutch settlement. In the late 1650s, the Dutch widened the path into their settlement. These improvements led the Dutch to refer to the path by the descriptive name "Breede Wegh," anglicized to "Broad Way." But these street and place names are the last vestiges of the Dutch presence in New York City. This essay examines the origins and development of the Dutch settlement of New Amsterdam and how the Dutch lost their North American colony to the English in September 1664. With the takeover of New Netherland, the English secured their hold on the eastern shores of North America and no longer feared any European threat from *within* their claims to coastal North America. Only the French in Canada loomed as a threat to the English holdings that stretched from Nova Scotia southward through the Chesapeake Bay.

In September 1609, Henry Hudson, an Englishman in the employ of the Dutch East India Company, reached the North American mainland north of Virginia. He guided his ship, *Da Halve Maen* (The Half Moon), into a navigable river that emptied into the Atlantic Ocean. He passed what would be known as Manhattan Island on his right and continued as far north as the river was navigable (to approximately the area of Albany). Along the way, Native Americans met his ship and traded tobacco, corn, and furs for trinkets, beads, and knives. That river bears this explorer's name, the Hudson River, and his company claimed the excellent port at the mouth of the river where the Dutch West India Company founded New Amsterdam in 1624. Yet Henry Hudson was not the first to "discover" the river. One hundred years before the founding of New Amsterdam, the Italian explorer Giovanni da Verrazano anchored at the narrow entrance to the river. Today, the elegant Verrazano Narrows Bridge connecting Staten Island and Brooklyn is named in his honor.

Henry Hudson had not set sail to find new peoples or to start new colonies; rather, in his quest for the riches of Asia, he searched for a northwest water passage through the land mass. In this goal he failed, but his later explorations took him farther north, where his name adorns Canada's Hudson Bay and Hudson Strait. His explorations proved controversial. Upon returning to Europe, Hudson put the *Half Moon* into Dartmouth, England, for repairs, and his mixed crew of Dutch and English spread the word about their discoveries. England's government viewed Hudson's actions as disloyal because he sailed for a potential competitor, the Dutch, and briefly imprisoned him. What bothered the English most was not Hudson's voyages but rather his claim for the Dutch of the entire Hudson River area. In particular, the Plymouth and Virginia Companies of London claimed the entire coastline in their royal charters even though they possessed no practical means to enforce those claims. As a result, the Dutch, the Swedes, the French to the north, and the Spanish to the south ignored English declarations of ownership and carved out areas of the new world for themselves.

Like their British rivals, the Dutch employed a particular form of organization to undertake their exploration and colonization ventures—the joint-stock corporation. In the late 16th and early 17th centuries, Dutch economic energies and banking successes resulted in a prosperous Holland. Because of their economic success, many Dutch had money to invest in risky but potentially lucrative overseas voyages. To spread the risk of such voyages, the Dutch (like the British) developed joint-stock companies. By allowing a large number of people to invest in their activities, companies could raise more capital to fund voyages than any one investor might be able to finance, and, if the voyage failed, no one investor lost all of his investment. Because of these economic advantages, Dutch and English authorities regularly chartered joint-stock companies for exploration and colonization purposes.

By October 1614, the Dutch East India Company had lost interest in the New World and concentrated its trade efforts in the fur trade with Moscow. As a result, the Dutch States-General chartered a new company, the New Netherland Company, to enter the North American fur trade. This company had a monopoly to make four voyages in the following three years, and the fur trade flourished. When the monopoly ended, in 1617, the proprietors of the New Netherland Company sought to renew its charter, but other investors lobbied the States-General and prevented the awarding of another charter until June 3, 1621. On that date, a competing group of investors, the Dutch West India Company, received a charter and the exclusive privileges to control Dutch trade with New Netherland. Under this 1621 charter, the Dutch West India Company possessed the authority to maintain military forces, to negotiate trade and peace terms with the local peoples, and to administer its own affairs in the Americas and in West Africa. As part of this charter, the Dutch States-General required the company to "advance the peopling of those fruitful and unsettled parts."

In April 1624, the ship *Nieu Nederlandt* reached the Hudson River. Captained by Cornelius Jacobsen May, the *Nieu Nederlandt* carried 30 families whose goal was to establish a Dutch colony in New Netherland. These families came from southern Holland, were Protestants, spoke French, and were known as the Walloons. May sent 18 of these families up the Hudson River to settle permanently at Fort Orange (near present-day Albany). He also dispatched settlers southward to Burlington Island in the Delaware River and others eastward to the Connecticut River Valley. Only a few families remained on Noten (Governor's) Island and on Manhattan Island. May scattered these people because of Holland's disputed claims to the Hudson River area. May and the company directors sought to show that the Dutch had occupied their claimed territory.

In 1625, the company sent out six relief ships carrying provisions and hundreds of new Dutch colonists. Willem Verhulst was the commander of this expedition, and, upon its arrival, he became the first director general of New Netherland. Verhulst had orders from the 19 Directors of the company to establish a permanent agricultural community in New Netherlands. To centralize his control, Verhulst recalled to New Amsterdam the outlying Walloon settlements; after 1626, those trading outposts were staffed only seasonally. Verhulst also ordered that any other directors of the company who might be in the colony serve as an advisory council to him, but, because few of the major investors ever visited the far-flung colony, the director general wielded almost unchecked power throughout the Dutch period.

Political power in the hands of one director general could become a problem, and Verhulst was the first to abuse his powers. He lost key support among the settlers by berating the settlers for not spending enough time working on the company's lands and for his harsh punishments for minor crimes. When it came to light that Verhulst had altered the company's books to enrich himself, the council banished him from the colony. Succeeding Verhulst was Peter Minuit, who had come to New Netherland to help Verhulst survey the area.

One of the persistent questions of this early period is how and when the Dutch "bought" Manhattan Island from the local Indians. The traditional account holds that Peter Minuit purchased the island for 60 florins' worth of trade goods from the local Mahican tribe in 1626. Historians challenge this story, arguing that Willem Verhulst actually arranged the exchange of goods for the Dutch settlement on Manhattan Island and that Minuit bought Manhattan. What actually occurred remains unclear. Because Indians did not think in terms of "owning" land as Europeans did but rather understood land as something that supported all people, one wonders whether the Mahicans considered their exchange for Manhattan a final "sale" or saw the exchange as a "gift" for the right of the Dutch to settle. What is clear is that, by the fall of 1627, New Netherland was taking shape, with its political and commercial center at New Amsterdam on Manhattan Island. In addition to 30 houses there, the colonists finished an unimpressive fort or blockhouse surrounded by a log and earthen palisades.

But all was not well. The Dutch West India Company, with its major investments in Africa and elsewhere in the Americas, expected the small colony to become self-sufficient quickly. Yet, the colony did not boom as investors hoped. Agricultural production failed to meet expectations, lumber proved expensive to harvest and ship, and the fur trade (the only true "cash crop" of the colony) slowed.

To address these problems, the Dutch West India Company loosened its hold over the colony and allowed more private initiative and investment. In 1629, the company implemented the patroonship plan, whereby a wealthy individual could acquire a large amount of land in return for recruiting colonists for New Netherland. Unfortunately for the Dutch, the patroonship plan did not prove successful. Few Dutch investors had the capital to establish patroonships, and few Dutch settlers were willing to work the large farms. The most successful of the patroonships, Kiliaen van Rensselaer's Rensselaerswyck, struggled during the 1630s, and most of the other patroons eventually sold their land back to the company. In the end, the patroonship plan failed to meet the key need of New Netherland—more colonists.

To meet this need the company revised its charter again in 1629 to allow less prominent people to receive land titles in New Netherland. Under these new terms, people who settled in the colony could receive title to a certain amount of land. This also failed to generate adequate immigration, so, in 1639, the company expanded its offer by granting as much land as people could cultivate. To sweeten the deal even further, the company granted colonists the right to control their property in perpetuity. In return, the settlers had to pay a tax, a quitrent, of one-tenth of the value of their produce and their cattle herds to the company. In 1640, building on these incentives, the company offered 200 acres of land to settlers who brought five immigrants to the colony and offered limited self-government to those who established towns or villages. One glitch in these plans was the Indian claims to the land that had to be cleared *before* the company recognized the settlers' land titles. This requirement led to widespread fraud and cheating by the Dutch settlers. Not surprisingly, this issue generated so much bad feeling between the Dutch and the Indians that, in 1652, Director General Peter Stuyvesant forbade private land purchases from the Indians without the consent of the company.

When experiments with land offerings failed to attract large numbers of Dutch settlers, New Netherland opened its doors to almost anyone willing to settle. Eventually the colony grew, but not necessarily with Dutch immigrants and certainly not quickly. New Netherland numbered about 300 people in 1630 and 500 in 1640; by 1664, when the English conquered New Amsterdam, the colony contained fewer than 9,000 settlers. At the same time, the English colony of Virginia had a population of approximately 40,000 people, and New England had 50,000. New Amsterdam attracted a wide diversity of people (Dutch, English, French) and religions (Protestants, Catholics, and even Jews), a tradition that has continued throughout New York City's rich history.

Dutch governance in New Netherland suffered from weak leadership. Director General Peter Minuit lasted until 1631, when the directors of the company recalled him after the controversy over the building of the *New Netherland*. After Minuit, Bastiaen Jansen Krol arrived but served only a year, and the alcoholic ex-company clerk Wouter Van Twiller followed him, in turn, in 1633. Van Twiller lasted five years, only to be followed in 1638 by the ambitious, heavy-handed, and imprudent Willem Kieft. Because of his rash policies and bad relations with the Native Americans, intermittent fighting with the Indians occurred. These attacks, combined with his harshness as director, led to a general call from within the colony for Kieft's removal, which occurred in 1646. New Netherland's last director general was the combative, pious military veteran Peter Stuyvesant, who arrived in New Amsterdam in May 1647. Stuyvesant's tenure was not without controversy, as he feuded with both his fellow Dutch settlers and his English neighbors, but he did bring stability and better leadership to the Dutch colony.

A principal area of simmering tension between the British and the Dutch lay to the northeast, in the Connecticut River Valley. Both the English in New England and the Dutch from New Netherland sought to control the lucrative Indian fur trade along that river. Their rivalry demonstrated the weakness of the Dutch and the determination of the English to claim the hinterlands of New England. What made the Connecticut River Valley so important to both groups was its geography—it flowed from deep in the heartland of New England. Indians used this natural highway to move their pelts of beaver and otter out of the countryside and down to the European trading posts. Dutch leaders and traders wanted control of the river so that the Connecticut River did not siphon trade away from the Hudson River; English leaders and traders hoped to cut into the Dutch trade by controlling the river.

In 1633, Director General Van Twiller sent Jacob van Curler and a company of soldiers to establish a Dutch presence on the Connecticut River. Van Curler and his men built a small fort and trading post a few miles up the river and named it the House of Good Hope. Soon Indians appeared, and the Dutch started doing a healthy business trading cloth, mirrors, and knives for furs.

Dutch advances into Connecticut caused concern in both the Pilgrim settlement of Plymouth and the Puritan settlements centered around Boston. Pilgrim governor Edward Winslow had opened negotiations with the Indians of the area but had not established a presence in the region. Upon hearing of the Dutch trading post, the Pilgrims began to outfit an expedition to establish their own presence on the river. Puritan governor John Winthrop did not openly support Winslow's more aggressive actions, but he did write a sharp letter to Van Twiller restating the English claim to the area and warning the Dutch not to build fortifications there. Van Twiller responded that the Dutch West India Company's claim to the Connecticut River Valley predated any English claim and that the House of Good Hope was only a trading post.

While Van Twiller and Winthrop exchanged letters, the Pilgrims sent a ship up the Connecticut River and set up their own trading post not far from the House of Good Hope. Van Twiller sent troops there with orders to eliminate the English. The Dutch commander, however, decided not to attack the English and withdrew to the House of Good Hope. More and more of the Indians took their furs to the English settlement for trading. This Dutch failure of nerve encouraged the English to continue their expansion in Connecticut. The House of Good Hope became merely a Dutch outpost amid a growing English colony.

Because of Van Twiller's alcoholism, the company recalled him in 1637 and appointed the strong-willed Willem Kieft the new director general for the colony. By appointing Kieft, the company sought to bring effective leadership to the colony and to place it on a better financial footing. In addition, the company tried to attract more settlers by liberalizing its policies on fur trading. Individual settlers could now enter into the lucrative trade, and private shippers could now handle the transportation of the furs.

As director general, Kieft caused more difficulties for the colony than he solved. Although he possessed some understanding of Indian culture and customs, he also believed that the Indians posed a problem for the Dutch fur trade. Kieft feared that the Indians would shift their trading relationship away from the Dutch to the English. In

1639, he placed a tax, a *contributie,* on Indians living within New Netherland, and he required that this tax be paid in pelts. His goal was to regularize the relationship between the Dutch and the Indians; instead, his policy resulted in a bloody war between the two peoples. There were misunderstandings about tax collection procedures and rumors about Indian raids on Dutch farms that prompted Kieft to order troops to destroy an Indian village and issue a proclamation offering a bounty for dead Indians. With this defiant attitude, Kieft virtually guaranteed that the conflict between the Dutch and the Indians would be neither short nor bloodless.

In 1641, the level of hostility increased after the brutal murder of a Dutch wheelwright, Claes Smits. Kieft prepared his troops for war, and, in February 1643, the Battle of Pavonia resulted in the deaths of 180 Indians, including women and children. That bloody event led to reprisals from Indians up and down the Hudson River in 1643 and 1644 in which numerous Dutch and English settlers on outlying farms were killed. Among them were the noted dissenter from the Massachusetts Bay Colony Anne Hutchinson and her children. Indian attacks so crippled the colony that the Dutch had to send food to New Amsterdam because so many Dutch farms had been abandoned.

After hearing numerous complaints about Kieft and the Indian war, the 19 Directors of the West India Company recalled the director general, instructed the remaining Dutch to sign a peace treaty with the Indians (which they did), and started a search for a new leader. Although they did not know it, their choice proved to be the colony's most colorful and important director general, Peter Stuyvesant.

On May 11, 1647, Stuyvesant arrived in New Amsterdam. The new director general cut quite a picture. A military man and an ardent Dutch nationalist, Stuyvesant had served in the Caribbean and in 1644 had led an assault on a Spanish fort on the island of Saint Martin. During the battle, a cannon shot cost him his right leg. He learned to walk again using a wooden peg leg that he adorned with silver bands. A devout Calvinist, Stuyvesant expected obedience and was both energetic and autocratic. These qualities made him an impressive and influential leader.

Although Stuyvesant brought stability to the colony, his personality and actions could not ultimately preserve New Netherland. International developments out of his control and the failure of the Dutch to people their North American claim caused the loss of New Netherland. But, for 17 years, Stuyvesant presided over the colony and sought to stem the rising tide of English colonies and colonists.

Boundary disputes between the Dutch and the Indians continued throughout Stuyvesant's administration, resulting in the Esopus War. This conflict started in 1659 at the Dutch village of Esopus (now Kingston), about halfway between New Amsterdam and Beverwyck. Tensions had been mounting in the area because some of the Dutch residents traded brandy for furs. Drunk Indians harassed the Dutch, invaded farms, and murdered one Dutch resident. Stuyvesant traveled to the area and spoke with the Indian leaders. He believed he had achieved an agreement for the Indians to move farther inland and to stop harassing the settlers, but, as soon as he left, the annoyances started again. On September 28, 1659, a local Dutch settler, Thomas Chambers, gave eight Indians brandy in exchange for their help in husking corn. They proceeded to get roaring drunk and spent the evening making a great noise just outside the Dutch settlement. Seizing the opportunity, the Dutch attacked, killing two Indians and capturing one. In retaliation, other Indians swept through the surrounding countryside destroying crops, killing livestock, and burning Dutch barns and houses. Heavily outnumbered, the Dutch drew up a petition to Stuyvesant imploring him to return to Esopus immediately and save them. Eighteen of the settlers, eight soldiers, and their sergeant made their way to the river and sent the petition downstream but were surrounded and captured; only seven of the men managed to return safely. Unable to defeat the Dutch in their defensive blockhouse, the Indians took out their frustrations on their prisoners by torturing them and eventually burning them to death. Dutch reprisals continued well into the summer of 1660 before the director general and the Indian leaders signed a new peace agreement.

Equally troubling throughout Stuyvesant's years as governor were his European neighbors. On September 23, 1650, Stuyvesant appeared in Hartford, Connecticut, to meet with representatives of the United Colonies (a defensive arrangement of the English New England colonies) in an effort to settle the boundary dispute between New Netherland and New England. Their first clash concerned Stuyvesant's reference in his opening statement to Hartford, Connecticut, as part of "New Netherland." This description irritated the English representatives, who asked him to stop using that label; he agreed, but only if the English stopped referring to Hartford and the Connecticut River Valley as "New England." Reluctantly they agreed and the meeting got down to serious negotiations. The Hartford Treaty that emerged from this meeting skirted the issue of which side had permanent claims to the disputed areas, but it did clarify the division of territory, especially on Long Island, where the English had been allowed to settle for some 20 years. Under this treaty, the representatives drew a line of demarcation from western Oyster Bay on the north shore of Long Island south across to the Atlantic Ocean. Another boundary line was drawn on the mainland north from Greenwich Bay, near present-day Stamford; the Dutch agreed not to settle within six miles of this line. Stuyvesant agreed to the loss of two-thirds of Long Island and the Dutch claims around Hartford and much of the Connecticut River Valley to protect Dutch holdings on the Hudson River. What the Hartford Treaty really accomplished was to describe and protect where the Dutch actually lived: Stuyvesant conceded no territory where the Dutch had permanent settlements. Although neither home government ratified the treaty promptly, New Englanders and New Netherlanders abided by its terms through the rest of the history of the Dutch colony.

In 1651, the economic rivalry between the British and the Dutch escalated when the British Parliament, in an effort to control its overseas trade, passed a Navigation Act requiring that all of its foreign trade be carried on in English ships with English crews. Directed at cutting into the Dutch trade, this 1651 Navigation Act led to a naval war between the two rivals. In North America, war panic emerged, with the English convincing themselves that the Dutch were arming the Indians against them, while the Dutch feared a full English assault. In the summer of 1653, New Netherland's last trading post in New England, the House of Good Hope, surrendered to the English. In June 1654, four English warships carrying troops and marines arrived in Boston with orders to invade New Netherland. But, just before the fleet was due to sail, a merchant ship arrived in Boston carrying news that the Anglo-Dutch War had ended. New Netherland had been saved—for now.

In 1660, the English civil war ended with the restoration of the British monarchy. Charles II returned to England and assumed his place as king. In early 1663, to reward his brother, James the Duke of York and Albany, for aiding him in regaining the throne,

Charles II gave James control of the area in North America claimed by the Dutch. This gift took the form of a proprietary grant that ignored Dutch claims and Dutch settlements and left James to figure out how to take possession of it. James and his friends developed a plan for the military invasion of New Netherland. While the plan was costly, James hoped that control of the fur trade would more than cover their expenses of taking over the Dutch colony.

Charles II's gift and James's plan dovetailed with international events. Economic rivalry persisted, and an undeclared naval and colonial war already existed between the British and the Dutch. On March 12, 1664, James received his grant from Charles II, officially giving him control of the Hudson River valley area. This enabled James to put his plan for the capture of New Netherland into operation. In May, he sent Colonel Richard Nicolls with a small fleet and two thousand soldiers to North America.

Storms and bad sailing luck scattered the fleet. Nicolls hoped to be assembled near eastern Long Island by late June, but all of his ships did not arrive until late July. Stuyvesant heard reports about the possible takeover of New Netherland and wrote the company for advice. The directors erroneously assured Stuyvesant that the English expedition sought only to bring the Puritans under greater English control.

Nicolls moved his flagship, the *Guinea,* and his fleet along the south shore of Long Island and on August 26 anchored in Graveshead Bay just south of the narrows between Long Island and Staten Island. At his disposal, Stuyvesant had about 150 soldiers, some of the local townspeople, and a dilapidated fort that could neither be adequately defended nor hold the town's 1,200 residents. Stuyvesant sent a messenger to Nicolls to inquire about the intentions of the British, and Nicolls demanded, quite simply, that Stuyvesant turn the town over to him. To emphasize his point, Nicolls moved his ships through the narrows and anchored them near Governor's Island. On September 2, 1664, Stuyvesant answered Nicolls's demand by declaring that the area had always been Dutch and would always remain Dutch. Nicolls brushed aside Stuyvesant's appeal to history and gave him 48 hours to surrender the city.

Between September 4 and September 6, Stuyvesant lost the support of burgomasters from the town. These prominent citizens were impressed with the generous terms offered by the English, whose spokesman, John Winthrop Jr., the governor of Massachusetts Bay Colony, promised that immigration from the United Provinces of Holland and Dutch trade with the colony could continue. The frustrated Stuyvesant hesitated as the English moved their ships into positions that would allow them to bombard New Amsterdam from the river. At that, the director general hurried to the fort and prepared to fire on the English, but cooler heads intervened. One of the most respected of the burgomasters, Dominie Megapolensis, and his son Samuel went to the fort, spoke briefly to Stuyvesant, and led him away before he ordered the cannons to fire.

Cornered and isolated, Stuyvesant now understood that his role had become one of carrying out the wishes of the people of New Amsterdam. He arranged a meeting of representatives of the English and the Dutch for the next day, September 6, at his own farm just outside the city, where they drew up a treaty surrendering the colony to the English. On September 8, 1664, Stuyvesant signed the document ending Dutch control of New Netherland, led his soldiers out of the fort, and marched them down to the Dutch ship, the *Gideon.* Once the Dutch had boarded their ship, Colonel Nicolls landed his forces and raised the Union Jack. New Amsterdam had become New York.

A few months after the fall of New Amsterdam, Great Britain and the United Provinces of Holland formally went to war in what is known as the Second Anglo-Dutch War of 1665–1667. England's victory in this war legitimized James's takeover of New Netherland. But the struggle for dominance was not quite over, as the Dutch and the English fought yet another conflict, the Third Anglo-Dutch War of 1672–1674. On August 8, 1673, eight Dutch warships entered New York City's harbor and anchored. They found the city with the English governor gone and the fort undermanned. The Dutch demanded the surrender of the fort, and, after a brief display of cannon fire, the English capitulated. The Dutch held New York for 15 months. Their occupation ended with the signing of the Second Treaty of Westminster on February 19, 1674; a section of the treaty promised that each side would return to the other "all lands, islands, towns, ports, castles and fortresses" taken during the war. On November 10, 1674, the Dutch administrator boarded a ship and left New York; the last gasp of Dutch control had ended.

With Dutch claims extinguished, England controlled the coastline of North America from the Chesapeake northward. While the Swedes and the Dutch had established claims to areas within Great Britain's interest, they had failed to populate their colonies adequately. In the case of the Dutch in New Netherland, inconsistent leadership, half-hearted support from the West India Company, and occasionally severe Indian troubles all combined to prevent the Dutch from succeeding with their North American colony. While Peter Stuyvesant brought order and stability to New Netherland, English encroachment from New England and Long Island could not be held back. In the end, only Stuyvesant stood alone on the battlements of New Amsterdam's rickety fort ready to defend Holland's possessions.

In the short run, the Dutch West India Company failed and the Dutch lost their toehold to an area of British North America; yet, their efforts in the long run were not in vain. From Henry Hudson to Peter Minuit's "purchase" of Manhattan Island to Peter Stuyvesant's last defense of the city, the Dutch formed a key part of the history of America's most important city.

## SELECTED BIBLIOGRAPHY

Burrows, Edwin G., and Mike Wallace. *Gotham: A History of New York City to 1898.* New York: Oxford University Press, 1999. Surveys the history of New York City from the Indian era through the late nineteenth century.

Irving, Washington. *Knickerbocker's History of New York.* Introduction by Andrew B. Myers. Tarrytown, NY: Sleepy Hollow Press, 1981. Washington Irving's delightful parody of the history of New York contains more sound history than the casual reader might imagine.

Kammen, Michael. *Colonial New York: A History.* New York: Charles Scribner's Sons, 1975. Provides important revisions to the story of early New York colonial history and continues to influence historians.

Kenney, Alice P. *Stubborn for Liberty: The Dutch in New York.* Syracuse, NY: Syracuse University Press, 1975. Covers the political history of Dutch New York as well as providing a social history of the colony.

Rink, Oliver A. *Holland on the Hudson: An Economic and Social History of Dutch New York.* Ithaca, NY: Cornell University Press, 1986. The most recent and important of the histories of Dutch New York building on and correcting Kammen's interpretation.

Ritchie, Robert C. *The Duke's Province: A Study of New York Politics and Society, 1664–1691.* Chapel Hill: University of North Carolina Press, 1977. Though the book is largely focused on the period after the English takeover, the early chapters provide an interesting and useful synthesis of the historical literature of Dutch New York.

Shorto, Russell. *The Island at the Center of the World: The Epic Story of Dutch Manhattan and the Forgotten Colony That Shaped America.* New York: Doubleday, 2004. A well-written account emphasizing the significance of the Dutch in American colonial development.

Smith, William, Jr. *The History of the Province of New-York.* Volume One: *From the First Discovery to the Year 1732.* Edited by Michael Kammen. Cambridge, MA: Harvard University Press, 1972. Reprint of one of the important early books on New York, reprinting some of the key Dutch and English documents while defending the English conquest of the colony.

Van Der Donck, Adriaen. *A Description of the New Netherlands.* Edited by Thomas F. O'Donnell. Syracuse, NY: Syracuse University Press, 1968. Originally published in 1656, this work describes and promotes the New Netherlands colony.

Van Der Zee, Henri, and Barbara Van Der Zee. *A Sweet and Alien Land: The Story of Dutch New York.* New York: Viking Press, 1978. A popular history of the Dutch in New York stressing the cultural and social conditions of the colony while providing some political history.

## ANGLO-DUTCH WARS

The Anglo-Dutch Wars were a series of three 17th-century conflicts fought between England and the United Provinces of Holland over the issue of European naval supremacy.

The first Anglo-Dutch War broke out in 1652 after the British Parliament passed the first Navigation Act, which limited the import of Dutch goods. In response, the Dutch government ordered its navy to fire on British ships. The Dutch Navy, however, was badly defeated in the English Channel in 1653, and a treaty of peace was signed in 1654.

The second Anglo-Dutch War was waged during 1664–1667 over the English seizure of New Amsterdam in 1664 and earlier clashes over trading rights in West Africa. Military encounters ended in a virtual stalemate, and, by 1667, both England and Holland were ready for an end to the conflict. The 1667 Treaty of Breda allowed the English to retain control of New Amsterdam but gave trading concessions to the Dutch that ameliorated provisions of the Navigation Act.

In 1672, the third Anglo-Dutch War began after French king Louis XIV invaded Holland, and England, committed to a secret alliance with France, found itself in another naval war with the United Provinces. The Dutch were victorious in the major naval engagements, but, when the treaty of peace was signed, in 1674, the Dutch acknowledged that New York (formerly New Amsterdam) was a British possession, while England ended its treaty of alliance with France.

After 1674, and as a direct result of the Anglo-Dutch Wars, the United Provinces of Holland did not have land holdings in North America and did not play a significant role in colonial affairs.

## DUTCH EAST INDIA COMPANY

The Dutch East India Company was chartered by the government of the Netherlands in 1602 to promote trade with Asia. By exploring new routes to Asia, establishing overseas colonies, and fostering trade, the Dutch East India Company brought substantial wealth to both the merchant community and the Crown during the 17th and 18th centuries. The company's charter granted it a monopoly on Dutch trade in Africa, South America, and Asia. Although the company's involvement in North American trade was limited, it contributed to the development of the continent in two ways: exploration and slavery.

In its search for a passage to Asia, the Dutch East India Company explored large portions of North America. In 1609, the company employed the Englishman Henry Hudson to locate the famed Northwest Passage from the Atlantic Ocean to the Pacific, which it was hoped would provide a shorter trade route between Europe and Asia than the treacherous journey around either the Cape of Good Hope or the tip of South America.

Hudson failed to find the elusive Northwest Passage but instead explored much of what is today the northern United States and Canada. During his journey, he discovered a large river in present-day New York (and which now bears his name). The river eventually became a vital means of transportation and trade for America. Hudson then sailed up the river to what is today Albany, New York, and traded with the local Mohawk Indians, establishing friendly relations with the Native Americans.

Once back in Europe, Hudson's journey spawned a series of travel narratives that encouraged further exploration in North America. In 1614, the company built trading posts at Manhattan and Albany, although its efforts to promote trade in the region remained halfhearted and it did not fund efforts to establish permanent settlements in the area. Nevertheless, Hudson's explorations and the establishment of the outposts aided the Dutch in gaining a foothold in America.

The Dutch East India Company also conducted a lucrative trade in slaves in North America, establishing a trade route between its colonies in Africa and the New World. A Dutch ship brought the first African slaves to the English colony of Virginia in 1619, and the company encouraged the growth of this trade throughout the 17th century, supplying colonists with desperately need labor for tobacco crops and fostering the growth of this labor system.

BRETT SCHMOLL AND ELIZABETH DUBRULLE

## DUTCH REFORMED CHURCH

The Dutch Reformed Church was the official church of the Netherlands, and it came to America when the Dutch East India and West India companies established settlements in what is today New York. It remained one of the foremost religious orders in the mid-Atlantic region during the colonial period.

The original impetus for the formation of the first Dutch settlements—Dutch East India and West India companies—was commercial, not religious. A decade and a half later, in 1628, however, those first settlers established the Dutch Reformed Church in New Amsterdam (present-day New York). The colony's Provisional Orders, a document written in 1624 as a guide for administering the Dutch colony, stated that the Dutch Reformed Church was the only allowable public form of worship, although dissenters were usually free to practice their beliefs in private. Unlike their English neighbors in New England, the Dutch colonists in America were primarily concerned with financial gain and with securing the Netherlands' hold over the colony, rather than with the formal establishment and practice of religion. Accordingly, the early history of the Dutch Reformed Church in America was less vibrant and not as well developed as that of the established religions in such colonies as New England, where religion was inseparable from the fundamental institutions of everyday life.

As the colony developed, however, more churches were established, and a prominent and active congregation was founded at Fort Orange in the 1640s by Johannes Megapolensis. By the end of the 17th century, more than 25 congregations of the Dutch Reformed Church were established in the region, although the Netherlands ceased to rule the colony in 1664 following its defeat by the British in the third Anglo-Dutch War. The treaty of surrender between the Dutch and the English guaranteed that the church would be allowed to continue in the colony without discrimination. That guarantee meant that some Dutch leaders in the colony continued to exercise a prominent role in the colony even after the area came under the control of the English Crown.

By the end of the 18th century, the Dutch Reformed Church began to wane due to a diminished interest in Dutch ethnic identity and an increased persistence in colonial identity, as well as the advent of the Great Awakening. The latter development, which was noted for the growth of homegrown American religions, including Presbyterianism, irrevocably altered the Dutch Reformed Church. As a result, the church broke into two splinter groups. A colonial-based religious faction wanted to incorporate English into its daily worship, to aid in church revivalism—a hallmark of Great Awakening itinerancy—as well as to form a college to train its ministers and to have greater autonomy from the established Dutch Reformed Church. Meanwhile, the conservative Dutch party wanted to maintain Dutch influence and leadership, including Dutch-trained pastors who had received an education in the Netherlands.

Eventually, the colonial party began to overtake the conservative arm of the church. In 1766, Queen's College (which later became Rutgers University) in New Brunswick, New Jersey, was established. Prior to the outbreak of the American Revolution, the two groups reunited in 1771, agreeing to allow authority to rest in the Netherlands while maintaining local power. Following the American Revolution, the Dutch Reformed Church formulated a constitution and broke all ties with Holland.

A vast influx of Dutch immigrants during the 1840s spurred church enrollment, although most of those immigrants settled in such areas of the Midwest as Michigan. The more recent wave of Dutch immigrants seemingly held to more traditional customs as they were more conservative than the older Dutch settlement of New York and New Jersey. In 1867, the church was renamed the Reformed Church in America. The church remains active today, and it currently has about 950 congregations in the United States and Canada and a total membership of more than 300,000.

BRETT SCHMOLL AND ELIZABETH DUBRULLE

## DUTCH WEST INDIA COMPANY

The Dutch West India Company established the only permanent Dutch colony in North America, named New Netherland (present-day New York State). Although the company maintained a hold on the colony for only 40 years, Dutch culture and society had a long-lasting impact on the region.

In 1621, William Usselinx proposed a plan for a permanent Dutch colony in North America to the States-General of the Netherlands. Despite the success of the Dutch East India Company, the government of the Netherlands had shied away from establishing permanent settlements in the New World because of the expense. Usselinx, however, persuasively argued that such a colony would provide a market for Dutch manufactured goods and would possibly bring riches in gold and silver. The Estates-General agreed but decided against a wholly state-supported venture. Instead, it chartered the Dutch West India Company in 1624 and encouraged merchants to fund, administer, and populate the new colony. The company was granted a 24-year charter, a monopoly on American trade, and 1 million florins (the Dutch monetary unit) to establish permanent settlements in the Americas.

In the late 1620s, the Dutch West India Company's colonizing efforts met with limited success in the Caribbean and on the coast of South America. It abandoned its South American holdings in 1654 after conflicts with the Portuguese, who controlled most of the area. Within a year of the granting of its charter, the company had also established a foothold in North America in the region surrounding the Hudson River, which had been discovered by Dutch-sponsored explorer Henry Hudson earlier in the century. Expanding on the Dutch East India Company's trading posts at Manhattan and Albany, the Dutch West India Company encouraged emigration and settlement to its colony, named New Netherland.

In 1625, 30 families arrived in New Netherland aboard a ship of the same name. The company drafted a document known as the Provisional Orders to provide a form of government for the colony. In addition to demanding that all colonists comply with the company's laws and muster in the company's militia for the colony's defense, the Provisional Orders allowed for freedom of religious belief, although it permitted public worship only in accordance with the Dutch Reformed Church.

Although the Dutch West India Company encouraged farmers to emigrate and consistently promoted agricultural efforts, it received most of its profits from the lucrative fur trade, assisted by the Netherlands' preeminence in trade over other European powers. Dutch ships used the colony as a base from which to conduct the fur trade and to trade with other European colonies in the New World.

In 1626, colonist Peter Minuit purchased the island of Manhattan from the local Indians and established the settlement of New Amsterdam (present-day New York City) as the capital of the new colony. The company elected Minuit governor. During Minuit's tenure, he encouraged settlement and worked diligently to bolster the colony's defenses against Indian attacks or encroachments from other European powers attempting to expand their power in the New World. Although he was successful in his efforts, internal dissension within the company prompted his dismissal from the governorship in 1631.

In 1629, the Dutch established a system to encourage emigration known as the patroonship system. Stockholders in the Dutch West India Company could receive large tracts of land in New Netherland by guaranteeing to bring 50 new emigrants to the colony within four years. These emigrants would become tenant farmers on the patroon's land and pay rent in a system reminiscent of the medieval European feudal system. In addition, patroons held enormous power within their domains. Only three patroonships were established in New Netherland—Pavonia, Swaanendael, and Rensselaerswyck—and only the last met with even limited success. Most emigrants elected to work their own land, which the company eventually encouraged by allowing anyone who improved land to receive ownership of it. The slow pace of emigration to New Netherland remained a disappointment to the company, however.

Emigration was only one challenge faced by the Dutch West India Company during the mid-17th century. Between 1640 and 1664, the company was involved in a series of wars (known collectively as the Dutch-Indian Wars) with local Indian tribes. These wars hindered the company's efforts to recruit settlers and severely damaged farming efforts and the fur trade in the colony.

In 1652, New Netherland faced its most serious challenge with the outbreak of the first Anglo-Dutch War. The conflict erupted between the English and Dutch because of England's attempt to impose restrictive trade acts on its colonies and their shipping. The Dutch generally ignored these laws and encouraged English colonists to smuggle their goods in Dutch ships. This war was the first of three wars between England and the Netherlands that eventually resulted in the Treaty of Westminister, in 1674, which granted New Netherland to the English. The Dutch West India Company went bankrupt shortly thereafter, and the Netherlands abandoned all efforts to colonize the New World.

BRETT SCHMOLL AND ELIZABETH DUBRULLE

## PETER MINUIT (1580–1638)

Peter Minuit, the third director general of the Dutch colony of New Netherland, led the famous purchase of Manhattan Island from the Indians for $24 in 1626. He was instrumental in shaping the new colony and acquired the necessary land so that the Europeans could settle and build their colony under the support of the Dutch West India Company.

It is believed that Minuit was born in 1580 in Wesel, a town in Prussia very close to the border with Holland. His father was Jean Minuit, a French-speaking Protestant refugee from what is now Belgium. Both men married natives of Wesel. In 1615, Minuit moved to Utrecht, Holland, where he became a diamond cutter. In search of greater fortune, he joined the Dutch West India Company, which incorporated in 1621.

The company owned and managed the colony of New Netherland in the New World. The colony stretched from the Connecticut to the Delaware rivers and was a commercial enterprise for the company. Outposts lined the rivers, including the Hudson River, which cut through the middle of the colony and was a major thoroughfare. The outposts received goods from Europe and the Caribbean and shipped out thousands of beaver furs.

Although Europeans started to settle in New Netherland in 1624, Minuit was not among them. When he arrived, in 1625, he organized the colonists, who were spread throughout the Hudson River valley from Beverwyck (present-day Albany) to New Amsterdam (present-day New York City). The risks to survival increased with the colony so spread out, and proper relations between Native Americans and Europeans could not be monitored. In 1626, after Minuit and the Native Americans in the area exchanged trade goods for the island of Manhattan, he gathered all the colonists to the tip of Manhattan (New Amsterdam), which provided greater security and allowed the land to develop.

Also in 1626, Minuit was appointed to succeed Willem Verhulst as director general of the colony. Minuit was directed to establish, supervise, and maintain healthy trade relations with the British colonies and the Native Americans, as this was the thrust of the colony's existence. Because of his critical position, Minuit became caught in political maneuvering between those who wanted to limit business to the fur trade and those who wanted to expand business through farming. In 1630, Minuit was brought to Amsterdam for questioning, and, in 1632, a new director general was named.

Because of his experience with the traders in New Netherland and along the northeastern seaboard, in 1638, Minuit went to work for the Swedish and led a settlement at the mouth of the Delaware River called New Sweden. He built Fort Christina, which lasted as an outpost until Peter Stuyvesant captured it, in 1655. Minuit perished in a hurricane in the West Indies in June 1638.

GRADY TURNER

## PETER STUYVESANT (1610–1672)

Peter Stuyvesant, a Dutch soldier and colonial official, was the last director general of the Dutch colony of New Netherland (present-day New York). Although he was an effective administrator, his religious intolerance and arbitrary methods made him an extremely unpopular governor.

Stuyvesant was born in Scherpenzeel, near Wolvega, Netherlands, around 1610. He was the son of Rev. Balthazar Johannes Stuyvesant, a Dutch Reformed Church pastor, and Margaretha Hardenstein Stuyvesant. Little is known about his youth except that he entered military service at an early age and attended Franeker University during 1629–1630. By 1632, he was serving in the Dutch West India Company, which sent him to Brazil in 1635.

In 1643, Stuyvesant was appointed governor of Curaçao and other Dutch possessions in the West Indies. While participating in a campaign against the Portuguese in the West Indies in 1644, he was wounded in his right leg, which was later amputated and replaced by a silver-ornamented wooden one. This elaborately decorated leg became popularly known as his "silver leg." Soon after returning to Holland from Curaçao, Stuyvesant married Judith Bayard in the Walloon Church of Breda on August 13, 1645.

On July 28, 1646, the States-General of the Netherlands commissioned Stuyvesant director general of "New Netherland and the places situated thereabout, as well as the islands of Curaçao, Buenaire, Aruba, and the dependencies and appurtenances thereof." That same year, Stuyvesant sailed to Curaçao then landed at New Amsterdam (present-day New York City) on May 11, 1647. Although Stuyvesant's acts as governor were often harsh and dictatorial, he made determined efforts to provide New Netherland with an honest and efficient administration.

Under his leadership, a marked change in the appearance of New Amsterdam soon occurred as a result of numerous public works projects. Stuyvesant also made extensive changes in the city government. He created the Board of Nine Men to assist him in governing the settlement on September 25, 1647. Stuyvesant soon proved to be so autocratic, however, that the citizens of New Amsterdam, aided by directors of the West India Company, forced him to grant independent municipal control of city on February 2, 1653.

Stuyvesant was also not very successful in settling a long-standing dispute between Connecticut and New Netherland. By way of the humiliating Treaty of Hartford in 1650, Stuyvesant virtually relinquished Dutch control of the Connecticut Valley. Pressures exerted by English colonists also resulted in Stuyvesant's granting to several Long Island towns the right to elect their own officials.

As a devout member of the Dutch Reformed Church, Stuyvesant was arbitrary in his religious policies. He regarded all nonconformists as likely to foment rebellion and therefore dealt harshly with them, particularly Lutherans and Quakers. With the West India Company on the verge of bankruptcy, Stuyvesant resorted to a policy of taxation to provide for badly needed improvements during his years as director general. Furthermore, he strove to eliminate smuggling to prevent loss of revenue. He also sought to improve relations with Native Americans by attempting to eliminate unscrupulous business practices long used by the merchants of New Amsterdam and Fort Orange (present-day Albany). Nonetheless, Stuyvesant was adamantly opposed to any governmental reforms that might lessen his own authority over New Netherland. Throughout his directorship, he rejected all demands for the creation of a popular legislative assembly.

From 1653 to 1664, Stuyvesant's primary concern was to prevent the decline of Dutch influence on Long Island. Despite his arduous efforts, Stuyvesant's success in achieving this objective varied greatly. His most notable achievement in the endeavor occurred in 1655 and involved a long-standing dispute over Swedish colonization of the Delaware Valley. To deal with this problem, he invaded New Sweden and forced its surrender. He was also able to keep the Native Americans restrained, as well.

Despite his successes with the Swedes and the Indians, Stuyvesant's dealings with aggressive colonists were far less successful. Increasing difficulties with the English over boundaries and trade eventually climaxed with the appearance of an English fleet in the harbor of New Amsterdam in 1664. The fleet, under the command of Col. Richard Nicolls, demanded that the city capitulate to the Duke of York, who had laid claim to all the land between the Connecticut River and the Delaware Valley. Stuyvesant, whose plans for the defense of the city were opposed by the local burghers, was compelled to surrender New Netherland to the English without resistance on September 8, 1664.

In October 1665, Stuyvesant arrived in the Netherlands to defend himself against charges of misconduct. He retired to New York in 1667 and lived on his farm, or *bouwerij*, from which New York City's Bowery takes its name. He died in February 1672 and was buried beneath the chapel on his farm, which is now the site of St. Mark's Episcopal Church.

# 10

# King Philip's War, 1675–1676

## INTRODUCTION

When New England was first settled, many of the area's Indians had died in a smallpox epidemic in 1616. Not until after 1630 and the great increase in European migration to New England did tensions begin to rise between white settlers and Indians, and these became particularly acute after 1630 with the settlement of Connecticut, which impinged on Pequot lands. This led to the bloody Pequot War of 1637.

In the 40 years between the Pequot War and King Philip's War, Europeans and Indians lived in a state of continuing tension. Some Indians abetted colonial economic growth by working for colonists, selling meat and fish, and trading in wampum currency. Some were converted to Christianity, and these "praying Indians" often became military allies in conflicts between colonists and other Indians.

Despite some degree of economic cooperation and religious conversion, however, Indian-white conflict continued in New England after the Pequot War. Expansion into Connecticut and the creation of the colony of Providence Plantations (Rhode Island) served only to whet colonists' thirst for more land, and everyone realized that if more land were placed under colonial jurisdiction, more land would be available for individual settlers. Thus efforts to assume dominion over additional land, whether occupied by Indians or not, played an important role in colonist-Indian relations in the mid-17th century. Intercolonial rivalry also exacerbated some of the moves to acquire more land.

In 1645, when the New Englanders denied the Narragansett Indians permission to attack the Mohegans and they did anyway, the colonists raised a force and brought about the capitulation of the Narragansetts. In the 1650s, the whites again put down an Indian force and obtained land from Indians in Connecticut as part of the settlement.

New England's colonies grew rapidly during the period between 1650 and 1675. The population doubled to some 50,000, and settlements spread into more backwater areas and encroached more and more on Indian lands. The Indians, bitter toward the English and unwilling to leave ancestral territory, became increasingly resentful. In the 1660s, the English forced the Wampanoag leader Metacom, whom they called King Philip, to recognize their sovereignty over all Indians. Many Indians came to the conclusion that armed resistance was the only way they could preserve their independence.

By the 1670s, English colonists particularly coveted the land of the large Narragansett tribe. It lay along the shore of what is now Rhode Island and southeastern Connecticut west from Narragansett Bay and included several islands in the bay. The English Crown

Indian wars in the 17th century featured fighting at close quarters, as seen in this engraving from the 19th century that shows American colonists fighting Wampanoag Indians in 1675. (Courtesy of the Library of Congress.)

had never granted a royal charter for this land to anyone, although some Englishmen, like Roger Williams, had moved there anyway. The Indians had tolerated this incursion, coming as it did fairly soon after the Pequot War. Moreover, Williams was known as an Indian ally in their struggles with the Massachusetts Bay and Connecticut colonies.

King Philip lived near the settlement of Bristol, in Rhode Island, at a place overlooking Narragansett Bay. In the early 1670s, militant Narragansett leaders approached him with an offer for the Wampanoags to join the Narragansetts in war against the land-hungry colonists, who were constantly trying to acquire more land in exchange for trinkets, liquor, or weapons. Indian attitudes grew more warlike, and Philip finally agreed that war was necessary. In June 1675, war broke out after an incident in which a farmer shot and wounded an Indian who had killed one of the farmer's oxen. Indians congregated in the area around Swansea, fighting began, and a number of settlers were killed. A force of 120, under Capt. Thomas Savage, went to Philip's home, surprised him, and killed 15 Indians. Although Philip himself managed to escape, Savage's force took his cattle and destroyed the rest of his property.

The Indian force under Philip then overran the colonial settlement of Mendan and almost took Brookfield, which was saved only by the timely arrival of additional colonial militia. At the same time, King Philip broadened his alliance; only the Mohegans, traditional enemies of the Narragansetts, refused to break a treaty made with settlers and join with Philip. It was a bad decision. The governor of Connecticut Colony, Edward Wilson, sent a force of colonial fighters to a fortified village of the Mohegans, and a major battle ensued. In what became known as the Great Swamp Fight, the village fell to the colonists, and more than 300 Indians, including women and children, were killed. The outcome of the Great Swamp Fight made the Indians even more determined to resist colonial encroachment, and, during the next several months, they attacked numerous white settlements throughout Massachusetts and Rhode Island, causing many casualties.

Philip next tried to lure the powerful Mohawk tribe into his alliance, but this effort failed and demoralized some of Philip's supporters. Nevertheless, the fighting continued with Philip's attack on Deerfield, a settlement in Massachusetts. At the same time, however, other Indians, weary of the warfare, were covertly seeking peace. They arranged for the capture of Philip's wife and child, who were shipped off to Bermuda as slaves, and Philip himself was killed by one of the dissenters.

Although the fighting continued for a few more months, King Philip's War was over by December 1676. Although accounts vary, it appears as though at least 800 colonists and more than 3,000 Indians died. The fighting also destroyed perhaps 25 English towns or about half of the European settlements in New England. But the colonists emerged from the war more unified, because of the cooperation utilized to subdue the Indians. New England Indian society, on the other hand, was weakened and fragmented, opening new lands for white settlement.

In the south, Jesuit and Franciscan missionaries worked to Christianize the Indians and to bring about some degree of allegiance to Spanish rule. Some 26,000 Indians had converted at midcentury, many doing so in return for the promise of protection and the advantages of trade. During the second half of the 17th century, however, conflict between the Spanish and English resulted in the virtual elimination of the Spanish and the arrival of English settlers and their African slaves.

During the Spanish era, the Indians had been given sovereignty over their land and freedom from enslavement in return for their souls and their loyalty to Spain. Indians chiefs received horses, swords, fancy clothes, and other symbols of social rank and distinction. This system worked particularly well among the Timucua and Apalachee tribes, where Christian missionaries became an integral part of Indian villages, and Indians were often induced to do the Spaniards' physical labor.

By about 1650, many Indians were becoming restless under this regimen, and many others died of European diseases that the Spanish had brought. In 1647, the Apalachees revolted against their Christian brethren in the hope of halting Spanish encroachment into their lives and liberties. Nine years later, the Timucua revolted after the Spanish forced several chiefs to perform physical tasks long considered beneath their dignity. Neither revolt succeeded, although that of the Timucua resulted in many priests leaving their Indian village posts and an end to Spanish gifts.

In 1680, English slave hunters sent their Indian allies out after rival Indians who could be sold as slaves. Most of the remaining Spanish missions closed during this time, while the remaining ones relocated to the relative safety of the area near Saint Augustine. The English continued to capture Indians in the south for the slave trade into the early 18th century.

In Virginia, the late 18th century was marked by the continued depopulation of the Powhatan confederacy. Remaining Indians lived on small reservations on the fringes of colonial settlement, and chiefs served at the pleasure of the colonial government in

Jamestown. African slaves in increasing numbers worked in tobacco fields that had once been Indian land. By 1700, only about 1,900 Indians still lived in eastern Virginia, down from nearly 70,000 when the English first came.

The English and Spanish regard for Indians was starkly different. The English regarded colonization as a business venture in which the Indians were an obstacle to be removed. They seldom recognized Indian land rights but simply claimed for themselves (and the king) all the land described in their royal charter. Except for Pocahontas, they were not much interested in converting Indians to Christianity; many thought that task was a useless endeavor. The Indians in Virginia made one major attempt to resist the English, that of Opechancanough's forces in 1644, and, after that failed, the Powhatans were of no social or economic consequence to the colony.

Around 1650, the English began trading with the natives who lived in the Piedmont region, farther to the west. These tribes, which had previously had very little contact with whites, were, like so many others, quickly decimated by disease and warfare. Often battles were fought between rival Indian tribes rather than between English militia and Indians; the English became skilled at pitting tribes against each other. After 1670, much of this activity was conducted from the more recently settled Charles Town (what is now Charleston, South Carolina), where the local economy was based on trade in furs and Indian slaves.

Clearly, no place in the area of English settlement in North America was pleasant for Indians in the late 17th century. Regarding colonization as primarily a business venture, the English treated Indians as economic assets for the slave trade or as obstacles to progress when more land was needed to meet the demands of the ever-increasing number of settlers.

## INTERPRETIVE ESSAY

STEVEN E. SIRY

In 1675, the long-standing alliance between the colony of Plymouth and the Wampanoag Indians came to an end. For years, advancing colonial settlements had gradually reduced the Indians' land base. Moreover, the increasing English population had driven away game, which greatly diminished the Indians' fur trade, and the colonists' livestock strayed into Indians' fields, destroying their crops. The Wampanoags were also alarmed at the influence of English culture on Indian children. Many of the tribal sachems especially resented the Christian missionaries. Metacom, known to the English as King Philip, supposedly told John Eliot, a leading missionary, that "he cared no more for the white man's gospel than he did for a button on Eliot's coat." Metacom, who succeeded his father, Massasoit, as the sachem of the Wampanoags, had also endured humiliations at the hands of the English. In 1671, colonial authorities had ordered him to surrender a large stock of guns, to pay a heavy fine, and to accept a treaty acknowledging Wampanoag submission to English law.

The Indians had limited options by the 1670s. They could sell their land to pay off trade debts and become laborers in the colonial settlements, they could move westward into areas controlled by the Five Nations of the Iroquois, or they could create a pan-Indian alliance to launch a war against the colonists. The decision for war was made after Wampanoag braves, allegedly under orders from Metacom, murdered John Sassamon, a Christianized, Harvard-educated Indian informer, though the chief denied responsibility. In January 1675, the informer had told Plymouth officials that the Wampanoags were planning an attack on colonial settlements. When the informer was murdered and stuffed under pond ice, the Plymouth government arrested and executed three Wampanoags. This action further outraged the Wampanoag Indians, who asserted that the English had violated Wampanoag sovereignty. By the end of the summer, they went to war against the English, who saw the conflict as an opportunity to seize more tribal lands and to subjugate the remaining powerful tribes in southern New England.

At the beginning of the conflict, the Wampanoags successfully carried out several raids on settlements in Plymouth and Massachusetts, and the colonial governments initially failed to create a unified front against the attacks. This led to numerous Algonquin tribes, including the Nipmucs, Narragansetts, Pocumtucks, and Pocassets, to become allies of the Wampanoags. Indian ambushes occurred in the late summer at Northfield and at Whalely. Survivors reported that the Indians had cut off soldiers' heads and put them on poles, had burned captives at the stake, and had hooked a chain into the under-jaw of one colonial prisoner and hung him from the bough of a tree.

By December, Metacom's forces had attacked along the New England frontier and destroyed settlements in the entire upper Connecticut River valley. But, on December 19, 1675, colonial forces attacked the Narragansetts' refuge, which lay hidden in a swamp in Rhode Island. What ensued has been called the "Great Swamp Fight." Despite suffering heavy losses, the colonial militia set fire to the Narragansett town. Most of the warriors escaped, but many of the noncombatants became casualties as more than 600 Narragansett men, women, and children perished in the battle. As Cotton Mather later phrased it, many had been "terribly Barbikew'd." This was one of at least two major battles where the English indiscriminately killed women, children, and old men.

In January 1676, Metacom led Indian forces into winter encampment approximately 50 miles from Albany, New York. Besides about 400 of Metacom's men, there were many hundreds of other Algonquin Indians from southern and northern New England, the largest number being Narragansetts who had survived the Great Swamp Fight. Promising weapons, food, clothing, and shelter, Gov. Edmund Andros of New York persuaded the Mohawks, always the most aggressive of the Iroquois, and some of their Iroquoian brethren to attack the Algonquins in early February and thus clear New York of this enemy. It was an extremely successful surprise attack. Only 40 of Metacom's 400 men survived, and many of them were badly wounded. The other Algonquins were dispersed. This was the key battle that prevented Metacom from emerging as the primary leader of the Algonquins and from creating a wider Indian alliance. Nevertheless, the war would continue to bear King Philip's name.

Despite the defeats at the Great Swamp Fight and near Albany, Algonquin forces by March 1676 were less than 20 miles from Providence and Boston. Refugees flooded into the coastal areas, profiteering in food supplies developed, and resistance to the colonial drafts became widespread. Nevertheless, the defeat at the hands of the Mohawks had eliminated the Algonquins' ability to attack the major New England towns.

Furthermore, in the spring of 1676, the Indians suffered from the spread of diseases and a lack of supplies.

In the summer, some Indians moved westward, while others surrendered. Indeed, during King Philip's War, the colonial governments were forced to deal with many Indian prisoners. Authorities in all of the New England colonies executed numerous enemy captives. Viewing the war as a rebellion instead of as a war between nations, the English felt that the "rebels" deserved to be executed. Moreover, in such a bloody conflict, the colonists believed that the execution of Indians was a just punishment and a good means to ensure the security of the colonial population. In the fall of 1675, Captain Samuel Moseley, described as a former buccaneer from the West Indies, reported the interrogation of a captured Indian woman, noting that the "aforesaid Indian was ordered to be torn to peeces by Doggs and she was soe dealt with."

But usually Indian prisoners were not killed until they had been given some form of a legal trial. Military commanders, however, sometimes were allowed to execute prisoners without a trial. Furthermore, occasionally private citizens would take the law into their own hands. For example, in Marblehead, Massachusetts, a group of women decapitated two Indian prisoners.

Public pressure could also affect the authorities' actions. At the end of the war, an Indian leader known as Chuff, who was badly wounded, arrived in a small Rhode Island settlement. Because the townspeople felt he had led attacks against Providence, they demanded his execution. The Town Council and the Council of War sentenced Chuff to death, and he was soon shot.

Even when the English had no desire to execute captive Indians, the colonists' Indian allies sought their deaths. In April 1676, Pequot warriors captured the Narragansett sachem Canonchet. After he was taken to Stonington, the English acceded to the Connecticut Indians' demand that he be executed. Before his death in front of an English firing squad, Canonchet asserted: "I like it well. I shall die before my heart is soft or I have said anything unworthy of myself."

The colonial authorities also sold numerous captive Indians into bonded servitude or slavery. No record exists of the exact number of Indians involved. But many were sent to slave markets in Spain, along the the Mediterranean coasts, in Virginia, or in the West Indies. Some areas, however, believing that North American Indians made poor slaves, refused to purchase them. The governments in Barbados and Jamaica even passed legislation barring their entrance.

Selling prisoners of war into slavery went far beyond the usual treatment. But the practice dated back to the Pequot War of 1637, and a 1641 Massachusetts law allowed the practice if it involved "lawful captives taken in just wars." Since many colonial officials claimed that the Indians were traitorous rebels, they viewed the punishment as just. However, not all the Indians sold into slavery had been hostile to the colonists. For example, in July 1675, soon after an attack on Dartmouth in Plymouth, 160 Indians who had not participated in the assault surrendered to colonial authorities when promised amnesty. Nevertheless, all but six of the Indians were sold into foreign slave markets. In short, sizable profits made from the slave trade also fostered the practice. A number of the colonists, however, unsuccessfully opposed the policy. Some had humanitarian concerns, while others wanted to use the captive Indians as a source of cheap labor in New England. Still other New Englanders noted that the Indians would continue the war even longer and fight more fiercely if they knew that slavery would result from defeat.

Using Indian scouts and tactics, colonial militia in early August 1676 attacked Metacom's camp. He escaped, but 173 Indians were killed or captured. The latter included Metacom's wife and nine-year-old son, who were subsequently sold into slavery in the West Indies. When Metacom learned of their fates, he declared: "My heart breaks. Now I am ready to die." On August 12, English forces, guided by one of Metacom's own men who had turned traitor, ambushed his sleeping camp, and Metacom was shot through the heart. The militia and their Indian allies then cut off his head and hands, quartered his body, and hung the parts in trees. After Metacom's death, sporadic fighting occurred for several months; a formal treaty, the Peace of Casco, was not signed until April 12, 1678.

A total defeat of the English had been impossible since the start of the war. Their much larger population, as well as their extensive network of logistical support from America to Europe, provided the English with a tremendous advantage over the Indian insurgents. Nevertheless, a stalemate might have been achieved if the tribes of southern New England throughout the war had gained the assistance of the Mohawks or the Abenakis, a powerful Algonquin tribe in northern New England that had ties with the French. But, without such allies, the Indians of southern New England were decisively defeated. The Algonquins succumbed to a two-front war against the English and the Mohawks.

New England experienced elation and relief at the end of King Philip's War. Yet, New Englanders also had to deal with the war's enormous destruction. Proportional to population, King Philip's War resulted in more casualties than any other war in American history. New England lost more than 800 colonists in the fighting, out of a total population of approximately 52,000 people. Thomas Hutchinson, nearly a century later, claimed that "Every person, almost, [in Massachusetts] lost a relation or near friend." Indeed, King Philip's War was the most destructive war ever fought in New England.

All New England colonies had suffered losses, with the frontier outposts experiencing the greatest destruction. The district of Maine, which had contained 13 towns and plantations at the beginning of the war, suffered such devastation that it did not recover for a half-century. Though New Hampshire suffered very little, Massachusetts experienced extensive losses. Overall, in New England, 16 towns were destroyed or deserted, and another 40 towns came under attack. Twenty years after the war, not all of the towns devastated in 1676 had been reestablished. For example, in Connecticut, few towns were started in the 1680s, and not until almost 1700 did a major westward advancement resume. When towns were rebuilt, the new communities often were more compact for defensive purposes.

The war had also very negatively affected New England's economy. The fur trade had nearly ended, 8,000 head of cattle had been killed, the import and export trade had often been interrupted, and the fishing industry had suffered a serious decline as sailors were recruited into the war effort. In addition, the United Colonies (Massachusetts Bay, Plymouth, and Connecticut) asserted that their wartime expenses totaled more than £80,000. This led to high taxes. Before 1675, Massachusetts colonists had paid a "country rate" or town levies, which were fairly light. But, in 1675, the Massachusetts government started using multiple rates that were much higher. These could be paid in money or corn. Not until 1775 in New England did per capita incomes recover their 1675 levels. The pre-1675 norm was not surpassed until after 1815. In part, this was because in the century between 1676 and 1776 the population increased 10-fold, primarily in the area settled before 1676. But the new settlers also often started from "scratch," which had not been the situation before 1676. King Philip's War had destroyed much of the previous generation's investments and placed significant restrictions on westward expansion.

Ironically, the Puritans' campaign against the New England Indians led to the Covenant Chain Conferences of 1677 between the English government and the Five Nations of the Iroquois. These conferences created a frontier line on the west and south between the colonists and the Iroquois that proved to be a solid barrier to colonial expansion. Furthermore, the New England colonies were now bordered on the north by Indian tribes backed by the French. As a result, the New England colonies, which had been very expansionistic before 1675, would remain territorially restricted until the American Revolution. In addition, both Algonquin and Iroquois Indians continued to attack New England's frontier settlements until the end of the French and Indian War, in 1763. For example, in 1704, Indians again destroyed towns in the Connecticut River valley that had been reestablished after King Philip's War.

Moreover, because many soldiers had served for extended periods, King Philip's War created America's first enormous problem that involved veterans. Indeed, in the aftermath of the war, veterans' organizations were created. The colonial governments usually provided relief to wounded veterans in the form of a one-time payment. But this could be supplemented with special privileges, including a tax-exempt status or the right to collect and keep all fines for violating liquor laws. In addition, some colonial legislatures and some towns provided benefits, especially land grants from areas vacated by the Indians, to survivors of deceased soldiers and to wounded or unwounded veterans. But not all veterans were compensated. More than 50 years after the end of King Philip's War, some veterans or their descendants were still pressuring colonial legislatures for tracts of land.

The war had also cost many people their homes or businesses. In Massachusetts alone, more than 2,000 colonists required assistance. To assist those in need of help, churches, charitable colonists, and sympathetic Europeans sent various types of aid. In addition, funds were raised to ransom colonists who had been captured by the Indians. For example, Mary Rowlandson and her son were ransomed when citizens in Boston and Portsmouth raised £27.

As a result of King Philip's War, the Algonquin Indians of southern New England had suffered a devastating defeat. Six thousand Indians, including most of the Narragansetts, the largest and most powerful tribe of the region, had died, were enslaved, or were reduced to becoming hired servants or poor farmers. But some Indians fled to New York, Virginia, the Susquehanna and Delaware valleys, or Canada as they sought to preserve their culture and their independence.

The New England colonies supervised all remaining Indians by limiting their daily activities. For example, in Rhode Island, the Indians were not allowed to gather in substantial numbers, and Rhode Island and Plymouth placed restrictions on the ownership or carrying of firearms. In addition, New England authorities assigned the Indians to various areas. This included the so-called praying Indians. Indeed, the Christian missionary movement in New England suffered a significant decline during the war. Many of the colonists distrusted the Christian Indians, and there was reason for some of this distrust. Most of the western Nipmucs, who had been exposed to Christianity for less than five years, had joined the Indian insurgents' uprising. But the colonists did not differentiate among the Christian Indians. Massachusetts authorities rounded up all the Bay Colony's praying Indians and relocated them to wind-swept Deer Island in Boston Harbor. Because of inadequate food, clothing, and shelter, a number of these Indians died during their imprisonment. Yet, numerous Christian Indians, despite all their suffering, remained devoted to their faith.

Four Christian Indian towns were rebuilt in postwar Massachusetts, but these were no longer just for the praying Indians. According to a 1677 law, these towns became reservations for the entire Indian population. But the towns were often headed by sachems and the churches headed by other Indians. In this way, the Algonquins, who adopted the European concept of land ownership and many other English ways, also maintained clan boundaries as the principal form of social organization and successfully preserved much of their culture, especially in crafts and trades. In short, these Indians' culture at the end of the 1600s became a combination of Algonquin and English. In the 1700s, however, the Indians increasingly lived more like the English, including adopting their styles of housing. Furthermore, by 1750, Indian languages had largely ceased to be used in New England, as more Native Americans spoke only English.

When King Philip's War ended, colonists commemorated their victory by distributing and displaying throughout New England many bloody reminders of the conflict. For example, colonists from across the region went to Plymouth to view Metacom's head. The colonists also published books and almanacs that listed the dates and provided detailed descriptions of significant wartime events. As the years went by, the descriptions became less detailed, but there remained just one interpretation of the cause of the war: the Indians were to blame.

Before King Philip's War, Puritan clergy condemned what they believed was a lack of discipline and numerous manifestations of ungodliness in New England. During the war, New England ministers asserted that Indian victories were indications of God's displeasure with the settlers and that the defeats inflicted on the Indians indicated a sense of penitence and spiritual regeneration among the colonists. Despite the colonists' victory in King Philip's War, the conflict helped to usher in a tension-filled era in New England. In the postwar period, the dislocations of individuals and groups of people brought about by the war adversely affected Puritan congregationalism's rigid discipline, which normally was under the control of church and state. Efforts by the church leaders to reverse this trend were in vain. The attitudes created by the uprootedness of the war would eventually contribute to the development of the Great Awakening, an extensive religious revival movement in the 1700s.

Besides the religious upheaval of the postwar era, New England's economic troubles prompted many colonists to become more involved in colonial politics and to challenge traditional authority. In some instances they placed new restrictions on the powers of government officials. Popular concern over government affairs would increase in 1686 with the creation of the Dominion of New England, which for four years brought under one government the colonies of Massachusetts, Connecticut, Plymouth, New Hampshire, Rhode Island, New York, and New Jersey.

In both its short- and long-term effects, King Philip's War had a dramatic impact on the development of New England. The Indians of the southern part of the region risked total defeat to stop the increasing colonial control over their societies. But the desperate gamble failed. In 1687, a visitor to New England asserted that there was nothing to fear from the Indians for the "last Wars they had with the English...have reduced them to a small number." The power of the tribes had been completely shattered, and a legacy of hatred had been created between the Indians and the colonists that would last for generations to come.

## SELECTED BIBLIOGRAPHY

Axtell, James. *The Indians' New South: Cultural Change in the Colonial Southeast.* Baton Rouge: Louisiana State University Press, 1997. A study of the impact of the Europeans on the southeastern Indians between 1500 and 1700.

Bourne, Russell. *The Red King's Rebellion: Racial Politics in New England, 1675–1678.* New York: Oxford University Press, 1990. Extensively covers the background and course of the war.

Calloway, Colin G. *New Worlds for All: Indians, Europeans, and the Remaking of Early America.* Baltimore: Johns Hopkins University Press, 1997. Attempts to integrate the Indians as important participants in the making of history and the shaping of societies in early America.

Cogley, Richard W. *John Eliot's Mission to the Indians before King Philip's War.* Cambridge, MA: Harvard University Press, 1999. Account of the well-known missionary's work with Massachusetts Indians in the mid-17th century.

Drake, James D. *King Philip's War: Civil War in New England, 1675–1676.* Amherst: University of Massachusetts Press, 1999. Argues that King Philip's War was, in actuality, a civil war that was not fought strictly along ethnic lines.

Ferling, John E. *A Wilderness of Miseries: War and Warriors in Early America.* Westport, CT: Greenwood Press, 1980. A topical study of war in colonial and Revolutionary America.

Hawke, David Freeman. *Everyday Life in Early America.* New York: Harper and Row, 1988. One chapter provides a brief overview of colonial warfare in the 17th century.

Jennings, Francis. *The Invasion of America: Indians, Colonialism, and the Cant of Conquest.* Chapel Hill: University of North Carolina Press, 1975. A revisionist work that portrays the war as an unjustified seizure of native territory by the English colonists.

Josephy, Alvin M., Jr. *The Patriot Chiefs: A Chronicle of American Indian Leadership.* New York: Viking Press, 1961. One chapter covers Metacom's role in the war.

———. *500 Nations: An Illustrated History of North American Indians.* New York: Knopf, 1994. Provides an overview of Indian history to the end of the 19th century.

Leach, Douglas E. *Flintlock and Tomahawk: New England in King Philip's War.* New York: W. W. Norton, 1958. Detailed study of the causes, course, and costs of the war.

Lepore, Jill. *The Name of War: King Philip's War and the Origins of American Identity.* New York: Knopf, 1998. Extensively covers certain aspects of the war, such as the experiences of captivity, confinement, and slavery. It also shows how participants and later generations portrayed the war in various types of literature.

Malone, Patrick M. *The Skulking Way of War: Technology and Tactics among the New England Indians.* Lanham, MD: Madison Books, 1991. Looks at combat in 17th-century New England and shows how the Indians' abilities in forest warfare, in combination with their mastery of firearms, made them into fearsome enemies of the English colonists.

Mathews, Lois Kimball. *The Expansion of New England: The Spread of New England Settlement and Institutions to the Mississippi River, 1620–1865.* New York: Russell and Russell, 1962.

Originally published in 1909, this book provides information about the war's effect on frontier settlements in New England.

Melvoin, Richard I. *New England Outpost: War and Society in Colonial Frontier Deerfield, Massachusetts.* New York: W. W. Norton, 1989. Shows the impact of King Philip's War on a frontier community.

Millett, Allan R., and Peter Maslowski. *For the Common Defense: A Military History of the United States of America.* Rev. ed. New York: Free Press, 1994. Places King Philip's War within the context of other colonial warfare.

Nash, Gary B. *Red, White, and Black: The Peoples of Early North America.* 3rd ed. Englewood Cliffs, NJ: Prentice-Hall, 1992. Contains a very concise overview of the war.

Puglisi, Michael J. *Puritans Besieged: The Legacies of King Philip's War in the Massachusetts Bay Colony.* Lanham, NY, and London: University Press of America, 1991. A very detailed study of the various costs of the war for the major colony in New England.

Webb, Stephen Saunders. *1676: The End of American Independence.* Syracuse, NY: Syracuse University Press, 1984. Argues that King Philip's War forestalled New England's expansion for almost a century.

## BENJAMIN CHURCH (1639–1718)

Benjamin Church was the first American-born war hero and an accomplished Indian fighter. His successful melding of Native American tactics and European warfare presaged the innovations of Robert Rogers by nearly a century and terminated New England's costliest colonial conflict, King Philip's War.

Church was born in 1639 in Plymouth, Massachusetts, where he worked as a carpenter. In 1675, he founded a colony in present-day Little Compton, Rhode Island, which placed him in almost daily contact with neighboring Indian tribes. Unlike many contemporaries, Church was friendly toward Native Americans, and he closely observed their methods of warfare. In his own words, he was held "in great esteem among them."

Since the founding of Plymouth colony, in 1620, the Europeans and Native Americans existed in a state of relative peace and coexistence. Massasoit, chief of the Wampanoag tribe, earnestly tried to maintain peaceful relations with his new neighbors, but this attitude was not shared by his descendants. The reason for mounting hostility was continuous white expansion into traditional Indian hunting grounds. This, coupled with a growing arrogance of the colonials toward their Native American neighbors, finally pushed relations to the breaking point. When the Wampanoag sachem Philip rose up against the colonialists in June 1675, Church became a captain in the Massachusetts militia. His first act was to boldly stride into the camp of the Sakonnet Indians and persuade the female sachem Awashonks to remain neutral. Church then attempted to convince his Puritan superiors to pursue the enemy and attack them in the field rather than simply build fortifications, but his advice was ignored. He did, however, conduct several successful forays against the Wampanoags and commanded a Plymouth company at the Great Swamp Fight of December 19, 1675. Church sustained two wounds, but the Indians suffered a crushing defeat.

In 1676, Gov. Josiah Winslow of Plymouth appointed Church commander of all militia forces. Church went about recruiting a special company composed of Europeans trained in Indian tactics, as well as large numbers of Indian volunteers who had joined the colonial side. Church then raided and burned Indian villages with great success, capturing Philip's wife and son on August 1, 1676. Philip himself was eventually cornered in present-day Bristol, Rhode Island, and shot dead by one of Church's Indian scouts on August 12. This act effectively ended the war and made Church a hero throughout New England.

Church returned to the field as a major in King William's War (1689–1697) and conducted four large-scale raids against Indian and French forces in Maine and Nova Scotia. His mixed European-Indian troops enjoyed some success but nothing on the scale of previous endeavors. In 1696, when the government of Massachusetts failed to grant what he considered adequate compensation for his efforts, Church retired in disgust.

Eight years later, Church tendered his services during Queen Anne's War (1702–1713) and was made a colonel. In this capacity, he led a large expedition against the French stronghold at Port Royal, Nova Scotia, in 1704 and succeeded in capturing and burning the town of Les Mines. Church warned the French authorities at Port Royal to cease raiding English settlements or he would return "with a thousand Indians and let them loose upon the frontiers of Canada to commit the like barbarities there." Despite this achievement, Church was criticized for allowing a group of French prisoners to be murdered. In 1705, he left the military under a cloud and returned to his home at Little Compton. Corpulent in his old age, Church died of injuries after falling from his horse on January 17, 1718.

JOHN C. FREDRIKSEN

## METACOM (ca. 1638–1676)

King Philip's War, in terms of numbers engaged and casualties sustained, was the single bloodiest Indian war in American history. Despite Metacom's diplomatic finesse in uniting with other tribes, it was a war that he could not win. His defeat presaged the ultimate removal of Native Americans from the New England region.

Metacom was born around 1638 in Massachusetts to the Wampanoag tribe, then a part of the great Algonquian-speaking confederacy. His father, Massasoit, was the tribal sachem during preliminary contacts with European colonists and labored many years to maintain peaceful relations with his new neighbors. Save for a brief outbreak of violence during the Pequot War in southern New England during 1636–1637, the two civilizations enjoyed relative tranquility.

When Massasoit died, Metacom's older brother Alexander (Wamsutta) succeeded him and also tried to maintain the status quo. However, the relentless expansion of white settlements into Indian land created tensions. At one point, Alexander was hauled before Puritan authorities in Plymouth to refute rumors that he was planning an uprising. This he did but died shortly after his release in 1662. Metacom, who was also known as "King Philip" by the English on account of his haughty demeanor, suspected his brother had been poisoned but took no overt action against the whites.

Like his predecessors, Metacom tried to accommodate his European neighbors, but conflict inevitably ensued over differing conceptions of land use. Whereas the Native Americans were willing to allow settlers to use the land, they had no concept of "ownership" and assumed that they too were entitled to free access for hunting and fishing. Unfortunately, these were rights the English proved unwilling to concede, a position based on their understanding of land titles. When they suspected Metacom of plotting an uprising in 1671, they made him appear before the General Court of Massachusetts and ordered his tribe to disarm and pay a fine. The chief tamely submitted to this humiliation, being aware of the strength of the Europeans and the relative weakness of the Wampanoags. Over the next five years, however, he sent runners out to neighboring tribes in an attempt to cement a military alliance against the whites.

The incident that triggered King Philip's War occurred in January 1675. John Sassamon, a Christian Indian who served as an informer, told the English of Metacom's plan for an uprising and was found murdered. The settlers, in turn, accused three Indians of the deed and executed them. This move infuriated Metacom, who began organizing a general insurrection. Initially, his alliance scored several local successes and engulfed the entire region.

Commencing in June 1675, warrior bands from the Wampanoag, Nipmuck, Sakonnet, and Pocasset tribes began raiding isolated settlements along the New England frontier, massacring the inhabitants. Numerous white settlements in New England were attacked, while perhaps 25 towns were completely destroyed. White casualties were estimated to run as high as 800 men, women, and children. Indian casualties were equally appalling. Once the various colonies began pooling their manpower and coordinating defenses, however, the tide invariably began to turn. A major contributor to battlefield success was Capt. Benjamin Church, who organized his men along Indian lines and waged an effective guerrilla war against them. He also employed Indian dissidents against the warring tribesmen with great effect.

In the course of heavy skirmishing, Metacom made several visits to the powerful Mohegan tribe of New York for their support, but they had already allied themselves with the English. They also provided several warrior bands to the army of Josiah Winslow when he crushed the Narragansetts in the Great Swamp Fight of December 1675. More than 600 Indians were slain in that battle and a like number captured at a cost of 20 English killed and 200 wounded. Throughout the winter, the displaced Indians, suffering greatly from hunger and attrition, began deserting Metacom's cause.

As Metacom's military fortunes began to wane, he returned to the solace of his traditional homelands near Bristol, Rhode Island, to await his fate. In May 1676, Church's men managed to capture Metacom's wife and son, an event that profoundly affected Metacom. Church's band then stalked the chief himself, aided by a former warrior of Metacom's whose brother had been executed for suggesting that he make peace with the English. On August 12, 1676, Church's men surprised Metacom in his camp, and he was shot down by an Indian auxiliary. His body was immediately drawn and quartered, and his head was displayed on a pole at Plymouth for more than two decades, a grisly warning against future uprisings. Sporadic fighting and raiding continued for another two years before peace was finally concluded in April 1678.

Metacom's defeat and death signaled the end of an era. Organized Native American resistance to white settlement of New England vanished. English control of the region was strengthened and consolidated, whereas Indian populations precipitously declined and in many instances disappeared. Many Indian captives, including Metacom's wife and son, were summarily sold into slavery in the West Indies and elsewhere.

Thus, a pattern of warfare, displacement, and annihilation was established and continued across North America for the next two centuries.

JOHN C. FREDRIKSEN

## NARRAGANSETTS

"Narragansett" means "People of the Small Point." It was the name of both a specific tribe and a group of tribes—including the Shawomets, Pawtuxets, Cowesets (Nipmucs), and eastern Niantics—dominated by Narragansett sachems. In the 16th century, at least 3,000 Narragansetts were located in south central Rhode Island, although the greater Narragansett territory extended throughout all but northwest and the extreme southwest of Rhode Island. Narragansetts spoke an eastern Algonquian language.

Cautantowwit, the supreme deity, lived to the southwest. There were also numerous other spirits or deities, who could and did communicate with people through dreams and visions. Priests or medicine men (powwows) were in charge of religious matters. They were usually men who realized their profession in a dream or a vision experience. Their main responsibilities included curing, bringing rain, and ensuring success in war. A harvest ritual was held in a longhouse near the sachem's house. At one important ceremony, possibly held in the winter, participants burned their material possessions.

Narragansetts recognized a dual (junior and senior) chief or sagamore. Power was shared with a council of elders, sachems, and other leaders. Sachems were responsible for seeing to the public welfare and defense and for administering punishment. The office of sagamore may have been inheritable and was occasionally held by a woman. Within the larger administrative body, there were smaller groups presided over by lesser sachems.

People changed their names at various life cycle ceremonies. They were generally monogamous. The dead were wrapped in skins or woven mats and then buried with tools and weapons to accompany them to an afterworld located to the southwest. Narragansetts lived in dome-shaped, circular wigwams about 10 to 20 feet in diameter, covered with birch and chestnut bark in the summer and with mats in the winter. Smoke passed through an opening at the top. Winter hunting lodges were small and built of bark and rushes. People erected temporary field houses where they stayed when guarding the crops. Villages were often stockaded.

Women grew corn, beans, squash, and sunflowers; men grew tobacco. The men also hunted moose, bear, deer, wolves, and other game, and they trapped beaver, squirrels, and other small animals and fowl. Deer were stalked and may have been hunted communally. People fished in freshwater and saltwater. They gathered much marine life, including the occasional stranded whale, as well as strawberries and a number of other wild foods.

The Narragansetts were notable traders. They dealt in wampum, skins, clay pots, carved bowls, and chestnuts. They imported carved stone and wooden pipes from the Mohawks. People generally wore deerskin breechclouts, skirts, and leggings. They might also wear turkey feather mantles and moccasins. In the winter they donned bear and rabbit skin robes, caps, and mittens.

This group may have originated well to the southwest of their historical territory. They were the most powerful New England tribe until 1675, dominating neighbors such as the Niantics and Nipmucs. They may have encountered non-Natives in 1524, although there was no significant contact for another century or so afterward.

Trade with the British and Dutch was under way by 1623. Although the Narragansetts largely avoided the epidemics of 1617–1619, smallpox and other diseases dramatically weakened the people in 1633 and thereafter. As British allies, some Narragansetts fought against the Indians in the Pequot War of 1636–1637. In 1636, the grand sachem Canonicus sold land to Roger Williams, on which he established the future state of Rhode Island.

In an effort to protect themselves from non-Native depredations, the tribe voluntarily submitted to Britain in 1644. Despite Williams's entreaties to treat the Indians fairly, many British remained extremely hostile. Eventually, they forced the Narragansett people to join the Nipmucs and Wampanoags in King Philip's War (1675–1676). A huge defeat in December 1675, in which more than 600 Narragansetts were killed and hundreds more captured and sold into slavery, signaled the beginning of the end of the war, as well as the virtual destruction of the tribe itself.

After the war, survivors dispersed among the Mohegans, Abenakis, and Niantics, the last group thenceforth assuming the name Narragansett. Some of the Mohegan joined the Brotherton Indians in 1788 and later moved with them to Wisconsin. Those who remained in Rhode Island (probably fewer than 100) worked as servants or slaves of the non-Native settlers, who moved quickly to occupy the vacated Narragansett lands.

The people underwent a general conversion to Christianity in the mid-18th century, at which time a Christian reservation community was established in Charlestown. After the last hereditary sachem died during that period, government changed to an elected president and council. The last Native speaker died in the early 19th century. A constitution was adopted in 1849. All of the Narragansett reservation, except for two acres, was sold in 1880, and the tribe was terminated by the state at that time. The Rhode Island Narragansetts incorporated in 1934 under the terms of the Indian Reorganization Act.

In 1985, the state of Rhode Island returned two pieces of land of about 900 acres each. The tribe's annual August meeting and powwow have been held for the past 250 or more years on the old meeting ground in Charlestown. Other ceremonies are both religious (such as the Fall Harvest Festival held in the longhouse) and secular (such as the commemoration of the 1675 battle) in nature. There are tribal programs for the elderly and for children. Tribal representatives are involved in local non-Native cultural and educational programs.

BARRY M. PRITZKER

## MARY ROWLANDSON (ca. 1635-ca. 1678)

Mary Rowlandson wrote the first published account of a New Englander captured by Native Americans. Born about 1635 in England, Rowlandson came with her parents to America as a child. She lived in Salem, Massachusetts, until 1653, at which time the family moved to Lancaster. In 1656, she married Rev. Joseph Rowlandson and lived quietly for the next 20 years. However, in 1676, she found herself in the middle of King

Philip's War. Five tribes—the Wampanoags, Mohegans, Narragansetts, Poduncks, and Nipmucks—felt the pressure of New England settlers' expansion. When Metacomet became chief of the Wampanoags, in 1662, tension mounted between the tribes and the settlers. On September 9, 1675, the New England Confederation declared war on the tribes. The war continued until 1676.

In February of that year, Rowlandson's house was attacked in retaliation for the massacre of more than 600 Narragansetts at their winter home in the swamps of central Rhode Island the previous November. "At length," Rowlandson wrote, "they came and beset our House, and quickly it was the dolefullest day that ever mine eyes say." She later wrote, "Some in our House were fighting for their Lives, others wallowing in their Blood; the House on fire over our Heads, and the bloddy Heathen ready to knock us on the Head if we stirred out."

Rowlandson, her 3 children, and 20 other captives were taken prisoner. In a forced march west, her young daughter died of starvation and a bullet wound. Rowlandson's sewing skills may have saved her own life; she was given some measure of respect and eventually was ransomed back to her husband. Her captivity narrative became a classic of captivity and colonial literature, contributing a great deal of information about her captors. In the second edition, it was titled *The Sovereignty & Goodness of God, Together, with the Faithfulness of His Promises Displayed: Being a Narrative of the Captivity and Restoration of Mrs. Mary Rowlandson.* Rowlandson died sometime after 1678.

## WAMPANOAGS

"Wampanoag" means "Eastern People." The Wampanoags were formerly known as Pokanokets, which originally was the name of Massasoit's village but which came to be the designation of all the territory and people under that great sachem. The Wampanoags or Pokanokets also included the Nausets of Cape Cod, the Sakonnets of Rhode Island, and various tribes of the offshore islands.

Traditionally, Wampanoags lived in southern New England from just north of Cape Cod, but including Nantucket and Martha's Vineyard, to Narragansett Bay. There were approximately 6,500 Wampanoags in 1600, including tributary island tribes. Wampanoags spoke the Massachusett dialect of an Algonquian language.

The people recognized a supreme deity and many lesser deities. Priests, or medicine men, provided religious leadership. Their duties included mediating with the spirit world to cure illnesses, to forecast the weather, and to conduct ceremonies.

A chief sachem led the tribe. In theory, his power was absolute, but in practice he was advised by a council of village and clan chiefs (sagamores). The village was the main political unit. Village leadership had a hereditary element, which may be responsible for the existence of women chiefs. Villages may have made their own temporary alliances. Overall political structure consolidated and became more hierarchical after the epidemics of 1616–1619.

Wampanoags were organized into a number of clans. Their annual round of activities took them from winter villages to gathering sites at summer fields. Women had clearly defined and significant political rights. Social stratification was reflected in leadership and marriage arrangements. Leading men might have more than one wife. The dead were wrapped in mats and buried with various possessions, mourners blackened their faces, and the souls of the dead were said to travel west.

There were at least 30 villages in the early 17th century, most of which were located by water. People lived in wigwams, both circular and rectangular. The largest measured up to 100 feet long; smaller ones were about 15 feet in diameter. The houses consisted of pole frames covered with birchbark, hickory bark, or woven mats.

Wigwams tended to have central fires, but longhouses featured rows of several fires. Some houses may have been palisaded. Their larger structures were probably built in winter villages. Mat beds stood on platforms against the walls or directly on the ground. Skins served as bedding. All towns featured a central open space that was used for ceremonies and meetings. The people also built sweathouses.

Men hunted fowl, as well as small and large game, with the white-tailed deer being the most important. They stalked, trapped, and snared deer and may have hunted them in communal drives. They also grew tobacco. The people ate seals and beached whales, and they gathered shellfish, often steaming them over hot rocks. They fished for freshwater and saltwater species in the winter (through the ice) and in the summer. Women gathered roots, wild fruits, berries, and nuts as well as maple sap for sugar. Women began growing corn, beans, and squash in the late prehistoric period. Fish may have been used as fertilizer.

Dugout canoes could hold up to 40 passengers, with the average being 10 to 15. There may also have been some number of birchbark canoes. Women wore skirts and poncho-style blouses, as well as soft-soled moccasins. They donned rabbit and beaver robes in cold weather. Men wore skin leggings and breechclouts and soft-soled moccasins. They also wore turkey feather cloaks and bone and shell necklaces. They tended to pull out all their hair except for a scalp lock.

Wampanoag/Pokanoket culture developed steadily in their approximate historical location for about 8,000 years. The tribe had already been weakened from disease and war with the Penobscots when it encountered non-Natives in the early 17th century. It had also been forced by the Narragansetts to accept tributary status.

The people greeted the Pilgrims in 1620, although there had been contact with the British some years earlier. The Grand Sachem Massasoit made a treaty of friendship with the British. His people helped the Europeans survive by showing them how to grow crops and otherwise survive in a land alien to them. Men named Squanto and Samoset are especially known in this regard. Largely as a result of Massasoit's influence, the Wampanoags remained neutral in the Pequot War of 1636. Many Indian residents of Cape Cod and the islands of Nantucket and Martha's Vineyard were Christianized during the mid-17th century.

Massasoit died in 1662. At that time, his second son, Metacomet, also known as Philip, renewed the peace. However, relations were strained by British abuses such as the illegal occupation of land; trickery, often involving the use of alcohol; and the destruction of resources, including forests and game. Diseases also continued to take a toll on the population.

Finally, local tribes reached the breaking point. The Pokanoket, now mainly relocated to the Bristol, Rhode Island, area and led by Metacomet, took the lead in uniting Indians from southern and central New England in King Philip's War (1675–1676). This was an attempt by the Wampanoag, Narragansett, and other tribes to drive the British out of their territory. However, the fighting began before all the preparations had been completed. In the end, hundreds of non-Native settlers died, but the two main Indian tribes were nearly exterminated. The tribal name of Pokanoket was also officially banned.

Most Wampanoags were either enslaved or killed. Survivors fled into the interior or onto the Cape and the islands, whose tribes had not participated in the war. Some also fled to the Great Lakes region or to Canada. For centuries following this event, local Indians were cheated, discriminated against, used as servants, or, at best, ignored.

The Indian population on Nantucket Island declined from possibly 1,500 in 1600 to 358 in 1763 to 20 in 1792, mainly owing to disease. The last of the indigenous population died in 1855. Indians at Mashpee, on Cape Cod, were assigned 50 square miles of land in 1660. Self-government continued until 1788, when the state of Massachusetts placed the Indians under its control. Most of their lands were allotted in 1842. Trespass by non-Natives was a large problem during the entire period. Near Mashpee, the 2,500-acre Herring Pond Reservation was allotted in 1850.

Indian land in Fall River was divided into lots in 1707, and a 160-acre reservation was created in 1709. The people's right of self-government was abrogated in the early 19th century. The reservation was eliminated entirely in 1907. Of the three reservations on Martha's Vineyard in the 19th century—Chappaquiddick, Christiantown, and Gay Head—only the latter remained by 1900. This group was never governed by non-Native overseers, and its isolation allowed the people to retain their identity and cohesion to a far greater extent than other Wampanoag communities.

Other groups of Wampanoag descendants maintained a separate existence until the 19th century, when most became fully assimilated. The Wampanoag Nation was founded in 1928 in response to the pan-Indian movement of the times.

Contemporary Wampanoag events, many of which have both sacred and secular/public components, include a powwow on the Fourth of July (Mashpee), Indian Day and Cranberry Day (Gay Head), and a new year's ceremony and a strawberry festival (Assonet). Many Gay Head people have left the island, but many also plan to return. The Mashpee people continue to seek a land base and hope that federal recognition will advance their prospects. The community is in the process of working out a fair relationship with the increasingly non-Native population of the town. The Pokanoket tribe, led by descendants of Massasoit, seeks federal recognition, as well as stewardship of 267 acres of land in Bristol, Rhode Island.

BARRY M. PRITZKER

## DOCUMENT: MASSASOIT PEACE TREATY, 1621

*The Wampanoag chief Massasoit was the first Indian leader to deal with the New England colonists shortly after the Pilgrims' arrival in Plymouth, Massachusetts, in late 1620. At the Pilgrims' request, Massasoit agreed to this treaty in March 1621. Both sides worked hard to maintain peace throughout Massasoit's life, despite bitter conflicts between Indians and colonists in other parts of New England. The chief died in 1662 and was succeeded by his son, Metacomet, who led the Wampanoags in King Philip's War against the colonists from 1676 to 1677.*

(*Massasoit Peace Treaty*, reprinted in *Mourt's Relation: A Journal of the Pilgrims at Plymouth* [London, 1622].)

1. That neither he nor any of his should injure or do hurt to any of our people.

2. And if any of his did hurt to any of ours, he should send the offender, that we might punish him.

3. That if any of our tools were taken away when our people were at work, he should cause them to be restored; and if ours did any harm to any of his, we would do the like to them.

4. If any did unjustly war against him, we would aid him; if any did war against us, he should aid us.

5. He should send to his neighbor confederates, to certify them of this, that they might not wrong us, but might be likewise comprised in the conditions of peace.

6. That when their men came to us, they should leave their bows and arrows behind them, as we should do our pieces when we came to them.

Lastly, that doing thus, King James would esteem of him as his friend and ally.

# 11

# The Glorious Revolution in America, 1688–1689

## INTRODUCTION

After 1660 and the restoration of Charles II to the English throne, American colonies grew more and more restive about political and religious questions. Josias Fendall attempted to oust the Catholic rulers of Maryland in 1660, political dissenters caused trouble in New Jersey in 1672, and William Davyes and John Pate rebelled against Lord Baltimore's absolutism in Maryland in 1676 but failed and were executed. These were fairly minor outbursts of colonial assertiveness; of far more concern was Bacon's Rebellion, in Virginia, in 1676.

The most serious challenge to colonial authority in the 17th century, Bacon's Rebellion came about in the midst of an effort by prominent Virginians in London to obtain a royal charter that would guarantee certain rights, including that of land ownership and taxation, only with the consent of those being taxed. Virginians wanted "the same liberties and privileges as Englishmen in England" (Clark, p. 243). Bacon's Rebellion, which complicated the charter effort, was ironic in that the rebels were making almost the same requests of the Virginia elite as the elite were making in London. Bacon and his supporters demanded protection from Indians, lower taxes, and rectification of local grievances.

Nathaniel Bacon's father had withdrawn his son from Cambridge University for having "broken into some extravagancies" (Clark, p. 244); after the young Bacon's arrival in Virginia, he was suspected of atheistic tendencies. He wanted to fight Indians, who were causing trouble on the frontier near his Henrico County plantation, but the governor would not sanction an Indian war. Bacon led an expedition in defiance of the governor and at different times found himself fighting both the Indians and the governor's troops. But he had a large following, and had he not died unexpectedly of natural causes in October 1676, his movement might have gone much further. After Bacon's death, the governor's forces easily subdued the rebellion.

Even before Bacon died, his movement prompted the convening of an assembly at Jamestown to discuss a variety of colonial grievances. Out of the assembly, at which Bacon himself had no particular influence, came several reforms, including one that allowed all freeholders to vote for members of the House of Burgesses, the Virginia colonial assembly. Another reform removed the tax-exempt status of council members. Soon afterward, the council (the upper house of the colonial legislature) repealed the

Portrait of Nathaniel Bacon, leader of Bacon's Rebellion in Virginia in 1676. This protest against royal authority was a precursor to the greater legislative power that resulted from the Glorious Revolution. (Courtesy of the Library of Congress.)

laws passed at the Jamestown assembly, and London sent over a team of royal commissioners and later a new royal governor to strengthen imperial authority over Virginia.

In New England, after years of contentiousness between England and the colonies, James II united all the New England colonies with New York and New Jersey into the Dominion of New England and appointed Sir Edmund Andros as governor in 1686. Andros, who had served as governor of New York, ruled with considerable more authority than the New Englanders wanted. He enforced the Navigation Acts, regularized colonial administration, and strengthened colonial defenses. James had decreed that no colonial assembly should meet nor denied towns the right to hold town meetings. Andros's ardent Anglicanism offended Puritan leaders, and, as his enforcement of trade regulations brought economic decline, moderate merchants joined with the Puritans to oppose the governor.

In England, James II had succeeded his brother, Charles II, in 1685. As king, James determined to advance the cause of Catholicism, out of favor in England since the reign of Henry VIII (1509–1547). In his first years on the throne, James managed to antagonize the Church of England in several ways. He established an ecclesiastical court, the Commissioners of Ecclesiastical Causes, that was designed to restrain the authority of Anglican priests and promote the appointment of Catholics to official posts. He issued two Declarations of Indulgence, seen as a ploy to legitimize Catholicism.

One of the early actions of the Commissioners of Ecclesiastical Causes was to suspend the bishop of London, Henry Compton, who also had jurisdiction over Anglicanism in the colonies. Compton had become bishop of London in 1675 and was also a member of the Council of Trade and Plantations, which had assumed control of colonial affairs the year before. As a member of the Lords of Trade, Compton worked to promote the Anglican Church in the colonies. On the basis of reports of the neglectful attitude of the colonists toward the church, Compton increased the authority of ministers in their parishes and ordered parishes to provide better financial support for their ministers. In 1679, Compton stipulated that all Anglican ministers bound for the colonies must obtain a certificate of appointment from him, and, by 1685, the bishop and his certified ministers had taken over many other ecclesiastical powers in the colonies.

Suspended early in James II's reign for not disciplining Anglican ministers who had been critical of the king, Compton saw his duties given over to a royal commission that the king could easily influence. Seven other Anglican bishops, including the bishop of Canterbury, who had publicly challenged the constitutionality of the second Declaration of Indulgence, were sent to the Tower of London to await trial on charges of sedition. After a month, the trial was held, and the seven were acquitted.

On June 30, 1688, the same day as the acquittal of the bishops, a group of prominent but aggrieved subjects of the Crown, including Bishop Compton, set the Glorious Revolution in motion. They invited William of Orange to come from the Netherlands and reign in England as William III with his wife, Mary, the oldest daughter of James II, who would become Mary II. Since James II's consort, whose name was also Mary, had just given birth to a son and heir, time was of the essence, and William was asked to come sooner rather than later.

In the early fall of 1688, William announced his intent to go to England to maintain Protestantism and a "free and lawful Parliament." He and his troops landed in England on November 5 and reached London within six weeks, forcing James to flee into exile in France. Englishmen in general rejoiced, although some were uneasy about the rapid changes occurring in their hallowed institutions. When a Scottish bishop rebuked a preacher for an enthusiastic pro-William sermon, the preacher replied, "He [who] is afraid of a fart will never stand thunder" (quoted in Lovejoy, p. 226).

Parliament met in January 1689 and passed measures that implemented the political agenda of the Glorious Revolution. The Mutiny Act, the Toleration Act, the Bill of Rights, and the Corporation Act were among the acts passed. For the American colonies, the Corporation Act was especially important, since it restored city and borough charters that James had suspended, including those in New England. As thankful as Parliament was to have William on the throne, the new monarch was not entirely supportive of what Parliament was trying to do. He and some of his supporters were reluctant to surrender some of their authority and to see the country move in the direction of republicanism. Many English moderates had liked James II's imposition of the Dominion of New England, because it made for more effective colonial administration and centralized imperial authority.

After news of the Glorious Revolution reached Boston, in early 1689, Andros's opponents armed themselves and overthrew the governor, jailing him and most of his officials. War with the French suspended colonial administration until 1691, when Massachusetts received a new charter from London. This charter provided for an elected assembly as well as an elected council, but the governor, who had veto power, was a Crown appointee. All of this struck a compromise between the virtually independent Massachusetts of pre-1686 days and the severely constricted colony under the Dominion of New England government. The new charter brought Massachusetts into rough conformity with the other colonies. It also brought an end to the waning Plymouth colony by merging it with Massachusetts. Plymouth had been in economic distress for many years, and the incorporation into the larger colony was not resisted.

Not long before the Glorious Revolution, the Virginia House of Burgesses petitioned James II to recall the colonial governor, Lord Howard of Effingham. James was overthrown before he could act on the petition, but William was sympathetic and placed royal authority in the hands of the lieutenant governor, Francis Nicholson. Lord Howard, who was in England when all of this was happening, did not return to Virginia, and relations between the assembly and Nicholson were peaceful.

In Maryland, a dissident named John Coode raised a force in 1689, seized public buildings and Lord Baltimore's plantation, and set up an interim government that excluded Catholics. Coode had been a Protestant activist well before the Glorious Revolution. In 1681, he and a friend, Josias Fendall, had tried to stir up sentiment against Catholics in Maryland. They were arrested, thrown in jail, and tried, in November 1681, on charges of mutiny and sedition. Coode was found not guilty, but Fendall was convicted, fined 40,000 pounds of tobacco, and banished from the colony.

Coode's government, in power after 1689, was not universally popular, although it legitimized itself with a convention in 1690. Many Marylanders thought it oppressive (any opponent of the government was deemed an opponent of William III), and even Coode said he favored a new royal government sent from London. Coode's past association with troublemakers like Fendall did not help his cause, and neither did assertions that he was using his power to enrich himself. Lord Baltimore, meanwhile, worked hard to regain his authority in Maryland, offering amnesty to Coode and consenting to have a Protestant governor appointed, but London was not sympathetic. William III appointed Lionel Copley as royal governor and sent him to Maryland to establish the Anglican Church there, as well as a fairly typical colonial administration and government. Under Copley, who died in 1694, and Francis Nicholson, who replaced him, Maryland returned to a semblance of normality.

Similarly, in New York, the local militia heard about the Glorious Revolution and the revolt in Massachusetts in the spring of 1689 and seized the royal fort from English troops. A rebel-formed group, the Committee of Safety, served as an interim government and appointed one of its members, Jacob Leisler, commander in chief of the colony. The members of the committee proclaimed their loyalty to William III and Mary and to Leisler, a German merchant who had never been part of the colony's ruling elite. All of this offended a number of Dutch landowners from the Albany area and socially prominent Englishmen from the New York City area, who also praised William III and Mary II but considered Leisler an illegitimate leader.

Leisler tried to get William III and Mary II to recognize his government by sending over personal representatives to lobby the court and Parliament, but those he sent did not serve him well. One of his agents, Joost Stoll, a liquor merchant, spent most of his time making business deals for himself, and the other, Matthew Clarkson, worked to get himself appointed to a royal position in the colonial government. Leisler's government, unlike those in Maryland and Massachusetts, was not recognized in London. Instead, William III appointed a new colonial government headed by Henry Slaughter, an English military officer. Slaughter came to New York in January 1691, expecting to find the colony in chaos. There was no chaos, but there was the strong-willed Leisler, who battled with Slaughter for authority from the time the new governor stepped on shore.

Leisler was suspicious of nearly everyone around him, and, when two companies of English troops showed up, he was convinced that a conspiracy against his rule had formed. In March, Leisler and his forces dug in at a fortress in New York City; the British troops challenged him, and a showdown was at hand. Firing from both sides resulted in the deaths of several men. Eventually, Leisler surrendered the fort, and Slaughter immediately arrested him, marking the end of the rebellion. Leisler and nine accomplices stood trial at the end of March; in early May, Leisler was convicted of "traitorously levying war" against William III and Mary and "feloniously murdering" one Josias Brown, a man killed in a skirmish during Leisler's resistance. Seven of Leisler's nine accomplices were also found guilty, and, two weeks after the verdict was announced, Leisler and his guilty accomplices were hanged.

Although rebellions like Leisler's and improvised governments like Coode's suggest that the Glorious Revolution brought substantial changes to the politics of the colonies, English authorities did not see it this way. William III tolerated the renewal of colonial autonomy because the North American colonies were not particularly important to him. The king continued to assert that he had ultimate authority over the colonies but that it was exercised through Parliament rather than directly. And members of Parliament believed that they could alter acts of colonial assemblies at their will. Thus the Glorious Revolution did not fundamentally change the relationship between England and its colonies in America.

Perhaps the Glorious Revolution more significantly affected colonial commerce. The Council of Trade and Plantations continued to exert some authority over the colonies, and a new Navigation Act in 1696 put stricter controls on commerce, in part by establishing Admiralty Courts, which sat in judgment of trade violations in the colonies. A new agency, the Board of Trade and Plantations, was created to oversee colonial affairs, but it was hampered by other parliamentary agencies, such as the War Office and the secretary of state for the Southern Department, both of which also bore some responsibility for colonial administration. Enforcement of commercial regulations was inefficient, however, and colonists were more inclined to be law-abiding because of the danger posed by England's rivals, France and Spain.

## INTERPRETIVE ESSAY

P. D. SWINEY

The revolution of 1688 in England is referred to as the "Glorious" Revolution because it created a constitutional settlement. Parliament, the representative assembly, became the sovereign power in English government. The Glorious Revolution in the American colonies was marked by three rebellions—in Massachusetts, New York, and Maryland. Rearrangements of power occurred in all the colonies, but with unforeseen and unexpected consequences. The colonists had been forcibly reminded that they were English, part of a growing empire. The Glorious Revolution in America was their declaration of indifference—that what was good for the British empire was not necessarily of interest or concern to the colonies. The colonists would move to defend the existing arrangements and practices that were of benefit to the individual settlements that dotted North America.

The restoration of the Stuart monarchy in 1660 was yet another attempt to provide stability and coherence to a government and society rent by religious, civil, and political strife. Contention between centralizing royal power and local government had torn England for decades. Parliament, the representative assembly of wealthy gentry and nobility, had struggled for supremacy with the autocratic Stuart kings. A growing national identification with Protestantism had led to a growing loathing of Catholics, and dissenting sects among the Protestants proposed radical revision of the distribution of land, property, and power. After the death, in 1658, of Oliver Cromwell, the Lord Protector, negotiations opened to bring back the heir of the beheaded Charles I. Charles II returned to England grateful to those who had shown loyalty to him during more than a decade of exile. Some of this gratitude would manifest itself in generous grants of land in the colonies of North America.

Those colonies already in existence had watched developments in England with considerable anxiety. The most successful of the colonies, Massachusetts Bay, had been founded and populated primarily by Puritans. As the Puritans in England had led the opposition to Charles I, rebelled against him, and executed him, it is understandable that Puritan colonies would view the accession of his son with considerable trepidation.

The change in government would require all the extant colonies to confirm their colonial charters with the new king. Only Virginia was a royal colony, with a royal governor appointed by the king. Virginia also had the House of Burgesses, a representative assembly, but the Burgesses were property holders, and only property holders could elect them. Maryland was a proprietary colony, founded as a haven for English Catholics by the Catholic Lord Baltimore. As proprietor, Lord Baltimore held title to all the land in his colony and could arrange the government as he saw fit. Massachusetts Bay Colony was a special case: a religious movement masquerading as a stock company. The original settlers/stockholders had migrated to Massachusetts to be a "city on a hill"—a moral example to the Church of England that would inspire it to reform. Massachusetts society and government had been organized around the Puritan version of the Church of England—Calvinist in theology, Congregationalist in organization. Congregations existed independently of one another and called their own ministers. But, very early, Massachusetts had extended participation in its General Court, or representative assembly, to all endorsed Church members. The governor of the colony was elected, yet the clergy were formally excluded from political affairs. This arrangement, peculiar as it may seem, was carried to a number of smaller settlements: Connecticut, Rhode Island, Providence Plantations, New Haven Plantation, and New Hampshire. None of these foundations had legal existence under the new regime.

The king's government in London was aware that political arrangements in the colonies were somewhat irregular, but, after years of uncertainty in the government in England, settlements now claimed the major attention of the king's ministers. After persistent petitions by agents sent by the colonists, the king made his dispositions over a period of several years. Massachusetts could continue under its original charter—for the present. Rhode Island and Providence Plantation were to combine but preserve their government. Connecticut and New Haven were to do the same. New Hampshire was chartered as a separate colony. Maine would be under the authority of Massachusetts. Virginia's claim to territory on its southern border was denied; the land would become part of a large grant to a group of the king's closest advisers, as proprietors.

They graciously christened their new enterprise Carolina, named after the king. After a successful war against the Dutch, major commercial rivals of England, the king would grant the acquired Dutch territories in the colonies to his brother, the Duke of York, who would then name them for himself—New York. The dual colonies of Jersey were awarded to separate proprietors, creating East and West Jersey. All the new colonies were expected to tolerate other Protestant sects (of which there were a considerable number) and to form some variety of a representative assembly to levy taxes. In 1681, Charles discharged an old debt by granting an enormous tract of land to William Penn, a prominent and wealthy member of the unorthodox and disturbing Quaker sect. As proprietor, Penn could rule as he pleased; he was pleased to found a colony for dissenting religious minorities and constructed an unusually liberal frame of government. Pennsylvania, after some bumpy adjustments, arrived at a consensual procedure in its assembly and became known as the Best Poor Man's Country.

Unfortunately, Charles's ignorance of colonial geography was as great as his largesse. Not only did his generous grants to friends and supporters collide, but the legal position of the settlers already in possession was jeopardized. The proprietors of New York, East and West Jersey, and the Carolinas proposed to sell these lands as a profit-making venture. Some wished to experiment with forms of government. None would follow any predictable pattern, thereby making administration from London more difficult. London was becoming more interested in the colonies as possible sources of increased revenue. Some of the laws from the Cromwell era were retained as part of a grand imperial design. The Navigation Acts, which were supposed to curtail trade among the colonies at increased profit to the mother country, required all English shipments to be carried on English ships, with an English crew. Contracting with carriers offering the most favorable terms was not permitted. All colonial exports and imports were to pass through England, with the accompanying duties and customs paid. Certain highly desirable products of the colonies, "enumerated goods" named by law, were to go only to England, to provide it with a monopoly on desirable exports.

The colonies were not at all fond of the Navigation Acts. They had evaded them and violated them and become proficient smugglers under Cromwell, and they were ready to do so again under Charles II. As the expected revenue fell short of expectations, a special committee of the Privy Council, the Lords of Trade, was created in 1675 to assist in the enforcement of the Navigation Acts. The king's brother, James, Duke of York, was particularly interested in consolidating and streamlining administration of the colonies, and he sponsored a major realignment of government. In 1684, Massachusetts's original charter was revoked, and various other New England colonies lost their patents to confer land titles and organize governments. The plan was to combine all the northern colonies with the administration of New York, creating the Dominion of New England. A similar plan was bruited for the southern colonies.

Unfortunately, the creation of the Dominion of New England coincided with the death of Charles II and his brother's accession to the throne. James II's province of New York automatically became a royal colony when he became king, but the orphaned colonies of New England did not learn of their consolidation with New York for months. James was busy securing his throne in the face of bitter opposition to his conversion to Catholicism and outright rebellion from Charles II's illegitimate (but Protestant) son. In 1686, Sir Edmund Andros was dispatched to administer a sullen Dominion of New England.

Sir Edmund was a soldier and courtier who had already served as governor of the king's province of New York. He was well acquainted with the sectional rivalries between the Albany frontier, which held a monopoly on the fur trade, and the port on Manhattan Island, which was rapidly acquiring a monopoly on regional shipping. The largest population was on Long Island, and it had a strong Puritan orientation. After 20 years of English occupation, the Dutch inhabitants had made some adjustment, but increasing English settlement had brought new tensions among Quakers, Anglicans, Lutherans, Dutch Reformed, and Puritans, who counted half a dozen nationalities among these congregations, a not uncommon circumstance in any port.

The New York assembly had been suspended in 1685 by James II, now king of England, and other regional assemblies were dissolved or relegated to local government business only. Andros was to govern with the aid of an appointed council. The suspiciously modest revenues from these thriving areas would be devoted to defense of the English empire in America, chiefly on the vulnerable New York border with French Canada.

Andros proposed to administer the dominion from Boston, and he also intended to institute observance of the English national church in the center of dissent from that church. The imposition of a tax, without the consent of the dissolved General Court, evoked bitter protest from the Puritans. But Andros's attempt to put the dominion on a self-supporting basis by charging fees to reconfirm land titles granted by the defunct previous charter and by collecting quitrents, a yearly charge for the land already purchased, was more than the Puritans could abide. Increase Mather, a prominent member of an eminent ministerial dynasty, was dispatched in 1688 to London to represent to the king Massachusetts's grievances. When he arrived there, Mather found a capital seething with anti-Catholic sentiment. The king had replaced royal officials with Catholic adherents (including the Lords of Trade), had issued a Declaration of Indulgence (or tolerance) for dissident sects, which was widely perceived as a means of reintroducing Catholicism to England, and had capped his folly by producing a male Catholic heir. Within six months, England had embarked on its Glorious Revolution. James II's Protestant firstborn, Mary, was married to a leading Protestant statesman in Europe, William of Orange. Parliament invited them to defend England from James's encroaching Catholicism. William landed with an army in November 1688, James fled to France in December, and by February William and Mary had accepted Parliament's offer of the throne of England and were crowned in April 1689. A profound change in England's political system had occurred in a breathless (and bloodless) six months.

Word of these dizzying events came sporadically and late to the colonies. By the time news of William's invasion arrived, he and Mary had accepted the throne. By the time the colonies heard of the change of monarchs, they had been crowned. Announcement of their coronation arrived six weeks later, but the Dominion of New England no longer existed. On April 18, leading Puritans of Boston, backed by a mob of excited Bostonians, arrested Gov. Edmund Andros and other royal officials as agents of the discarded King James. A Council of Safety was formed, composed chiefly of members of the former charter government. As word spread of Massachusetts's action, other portions of the dominion followed suit, and New England fragmented back into the colonies of Connecticut, Rhode Island, Plymouth, and Massachusetts Bay.

Andros's deputy in New York, Francis Nicholson, was in a peculiar position. Word of Massachusetts's Glorious Revolution had come far more quickly than England's.

Indeed, Nicholson had received word of William and Mary's accession in March, but he had not proclaimed it. Massachusetts had successfully challenged the origin of the authority Nicholson held. While Nicholson waited for some instruction from London and warned Albany to expect an attack from the French, the divisions in New York society manifested themselves.

At the end of May 1689, the commander of the militia, Jacob Leisler, seized Fort James, the fortress of New York City. Rather than confront him (and the large portion of militia at his back), Nicholson sailed for England in June. Upon the deputy's departure, Leisler proclaimed the coronation of William III and Mary II and declared that he had secured the Anglo-Dutch colony of New York for a Dutch king of England.

In Maryland, a similar set of circumstances occurred. Lord Baltimore had been in England since 1684. The council appointed to govern in his absence made two fatal errors: it dismissed the assembly for two consecutive sessions, and it made Maryland conspicuous in its lack of support for the new king and queen. The council may have regretted the departure of the Catholic James, but the majority of the population in this Catholic proprietor's colony was staunchly Protestant. John Coode seized the opportunity and led a rebellion in 1689 on behalf of a Protestant Association against the autocratic Catholic proprietor. Having seized power, Coode called an increasingly uneasy representative assembly to proclaim William and Mary sovereigns of England and Maryland's loyalty to them. These three rebellions, one reputedly against Catholic tyranny and all supposedly in defense of representative government, were not precisely what they proclaimed themselves.

By no stretch of the 21st-century imagination can these assemblies be considered "representative" in the sense of considering the interests of the entire population. English political institutions had been carried to the colonies without the accompanying social hierarchies to support them. In England, local government was administered and representatives sent to Parliament by the land-owning elite. Political authority was supported by social status, which was based on the holding of land. The longer the land was held by a single family, the higher the family's social status and political influence. Even the townsmen based status on generations of occupancy, accompanied by wealth. Political power was divided and local government administered by these long-dominant families, their allies, and their kin.

But, in America, a similar political structure was transplanted without the centuries of land tenure dominance. Many a "new man" made a fortune in the colonies, and in the colonies it was wealth that conferred social status. The presumption of political power that accompanied social status developed in a different pattern. Land was far easier to come by in the colonies, and men could quickly accumulate wealth without owning large tracts of land. The dominant men of the local governments, who sent certain of their number to the assemblies, might not have been accepted as the elite in England, but they were certainly the elite of the colonies.

But, in a social structure that creates a self-defined elite, a certain number of people will predictably be excluded from what they consider their just portion of political power and the accompanying appointments in government where money is made. This was a contributing factor in Jacob Leisler's seizure of Fort James in New York. Leisler himself was a member of the second rank of the Dutch hierarchy who had submitted to English rule. Leisler and his supporters had failed to achieve the highest positions available in the new English administration. Some Dutch had quickly accommodated themselves to English rule and become a part of the ruling coterie in the English administration of New York, with the accompanying monetary rewards. The Dutch community, still in the majority after 20 years of English rule, was deeply divided among political factions based in kinship networks that were in a continual state of flux. These wealthy families were accustomed to apportioning political power among themselves. Leisler had arrived in New Amsterdam just before it surrendered to the English and had married into a political faction that did not flourish in the Duke of York's government.

Leisler's seizure of power was precisely that—an attempt to move himself, and the factions backing him, to a more prominent place in local government. A Committee of Safety called delegates from various settlements in New York and proclaimed Leisler commander in chief. Under this title, Leisler set about dismantling the former government. He was blocked somewhat by Albany, which supported King William but also sustained an ongoing enmity with its downstream rival. Albany simply ignored Leisler's command. A letter sent from the Privy Council addressed to Nicholson stated, "and in his absence such as for the time being take care for preserving the peace and administering the laws," which was all Leisler needed to proclaim himself deputy governor. He ruled as ultimate authority in New York for two years, with large portions of opposing factions, both in the city and up the Hudson Valley to Albany, jailed, exiled, or silenced. However, Leisler was not capable of ceding the power he had coveted for so long. When the duly appointed royal governor arrived from England in 1691, Leisler initially refused to surrender the fort. When he did so, he found himself in chains, accused of treason. The opposing factions rushed to fill the vacancies in government left by Liesler's adherents and pressed for a trial for treason. After a long and contentious legal process, Leisler and his son-in-law were condemned to death. The death penalty was not uncommon in Dutch practice, but death sentences were almost always commuted. The opposition's insistence on his execution sowed permanent bitter divisions in the ruling families of the province of New York.

Maryland's rebellion had similar antecedents. It was a proprietary colony, meaning that all the land was owned by Lord Baltimore and the Calvert family and was sold to settlers for profit. Maryland, like Pennsylvania, had been founded as a haven for a persecuted minority, in this case English Catholics. But Catholicism had been viewed in England as a form of treason for more than a century, and Lord Baltimore's haven for Catholics was quickly settled by a majority of Protestants. Instead of the complex divisions that characterized New York politics, Maryland featured a proprietary party, composed of the proprietor, his Council, members of his administration, and all their marital and political allies. The proprietary party kept an iron grip on lucrative government positions, and Catholicism and kinship seemed the only entries.

An overwhelmingly Protestant majority vastly outnumbered the proprietary party. Unfortunately, Lord Baltimore confirmed every English Protestant prejudice about the equation of Catholicism and tyranny by raising taxes, cutting tobacco prices, awarding monopolies to the proprietor's party, and abolishing the head right system (an easy way to obtain land grants by bringing settlers into the colony; a number of acres was awarded per head). His greatest error, the one that would cost him his government, was the exclusion of Protestant politicians from any advancement in his government. In 1684, Lord Baltimore sailed for England to defend both his charter and his boundary, disputed by the new colony of Pennsylvania. While he was gone, his deputies repeatedly dismissed a defiant and angry General Assembly. In 1689, news that a Protestant prince was ascending the English throne was a gift to the disgruntled Protestants of Maryland. While the council declined to proclaim and swear allegiance to the new monarchs, the antiproprietary party was organizing a Protestant Association to declare William and Mary the rulers of England. However, these "associators" had been ringleaders in repeated insurrections long before any change in the monarchy. Charles II and James II had repeatedly upheld the proprietor's regime. William would not be so supportive of a Catholic dissident.

In July 1689, John Coode's armed force seized the capital, St. Mary's, and convened an assembly. In September, it proclaimed King William III and Queen Mary II. In 1690, the rebels sailed for England to confront Lord Baltimore. The new sovereigns found in favor of the rebels, Baltimore lost the government of his colony (but not ownership of the land), and Maryland gained a royally appointed governor. Catholics in Maryland, their former haven and hegemony, were relegated to the status of Catholics in the mother country—fined, disenfranchised, sidelined.

Massachusetts was again an exceptional case. Once the hated Andros was incarcerated, the Council of Safety tried to reestablish the original charter government and recalled its last elected governor to office. But Massachusetts was divided against itself—though many hoped for the restoration of the original charter, in which political structures were intertwined with religious position, not all were confident that such a restoration was possible or even desirable. The fervor that had sent 30,000 Puritans to a wilderness to create a godly society had waned in the intervening half-century. Some were troubled at the equivocal legal position of the colony. Andros could be accused of little but attempting to enforce imperial policy; the same independent spirit that had resisted him resisted the new government that rested on such tenuous authority. For three long years, there was no clear central authority in Massachusetts. Andros was returned to England, accompanied by more agents for the Massachusetts colony. Increase Mather had been pleading, cajoling, and lobbying in London since 1688, and his advocates and advisers convinced him that the new king would not tolerate the self-government built into the old charter. The General Court—the representative assembly that had governed the colony since its founding—was restored. But its composition would be permanently altered by the decision to extend the franchise to property holders, rather than members of the church. The king appointed the governor. Massachusetts was no longer God's "city on a hill"; it was another royal colony of North America. But the self-regard that had established the colony as the province of God's elect would not bend readily to imperial imperatives.

By 1696, all the colonies had royally appointed governors. New York gained a representative assembly populated largely by the competing, jealous factions that harbored residual enmity from Leisler's rebellion. The proprietary families of Maryland and Pennsylvania retained land titles to their colonies until the Revolution, but the governments were no longer in their control. Voting privileges in all the colonies were standardized.

The Glorious Revolution in America served, in the long run, to undermine seriously the ties between England and its North American colonies. From the English viewpoint, two laws enacted in 1696 to support and enforce the Navigation Acts would streamline administration, communication, and control of the colonies, thereby increasing English trade and English power. However, avoidance and, later, defiance of these two provisions would increase the distance between imperial and colonial objectives.

The Board of Trade was created to oversee government and administration in the colonies. It functioned as a clearinghouse for all kinds of colonial affairs, dispatching colonial legislation, customs documents, and military reports to the appropriate offices in the British government for review. It was also an advisory panel for the Privy Council, which made all appointments of colonial officers.

Parliament also found it necessary to extend jurisdiction to vice admiralty courts for violations of the Navigation Acts. Woefully few smugglers were actually convicted in the North American colonies after trial by a jury of their peers. The vice admiralty courts established in those colonies could circumvent that problem, as they had no juries. But the law establishing the vice admiralty courts did not eliminate jury trials, and therefore colonial juries continued to acquit their smuggling peers.

In 1701, the Society for the Propagation of the Gospel was founded to convey Anglican missionaries to North America. Only Virginia had established the state Church of England as the state church of Virginia. Some partial establishment (payment of a tax to support the "established," or government-endorsed, religion) had taken place in some sectors of New York, Maryland, and North and South Carolina. The other colonies had been founded by or on behalf of religious dissenters, who formed the bulk of the colonial population. As more colonial officials and administrators came to the colonies, they brought their Anglicanism with them, contributing to an increasingly diverse religious observance.

Also in 1701, the cultural and economic differences between the northern and southern portions of Carolina were recognized, and their division became formal. The following year, East and West Jersey were united. The unexpected consequence of the Glorious Revolution in the colonies was the echo of parliamentary sovereignty found in the colonial assemblies. As Parliament triumphed at home, so did the colonial assemblies in America. London's neglect of the colonies and the absorption in European affairs that led to colonial autonomy in the 17th century would permit the disregard of imperial decrees in the 18th. Colonial assemblies repeatedly refused to post their militias or spend their money to aid other colonies—Virginia, Maryland, Massachusetts, and Pennsylvania all refused royal directives in the first decade of the 1700s. In addition, whenever war broke out between England and France, the colonies were expected to strike at French Canada. Wartime expenses were a burden to each of the colonies; in matters of defense, the colonies were on their own. Paper money issued in the wake of various wars by various colonial governments to pay their local debt was a continual problem for both the local economy and the local government. This circumstance would lead to serious repercussions at the conclusion of the Seven Years' War (known in America as the French and Indian War) in 1763, when London decided to station an English army permanently in North America. Colonists who had managed their own defense (and taken on the accompanying financial burden) for decades were not at all interested in paying for the maintenance of a standing army. The protests over taxation imposed by Parliament would lead to the Revolution.

Colonial assemblies, holding the "power of the purse," regularly expressed their displeasure with imperial administration by declining to fund royal officials' salaries. One such dispute is best known as the Zenger case; it involved newspaper editor John Peter

Zenger of New York, who was charged, in 1740, with sedition for supporting the New York Assembly in its dispute with the royal governor. A jury of sympathetic New Yorkers acquitted him. This case is often held up as an early freedom-of-the-press case, because Zenger argued that he could not be publishing treasonous material if it could be proved true. However, it is more accurately an illustration of the power of the colonial legislatures a half-century after the Glorious Revolution. Despite the intermittent desire of the imperial government to increase and centralize control over the American colonies, the refusal of the local legislatures to obey instruction and even to pay the salaries of royal officials demonstrates that the colonists viewed their assemblies as "mini-Parliaments," and the Glorious Revolution had made Parliament sovereign. The insistence on the powers of their local governments would lead the colonists to their own revolution in 1776.

## SELECTED BIBLIOGRAPHY

Arch, Stephen Carl. "The Glorious Revolution and the Rhetoric of Puritan History." *Early American Literature* 27 (1992): 61–74. How the Puritans convinced themselves their rebellion was not treasonous.

Archdeacon, Thomas J. *New York City, 1664–1710: Conquest and Change.* Ithaca, NY: Cornell University Press, 1976. A population analysis and study of popular politics, with emphasis on Dutch-English conflict.

Bailyn, Bernard. "Politics and Social Structure in Virginia." In *Seventeenth Century American: Essays in Colonial History,* edited by James M. Smith. New York: W. W. Norton, 1959. How fluid social mobility affected the allotment of political power.

Bonomi, Patricia U. *A Factious People: Politics and Society in Colonial New York.* New York: Columbia University Press, 1971. A lucid untangling of political rivalries and alliances in colonial New York over an extensive period.

Clark, J. C. D. *The Language of Liberty.* Cambridge: Cambridge University Press, 1994. A work that analyzes the themes of religion and law in the political discourse between England and America between 1660 and 1832.

Craven, Wesley Frank. *The Colonies in Transition: 1660–1713.* New York: Harper and Row, 1968. A thorough narrative of the crucial period bracketing the Glorious Revolution.

Greene, Jack. "Metropolis and Colonies: Changing Patterns of Constitutional Conflict in the Early Modern British Empire, 1607–1763." In *Negotiated Authorities: Essays in Colonial Political and Constitutional History.* Charlottesville: University Press of Virginia, 1994. The conflict between British imperial policy and colonial interests.

———. *The Quest for Power: The Lower Houses of Assembly in the Southern Royal Colonies 1689–1776.* Chapel Hill: University of North Carolina Press, 1963. How the lower assemblies achieved the upper hand.

Hall, Michael G., Lawrence H. Leder, and Michael G. Kammen, eds. *The Glorious Revolution in America: Documents on the Colonial Crisis of 1689.* Chapel Hill: University of North Carolina Press, 1964. A documentary chronicle of events in New England, New York, and Maryland.

James, Sidney V. *Colonial Rhode Island: A History.* New York: Charles Scribner's Sons, 1975. An enjoyable explanation of why Rhode Island is known as "the land of the otherwise-minded."

Kammen, Michael. "The Causes of the Maryland Revolution of 1689." *Maryland Historical Magazine* (December 1960): 293–333. Poor policy of the Calverts led to popular support for a small, ambitious group of opponents to proprietary rule.

———. *Colonial New York.* New York: Charles Scribner's Sons, 1975. Leisler's rebellion in a comprehensive context.

Lovejoy, David S. *The Glorious Revolution in America.* New York: Harper and Row, 1972. A comprehensive study emphasizing the colonies as part of the British empire.

Miller, Perry. *The New England Mind: From Colony to Province.* Cambridge, MA: Harvard University Press, 1953. An interesting history by the premier authority on Puritan society. Any study of colonial New England must begin with Perry Miller.

Sewall, Samuel. *The Diary and Life of Samuel Sewall.* Edited by Mel Yazawa. New York: Bedford Books, 1998. The events in Boston as recounted by a prominent participant.

Sosin, Jack M. *English America and the Revolution of 1688.* Lincoln: University of Nebraska Press, 1982. The impact of the Glorious Revolution on American political structures.

Stout, Harry O. *The New England Soul: Preaching and Religious Culture in Colonial New England.* New York: Oxford University Press, 1986. A study drawn from sermons that demonstrates the strong influence of Puritanism in politics.

Ver Steeg, Clarence L. *The Formative Years 1697–1763.* New York: Hill and Wang, 1964. The transition from English colonies to American provinces.

## SIR EDMUND ANDROS (1637–1714)

Sir Edmund Andros was a prominent colonial governor of New York, the Dominion of New England, and New Jersey and governor of Virginia. As he was appointed by the Crown and believed in exercising royal prerogatives, Andros was overthrown by colonists in Massachusetts during the Glorious Revolution of 1688–1689.

Andros was born in London on December 6, 1637, the second son of Amice Andros and Elizabeth Stone. The family had strong connections to the ruling Stuart family, monarchs of England. When the Stuart king Charles I was overthrown and executed in the English Civil War, the senior Andros took his family into exile in Holland in December 1651. There, Andros studied Dutch and French and joined the Dutch Army when he turned 18. After Charles's son was restored to the throne as King Charles II, in 1660, the Andros family returned to England, where the family's loyalty to the Stuarts made them influential. In 1674, the Duke of York (Charles II's brother James) appointed Andros to be governor of the province of New York, a post that he held until 1681. For his services in the New World, Andros was knighted in 1678.

When James ascended the throne, in 1685, as King James II, the Lords of Trade and Plantations (a committee established by Charles II in 1660 to formulate colonial policy) was already consolidating royal power in the colonies. The committee expanded royal authority even more in 1686 when it formed the Dominion of New England out of the colonies of Connecticut, Rhode Island, Massachusetts Bay, part of Maine, and Plymouth. In March 1686, the Lords of Trade added New York and New Jersey to the new royal province. The Dominion of New England, as one historian remarked, became a "new authoritarian model of colonial administration." In May 1686, James II appointed Andros as the vast dominion's governor.

Andros moved quickly to dismantle preexisting colonial institutions that he believed denied the Crown of its ability to rule by granting too many privileges for self-rule in the colonies. He carried out the Crown's orders to eliminate legislative assemblies and, over the strenuous objections of leading colonial authorities, began to impose measures that would raise revenue (levying heavier taxes), make the Church of England a larger presence (which dismayed the Puritans), and prohibit town meetings (which undercut local autonomy). Moreover, he challenged the validity of all land titles granted under the original Massachusetts charter. Thus, most colonists faced the frightening prospect of losing their lands.

Andros's days as the dominion's governor, however, were numbered. By 1688, the colonists had sent a deputation led by the auspicious Rev. Increase Mather to London to present the colonists' grievances against Andros. In England, however, a more serious governing crisis had arisen. In 1688, King James II was forced to abdicate in what became known as the Glorious Revolution, a bloodless coup that resulted in critical changes in royal authority and the Crown's relationship with Parliament. When Protestants Queen Mary II (James II's daughter) and King William III (Mary's husband) assumed the throne, they agreed to rule as constitutional monarchs. They accepted a bill of rights that limited the authority of the monarchy and gave subjects and Parliament more freedom and power.

When word of England's Glorious Revolution reached America, the colonists did not waste time ridding themselves of their own hated ruler, Andros. With Massachusetts leading the way, colonists throughout New England vowed to depose Andros. Puritan ministers called on the townspeople to "seize the vile persons who oppressed us," and the local militia captured Andros and other English officials on April 18, 1689, holding them prisoner.

Shortly thereafter, Andros was forced to return to England. William and Mary were reluctant to dismantle the Dominion of New England but agreed to do so if they could maintain close control of the colonies. The colonists accepted the arrangement on the grounds that it was better than the system that had been in place before. In 1691, the new royal colony of Massachusetts was created from the old charter colonies of Massachusetts Bay, Plymouth, and Maine.

In July 1692, Andros returned to America to serve as governor of Virginia. During his six-year tenure, he founded the College of William and Mary and promoted agriculture and industry. He clashed with colonial church authorities, however, and was recalled by the Crown in 1698. Andros held his fourth and last governorship, in New Jersey, between 1704 and 1706. He spent his remaining years in London and died on February 24, 1714.

## BACON'S REBELLION (1676)

A controversial episode in Virginia history, Bacon's Rebellion was actually an outgrowth of the Indian War of 1675–1676, which began as a dispute between some Maryland Nanticoke (Doeg) Indians and a Virginia planter named Thomas Mathew. Convinced that the planter had cheated them, the Indians murdered him, thereby triggering reprisals from both sides, including an accidental attack on a friendly Susquehannock village, which was actually a palisaded settlement located on Piscataway Creek. That attack, known as the siege of Fort Piscataway, was carried out by Virginia militia and caused the death of five Susquehannock chiefs under a flag of truce.

A full-scale investigation was immediately launched by Virginia's governor, William Berkeley, who feared that the situation might escalate into a broader conflict like King Philip's War, then raging in New England. Berkeley addressed the crisis by adopting a defensive strategy, which included constructing a series of forts into which colonists could retire when threatened. Berkeley also prohibited unauthorized campaigns against the Indians, a departure from the more aggressive posture he had adopted during the Powhatan War. Berkeley drew the ire of many colonists with the order forbidding independent campaigns, which some chose to ignore regardless. Those events set the stage for one Nathaniel Bacon, a wealthy young planter from Henrico County and a member of the Virginia Council who was related to the governor by marriage.

In the spring of 1676, Bacon presented himself to the governor in Jamestown, requested a commission, and offered to lead an expedition against the Indians. The request was denied, but Bacon nevertheless organized and led a force of 200 men against some alleged Susquehannock raiders. Unsuccessful in locating his quarry, Bacon then entered an alliance of sorts with some Occaneechees who offered to attack their old enemy, the Susquehannock. They subsequently did so and captured some 30 in the process. After torturing the Susquehannock, Bacon suddenly turned on the Occaneechee, apparently in a dispute over captured booty, and killed 50 men while losing 12 himself. As a result, Berkeley declared Bacon to be in rebellion and removed him from the Virginia Council. Notwithstanding his public censure, Bacon savored the adulation accorded a popular hero.

Although he was elected to the new Virginia Council, Bacon was captured by Berkeley and persuaded to admit the error of his ways, whereupon he was pardoned. Berkeley's victory, however, was only temporary, because Bacon returned to Jamestown in June accompanied by 500 followers. Confronted by this show of support for Bacon, Berkeley reluctantly issued him a commission. Now backed by the force of a coerced commission, Bacon launched a campaign against area Indians and even attacked a village of friendly Pamunkeys, many of whom were killed. Although Bacon's ruthless and indiscriminate behavior was supported by some council members who favored enslaving the Indians, Berkeley repudiated the act and repealed Bacon's commission. Learning of the governor's action against him, Bacon returned and laid siege to Jamestown. Using hostages, he forced Berkeley out of the stockaded settlement and into exile on Virginia's Eastern Shore; he then put Jamestown to the torch.

In October, Bacon succumbed to the effects of dysentery, and, without his leadership, the movement lost much of its impetus. By January, Berkeley had mustered enough support to end what was left of the rebellion. Bacon's leaders were executed and their property confiscated. Any servant who was found guilty of aiding the rebellion had his term of indenture extended.

The effects of Bacon's uprising were far-reaching. For all practical purposes, the Occaneechee ceased to be a presence of any importance in the area, and, as a consequence, the Virginia settlements then had direct access to the Cherokee villages to the south. The rebellion also prompted an inquiry that subsequently resulted in Berkeley's dismissal as governor. In addition, the Virginia Council authorized the sale of Indian lands to underwrite the cost of the war and also sanctioned the sale and enslavement of Indians. Those laws were repealed by the Treaty of Middle Plantation (1677).

## KING WILLIAM'S WAR (1689–1697)

The first of the intercolonial wars between France and England in North America, King William's War is sometimes referred to as the Abnaki War because it pitted the English and their Iroquois allies against the French and their Abnaki allies. The European

component of the conflict was known as the War of the League of Augsburg. A deterio-
rating situation in northern New England set the stage for the North American phase
of the European war.

In the years following the Dutch departure from New York, the Iroquois Confederacy established new economic ties with the English, an alliance that was largely to
remain steadfast during the next century. Despite the reassurance of their relationship with the Iroquois, however, the British were concerned over an alliance between
France and the Abnakis, a powerful Algonquian tribe from Maine, who in turn were allied with Pennacooks, Penobscots, Micmacs, and others. In large part, the concern was
based simply on the increasing rivalry between France and England for control of North
America. In addition, there was also a fear that Catholicism (epitomized by Louis XIV
of France) was on the rise and threatening Protestantism. In North America, there was
a disturbing rumor to the effect that French Catholics were preparing a savage alliance
with the Indians to take over the colonies and install Catholicism.

In Massachusetts, British colonists upset an uneasy peace by taking Abnaki prisoners in response to the killing of English cattle. Abnaki raids followed, and, in April 1688,
Sir Edmund Andros, recently appointed governor of all the northern colonies (called
the Dominion of New England), launched a retaliatory strike and captured a French
outpost on Penobscot Bay on the pretext that it was British property. Aside from that,
Andros concentrated on building forts and employing a largely defensive strategy to
deal with the Abnaki raids. His tenure as governor was short-lived, however, and he was
deposed as a result of the Glorious Revolution in England in the spring of 1689, which
saw James II replaced by William of Orange and Mary II.

With the war in Europe officially under way, Louis XIV chose the aging Louis de
Baude, Comte de Frontenac, to govern New France. A 70-year-old curmudgeon, Frontenac decided to move south from Canada and invade British New York, an unwise
move since Frontenac lacked the necessary resources to execute his strategy. In July
1689, in the first real strike of the war, a large contingent of Iroquois attacked Lachine, a
French settlement near Montreal, virtually destroyed the settlement, and killed many of
its inhabitants. As a result of the Lachine Massacre, Frontenac decided to adopt guerrilla tactics. No quarter was asked, and none was given. As the Iroquois terrorized the
French, the Abnakis and their allies retaliated in like form against the English.

During the winter of 1689–1690, Frontenac led a force from Montreal down into New
England, struck Schenectady, and slaughtered many settlers in retaliation for Iroquois
raids. That was followed in March by a similar attack on Salmon Falls, New Hampshire.
In an effort to gain the initiative, a British squadron under the command of Maine-born
frontiersman Sir William Phips captured the lightly defended Port Royal, Maine, in the
spring of 1690. Buoyed by that success, the British decided to launch an invasion of Canada in August 1689, with Phips in command. However, beset by a number of military
and logistical problems and with the ranks devastated by smallpox, the offensive came
to naught. Although Frontenac's guerrilla tactics spread terror through the northern
colonies, they had accomplished little of real substance for the French cause.

In 1691, an aging and barely mobile Capt. Benjamin Church, hero of earlier troubles,
was called on to help counter the Abnaki raids. Church's efforts produced some success,
but the raids continued. In 1692, Wells, Maine, and Deerfield, Massachusetts, were victims of raids, and similar attacks continued for the next several years.

In a March 1697 raid on Haverhill, Massachusetts, Abnakis captured Hannah Dustin, mother of eight and one of the most famous of New England's Indian captives. After their capture, Dustin and a companion attacked their captors, killed all but two as they slept, and made their escape.

In September 1697, the Treaty of Ryswick ended the European war, which in turn brought an end to the conflict in North America, though New England continued to see sporadic fighting for some time. As a postscript to King William's War, the Iroquois Confederacy and western tribes allied with the French continued their struggle. Near the end of the century, most likely in 1698 or 1699, a major battle took place between those factions on the shores of Lake Erie and resulted in an Iroquois defeat.

JERRY KEENAN

## JACOB LEISLER (1640–1691)

Jacob Leisler led a rebellion against royal authority in the colony of New York from 1689 to 1691. Jacob was born in 1640 in Frankenthal, Palatine, Germany, to the Calvinist family of Rev. Jacob Victorian Leisler and Susanne Adelheid Wissenbach. He grew up in a bilingual household, speaking both French and German, and in later years learned to read and write English and Dutch. He also studied math, logic, and the Bible. When his mother moved to Hanau after his father died, in 1653, Jacob continued his education at a military academy.

Leisler moved to Amsterdam in the winter of 1658–1659. He began to consider the idea of seeking a new life in America, and his chance came in 1660, when the Dutch West India Company sent the young officer to the Dutch colony of New Netherland (present-day New York). Two years later, Leisler was enjoying a prosperous business in the fur and tobacco trades in New Amsterdam. Over the next 12 years, he expanded his ventures to include wine, beer, salt, grains, fish, horses, cloth, spices, and humans (indentured and slave), as well as owning shares in many ships and investing in land. As one historian noted, Leisler "was among the richest merchants in the duke of York's province."

On April 11, 1663, Leisler married Elsie Tymens, the widow of Pieter Cornelisse Van der Veen, a prosperous merchant. His marriage enabled him to make even more important contacts among the leading families in New York and increased his commercial opportunities. He and Elsie eventually had three daughters—Catharina, Susannah, and Mary.

Leisler did not serve in any political posts during the Dutch administration of New Netherland, but he became more publicly involved when the colony fell under English rule and became the colony of New York. He often served as a juror or arbitrator in civil and criminal cases. Gov. Francis Nicholson appointed Leisler to a council in the spring of 1689, shortly after the Glorious Revolution had spread its fervor to Boston. Nicholson directed Leisler to prevent the growing rebellion from spilling into New York, but Leisler turned against Nicholson when he became convinced that Nicholson, despite his Protestant background, would continue to support the Catholic King James II instead of the Protestant King William and Queen Mary for the English Crown.

In May 1689, one month after an uprising in Massachusetts in which colonists overthrew Gov. Sir Edmund Andros, Leisler led a revolt against royal authority in New York. Assisted by the New York militia, which was made up primarily of Dutch artisans and

Puritan farmers, Leisler and the rebels ousted Nicholson and other royally appointed officials in the administration. Leisler assumed the title of lieutenant governor, hailed the authority of William and Mary, and solicited support from the other rebel governments of Maryland, Massachusetts, and Connecticut. In New York, Leisler organized a convention with head officials from other towns, at which delegates discussed their concerns and appointed a committee of safety, with Leisler as its head. Leisler was given full legal, administrative, and military responsibility over the colony.

In the meantime, William sent a letter to Nicholson giving him royal authorization to run the New York government. Since Nicholson had returned to England, however, the letter was also addressed to an unnamed person who would "Preserv[e] the Peace and administer the Lawes of our said Province in New York In America." Leisler assumed that William meant for him to see the letter, and, for the remainder of his tenure, Leisler considered himself as the legitimate head of the New York government.

Leisler's regime revealed that he was an active and capable public administrator. As one historian admiringly noted, the Leisler administration "organized a government and raised funds, issued commissions, created courts, suppressed riots, appointed military officers, created a commission that sat as a court of vice-admiralty, and sent agents to England." Leisler also sought to improve intercolonial affairs. In the spring of 1690, for example, he organized an intercolonial conference to discuss the French and Indian attacks in northern New York.

Leisler enjoyed support from people of different socioeconomic backgrounds, but that support dwindled when he freed debtors from prison and advocated the formation of a more democratic form of government. Dutch artisans aligned with Leisler, while the wealthier merchants withdrew their support and openly criticized him. Merchants and town leaders began to complain against his rule, and some sent letters to England.

In March 1691, William's new governor, Col. Henry Sloughter, and English troops led by Maj. Robert Ingoldesby arrived in New York to remove Leisler. At first, Leisler resisted and refused to relinquish his power, but he eventually surrendered to Sloughter. Leisler and nine other men were charged with treason and murder. The trial lasted just over two weeks. Two men were acquitted, but the rest were sentenced to hang. In the end, only Leisler and his son-in-law, Jacob Milburne, were executed, as the other six gained a stay in execution and were eventually pardoned. The original order for the execution of Leisler and Milburne stated that they be hanged "by the Neck and being Alive their bodys be Cutt downe to the Earth and Their Bowells be taken out and they being Alive, burnt before their faces; that their heads shall be struck off and their Body's Cutt in four parts." The records indicate, however, that the two men were simply hanged and then decapitated in May 1691. Even after his death, Leisler did not entirely disappear from the New York landscape. The political battles between Leisler and anti-Leisler forces would last through the first decade of the 18th century.

## DOCUMENT: ENGLISH BILL OF RIGHTS, 1689

*While early English history consisted of a struggle between the monarch and the Parliament, the English Bill of Rights of 1689 marked the triumph of parliamentary sovereignty. Drafted by the English Parliament in the wake of the Glorious Revolution that had replaced on the throne the autocratic King James II with the more liberal King William III and Queen Mary II, the Bill of Rights sought to protect the "ancient rights and liberties" to which the people considered themselves entitled. A large number of the concerns raised in the English Bill of Rights would later be specifically reflected in the U.S. Constitution and in America's own Bill of Rights.* (English Bill of Rights, 1689 [Am. Legal System].)

WHEREAS the late King James the Second, by the assistance of divers evil counsellors, judges and ministers employed by him, did endeavor to subvert and extirpate the protestant religion, and the laws and liberties of this kingdom.

1. By assuming and exercising a power of dispensing with and suspending of laws, and the execution of laws, without consent of parliament.

2. By committing and prosecuting divers worthy prelates, for humbly petitioning to be excused from concurring to the said assumed power.

3. By issuing and causing to be executed a commission under the great seal for erecting a court called the Court of Commissioners for Ecclesiastical Causes.

4. By levying money for and to the use of the crown, by pretence of prerogative, for other time, and in other manner, than the same was granted by parliament.

5. By raising and keeping a standing army within this kingdom in time of peace, without consent of parliament, and quartering soldiers contrary to law.

6. By causing several good subjects, being protestants, to be disarmed, at the same time when papists were both armed and employed, contrary to law.

7. By violating the freedom of election of members to serve in parliament.

8. By prosecutions in the court of King's bench, for matters and causes cognizable only in parliament; and by divers other arbitrary and illegal courses.

9. And whereas of late years, partial, corrupt, and unqualified persons have been returned and served on juries in trials, and particularly divers jurors in trials for high treason, which were not freeholders.

10. And excessive bail hath been required of persons committed in criminal cases, to elude the benefit of the laws made for the liberty of the subjects.

11. And excessive fines have been imposed; and illegal and cruel punishments have been inflicted.

12. And several grants and promises made of fines and forfeitures, before any conviction or judgement against the persons, upon whom the same were to be levied.

All which are utterly and directly contrary to the known laws and statutes, and freedom of this realm.

And whereas the said late king James the Second having abdicated the government, and the throne being thereby vacant…the said lords spiritual and temporal, and commons…do in the first place (as their ancestors in like case have usually done) for the vindicating and asserting their ancient rights and liberties, declare;

1. That the pretended power of suspending of laws, or the execution of laws, by regal authority, without consent of parliament, is illegal.

2.  That the pretended power of dispensing with laws, or the execution of laws, by regal authority, as it hath been assumed and exercised of late, is illegal.

3.  That the commission for erecting the late court of commissioners for ecclesiastical causes, and all other commissions and courts of like nature are illegal and pernicious.

4.  That levying money for or to the use of the crown, by pretence of prerogative, without grant of parliament, for longer time, or in other manner than the same is or shall be granted, is illegal.

5.  That it is the right of the subjects to petition the King, and all committments and prosecutions for such petitioning are illegal.

6.  That the raising or keeping a standing army within the kingdom in time of peace, unless it be with consent of parliament, is against law.

7.  That the subjects which are protestants, may have arms for their defence suitable to their conditions, and as allowed by law.

8.  That election of members of parliament ought to be free.

9.  That the freedom of speech, and debates or proceedings in parliament, ought not to be impeached or questioned in any court or place out of parliament.

10.  That excessive bail ought not to be required, nor excessive fines imposed; nor cruel and unusual punishments inflicted.

11.  That jurors ought to be duly impanelled and returned, and jurors which pass upon men in trials for high treason ought to be freeholders.

12.  That all grants and promises of fines and forfeitures of particular persons before conviction, are illegal and void.

13.  And that for redress of all grievances, and for the amending, strengthening, and preserving of the laws, parliaments ought to be held frequently.

And they do claim, demand, and insist upon all and singular the premises, as their undoubted rights and liberties; and that no declarations, judgements, doings or proceedings, ought in any wise to be drawn hereafter into consequence or example.

# 12

# The Salem Witch Trials, 1692

## INTRODUCTION

The witch trials of Salem Village, Massachusetts (March–September 1692) were America's most notorious episode of witchcraft hysteria. The belief in witchcraft was carried to colonial America from Europe, where thousands had been executed as witches in the two centuries before 1650. The Salem incident began when two young girls in the household of Rev. Samuel Parris began to behave oddly. One of the girls was Reverend Parris's daughter, Betty. She was nine years old. The other girl was 11-year-old Abigail Williams, Betty Parris's cousin.

Apparently, the girls had been feeling guilty for dropping an egg in a glass and looking at it in the style of crystal-ball gazing, a forbidden behavior, to see what the trade of their sweethearts would be. Looking at an egg in a glass in this fashion was considered a fairly benign and common form of witchcraft, so-called white witchcraft. When they thought they saw a coffin in the glass, their guilt turned to terror.

In February 1692, Betty Parris and Abigail Williams began slipping into trances, blurting nonsensical phrases, cowering in corners, and collapsing in epileptic-like fits. Their bodies were supposedly twisted as if their bones were made out of putty. Reverend Parris invited many doctors to examine the children. No doctor knew what to make of the situation until Doctor William Griggs examined the girls and diagnosed witchcraft.

Reverend Parris asked his congregation to pray and fast, hoping that this would end the witchcraft. They prayed for weeks, but the girls still babbled nonsense and had fits. As more members of the congregation became aware of the problem, the behavior spread to other girls who might also have been experimenting with the occult. Among them were Ann Putnam Jr., 12, Mary Warren, 20, Mercy Lewis, 19, Mary Walcott, 16, and Elizabeth Hubbard, 17.

The symptoms exhibited have been called "hysteria," but there is confusion about what this term means. In its common usage, it is understood to mean a temporary state of excitement in which the victim loses self-control. However, the term in medicine is far more serious and may include the types of fits observed at the time, as well as temporary loss of hearing, sight, speech, and memory. Symptoms may extend to a choking sensation in the throat, hallucinations, and feelings of being pinched or bitten; marks may even appear on the skin.

In more modern times, such fits have been reported. During World War II, British military hospitals reported that seizures in connection with hysteria occurred in only six cases of hysteria out of 161, while, during the same time period, the behavior was the most common symptom among hysterics in Delhi, India. Fear of witchcraft, rather than its practice, seems the most likely cause of the behavior that occurred in Salem.

As Reverend Parris questioned the girls further, they told him that Tituba was the witch. Tituba was the minister's slave, who was from Barbados. While Reverend Parris seems to have been hesitant to believe the doctor's diagnosis, his neighbors were more ready to believe it. On February 25, Mary Sibley, the aunt of Mary Walcott, went to Tituba and asked her to prepare a witch cake—meal mixed with the children's urine and baked in fire—that was fed to the Parrises' dog. The dog was a "familiar"—a messenger assigned to a witch by the devil. This also was considered white magic, but Reverend Parris was appalled when he found out a month later because he felt the community should go to God, not the devil, even in a good cause.

However, the magic worked—the girls were able to name those afflicting them as Sarah Good and Sarah Osborne. On March 1, 1692, Tituba, Sarah Good, and Sarah Osborne were arrested for practicing witchcraft. Two Salem magistrates who would conduct most of the preliminary examinations, John Hathorne and Jonathan Corwin, questioned the women. John Hathorne asked most of the questions and acted more like a prosecuting attorney than an impartial investigator, as had been the case in past investigations in New England. Hathorne also asked the girls to confront Sarah Good. When they accused her to her face, they immediately were beset by fits, which they said were caused by Good's specter.

This 19th-century engraving illustrates one of the often dramatic judicial proceedings in the Salem witch trials of 1692. (Courtesy of the Library of Congress.)

Tituba eventually confessed, naming four other witches: Good, Osborne, and two others she did not know. She described the devil as a tall man in a black suit who had a yellow bird, and he carried a book he urged Tituba to sign. There were nine marks in the book, two by Good and Osborne. The devil promised to give her nice things if she obeyed him, but he also threatened to hurt her if she disobeyed him. Tituba then confessed to trying to kill children while she was in the form of a specter, a ghostly image, a visible disembodied spirit that haunts the mind. Tituba's confession affected the outcome of the witch trials, because she supported the girls' claims that they had seen specters, which made it possible for them to identify witches.

The three women were sent to the Boston jail to await trial, but the magistrates in Salem Village continued to question the afflicted until the names of other witches and the grand wizard were revealed. Two weeks later, Ann Putnam Jr. and Abigail Williams named Martha Corey as a witch. Martha Corey was a woman who was respected in the village, and she attended church every Sabbath. She was arrested the day after Abigail Williams pointed out her specter.

Martha Corey's husband, Giles, was called to testify. He said that he found it hard to pray when she was around. He also said he would find her late at night by the hearth, kneeling mysteriously. This testimony was accepted as proof that Mrs. Corey was a witch. Mrs. Corey soon joined Tituba, Sarah Good, and Sarah Osborne in the Boston jail. She was the first "gospel woman" to be marked as a witch.

Soon, Mary Warren was arrested. Abigail Williams said she had seen Mary sign the devil's book. She said she had also seen her in specter form and that Warren had pinched and hurt her. Abigail and the others also accused John Proctor's, wife, Elizabeth. When Proctor came to his wife's defense, he also was arrested. Rebecca Nurse and her sisters Sarah Cloyce and Mary Easty also were arrested. All three were educated, devout Christians. In April 1692, Sarah Good gave birth, and, a few weeks later, the baby died. Sarah Osborne also died while in jail. By the end of May 1692, nearly 100 people had been arrested on charges of witchcraft. Bail was denied, and no one yet had been tried by a jury.

Because Massachusetts Colony had just received a new charter from England in May 1692, after eight years without one, no courts were established yet. The new governor, Sir William Phips, realized that the witchcraft trials could not wait until the previously planned date of January 1693. So, on May 27, Governor Phips established a special Court of Oyer and Terminer with seven experienced and distinguished judges, headed by William Stoughton, Phips's lieutenant governor.

The court met June 2 and tried one person—Bridget Bishop. She had been charged of using witchcraft in April. She was a woman in her fifties who was twice widowed and who was married to a third husband. Rumor had it that she had been unfaithful to all three of her husbands. She had been accused with spectral evidence (two women testified that they had seen the devil enter her body), but that alone was not enough. Two laborers who had worked for her had found dolls with pins in them stuffed into holes in the cellar walls of her previous house. This was concrete evidence of the practice of witchcraft and made her conviction relatively easy. She was hanged on June 10, 1692.

However, such concrete evidence did not exist against the other accused witches. Apparently, other types of evidence were enough to convince the judges. Evidence accepted by the court included self-confession; accusation by others, including other accused witches; being caught in lies; inability to say the Lord's Prayer without error; spectral evidence provided by the afflicted girls; and marks of the devil on the bodies of the accused.

On June 30, five people were tried, convicted, and condemned to death—Sarah Good, Rebecca Nurse, Susannah Martin, Elizabeth Howe, and Sarah Wildes. On July 19, they were all executed. The morning after, Rebecca Nurse's body was missing. Her family had come and taken it for a secret Christian burial, although it was against the law to have a Christian burial for a condemned person. The other four bodies were dumped in a shallow grave near the gallows, at a place known as Gallows Hill.

On August 6, the court sat again to consider the cases of six people—John and Elizabeth Proctor, George Burroughs, John Willard, George Jacobs Sr., and Martha Carrier. All were found guilty and sentenced to death. Elizabeth Proctor's death was delayed because she was pregnant. By the time her baby was born, in January 1693, the witch trials were over, so her life was spared.

John Proctor wrote a letter to five area ministers on July 23, on behalf of himself and the other prisoners. He said that the community had condemned them before their trials and asked that the ministers intercede to have the venue of the trials or the judges changed. Governor Phips was the only one who could make any changes, but Proctor hoped to gain more influence than had been the case with Rebecca Nurse's family, which had also sent a petition to the governor.

Eight more people were hanged on September 22, 1692, including Martha Corey. Giles Corey, her husband, had been crushed to death just three days earlier for refusing to enter a plea. They laid him down, placed a board over him, and stacked large flat rocks on top of him. They placed the rocks one on top of the other until his rib cage caved in, an agonizing death that took two days. Although there has been debate on the reasons he chose to die this way, it seems clear that it was done in protest against the court and its proceedings, since none of the accused witches had yet been found not guilty and he was bound to die in any case.

The tide began to turn against the witch hunt for a number of reasons, including sympathy among the public for some of those condemned, such as Proctor, Corey, and George Burroughs, who was able to recite the Lord's Prayer without error. Also, the afflicted girls began to accuse influential people, including the wife of Increase Mather, the president of Harvard College. He responded by writing *Cases of Conscience*. He warned of the danger of accusing innocent people of witchcraft, especially those in good standing in the church.

A third reason was that the court was not accomplishing its purpose, which was to clear the jails. The more the court sat, the more crowded the jails became and the greater the disturbances in the community. The afflicted girls had gotten not better but worse. In the nearby town of Andover, where witchcraft accusations were spreading fast, an accused man of means sent friends around town to inquire who his accusers were so that he could sue them for defamation of character. Shortly thereafter, accusations were halted.

The witch trial era lasted less than a year. The first arrests were made in March 1692, and the final hanging day was September 22, 1692. Jurors and magistrates apologized. Restitution was made to the victims' families, and a Day of Fasting and Remembrance was instituted. Many of the girls, such as Ann Putnam Jr., later admitted that no evil hand had touched them. The girls had been enmeshed in the beliefs of the community and had become convinced that evil forces had bewitched them.

To understand the issues of the Salem witch trials, it is important to place them into a broader historical context. As early as the fifth century, Saint Augustine saw sorcery and white magic as being dependent on the help of the devil. In the mid-13th century, Saint Thomas Aquinas agreed with Saint Augustine. At this time, the Inquisition, composed mainly of members of the newly formed Dominican order, was formed to deal with heresy. The Dominicans were the first to use torture to gain confessions, and, by the late 14th century, this policy became the norm in secular courts as well.

In 1486, Heinrich Kramer and Jacob Sprenger published *Malleus Maleficarum,* or *The Witches' Hammer.* They had been involved for more than five years in witchcraft trials that had resulted in nearly 50 executions. *The Witches' Hammer* was written in the form of a handbook and was convenient for use by judges. It remained an important work for more than 200 years.

Statistics vary, but the pace of prosecutions picked up in the last three-quarters of the 15th century and then skyrocketed from the last half of the 16th through the 17th centuries, reaching a peak in the last half of the 17th century. Between 1365 and 1428, there were 84 verified prosecutions, and this number increased to 354 between 1428 and 1500. In Europe, figures range as high as 10,000 executions for witchcraft, with 900 in the city of Bamburg and 5,000 in the province of Alsace, 368 in Trier, 274 in Eichstatt, and 390 in Ellwangen. The English and Swiss were more restrained, as were the American colonies. There were fewer than 50 executions in the American colonies during the 17th century, including those in Salem. The parallels between the Salem witch trials and more modern examples such as the McCarthy hearings of the 1950s have also been studied.

In 1992, the town of Salem observed the tercentenary of the Salem witch trials. Among the many events in Salem that year, a memorial was dedicated, and Prof. Joseph Flibbert of Salem State College organized a conference that brought scholars to Salem from around the world to discuss the trials and other topics related to witchcraft. On September 20, 1992, the First Church in Salem readmitted Giles Corey and Rebecca Nurse to church membership.

## INTERPRETIVE ESSAY

FREDERICK M. STOWELL

At the beginning of the 21st century, American society has become jaded by stories of violence and the persistent images of this violence on television and in the media. Whether the images are generated by war, social unrest, or natural disaster, they have become commonplace as Americans expect more realism and graphic details in the reporting of current events. In this environment of information overload, the Salem witchcraft trials of 1692 still hold the interest of the general public and generate analysis by social scientists, historians, and researchers. The events that occurred more than 300 years ago and affected a relatively small number of people have made Salem synonymous with witch hunts and mass hysteria. The significance of the trials in Salem,

Massachusetts, is not earthshaking but subtle. It did not have the effect on society of the Declaration of Independence or the War of 1812, yet it is still used as a benchmark by which to judge other occurrences of group hysteria. This traditional interpretation of a Massachusetts community in turmoil, generated more than a century ago, has become the popular image of the colonial witch hunt craze.

The significance of the Salem witchcraft trials, however, is more than just the traditional interpretation of group hysteria. The trials are an opportunity to view the dynamics of a primitive frontier culture, established in a hostile environment, clinging to its European beliefs, and restricted by its dogmatic religious beliefs. While group hysteria played a part in the accusations of witchcraft and the resulting trials, the actual causes of the witch craze were rooted in the frontier society of the colony and its European traditions. Political instability, economic uncertainty and conflict, and the threat of war with the local Native American nations were clear and present concerns to the residents of Salem. Add to this the ingrained fear of a demonic presence and the dominant view among men that women were a threat to the church, the government, and the society, and it becomes apparent how an atmosphere of hysteria could develop and grow.

To understand fully the significance of the 1692 Salem witchcraft trials, it is necessary to understand the variety of historical interpretations and the influence of the period during which the interpretations were written. The earliest writings on the trials occurred shortly after the trials ended, in 1692. Rev. Cotton Mather, a member of the Puritan hierarchy in Massachusetts, recorded the events leading up to the trials and the accusations and testimonies of the trials in an attempt to justify the verdicts. His own position was that the trials were justified and carried out within the laws of the colony and Christianity. His view was different from that of his father, Increase Mather, who preached moderation and rationality. A counterpoint to Cotton Mather's writings was the work of Robert Calef, a Boston merchant who witnessed the trials and executions. In his book *More Wonders of the Invisible World* (1701), Calef suggests that the evil could be found not in the witchcraft but in the very trials themselves. In his view, the witch hunts and trials were "bigoted zeal" directed toward "virtuous and religious people."

The traditional view that attempted to fix blame for the trials developed from the writings of Charles Upham in 1867. *Salem Witchcraft,* Upham's two-volume interpretation of the original trial transcripts, attempted to focus blame on the "afflicted" girls as the leaders of a larger conspiracy against the accused witches. His contention became the popular cultural view that would influence the teaching of the event in American public schools for the next 100-odd years.

In 1953, Perry Miller delved into the meaning of being a Puritan and how that faith affected the lives of the colonists and laid the basis for the trials. This was an important connection for writers attempting to fully understand the reasons for the witch craze in New England and specifically Salem. Miller focused on the covenant or relationship the Puritans believed they had with God. As the Puritans worked to serve God and establish a community to do his will on earth, they truly believed that seeking out witches and destroying them was part of that covenant. When they realized that something had gone wrong with the trials, the foundation of this relationship with God came into question. Miller's interpretation of this relationship and the resulting confusion of belief added to an increased understanding of the events.

By the late 1960s, other researchers began to take different approaches to the cause of the witch craze. Chadwick Hansen, in *Witchcraft at Salem* (1969), argued that witchcraft really did exist in Salem, as well as in other parts of New England. Folk magic was widely used by the early colonists, and the activities of the first afflicted girls in Salem were not out of the ordinary. Since the community believed in the power of magic and since some of the accused were admitted witches, then witchcraft must have existed. According to Hanson, the trials were justified in that context.

Other views about the cause of the craze include a virus among the afflicted, the dominance of men and the low position of women in the society, the economic struggle between the rural and commercial centers of Salem Village and Salem Town, the demographics of the affected regions, and the power struggle within the community. All of these theories have developed since the 1960s as more researchers have attempted to go beyond the trials and to look at the complex issues of the community. The idea that a virus was the cause was posited in 1976 and has largely been discredited. The feminist approach, which Carol Karlsen first developed in *Devil in the Shape of a Woman* (1987), attempted to analyze the trial and accusations in light of late-20th-century concepts about the treatment of women. From this point of view, the author expands the descriptions of the accused witches from disagreeable old hags to women who were guilty because they were different. She states that gender issues merged with religious issues and that these were seen to be transgressions against God. Displays of anger, temper, and discontent with the church all were seen as signs of an alliance with the devil. Additionally, women who practiced healing and midwifery, assisting in the birth process, were seen as threats to the developing male medical profession. Although midwifery was not a sign of demonic involvement, it was enough to bring suspicion upon the accused.

Three researchers, John Demos, Paul Boyer, and Stephen Nissenbaum, attempted to go outside the actual trial and to look at the social environment of the community. Through their research, they developed a full picture of a community in turmoil. Taken together, their works explain why certain people became accusers and others became victims. The authors paint a picture of old animosities, lawsuits, and rivalries. It is through the view of these authors that a more detailed perspective of the community and the trials emerges.

Even the heritage of Tituba, the Indian slave of Samuel Parris, has been traced as far back as her documented origin in the Caribbean. Details of plantation life in the islands that influenced Tituba and, ultimately, Salem have been reconstructed through diligent research.

The events of 1692 in Salem, Massachusetts, have provided Americans with an example of a community gripped by group hysteria. This traditional and very general view was originally created in the writing of Charles Upham in 1867 and then incorporated into the massive *History of the United States* (1883–1885), by George Bancroft. From there it found its way into the history texts of American public schools and into American popular culture. The image of young girls writhing in pain, afflicted by unknown demons, and stern-faced Puritan men in austere black clothing sitting in judgment of haggard old women made its way into American culture in art, in literature, and on stage. Instilled into the collective memory of Americans, the Salem trials have become a benchmark for any similar event where unfounded accusations lead to the suffering of innocent victims. It has provided a perfect example of people who are seen as guilty until proved innocent. The playwright Arthur Miller used it for the theme of his play *The Crucible* (1953), which was also an analogy for the anticommunist movement of the early 1950s. The image of the "witch hunt" has been used to refer to the anticommunist Red Scare of both the post–World War I years and the McCarthyism of the early 1950s. In the former event, Americans were accused of association with the Communist Party and, in some cases, deported. During the latter, those accused of communist ties were hounded out of positions of authority in the government or jobs in the private sector. McCarthyism, named for the U.S. senator who led the anticommunist movement, has come to mean accusations lodged publicly against a person for which there is either no evidence of guilt or only evidence of guilt by association.

Additionally, the Salem trials have provided an intimate view of the much greater witch craze that had gripped Europe during the 15th and 17th centuries. The accusations of 150 people and the deaths of 20 accused witches in Salem was much more personal than the deaths of an estimated 200,000 people in Europe. The accused, the accusers, and the magistrates in Salem are known by name, and their words reverberate from the trial transcripts. The examinations by William Stoughton, chief justice of the Court of Oyer and Terminer, the accusations of Ann Putnam Jr., the denials of Mary Easty, and even the silence of Giles Corey all provide a personal view of the participants. The events of Salem also show the influence of the European-based superstitions on the colonists. The actions of the first accusers, Betty Parris, Abigail Williams, and Ann Putnam Jr., were based on European superstition and not the supposed voodoo of Tituba, Samuel Parris's Caribbean Indian slave. The practice of fortune-telling through the reading of eggs dropped in a glass was part of English folklore and not unusual in the Puritan communities of North America. So the girls were simply following an established magical practice that had migrated with the Puritans from England.

If the popular view of Salem has been one of mass hysteria, the reality of the situation was somewhat different. The events of Salem can be viewed as the result of an unstable environment, composed of political uncertainty, threats of war, and the fear of change, that generated an atmosphere of fear within the community. That fear found its focal point in the witch hunts and trials.

At the beginning of the Salem witch craze, the Massachusetts colony was without a charter, a governor, or a legally recognized government. The original charter, issued in 1630, had been revoked by King Charles II in 1684 in an attempt to increase English control over the profitable American colonies. With the ascension of James II, brother of King Charles II, to the throne, Massachusetts became part of the Dominion of New England, made up of New York, New Jersey, New Hampshire, Rhode Island, Connecticut, Plymouth, and part of Maine. In 1686, King James II appointed Sir Edmund Andros to govern the new dominion. Andros began to govern with a heavy hand, imposing taxes without legislative approval, challenging all land titles, and allowing religious dissent in the formerly Puritan stronghold of Massachusetts. This threat of change caused a fear within the Puritan leadership as it saw its control slipping away. With the Glorious Revolution in England and Parliament's overthrow of James II, in 1689, the colonists who hoped for a return to the status quo ousted Andros. The interim government, called the Council of Safety and made up of Boston merchants and magistrates, would lead the colony until the arrival of the new governor and charter in 1692, four months after the start of the witch hunt. In this environment of political instability, the accusations and arrests of witches took place in a vacuum lacking a legal framework. Without the guidance and justification of law, the magistrates found the necessary validation for their actions in the word of God.

Throughout the colony, fear of impending war with the local Native American Nations was also spreading. King Philip's War of 1675–1676, massacres at Lancaster in 1676, and the Native American involvement in King William's War, in 1688, were all part of recent memory. Rumors were rampant in 1692 that the Native Americans were preparing to mount another assault on the colonists. In addition, early settlers believed that there was a Satanic presence that permeated Native American life. This belief even spilled over into the accusation of Capt. John Alden as a witch. He became suspect of witchcraft through his association with the Native Americans. Prior to the trials, he had worked to create a better relationship between the colonists and the Native Americans. Add to this the belief that the Native Americans were in league with the devil, and there is little wonder that the residents of Salem were on edge.

Fear was also part of the Puritan faith. Fear of the devil was instilled through the sermons of the church leaders and parish preachers. In Boston, the sermons of Cotton Mather were filled with warnings of the power of the devil and the existence of evil in the world, an evil that was a direct threat to the Puritan vision of a holy utopia in the new world. The Salem preacher, Rev. Samuel Parris, invoked the threat of the devil in his sermons to explain the turmoil within his own parish prior to the witch hunts. And it was not difficult to maintain this fear of evil: the belief in the devil and witchcraft was real for the European settlers. On the basis of biblical passages, Puritans were certain that the devil walked the earth and, in particular, Massachusetts. Worse yet, they believed that women, weak and easily coerced, could be seduced by the devil. According to Puritan beliefs, women were unable to resist the devil and therefore were subject to the ways of witchcraft. Finding its roots in the Bible, this belief dated from the telling of the story of Eve, the snake, and the Garden of Eden. This belief explains the fact that the majority of the accused and convicted witches in Salem, in the rest of the colonies, and in Europe were women.

Finally, the fear of change infected the participants. The arrival of Gov. William Phips and the new charter, in May 1692, signaled that the Puritans had lost local political control. Not only were the Puritan leaders concerned over the loss of political power, but they also worried about the threat posed by women. The male-dominated Puritan society was afraid of any woman who was different, strong-willed, questioning of authority, even argumentative. Anne Hutchinson, who had questioned the authority of the Puritan church in Massachusetts, had been excommunicated and exiled to Rhode Island in 1638. This would be an omen for the deadly events of 1692. The male leadership also feared the change that was apparent in the commercial success that Salem Town was undergoing while the members of the rural Salem Village languished in an economic backwater. Finally, the Puritans were grasped by fear caused by the loss of control as non-Puritans migrated to the colony and began to demand equal authority and rights. This loss of control began with the heavy-handed authority of Gov. Sir Edmund Andros. He attempted to established the presence of the Anglican Church in Boston, the seat of Puritanism, and to legislate religious tolerance in the colony. His actions would be an omen for the change that would come. All of this fear added to the desire to find a reason why God had apparently forsaken his people and allowed the devil to reign in Massachusetts.

The events of 1692 also provide the validation for the theory of separation of church and state. The Massachusetts colony has been referred to as a theocracy, a governmental form where the state religion provides the leadership for the government. This was not quite true of Massachusetts. Elected officials did not have to be members of the clergy. However, the right to vote was restricted to male members of the Puritan Church, and the laws were filled with scriptural references to justify this arrangement. Scripture was used to validate beliefs not only in male dominance and the divine right of the Puritans, as they saw it, but also in the evil incarnate in women.

This merging of law and scripture allowed for the most flagrant violation of individual rights during the Salem witchcraft trials, the use of spectral evidence in the accusation of the afflicted. Spectral evidence, the concept that the afflicted had been visited by an image of the accused, was the basis for all of the guilty judgments save those accused persons who admitted their guilt. Founded in English law, it allowed for the unsubstantiated claim of one individual against another without the opportunity for the victim to prove otherwise. Because witchcraft was considered a capital offense, the accused were denied the right to legal counsel. As one author put it, the accused were required to "defend against the indefensible." The judges sincerely believed that the trials were held in an enlightened and rational manner, using scientific principles of law and humane behavior. Besides the spectral evidence, the presence of physical marks, called the devil's mark, on the bodies of the accused was used to prove guilt. Finally, the existence of the witch's teat, a third nipple allegedly used to suckle the witch's "familiar," was certain evidence that the accused was part of the devil's coven. Familiars were usually cats, dogs, or even toads who helped the witch in her work with the devil. Accused witches were forced to submit to humiliating searches by female matrons as the magistrates sought solid evidence. In late May 1692, physical searches were made of six of the accused. Bridget Bishop, Rebecca Nurse, and Elizabeth Proctor were all found to have marks. The other three, Susannah Martin, Sarah Good, and Alice Parker, were free of blemishes. In a second search later in the day, the marks on Bishop and Proctor had disappeared. This remarkable discovery was seen as further proof that the women were witches. Of these six women, only Elizabeth Proctor would escape execution, and then only because she was pregnant.

One major influence on the trials was the Puritan concept of redemption through repentance. Sinners who asked forgiveness and admitted their failings were perceived as able to return to God's grace. Individuals who stood by their faith and denied any failings were seen as denying the grace of God. During the witchcraft trials, the accused who admitted their guilt were spared execution. Some even became witnesses against other accused witches, including their wives and husbands. Those who denied their guilt, as did Rebecca Nurse, were found guilty and punished. In the case of Giles Corey, who refused to plead innocent or guilty, English law and not Puritan beliefs sealed his fate. Corey was crushed to death from the weight of rocks placed upon his chest. The rocks that were intended to force a plea from him resulted only in his silent death.

Finally, and perhaps most important, the events of Salem provided a documented example of community life and relations in colonial America. Initially, this view was limited to the analysis of the trial documents, which illustrated the activities of the legal system and the Puritan views on witchcraft. With the passing of time, Salem became the laboratory for social scientists who investigated other aspects of community life in search of causes for the witch craze. The influence of Puritan belief, the effects of sermons, and the influence of the clergy on the lives of people were studied. In particular, the sermons and writings of Cotton Mather and Samuel Parris were analyzed. Mather and Parris have both been held responsible for helping to create the atmosphere of fear that permeated Massachusetts. The responses of Robert Calef and John Hale provided the opposing view of clergy who questioned the trials and the guilt of the accused. The writings of each of the clergy provided an intimate view of the dominance of religion in local life.

Local politics, which illustrated the conflict between the agricultural Salem Village and the commercial Salem Town, became the focus of interest in the 1960s as researchers sought further causes for the craze. The people of Salem Village felt that they were losing control and were being overshadowed by the economically successful Salem Town. Researchers found that a pattern of accusations of witches correlated with times of economic troubles. Also apparent were the local power struggles between groups within the village that supported or disliked Rev. Samuel Parris. Documents describing lawsuits, land claims, and debts created a network that also followed the network of accusers, accused, witnesses, and supporters. Researchers have prepared maps defining the residence of each participant in the witch craze and genealogical charts showing the family relationships. Of the 22 men accused, 11 were closely related to the accused women. Eight other men were accused through more casual association with the women. The relative position of people in Massachusetts society also became apparent. At first, the list of the accused included only the poor and widowed. As the spring of 1692 turned into summer, the list began to include members of the economic elite whose piety and status were firmly established. Rebecca Nurse, wife of a respected landowner, was accused and executed despite her piety and her reputation within the community. George Burroughs, the former Salem Village minister, also became a victim of the trials. When this pattern started to develop, it became apparent that the accusers could no longer be believed, and something had to be done. When Gov. William Phips's wife was accused, he called a halt to the proceedings, disbanded the Court of Oyer and Terminer, ceased all executions, and finally pardoned those still in jail.

The Salem witch craze and the ensuing trials may have had neither the devastating effect on people that the European witch hunts did nor a direct effect on the overall social, economic, political, legal, or international climate in colonial America. However, the trials did provide a traditional example for group hysteria that found its way into the American self-image. Beyond that, the trials have continued to provide an intimate and detailed view of early colonial America and the difficulties of living on the frontier far from the accepted way of life.

## SELECTED BIBLIOGRAPHY

Boyer, Paul, and Stephen Nissenbaum. *Salem Possessed: The Social Origins of Witchcraft*. Cambridge, MA: Harvard University Press, 1974. An excellent source for understanding the social background of the witch craze and trials.

———. *The Salem Witchcraft Papers: Verbatim Transcripts of the Legal Documents of the Salem Witchcraft Outbreak of 1692*. New York: Da Capo, 1977. The currently accepted source for the official trial transcripts.

Breslaw, Elaine G. *Tituba, Reluctant Witch of Salem—Devilish Indians and Puritan Fantasies.* New York: New York University Press, 1996. A well-researched book on the origins of the slave Tituba and an interpretation of her part in the witch craze and trials.

Demos, John P. *Entertaining Satan: Witchcraft and the Culture of Early New England.* New York: Oxford University Press, 1982. A view of witchcraft in 17th-century New England from the historical, sociological, psychological, and biographical perspectives.

Drake, Samuel, G., comp. *The Witchcraft Delusion in New England.* New York: B. Franklin, 1970. This volume includes Robert Calef, *More Wonders of the Invisible World,* an early (1701) account of the Salem witch trials by one who considered them to be evil.

Hall, David D., ed. *Puritanism in Seventeenth Century Massachusetts.* New York: Holt, Rinehart and Winston, 1968. A collection of essays by various authors on Puritan beliefs in Massachusetts.

Hansen, Chadwick. *Witchcraft at Salem.* New York: George Braziller, 1969. Takes the view that witchcraft did exist in Salem and that the hysteria was a real affliction for the accusers.

Hill, Frances. *A Delusion of Satan: The Full Story of the Salem Witch Trials.* New York: Da Capo, 1997. A recent retelling of the story that is very subjective but does not break any new ground or provide a substantially different interpretation.

Karlsen, Carol F. *The Devil in the Shape of a Woman.* New York: W. W. Norton, 1987. Provides a feminist view of the trials, emphasizing a male dominant society and its effect on the outcome of the trials.

Klaits, Joseph. *Servants of Satan: The Age of the Witch Hunts.* Bloomington: Indiana University Press, 1985. A good source for the broader historical context of the Salem witch trials.

Mappen, Marc, ed. *Witches and Historians: Interpretations of Salem.* Huntington, CA: Robert E. Krieger, 1980. A series of essays by various historians comparing the shifting interpretations of the causes of the Salem witch trials.

Marshall, Richard. *Witchcraft: The History and Mythology.* New York: Crescent Books, 1995. An illustrated volume on the history of witchcraft to the present that includes a chapter on the Salem trial.

Miller, Arthur. *The Crucible, a Play in Four Acts.* New York: Viking, 1953. The celebrated stageplay about the Salem witch trials that many saw as a commentary on contemporary McCarthyism and its "witch" hunts.

Miller, Perry. *The New England Mind: From Colony to Province.* Cambridge, MA: Harvard University Press, 1953. An explanation of the Puritan intellectual and social world of the 17th century.

Morrison, Dane Anthony, and Nancy Lusignan Schultz, eds. *Salem: Place, Myth, and Memory.* Boston: Northeastern University Press, 2004. Collection of essays about Salem that goes well beyond the witch trials.

Norton, Mary Beth. *In the Devil's Snare: The Salem Witchcraft Crisis of 1692.* New York: Knopf, 2002. A leading feminist historian's analysis of the Salem witch trials and their possible connection with the Indian wars of the time.

Upham, Charles W. *Salem Witchcraft.* New York: Frederick Ungar, 1959. Originally published in 1867, this is the traditional view of the Salem event from the group hysteria standpoint.

## COTTON MATHER (1663-1728)

Father and son, Increase Mather and Cotton Mather were prominent Puritan leaders and ministers. Of the two, Cotton was the more famous—indeed, perhaps the most famous of all the Puritans. He played a leading role in the transition from extreme religious orthodoxy to a more secular outlook in New England.

Mather was born on February 12, 1663, in Boston. By his own account, he "began to pray, even when [he] began to speak." Entering Harvard College at the age of 12 (the youngest student the college had ever admitted), he graduated in 1678. Fearful that his habit of stammering would interfere with his preaching, he studied medicine for a time before earning his master's degree from Harvard in 1681. By 1680, he had overcome his stammer enough to begin preaching. Five years later, he was ordained and joined his father in the pulpit of the Second Church of Boston, holding this position until his death.

As minister of this church, one of the largest in Boston, Mather earned a reputation for his pastoral care. He was the first American minister to organize clubs for young people, and he started the practice of making regular calls on elderly and ill church members and on prisoners. He also helped set up a school for the education of slaves and organized efforts to promote peace, build churches in poor communities, provide relief for needy ministers, and establish missions among the Native Americans.

Mather's role in the Salem witchcraft trials of 1692 has been much debated. An intensely religious and introspective man given to swooning and to moments of sudden illumination, he had a strong sense of evil and of the power of the devil, which he believed could result in diabolical possession. In 1689, he published *Memorable Providences, Relating to Witchcrafts and Possessions,* which, along with two other works on the subject, probably helped foster an awareness of witchcraft that may have contributed to the Salem hysteria. Yet, at the time of the actual trials, Mather wrote a statement to the judges, warning them about the overuse of "spectral evidence" (whereby witnesses claimed to see specters of accused witches, and judges accepted their testimony without question) and advising punishments milder than execution. Nevertheless, he gave his full support to the proceedings.

After the trials and executions ended in late 1692, Mather vehemently defended the verdicts, both in speech and in print, particularly in his book *Wonders of the Invisible World* (1693). Yet, later still, in his most famous work, *Magnalia Christi Americana* (1702), a monumental ecclesiastical history of New England, Mather presented the Salem witchcraft trials as having unjustly condemned to death many innocent people.

After 1692, Mather's influence diminished somewhat because of the trend away from Puritan dominance and also because of his own hot temper and arrogance. Although he had hoped to follow in his father's footsteps as president of Harvard, Mather was denied this honor. In 1703, when the lower house of the Massachusetts legislature, consisting largely of religious conservatives, appointed Mather president, their action was overruled by the more liberal upper house. Thereafter, Mather looked to a new educational institution to be the stronghold of Congregational orthodoxy, persuading Elihu Yale to contribute generously to it and convincing the governor of Connecticut to name the college after Yale.

Although at the outset of his career Mather bitterly attacked those with differing religious beliefs, he grew more tolerant with age. He even boasted that his church had welcomed into the fold not only Anglicans but also Baptists, Presbyterians, and Lutherans. Also, toward the end of his life, Mather began to expound doctrines that placed him at a distance from the strict Calvinism of his youth and closer to the deism of the 18th century with its emphasis on a rationally ordered universe and a benevolent God.

An even more prolific author than his father, Mather wrote more than 450 books, cementing his reputation not only as a religious leader but also as a man of letters and a scientist, made evident in *The Christian Philosopher* (1721) and other works. He had a wide-ranging curiosity about the natural world and saw no conflict between his religious beliefs and science, because, in his view, an understanding of nature was the best cure for atheism. He conducted many experiments of his own and published the results, including one of the earliest known descriptions of plant hybridization. Mather's concern with the useful in everyday life produced such observations as "The very wheelbarrow is to be with respect looked upon." In this, he anticipated Benjamin Franklin, who claimed that Mather's essays had provided the inspiration for many of his own practical devices.

Mather corresponded with some of Europe's leading scientists and was a great admirer of Sir Isaac Newton. In 1712, he became one of the few American colonists to be elected to the Royal Society of London. In 1721, when smallpox broke out in Boston, Mather advocated inoculation despite the protests of most physicians, the general populace, and some clergy, who regarded it as both a dangerous and a godless practice. Mather's role in the inoculation campaign, together with his many other activities, reflected the tireless zeal with which he worked for what he considered to be the best interests of others. Mather died in Boston on February 13, 1728, at the age of 65.

WILLIAM MCGUIRE AND LESLIE WHEELER

## INCREASE MATHER (1639–1723)

Increase Mather, father of the prominent Puritan leader Cotton Mather, was, like his more famous son, well regarded in his lifetime; he gained tremendous influence and respect for his judgment and intellect.

Increase was born on June 21, 1639, in Dorchester, Massachusetts, the son of Richard Mather, first pastor of the Dorchester Church. Raised a strict Puritan, he graduated from Harvard College in 1656 and received his master's degree from Trinity College in Dublin, Ireland, in 1658. After preaching in England and on the island of Guernsey, he returned to Boston in 1661. In 1664, he became minister of the Second Church of Boston, a position he held for the rest of his life.

Chosen a fellow of Harvard in 1674, Mather served as president with the title of rector from 1685 to 1701. He encouraged the study of science at Harvard but stood firm against efforts to undermine the college's strict Congregationalism. From 1688 to 1692, Mather served as an able ambassador for the Massachusetts Bay Colony at the courts of Kings James II and William III while the colony's original charter was being renegotiated.

A prolific writer, Mather produced more than 100 books and pamphlets, including *A Brief History of the War with the Indians* (1676) and *Remarkable Providences* (1684). Unlike his son, Mather was cautious during the Salem witchcraft trials of 1692 and 1693. In *Cases of Conscience Concerning Evil Spirits* (1693), he argued against the use of "spectral evidence," maintaining that it was better for 10 guilty witches to escape than for 1 innocent person to die. The tract made an impression on Gov. William Phips and helped end the trials.

In 1721, Mather joined his son Cotton in advocating inoculation for smallpox despite the opposition of laypersons and many doctors. He died in Boston two years later, on August 23, 1723, at the age of 84.

WILLIAM MCGUIRE AND LESLIE WHEELER

## PURITAN FAMILY

The Puritans' concept of covenant helps to explain their understanding of the family and the role and rights of women within the family and society. The Puritans rejected the Catholic idea—also shared by the Church of England and most Protestants—that marriage was a sacrament, but morality had a firm place in their concept of marriage. For the Puritans, marriage was a contract and a set of mutual obligations and responsibilities, and the home—which included extended family, servants, and others who lived with it—was a symbol in miniature of their idea of community. In Connecticut and in Plymouth, Massachusetts, it was illegal for any single person to live alone, and, if anyone was found doing so, he or she would be assigned to a family in the community. Hierarchy also existed within Puritan families and is reflected in the Puritan custom that parents and children would not eat together. Children whose parents could not control them would be removed to other families that could.

It is widely believed that men and women married early in life during the early modern period, but Puritans did not tend to do so. In the first century of their settlement in New England, the average age at marriage for Puritan men was 26 years, and for women it was about 23 years. The percentage of the New England Puritan population that entered into marriage was also extremely high: less than 6 percent of women and 2 percent of men remained single; in contrast, up to 27 percent of the non-Puritan English population were unable or unwilling to marry during this same era. For the Puritans, marriage was a contract that should be performed in front of a civil, not a religious, authority, and both parties had the right to divorce if the terms of the marriage covenant were violated. Marriage carried serious social obligations, and families were tightly knit through a complex web of relationships. Yet, marriages were not arranged by parents, though parental approval was required. However, the law stipulated that children could sue their parents for unreasonably withholding permission to marry. The prolonged absence of a spouse, physical mistreatment, abuse of children, neglect, and adultery were all grounds for divorce within Puritan law, and women were allowed to hold property independently, even after marriage. Sexuality was regarded as an important and healthy part of marriage, though contraception was condemned, and the civil punishment for fornication, for which men were often punished more severely than women, was harsh. Sexual deviancy of any kind was not tolerated and was often punishable by death.

Although women were the majority among those admitted to church congregations in Puritan New England and were regarded as equally capable of holiness and salvation, the ministry was restricted to men only. Men and women were punished equally for the same crimes, as court records from the period reveal, and communities were intolerant of domestic quarrels, often stepping in to intervene. Disciplining children, often through public humiliation, was also an essential part of Puritan culture. Again, these attitudes all reflect the Puritan concern with covenant—that the behavior of individuals in the community affects their collective relationship before God. Civil authorities in early New England passed laws forbidding not just sexual crimes but also blasphemy, drunkenness, gambling, and violations of the sanctity of the Sabbath through inappropriate behavior. Rooting out ungodly behavior among the citizenry was an important concern if the community as a whole was going to keep its communal covenant with God.

Puritans are often represented in illustrations as wearing only black and gray, but in reality they seldom wore black and instead preferred what they called "sadd" colors. This included green, rust, orange, purple, brown, and other dark colors. In the 17th century, black was the color of formal garments and was thought to be inappropriate to the simplicity preferred by the Puritans. The Puritans, unlike their Quaker neighbors who arrived to the south in Pennsylvania during the 1680s, used clothing as a marker of social status. Black was appropriate to the leaders of the colony, including ministers, who often added lace and other indicators of privilege to their costumes. Sumptuary laws were even passed by the leaders of the colony, specifically banning the wearing of gold and silver or silk lace and of certain other popular fashions from Europe. Eventually, these sumptuary laws forbade those of the lower social classes to wear clothing inappropriate to their station. In general, Puritans emphasized simplicity and modesty in their clothing, though these standards shifted during the late 17th and early 18th centuries.

This ideal of simplicity extended beyond clothing to architectural styles and to the decoration—or, rather, lack of it—in Puritan churches, which included no artwork and were built in the most severe, plain form possible. An unusual exception to this prohibition against religious art, which was seen as an excess deriving from Catholicism, was tombstone art, which is one of the most interesting and distinctive Puritan cultural contributions. Primitive-looking angel faces or skulls—sometimes with wings attached—were often carved into tombstones in Puritan cemeteries, many of which can still be seen today.

Puritan conceptions of time and work also help illustrate the values that were most important to them. The government of the Massachusetts Bay colony went so far as to make time wasting illegal in 1633 and prosecuted several persons for this crime over the next few years. Time was a commodity to Puritans, who placed much emphasis on material success in this life, which they believed to be a sign of God's favor. Another important time-related value was "improving the time," which was quite distinctive among the Puritans. Life was clearly marked by minutes, hours, days, and seasons. The most important among these periods of time was the Sabbath, the violation of which was punishable by law. Offenses against the Sabbath could include intercourse between married couples, fruit picking, tobacco smoking, and even performing excess work, including brewing one's beer.

While Puritans observed the Sabbath and held public thanksgivings, they did not celebrate Christmas, believing it to be too much a remnant of Catholic-style feasts. By 1676, Thanksgiving Day became a regular, annual holiday, the first such feast having been held in 1621. By the late 1670s, however, this celebration was moved to the fall and included fasting, which was followed by a feast. Alcoholic beverages, especially hard cider and other forms of beer, were usually served at these events, but drunkenness, condemned in the Bible, was never acceptable to the Puritans.

Nathaniel Hawthorne's novel *The Scarlet Letter* is accurate at least in its depiction of the fictional character Hester Prynne, who is forced to wear a letter "A" as a punishment for her crime of adultery. Those convicted of committing such sins were regularly forced to wear such badges: a D for drunkenness, a B for blasphemy, and so on. Punishment often included being locked in the stocks, a device located in a public place that locked the head, hands, and feet while townspeople heaped humiliation on the criminal. Whipping, scarring, and maiming—including the cutting off of ears or other mutilations of the face—were also forms of punishment handed down by Puritan authorities, who used hanging as the most extreme form of punishment. Heresy, blasphemy, and witchcraft were among the crimes that received capital punishment.

JOHN A. GRIGG

## SAMUEL SEWALL (1652–1730)

A prominent Puritan merchant and judge, Samuel Sewall presided over the Salem witchcraft trials and was the only judge to later admit the error of his decisions that sent 19 people to their deaths. The voluminous diary he left behind has made him the focus of many historical studies and provides an invaluable record of early colonial life.

Sewall was born in Bishopstoke, Hampshire, England, on March 28, 1652. He sailed with his family to Boston when he was nine years old. His father, Henry Sewall, and mother, Jane Dummer Sewall, quickly became enmeshed in the upper-class life of the Massachusetts colony. They sent their son to Harvard College, from which he graduated in 1671. Like many other scholars at the school, Sewall devoted most of his time to the study of law and divinity and very nearly became a minister. His deep affection for the Puritan religion would always remain with him.

With background and connections, Sewall was able to secure many important positions in Massachusetts, including manager of the colonial printing press (1681–1684), member of the Governor's Council (1684–1725), and chief justice of the Superior Court (1718–1728). He also served as captain of the Ancient and Honorable Artillery Company and as an overseer of Harvard College.

Sewall's marriage to Hannah Hull on February 28, 1675, sealed his place in Boston society. His wife's father, John Hull, was the colony's mint master and probably the richest and most powerful man in the city at the time. The couple eventually had 14 children, although many of them died at an early age. When his father-in-law died, in 1683, Sewall became a very wealthy man, as he took control of his wife's family estate and the merchandising business. He continued in the business for nearly a decade before his other duties took precedence, and then neglected his merchant business.

In 1692, Massachusetts governor William Phips, on being informed about suspected witches in the town of Salem, named seven special commissioners to investigate the charges. William Stoughton was named chief justice of the court, and Sewall was one of the seven named to sit on the bench. Most Puritans and other religious people of the time believed wholeheartedly in the existence of witches who served the devil. Therefore, Sewall felt it his duty to serve on the court.

The judges heard case after case of hysterical or "crazed" children in the town who were supposedly being pursued by witches. The minister's own daughter and niece were among the accusers. Although history has treated harshly those judges and villagers who, in a paranoid fashion, condemned to death the 19 accused witches, it seems that the children may have been convincing actors. Among other strange actions, they would shake and convulse whenever they were shown a book of catechism or other religious works.

As time passed, though, and Sewall looked back on his actions, he felt more and more strongly that he and the other judges had been swept up by the hysteria of the trials and had condemned to death innocent people. On January 14, 1697, he stood before the congregation at the Old South Church in Boston while his confession of guilt was read aloud by the pastor: "Samuel Sewall, sensible of the reiterated strokes of God upon himself and family; and being sensible, that as to the Guilt contracted upon the opening of the late Commission of Oyer and Terminer at Salem…he is, upon many accounts, more concerned than any that he knows of, Desires to take the Blame and shame of it, Asking pardon of men."

After the trials, Sewall took his seat on the Massachusetts Superior Court, which meant he had to ride the circuit to hear cases around the Boston area. He was always welcomed throughout the colony and was often invited to address local Puritan congregations.

His wife, Hannah, died on October 19, 1717, after nearly 42 years of marriage. Sewall remarried the widow Tilly soon after Hannah's death, but Tilly died unexpectedly after just eight months of marriage. He was next wed to Mary Gibbs, also a widow, on March 29, 1722. She would outlive him.

To the delight of historians, Sewall committed his thoughts to his diary for more than a half-century. Sewall kept the diary from December 1673 through October 1729, although one book, covering about seven years, has never been discovered. The diary is truly one of the most important documents that has survived from its time. Not only is the reader able to follow the events of Sewall's life, but one can also understand what it was like to be a colonial Puritan. Sewall writes of the everyday events of Boston: the deaths and births, the controversies and celebrations, and the sicknesses that often swept through town.

Sewall wrote other books, too, including one of the earliest appeals against slavery, *The Selling of Joseph,* published in 1700. Sewall also argued for the humane treatment of Native Americans and put many of his thoughts down in *A Memorial Relating to the Kennebeck Indians,* published in 1721.

A man in his seventies at the time of his third marriage, Sewall began to cut back on his duties. He died at the age of 77 on January 1, 1730, and was buried in the Hull tomb in the Old Granary Burying Ground in Boston, where his parents and wife were also buried.

JOHN VILE

# DOCUMENT: COTTON MATHER: *WONDERS OF THE INVISIBLE WORLD,* 1693

*The leading minister in colonial New England, Cotton Mather distinguished himself as a theologian, scholar, author, public speaker, and popular leader. His 1693 book* Wonders of the Invisible World *was widely considered throughout New England as the most important scholarly work on witch-craft ever to appear in print. Mather was an ardent believer in the perva-siveness of witchcraft in colonial society and had vigorously supported the Salem witchcraft trials of the previous year. An excerpt of the book appears below.* (Mather, Cotton, *The Wonders of the Invisible World* [Boston: Harris for Phillips, 1693].)

Martha Carrier was indicted for the bewitching of certain persons, according to the form usual in such cases, pleading not guilty to her indictment. There were first brought in a considerable number of the bewitched persons, who not only made the court sensible of an horrid witchcraft committed upon them, but also deposed that it was Martha Carrier or her shape that grievously tormented them by biting, pricking, pinching, and choking of them. It was further deposed that while this Carrier was on her examination before the magistrates, the poor people were so tortured that everyone expected their death upon the very spot, but that upon the binding of Carrier they were eased....

Benjamin Abbot gave in his testimony that last March was a twelve-month this Carrier was very angry with him upon laying out some land near her husband's.... Presently after this he was taken with a swelling in his foot, and then with a pain in his side, and exceedingly tormented. It bred unto a sore, which was lanced by Doctor Prescot, and several gallons of corruption ran out of it. For six weeks it continued very bad; and then another sore bred in his groin, which was also lanced by Doctor Prescot. Another sore then bred in his groin, which was likewise cut, and put him to very great misery. He was brought unto death's door and so remained until Carrier was taken and carried away by the constable, from which very day he began to mend and so grew better every day and is well ever since.

Allin Toothaker testified that Richard, the son of Martha Carrier, having some difference with him, pulled him down by the hair of the head. When he rose again, he was going to strike at Richard Carrier, but fell down flat on his back to the ground and had not power to stir hand or foot until he told Carrier he yielded; and then he saw the shape of Martha Carrier go off his breast....

Phebe Chandler testified that about a fortnight before the apprehension of Martha Carrier, on a Lord's day while the psalm was singing in the church, this Carrier then took her by the shoulder and shaking her asked her where she lived. She made no answer, although as Carrier, who lived next door to her father's house, could not in reason but know who she was. Quickly after this, as she was at several times crossing the fields, she heard a voice that she took to be Martha Carrier's; and it seemed as if it was over her head. The voice told her she should within two or three days be poisoned. Accordingly, within such a little time, one half of her right hand became greatly swollen and very painful, as also part of her face—whereof she can give no account how it came. It continued very bad for some days, and several times since she has had a greater pain in her breast and been so seized on her legs that she has hardly been able to go. She added that lately, going well to the house of God, Richard, the son of Martha Carrier, looked very earnestly upon her; and immediately her hand, which had formerly been poisoned, as is said above, began to pain her greatly; and she had a strange burning at her stomach, but was then struck deaf so that she could not hear any of the prayer or singing till the two or three last words of the psalm....

One Lacy, who likewise confessed her share in this witchcraft, now testified that she and the prisoner were once bodily present at a witch meeting in Salem village, and that she knew the prisoner to be a witch and to have been at a diabolical sacrament, and that the prisoner was the undoing of her and her children by enticing them into the snare of the devil....

In the time of this prisoner's trial, one Susanna Sheldon in open court had her hands unaccountable tied together with a wheel band so fast that without cutting it could not be loosened. It was done by a specter, and the sufferer affirmed that it was the prisoner's.

Memorandum: This rampant hag, Martha Carrier, was the person of whom the confession of the witches and of her own children among them are agreed that the devil had promised she should be queen of hell.

## DOCUMENT: DEATH WARRANT OF FIVE WOMEN CONVICTED OF WITCHCRAFT IN SALEM, 1692

*This death warrant for Sarah Good, Rebecca Nurse, Susanna Martin, Elizabeth How, and Sarah Wild was one of several handed down during the Salem witchcraft trials of 1692 in Salem, Massachusetts. All of these women had been condemned to hang for being witches. Their executions, later in the month of July, caused a storm of controversy, particularly as Nurse was a well-respected member of the church whom many had difficulty in believing was guilty of witchcraft. In all, 19 people were hanged as witches and 1 person was pressed to death by heavy stones during questioning before the trials ended in October 1692.* (Boyer, Paul, and Stephen Nissenbaum, eds., *The Salem Witchcraft Papers: Verbatim Transcripts of the Legal Documents of the Salem Witchcraft Outbreak of 1692*, vol. II [New York: Da Capo Press, 1977].)

To George Corwine Gent'n High Sheriff of the county of Essex
Whereas Sarah Good Wife of William Good of Salem Village Rebecka Nurse wife of Francis Nurse of Salem Village Susanna Martin of Amesbury Widow Elizabeth How wife of James How of Ipswich Sarah Wild wife of John Wild of Topsfield all of the County of Essex in thier Maj'ts Province of the Massachusetts Bay in New England Att A Court of Oyer & Terminer held by Adjournment for Our Severaign Lord & Lady Kind Wiliam & Queen Mary for the said County of Essex at Salem in the s'd County onf the 29th day of June [torn] were Severaly arrigned on Several Indictments for the horrible Crime of Witchcraft by them practised & Committed On Severall persons and pleading not guilty did for thier Tryall put themselves on God & Thier Countery whereupon they were Each of them found & brought in Guilty by the Jury that passed On them according to their respective Indictments and Sentence of death did then pass upon them as the Law directs Execution whereof yet remains to be done: Those are Therefore in thier Maj'ties name William & Mary now King & Queen over England &ca: to will & Command you that upon Tuesday next being the 19th day for [torn] Instant July between the houres of Eight & [torn] in [torn] forenoon the same day you Safely conduct the s'd

Sarah Good Rebecka Nurse Susann Martin Elizabeth Howe & Sarah Wild From thier Maj'ties goal in Salem afores'd to the place of Execution & there Cause them & Every of them to be hanged by the Neck untill they be dead and of the doings herein make return to the Clerke of the said Court & this precept and hereof you are not to fail at your per-ill and this Shall be your sufficient Warrant given under my hand & seale at Boston th 12't day of July in the fourth year of Reign of our Soveraigne Lord & Layd Wm & Mary King and Queen &ca:

[signed] Wm Stoughton

Annoq Dom. 1692

[Reverse]

Salem July 19th 1692

I caused the within mentioned persons to be Executed according to the Tenour of the with[in] warrant

[signed] George Corwin Sherif

# APPENDIX A: GLOSSARY OF TERMS AND PEOPLE

**Act of Toleration (1688).** During the Glorious Revolution, Parliament approved this measure, which allowed dissenting Protestants freedom from attending Church of England services and the right to attend their own church. The act granted other rights to Protestant dissenters and their ministers, but Roman Catholics were not covered under its provisions.

**Baltimore, Lord [Charles Calvert] (1637–1715).** Charles Calvert, the third Lord Baltimore, was the Catholic proprietor of Maryland from 1675 to 1715, although much of his political power was removed after the Glorious Revolution. He was the grandson of George Calvert, the first Lord Baltimore, to whom King Charles I granted the territory in the 1630s.

**Charles II (1630–1685).** King of England (1660–1685) after the end of the English Civil War (1649–1660). He worked to reunify England after the civil war, fought trade wars with the Dutch, and battled with Parliament over questions of religious toleration.

**Charles IX (1550–1574).** Short-lived, weak-minded King of France (1560–1574), Charles IX was on the throne when Admiral Gaspard de Coligny sent a Huguenot expedition to establish a colony in Florida.

**Council of Trade and Plantations.** Established by King Charles II in 1674 to handle colonial matters but replaced by the Board of Trade and Plantations, a Parliamentary committee, after the Glorious Revolution.

**Declaration of Indulgence (1687).** Issued by King James II of England, this granted Catholics freedom from penalties to which they had been liable if they practiced their religion. This and subsequent pro-Catholic actions of the king led to the Glorious Revolution.

**English Civil War.** From 1642 to 1649, the English fought a civil war to settle the question of who was to rule: the king in an absolute manner or a combination of the king and Parliament sharing power. Religious issues also figured prominently. Parliamentary forces triumphed, culminating in the execution of King Charles I in 1649. After a decade or so of Parliamentary rule, royal forces regained the upper hand, only to relinquish it permanently in the Glorious Revolution of 1688–1689.

**Ferdinand II (1452–1516) and Isabella I (1451–1504).** King and queen of Spain following the union of the kingdoms of Castile and Aragon, in 1469. They sponsored Columbus's first three voyages, drove Jews who would not convert to Catholicism from Spain, and finished the *reconquista*, the process of expelling Muslims, or Moors, from Spain.

**Fox, George (1624–1691).** Born into England's turbulent 17th century, Fox, the son of a successful weaver, rejected all the common religious variations of his day, including Roman Catholicism, Anglicanism, and Puritanism. Instead, he founded the Religious Society of Friends, or Quakers, a religious movement that emphasized an individual's relationship with God and refused to discriminate on the basis of either class or sex.

**Hakluyt, Richard (1552–1616).** An English geographer and chronicler, Hakluyt published between 1582 and 1600 a number of important accounts of voyages to America and helped popularize the notion of English imperial expansion. Sometimes he is referred to as Richard Hakluyt the Younger to distinguish him from his cousin, Richard Hakluyt the Elder, who raised him and inspired his love of geography.

**Henry VII (1457–1509).** King of England (1485–1509) during the earliest voyages of exploration, Henry did much to unify England under his rule and to broaden its commercial outlook and contacts.

**Huguenots.** This is the name applied to French Protestants, who lost their civil and religious freedom (and, in some cases, their lives) in 1685, when Louis XIV issued a decree known as the Edict of Nantes. Many immigrated to the North American colonies, following a practice that had begun in the 1560s.

**James I (1566–1625).** King of England (1603–1625) and, as James VI, King of Scotland (1567–1625). James was the monarch for whom the settlement of Jamestown was named and in whose name other settlements were founded. He achieved popularity at the end of his reign when he requested that Parliament declare war on Spain after the Spanish court rejected a marriage offer between his son Charles and the daughter of the Spanish king.

**James II (1633–1701).** King of England (1685–1688) and brother of Charles II. James's adherence to Catholicism led to the Glorious Revolution in 1688 and his subsequent exile in France.

**Jesuits.** The Jesuits, officially known as the Society of Jesus, are a Roman Catholic religious order founded by Ignatius Loyola in 1540. The Jesuits were known for obeying religious authority, emphasizing education, and aggressively spreading Roman Catholicism to non-Christian peoples throughout the globe.

**King Philip's War (1675–1676).** This was a war between Indians living in New England, led by "King" Philip, and colonists of the region. The Indians frightened the colonists with their strategy of swiftly executed raids on Massachusetts towns, and the colonist counterattack failed because the Indians were too mobile. After a year and further losses, the colonists gained the advantage and killed Philip in August 1676. A peace treaty, providing for a prisoner-of-war exchange, was signed in April 1678.

**Mary II (1662–1694).** Queen of England (1689–1694) who reigned with her husband, William III. The daughter of James II, she deferred to William on most state matters and died of smallpox at a young age, leaving no children.

**McCarthy hearings (1950–1954).** Senator Joseph McCarthy (R-WI) made a name for himself in the Cold War era through his leadership of an anticommunist crusade that many critics called a "witch hunt." Some of the more celebrated "witches" were "hunted" by means of congressional hearings.

**Mutiny Act (1689).** A consequence of the Glorious Revolution, this act of Parliament limited the size of the military and authorized the use of the court-martial to enforce military justice. The act had to be renewed annually, thus helping to guarantee frequent sessions of Parliament.

**Navigation Act (1651).** Part of English imperial trade policy sometimes referred to as mercantilism. This act of Parliament barred foreign ships from trading with English colonies and prohibited imports that did not arrive in England on either English ships or those of the country of origin. Certain "enumerated" colonial products, like tobacco, could be sent only to English ports. This and other navigation acts were designed to limit the ability of the Dutch and other European rivals to trade with the American colonies.

**Powhatan (1550–1618).** Also known as Wahunsunacock, he was chief of the Powhatan federation when the first settlers came to Virginia. A strong leader, Powhatan became more friendly and tolerant of the colonists after the marriage of his daughter Pocahontas to John Rolfe.

**Richelieu, Cardinal (1585–1642).** Although a cardinal in the Roman Catholic Church, Richelieu is best known for being the power behind the French throne during the reign of Louis XIII. As the king's chief minister, he is credited with strengthening monarchical power at home and making France the dominant country in Europe.

**Salem Witch Trials.** Well into the 18th century—if not later—most Christians believed in witches, seeing in them the handmaidens of the devil. Persecution of witches was common, and England's North American colonies were no exception. In 1692, witch hysteria reached its height at Salem, Massachusetts, where more than 100 were accused of witchcraft and 19 were executed before the panic abated.

**Spanish Armada (1588).** The name given to a fleet of 130 ships sent to participate in an invasion of England in 1588. In a major naval battle in the English Channel in late July and early August, England's more maneuverable ships and better guns led to the rout of the Spanish fleet. The defeat of the armada was a major boost to England's imperial ambitions and a severe blow to Spain's international prestige.

**William III (1650–1702).** A native of the Netherlands, he became King of England (1689–1702) as a result of his marriage to Mary, the oldest child of James II, and the Glorious Revolution, which drove his father-in-law from power. As king, he was staunchly Protestant and fought a lengthy war against the French that distracted him from concern about the English colonies in North America.

**Winthrop, John (1588–1649).** Winthrop, a leading English Puritan, played a major role in the founding of the Massachusetts Bay Colony, in 1630. From that time until his death, he served as governor of the Puritan colony. While a successful leader, he displayed a lack of flexibility that caused friction among the colonists.

# APPENDIX B: TIMELINE

**ca. 40,000 BCE:** First people arrive in North America from Asia.

**ca. 5000 BCE:** Crop cultivation begins in Mexico and spreads throughout North America.

**ca. 800:** Norse colonies established in Iceland.

**ca. 1000:** Leif Eriksson leads voyage to east coast of Canada.

**1325:** Founding of Aztec capital, Tenochtitlán.

**1492:** First voyage of Christopher Columbus.

**1493:** First permanent Spanish settlement in New World.

**1497:** John Cabot's first voyage to eastern coast of Canada.

**1508–1511:** Decimation of Native population of West Indies by disease and warfare.

**1513:** Juan Ponce de León arrives in and names Florida.

**1517:** Spanish begin bringing African slaves to South and Central America.

**1519:** Hernán Cortés begins conquest of Aztec society in Mexico.

**1527–1528:** Pánfilo de Narváez leads expedition to Gulf Coast region.

**1539–1542:** Hernando de Soto leads expedition to Gulf Coast region.

**1540–1542:** Coronado leads expedition to present-day southwestern United States.

**1561:** Tristán de Luna heads an expedition that attempts to settle near Pensacola.

**1564:** Laudonnière establishes French colony near Atlantic coast of Florida.

**1565:** Spanish establish colony of Saint Augustine, Florida.

**1584:** First English attempt to plant a colony in North America.

**1588:** Defeat of the Spanish Armada.

**1607:** English establish first permanent colony at Jamestown.

**1609:** Henry Hudson sails up Hudson River; claims area for Dutch.

**1612:** Powhatan teaches English in Virginia to cultivate tobacco.

**1614:** Pocahontas and John Rolfe marry.

**1616–1617:** Smallpox epidemic kills many New England Indians.

**1619:** First Africans brought to Virginia as slaves.

**1620:** Pilgrims establish colony at Plymouth, Massachusetts.

**1624:** First permanent Dutch colony established at New Netherland.

**1630:** Puritan colony established in Massachusetts under John Winthrop.

**1634:** Lord Baltimore establishes Catholic colony of Maryland.

**1636:** Roger Williams establishes colony of Rhode Island.

**1637:** Pequot War in New England.

**1644:** Final significant Indian uprising in Virginia.

**1651:** Parliament approves first of several Navigation Acts.

**1658:** Esopus rebellion against Dutch in New Netherland.

**1664:** English force Dutch surrender of New Netherland.

**1675–1676:** King Philip's War in New England.

**1676:** Bacon's Rebellion in Virginia.

**1681:** William Penn given land grant and charter to establish Pennsylvania.

**1688–1689:** Glorious Revolution in England.

**1691:** Leisler's Rebellion defeated in New York.

**1692:** Salem witch trials in Massachusetts.

# ABOUT THE EDITORS AND CONTRIBUTORS

## EDITORS

JOHN E. FINDLING is professor emeritus of history at Indiana University Southeast. He earned his PhD in history from the University of Texas and has pursued research interests in world's fairs and the modern Olympic movement for nearly 30 years. Among his recent publications are *Fair America* (2000), coauthored with Robert Rydell and Kimberly Pelle, and *Encyclopedia of the Modern Olympic Movement* (2004) and *Encyclopedia of World's Fairs and Expositions* (2008), both coedited with Kimberly Pelle. In retirement, he sells stamps and vintage postcards at Collectors' Stamps, Ltd., in Louisville, Kentucky.

FRANK W. THACKERAY is professor emeritus of history at Indiana University Southeast. A former Fulbright scholar in Poland, he received his PhD from Temple University. Specializing in Russian-Polish relations in the 19th and 20th centuries, he is the author of *Antecedents of Revolution: Alexander I and the Polish Congress Kingdom* (1980). He also edited *Events That Changed Russia since 1855* (2007) and *Events That Changed Germany* (2004). Currently, he is term professor of history at the University of Louisville.

## CONTRIBUTORS

BLAKE BEATTIE is associate professor of history at the University of Louisville. He received his PhD from the University of Toronto in 1992. A specialist in the history of the Medieval Church and the Avignon Papacy, he is the author of *Angelus Pacis: The Legation of Cardinal Giovanni Gaetano Orsini, 1326–1334* (2007).

THOMAS CLARKIN received his doctorate in U.S. history from the University of Texas at Austin in 1998. He has completed a manuscript on federal Indian policy during the Kennedy and Johnson administrations, and he currently teaches at San Antonio College.

ANDREW FRANK is an assistant professor of history at Florida State University. He received his BA degree from Brandeis and his MA and PhD from the University of Florida.

He is the author of *Creeks and Southerners: Biculturalism in the Early American Frontier* (2005) and the editor of *The Routledge Historical Atlas of the American South* (1996); *The Birth of Black America: The Age of Discovery and the Slave Trade* (1998), *The American Republic: People and Perspectives* (2007), and *The Early Republic: People and Perspectives* (2009). He is currently working on projects involving the Indians of Florida.

JOHN M. HUNT is visiting assistant professor of history at the University of Louisville. He received his PhD from The Ohio State University. He is the recipient of a Fulbright award for study in Italy and is currently completing a manuscript on disorder in 16th- and 17th-century Rome during periods of papal interregnum.

RICK KENNEDY is professor of history at Point Loma Nazarene University, San Diego, California. He received his PhD from the University of California at Santa Barbara. He is the author of *A History of Reasonableness: Testimony and Authority in the Art of Thinking* (2004) and has contributed to *The Encyclopedia of American Cultural and Intellectual History*.

THOMAS A. MACKEY is professor of history at the University of Louisville and adjunct professor of law at the Brandeis School of Law, University of Louisville. He earned his PhD at Rice University. He is the author of *Pursuing Johns* (2005), *Pornography on Trail* (2002), and *Red Lights Out: A Legal History of Prostitution, Disorderly Houses, and Vice Districts, 1870–1917* (1987).

KATHLEEN PERDISATT graduated from Point Loma Nazarene University in 1999 and currently teaches second grade in the Saugus Union School District, Santa Clarita, California.

BARRY M. PRITZKER is director of foundation and corporate relations at Skidmore College, Saratoga Springs, NY. His published works include ABC-CLIO's *Native America Today: A Guide to Community Politics and Culture* and *Native Americans: An Encyclopedia of History, Culture, and Peoples*.

STEVEN E. SIRY is professor of history at Baldwin-Wallace College. He received his PhD from the University of Cincinnati, and he is the author of *Greene: Revolutionary General* (2006).

FREDERICK M. STOWELL holds an MA in military history and studies. He has taught at Tulsa Community College and Langston University. Currently, he is writing in the area of fire protection and has published *Safety Officers* (1998) and *Fire and Emergency Services Company Officer* (4th ed., 2007), under the auspices of the International Fire Service Training Association.

P. D. SWINEY is associate professor of history at Tulsa Community College. She teaches the American survey, African American history, and history of film. She earned her MA from Oklahoma State University, where she continues work on the PhD. Her undergraduate degree is from St. Mary's of Notre Dame. Her interests include legal history and Alexander Hamilton.

TIMOTHY L. WOOD is an associate professor of history at Southwest Baptist University. He holds an MA from the University of Louisville and a PhD in American history from Marquette University. He is the author of *Agents of Wrath, Sowers of Discord: Authority and Dissent in Puritan Massachusetts* (2006).

JULIA A. WOODS received her MA and PhD in history from the University of Texas at Austin and a law degree from the University of North Carolina at Chapel Hill. Her dissertation dealt with Southern lawyers before the Civil War.

# INDEX

Abenakis tribe, **1:**227

Abnaki War. *See* King William's War

Abolition (abolitionism), **3:65–85**
  American Anti-Slavery Society, **3:78–79**
  Birney, James G., **3:**67, 73, 79
  Child, Lydia Maria, **3:**78, **79–82**
  Clarkin's interpretive essay, **3:69–76**
  Douglass, Frederick, **3:**67, 75, 224
  of France, **1:**152
  Garrison, William Lloyd, **3:**66–67, 72–73, 75, 79
  of Great Britain, **1:**152
  Grimké, Angelina and Sarah, **3:**73
  John Brown's Final Statement to Virginia Court, **3:84–85**
  *The Liberator* First Edition excerpt, **3:83–84**
  Liberty Party, **3:**65, 67, 75, 79, **81–82**
  Nat Turner's Rebellion, **1:**152, 158–159, **3:**72
  overview, **3:65–69**
  participation by African Americans, **3:**71
  Pennsylvania Society for Abolition, **2:**194
  during the Progressive era, **4:**9
  Southern states hatred of, **3:**68, 69
  Tappan, Arthur, **3:**73, 75–76
  Tubman, Harriet, **3:82–83**
  *See also* Douglass, Frederick; Slaves/slavery

Académie des Sciences of Paris, **2:**25, 28

Acheson, Dean, **4:**182–183

Act of Toleration (1649), **1:**170, 183

Act to Prohibit the Importation of Slaves (1807), **1:**152

Acts of Confiscation (1861, 1862), **3:**193

Acts of Trade (1660), **2:**7

Adams, Abigail (wife of John, mother of John Quincy), **2:**189, 197, **200–202, 209**
  *See also* "Remember the Ladies" letter

Adams, Henry, **3:**262

Adams, John, **1:**109, **2:**95, 124, **3:**142
  abrogation of 1778 treaties, **2:**251
  American Academy of Arts and Sciences, **2:**28
  American Revolution involvement, **2:**143

arrest of, **2:**178
biographical data, **2:252–255**
commercial interests, **2:**263
Continental Congress participation, **2:**162, 163, 253
Convention of 1800, **2:**243
Declaration of Independence role, **2:**253
denunciation of French, **2:**245
1800 presidential election, **2:**263
Federalist opposition to, **2:**244
as Founding Father, **2:**25
Hamilton's opposition to, **2:**271
Jefferson's association with, **2:**174
Judiciary Act (1801), **2:**265
letter of attack by Hamilton, **2:**250
Naturalization Act, **2:**241, 246
political experience of, **2:**239
role in XYZ Affair, **2:**247–248, **252–255**
Second Continental Congress participation, **2:**173
slavery opposed by, **3:**69
split 1800 election, **2:**276
Talleyrand's interactions with, **2:**249

Adams, John Quincy (son of John Adams), **2:**201, 278, **3:**89, 92, **99–101,** 109, 146
  *See also* Monroe Doctrine

Adams, Samuel (1722–1803), **1:**109, 226
  Boston Tea Party instigation, **2:126–128,** 217
  British plans for capturing, **2:**131
  Committees of Correspondence and, **2:**117, 120
  Constitutional Convention participation, **2:**217
  Continental Congress participation, **2:**127, 162
  Declaration of Independence signatory, **2:**185
  Franklin's warnings against, **2:**35
  Hutchinson's confrontations with, **2:**107
  "Innocent Blood Crying to God from the Streets of Boston" pamphlet, **2:**116
  North Caucus Club formation, **2:**130
  Sons of Liberty movement formation, **2:**108
  Stamp Act Riots participation, **2:**110

Adams-Onis Treaty, **3:**47, 51, 137
Addams, Jane, **3:**170, 257, 279
Adler, Dankmar, **3:**255
Administration of Justice Act, **2:**118
Admittance into the Company of Eleven of the
    Daughters of Liberty, **2:**194–195
Adopting Act (1729), **2:**52
Adros, Gov. Edmund, **1:**217
Africa, slave-trading history, **1:**140–141, **148–153**
African Americans
    black colleges, **4:**52
    "Colored People's Day" (Columbian
      Exposition), **3:**261
    effects of war on, **2:**145
    emancipation of, **4:**51
    freedom movement, **4:**263
    Great Migration (1920), **2:**145, 53, 54
    Industrial Revolution era, **3:**166
    Niagara Movement (1905), **4:13**
    post-WW I influx of, **4:**53
    rejection as equals, **2:**220–221
    suburbanization efforts, **4:**134, 138
    suffrage rights, **3:**214
    support for American Revolution, **2:**192
    votes for Grant for presidency, **3:**215
    World War I service, **4:**54, 58
    *See also* Emancipation Proclamation; Harlem
      Renaissance; National Association for the
      Advancement of Colored People; Slaves/slavery
African Methodist Episcopal Church, **3:**13
Age of Reason, **2:**25
Agricultural Adjustment Act (AAA), **4:**78
Agricultural Adjustment Administration (AAA),
    **4:**82–83, 84
Agriculture
    European benefit from, **1:**11
    Farmer's Alliance, **1:**95
    Hopewell's contributions, **1:**17
    Hopi technology, **1:**72
    influence of Columbian exchange, **1:**8–9
    slash-and-burn method, **1:**5
Aguinaldo, Emilio, **3:**274–275, 278
Ahlstrom, Sydney, **3:**1
Aircraft inventions (Bell), **3:**175
Albany Plan of Union (document, 1754), **2:90–92**
Alden, Capt. John, **1:**263
Aldrich, Nelson, **3:**279
Algonquins, **1:12–13,** 40, 42, 47, 117, 217–218,
    220–221
Alien and Sedition Acts (1798), **2:**174–175, 231,
    241, 246–247, 254, **259–261,** 265, 280, **3:**2
Alien Enemies Act (from Alien and Sedition Acts),
    **2:**242, 259–260
*All in the Family* (TV show), **4:**202

Allen, Ethan, **2:**152
Alliance, Treaty of, **2:**142, 146
Alvarado, Hernando, **1:**63
Amadas, Philip, **1:**115
Ambrister, Robert C., **3:**23
American Academy of Arts and Sciences, **2:**29
American Anti-Slavery Society, **3:**65, 66–67,
    72–74, **78–79**
American Broadcasting Company (ABC), **4:**206
American Colonization Society, **3:**65–66, 105
American Dream, **4:**5, 85, 132, 136, 141
American Enterprise Institute, **4:**278
American Expeditionary Force (AEF), **4:**26, 40–43
    *See also* Pershing, Gen. John J.
American Federation of Labor (AFL), **3:**162, **4:**38
American Historical Association meeting (1893),
    **3:**240
American Independence Day, **3:**143
American Letter of Marque (1812, document),
    **3:62–63**
*American Magazine* (American Revolution era),
    **2:**188
*The American Nation Series* (Frederick Jackson
    Turner), **3:**250
American Philosophical Society, **2:**29, **33–34,** 176
American Protective League (vigilante group),
    **4:**33
American Revolution, **1:**44, 92–93, 159, 208,
    **2:**5–6, 30, **139–157**
    Adams, John, involvement, **2:**143
    America's invasion of Canada, **2:152–153**
    Bunker Hill, Battle of, **2:153–154**
    causes of, **2:**80
    Continental Army, **2:154–155**
    Dulany's role, **2:**106
    Franklin's contributions, **2:**34
    George III's Proclamation of Rebellion,
      **2:155–156**
    Lord Dunmore's Proclamation, **2:156–157**
    magazines of the era, **2:**188–189
    overview, **2:139–143**
    role of women, **2:**196, 198
    Siry's interpretive essay, **2:143–150**
    Sons of Liberty's role, 108–109
    Yorktown, Battle of, **2:**154
American Socialist Party, **4:**38
American Society for Colonizing the Free People
    of Color of the United States, **3:**70
*The American Spelling Book* (Webster), **2:**148–149
American Temperance Union (1836), **3:**5
Americas
    Columbus's expeditions to, **1:**6–8, 15–16
    early diseases, **1:**4
    flourishing of agriculture, **1:**11

hunters and gatherers, **1:**1, 5
Italian expeditions to, **1:**99
pre-1492 population, **1:**1–2
Spanish colonization of, **1:73–76,** 83, 87–90,
    **2:**1–2
Amerindians, **1:**4
*Amistad* legal case (1841), **3:**101
Amity and Commerce, Treaty of, **2:**146
*Amusing Ourselves to Death* (Postman), **4:**207
Anasazi culture, **1:13–15**
*Andrew Jackson and the Course of American
    Democracy* (Remini), **3:**120
Andros, Sir Edmund, **1:**234, 239–240, **246–247,**
    250–251, 263, **2:**3
Anglican Church, **1:**234–235, 244, **2:**27, 47, 51,
    55, **3:**8
    *See also* Society for the Propagation of the
        Gospel
Anglican Society for the Propagation of the
    Gospel in Foreign Parts (1701), **2:**63
Anglo-American Convention (1818), **3:**26
Anglo-American treaty, **2:**147
Anglo-Dutch Wars, **1:**205, **206**
Anglo-Soviet-U.S. alliance, **4:**174–175
Angola slave trading posts, **1:**151
*Anschluss* policy (German), **4:**86
Anthony, Susan B., **3:**257
Anti-Federalists, **2:224–225**
Anti-Imperialist League (Boston, 1898), **3:**279
Anti-Masonic Party (1831), **3:**116–117
Anticommunist movement (1950s), **1:**262
Antiem Creek, Battle of, **3:**194
Antislavery Whigs, **3:**148
Antiwar movement (1960s), **4:231–232**
Anzaldua, Gloria, **4:**265
Apalachee tribe, **1:**79
*Apocalypse Now* (war movie), **4:**228
*An Appeal in Favor of That Class of Americans
    Called Africans* (Child), **3:**79–80
*An Appeal to the Public for Religious Liberty*
    (Backus), **3:**16
Appy, Christian G., **4:**225
Arbuthnot, Alexander, **3:**23–24
*Architecture of the World's Columbian Exposition*
    (Brunt), **3:**260
Arkansas territory, **3:**26–27
Armstrong, John, **3:**55
Armstrong, Louis, **4:**55
Army of the Potomac, **3:**194
Army of the Potomac (Union Army), **3:**194, 201
Army of the Republic of Vietnam (ARVN),
    **4:**222–223
Arnold, Benedict, **2:**153
Articles of Confederation (1776), **2:**144, 147, 179

Continental Congress adoption, **2:**215
function of, **3:**46
Hamilton's criticism of, **2:**227
inadequacy of, **2:**215–216
signers, **2:**217
Asbury, Francis, **2:**150
Ashburton, Lord, **1:**152–153
Atomic bomb, **4:**107, 116, 150, 154
    *See also* Manhattan Project
Atomic Energy Act (1954), **4:**152
Atomic Energy Commission (AEC), **4:**150, 152,
    **163–164**
Atomic energy development (1945–1995), **4:149–
    167**
    atomic bomb, **4:**107, 116, 150, 154
    Atomic Energy Commission, **4:**150, 152,
        **163–164**
    Baruch Plan, **4:**149
    Cuban Missile Crisis, **4:**151, 175–176, **186–188**
    Cuban Missile Crisis (1962), **4:**151
    hydrogen bomb, **4:**175
    Kunetka's interpretive essay, **4:153–161**
    Manhattan Project, **4:**149
    nuclear freeze movement, **4:164**
    Oppenheimer, J. Robert, **4:**160, **165–166**
    overview, **4:149–153**
    Three Mile Island nuclear accident, **4:**153, 157,
        167
    U-2 incident (1960), **4:**151
Atoms for Peace proposal (Eisenhower), **4:**151
Austrian Succession, War of (1740–1748), **2:**9, 12
Automobile vs. streetcar suburbs, **4:**131–132
Aztec Empire (Mexico), **1:**98

*Baby and Child Care* (Spock), **4:**257
Backus, Isaac, **3:15–16**
Bacon, Nathaniel, **1:**233–234, 247–248
Bacon's Rebellion (1676), **1:**112, **1:**233, **247–248**
Bagdikina, Ben H., **4:**205
Bailyn, Bernard, **2:**11
Baker, Josephine, **4:**55
Balboa, Vasco Núñez de, **1:**93
Bancroft, George, **3:**153
Bancroft, Hubert Howe, **3:**256
Bank of the United States, **3:**111–112, **122–125**
Bank War (Jackson), **3:**129
Banking acts, **3:**197
Baptist Church, **2:**48, 150, **3:**6, 7, 12, 15–16
    *See also* Backus, Isaac
Baptiste de Rochambeau, Gen. Jean, **2:**154
Barbary pirates, **3:**21
Barlow, Joel, **2:**149
Barlowe, Arthur, **1:115–116**
Barnard, Henry, **2:**209

Barney, Joshua, **3**:57

Barré, Isaac, **2**:108

Bartram, John, **2**:33

Baruch, Bernard, **4**:25, 149

Beattie, Blake, **1:82–90**

Beaver trade, **1**:38–39

Beaver Wars, **1**:40

Beecher, Henry Ward, **3**:258

Beecher, Lyman, **3**:2, 4, 9

Bell, Gen. J. Franklin, **3**:275

Bell, John, **3**:191

Bell Telephone Company, **3**:174

Bellamy, Edward, **3**:163

Benson, Thomas Hart, **3**:117

Bering Strait, **1**:4

Beringia, **1**:1, 4

Berkeley, Gov. William, 247–248

Berle, Milton (1908–2002), **4:212–214**

Berlin Wall, **4**:171, 172, 174

Bessemer, Sir Henry, **3**:176

Bett, Mum, **2**:198

Biddle, Nicholas, **3**:112, 124, 128

    *See also* Bank of the United States

Big Horn, Battle of, **3**:29

"Big Three." *See* Churchill, Winston; Roosevelt,

    Franklin D.; Stalin, Joseph

"Bill for Establishing Religious Freedom"

    (Jefferson), **2**:57

Bill for More General Diffusion of Knowledge

    (Jefferson), **2**:173

Bill of Rights (document, U.S. Constitution),

    **1**:180, **2**:32, 230, **236–238**

Billings, William, **2**:148

Bingham, Anne Willing, **2**:28

Birney, James G., **3**:67, 73, 79

    *See also* Liberty Party

Bishop, Bridget, **1**:264

Bishop, Maurice, **4**:281

"Black Codes" (Johnson), **3**:213, 218, 220

Black Diaspora, **1**:141

Black Hawk War, **3**:156, **204**

Black Hills Dakota Territory, **3**:29

Black Muslims, **4**:240

Black Panthers, **4**:240

Black Power movement, **4**:247, 265

    *See also* Davis, Angela

Black Thursday, **4**:80

Blaine, James, **3**:255

Blair, Frank, Sr., **3**:117

Blake, Eubie, **4**:55

"Bleeding Kansas" territory, **3**:28

Bloody Marsh, Battle of (1742), **1**:95

*Bloudy Tenent of Persecution* (Williams),

    **1:187–189**

Blount, William, **3**:125

Board of Lady Managers (Columbian Exposition),

    **3**:260

Board of Nine Men (New Netherland Colony),

    **1**:211–212

Board of Trade and Plantations, **2**:3, 8, **13–14**

Boas, Franz, **3**:256

Bolívar, Simón, **3:101–103**

Bonaparte, Napoleon, **2**:242, 251, 257, 266, **3**:21,

    36, 43, 87

Bonus Army (post-WW I), **4**:77, 81

*Book of Mormon* (Smith), **3**:13

*The Book of Negro Poetry* (Jams Weldon Johnson),

    **4**:59

*The Book of the Fair* (Bancroft), **3**:256

Boone, Daniel, **3**:242

Booth, John Wilkes, **3**:207

*The Boston Evening Post* newspaper, **2**:193

Boston Massacre (1770), **2**:116, 122, 239, 253

Boston Port Act, **2**:118

Boston Port Bill, 123

Boston Tea Party, **2**:108, **115–138**

    Adams, Samuel, organization of, **2:126–128**

    East India Company, **2**:112, 120, 123, 125,

        **128–129**

    First Continental Congress, **2**:129–130

    Hewess's account of (document), **2:136–138**

    Mattox's interpretive essay, **2:119–126**

    overview, **2:115–119**

    Revere, Paul, **2:130–132**

    Tea Act (1773) document, **2:132–135**

    vessels (ships) involved, **2**:121–122

Boy Spies of America (vigilante group), **4**:33

Boycotts and protests, by women, **2**:187, 191

Braddock's (Gen. Edward) Campaign (1755), **2**:72,

    74–75, **83**

Bradford, Sarah, **3**:82–83

Bradley, Omar (1893–1981), **4:120–121**

"Brain Trust" advisory (of FDR), **4**:82

Brandeis, Louis, **4**:4, 84

Breckinridge, John, **3**:26

Brendan (Saint, Irish monk), **1**:2

Brezhnev, Leonid, **4**:176

*A Brief History of the War with the Indians*

    (Increase Mather), **1**:268

British West Indies, **2**:4

Bronxville, New York, **4**:131

Broward, Napoleon Bonaparte, **1**:96

Brown, Charles Brockden, **2**:149

Brown, James, **4**:54

Brown, Joseph, **3**:193

*Brown v. Board of Education of Topeka* (Supreme

    Court decision), **4**:237–239, 244

Bryan, William Jennings, **3**:30, 279

Buade, Louis de, **1:**48–50

Bubble Act, **2:**7

Buchanan, James, **3:**147

Buckley, William F., **4:**278

Buena Vista, Battle of (1847), **3:**138, 140–141, 144, **152,** 157, 203

Bulge, Battle of the (1944), **4: 119–120,** 121

Bull Moose Party. *See* Progressivism

Bunker Hill, Battle of (1775), **2:153–154,** 159

Bureau of Refugees, **3:**217

Burger, Warren E., **4:**275

Burgoyne, Gen. John, **2:**140, 141, 148, **3:**55

Burke, Edmund, **2:**5–6

Burnham, Daniel, **3:**254–25, **3:**254–255, 259, **264–265**

Burr, Aaron, **2:**175, 229, 263, 271–273, **275–277,** **3:**23

Burroughs, George, **1:**258

Bus boycott (Montgomery, Alabama), **4:**238

Bush, George H. W., **4:**174, 228–229, 240, 247, 261, 277, 283, **285–287**

Bush, George W., **4:**284

Cabeza de Vaca, Álvar Núñez, **1:**57, 65, **67–68,** 70, 75

Cable News Network (CNN), **4:**208

Cabot, John (Giovanni Caboto), **1:**99, **110–111**

Calef, Robert, **1:**260, 265

Calhoun, John C., **2:**278, 45, 51, 92, 126, 130, 146, 190

Calvert, Cecil, **1:**177, **181–183**

Calvert, George, **1:**176–177

Calvert, Leonard, **1:**177, 182–183

Calvin, John, **1:**34, 84, 172

Calvinism, **1:**34, 172, **2:**27, 49, **2:**66, **3:**1, 9

Calvinist Puritans, **1:**168–169

Cambodia, **4:**219

Cambodian incursion (1970), **4:232–233**

Campbell, John (Lord Loudon), **2:**76–78

Canada

    Algonquins, **1:12–13,** 40, 42, 47, 117, 220–221

    American invasion of, **2:152–153**

    Buade's stand for Quebec, **1:**48

    Cartier's visits, **1:**45–46

    Champlain's visits, **1:**47–48

    dependence on France, **2:**69

    exploration aid by slaves, **1:**135

    Great Treaty of Montreal, **1:**41

    Joliet in, **1:**50–51

    Quebec City, founding of, **1:**38

    siege of Quebec, **1:**48, 50

    Tecumsah supplied by, **3:**44

Cancer de Barbastro, Fray Luis, **1:**80

*Cane* (Toomer), **4:**59

Canning, George, **3:**88–89

Cape Cod/ranch-style homes, **4:**132, 134, 137

    *See also* Levittowns (NY, NJ, PA)

Cárdenas, Garciá López de, **1:**62, 65

Cardozo, Benjamin, **4:**84

Carleton, Sir Guy, **2:**152–153

Carmichael, Stokely, **4:**247

Carnegie, Andrew (1835–1919), **3:**163, **175–178,** 279, 6

Carnegie Endowment for International Peace (1910), **3:**178

Carnegie Steel, **3:**163

Carson, Rachel, **4:**142

Carter, Jimmy, **4:**173, 273–274, 275, 278

Cartier, Jacques, **1:**35, 37, **45–46,** 84

Cartwright, Peter, **3:**5–6, 8, **16–17,** 19

Case, Lewis, **3:**190

*Cases of Conscience* (Mather), **1:**258

*Cases of Conscience Concerning Evil Spirits* (Increase Mather), **1:**268

Castillo de San Marcos (in St. Augustine), **1:92–93**

Castro, Fidel, **4:**172

Cateau-Cambresis Treaty, **1:**33

Cato Institute, **4:**278

Cattle ranching, **3:**30–31

Cavelier, René-Robert, **1:**36, 40–41, 49, 50

CCC. See Civilian Conservation Corps

Census Bureau (U.S.), pre-1890 report, **3:**239

Central America

    Contras/Sandinistas, **4:**275

    Court of Justice, **3:**178

Central American Court of Justice, **3:**178

Ceremonial cycles (Native Americans), **1:**71, 73, 77

Cervera, Adm. Pascual, **3:**277

Champlain, Samuel de, **1:**38, 47, **47–48, 2:**69

Channing, William, **3:**3

Charles I (King of England), **1:**169–170, 176–177, 181–182, 246

Charles II (King of England), **1:**137, 169–170, 196–197, 203–204, 233, 246, 262, **2:**50, 177

Charles IX (French King), **1:**33, 81

Charles of Habsburg (Spain), **1:**83–84

Charles V (Spanish Emperor), **1:**68, 93, 168

*Charlie's Angels* (TV show), **4:**202

Charter of Liberties (England, 1701), **1:**171

Chauncy, Pastor Charles, **2:**54

*Cheers* (TV show), **4:**202

Cherokee Indians, **1:**5–6, **3:**127, 132

*Chesapeake* naval affair, **3:**42–43, 100

Cheves, Langdon, **3:**124

Chiang Kai-shek, **4:**171

Chicago, Illinois. *See* Burnham, Daniel; World's Columbian Exposition (1893)

Chickahominy Indians, **1:**130
Chickasaw tribes, **3:**49
Child, Lydia Maria (1802–1880), **3:**78, **79–82**
Child labor laws, **3:**164–165
China
   war with Japan, **4:**106
Choctaw tribes, **3:**49
*The Christian Philosopher* (Cotton Mather), **1:**268
Christianity
   abolition and, **3:**68
   ascendancy of Church, **2:**21
   banning of, **2:**268
   British/U.S. evangelicals, **1:**152
   Columbus era missionaries, **1:**10–11
   defense of slavery, **3:**3
   Dwight's lectures on, **3:**2
   English North America, **1:**167
   Indian women conversions, **1:**43
   slave conversion attempts, **2:**62
*Chubb* British warship, **3:**56
Church, Benjamin, **1:223–224,** 249
Church of England, **1:**113, 168, 172, **1:**172, 234,
   **2:**26, **3:**8
Church of Jesus Christ of Latter-Day Saints,
   **3:**13–14
Churchill, Winston, **3:**56–57, **4:**105, 178
   Atlantic Charter, **4:**110
   "iron curtain" speech, **4:**175
Cities, Industrial Revolution growth, **3:**165–167,
   171
City Beautiful movement (Burnam), **3:**264–265
"Civil Disobedience" essay (Thoreau), **2:**167
Civil Rights Act (1866), **3:**198, **3:**198, 219
Civil Rights Act (1964), **4:**226, 239, 245, 259
Civil Rights Act (1968), **4:**239, 240
Civil Rights Movement (ca. 1954-Present),
   **4:237–256**
   Black Power movement, **4:**247
   *Brown v. Board of Education of Topeka,*
      **4:**237–239, 244
   Civil Rights Act (1964), **4:**226, 239, 245
   Civil Rights Act (1968), **4:**239, 240
   Clarkin's interpretive essay, **4:240–249**
   Freedom Riders, **4:**239
   Freedom Summer, **4:**247, **252–253**
   Greensboro Sit-Ins, **4:251–252**
   King, Martin Luther, Jr., **4:**239, 244,
      245–246, **253–255**
   Los Angeles Riots, **4:**247, **256**
   March on Washington (1963), **4:**239
   Montgomery bus boycott, **4:**238, **251**
   overview, **4:237–240**
   *Plessy v. Ferguson,* **4:**12, 237, 241
   Project C (confrontation), **4:**246

SNCC, **4:**225, 240, 245, 247
Voting Rights Act, **4:**234, 239, 247
*See also* National Association for the
   Advancement of Colored People
Civil Service Commission (U.S.), **4:**1
Civil War (1861–1865), **1:**77, 95, 153, **3:185–209**
   Army of the Potomac, **3:**194, 201
   commercial cattle ranching, **3:**30
   Confederate States of America, **3:**143, 185,
      **200–202**
   Conscription Act, **3:**195
   Davis, Jefferson, **3:**193, **202–204**
   Dred Scott decision, **3:**191
   economic impact of, **3:**195–196
   Emancipation Proclamation, **1:**160, **3:**194, 195,
      196, 206
   Gettysburg Address, **1:**167, **2:**167, **3:**198, 207
   Harper's Ferry raid, **3:**191
   Indian revolts, **3:**28
   issues resolved by, **3:**216
   Kramer's interpretive essay, **3:189–198**
   Lee's surrender to Grant, **3:**202, 207
   Lincoln, Abraham, **3:204–207**
   Lincoln on cause of, **1:**160
   National Banking Acts, **3:**197
   Ordinance of Secession (South Carolina),
      **3:208–209**
   overview, **3:185–189**
   Radical Republican view of, **3:**218–219
   role in Industrial Revolution, **3:**159
   Sanitary Commission, **3:**198
   Sherman's March to the Sea, **3:207–208**
   United States Military Railroads, **3:**196
   *See also* Abolition
Civilian Conservation Corps (CCC), **4:**77, 87
Clark, William, **3:**25, 35
   *See also* Lewis and Clark expedition
Clark, York (d. 1770-ca. 1832), **3:33–35**
Clarke, John, **1:**169
Clarkin, Thomas, interpretive essays
   Abolition, **3:69–76**
   Expedition of Coronado, **1:58–66**
   French and Indian War, **2:73–81**
Clay, Henry, **2:**278, **3:**44, 45, 70, 81, 87, 92, 109,
   111, 114, 126, 139
   *See also* Whig Party
Clayton Anti-Trust Act (1914), **4:**4
Clayton-Bulwer agreement, **3:**144
Clement VII (Pope), **1:**168, 172
Cleveland, Grover, **3:**96, 239, 259
Clinton, Bill, **4:**229, 284
Clinton, Gov. DeWitt, **2:**208, **3:**130
Clinton, Gov. George, **2:**224, 276
Clooney, George, **4:**206

Closing of the frontier (ca. 1890s), **3:233–251**
   costs of settlement, **3:**238
   Devine's interpretive essay, **3:237–242**
   Ghost Dance movement, **3:**29, 235, **243–245,** 248, 250, 251
   Immigration Reduction League, **3:**239
   Little Big Horn, Battle of, **3:**234
   mining phase, **3:**233
   myths about the frontier, **3:**242
   "New Frontier" slogan, **3:**242
   overview, **3:233–237**
   Sand Creek Massacre, **3:**234
   Sioux Indian War, **3:245–246,** 247
   Sitting Bull, **3:**29, 235, **246–248**
   Turner, Frederick Jackson, **3:248–250**
   Wounded Knee Massacre, **3:**245, **250–251**
Cochrane, Sir Alexander, **3:**54, 57
Cockburn, Sir George, **3:**57
Cody, William F. "Buffalo Bill," **3:**30, 242
Coercive Acts (1774), **2:**104, 127, 129
Coetus party (of Frelinghuysen), **2:**61
Cohen, Lizabaeth
   "Consumers' Republic," **4:**140
   "Purchaser Citizens," **4:**136
Coit, Mehetabel Chandler, **2:**203
Cold War, **4:**115–117, 121, **169–197**
   atomic energy cause, **4:**151
   "Consumers' Republic," **4:**140
   Cuban Missile Crisis, **4:**151, 175–176, **186–188**
   Eisenhower, Dwight D., **4:**171–172, **188–190**
   Far East involvement, **4:**171
   inevitability of, **4:**178–179
   Korean War, **4:**171, 175, **190–193**
   length of (1946–1991), **4:**180
   Mayers' interpretive essay, **4:174–184**
   name derivation, **4:**174–175
   North-South Korea engagement, **4:**124
   nuclear arsenals, **4:**155
   overview, **4:169–174**
   Stalin's inflammatory rhetoric, **4:**170
   Trotsky's characterization of, **4:**176
   Truman, Harry, **4:**169–170, 175, 178, **193–196**
Colden, Cadwallader, **2:**108
Cole, Donald B., **3:**117
Coligny, Gaspard de, **1:**34, 84
College of William and Mary (Virginia), **2:**27
Colonial National Historic Park System, **1:**112
Colonial Virginia, slavery (mid-18th century), **1:161–163**
"Colored People's Day" (Columbian Exposition), **3:**261
Columbia Broadcasting System (CBS), **4:**200, 206
Columbian Exposition. *See* World's Columbian Exposition

*Columbian Magazine* (American Revolution era), **2:**188–189
Columbine High School shooting, **4:**209
Columbus, Christopher, **1:2, 15–16**
   childhood years, **1:**2–3, 15
   Document: journal (1492), **1:18–32**
   inspirational sources for, **1:**15
   Native Americans and, **1:**6–8
   plants/animals introduced by, **1:**8–9
   voyages/explorations, **1:**3–4, 6–8, 15–16
   *See also* Ferdinand V; Isabella I; World's Columbian Exposition
Commissioners of Ecclesiastical Causes, **1:**234
Committee for Postponed Matters, **2:**221
Committee of Correspondence, **2:**108, 117
Committee of Safety, **1:**242
Committee on Public Information (CPI), **4:**25, 32, **37–38**
Committee on the Conduct of the War (1861), **3:**229
*Common Sense* pamphlet (Paine), **2:**125, 161
Communist doctrine, **4:**177
*The Communist Manifesto,* **4:**117
Community antenna television (CATV), **4:**201
Compact discs (CDs), **4:**201
Compromise of 1850, **3:**68, 133, 158
Compton, Henry, **1:**234–235
Comte de Frontenac. *See* Buade, Louis de
Confederate States of America (CSA), **3:**143, 185, 191, **200–202**
   post-Civil War turmoil, **3:**213
   *See also* Davis, Jefferson
*Confiance* British warship, **3:**56
Congregational Churches (New England), **1:**82, **2:**149–150, **3:**7
Congregationalists ("Old Lights"), **2:**48
Congress (U.S.)
   arms appropriation for McKinley, **3:**276
   Bureau of Refugees, creation of, **3:**217
   Consumer Product Safety Act, **4:**135
   Federal Cigarette Labeling and Advertising Act, **4:**135
   Federal Highway Act, **4:**139
   Freedman's Bureau, **3:**212, 217
   Lend-Lease military aid bill, **4:**105
   Macon's Bill No. 2, **3:**43
   Meat Inspection Act, **4:**2
   National Traffic and Motor Vehicle Safety Act, **4:**135
   negative view of Confederacy, **3:**211
   Payne-Aldrich Tariff, **4:**3
   Prohibition legislation, **4:**34
   Pure Food and Drug Act, **4:**2
   Reconstruction passed by, **3:**212, 214

Revenue Act (1942), **4:**108
Smoot-Hartley tariff bill, **4:**76
support for FDR's reforms, **4:**84
Voting Rights Act, **4:**239
War of 1812 actions, **3:**44
Congress of Industrial Organizations (CIO), **4:**39
Congress of Racial Equality (CORE), **4:**243, 245
Congress of Vienna, **2:**257
Connecticut Indians, **1:**218
"Conscience Whigs," **3:**148
Conscription Act (1863), **3:**195
*Considerations on the Propriety of imposing Taxes in the British Colonies, for the Purpose of raising a Revenue, by Act of Parliament* (Dulany), **2:**106
Constitution (U.S.), **2:**30
    Bill of Rights, **1:**180, **2:**32, **236–238**
    Eighteenth Amendment, **4:**34
    Electoral College, **2:**221, **225–226,** 263
    Fifteenth Amendment, **3:**22, 198, **4:**51
    First Amendment, **1:**180, **2:**269
    Fourteenth Amendment, **3:**198, 212
    Nineteenth Amendment, **4:**4, 34, 263
    Seventeenth Amendment, **4:**2–3
    Sixteenth Amendment, **4:**2–3, 11–12
    Thirteenth Amendment, **1:**156, 160, **3:**198, **3:**212, 219, 227, **4:**51
    Three-Fifths Compromise, **2:**274
    Twelfth Amendment, **2:**175, 221, 264, **281–282**
    Twentieth Amendment, **4:**77
    Twenty-First Amendment, **4:**5
    "We the people" preamble, **2:**31
Constitutional Convention (1787), **1:**150, 159, 34, 106, **211–238**
    Anti-Federalists, **2:**224–225
    Bill of Rights (document), **2:**236–238
    Committee for Postponed Matters, **2:**221
    Committee of Style review, **2:**222
    Electoral College, **2:**221, **225–226,** 263
    European observer experiences, **2:**215
    Franklin's participation, **2:**218, 220
    Hamilton, Alexander, role, **2:226–229**
    Madison, James, role, **2:**217, 218, 227, **229–232**
    New Jersey Plan (document), **2:**220, **234–236**
    overview, **2:211–214**
    presidency discussions, **2:**221
    Supreme Court creation discussions, **2:**219, 221
    trade regulation discussions, **2:**216
    Virginia Plan (document), **2:**218–219, 222, **232–234**
    Woods' interpretive essay, **2:215–222**
Consumer Product Safety Act (1970), **4:**135
Continental Army, **2:**125, 139, **154–155,** 159–160
Continental Association (1774), **2:**124, 130

Continental Congress (1776), **2:**30, 36
    Articles of Confederation adoption, **2:**215
    mission to France, **2:**140
    money plan, **2:**144
Convention of 1800, **2:**243, 252
Convention of 1818, **3:**44
Convention of Pardo (1739), **2:**9
Coode, John, **1:**236–237, 241, 243
Cooker, Jay, **3:**197
Cooper, James Fenimore, **3:**242
Copernicus, **2:**22–23
Copley, John Singleton, **2:**148
Copley, Lionel, **1:**236
*Copper Sun* (Cullen), 59
Corey, Giles, **1:**259, 262, 264
Cornwallis, Lord Charles, **2:**142, 147, 154
Coronado, Francisco Vásques de, **1:68–69**
    abandonment by followers, **1:**69
    appointment as governor, **1:**57
    interactions with Native Americans, **1:**58, 62, 63, 72–73
    *la Tierra Nueva* expedition, **1:**58–60
    loyalty of army to, **1:**59
    search for Quivira, **1:**58, 63–64, 69
    search for Seven Cities of Cíbola, **1:**57, 59–61, 68, 75–76
Coronado Expedition (1540–1542), **1:55–78**
    background information, **1:55–58**
    Cabeza de Vaca, Álvar Núñez, **1:67–68**
    Clarkin's interpretive essay, **1:58–66**
    Esteban, **1:69–71**
    Hopi Indians, **1:71–73**
    Spanish colonization of Americas, **1:73–76**
    Zuni Indians, **1:**61, 68–69, **76–78**
Corporation Act, **1:**235
"Corps of Discovery" exploration, **3:**25
Cortés, Hernán, **1:**55–56, 74
*The Cosby Show* (TV show), **4:**202
Cotton Club jazz club, **4:**58
Cotton gin, **1:**150–151, 160
*The Cotton Kingdom* (Olmsted), **3:**267
"Cotton Whigs," **3:**148
Coughlin, Charles E. "Radio Priest," **4:**79
Council for National Defense (CND, 1916), **4:**24–25, 29, 30
Council of Trade and Plantations, **1:**234–235, 237
Council of Trent, **1:**43
Council of War (Rhode Island colony), **1:**218
Court of Honor (Columbian Exposition), **3:**254–255, 259, 261
Court of Oyer and Terminer (Massachusetts Bay Colony), **1:**257, 262
Cowboy life, **3:**30
Cowpens, Battle of, **2:**146

*Crabgrass Frontier* (Jackson), **4:**131

Crandall, Prudence, **3:**73

Crawford, William H., **3:**92, **3:**130

Crazy Horse (Native American chief), **3:**29

Credit cards, introduction of, **4:**134

Credit Mobilier scandal, **4:**5

Creek Indians, **3:**47, 49, 125, 234

Creel, George, **4:**32

Crevecoeur, St. John de, **3:**238

*The Crisis* (Du Bois), **4:**54, 60

Crittenden, John J., **3:**191

Crockett, Davy, **3:**242

Cromwell, Oliver, **1:**169, 178, 183

Cronkite, Walter (1916–2009), **4:214–216**

Crothers, A. Glenn, **3:5–14**

Cruger, Nicholas, **2:**226

Cuban Missile Crisis (1962), **4:**151, 175–176, **186–188**

Cuban Revolution (late 1950s), **1:**96

Cullen, Countee, **4:**55, 58, 59–60

Cullom, Shelby, **3:**162

Currency Act (1751), **2:**4, 99

Custer, George A., **3:**234, 246

Custer's Last Stand, **3:**246

Cutler, Timothy, **2:**54


D-Day invasion (northern France), **4:**106

Danbury Baptist Association, **1:**171

Darwin, Charles, **3:**168, 273

Davenport, James, **2:**53–54

Davie, William R., **2:**250–251

Davis, Angela, **4:**265

Davis, Jefferson, **3:**193, **202–204, 3:**217

Davis, Joseph (brother of Jefferson Davis), **3:**217

Davyes, William, **1:**233

Dawes, Phillip, **2:**192

Dawes Act (1887), **1:**73

Dawes Severalty Act, **3:**234–235

*The Day the Earth Stood Still* (war movie), **4:**224

De Delon, Daniel, **4:**38

De Loet, Johannes, **1:**193

De Soto, Hernando, **1:**57, 75, **93–94**

    battles with indigenous peoples, **1:**75, 86, 94

    expedition failures, **1:**80, 83

    Gulf Coast exploration, **1:**57

    search for gold, **1:**7

    search for Seven Cities, **1:**60

Deane, Silas, **2:**140

Death Warrant of Five Women Convicted of Witchcraft (document), **1:274–275**

Debs, Eugene V., **4:**34, 38

Decapitation of Native American women prisoners, **1:**218

Declaration of Causes and Necessity of Taking Up Arms (Washington and Jefferson), **2:**125, 179

Declaration of Colonial Rights and Grievances conceded to Parliament, **2:**124

Declaration of Independence, **1:**260, 139, 141, **159–185**

    Adams, Samuel, as signatory, **2:**117

    African Americans and, **2:**169

    Declaration of Independence (document), **2:182–185**

    diminishing power of, **2:**169–170

    Franklin's involvement, **2:**30, 34, 161–164, 173, 179, 182

    George III, **2:171–172**

    God's inclusion in, **2:**23

    Jefferson, Thomas, **2:172–176**

    Kennedy's interpretive essay, **2:163–170**

    Lee's proposal resolution, **2:**161, 163, **182**

    Lincoln's thoughts on, **2:**167

    Locke, John, **2:176–178**

    major premise of, **2:**166

    Olive Branch Petition, **2:**125, **179–181**

    overview, **2:159–163**

    Second Continental Congress, **2:178–179**

    structural components, **2:**165

    Washington's reading to troops, **2:**164

    *See also* Enlightenment in North America

"Declaration of Intellectual Independence" speech (Emerson), **2:**166–167

Declaration of Liberated Europe (1945), **4:**169

Declaration of Sentiments (American Anti-Slavery Society), **3:**73

"Declaration of Sentiments and Resolutions" (Stanton), **2:**167

"Declaration of the Rights and Grievances of the Colonies" (Stamp Act Congress), **2:**103, 129–130

Declaratory Act (1776), **2:**95, 104

Deism, **3:**7

*Democracy Triumphant* (Carnegie), **3:**178

Democratic Republic of Vietnam, **4:**219–220

    *See also* Vietnam War

Democratic-Republican Party, **2:**174, 228, 231, 254, 263, **277–278,** 279, **3:**7, 26, 36, 104, 126

Descartes, René, **2:**176

"Detente" policy, **4:**151, 173

*Devil in the Shape of a Woman* (Karlsen), **1:**261

Dewey, George, **3:**277, **283**

    *See also* Spanish-American War; U.S. Navy

Dexter, Samuel, **2:**250

Diaz, Melchior, **1:**62

Dickens, Charles, **3:**239

Diem, Ngo Dinh (South Vietnam prime minister), **4:**220–221

Dien Bien Phu (Vietnam village), **4:**219

Diggers (communistic group), **1:**170

*Discourse on the Origin of Inequality* (Rousseau), **2:**41–42

*A Discourse on the Sciences and the Arts* (Rousseau), **2:**41

*The Distinguishing Marks of a Work of the Spirit God* (Edwards), **2:**60

"Distributor of Stamps for Massachusetts." *See* Oliver, Andrew

Dominion of New England
   creation of, **1:**239
   dismantling of, **1:**247

Domino Theory, **4:**220

Donnelly, Ignatius, **3:**239–240

Dorantes, Esteban de, **1:**57

Dorantes de Carranza, Andrés de, **1:**67–68, 70

Douglas, Aaron, **4:**58

Douglas, Stephen A., **3:**27, 190

Douglass, Frederick, **3:**67, 75, 224, 261

Dow Chemical Company, **4:**141

*Dr. Strangelove* (war movie), **4:**224

Drake, Sir Francis, **1:**100–101

Dreamer Religion (Native Americans), **3:**244

Dred Scott decision, **3:**191

Drinker, Elizabeth, **2:**203

Du Bois, W.E.B., **1:**135, **4:**52–54, 56, 58

Dulaney, Daniel, **2:105–107**

Dulles, John Foster, **4:**172

Dunk, George (Earl of Halifax), **2:**14

Dunlap, William, **2:**148

Dunmore's Proclamation (document, 1776), **2:156–157**

Dupey de Lôme, Enrique, **3:**274, 276

Dutch East India Company, **1:**198, **206–207**

Dutch Reformed Church, **1:207–208**, 212, **2:**49, 61

Dutch West India Company, **1:**118, 136, 193–194, 196, 198, 200, **208–210**

DVD (digital video disc), **4:**201

Dwight, Timothy, **2:**149, **3:**2, 9

*Eagle* warship, **3:**56

Earl of Chatham. *See* Pitt, William

East India Company, **2:**112, 117, 120, 123, 125

Eaton, John H. and Peggy, **3:**127

Edenton (North Carolina) women, **2:**191–192

Edison, Thomas, **3:**159–160, 262

Education
   black colleges, **4:**52
   Progressive Era importance, **4:**8–9
   in Puritan communities, **2:**205
   push for academies for, **2:**197
   in Quaker communities, **2:**189, 205

   Willard's role, **2:**208–209
   for women, **2:**190
   World Education Convention, **2:**209

Edwards, Jonathan (1703–1758), **2:**52, 55, **59–60,** **3:**2, 6–7

Egypt, **4:**172

Eighteenth Amendment (Constitution), **4:**34

Eisenhower, Dwight D., **4:**120, 150–151, 171–172, **188–190,** 209–210, 244

Election of 1876, **3:**225

Electoral College, **2:**221, **225–226,** 263, 271–272

Eliot, John, **1:**117, 216

Elizabeth I (Queen of England), **1:**84, 100, 168, 172

Elizabethan Compromise (17th Century), **1:**168

Elkins Act (1903), **4:**2

Ellington, Duke, **4:**55, 58

Ellsberg, Daniel, **4:**226

Ellsworth, Oliver, **2:**250

Ely, Richard, **3:**239

Emancipation Proclamation (1862), **1:**160, **3:**194, 195, 196, 206, 216

Embargo Act (1807), **2:**175, **3:**43

Emergency Banking Act, **4:**82

Emerson, Ralph Waldo, **2:**166, **3:**3

*The Empire of Business* (Carnegie), **3:**178

*The End of Victory Culture* (Engelhardt), **4:**227

Energy Research and Development Administration (ERDA), **4:**150

Engels, Friedrich, **3:**169–170

Englehardt, Tom, **4:**227

English Bill of Rights (document, 1689), **1:251–253**

English Civil War, **1:**177–178, 246

English Colonization Efforts (ca. 1584–1630), **1:99–116**
   Cabot, John, **1:110–111**
   "First Voyage to Roanoke" excerpt, **1:115–116**
   Jamestown, founding of, **1:**82, **112**
   Kennedy's interpretive essay, **1:103–109**
   overview, **1:99–103**
   Pilgrims, **1:112–113**
   Raleigh, Sir Walter, **1:113–114**
   reasons for, **1:**140
   religious influences, **1:**100
   Roanoke Colonies, **1:114–115**

English Reformation, **1:**176

English Royal African Company, **1:**138

Enlightenment in North America (1727–1790), **2:21–44**
   American Philosophical Society, **2:33–34**
   Franklin, Benjamin, **2:34–36**
   Junto, **2:36–37**
   *Letter on Science and the Perfectibility of Men* (Jefferson), **2:43–44**

overview, **2:21–24**
Priestley, Joseph, **2:37–40**
Rousseau, Jean-Jacques, **2:40–42**
Skillin's interpretive essay, **2:25–32**
*See also* Declaration of Independence
Epidemic diseases, **1:**4
  of Native Americans, **1:**6–7, 40
  in New England, **1:**120
  in St. Augustine, Florida, **1:**82
Equal Employment Opportunity Commission
  (EEOC), **4:**239, 259
Equal Pay Act (1963), **4:**259
Equal Rights Amendment (ERA), **4:**257, 262, 264,
  **271,** 275
Equal Rights Party, **3:**129
Equiano, Olaudah, **1:**148, 150, 153
"Era of Good Feelings" (1817–1825), **2:**278, **3:**103,
  104, 105
Erie Canal construction, **3:**130
Eriksson, Leif, **1:**2
Espionage Act (1917), **4:**33
*An Essay Concerning Human Understanding*
  (Locke), **2:**177
*Essay on a Course of Liberal Education for Civil*
  *and Active Life* (Priestley), **2:**38
*Essex* legal case, **3:**41
Establishing Religious Freedom bill (Jefferson),
  **2:**173
Esteban (Estevánico the Moor), **1:**60, 67–68,
  **69–71**
European Age of Discovery, **1:**33
European-Native American encounters
  (1607–1637), **1:117–134**
  Kennedy/Perdisatt's interpretive essay,
    **1:120–127**
  Opechancanough, **1:129–130**
  overview, **1:117–120**
  Pequot War, **1:130–131**
  Pocahontas, **1:131–132**
  smallpox epidemic, **1:**4, 40, 120, **128–129**
  Smith, John, **1:133–134**
  Squanto (Patuxet Indian), **1:134**
European Renaissance, **1:**135
Evans, George Henry, **3:**129
Evarts, William M., **3:**271
"Evil Empire" (Soviet Union), **4:**152, 227–228
Excise Bill (1733), **2:**10
*Exposition and Protest* pamphlet (Calhoun), **3:**51

*Fail Safe* (war movie), **4:**224
Fair Employment Congress of Racial Equality
  (CORE), **4:**243
*A Faithful Narrative of the Surprising Work of God*
  (Edwards), **2:**59

Falwell, Jerry, **4:**279
Farmer's Alliance, **1:**95
Fascism, rise of, **4:**85
Faust, Jessie, **4:**58, 60
Federal Cigarette Labeling and Advertising Act
  (1965), **4:**135
Federal Communications Commission (FCC),
  **4:**199, 201, 206
Federal Deposit Insurance Corporation (FDIC),
  **4:**78, 280
Federal Emergency Relief Administration (FERA),
  **4:**77
Federal Highway Act (1956), **4:**139
Federal Housing Authority (FHA), **4:**132, 133, 139
Federal Reserve Act (1913), **4:**4
Federal Reserve Bank, **3:**125
Federal Trade Commission Act (1914), **4:**4
*Federalist Papers* (Hamilton, Madison, Jay), **2:**228,
  230
Federalist Party, **2:**174–175, 228, 229, 231, 239,
  243
  background/description, **2:278–280**
  commercial interests, **2:**263
  dissent within, **2:**269
  end of (1812), **3:**44–45
  Hamilton's intellectual guidance, **2:**79
  Jefferson/Madison opposition to, **2:**267–268,
    **3:**50
  War of 1812 opposed by, **2:**280
  Washington's leadership of, **2:**279
  XYZ Affair issues, **2:**246, 249
  *See also* Adams, John
*The Female Review* (Sampson), **2:**207
*The Feminine Mystique* (Friedan), **4:**259, 264–265,
  267–269
Feminist activism, **4:**262–263
  *See also* Women's Rights Movement
Feminist Majority, **4:267**
Fendall, Josias, **1:**233
Ferdinand V (King of Spain), **1:**4, 15–16, 55,
  73–74, 83
Ferdinand VII (King of Spain), **3:**87, 88–89
Ferraro, Geraldine, **4:**262
Ferris, George (1859–1896), **3:**255, **265–267**
Fessenden, William Pitt, **3:**231
Fifteenth Amendment (Constitution), **3:**22, 198,
  **4:**51
Fifth Monarchy Men, **1:**170
Filene, Edward, **4:**134
Fillmore, Millard, **3:**158
*Finch* British warship, **3:**56
Fine Arts Building (Columbian Exposition),
  **3:**254–255
Finney, Charles Grandison, **3:**2–3, 4, 6, 13, **17–18**

First Amendment (Constitution), **1:**180, **2:**269

First Anglo-Dutch War (1652), **1:**206

*First Blood* (war movie), **4:**228

First Church of Boston, **2:**54

First Continental Congress (1774), **2:**106, 119, 124, **129–130,** 152, 159, 178, 200, 209, 253
  *See also* Intolerable Acts

First Encounters, ca. 40,000 (BCE-CE 1492), **1:1–32**
  Algonquin, **1:12–13**
  Anasazi culture, **1:13–15**
  background information, **1:**1–4
  Columbus, Christopher, **1:15–16**
  Frank's interpretive essay, **1:**4–11
  Hopewell culture, **1:17**
  *Journal of Christopher Columbus (1492),* **1:18–32**
  Mississippian culture, **1:17–18**

First Great Awakening, **2:**66, **3:**1, 7–8
  *See also* Second Great Awakening

First Hundred Days (FDR Presidency), **4:89–90**

First Seminole War, **1:**95

"First Voyage to Roanoke" (Barlowe) excerpt, **1:115–116**

Fisk College, **4:**52

Fithian, Philip Vickers, **1:**161–163

Five Nations of the Iroquois, **1:**216–217

Flagler, Henry, **1:**96, **3:**182–183

Florentine Renaissance, **2:**143

Florida, **1:94–97**
  Caribbean refugees in, **1:**96–97
  ceding of to Great Britain, **1:**95
  colonization attempts, **1:**80, 81
  Gulf Coast discovery, **1:**74, 79, 83
  Jesuit conversions in, **1:**82
  Luna y Arellano's settlement attempts, **1:**83
  naming, by Ponce de Léon, **1:**94
  Philip II's involvement in, **1:**80–81, 83
  post-WW II population changes, **1:**96
  *See also* St. Augustine, founding of

Flynn, Elizabeth Gurley, **4:**38

Folk magic, **1:**261

Food Administration, **4:**25

Ford, Henry, **4:**133

Foreign Anti-Slavery Society, **3:**74

Forrest, Nathan Bedford, **3:**213
  *See also* Ku Klux Klan

Fort Laramie Treaty (1851), **3:**27, 234, 247

Fort Wayne, Treaty of, **3:**48

Fort Wilson riot, **2:**144–145

*Fortune* magazine, **4:**141–142

Founding Fathers (of the U.S.)
  Electoral College and distrust of, **2:**225
  engagement with Age of Reason, **2:**32

fears of "factions," **2:**267
hierarchical/controlled systems, **2:**166
role in Enlightenment of America, **2:**25, 30

Fountain of Youth, **1:**74

Fourteen Points (Wilson), **4:**26, **47–49**

Fourteenth Amendment (Constitution), **3:**198, 212, 214

Fox, George, **1:**178, 184–185
  *See also* Quakers (Society of Friends)

France
  abolitionists of, **1:**152
  Académie des Sciences of Paris, **2:**25, 28
  Canada claimed for, **1:**46
  Cavalier's land claims for, **1:**36
  D-Day invasion, **4:**106
  five-man committee rulership, **2:**240
  Franklin's mission to, **2:**25, 140–142, 147
  Jay's mission to, **2:**142, 147
  Jefferson's mission to, **2:**147
  Louis XIV, **1:**49, 249
  Louis XV, **2:**256
  Louis XVIII, **2:**257–258
  Murray's mission to, **2:**249–250
  Oswald's mission to, **2:**147
  Quadruple Alliance membership, **3:**87
  reign of Francis I, **1:**33, 45
  Revolutionary War aid to U.S., **2:**239
  Roman Catholic Church, **1:**34
  Spain vs., for North America, **1:**83
  Treaty of Alliance, **2:**142, 146
  Treaty of Paris signing, **1:**44, **2:**12, 72, 79, 87
  West Africa's wars with, **1:**137
  XYZ Affair (France), **2:**201, **239–261**
  *See also* Cartier, Jacques; Coligny, Gaspard de; Marquette, Jacques; New France

Francis I (French King), **1:**33, 37, 46

Franciscan missionaries, **1:**215

Franco-American alliance, **2:**141

Frank, Andrew, **1:**4–11

Franklin, Benjamin (1706–1790), **2:34–36**
  Adam's jealousy of, **2:**253
  American Philosophical Society founded by, **2:**29, **33–34**
  biographical information, **2:**24, **34–36,** 122
  Constitutional Convention participation, **2:**218, 220
  Declaration of Independence involvement, **2:**30, 34, 161–164, 173, 179, 182
  electricity experiments, **2:**29, 34–35
  French and Indian War involvement, **2:**75
  Junto established by, **2:**27–28, **36–37**
  mission to France, **2:**25, 140–142, 147
  Second Continental Congress participation, **2:**173

slavery opposed by, **3:**69
stance for Native Americans, **2:**35
Franklin, John Hope, **1:**135
Franks, Abigail Bilhah Levy, **2:**204
Fray Marcos, **1:**60–61, 70–71
Frederick the Great (of Prussia), **2:**139
Free Soil Party, **3:**132, 157
Free Speech Movement (UC Berkeley), **4:**225
Freedman's Bureau, **3:**212, 217, 219, 220
*Freedom of the Will* (Edwards), **2:**60
Freedom Riders, **4:**239, 245
Freedom Summer (1964), **4:**247, **252–253**
Freethinkers, **3:**7
Frelinghuysen, Theodorus (1691-ca. 1747), **2:**47, 52, **60–62**
Fremont, Gen. John C., **3:**192
French and Indian War (1756–1763), **1:**41, 44, 92–93, **2:**5, **69–92**
  Albany Plan of Union (document), **2:90–92**
  Braddock's campaign, **2:**72, 74–75, **83**
  Clarkin's interpretive essay, **2:73–81**
  Great Britain and, **2:**69–70
  guerilla warfare, **2:**71
  Kentucky rifle introduction, **2:**71
  Montcalm-Gozon, Louis-Joseph de, **2:84–85**
  overview, **2:69–73**
  Pitt, William, **2:**18, 72, 73, 78, 80, **85–87**
  problems created by, **2:**93
  Rogers, Robert, **1:**223, **2:87–89**
  segmented state banner symbol, **2:**160
  Wolfe, James, **2:**72, 78, 84–85, **89–90**
French Company of the West Indies (company), **1:**137
French in North America (1534–1701), **1:33–53**
  beaver trade, **1:**38–39
  Buade, Louis de, **1:48–50**
  Cartier, Jacques, **1:45–46**
  Champlain, Samuel de, **1:47–48**
  conversion of Indians to Catholicism, **1:**41–42
  fur trade, environmental consequences, **1:**48
  Hunt's interpretive essay, **1:37–44**
  interactions with Native Americans, **1:**35, 38, 39–40
  Joliet, Louis, **1:50–51**
  King William's War, **1:**49–50
  Marquette, Jacques, **1:51–53**
  "Middle Ground" legacy, **1:**41
  Mississippi River Valley exploration, **1:**51–52
  North America resettlement, **1:**37
  overview, **1:33–36**
  Thirty Years War, **1:**49
French Indochina, **4:**219–220
French Wars of Religion (1589), **1:**37–38
French West Indies, **2:**4

Friedan, Betty (1921–2006), **4:**259, 264–265, **267–269**
Friedman, Milton, **4:**278
Friends of Equal Rights group, **3:**129
Frobisher, Martin, **1:**100–101
Frontenac, Comte de. *See* Buade, Louis de
Frontier. *See* Closing of the frontier (ca. 1890s)
*The Frugal Housewife* (Child), **3:**80
Fuel Administration, **4:**25
Fuller, Margaret, **3:**3
Fuller, William, **1:**178
Fulton, Robert, **3:**36
Fur trade (17th/18th centuries), **1:**48
Fur Trade Wars, **1:**40, 43

Gabriel's Rebellion (1800), **1:**152
Gadsden Purchase, **3:**203, 233
Gage, Thomas, **2:**75–76, 88, 107, 118–119, 123–125, 129, 159
  *See also* Bunker Hill, Battle of (1775)
Galileo, **2:**22–23
Gallatin, Albert, **2:**246–247, 265, **3:**52
Galloway, Joseph, **2:**129
Gallup, John, **1:**119
Garay, Francisco de, **1:**55–56
Garfield, James, **3:**174
Garland, Hamlin, **3:**29
Garrison, William Lloyd, **3:**66–67, 72–73, 75
  *See also* American Anti-Slavery Society
Garvey, Marcus, **4:**55
  *See also* Universal Negro Improvement Association
Gates, Gen. Horatio, **2:**140
*The Generall Historie of Virginia, New-England, and the Summer Isles* (Smith, 1624), **1:**133–134
Geneva Accords conference, **4:**220–221
*Gentleman and Lady's Town and Country Magazine* (Murray), **2:**206
George, Henry, **3:**162
*George Fox Digg'd Out of His Burrowes* (Williams), **1:**187
George I (King of England), **2:**6, 17–18
George II (King of England), **2:**7, 9, 18, 93, 171
George III (King of England), **2:**73, 87, 93, 109, 123, 125, 130, 140, 160, **171–172**
  *See also* Declaration of Independence; Olive Branch Petition
George IV (King of England), **2:**172
Germany
  Battle of the Bulge defeat, **4: 119–120**
  Berlin blockade, **4:**171
  British attacks on, **4:**105
  Nazi-Soviet Nonaggression Pact, **4:**86, 179

response to Great Depression, **4:**85

rise of Hitler, **4:**85–86

submarine attacks by, **4:**110

weapons development, **4:** 154

World War II surrender, **4:**169

Gerry, Elbridge, **2:**222, 240–241, 243, **255–256**

Gettysburg Address (Lincoln), **2:**167, **3:**198, 207

Ghana slave trading posts, **1:**151

Ghent, Treaty of (1814), **2:**232, **3:**44, 47, 49, 54, 55, 60, 100

Ghost Dance religion (Native Americans), **3:**29, 235, **243–245,** 248, 250, 251

GI Bill, **4:**136, 137

Gilded Age (1877–1901), **3:**159, 161

Glass-Steagall Banking Act (1933), **4:**78

*The Gleaner* (Murray), **2:**206

*Glee* TV show, **4:**204

*The Glorious Cause* (Middlekauff), **2:**165

Glorious Revolution in America (1688–1689), **1:**168, **233–253**

  Andros, Sir Edmund, **1:246–247**

  Bacon's Rebellion, **1:247–248**

  English Bill of Rights (document), **1:251–253**

  King William's War, **1:248–250**

  Leisler, Jacob, **1:**236–237, **250–251**

  Locke's justification for, **2:**162

  origins of, **1:**235, 247, **2:**6–7

  overview, **1:233–237**

  Swiney's interpretive essay, **1:237–245**

Gold and silver mining, **3:**27, 233

Good, Sarah, **1:**256, 258, 264

*Good-Bye Columbus* (Roth), **4:**138

Good Neighbor Policy, **4:**85–86

Gorbachev, Mikhail, **4:**152, 174, 176, 277, 281–282

Gordon, William, **2:**149

Gorgas, Gen. Josiah, **3:**196

Gorton, Samuel, **1:**175

Gosnold, Captain Bartholomew, **1:**101, 112

"The Gospel of Wealth" (Carnegie), **3:**177

Goulaine de Laudonnière, René, **1:**81, 84

Gould, Jay, **3:**163

Gradualism, **3:**71–72

Graeme, Elizabeth, **2:**28

Graham, Sylvester, **3:**65

Grand Itinerants, **2:**54

Grant, Gen. Ulysses S., **3:**95, 143, 192, 201–202, 207, 215, 222, 223

Grasse, Admiral François de, **2:**154

Great American Desert, **3:**25

Great Awakening (ca. 1730s-1760), **1:**208, 221, **2:45–67**

  Congregationalists ("Old Lights"), **2:**48

  controversy created during, **2:**47–48

  Edwards, Jonathan, **2:**51, **59–60**

Frelinghuysen, Theodorus, **2:**51, **60–62**

  Halfway Covenant (1662), **2:**45, 51

  intellectual side of, **2:**48–49

  Kramer's interpretive essay, **2:49–57**

  "Old Lights"/"New Lights," **2:**54–55

  origins of, **2:**51

  overview, **2:45–49**

  pietism/revivalism during, **2:**46–47, 49

  Presbyterianism, **2:**48–49, 52

  slave religion during, **2:62–63**

  Stoddard, Solomon, **2:**45, 51

  Tennent, GIlbert, **2:63–65**

  Whitefield, George, **2:65–66**

  women in, **2:66–67**

  *See also* Religious traditions

Great Britain

  abolitionists of, **1:**152

  Atlantic Charter, **4:**110

  attacks on Germany, **4:**105

  capture of Washington, D.C., **3:57–58**

  Coercive Acts (1774), **2:**104

  Currency Act (1751), **2:**4, 99

  Declaratory Act, **2:**95, 104

  Florida ceded by Spain to, **1:**95

  French and Indian War and, **2:**69–70

  Intolerable Acts, **2:**123

  Jay's Treaty, **2:**147, 239, 251

  losses at Bunker Hill, **2:**153–154

  Madison's sanctions against, **3:**25–26

  mercantilist policies, **2:**3

  Molasses Act (1733), **2:**4, 5, 8, 94

  North American takeover by, **1:**74

  occupation of Oregon territory, **3:**139

  Orders-in-Council decrees, **3:**41

  Proclamation of 1763, **2:**93–94, 97

  Quadruple Alliance membership, **3:**87

  Quartering Act (1765), **2:**102

  salutary neglect policy, **2:**70

  Seven Years' War (with France), **2:**71

  Sugar Act (1764), **2:**5, 93–94, 99

  Townshend Duties (1776), **2:**104

  Treaty of Alliance, **2:**142, 146

  Treaty of Ghent, **3:**44

  Treaty of Paris signing, **1:**44, **2:**12, 72, 79, 87

  war with Holland, **1:**205

  Weber-Ashburton Treaty, **1:**152–153

  World War II involvement, **4:**110

  Yorktown, Battle of, **2:**154

  *See also* Stamp Act (1765)

Great Commoner. *See* Pitt, William

Great Depression (1929-ca. 1939), **4:**39, 56, **75–103**

  Agricultural Adjustment Administration, **4:**82–83, 84

events leading up to, **4:**80
First Hundred Days (FDR Presidency), **4:89–90**
Greenspan's interpretive essay, **4:79–87**
Hoover, Herbert, **4:**76–77, 79–80, **90–92**
Long, Huey "Kingfish," **4:**79, 83–84, **92–93**
National Recovery Administration, **4:**78, 82, 84
overview, **4:75–79**
post-WW I origins, **4:**75
Reconstruction Finance Corporation, **4:**76–77, 81
Social Security Act, **4:**84
stock market crash, **4:**75, 80, **102–103**
suburban housing boom, **4:**132
Works Progress Administration, **4:**78, 79, 84
*See also* New Deal; Roosevelt, Franklin D.
Great Migration (of African-Americans, 1920), **2:**145, 53, 54
Great Plains territory, **3:**29–30
Great Society (Lyndon Johnson), **4:**234
Great Swamp Fight, 23, **1:**215, 217–218, 223, 225
Great Treaty of Montreal, **1:**41
Great War for Empire, **2:**71
*See also* Seven Years' War
Green, Nancy, **3:**261
Green Party USA (political party), **4:**146
Greene, Gen. Nathaniel, **2:**202
Greenleaf, Stephen, **2:**97
Greensboro Four activists, **4:**141
Greensboro (North Caroline) Sit-Ins (1960), **4:251–252**
Greenspan, Anders, **4:79–87**
Greenwich Village (New York City), **4:**59
Grenville, George, **2:**73, 93, 98
Grenville, Richard, **1:**101, 114
Grimké, Angelina and Sarah, **3:**73, 78
Guadalupe Hidalgo, Treaty of, **3:**141, 143, 149, 154, 190, 233
Guerilla warfare (French and Indian War), **2:**71
Guilford Courthouse, Battle of, **2:**146–147
Gulf War (1990), **4:**229

Hague, Laura, **4:5–13**
Hague Peace Palace (Netherlands), **3:**178
Haitian Revolution (1791), **1:**152
Hakluyt, Richard, **1:**101
Hale, John, **1:**265
Halfway Covenant (1662), **2:**45, 51, 55
Hall of Manufactures (Columbian Exposition), **3:**256
Hamilton, Alexander, **2:**25, 174, 219, **226–229,** 239
Bank of the United States actions, **3:**123
commercial interests, **2:**263
*Federalist Papers,* **2:**228, 230

hatred of/duel with Aaron Burr, **2:**273
intellectual guidance of Federalists, **2:**79
letter attacking John Adams, **2:**250
opposition to Murray's French mission, **2:**249–250
"The Stand" newspaper, **2:**245
warrior ambitions of, **2:**248
*See also Federalist Papers;* Federalist Party; Yorktown, Battle of (1781)
Hampton Institute, **4:**52
Hancock, John, **2:**35, 102, 164, 178
Handy, Moses P., **3:**258
Hanikuh (Zuni leader), **1:**70
Hanoverian monarchy, **2:**6–7, 8, 15–17, 73, 85–86
Hansen, Chadwick, **1:**261
"The Harlem Dancer" (McKay), **4:**59
Harlem Renaissance (1917–1935), **4:51–73**
Beeby's interpretive essay, **4:56–63**
Hughes, Langston, **4:**55, 56–58, **68–69**
Hurston, Zora Neale, **4:**57, 58, **69–70**
Johnson, James Weldon, **4:**58, 59, **70–72**
McKay, Claude, **4:**54, 57, 59, **72–73**
NAACP, **4:**13, 52, 58–60, 71–72
overview, **4:51–56**
*Harlem Shadows* (McKay), **4:**59
Harper's Ferry raid (1859), **3:**191
*Harriet, the Moses of Her People* (Bradford), **3:**83
Harrison, William Henry, **3:**43–44, 46, 48
Hartford Convention (1814), **3:**44–45, 50, 52, **58–60**
Hartford Treaty, **1:**203
Harvard College, **2:**24, 26, 53, 116, 126, 205, 241
Harvey, William, **2:**22–23
Hat Act (1732), **2:**3
Hatch Act (1939), **4:**78
Hay, John, **3:**275–276, 278
Hayden, Tom, **4:**140
Hayes, Rutherford, **3:**211, 215, 223, 225
Haymarket Riot (1886, Chicago), **4:**7
Hays, John, **2:**202
Hays, Mary Ludwig, **2:202–203**
Haywood, Bill, **4:**38
Hazel Bishop cosmetics, TV advertising, **4:**205
Head Start program, **4:**234
Hearst, William Randolph, **3:**274, 276, **283–285**
Henderson, Francis, **3:**12
Henry, Patrick, **2:**102–103, 117, 129, 226, 230, **3:**69
Henry II (French King), **1:**33
Henry IV (French King), **1:**34, 36, 47
Henry VII (French King), **1:**167, 172
Henry VII (King of England), **1:**99, 111
Henry VIII (King of England), **1:**100, 167–168, 172, 176, 234

Hepburn Act (1906), **4:**2, 18

Heritage Foundation, **4:**278

Hernández de Córdoba, Francisco, **1:**75

Hewes, George, account of Boston Tea Party (1773), **2:136–138**

Hiacoomes (Native American), **1:**121, 124–126

*Hidden Persuaders* (Packard), **4:**140

Higher law, **2:**168

Highway Revenue Act, **4:**279

Hill, Anita, **4:**263, 265–266

*Hill Street Blues* (TV show), **4:**202

"Hippie" movement, **4:**141

*The History and Present State of Discoveries relating to Vision, Light and Colours* (Priestley), **2:**39

*The History and Present State of Electricity with Original Experiments* (Priestley), **2:**38

*The History of all the Branches of Experimental Philosophy* (Priestley), **2:**39

*A History of New England with Particular Reference to the Denomination of Christians Called Baptists* (Backus), **3:**16

*History of the American Revolution* (Ramsay), **2:**149

*The History of the Colony of Massachusetts Bay* (Thomas Hutchinson), **2:**108

*History of the Standard Oil Company* (Tarbell), **3:**184

*History of the United States* (Bancroft), **1:**261

*History of the World* (Raleigh), **1:**113

Hitler, Adolf, **4:**85–86, 181, 242

Ho Chi Minh (Vietnam leader), **4:**219–220, 224

Hohokam culture, **1:**14

Holy Alliance
   Latin America ambitions, **3:**92–93
   Monroe's warnings against, **3:**94

Holy Roman Emperor, **1:**83

*Home to Harlem* (McKay), **4:**57

Homestead Act (1862), **3:**28, 196, 236

Homestead Strike (1892, Pennsylvania), **4:**7

Hong, Stephen H., **3:**25

Hoover, Herbert, **4:**76–77, 79–80, **90–92**
   presidency of, **4:**79–80
   Reconstruction Finance Corporation, **4:**76–77
   Roosevelt vs. (presidential election), **4:**77

Hopewell culture, **1:**17

Hopi Indians ("Peaceful People"), **1:**68, **71–73**

Hopkins, Lemuel, **2:**149

Hopkinson, Francis, **2:**148

Horseshoe Bend, Battle of, **3:**47

House Committee on Un-American Activities, **4:**182

House of Burgesses (Virginia), **1:**157, **2:**102

House of Commons, **1:**176

Boston Tea Party role, **2:**118

Grenville's role, **2:**100–101, 103

Newcastle's role, **2:**15, 16–18

Pitt's role, **2:**85–86, 103

repeal of Stamp Act, Declaratory bill, **2:**104

Walpole's role, **2:**9–10

Houston, Charles, **4:**237

Houston, Sam, **3:**138

Howard (Lord of Effingham), **1:**236

Howard University, **4:**52, 54

Howe, Elizabeth, **1:**258

Howe, Gen. Sir William, **2:**153–154

Howells, William Dean, **3:**272

Hudson, Henry, **1:**193, 197–198

Hughes, Langston, **4:**55, 56–57, 56–58, 58, **68–69**

Huguenots, **1:**34, 37, 81, 84

Hull House (Jane Addams), **3:**170

*Hulu* Web site, **4:**204

Humphreys, David, **2:**149

Hungarian Revolution, **4:**175

Hunt, Capt. Thomas, **1:**118

Hunt, John M., **1:37–44**

Hunt, Richard, **3:**255

Hunters and gatherers, **1:**1, 5

Huron nation, **1:**38, 47

Hurston, Zora Neale, **4:**57, 58, **69–70**

Hutchinson, Anne, **1:**174–175, **183–184**, 263, **2:**49–50

Hutchinson, Thomas, **2:**35, 90, 95, **107–108,** 121–12

Hutchinson, William, **1:**174–175

"Hydra of corruption" (of Biddle), **3:**112

ICBMs (intercontinental ballistic missiles), **4:**154

"If We Must Die" (McKay), **4:**54

Igbo language (Africa), **1:**148

Immigration Reduction League (1894), **3:**239

Independent Treasury Act (1846), **3:**154

Indian War (1675–1676), **1:**247

Indians. *See* Native Americans

Indigenous peoples
   Cabeza de Vaca and, **1:**57
   early North America, **1:**1
   Ponce de Léon confrontations with, **1:**75

Industrial, northern states, **3:**65

Industrial Revolution (ca. 1860s-1890s), **3:159–184**
   American Federation of Labor, **3:**162
   Bell, Alexander Graham, **3:173–175**
   Carnegie, Andrew, **3:175–178**
   child labor laws, **3:**164–165
   Edison's inventions, **3:**159–160
   growth of cities, **3:**165–167, 171
   Knights of Labor (labor union), **3:**161–162

labor practices/unions, **3:**161, 168, 170, **178–179**

meat packing plants, **3:**160

Morgan, J. P., **3:179–181**

onset of (1794), **1:**151

overview, **3:159–163**

railroads, **3:**165, 175

Rockefeller, John D., **3:181–184**

steel industry, **3:**160–161, 163, 171

women's movements, **3:**170–171

Woods' interpretive essay, **3:163–171**

World's Columbian Exposition and, **3:**257, 263

Industrial Workers of the World (IWW), **4:**34, **38–39**

*The Influence of Sea Power upon History* (Mahan), **3:**272

Ingoldesby, Maj. Robert, **1:**251

"Innocent Blood Crying to God from the Streets of Boston" pamphlet (Sam Adams), **2:**116

Intercolonial congress. *See* First Continental Congress (1774)

Intermediate Nuclear Force (INF) treaty (1987), **4:**152, 174, 277, 281–282

International Campaign to Ban Landmines, **4:**229

Internment camps, of Japanese, in U.S., **4:**109, 114

Interstate Commerce Act (1887), **3:**162, 163

Interstate Commerce Commission (ICC), **3:**162, **4:**2, 18

Intolerable Acts, **2:**123, 159

Iran, **4:**169

Iran-Contra Scandal, **4:**276, **288**

Iron Act (1750), **2:**3

Iroquois nations, **1:**38

Irvine, Col. William, **2:**202

Isabella I (Queen of Spain), **1:**4, 15–16, 83

Italian expeditions to America, **1:**99

*See also* Cabot, John (Giovanni Caboto)

Izard, George, **3:**55


Jackson, Andrew (1767–1845)

admission to bar, **3:**125

Bank of America favored by, **3:**111–112

Battle of New Orleans actions, **3:**110

biographical data, **3:125–128**

"Kitchen Cabinet" of, **3:**126

presidency of, **3:**114, 116, 124

Texas annexation, **3:**138

Trail of Tears against Cherokees, **3:**127

War of 1812 participation, **3:**23–24, 45, 47, 54, 92, **3:**109

Jacksonian Democracy (1828–1840), **3:109–135**

Bank of the United States, **3:**111–112, **122–125**

Bank War, **3:**129

codification of common law, **3:**119–120

Equal Rights Party, **3:**129

Free Soil Party, **3:**132

Friends of Equal Rights group, **3:**129

Jackson, Andrew, **3:125–128**

Locofoco Party, **3:128–129**

Mackey's interpretive essay, **3:113–121**

Nullification Document (Jackson), **3:134–135**

overview, **3:109–113**

Van Buren, Martin, **3:129–132**

Whig Party, **2:**278, **3:**67, 81, **132–134**

Workingman's Party, **3:**128

Jacobite rebellion (1715), **2:**7, 249

Jacobs, George, Sr., **1:**258

Jacobsen, Capt. Cornelius, **1:**199

James (Duke of York), **1:**239

James, Henry, **3:**272

James, William, **2:**60

James I (King of England), **1:**101, 137, 169, 170, 196, **2:**112

James II (King of England), **1:**234, 239, 249, 250, **2:**6–7

Jamestown

arrival of slaves, **1:**136

founding (1607), **1:**82, **112,** 121

naming of, **1:**101

Opechancanough attack on, **1:**130

Tercentenary Exposition, **1:**100

Japan

atomic bombing of, **4:**107, 116, 150, 154, 159

internment order (1942), **4:**109, 114, **128–129**

Pearl Harbor attack, **4:**106, 107, 110–111, **126–127**

war with China, **4:**106

Jarratt, Devereux, **2:**55–56

Jay, John, **2:**129, 142, 147, **3:**36

*See also Federalist Papers*

Jay's Treaty (1795), **2:**147, 239, 251

Jefferson, Thomas, **1:**145–146, 160, **3:**142, 190

Adams, John, association with, **2:**174

American Philosophical Society activities, **2:**176

anti-Federalist stance, **2:**263

anti-slavery document signing, **2:**221

anti-slavery stance, **3:**70

Bible edited by, **2:**26

"Bill for Establishing Religious Freedom," **2:**57

Committees of Correspondence and, **2:**117

Continental Congress participation, **2:**173, 174

Danbury Baptist Association speech, **1:**171

Declaration of Independence role, **2:**162, 164, **172–176**

1800 presidential election, **2:**263

election of 1800 viewpoint, **2:**266–267

election to vice-presidency, **2:**28

embargo on East India Company, **2:**129

*Essex* legal case, **3:**41
Establishing Religious Freedom bill, **2:**173
Federalists opposed by, **2:**267
as Founding Father, **2:**25
higher law and, **2:**168
Kentucky Resolution, **2:**175, 247, 269
*Letter on Science and the Perfectibility of Men,*
    **2:43–44**
Louisiana Purchase viewpoint, **2:**266
mission to France, **2:**147
Monroe's studies with, **3:103**
More General Diffusion of Knowledge Bill,
    **2:**173
*Notes on the State of Virginia,* **2:**30, 174, **3:**169
presidency of, **2:**273, **3:**21
Quasi-War affair viewpoint, **2:**250
*Report of Government for the Western Territory,*
    **2:**174
resolutions penned by, **2:**247
*A Summary View of the Rights of British
    America,* **2:**164, 172
vice-presidency of, **2:**265
Virginia State of Religious Freedom, **2:**172
Washington's association with, **2:**174
*See also* Louisiana Purchase
*The Jeffersonian Image in the American Mind*
    (Peterson), **3:**31
Jenkin's Ear, War of, **2:**9
Jennings, William Sherman, **1:**96
Jesuits (Society of Jesus)
    Beaver Wars and, **1:**40
    Canadian settlements, **1:**38
    college in Quebec, **1:**50
    conversion of Native Americans, **1:**36, 40,
        42–43, 215
    conversions in Florida, **1:**82
    New France missions, **1:**42
Jewish people, **1:**170, 175
Jim Crow Laws, **4:**54, 241–242
John Brown's Final Statement to Virginia Court,
    **3:84–85**
John I (King of England), **1:**167
Johnson, Andrew, **3:**95
    biographical background, **3:226–228**
    Black Codes enactment, **3:**213
    Reconstruction ideas of, **3:**211–212, 217–218
    resistance to Fourteenth Amendment, **3:**212
Johnson, James Weldon, **4:**58, 59, **70–72**
Johnson, Lyndon, **4:**135, 221–222, 233–234,
    239–240
Johnson, Sir William, **2:**75, 87–88
Joint Congressional Committee on Atomic Energy
    (JCAE), **4:**150
Joliet, Louis, **1:50–51**

Jones, Mary Harris (Mother Jones), **4:**38
*Journal of Christopher Columbus (1492),* **1:**18–32
"A Journal of the Times" newspaper series, **2:**194
Journals of Lewis and Clark, **3:38–39**
*A Journey in the Back Country* (Olmsted), **3:**267
*A Journey in the Seaboard Slave States* (Olmsted),
    **3:**267
*A Journey through Texas* (Olmsted), **3:**267
Judiciary Act (1789), **2:**266
Judiciary Act (1801), **2:**265
*The Jungle* (Sinclair), **4:**2, 20

Kalman, Laura, **2:**168–169
Kansas-Nebraska Act, **3:**28
Karlsen, Carol, **1:**261
Katsinas (ceremonial spirits), **1:**71
Kelly, Abby, **3:**74
Kennan, George, **4:**170, 182
Kennedy, Anthony M., **4:**275, 280
Kennedy, John F., **3:**242, **4:**172–173, 202, 208, 210,
    220, 259
Kennedy, Rick, **1:103–109, 120–127, 2:163–170**
Kennedy, Robert F., **4:**234
Kentucky Resolution (Jefferson), **2:**175, 247, **2:**247,
    269, **3:**190
Kentucky rifle introduction, **2:**71
Kerber, Linda, **2:**189, 196
Kerner Commission Report, **4:**240
Kerry, John, **4:**229
*A Key into the Language of America* (Williams),
    **1:**186
Khrushchev, Nikita, **4:**172–173
Kieft, Willem, **1:**201–202
King, Martin Luther, Jr., **2:**169, 225, 239, 244,
    245–246, **253–255,** 264
King George's War (1743–1748), **2:**73, 87
King Philip's War (1675–1676), **1:**186, **213–231, 263**
    Bacon's Rebellion association with, **1:**247
    Church, Benjamin, **1:223–224**
    defeat of Algonquins, **1:**220–221
    Great Swamp Fight, **1:**215, 217–218, 223, 225
    Massasoit Peace Treaty (document), **1:230–231**
    Metacom (ca. 1638–1676), **1:224–226**
    Mohawk Indians and, **1:**215
    Narragansett Indians and, **1:**213–214
    Narragansetts, **1:226–227**
    overview, **1:213–216**
    Powhatan confederacy depopulation, 215–216
    Rowlandson, Mary, **1:227–228**
    Savage, Thomas Savage, **1:**214
    Siry's interpretive essay, **1:216–222**
    triggering event, **1:**223
    Wampanoag Indians, **1:**126, 214, 217, 223,
        **228–230**

King William's War (1689–1697), **1:**49–50, **248–250, 2:**73

King's Mountain (NC) battle, **2:**146

Kinnersley, Ebenezer, **2:**29

Kinsey, Alfred, **4:**257

Kipling, Rudyard, **3:**273

Kissinger, Henry, **4:**173, 222, 282

"Kitchen Cabinet" (of Jackson), **3:**126

Kiva ceremony (Hopis), **1:**71

Knights of Labor (labor union), **3:**161–162

Knox, Hugh, **2:**226

Knox, Lucy Flucker, **2:**195

Kongo Empire slave trading posts, **1:**151

Korean War, **4:**171, 175, **190–193,** 202, 219

Kramer, Carl E., **2:49–57**

Kramer, Heinrich, **1:**259

Krol, Bastiaen Jansen, **1:**194

Ku Klux Klan (KKK), **3:**213, 221

La Farge, Oliver, **1:**72

La Follette, Robert "Fighting Bob" (1855–1925), **4:15–16**

Labor practices/unions, Industrial Revolution era, **3:**161, 168, 170, **178–179**

Lachine Massacre, **1:**249

Ladies Association of Philadelphia, **2:**145

"A Lady's Adieu to Her Tea-Table" poem, **2:**194

Lake George, Battle of, **2:**75

Lamb, John, **2:**108

Laos, **4:**219

Larsen, Nella, **4:**58

Latin America, **1:**96, **2:**2

anti-Napoleonic movements, **3:**87

Franco-Spanish military expedition, **3:**89

Holy Alliance interest in, **3:**92–93

progressive revolutionaries, **2:**166

Roosevelt's involvement with, **3:**96

slave labor colonies in, **1:**156

Spanish-American War origination, **3:**274

U.S. protection for, **3:**104

U.S./Great Britain's interests, **3:**88, 91

*See also* Bolívar, Simón; Monroe Doctrine

Latin Christian Church, **1:**167

Laurens, Henry, **2:**147

Lawrence, William Van Duzer, **4:**131

Lay, Benjamin, **3:**69

League of Nations, **4:**16, 25–26, 26, **39–40,** 85

Lecompton Constitution, **3:**191

*Lectures on History and General Policy* (Priestley), **2:**38

*Lectures on Revivals* (Finney), **3:**18

*Lectures on Systematic Theology* (Finney), **3:**18

Lee, Arthur, **2:**140

Lee, Gen. Charles, **2:**202

Lee, Gen. Robert E., 194, 201–202, 207

Lee, Richard Henry, **2:**161, 163, **182, 253**

*See also* Resolution Proposing a Declaration of Independence

Lee, Robert E., **3:**143

LeFeber, Walter, **3:**240

Legal Defense Fund (NAACP), **4:**237

*Legal Realism at Yale, 1927–1960* (Kalman), **2:**168–169

Legal Tender Act (1862), **3:**197

Leibniz, Gottfried Wilhelm, **2:**177

Leisler, Jacob, **1:**236–237, 241–242, **250–251**

Lend-Lease military aid bill, **4:**105, 178

*Leopard* (British ship), **3:**42–43

*A Letter Concerning Toleration* (Locke), **2:**177

*Letter on Science and the Perfectibility of Men* (Jefferson), **2:43–44**

*Letters and Sketches of Sermons* (Murray), **2:**206

*Letters from an American Farmer* (Crevecoeur), **3:**238–239

Levitt, Alfred and William, **4:**132–134, 136–138

Levittowns (NY, NJ, PA), **4:**132–134, 136–137, **144**

Lewis, David Levering, **4:**59

Lewis, Meriwether, **3:**25, 35

*See also* Lewis and Clark expedition

Lewis and Clark expedition (1803–1806), **3:35–36**

"Corps of Discovery" exploration, **3:**25, 35

journal excerpts, **3:38–39**

Sacajawea's assistance, **3:**34, **37–38**

York Clark's assistance, **3:33–35**

Lexington and Concord, Battle of,, **2:**30, 35, 124–125, 130, 131–132, 153, 159, 171, 172

*The Liberator* (First Edition) excerpt, **3:**66–67, 72, 78, **83–84**

Liberia, **3:**65–66

Liberty Bonds, **4:**32

Liberty Party, **3:**65, 67, 75, 79, **81–82**

Light Brigade, **3:**57

Limerick, Patricia Nelson, **3:**241

Limited Test Ban Treaty (1963), **4:**156

Lincoln, Abraham, **1:**77, **3:204–207**

Acts of Confiscation, **3:**193

Amnesty and Reconstruction Proclamation, **3:**211

appointment of Johnson, **3:**226

assassination of, **3:**207, 211, 218

on cause of Civil War, **1:**160

Democratic Party vs., **3:**185, 206

1860 presidential election, **3:**191

Emancipation Proclamation, **1:**160, **3:**194, 195, 196, 206, 216

Gettysburg Address, **2:**167, **3:**198, 207

inauguration (1861), **3:**192

Mexican-American War opposition, 3:205
Republican abolitionist support, 3:194
rivalry with Cartwright, 3:16
Ten Percent Plan, 3:211
thoughts on Declaration of Independence, 2:167
Lindbergh, Charles, 4:134
Linnaeus, Carl, 2:29
*Linnet* British warship, 3:56
*Little Belt* (American vessel), 3:44
Little Big Horn, Battle of, 3:234, 245
Livingston, Robert R. (1746–1813), 2:173, 3:22, **36–37**, 104
Lloyd, Henry D., 3:163
Locke, Alain, 4:58
Locke, John, 2:59, 143, 162, **176–178**
    See also Declaration of Independence
Lockwood, W. J., 4:139
Locofoco Party, **3:128–129**
Lodge, Henry Cabot, 3:271, 279
Logan, James, 2:25
Long, Huey "Kingfish," 4:79, 83–84
Long Island (NY) suburbanization, 4:132–134
*Looking Backward* (Bellamy), 3:163
Lord Dunmore's Proclamation (document, 1776), **2:156–157**
Lords of Trade (1675), 1:239
Lords of Trade and Plantations, 1:246
Los Alamos, New Mexico (Manhattan Project), 4:149
Los Angeles Riots (1992), 4:247, **256**
Louis XIV (French King), 1:49, 249
Louis XV (French King), 2:256
Louis XVIII (French King), 2:257–258
Louisiana Purchase (1803), 2:266, **3:21–39**, 233
    Clark, York, **3:33–35**
    initial steps, 3:24
    Journals of Lewis and Clark, **3:38–39**
    land acquisitions, 3:26
    Lewis and Clark expedition, 3:35–36
    Livingston, Robert R., **3:36–37**
    overview, **3:21–24**
    role of Jefferson, 3:21
    Sacajawea, **3:37–38**
    Siry's interpretive essay, **3:24–31**
Louisiana Purchase Exposition (1904, St. Louis), 3:267
Louisiana Territory, 2:175, 251
L'Ouverture, Toussaint, 2:266, 3:21–22, 261
Loyola, Ignatius, 1:52
Luna y Arellano, Tristán de, 1:80, 83
Lundy's Lane, Battle of (1814), 3:154
Luther, Martin, 1:83–84, 167, 172, 2:22
Lutheranism, 1:83–84, 2:50
Lyon, Matthew, 2:242, 269

Mabila, Battle of (Florida), 1:94
MacArthur, Douglas, 4:81–82, **122–125**
MacArthur, Gen. Arthur, 3:275
MacArthur, Gen. Douglas, 4:81–82
Mackey, Thomas A.
    Jacksonian Democracy, **3:113–121**
    Stamp Act, **2:96–105**
    surrender of New Amsterdam, **1:197–205**
Macomb, Alexander, 3:55, 56
Macon's Bill No. 2, 3:43
Madison, James
    Federalists opposed by, 2:267, 3:50
    resolutions penned by, 2:247
    role in War of 1812, 3:45
    sanctions against Great Britain, 3:25–26
    Treaty of Ghent accepted by, 3:51
    view of federal government, 3:123
    Virginia Resolution, 2:247, 269
Madison, James (1751–1836), 2:217, 218, 227, **229–232**
Magazines, American Revolution era, 2:188–189
Magic Electric Button (Columbian Exposition), 3:259
*Magnalia Christi Americana* (Cotton Mather), 1:267
Mahan, Alfred Thayer, 3:272, 280
*Main-Travelled Roads* (Garland), 3:29
Malcolm, Pulteney, 3:57
Malcolm X, 4:247
Malenkov, George, 4:175
Manhattan Project (atomic bomb), 4:149, 161
Manifest destiny (1840s), 3:46
Manila Bay, Battle of, 3:283
Manufactures and Liberal Arts Building (Columbian Exposition), 3:261
Manufacturing Acts, 2:3
Mao Zedong, 4:171, 182–183
*Marbury v. Madison,* (Supreme Court decision), 2:265–266
March to the Sea (Sherman, 1864), **3:207–208**
Marcos de Niza, Fray. *See* Fray Marcos
Marcy, William L., 3:117–118
Marital rape, criminalization of, 4:260–261
Markham, Sir Clements Robert, 1:18
    See also *Journal of Christopher Columbus (1492)*
Marquette, Jacques, 1:36, **51–53**
Marshall, George, 4:170, 182–183
Marshall, John, 2:240, 250, 266, 3:25, 70
Marshall, Thurgood, 4:237, 242
Marshall Plan, 4:115, 170–171, 175, 181
Martha's Vineyard (Massachusetts), 1:117, 125
Martial law, 3:214
Martin, Joseph Plumb, 2:196

Martin, Susannah, **1:**258, 264

Marx, Karl (Marxism), **3:**169–170, **4:**177, 180

Mary II (English monarch), **1:**236, 241, 243, 247

Mary III (English monarch), **1:**178

*The Mary Tyler Moore Show* (TV show), **4:**202

*Maryland Act of Toleration* (Lord Baltimore, 1649), **1:189–192**

*M\*A\*S\*H* (TV show), **4:**202, 204

Massachusetts Bay Colony
    Court of Oyer and Terminer, **1:**257, 262
    founding by Puritans, **1:**113
    Gorton's expulsion from, **1:**175
    growth phase, **1:**102
    Hutchinson's expulsion from, **1:**183
    Phips' service to, **1:**249, 257, 258, 263, 271
    Plymouth Colony merge with, **1:**235–236
    Puritan founding of, **1:**113, 238
    ruling by self-proclaimed "saints," **1:**168
    separation of church and state, **1:**264
    Stone's expulsion from, **1:**119
    structure/purpose of, **1:**107
    Williams's expulsion from, **1:**173, 187

Massachusetts Bay Company, **1:**10, 102–105, 130–131, 168, **2:**50

Massachusetts Government Act, **2:**118

Massachusetts Justice Act, **2:**123

Massasoit Peace Treaty (document), **1:230–231**

Matanzas (Place of Killing), in Florida, **1:**81

Mateo Sagasta, Praxedes, **3:**276

Mather, Cotton (son of Increase), **1:**123, 217, 260, 265, **266–268**, **2:**50

Mather, Increase (father of Cotton), **1:**258, **268–269**

Mattox, Henry E., **2:119–126**

Maximilian I (Spanish Emperor), **1:**83, 95

Mayhew, Thomas, **1:**117, 124–126

McCain, John, **4:**229

*McCall's* women's magazines, **4:**258

McCarthy, Eugene, **4:**234

McCarthy, Joseph, **1:**259, 262, **4:**150, 160, 171, 182, 202

McCarthyism, **4:**150, 171, 258

McCauley, Mary Ludwig Hays, **2:**196

McClellan, Gen. George B., **3:**156, 194, 201, 206, 229

McDougall, Alexander, **2:**108

McFarlane, Robert, **4:**276

McGinniss, Joe, **4:**210

McGovern, George, **4:**226

McGready, James, **3:**8, **18–19**

McHenry, James, **2:**229, 244, 250

McKay, Claude, **4:**54, 57, 59, **72–73**

McKinley, William, **3:**96, 274, 276–277, 279, **285–287**, **4:**1

*McLaurin v. Oklahoma* (Supreme Court decision), **4:**243

McLuhan, Marshall, **4:**207

McNamara, Robert, **4:**220

Measles epidemic, **1:**4

Meat Inspection Act (1906), **4:**2, 18

Meat packing plants, **3:**160

*The Medium, or A Happy Teaparty* play (Murray), **2:**206

Megapolensis, Johannes, **1:**208

*Memorable Providences, Relating to Witchcraft and Possessions* (Cotton Mather), **1:**267

*A Memorial Relating to the Kennebeck Indians* (Sewall), **1:**272

Mendoza, Antonio de, **1:**57

Menéndez de Avilés, Pedro, **1:**81, 85
    colony maintained by, **1:**87–88
    defeat of French in St. Augustine, **1:**86
    expedition to Florida, **1:**81, 85
    post-death succession of, **1:**90
    St. Augustine christened by, **1:**83, 85

Mennonites, **2:**50

Mercantilism, **2:14**
    Acts of Trade (1660), **2:**7
    colonies development of, **2:**1–2
    described, **2:**14
    Great Britain's policies, **2:**3
    Hat Act (1732), **2:**3
    Iron Act (1750), **2:**3
    Molasses Act (1733), **2:**4, 5
    Sugar Act (1764), **2:**5
    Woolens Act (1699), **2:**3
    *See also* Navigation Acts

Meredith, James, **4:**245

Metacom (ca. 1638–1676), **1:**217, **224–226**
    attack of camp of, **1:**219
    English humiliation of, **1:**216
    murder of, **1:**219
    poisoning of brother of, **1:**124
    war with Puritans, **1:**126, 217

Methodism, **2:**47, 53, 56, 65, 150, **3:**1, 2
    *See also* Wesley, John

Mexican-American War, **3:**132, **137–158**
    Buena Vista, Battle of, **3:**138, 140–141, 144, **152**, 157, 203
    Confederate involvement, **3:**143
    Guadalupe Hidalgo, Treaty of, **3:**141, 143, 149, 154, 190
    overview, **3:**137–141
    Polk, James, **3:**152–154
    Rakestraw's interpretive essay, **3:141–149**
    Scott, Winfield, **3:154–156**
    Taylor, Zachary, **3:**132, 133, **156–158**
    Wilmot Proviso (document), **3:158**

Mexico
   Aztec Empire, **1:**98
   gold and silver resources, **1:**140
   independence won from Spain, **3:**137
"Middle Ground" legacy (French colonialism),
   **1:**41
Middle Passage (of slave trade journey), **1:**149–
   150, 158
Middle Plantation Treaty (1677), **1:**248
Middlekauff, Robert, **2:**165
Midway, Battle of, **4:**106
Military Affairs Committee, **4:**42
Military Reconstruction Act of March 1867, **3:**214
Miller, Perry, **1:**260
Mining phase of Western settlement, **3:**233–234
Minor, Elizabeth Montague, **2:**203–204
Minuit, Peter, **1:**193, **210–211**
   New Netherland Colony service, **1:**193, 199, 200
   purchase of Manhattan Island, **1:**209
   Swedish South Company service, **1:**195
Mississippi Rifles Unit (Civil War), **3:**203
Mississippi River Valley exploration, **1:**50–52
Mississippian culture, **1:17–18**
Missouri Compromise (1820), **1:**160, **3:**27–28,
   148, 191–192
*Missouri ex rel. Gaines v. Canada,* **4:**242
"Model of Christian Charity" essay (Winthrop),
   **1:**103, 104, 106, 108, 109
*Modern Woman: The Lost Sex* (Farnham), **4:**257
Mogollon culture, **1:**14
Mohawk Indians, **1:**118, 215
Mohawk tribe (of Iroquois nation), **1:**42
Mohegan tribe, **1:**227
Moki (Moqui) Indians. *See* Hopi Indians
   ("Peaceful People")
Molasses Act document (1733), **2:**4, 5, 8, **18–20,**
   94
Monmouth, Battle of, **2:**196, 202
Monroe, James, **2:**278, **3:**22, **26,** 36, **103–105,** 126
Monroe Doctrine (1823), **3:87–107**
   Adams, John Quincy, **3:99–101**
   basic points, **3:**89–90
   Bolívar, Simón, **3:101–103**
   Felten's interpretive essay, **3:90–97**
   Monroe, James, **3:103–105**
   Monroe Doctrine document, **3:105–107**
   overview, **3:87–90,** 171
   Roosevelt, Theodore, **3:**96–97
   Roosevelt Corollary, **3:**96
Montcalm-Gozon, Louis-Joseph de, **2:**72, 77,
   **84–85**
Montesquieu, Baron de, **2:**215
Montgomery, Richard, **2:**152–153
Montgomery bus boycott (1955–1956), **4:**238, **251**

Moore, James, **1:**92
Moral Majority (Falwell), **4:**279
Moravians, **2:**50, 189
*More Wonders of the Invisible World* (Calef), **1:**260
Morgan, Edmund S., **1:**121
Morgan, J. P., **3:**163–164, **4:**2, 6
Mormonism, **3:**13–14
Morrill Land-Grant College Act, **3:**196–197
Morris, Gouverneur (NY State), **3:**36
Morse, Jedediah, **2:**149
Môrtefontaine, Treaty of (1800), **2:**252
Morton, Levi, **3:**259
Moseley, Capt. Samuel, **1:**218
Motherhood in the colonial era, **2:203–205**
Mott, Lucretia, **3:**78
Moyne, Pierre le, **1:**36
*Mr. Cotton's Letter Lately Printed, Examined, and
   Answered* (Williams), **1:**186
MTV TV show, **4:**207
Muckrakers, **4:**1
Munford, Robert, **2:**148
Murray, Donald Gaines, **4:**242
Murray, Judith Sargent, **2:**189, 198, **205–206**
Murray, William Vans, **2:**249
*Murray v. Maryland* (Supreme Court decision),
   **4:**237, 242
Murrow, Edward R., **4:**206
Mutiny Act, **1:**235
Mutually Assured Destruction (MAD), **4:**155–156
My Lai massacre (Vietnam War), **4:**227
*The Myth of Media Violence: A Critical
   Introduction* (Trend), **4:**209

Nader, Ralph, **4:**142, **144–146**
Napoleon III, **3:**95
Napoleonic Wars (1803–1805), **1:**152, **3:**41, 87
Narragansett tribe/group of tribes, **1:**213–214,
   **226–227**
Narváez, Pánfilo de, **1:**56–57, 75
Nasser, Gamal Abdel, **4:**172
Nat Turner's Rebellion (1831), **1:**152, 158–159, **3:**72
National Association for the Advancement of
   Colored People (NAACP), **2:**169, **4:**13, 52,
   58–60, 59, 71–72, 237, 242
National Association Opposed to Women
   Suffrage (1911), **4:**2
National Banking Acts (1863, 1864), **3:**197
National Broadcasting Company (NBC), **4:**201
National Educational Television (NET), **4:**201
*National Intelligencer* Offices, **3:**58
National Labor Relations (or Wagner) Act (1935),
   **4:**78
National Organization for Women (NOW),
   **4:**259–260, 269

National Park Service (1916), **4:**13

National People's Party (1892), **3:**30

National Recovery Administration (NRA), **4:**78, 82, 84, 87

National Right to Life Committee, **4:**261

National Security Council (NSC), **4:**276

National Traffic and Motor Vehicle Safety Act (1966), **4:**135, 142

National Urban League (NUL), **4:**58, 59

Native Americans

    Algonquins, **1:12–13,** 40, 42, 47, 117, 217–218, 220–221

    Anasazi culture, **1:13–15**

    Battle of Pavonia, **1:**202

    Cabeza de Vaca's interactions with, **1:**67

    Cartier's interactions with, **1:**45–46

    CCC programs for, **4:**77

    Christianity and, **1:**10–11

    Connecticut Indians, **1:**218

    conversion to Roman Catholicism, **1:**41–42

    Coronado's interactions with, **1:**58, 62, 63

    decapitation of women prisoners, **1:**218

    displacement threats, **2:**11

    Dreamer Religion, **3:**244

    English thoughts about, **1:**216

    epidemic diseases of, **1:**4, 6–7, 11, 40, **128–129**

    Five Nations of the Iroquois, **1:**216–217

    Florida tribes, **1:**79

    French interaction with, **1:**35, 38, 39–40

    Ghost Dance religion, **3:**29, 235, **243–245,** 248, 250, 251

    Hopi Indians, **1:**68, **71–73**

    Huron nation, **1:**38, 47

    impact of gold prospecting on, **3:**29

    impact of War of 1812, **3:**45

    Indian War (1675–1676), **1:**247

    Iroquois nations, **1:**38, 42

    Jesuit missionaries and, **1:**36, 40, 42–43

    Louisiana Purchase era, **3:**27

    Mohawk tribe, **1:**42, 118, 215

    new animals incorporated by, **1:**9–10

    Pawnee Indians, **1:**58, 63

    Peoria Indians, **1:**51

    Prophet Dances, **3:**244

    Pueblo Revolt, **1:**72–73, 76

    religious traditions, **1:**5–6

    Rowlandson captured by, **1:**228

    Seminole Indians, **3:**47

    Seminole Wars, **1:**95

    slash-and-burn agriculture, **1:**5

    tribal intermarriages, **1:**10

    tribal-restructuring, **1:**7–8

    Wampanoag Indians, **1:**126, 214, 217, 223, **228–230**

    Wichita Indians, **1:**64

    Wounded Knee massacre, **3:**245

    Zuni Indians, **1:**68–69, **76–78**

    *See also* French and Indian War

Native Americans, European encounters with, **1:117–134**

Naturalization Act, **2:**241, 246

Naval War College (U.S.), **3:**272

Navigation Act (1651), **1:**203, 234, **2:**2

Navigation Act (1660), **2:**2, 14

Navigation Act (1696), **1:**237, 243–244, **2:**2, 7

Nazi-Soviet Nonaggression Pact (1939), **4:**86, 179

"The Negro Artist and the Racial Mountain" (Hughes), **4:**55

Nelson, Horatio, **3:**41

Neutrality Acts, **4:**86, 105

Neutrality theories, **3:**45–46

New Amsterdam, surrender of (1664), **1:193–212**

    Anglo-Dutch Wars, **1:206**

    Dutch East India Company, **1:206–207**

    Dutch Reformed Church, **1:207–208,** 212

    Dutch West India Company, **1:**118, 136, **208–210**

    Mackey's interpretive essay, **1:197–205**

    Minuit, Peter, **1:210–211**

    overview, **1:193–197**

    Stuyvesant, Peter, **1:**195–196, 200–205, **211–212**

New Deal (1930s, FDR), **4:**12, **77, 93–98**

    Agricultural Adjustment Administration, **4:**82–83, 84

    Civilian Conservation Corps, **4:**77, 87

    National Recovery Administration, **4:**78, 82, 84, 87

    opposition to, **4:**79

    programs created by, **4:**77–78, 82–85

    Social Security Act, **4:**84

    suburban housing boom, **4:**132

    weakening policies of, **4:**83

    Works Progress Administration, **4:**78, 79, 84, 87

New England

    centrality of religion in, **1:**82, 101

    Champlain's voyages, **1:**47

    conversions of Native Americans, **1:**10–11

    Dominion of, creation of, **1:**239

    Indian-white distrust, **1:**118

    King Philip's War and, **1:**186, **213–231**

    Narragansett tribe/group of tribes, **1:**213–214, **226–227**

    Native American tribes, **1:**5, 8–9, 118–119

    Pequot Indians-white battles, **1:**120

    Pilgrim settlements, **1:**102, 113

    Puritan colonies in, **1:**103, 113

    Quakers, **1:**106

Salem witch trials, **1:**82

slavery population, **1:**138

smallpox epidemic, **1:**120

New England Anti-Slavery Society (1832), **3:**67

New France, **1:**35–36, 38–44, **2:**69, 72, 80

    *See also* Buade, Louis de; Champlain, Samuel de

New Freedom program (Wilson), **4:**3

"New Frontier" slogan (JFK), **3:**242

New Harmony community, **3:**5

New Jersey Plan (document), **2:**220, **234–236**

New Jewel Movement (Grenada), **4:**281

New Left activism, **4:**141

New Light Party, **2:**54–55, 57

New Light Presbyterians, **2:**38, 55, 56–57, **3:**7, **15**

*The New Negro* (Locke), **4:**54

New Negro Movement. *See* Harlem Renaissance

New Netherland Colony, **1:**7, 118

    Dutch vs. English in, **1:**196–197, 201, 203–205

    Dutch West India Company and, **1:**193–194, 200, 208–209

    English takeover of, **1:**197

    establishment of, **1:**199

    Kieft's service in, **1:**201–202

    Minuit's service in, **1:**199, 200, 210–211

    patroonships in, **1:**210

    relations with Native Americans, **1:**118, 202

    slavery in, **1:**137

    Stuyvesant's service in, **1:**211–212

    Van Twiller's service in, **1:**195, 200–201

    Verhurst's service in, **1:**199

New Netherland Company, **1:**198

New Orleans, Battle of (1815), **3:**51–52, **54–55,** 60, 110–111, 125, 145

New Orleans, settlement of, **1:**36

New Sweden Colony, **1:**194, 195, 197, 211–212

New World

    Cartier's voyages to, **1:**37, 45–46

    Champlain's voyages to, **1:**47

    Christianity in, **1:**10

    Columbian exchange and, **1:**8–10

    Columbus's voyages to, **1:**3, 4

    Cortez's plundering of, **1:**59–60

    epidemic diseases in, **1:**11, 40

    French colonization, **1:**33, 37, 39–41

    Italian expeditions to, **1:**99

    Marquette's voyages to, **1:**52

    plantation economy, **1:**149

    Spanish colonization, **1:73–76,** 83, 87–90

    *See also Journal of Christopher Columbus* *(1492)*

*New York Gazette* article (1764), **2:**94

New York Stock Exchange, **4:**80

Newton, Sir Isaac, **1:**268, **2:**22–23, 59

Niagara Movement (1905), **4:**13

Niantic Indians, **1:**131, **1:**227

Nicholson, Francis, **1:**236, 240–241, 250–251

Nicolls, Colonel Richard, **1:**204

Nielsen, A. C. (1897–1980), **4:217–218**

Nielsen (TV rating) Company, **4:**203–204, 207

*Niña* (ship of Columbus), **1:**4, 16

Nineteenth Amendment (Constitution), **4:**4, 34, 263

Nixon, Richard, **4:**209–211, 239

    Consumer Product Safety Act, **4:**135

    "detente" policy, **4:**173

    Moscow mission, **4:**140

    SALT I treaty, **4:**176

Nixon Doctrine, **4:**183

No Child Left Behind Act (2001), **4:**284

Norse people, **1:**2

North, Col. Oliver, **4:**276

    *See also* Iran-Contra Scandal

North, Lord Frederick, **2:**108, 115, 128, 142

    *See also* East India Company

North America

    archaeological evidence, **1:**2

    Cabeza de Vaca's crossing of, **1:**67

    England's colonization efforts, **1:99–116**

    English NA, religious toleration, **1:167–192**

    English resettlement in, **1:**35

    French resettlement in, **1:**37

    indigenous peoples of, **1:**1

    introduction of slavery, **1:135–165**

    smallpox epidemic, **1:**4, 40, **128–129**

    *See also* Enlightenment in North America; Religious toleration, English North America

North American Free Trade Agreement (NAFTA), **4:**284

North Atlantic Treaty Organization (NATO), **4:**115, 171, 177, 180

North Caucus Club (political group), **2:**130

*North Star* periodical (Douglass), **3:**67

Northern Securities Company railroad trust, **4:**2

Northwest Indians, **3:**49

Northwest Passage, **1:**207

*Notes on the State of Virginia* (Jefferson), **2:**174, **3:**169

Noyes, John Humphrey, **3:**5

Nuclear freeze movement, **4:164**

Nuclear Non-Proliferation Treaty (1968), **4:**151, 158

Nuclear Regulatory Commission (NRC), **4:**150

Nullification Document (document, 1832), **3:**134–135

Nurse, Rebecca, **1:**258, **1:**259, 264–265

Oberlin College, **3:**73

O'Connor, Sandra Day, **4:**262, 275, 280, **288–290**

Office of Price Administration (OPA, WW II), **4**:108

Office of War Information (WW II), **4**:113

Office of War Mobilization (OWN, WW II), **4**:107–108

O'Higgins, Bernardo, **3**:87

Okeechobee, Battle of, **3**:156

Old Fuss and Feathers. *See* Scott, Winfield

Old Light Party, **2**:54–55, 57, 63

Old Northwest Territory, **3**:2

Old Rough and Ready. *See* Taylor, Zachary

Oldham, John, **1**:119

Olive Branch Petition (1775), **2**:125, 160, 171, **179–181**

Oliver, Andrew, **2**:96–97, 127

Olmsted, Frederick Law, **3**:253, 259–260, **267–269**

Olney, Richard, **3**:96

Omnibus Budget Reconciliation Act (1987), **4**:279

"On the Danger of an Unconverted Ministry" sermon (Tennent), **2**:53, 55

"On the Equality of the Sexes" essay (Murray), **2**:189, 198

Opechancanough, **1**:121, 122, **129–130**, 216

Open Door note (1900), **3**:278–279

Open Door Policy (Eastern Europe), **4**:177

Oppenheimer, J. Robert, **4**:160, **165–166**

Orange County Revolutionary Committee of Safety, **2**:230

Orders-in-Council decrees, **3**:41

Ordinance of Secession (South Carolina, 1860), **3**:208–209

Oregon Territory, **3**:44, 94, 148

Oregon Trail, **3**:143

Oregon Treaty (1864), **3**:233

*Origin of Species* (Darwin), **3**:273

*The Origins of American Politics* (Bailyn), **2**:11

O'Sullivan, John L., **3**:137, 142, 237

Oswald, Richard, **2**:147

Otis, James, **2**:107

*Our Country: It's Possible Future and Its Present Crisis* (Strong), **3**:273

L'Ouverture, Toussaint, **2**:266, **3**:21–22, 261

Owen, Robert, **2**:166, 167

Owens, Robert Dale, **3**:128
    *See also* Locofoco Party

Pacific Railroad Act, **3**:197

Packard, Vance, **4**:138, 140

Paine, Thomas, **2**:125, 161, 226, **3**:99, 103
    *See also Common Sense* pamphlet

Pakenham, Sir Edward, **3**:54, 55

Palmer, Bertha, **3**:256, 260

Pan-Americanism, **3**:255

Panama Canal, **3**:279, 280, **4**:18

Paris, Treaty of (1763), **1**:44, **2**:12, 72, 79, 87, 140, 171, 239, 253, **3**:36

Paris, Treaty of (1898), **3**:274, 278

Paris Peace Agreement, **4**:222

Parker, Alice, **1**:264

Parks, Rosa, **4**:258

Parris, Betty, **1**:255, 262

Parris, Reverend Samuel, **1**:255–256, 262, 265

Partial Nuclear Test Ban Treaty (1963), **4**:151

Pate, John, **1**:233

*Paths of Glory* (war movie), **4**:224

Patterson, Daniel Todd, **3**:55

Pavonia, Battle of (1643), **1**:202

Pawnee Indians, **1**:58, 63

PAYGO system (Bush, G.H.W.), **4**:283–284

Payne-Aldrich Tariff (1909), **4**:3

Peace Democrats, **3**:218

Peace of Amboise (1563), **1**:84

Pearl Harbor attack, **4**:106, 107, 110–111, **126–127**

Pelham-Holles, Thomas, **2**:6, **14–16**

Penn, William
    adoption of *Pennsylvania Charter of Privileges,* **1**:191
    founding of Pennsylvania, **1**:178
    landownership rights and, **1**:106, 170–171, 179, 239
    slavery views of, **1**:138
    *See also* Quakers (Society of Friends)

Pennsylvania
    emancipation statute, **2**:145–146
    Ladies Association (Philadelphia), **2**:145

*Pennsylvania Charter of Privileges* (1701), **1:191**

Pennsylvania Railroad, **3**:175

Pennsylvania Society for Abolition, **2**:194

Pentecostal Protestants, **2**:56

People's Party (Populist Party), **1**:95

Peoria Indians, **1**:51

Pequot Indian tribe (Connecticut), **1**:118–119, 120

Pequot War (1636–1637), **1**:118, **130–131,** 156, 213, 218

Perdisatt, Kathleen, **1**:120–127

Perry, Oliver Hazard (1785–1819), **3:60–62**

Pershing, Gen. John J. (1860–1948), **4**:26, **40–43**
    *See also* American Expeditionary Force

Peterson, Merrill, **3**:31

Philadelphia Young Ladies' Academy, **2**:190

Philip II (Spanish King), **1**:80–81, 83–85

Philippine-American War (1899–1902), **3:287–288**

Philippines. *See* Spanish-American War (1898–1910)

*Philips vs. Martin Marietta* (Supreme Court decision), **4:**261

Phillips, Wendell, **3:**78

Phips, Sir William, **1:**249, 257, 258, 263, 265, 271

Pickering, Timothy, **2:**229, 244, 249–250, 250

Pierce, Franklin, **3:**155, 203

Pietism, **2:**46–47, 49, 50

Pike, Zebulon, **3:**25

"Pikes Beak or Bust!" slogan, **3:**233

Pilgrims, **1:112–113**

  break with Church of England, **1:**112

  New England settlements, **1:**102

  Plymouth Rock landing, **1:**82, 113

Pinckney, Charles Cotesworth, **2:**240, 243, 244, 263, 271, **280–281**

Pinckney's Treaty (1795), **3:**22

*Pinta* (ship of Columbus), **1:**4, 16

Pitcher, Molly. *See* McCauley, Mary Ludwig Hays

Pitt, William, **2:**5, 18, 72, 73, 78, 80, **85–87,** 103

Pizarro, Francisco, **1:**74

Plains Indians, **1:**6

*Plan for Improving Female Education* (Clinton), **2:**208

"Plan of Chicago" (Burnham), **3:**265

*Planned Parenthood of Southern Pennsylvania v. Casey* (Supreme Court decision), **4:**261–262

Plantation economy (New World), **1:**149

Platt Amendment, **3:**96

Plattsburgh, Battle of (1814), **3:55–57**

*Plessy v. Ferguson* (Supreme Court decision), **4:**12, 237, 241

Plymouth Colony (Massachusetts), **1:**82, 102, 117, 120, 123–124, 134, 223, 235–236

Pochahontas, **1:**82, 121–122, **131–132**

  *See also* Rolfe, John; Smith, Capt. John

Poetry, of Phillis Wheatley, **2:**193–194

Poindexter, John, **4:**276

  *See also* Iran-Contra Scandal

Polk, Gen. Leonidas, **3:**192

Polk, James K., **3:**117

  biographical information, **3:152–154**

  Buena Vista, Battle of, **3:**153

  Davis' support of, **3:**203

  expansionist ideas, **3:**139

  Independent Treasury Act, **3:**154

  Mexican-American War association, **3:**143–149

  Monroe Doctrine association, **3:**90, **96,** 144–149

  presidency, **3:**67, 81, 94–95, 131, 139

  protection of Texas, **3:**140

  *See also* Guadalupe Hidalgo, Treaty of

Ponce de Léon, Juan, **1:97–98**

  arrival in West Indies, **1:**55

  financial ruin of, **1:**83

Gulf Coast Florida discovery, **1:**74, 79, 83

indigenous people confrontations, **1:**75

naming of Florida, **1:**94

Pontiac (Indian Chief), **2:**93, 97

*Poor Richard's Almanack* (Franklin), **2:**34

Populist Party (1892), **3:**30, 239

Port Bill (Boston), **2:**123

Port Huron Statement, **4:**140, 141

Portuguese slave trade, **1:**70, 149–150

Post, George B., **3:**255

*Posterior Analytics* (Aristotle), **2:**168

Postman, Neil, **4:**207

Potsdam Conference, **4:**178

Powhatan Confederacy, **1:**131, 143, 215–216

Powhatan Indians, **1:**121–122, 129, 130–133

  *See also* Opechancanough

Powhatan War, **1:**248

Prasch, Thomas A., **2:5–12**

Pratt, Julius W., **3:**280

*Preble* warship, **3:**56

Presbyterianism, **2:**48–49, 52–53, 53, **3:**1

Prescott, Col. William, **2:**153

*The Presidency of Andrew Jackson* (Cole), **3:**117

*President* (American vessel), **3:**44

President's Commission on the Status of Women, **4:269–271**

Prevost, Sir George, **3:**55

Price-Anderson Act (1957), **4:**152

Priestley, Joseph (1733–1804), **2:37–40**

Princeton, Battle of, **2:**148

Prisoner of War/Missing in Action (POW/MIA) issue, **4:**228

Privy Council, **1:**239, 242

Proclamation of 1763, **2:**93–94, 97

Proclamation of Amnesty and Reconstruction (Lincoln), **3:**211

Proclamation of Neutrality (Washington, 1793), **2:258–259**

Proclamation of Rebellion (1775, George III), **2:**155–156

Proctor, John and Elizabeth, **1:**258, 264

*Progress and Poverty* (George), **3:**162

Progressive Party, **4:**3, **16,** 44

Progressivism (1901–1914), **3:**170, **4:1–21**

  anti-corruption mayors, **4:1**

  anti-suffrage movement, **4:**2

  Credit Mobilier scandal, **4:**5

  education's importance, **4:**8–9

  growth of national wealth, **4:**8

  Hague's interpretive essay, **4:5–13**

  La Follette, Robert "Fighting Bob," **4:15–16**

  overview, **4:1–5**

  Payne-Aldrich Tariff, **4:**3

  political reforms, **4:**4, 10–11, 11–12

Progressive Party, **4:**3, **16,** 44

Roosevelt, Theodore, **4:**3, 13, **16–18**

Settlement House movement, **4:**11, **18–19**

Sinclair, Upton, **4:**1–2, **19–21**

Social Gospel movement, **4:**7, 9

Underwood Tariff, **4:**3

Prohibition legislation, **4:**34

Project C (confrontation), **4:**246

Prophet Dances (Native Americans), **3:**244

Prosser, Gabriel, **1:**152

Protestant-Catholic War (1593–1598), **1:**47

Protestant Reformation, **1:**100

Protestantism, **1:**34, 140, 169, 235, 239, 243, **2:**67, **3:**5, 7, 17

Protests, by women, **2:**187, 191

Prussia, Quadruple Alliance membership, **3:**87

Public Broadcasting System (PBS), **4:**201

Public Interest Research Group (Nader), **4:**145

Pueblo Revolt (1680), **1:**72–73, 76

Pulitzer, Joseph, **3:**274, 276

Pullman Strike (1894, Chicago suburbs), **4:**7

Pure Food and Drug Act, **4:**18

Puritan Revolution, **2:**50

Puritans

  Act of Toleration accepted by, **1:**183

  Andros' leadership of, **1:**240

  Calvinist Puritans, **1:**168–169

  campaign against Indians, **1:**220

  conflict with Catholicism, **1:**102

  dissatisfaction with Elizabethan Compromise, **1:**168

  education valued by, **1:**107–108

  "experimental" Puritanism, **2:**52

  King Philip's War and, **1:**221

  Massachusetts Bay Colony founded by, **1:**113, 238

  Massachusetts covenants, **1:**107

  Metacom's war with, **1:**126

  New England colonies, **1:**103, 113

  non-Puritans vs., **2:**45

  "praying towns" established by, **1:**10

  Rogers' ideas rejected by, **1:**169

  Salem witch trials and, **1:**260, **269–271**

  slavery justified by, **1:**138

  *See also* Cromwell, Oliver; Edwards, Jonathan; Winthrop, John

Putnam, Ann, Jr., **1:**262

Putnam, Frederick War, **3:**256

Quadruple Alliance (in Europe), **3:**87

Quakers (Society of Friends), **1:**170, **184–185**

  anti-slavery stance, **1:**138, **3:**69

  beliefs of, **1:**138, 178–180

  emergence of, **1:**178

Fox's founding of, **1:**184–185

friendship with Indians, **1:**106

girls schools, **2:**189

opposition to Penn, **1:**171

Stuyvesant's opposition to, **1:**212

Williams' defense of, **1:**187

  *See also* Penn, William

Quartering Act (1765), **2:**102, 118

Quasi-War (1798–1800), **2:**241, 248, 250–251, **256,** 263, **3:**60

Quebec Act, **2:**118

Queen Anne's War (1702–1713), **1:**224, **2:**9, 73

Quivira (golden city), **1:**58, 63–64, 65, 69

Race riots, **4:**53

Radical Republicans, **3:**213–214, 218, **228–230**

*The Radicalism of the American Revolution* (Wood), **2:**166

Radio Corporation of American (RCA), **4:**200

Railroad Administration, **4:**25

Railroads, **3:**165, 175, 196, 197, 221, 237

Rain-in-the-Face (Native American chief), **3:**29

Rainey, Ma, **4:**55

Rakestraw, Donald A., **3:141–149**

Raleigh, Sir Walter, **1:**101, **113–114**

Ramsay, David, **2:**149

Randolph, A. Philip, **4:**58

Randolph, Gov. Edmund, **2:**218

Rawls, John, **2:**169

Reagan, Ronald, **3:**242, **4:**143, 146, 152, 155, 227, 240, **288–290**

Reagan Revolution (1981–1989), **4:273–293**

  attacks on communism, **4:**275

  criticism of Carter, **4:**275

  INF treaty, **4:**152, 174, 277

  Iran-Contra Scandal, **4:**276, **288**

  legislation, **4:**279

  meeting with Gorbachev, **4:**277

  myth vs. fact basis, **4:**283

  O'Connor, Sandra Day, **4:**262, 275, 280, **288–290**

  overview, **4:273–277**

  Staten's interpretive essay, **4:277–284**

  Strategic Defense Initiative, **4:**152, 155, 174, 276, 282

  *See also* Bush, George H. W.; Strategic Defense Initiative (Star Wars)

"Reaganomics" (economics), **4:**274

*The Reasonableness of Christianity as Delivered in the Scriptures* (Locke), **2:**178

"Reconcentrado" camps (Spanish-American War), **3:**275

Reconstruction era (1863–1876), **3:211–231**

  Black Codes, **3:**213, 218, 220

Civil Rights Act (1866), **3:198,** 219
Committee on the Conduct of the War, 3:229
election of 1876, **3:225**
Freedman's Bureau, 3:212, 219, 220
Hayes, Rutherford, 3:211, 215, 223, 225
Johnson, Andrew, **3:226–228**
Ku Klux Klan, 3:213, 221
overview, **3:216–224**
Peace Democrats, 3:218
Radical Republicans, 3:213–214, 218, **228–230**
Redemption Democrats, 3:215
"Rehearsal for Reconstruction," 3:217
Stevens, Thaddeus, **3:230–231**
term derivation, 3:216
Tilden, Samuel J., 3:25, 215, 223
Wade-Davis Bill, 3:211, 227
Reconstruction Finance Corporation (RFC),
    4:76–77
Red Fox of Kinderhook. *See* Van Buren, Martin
Red Scare (communist scare), **1:**262
Reed, Ester DeBert, 2:196
Reform Act (1832), 2:10
Rehnquist, William, 4:275
*Relación de la Jornada de Cíbola* (Castañeda),
    **1:**70
Religion
    Calvinism, 1:34, 172, 2:27, 49, 66, 3:1
    Deism, 3:7
    Jewish people, 1:170, 175
    Presbyterianism, 2:48–49, 52–53, 3:1
    Protestantism, 1:34, 140, 169, 235, 239, 2:67,
        3:5, 7, 17
    Unitarianism, 3:3
    *See also* Christianity; Religious revivalism;
        Roman Catholic Church
*Religious History of the American People*
    (Ahlstrom), 3:1
Religious revivalism, 2:46–47, 66, 3:3, 4
    appeal of, **3:10–13**
    consequences of, **3:13–14**
    Finney's writings on, 3:18
    origins/spread of, **3:6–10, 71**
    women and, 3:12
    *See also* Cartwright, Peter; Edwards, Jonathan;
        Finney, Charles Grandison
Religious Right politics (U.S.), 4:263, 279
Religious toleration, English North America
    (1636–1701), **1:167–192**
    *Bloudy Tenet of Persecution* excerpt, **1:**187–189
    Calvert, Cecil, **1:**181–183
    Hutchinson, Anne, **1:**183–184
    Maryland Act of Toleration (document),
        **1:**189–192
    overview, **1:167–171**

Pennsylvania Charter of Privileges excerpt,
    **1:192**
Rhode Island colony, **1:**169, 171–173, 175–176
Society of Friends (Quakers), **1:184–185**
Woods' interpretive essay, **1:171–180**
*See also* Williams, Roger
Religious traditions
    Anglican Church, 1:234–235, 244, 2:27, 47,
        51, 55
    Baptist Church, 2:48
    Calvinism, 1:34, 172, 2:27, 49
    Congregationalists ("Old Lights"), 2:48
    Dutch Reformed Church, **1:**207–208, 212,
        2:49, 61
    early Native Americans, 1:5–6
    Halfway Covenant, 2:45, 51, 55
    Methodism, 2:47, 53, 56, 65
    New Light Presbyterians, 2:38, 55, 56–57
    Pentecostal Protestants, 2:56
    pietism, 2:46–47
    Presbyterianism, 2:48–49, 52, 53
    Protestantism, 1:34, 140, 169, 235, 239, 2:67
    revivalism, 2:46–47
    of slaves, Great Awakening era, **2:62–63**
*Remarkable Providences* (Increase Mather), 1:268
"Remember the Ladies" letter (Adams), **2:209**
Remini, Robert V., 3:120
Renaissance (Europe), 1:135, 2:22–23
*Report of Government for the Western Territory*
    (Jefferson), 2:174
Report on Manufactures (Hamilton, 1791), 2:228
Republican Motherhood (1780–1820), **2:187–209**
    Adams, Abigail, **2:200–202,** 209
    Hays, Mary Ludwig, **2:202–203**
    motherhood in the colonial era, **2:203–205**
    Murray, Judith Sargent, **2:205–206**
    name derivation, 2:187
    overview, **2:187–191**
    religious links, 2:190–191
    "Remember the Ladies" letter (Adams), **2:209**
    Ryan's interpretive essay, **2:191–198**
    Sampson, Deborah, **2:206–207**
    Willard, Emma, **2:207–209**
Resolution Proposing a Declaration of
    Independence (Richard Henry Lee), **2:182**
Resolutions of Stamp Act Congress (document,
    1765), **2:110–112**
Revenue Act (1762), 2:5
Revenue Act (1942), 4:108
Revere, Paul, 2:119, **130–132**
Revivalism. *See* Religious revivalism
Revolution of 1800, **2:263–282**
    Burr, Aaron, role, **2:275–277**
    Democratic-Republican Party, **2:277–278**

Federalist Party, **2:278–280**
  Felten's interpretive essay, **2:266–274**
  Jefferson's viewpoint, **2:**266–267
  name derivation, **2:**264
  overview, **2:263–266**
  Pinckney, Charles Cotesworth, **2:280–281**
  Twelfth Amendment (document), **2:281–282**
Revolving Old Age Pension Plan (Townsend), **4:**79
Rhode Island colony, **1:**169
  Council of War/Town Council, **1:**218
  founding of, **1:**171–173
  governing difficulties, **1:**175–176
Ribault, Jean, **1:**34, 81, 84
*Rights of Man* (Paine), **3:**99
*The Rise and Fall of the Confederate Government* (Davis), **3:**204
*The Rise of the New West* (Frederick Jackson Turner), **3:**250
Rittenhouse, David, **2:**25, 29
Roanoke (Virginia) Colonies (1585, 1587), **1:114–115**
"Robber barons." *See* Carnegie, Andrew; Morgan, J. P.; Rockefeller, John D.
Roberval, Jean-François de La Rocque de, **1:**46
Robeson, Paul, **4:**55
Robespierre, Maximilien, **2:**257
Robinson, Bill "Bojangles," **4:**55
Rockefeller, John D., **4:**6
Rockingham, Marquis of, **2:**103–104
*Roe v. Wade* (Supreme Court decision), **4:**261
Rogers, Robert (1731–1795), **1:**223, **2:87–89**
Rolfe, John, **1:**132, 139, 156
  *See also* Pochahontas
*Rolling Stone* magazine, **4:**141
Roman Catholic Church, **1:**34, **36**
  encumbrances of, **2:**51
  England, 16th century, **1:**167–168, 170, 172
  James' conversion to, **1:**239
  Native American's conversions, **1:**41–42
  Protestant Church vs., **1:**47
  Spanish colonization and, **1:**74
Roosevelt, Franklin D. (FDR, 1882–1945), **3:**241, 275, **98–102**
  Atlantic Charter, **4:**110
  "bank holiday" declared by, **4:**77
  Executive Order 9066 (1942), **4:**109
  federal judge appointments, **4:**84–85
  initial view on WW II, **4:**110
  Lend-Lease bill, **4:**105–106
  Manhattan Project authorization, **4:**149
  Neutrality Acts, **4:**86, 105
  presidential victory, **4:**79, 82
  Victory Program (WW II), **4:**112
  *See also* New Deal

Roosevelt, Theodore, **3:**96–97, 145, 240, 279, 283, **4:**3, 13, **16–18**
  *See also* Rough Riders
Roosevelt Corollary to the Monroe Doctrine, **3:**96
Roosevelt Field Shopping Center (LI, NY), **4:**134
Root, John Welborn, **3:**254
Rosenberg, Ethel and Julius, **4:**171
Roth, Philip, **4:**138
Rough Riders, **3:288–289, 4:**42
  *See also* Roosevelt, Theodore
Rousseau, Jean-Jacques (1712–1778), **2:40–42**
Rowlandson, Mary, **1:**220, **227–228**
Royal Society of London, **2:**25, 28, 33
*Rudiments of English Grammar* (Priestley), **2:**38
Runaway servants, **1:154–156**
Rush, Dr. Benjamin, **2:**187, 190
Rush-Bagot Agreement (1817), **3:**44
Russia
  defeat by Napoleon, **2:**257
  Holy Alliance membership, **3:**92
  Monroe's warnings to, **3:**93–94
  Pitt's aid to, **2:**72
  Quadruple Alliance membership, **3:**88
  U.S. tensions with, **3:**91
Russian Revolution (1917), **4:**39
Russo-Japanese War, **4:**18, 42
Ryan, Kelly A., **2:191–198**
Ryswick Treaty, **1:**250

Sacajawea (d. 1812), **3:**34, **37–38**
Saint Bartholomew's Day Massacre (1572), **1:**34
Salem witch trials (1692), **1:**82, **255–275**
  Death Warrant of Five Women Convicted of Witchcraft, **1:274–275**
  Mather, Cotton, **1:266–268**
  Mather, Increase, **1:268–269**
  overview, **1:255–259**
  Puritan family, **1:269–271**
  Sewall, Samuel, **1:271–272**
  Stowell's interpretive essay, **1:259–265**
  women tries as witches, **1:**257–258, 264
  *Wonders of the Invisible World* (Mather), **1:272–274**
*Salem Witchcraft* (Upham), **1:**260
Salons, establishment of, **2:**28
SALT (Strategic Arms Limitations Talks), **4:**151–152, 156
SALT I (Strategic Arms Limitations Talks), **4:**151–152, 156
SALT II (Strategic Arms Limitations Talks), **4:**151–152, 156, 173
Salutary Neglect, Era of (1720s-1750), **2:1–20**
  Board of Trade and Plantations, **2:13–14**
  Burke's speech, **2:**5–6

mercantilism, **2:**14

Molasses Act document, **2:18–20**

overview, **2:1–5**

Pelham-Holles, Thomas, **2:14–16**

Prasch's interpretive essay, **2:5–12**

Walpole, Robert, **2:16–18**

Sampson, Deborah, **2:206–207**

Sampson, William T., **3:**277

San Jacinto, Battle of, **3:**138

San Martín, José de, **3:**87, 102

Sand Creek Massacre, **3:**234

*Sands of Iwo Jima* (war movie), **4:**224

Sanitary Commission (U.S.), **3:**198, 268

Santa Anna, Antonio López de, **3:**138

Santa Domingo (Haiti) naval base, **3:**21–22

*Santa Maria,* **1:**3, 16

Saratoga, Battle of (1777), **2:**36, 146, 147, 148

*Saratoga* warship, **3:**56

Sassacus (Pequot chief), **1:**119

Savage, Capt. Thomas, **1:**214

Scalia, Antonin, **4:**275, 280

*Scenes in the Life of Harriet Tubman* (Bradford), **3:**82–83

*Schechter v. U.S.* (Supreme Court decision), **4:**78, 84

Schlafly, Phyllis, **4:**262, 264

Schley, Winfield Scott, **3:**277

Schuyler, Gen. Philip John, **2:**152

Schwenkfelders, **2:**50

Scientific Revolution, **2:**22–23, 28–30

See also Priestley, Joseph; Royal Society of London

Scott, Thomas A., **3:**175–176

Scott, Winfield, **3:**134, 144, 152

See also Whig Party

Searles, Robert, **1:**92

Second Anglo-Dutch War (1665–1667), **1:**205

Second Bank of the United States, **3:**124–125

Second Continental Congress (1775), **2:**125, 128, 144, 146, 155, 159, 160, 163, 172–173, **178–179,** 182, 211, 230, 239, 253, 255, 285

See also Declaration of Independence

Second Continental Congress (1776), **2:**35, 88, **3:**36

Second Great Awakening, **2:**54–55, 191, **3:1–19**

Backus, Isaac, **3:15–16**

Cartwright, Peter, **3:16–17**

Crothers' interpretive essay, **3:5–14**

Finney, Charles Grandison, **3:17–18**

McGready, James, **3:18–19**

Old Northwest Territory, **3:**2

origins, **3:**1–2

overview, **3:1–5**

revivalism during, **3:**3, 4

upstate New York, **3:**2, 5, 13

Second Seminole War, **1:**95

Securities Exchange Commission (SEC), **4:**78

Sedgewick, Theodore, **2:**198

Sedition Act, **2:**242, 246

Sedition Act (from Alien and Sedition Acts), **2:260–261**

Sedition Slammers (vigilante group), **4:**33

Selective Service Act (1917), **4:**25–26

*The Selling of Joseph* (Sewall), **1:163–165,** 272

*The Selling of the President* (McGinniss), **4:**210

Seminole Indians, **3:**47, 156

Seneca Falls Woman's Rights Convention (1848), **4:**263

Settlement House movement, **4:**11, **18–19**

Settlement houses, **4:**11

Seven Cities of Antillia, **1:**59

Seven Cities of Cíbola, **1:**57, 59–61, 68, 75–76

Seven Year's War. See French and Indian War (1756–1763)

Seventeenth Amendment (Constitution), **4:**2–3

Sewall, Samuel, **1:**163–165, **271–272**

Seward, William Henry, **2:**167, **3:**95, 194

*Sexual Behavior in the Human Female* (Kinsey), **4:**257

Shafter, Gen. William, **3:**272, 277

"Share the Wealth" program (Long), **4:**79

Shay's Rebellion, **2:**216, 227

*Shelley v. Kraemer* (Supreme Court decision), **4:**139

Sherman, Gen. William T., **3:**201

capture of Atlanta, **3:**206

March to the Sea (1864), **3:207–208**

Special Field Order No. 15, **3:**217

Sherman, Roger, **2:**173

Sherman Anti-Trust Act (1890), **3:**163, **4:**2, 4

Shirley, Gov. William, **2:**75, 77, 88

Shopping center development, **4:**134

*The Significance of Sections in American History* (Frederick Jackson Turner), **3:**240

*The Significance of the Frontier in American History* (Frederick Jackson Turner), **3:**240, 248–249

Sigur, Hannah, **3:257–263**

*Silent Spring* (Carson), **4:**142

Sinclair, Upton, **4:**1–2, 2, **19–21**

"Sinners in the Hands of an Angry God" speech (Edwards), **2:**46, 59–60

Sioux Indian War (1876–1877), **3:**235, **245–246,** 247

See also Sitting Bull (Native American chief)

Siry, Steven E.

American Revolution essay, **2:143–150**

King Philip's War essay, **1:216–222**

Lewis and Clark essay, **3:24–31**

Sitting Bull (Native American chief), **3:**29, 235, **246–248**
*See also* Sioux Indian War
Sixteenth Amendment (Constitution), **4:**2–3, 11–12
*Sixty Minutest* (TV show), **4:**203
Slash-and-burn agriculture, **1:**5
Slaughter, Henry, **1:**236
Slave religion, during the Great Awakening, **2:62–63**
Slavery, North American introduction (1619), **1:135–165,** 215
  accidental introduction, **1:**138–139
  African slave trade, **1:**140–141, **148–153**
  arrival in Jamestown, **1:**136
  colonial Virginia, mid-18th century, **1:161–163**
  end of, in America, **3:**217
  initial English resistance, **1:**141
  in Missouri, **3:26**
  in New Netherlands, **1:**137
  newspaper advertisements, **1:**154
  Puritan justification of slavery, **1:**138
  Quaker influence, **1:**138
  runaway servants, **1:154–156**
  *The Selling of Joseph* excerpt, **1:163–165**
  slavery, **1:156–161**
  Woods' interpretive essay, **1:138–146**
Slaves/slavery, **1:156–161**
  African slave trade, **1:**148–153
  Cartwright's opposition to, **3:**17
  Christian conversion attempts, **2:**62
  Christian defense of, **3:**3
  effects of American Revolution on, **2:**145
  freeing of, **1:**95
  Ghana slave trading posts, **1:**151
  Haitian Revolution (1791), **1:**152
  historical background, **1:**141–142, 145
  indentured servitude vs., **1:**144
  Jefferson's feelings about, **1:**145–146, **2:**221
  of John Smith, **1:**133
  Middle Passage (of journey), **1:**149–150, 158
  Portuguese sale of, **1:**70, 149
  Portuguese slave trade, **1:**70, 149–150
  Quaker opposition to, **3:**69
  racism relation to, **1:**141
  rise of, **1:**36
  runaways, **1:**154–156
  Sewall's opposition to, **1:**272
  Spanish capture/forcing of, **1:**75
  of Squanto, **1:**134
  Thirteenth Amendment and, **1:**156, 160, **3:**212, 219
  *See also* Abolition; Bett, Mum; Civil War
Slaughter, Col. Henry, **1:**251

Smallpox epidemic, **1:**4, 40, **128–129**
Smith, Adam, **2:**7
Smith, Bessie, **4:**55
Smith, Capt. John, **1:133–134**
  Congressional Church guidance, **1:**82
  interactions with Indians, **1:**121, 126, 129
  opposition to Wingfield, **1:**112
  voyage to Cape Cod, **1:**123
  *See also* Pochahontas legend
Smith, Gen. Jacob H. "Hell-Roarin," **3:**275
Smith, Gerrit, **3:**78
Smith, Joseph, **3:**13
Smith, William, **2:**25
Smith, Willie "The Lion," **4:**55
Smohalla (Wanamum Prophet), **3:**244
Smoot-Hartley tariff bill, **4:**76
*The Social Contract* (Rousseau), **2:**42
Social Darwinism, **3:**168, 273
Social Gospel movement (Progressive era), **4:**7, 9
Social Security Act (1935), **4:**84
Social Security Reform Act (1983), **4:**279
Socialism, **3:**169–170
Socialist Labor Party, **4:**38
Society for the Propagation of the Gospel, **1:**244
Society of Friends. *See* Quakers (Society of Friends)
Solemn League and Covenant, **2:**124
*Some Thoughts Concerning the Present Revival of Religion in New England* (Edwards), **2:**60
Sons of Liberty Movement, **2:**95, 103, **108–109,** 193
"The Sources of Soviet Conduct" (Kennan), **4:**170
South Carolina, Ordinance of Secession (1860), **3:**208–209
South Sea Bubble crisis (1720), **2:**7, 8, 17
Southern States
  class warfare, **3:**195
  end of military rule, **3:**214
  pro-slavery stance, **3:**68, 69, 73
Soviet Union
  Afghanistan invasion, **4:**273
  aid to Ho Chi Minh, **4:**219
  atom bomb detonation, **4:**154
  Baruch Plan rejection, **4:**149–150
  Chernobyl nuclear accident, **4:**157
  detente with, **4:**173
  European occupations, **4:**169
  as "evil empire," **4:**152, 227–228
  Gorbachev, Mikhail, **4:**152
  Nazi-Soviet Nonaggression Pact, **4:**86, 179
  response to Marshall Plan, **4:**170–171
  SALT I treaty, **4:**176
  Yalta Conference, **4:**107

Spain (Spanish)
  Charles of Habsburg, **1:**83–84
  colonization of the Americas, **1:73–76,** 83,
    87–90, **2:**1–2
  indigenous Indians enslaved by, **1:**135–136
  interactions with Native Americans, **1:**117
  Latin America and, **3:**89, 91
  Maximilian I, **1:**83
  Mexico's independence from, **3:**137
  Philip II, **1:**80–81, 83–85
Spanish-American War (1898–1910), **3:**144, 198,
    **271–289**
  Cuban blockade, **3:**277
  Dewey, George, **3:**277, **283**
  Hay, John, **3:**275–276, 278
  Hearst, William Randolph, **3:**274, 276, **283–285**
  as historical turning point for U.S., **3:**279
  Manila Bay, Battle of, **3:**283
  Mattox's interpretive essay, **3:275–281**
  McKinley, William, **3:**274, 276–277, 279,
    **285–287**
  Open Door note (1900), **3:**278–279
  overview, **3:**271–275
  Paris, Treaty of (1898), **3:**274, 278
  Philippine-American War, **3:287–2888**
  "reconcentrado" camps, **3:**275
  Roosevelt, Theodore, **3:**279, 283
  Rough Riders, **3:288–289**
  USS *Maine* battleship, **3:**274, 276, 280, 287, **289**
Spanish Succession, War of, **2:**16
Special Field Order No. 15 (Sherman), **3:**217
Specie Circular (Jackson), **3:**112
*Speech on Conciliation with America* speech
    (Burke), **2:**5–6
Spencer, Herbert, **3:**273
Spock, Dr. Benjamin, **4:**257
Sporting events (on TV), **4:**203, 204
Sprenger, Jacob, **1:**259
Squanto (1580–1622), **1:**118, 121, 123–124, **134**
St. Augustine, founding of (1565), **1:79–98**
  attack by Searles, **1:**92
  attempts by Spain, **1:**83
  Beattie's interpretive essay, **1:82–90**
  Castillo de San Marcos, **1:92–93**
  De Soto, Hernando, **1:93–94**
  demographics, **1:**87
  disease epidemics, **1:**82
  Florida, **1:94–97**
  Menéndez de Avilés and, **1:**81, 83, 85–88, 90
  overview, **1:79–82**
  Ponce de Léon, Juan, **1:97–98**
Stalin, Joseph, **4:**106–107, 170, 175, 177, 178
Stamp Act (1765), **2:93–113**
  description, **2:**94–95, 101

Dulaney, Daniel, **2:105–107**
Grenville, George, **2:**73, 93, 98, 101
Hutchinson, Thomas, 4, **2:**35, 97, **107–108**
Mackey's interpretive essay, **2:96–105**
modification/repeal appeals, **2:**95
Oliver, Andrew, **2:**96–97
opposition of John Adams, **2:**253
overview, **2:93–95**
Resolutions of Stamp Act Congress, **2:110–112**
Sons of Liberty Movement, **2:**95, **108–109**
Virginia Stamp Act Resolutions, **2:112–113**
"virtual representation" discussions, **2:**116
Stamp Act Congress (1765), **2:**103, **109**
Stamp Act Crisis (1765–1766), **2:**86, 98, 104–105
Stamp Act Riots (1765), **2:**96, 102, **109–110**
"The Stand" newspaper (Hamilton), **2:**245
Standard Oil Company (Rockefeller), **3:**164, 181,
    184, **4:**1
Standish, Miles, **1:**124
Stanton, Elizabeth Cady, **2:**167, **3:**257
Stanton, Theodore, **3:**276
Staple Act (1663), **2:**2
START (Strategic Arms Reductions Talks), **4:**152
*The Status Seekers* (Packard), **4:**138
Steamship invention, **3:**36
Steel industry, **3:**160–161, 163, 171, 176, **4:**6
  *See also* Carnegie, Andrew
Steffens, Lincoln, **4:**1
Stephens, Alexander, **3:**193, **212**
Stevens, Thaddeus (1792–1868), **3:**214, **230–231**
Stock market crash (1929), **4:**75, 80, **102–103**
  *See also* Great Depression
Stoddard, Solomon, **2:**45, 51, 55, 59
Stone, Capt. John, **1:**119, **133–134**
Stone, Harlan, **4:**84
Stone, Lucy, **3:**257
Stono Rebellion (1739), **1:**158
STOP ERA movement, **4:**262
Stoughton, William, **1:**262
Stowell, Frederick M., **1:259–265**
Strategic Arms Reduction Treaty (1991), **4:**282
Strategic Defense Initiative (Star Wars), **4:**152,
    155, 174, 276, 282
Strayhorn, Billy, **4:**55
Streetcare vs. automobile suburbs, **4:**131–132
Strong, Josiah, **3:**273
Stuart monarchy restoration (1660), **1:**238, **2:**50
Student Nonviolent Coordinating Committee,
    **4:**225, 240, 245, 247
Students for a Democratic Society (SDS),
    **4:**140–141, 225–226
Stuyvesant, Peter, **1:211–212**
  creation of Board of Nine Men, **1:**211–212
  Dutch West India Company employment, **1:**196

feuds with Dutch/English, **1:**200–201

relations with Indians, **1:**200

service in New Netherland Colony, **1:**195, 200, 202–205, 211–212

surrender of power to Nicolls, **1:**197

Suburbanization and consumerism (1945–1990), **4:131–147**

American Dream, **4:**5, 85, 132, 136, 141

automobile vs. streetcar suburbs, **4:**131–132

credit cards, introduction of, **4:**134

Dunak's interpretive essay, **4:135–143**

Federal Housing Authority, **4:**132, 133, 139

government-forced segregation, **4:**138

"hippie" movement, **4:**141

Levittowns (NY, NJ, PA), **4:**132–134, 136–137, **144**

Nader, Ralph, **4:**142, **144–146**

overview, **4:131–135**

post-WW II embrace of, **4:**136

post-WW II onset of, **4:**131

"Purchaser Citizens" (Cohen), **4:**136

shopping center development, **4:**134

Thompson, Joe, Jr., **4:146–147**

Suez Canal crisis, **4:**172, 175

Suffrage, for African Americans, **3:**214

Sugar Act (1764), **2:**5, 93–94, 99

Sullivan, Louis, **3:**255, 260, **3:**261

*A Summary View of the Rights of British America* (Jefferson), **2:**164, 172

Sumner, Charles, **3:**214, 231

Supreme Court, **4:**42

Cherokee decision, **3:**127, 132

creation discussions, **2:**219, 221

justice opposition to New Deal, **4:84**

Thomas, Clarence, **4:**263

*See also* individual Supreme Court decisions

Supreme Court creation discussions, **2:**219, 221

Swartout, Samuel, **3:**111

*Sweatt v. Painter* (Supreme Court decision), **4:**243

Swedish South Company, **1:**195

Swiney, P. D., **1:237–245**

Taft, William Howard, **3:**265, **4:**2–3, 18

"Take the A Train" music (Strayhorn), **4:**55

Talleyrand, Charles Maurice de

Adam's interactions with, **2:**242

burning of, in effigy, **2:**246

committee rulership of France, **2:**240

role in XYZ Affair, **2:**249, **256–258**

Tallmadge, James, Jr., **3:**26

Talon, Intendant, **1:**50

Taney, Roger B., **3:**128

Tappan, Arthur, **3:**73, 75–76

Tarbell, Ida, **3:**181, **4:**1

Tax Equity and Fiscal Responsibility Act (TEFRA), **4:**279

Taylor, Nathaniel William, **3:**2

Taylor, Zachary (1784–1850), **3:**132, 133, 144, 148, 153–154, **156–158**

Taylor-Rostow mission (to Vietnam), **4:**220–221

Tea Act (1773), **2:**120–121

Tea Act document (1773), **2:132–1135**

Tecumseh (Indian leader), **3:**42, 43–44, 48

Teheran Conference, **4:**106

Tekesta Indians, **1:**79

Telephone, invention of, **3:**173, **4:**204–205

Television, rise of (1948–2010), **4:199–218**

Berle, Milton, **4:212–214**

Clair's interpretive essay, **4:203–211**

Cronkite, Walter, **4:214–216**

Federal Communications Commission, **4:**199

overview, **4:199–203**

post-WW II experimentation, **4:**199

Teller, Henry M., **3:**277

Ten Percent Plan (Lincoln), **3:**211

Tennent, Gilbert (1703–1764), **2:63–65**

Tennent, William, Sr., **2:**52

Tenure of Office Act, 28, **3:**214

Tet Offensive (Vietnam War), **4:**221–222, **234–236**

Texas

admission to statehood, **3:**138–139

independence from Mexico, **3:**138

Textile manufacturing, **3:**159

*A Theory of Justice* (Rawls), **2:**169

*Theory of Language and Universal Grammar* (Priestley), **2:**38

*There is Confusion* (Faust), **4:**60

Third Anglo-Dutch War (1672–1674), **1:**205

Third-wave consumerism, **4:**135

Thirteenth Amendment (Constitution), **1:**156, 160, **3:**212, 219, 227, **4:**51

Thirty-Nine Articles (England, 1563), **1:**168

Thirty Years War, **1:**49

Thomas, Clarence, **4:**263, 265–266

Thompson, Joe, Jr. (1901–1961), **4:146–147**

Thomson, Charles, **2:**164

Thoreau, Henry David, **2:**167, 168

Thornton, Larry, **4:109–117**

Thornton, Matthew, **2:**164

Thornton, Sir William, **3:**55

Three-Fifths Compromise (Constitution), **2:**274

Three Mile Island nuclear accident, **4:**153, 157, **167**

Thurman, Wallace, **4:**56–57, 58

*Ticonderoga* warship, **3:**56

Tilden, Samuel J., 25, **3:**215, 223

Timber Culture Act (1873), **3:**28, 236

Timucua indigenous culture, **1:**79

Tingey, Thomas, **3:**58

Tippecanoe, Battle of, **3:**43–44

Tituba (Rev. Parris's slave), **1:**256–257, 262

Tobacco advertising (on TV), **4:**202

Tocqueville, Alexis de, **3:**239

Toleration Act, **1:**235

Tonkin Gulf Resolution, **4:**221, 224

Toomer, Jean, **4:**59

Toral, Gen. Jose, **3:**272

Town Council (Rhode Island), **1:**218

Townsend, Francis E., **4:**79

Townshend, Charles, **2:**115

Townshend Acts (Duties) (1776), **2:**104, 116, 120, 127, 194

Trafalgar, Battle of, **3:**41

Trail of Tears, **3:**127

*The Traveller Returned* play (Murray), **2:**206

*A Treatise Concerning Religious Affections* (Edwards), **2:**60

Trend, David, **4:**209

Trenton, Battle of, **2:**139, 148

Trotsky, Leon, **4:**176

Truman, Harry, **4:**107, 121, 158, 169–170, 175, 178, **193–196**

Truman Doctrine, **4:**115, 181

Trumbull, John, **2:**147–148, 149

Trumbull, Lyman, **3:**231

Tubman, Harriet (ca. 1820–1913), **3:82–83**

Tudor dynasty, **1:**167

Turner, Frederick Jackson (1861–1932), **3:248–250,** 256

Turner, Jackson, **3:**240–241

Turner, Nat, **1:**152, 68, 72

Tuskegee Normal and Industrial Institute, **3:**220, **4:**52

*TV Guide* study, **4:**208

Twain, Mark, **3:**272, 279

Twelfth Amendment (U.S. Constitution), **2:**175, 221, 264, **281–282**

Twentieth Amendment (Constitution), **4:**77

Twenty-First Amendment (Constitution), **4:**5

*Two Treatises of Government* (Locke), **2:**178

Tyler, John, **3:**94, 138

Tyler, Royall, **2:**148

U-2 incident (1960), **4:**151, 172, **196–197**

Ubeda Friar Luis de, **1:**65–66

UHF (Ultra High Frequency) stations, **4:**201

Underwood Tariff (1913), **4:**3

Unitarianism, **3:**3, 4, 7, 9

United Auto Workers (UAW), Women's Bureau, **4:**259

United Nations (UN)

  atomic energy control dispute, **4:**169

  Lebanon peacekeeping, **4:**275–276

  Universal Declaration of Human Rights, **2:**169–170

  woman's conferences, **4:**265

United Nations (UN) Charter, **2:**169

United Nations Security Council, **4:**169

United Negro Improvement Association (UNIA), **4:**55, 57

United States (U.S.)

  Act to Prohibit the Importation of Slaves, **1:**152

  as "American Eden," **3:**239

  American Independence Day, **3:**143

  anti-Catholic/anti-Semitic sentiment, **3:**169

  anti-Communist hysteria, **4:**160

  Atomic Energy Commission, **4:**150

  cities, Industrial Revolution era, **3:**165–167

  Civil Service Commission, **4:**1

  closing of the frontier (ca. 1890s), **3:233–251**

  Constitutional Convention, **1:**150

  early history, **1:**1

  Emancipation Proclamation, **1:**160

  France's Revolutionary War aid, **2:**239

  Good Neighbor Policy, **4:**85–86

  Green Party USA, **4:**146

  introduction of slavery, **1:135–165**

  Jay's Treaty, **2:**239

  Missouri Compromise, **1:**160

  Naval War College, **3:**272

  occupation of Oregon territory, **3:**139

  "Religious Right" politics, **4:**263

  Sanitary Commission, **3:**198

  Three Mile Island nuclear accident, **4:**153, 157

  Weber-Ashburton Treaty, **1:**152–153

  World War I costs, **4:**25

  XYZ Affair, **2:**201, **239–261**

  Yalta Conference, **4:**107

  *See also* Industrial Revolution; Mexican-American War

*The United States 1830–1850* (Frederick Jackson Turner), **3:**240

*United States Magazine* (American Revolution era), **2:**188

United States Military Railroads (USMRR), **3:**196

*United States Telegraph* Pro-Jackson newspaper, **3:**117

Universal Declaration of Human Rights (UN), **2:**169

Universal Negro Improvement Association (UNIA), **4:**55

  *See also* Garvey, Marcus

*Unsafe at Any Speed* (Nader), **4:**142, 145

Upham, Charles, **1:**260

U.S. Navy, **3:**272, 277, 283
  *See also* Dewey, George
U.S. Shipping Board, **4:**25
*U.S. v. Butler* (Supreme Court decision), **4:**78
USS *Constellation,* **2:**247–248
USS *Maine* battleship, **3:**274, 276, 280, 287, 289
USS *Nautilus* nuclear submarine, **4:**152
USS *Olympia* battleship, **3:**277
Utopian communities, **2:**166
Utrecht, Treaty of, **2:**7, 9

Valley Forge, Battle of, **2:**155
Van Buren, Martin, **3:**112–113, 127, **129–132,**
  148, 153
Van Twiller, Wouter, **1:**95, 200–201
Vance, Zebulon, **3:**193
Vane, Governor Henry, **1:**120
*The Varieties of Religious Experiences* (James), **2:**60
Velásquez, Gov. Diego, **1:**55–56
Vergennes, Count Charles, **2:**140
Verhurst, Willem, **1:**199
Verin, Joshua, **1:**173–174
Verrazano, Giovanni de, **1:**35
Versailles, Treaty of, **4:**16, 26, 86
Victory Program (WW II, 1943), **4:**112
Video cassette recorders (VCRs), **4:**201
Video Home System (VHS) tapes, **4:**201
Vietnam Veterans against the War, **4:**229
Vietnam War (1960s), **3:**280, 141, 176, 183,
  **219–236**
  Abbott's interpretive essay, **4:223–229**
  antiwar movement, **4:231–232**
  Cambodian incursion, **4:232–233**
  Johnson, Lyndon, **4:**221–222
  Kissinger, Henry, **4:**222
  My Lai massacre, **4:**227
  overview, **4:219–223**
  POW/MIA issue, **4:**228
  Taylor-Rostow mission, **4:**220–221
  Tet Offensive, **4:**221–222
  Tonkin Gulf Resolution, **4:**221
  U.S. citizen skepticism about, **4:**226–227
  U.S. death figures, **4:**224–225
  war movies, **4:**224, 227–228
Virginia Company (of London)
  formation (1606), **1:**101
  New World colonization plans, **1:**112
  Pilgrims' relationship with, **1:**102
  relation to slavery, **1:**139
Virginia Constitutional Convention, **3:**105
"Virginia Dynasty" (presidents from Virginia),
  **2:**278
Virginia Plan (document), **2:**218–219, 222,
  **232–234**

Virginia Resolution (Madison), **2:**247, 269, **3:**190
Virginia Stamp Act Resolutions (document, 1965),
  **2:112–113**
Virginia State of Religious Freedom (Jefferson),
  **2:**172
Voter literacy test (Mississippi), **4:**241
Voting Rights Act (1965), **4:**234, 239, 247

Wade-Davis Bill (1864), **3:**211, 227
Wadsworth, Benjamin, **2:**192
Wahunsonacock (Native American), **1:**121–122
Walker, Alice, **4:**265
Walker, Robert J., **3:**147
Walker River Reservation (Native Americans),
  **3:**244
*Walks and Talks of an American Farmer in
  England* (Olmsted), **3:**267
Waller, "Fats," **4:**55
Walpole, Robert, **2:**1–2
  financial management skills, **2:**7
  patronage system of, **2:**3–4
  political ascendancy of, **2:**6
  war avoidance efforts, **2:**8, 9, 12
  withdrawal of Excise Bill, **2:**10
  *See also* Salutary Neglect, Era of
Wampanoag Indians (Martha's Vineyard), **1:**126,
  214, 217, 223, **228–230**
  *See also* Metacom
War Industries Board, **4:**25, 31
War Labor Board (WW II), **4:**108
War Manpower Board (WW II), **4:**108
War movies, **4:**224, 227–228
War of 1812, **1:**95, 260, **2:**264, **3:41–63**
  American Letter of Marque document, **3:62–63**
  British capture of Washington D.C., **3:57–58**
  as end of Federalist Party, **3:**44–45
  as "forgotten conflict," **3:**45
  Hadden's interpretive essay, **3:45–52**
  Hartford Convention, **3:**44–45, 50, 52, **58–60**
  Jackson's commission, **3:**125
  neutrality theories, **3:**45–46
  New Orleans, Battle of, **3:**51–52, **54–55**
  overview, **3:41–45**
  Perry, Oliver Hazard, **3:60–62**
  Plattsburgh, Battle of, **3:55–57**
  role in Industrial Revolution, **3:**159
  U.S. expansionist dreams, **3:**47–48
  *See also* Jackson, Andrew
War of Jenkin's Ear, **2:**9, 47
War of the Austrian Succession (1740–1748), **2:**9,
  12, 47, 84, 85
War of the League of Augsburg, **1:**249
War of the Polish Succession (1733–1735), **2:**9, 84
War of the Spanish Succession, **2:**16

Warren, Dr. Joseph, **2:**131

Warren, Earl, **4:**238, 244

Warren, Helen Frances, **4:**42

Warren, Mary Otis, **2:**189

Warren, Mercy Otis, **2:**148, 149, 200

Warren Association, **3:**16

Warsaw Pact, **4:**171

Washington, Booker T., **3:**220, **4:**52, 53–54

Washington, George, **1:**146, **2:**72, 74, 76, 83, 125, 129

  cabinet divisions, **2:**267

  comments on American Revolution, **2:**166

  commercial interests, **2:**263

  Constitutional Convention participation, **2:**217–218

  Continental Army leadership, **2:**139, 159–160

  Copley's portrait of, **2:**148

  death of, **2:**270

  Declaration of Independence reading to troops, **2:**164

  Farewell Address, **3:**93, 280

  Federalist Party leadership, **2:**279

  Hamilton's association with, **2:**227

  Jefferson's association with, **2:**174

  positive opinions of women, **2:**196

  power transfer to John Adams, **2:**243

  Proclamation of Neutrality document, **2:258–259**

  second presidential term, **2:**268

  XYZ Affair role, **2:**241

Watergate Scandal (Nixon administration), **4:**223

Waterloo, Battle of, **2:**257

Watson, Thomas, **3:**174

*Wealth against Commonwealth* (Lloyd), **3:**163

*The Wealth of Nations* (Smith), **2:**7

*The Weary Blues* (Hughes), **4:**60

Webster, Daniel, **1:**152–153, 148–149, **3:**112

Webster-Ashburton Treaty (1842), **1:**152–153, **3:**155

Weld, Theodore, **3:**73, 78

"A Well Ordered Family" essay (Wadsworth), **2:**192

Wells, Rachel, **2:**196

Wesley, Charles, **2:**53, 55–56, 65

Wesley, John, **1:**11, **2:**47, 53, 55, 65, **3:**8

West Africa, slavery and, **1:**137, 141, 153

Western Federation of Miners, **4:**38

Westminster Confession, **2:**52

Weyler, Gen. Valeriano, **3:**274, 276

Wheatley, Phillis, **2:**193

Whig Party, **2:**278, **3:**67, 81, **132–134,** 144, 145

  *See also* Antislavery Whigs

Whiskey Rebellion, **2:**228, **3:**2

White, Richard, **3:**241

White, Walter, **4:**58

White City (Columbian Exposition), **3:**254, 257, 259–262, 265

"White Man's Burden" (Kipling), **3:**273

White resistance, Reconstruction era, **3:**215

  *See also* Ku Klux Klan

Whitefield, George (1714–1770), **2:**46–47, 54, 55, **65–66, 3:**6–7

Whitney, Eli, **1:**150–151, 160

Wholesome Meat Act (1967), **4:**145

Wichita Indians, **1:**64

Wild West shows, **3:**30

Wildes, Sarah, **1:**258

Willard, Emma, **2:207–209**

Willard, Frances, **3:**170, **3:**257

Willard, John, **1:**258

Willard Association for the Mutual Improvement of Female Teachers, **2:**208

William III (English monarch), **1:**178, 235, 236–237, 241, 243, 249, **2:**13

William of Orange. *See* William III (English monarch)

Williams, Abigail, **1:**255, 262

Williams, Roger, **1:**86, **185–187,** 214

  expulsion from Massachusetts colony, **1:**173, 187

  founding of Rhode Island, **1:**172–173, 175, **2:**49–50

  governing attempts by, **1:**176, 180

  Pequot War and, **1:**131, 227

  Puritans challenged by, **1:**168–169

  writings of, **1:**186, **187–189**

Wilmot, David, **3:**147–148

Wilmot Proviso document (1846), **3:**147, 149, **158,** 190, 203

Wilson, Governor Edward, **1:**214–215

Wilson, James, **2:**144–145

Wilson, Woodrow, **3:**240, **4:**23–27

  biographical information, **4:43–46**

  Clayton Anti-Trust Act, **4:**4

  Committee on Public Information, **4:**25, 32

  Federal Reserve Act, **4:**4

  Federal Trade Commission Act, **4:**4

  Fourteen Points, **4:**26

  on German submarine attacks, **4:**110

  League of Nations, **4:**16, 25–26

  National Park Service, **4:**13

  Underwood Tariff, **4:**3

  winning presidential election, **4:**29

  World War I actions, **4:**23–27, **43–46**

  *See also* Fourteen Points

Wingfield, Edward Maria, **1:**112

Winslow, Josiah, **1:**225

Winthrop, John, **1:**102–109

"city on a hill" quote, **1:**105

land giveaways to immigrants, **1:**106

law delineations, **1:**107

"Model of Christian Charity" essay, **1:**103, 104, 106, 108, 109

Puritan friends membership, **1:**104

Van Twiller's correspondence with, **1:**201

*See also* Massachusetts Bay Company; Puritans

*Witchcraft at Salem* (Hansen), **1:**261

Witchcraft hysteria. *See* Salem witch trials (1692)

*The Witches' Hammer* (Kramer & Sprenger), **1:**259

Wolcott, Oliver, **2:**229, 244

Wolfe, James (1727–1759), **2:**72, 78, 84–85, **89–90**

Woman's Christian Temperance Union (WCTU), **3:**170–171

"Woman's lib" movement, **4:**263

Women

    AFL union workers, **4:**39

    African America, **2:**192, 195

    boycotts and protests by, **2:**187, 191

    caretaker roles, **2:**195

    colonial era motherhood, **2:203–205**

    education for, **2:**190

    in the Great Awakening, **2:66–67**

    poetry of Phillis Wheatley, **2:**193–194

    religious revivalism and, **3:**12

    Victorian vs. Progressive eras, **4:**8–9

    Washington's positive opinion of, **2:**196

    "A Well Ordered Family" essay, **2:**192

    white, middle-/upper-class, **2:**197

    *See also* Republican Motherhood

*Women of the Republic* (Kerber), **2:**189

Women's Building (Columbian Exposition), **3:**256, 260

Women's Rights Movement (1961–1991), **4:257–271**

    Equal Rights Amendment, **4:**257, 262, 264, **271**

    Feminist Majority, **4:**267

    Fosl's interpretive essay, **4:263–266**

    Friedan, Betty, **4:**259, 264–265, **267–269**

    National Organization for Women, **4:**259–260, 269

    overview, **4:257–263**

    President's Commission on the Status of Women, **4:269–271**

*Wonders of the Invisible World* (Cotton Mather, 1693), 267, **1:272–274**

Wood, Gordon, **2:**166, 168

Wood, Timothy L., **1:171–180**

Woods, Julia A., **1:138–146, 2:215–222, 3:163–171**

Wool, Gen. John E., **3:**152

Woolens Act (1699), **2:**3

Woolman, John, **3:**69

*Working Class War* (Appy), **4:**225

*The Working Man's Advocate* (Evans), **3:**129

Workingman's Party, **3:**128

Works Progress Administration (WPA), **4:**78, 79, 84, 87

World Court, **4:**27

World Education Convention (London), **2:**209

World Trade Organization, **4:**284

World War I (1914–1918), **4:23–48**

    African American soldiers, **4:**54, 58

    Committee on Public Information, **4:**25, 32, **37–38**

    costs to U.S., **4:**25

    Council for National Defense, **4:**29, 30–31

    Espionage Act, **4:**33

    Fourteen Points (Wilson), **4:**26, **47–49**

    Industrial Workers of the World, **4:**34, **38–39**

    influx of African-Americans (U.S.), **4:**53

    League of Nations, **4:**16, 25–26, **39–40**

    Liberty Bonds, **4:**32

    obstacles to presidential policies, **4:**28–29

    overview, **4:23–27**

    Pershing, Gen. John J., **4:**26, **40–43**

    post-war "bonus army," **4:**77

    Russian Revolution, **4:**39

    Selective Service Act, **4:**25–26

    Treaty of Versailles ending, **4:**16, 26, 86

    U.S. unity building, **4:**28

    Vander Meulen's interpretive essay, **4:27–35**

    vigilante groups, **4:**33

    War Industries Board, **4:**25, 31

    Wilson, Woodrow, **4:23–27**

    women union workers, **4:**39

    World Court, **4:**27

    Zimmerman Note, **4:**23–24, **46–47**

World War II (1939–1945), **4:105–129**

    atomic bombing of Japan, **4:**107, 116, 149

    Battle of Midway, **4:**106

    Bradley, Omar, **4:120–121**

    Bulge, Battle of the, **4:** **119–120**

    economic impact, in U.S., of, **4:**112

    German's surrender, **4:**169

    industrial component of, **4:**111

    Japanese internment order, **4:**109, 114, **128–129**

    MacArthur, Douglas, **4:**81–82, **122–125**

    Navajo Code Talkers, **4:125–126**

    Office of War Information, **4:**113

    overview, **4:105–109**

    Pearl Harbor attack, **4:**106, 107, 110–111, **126–127**

    propaganda by entertainers, **4:**113

Teheran Conference, **4:**106
Thornton's interpretive essay, **4:109–117**
Truman Doctrine, **4:**115
Victory Program (1943), **4:**112
Yalta Conference, **4:**106–107
Zoot Suit Riots, **4:127–128**
World's Columbian Exposition (1893),
    **3:253–269**
  architectural ideas, **3:**253–254
  Burnham, Daniel, **3:**254–25, 259, **264–265**
  Ferris, George, **3:**255, **265–267**
  global transformation effect, **3:**262–263
  Industrial Revolution's inspiration, **3:**257, 263
  Japan's contributions, **3:**255–256
  Olmsted, Frederick Law, **3:**253, 259–260,
    **267–269**
  overview, **3:253–257**
  Sigur's interpretive essay, **3:257–263**
  time spend building, **3:**255
  White City, **3:**254, 257, 259–262, 265
  women's representation, **3:**256–257
World's Congress Auxiliary, **3:**256
World's Congress of Representative Women
    (1898), **3:**256–257
Worster, Donald, **3:**241
Wounded Knee Massacre, **3:**245, **250–251**
Wright, Francis, **3:**128
Wright, Frank Lloyd, **3:**255

X, Malcolm, **4:**247
XYZ Affair (France), **2:**201, **239–261**
  Adams, John, role, **2:**47, **252–255**
  Alien and Sedition Acts document, **2:259–261**
  Bonaparte, Napoleon, role, **2:**242, 251
  Elbridge, Gerry, role, **2:255–256**
  Federalist Party issues, **2:**246, 249
  name derivation, **2:**241, 254
  overview, **2:239–243**
  Proclamation of Neutrality document,
    **2:258–259**
  Quasi-War, **2:**241, 248, 250–251, **256**
  Rakestraw's interpretive essay, **2:243–252**
  Talleyrand, Charles Maurice de, **2:256–258**

Yale College, **2:**24, 26, 51, 53, 241
Yalta Conference, **4:**106–107
Yarmouth Stone (Nova Scotia), **1:**2
Yeltsin, Boris, **4:**174
Yorktown, Battle of (1781), **2:**141, **154**, 206, 226
Young Ladies Academy, **2:**190
"Yuppies" movement, **4:**143

Zapata, Emiliano, **4:**54
Zenger, Peter, **1:**244–245
Zimmerman Note (1917), **4:**23–24, **46–47**
Zoot Suit Riots (1943), **4:127–128**
Zuni Indians, **1:**68–69, **76–78**